Paul and the Rhetoric of Reconciliation

Paul and the Rhetoric of Reconciliation

An Exegetical Investigation of the Language and Composition of 1 Corinthians

Margaret M. Mitchell

Westminster/John Knox Press
Louisville, Kentucky

First published in Tübingen, Germany, by J. C. B. Mohr (Paul Siebeck) in 1992

First American edition

Published by Westminster/John Knox Press
Louisville, Kentucky

PRINTED IN THE UNITED STATES OF AMERICA
9 8 7 6 5 4 3 2 1

Library of Congress Cataloging-in-Publication Data

Mitchell, Margaret Mary, 1956–
Paul and the rhetoric of reconciliation : an exegetical investigation of the language and composition of 1 Corinthians / Margaret M. Mitchell. — 1st American ed.
p. cm.
Revision of the author's thesis (doctoral—Chicago) , 1989.
Includes bibliographical references and index.
ISBN 0-664-22177-7 (pbk)

1. Bible. N.T. Corinthians, 1st—Criticism, interpretation, etc.
2. Rhetoric in the Bible. I. Title.
BS2675.2.M58 1993
277'.2066—dc20 92-30364

Margaret Brennan Mitchell
† Walter Booth James Mitchell, Jr.

Acknowledgements

This book is a revised version of my doctoral dissertation, which was accepted by the faculty of the University of Chicago Divinity School in the fall of 1989. I would like to thank the editors of Hermeneutische Untersuchungen zur Theologie, Hans Dieter Betz, Pierre Bühler, Dietz Lange and Walter Mostert, for including the book in this fine series, and publisher Georg Siebeck for most kind assistance throughout the publication process. I also thank Ilse König and the production staff for accomplishing miracles in the computer conversion of a difficult manuscript.

In terms of the content of the book, a study on the composition of 1 Corinthians, I have especially to thank Hans Dieter Betz, the advisor of the dissertation, who contributed to my learning and research through his careful teaching, his example of scholarly depth and precision, and his continual encouragement and support. In particular I thank him for assuring (and reminding) me that in taking on this project I was not doing a commentary on 1 Corinthians! I would also like to thank Elizabeth Asmis of the Classics Department of the University of Chicago, who has been an invaluable resource to me as a teacher of Hellenistic rhetoric, and as a very careful reader of the dissertation. I also express my gratitude to the late David J. Wilmot for excellent instruction in Greek and in methods and resources for studying ancient texts. I have learned much also from the many scholars whose works on 1 Corinthians I have read and studied, perhaps especially those with whom I disagree. I thank them all, and look forward to continuing the debate.

Much of this work was written while I have been on the faculty of McCormick Theological Seminary. I thank the Seminary for a research leave in the fall of 1988, and other generous assistance along the way. Special thanks go to Karl J. Frantz, who completed the arduous task of the indices with exquisite care.

My family, Mitchells and Rosengartens, has given me unbounded encouragement and much more. My husband, Richard A. Rosengarten, deserves more than any thanks I could possibly offer here, but I express my gratitude here especially for his excellent editorial and proofreading assistance. Finally, it is my honor to dedicate this study to my parents, with love, gratitude and respect.

Chicago, June 1991 Margaret M. Mitchell

Table of Contents

Note on Citations

This investigation follows these standards for abbreviations, citations, texts and translations:

Abbreviations of biblical, apocryphal, intertestamental, rabbinic books, early patristic writings, and periodicals and series, follow those listed in the *Journal of Biblical Literature*'s "Instructions for Contributors" (*JBL* 107 [1988] 579–96).

References to classical texts (and some periodicals and series) follow the abbreviations listed in the *Oxford Classical Dictionary*. Where authors, texts or periodicals and series are not found in that list, I follow those of Liddell, Scott and Jones, *A Greek-English Lexicon* for Greek texts, and Glare, *Oxford Latin Dictionary* for Latin texts. Patristic Greek texts are cited according to the abbreviations in Lampe, *A Patristic Greek Lexicon*.

Classical texts are cited according to the text and translation of the Loeb Classical Library editions where available. All are listed in the bibliography. I cite this text and translation first, even if I disagree with it on a given passage (my proposed alterations are noted in such cases). Works not included in that series will, at first citation, refer to the edition of the text and translation followed. All will also be found in the bibliography. My own translations are so marked.

The Greek New Testament is cited from *Novum Testamentum Graece*, the Nestle-Aland 26th edition. All translations are my own, except where otherwise noted.

Chapter I

Introduction to the Task and Methodology

The subject of this inquiry is the overall genre, function and composition of Paul's first letter to the Corinthians. The thesis which will be propounded, on the basis of an exegetical investigation including a rhetorical analysis of the text, is that 1 Corinthians is a single letter of unitary composition which contains a deliberative argument persuading the Christian community at Corinth to become reunified.[1] 1 Corinthians is throughout an argument for ecclesial unity, as centered in the πρόθεσις, or thesis statement of the argument, in 1:10: "I urge you, brothers and sisters, through the name of our Lord Jesus Christ, to all say the same thing, and to let there not be factions among you, but to be reconciled in the same mind and in the same opinion." Factionalism, an inherently political problem which is often, as here, intertwined with religious issues and motivations, is combatted by Paul throughout 1 Corinthians[2] by employing appropriate political terms and *topoi* about factionalism and the appropriate rhetorical genre for urging its cessation, deliberative rhetoric.

The arrangement of 1 Corinthians conforms to expectations for deliberative discourse. Paul's response to the Corinthian situation of which he had been variously informed (1:11; 5:1; 7:1; 11:18; 16:17), likely by several parties soliciting his support for their own position, is an argument in which each of the topics of Corinthian debate (sexual morality, civil procedures, marital relations, the

---

[1] Historically, the church at Corinth may never have been an actual unity before Paul wrote this letter, but it may have been a collection of disparate house churches from its very inception (see ch. III n. 62 for scholarly discussion on this point). Nevertheless, Paul's rhetorical stance throughout 1 Cor is to argue that Christian unity is the theological and sociological expectation from which the Corinthians have fallen short, and to which they must return. Thus we may speak of his urging the church to become "reunified."

[2] This thesis is directly contrary to the position of J. Munck, "The Church Without Factions. Studies in I Corinthians 1–4," chap. in *Paul and the Salvation of Mankind*, trans. F. Clarke (Richmond: John Knox, 1959) 135–67, recently revived in the commentary by G. D. Fee, *The First Epistle to the Corinthians*, NIC (Grand Rapids, MI: Eerdmans, 1987), denying that there were factions in the Corinthian church. That factionalism is the "Grundübel" which Paul confronts throughout 1 Corinthians was suggested in the important but neglected article by K. Prümm, "Die pastorale Einheit des ersten Korintherbriefes," *ZKT* 64 (1940) 202–14 (but that on theological, not historical and rhetorical grounds, as will be argued here; see below).

consumption of idol meats, hairstyles, the Lord's supper, the meaning and use of spiritual gifts, the resurrection) is subsumed under a discussion of what *he* considers to be the seminal problem at Corinth – factionalism – which is the innate cause and further result of these specific contentions. The various questions of Corinthian debate thus become transformed into subordinate arguments in Paul's larger argument throughout 1 Corinthians for the reunification of the church.[3] Instead of supporting one group over another, Paul exhorts all to a course of unity. He does this by persuading the Corinthians that reunification is the most advantageous course for them to follow. In order to do this he redefines the standards in relation to which the Corinthians should choose their future course of action. Paul then offers, throughout the letter, himself as a living example, a living παράδειγμα, of the non-factionalist, non-divisive course to which he counsels them.

This investigation, through its understanding of 1 Corinthians as deliberative rhetoric, renders a fully coherent reading of the letter in its present literary form, and thus constitutes a sustained defense of the compositional integrity of 1 Corinthians.[4] This work enters into the current (and longstanding) debate among New Testament scholars about the compositional integrity of 1 Corinthians. The unity of the letter in our canonical 1 Corinthians has been questioned, especially since Johannes Weiss published his commentary on 1 Corinthians in 1910.[5] The last forty years have seen a proliferation of partition theories which divide the canonical letter into from two to four letters or letter frag-

[3] Three things must be differentiated: 1. Paul's way of describing the situation at Corinth, which draws upon political terms and *topoi* which depict factionalism; 2. the way the church members at Corinth would have described their behavior; and 3. the real social conditions in the Corinthian church apart from the various viewpoints. This study will focus on the first point: Paul's own rhetorical stance in 1 Cor. The implications of this analysis for the second and third points, the problems of historical reconstruction, will be taken up in chap. V.

[4] Other scholars have been able to make sense of the text and argue for its unity (e. g., C. K. Barrett, *The First Epistle to the Corinthians*, HNTC [New York/Evanston: Harper & Row, 1968] 17; see the discussion below). This inquiry responds to the objection that "unity is in the eye of the beholder" by demonstrating the correspondence throughout this argument with contemporary Greco-Roman texts, thus providing an historical control for the literary analysis. See the statement of this methodological principle by S. K. Stowers: "When interpreters must rely solely on reconstructing a historical occasion for letters from clues within the letters themselves, they are caught in a vicious circle ... If, however, researchers can show through the comparative study of Greco-Roman letters that a New Testament letter follows or adapts certain conventions, is a certain type, or functions in a certain way, then the researcher has introduced an outside control over that vicious circle" (*Letter Writing in Greco-Roman Antiquity*, Library of Early Christianity 5 [Philadelphia: Westminster, 1986] 25).

[5] J. Weiss, *Der erste Korintherbrief*, MeyerK vol. 7, 9th ed. (Göttingen: Vandenhoeck & Ruprecht, 1910), especially his suggestions on xl-xliii. Weiss revised this theory somewhat in his later work, *Earliest Christianity*, ed. and trans. F. C. Grant (New York: Harper, 1959) 2.323–57. See also P. Vielhauer's note that later theories are mostly variations on Weiss's insights (*Geschichte der urchristlichen Literatur* [Berlin/New York: de Gruyter, 1975] 141). For discussion on the unity of 1 Corinthians before Weiss, see C. F. G. Heinrici, *Der erste Brief an die Korinther*, MeyerK vol. 7, 8th ed. (Göttingen: Vandenhoeck & Ruprecht, 1896) 27–31; P. Bach-

ments, usually in concert with theories on 2 Corinthians.[6] These theories reject the original unity of this letter on the basis of perceived inconsistencies, different epistolary situations, harsh transitions, and some observations which are deemed formal.[7] Each partition hypothesis is buttressed by an historical scenario of Paul's stormy relationship with the church at Corinth which might account for the array of letters thus produced, and in some cases reconstructions of the redactor's work, with accompanying speculation on his or her theological and sociological motives.[8]

Despite the proliferation of partition theories, some scholars have held to the

mann, *Der erste Brief des Paulus an die Korinther*, KNT 7 (Leipzig: Deichert, 1905) 28–29; M. Goguel, *Introduction au Nouveau Testament*, vol. 4, pt. 2 (Paris: Leroux, 1926) 86 n. 1.

[6] The varied works of W. Schmithals have had particular influence (*Gnosticism in Corinth*, trans. J. E. Steely [Nashville: Abingdon, 1971]; "Die Korintherbriefe als Briefsammlung," *ZNW* 64 [1973] 263–88; *Die Briefe des Paulus in ihrer ursprünglichen Form* [Zurich: Theologischer Verlag, 1984]). Other scholars who partition 1 Cor are Goguel, 72–78, 86; J. Héring, *The First Epistle of Saint Paul to the Corinthians*, trans. A. W. Heathcote and P. J. Allcock (London: Epworth, 1962); E. Dinkler, "Korintherbriefe," *RGG*[3] 4 (1960) 17–23; W. Schenk, "Der 1. Korintherbrief als Briefsammlung," *ZNW* 60 (1969) 219–43; R. Jewett, *Paul's Anthropological Terms. A Study of their Use in Conflict Settings*, AGJU 10 (Leiden: Brill, 1971) 23–40; A. Suhl, *Paulus und seine Briefe. Ein Beitrag zur paulinischen Chronologie*, SNT 11 (Gütersloh: Mohn, 1975) 203–13; Vielhauer, 140–41; H.-M. Schenke and K. M. Fischer, *Einleitung in die Schriften des Neuen Testaments I. Die Briefe des Paulus und Schriften des Paulinismus* (Gütersloh: Mohn, 1978) 92–107; W. Marxsen, *Einleitung in das Neue Testament. Eine Einführung in ihre Probleme* (Gütersloh: Mohn, 1978[4]) 84–95 (in earlier editions he held to the unity of 1 Corinthians); C. Senft, *La première Epître de saint-Paul aux Corinthiens*, CNT n. s. vol. 7 (Neuchâtel/Paris: Delachaux & Niestlé, 1979); H.-J. Klauck, *Herrenmahl und hellenistischer Kult. Eine religionsgeschichtliche Untersuchung zum ersten Korintherbrief*, NTAbh n. s. 15 (Münster: Aschendorff, 1982), and *idem*, *1. Korintherbrief*, Die Neue Echter Bibel, vol. 7 (Würzburg: Echter Verlag, 1984) (with some caution; see p. 11); R. Pesch, *Paulus ringt um die Lebensform der Kirche. Vier Briefe an die Gemeinde Gottes in Korinth*, Herderbücherei 1291 (Freiburg/Basel/Vienna: Herder, 1986); cf. the very tentative observations of G. Bornkamm on 6:12–20 and 6:1–12, who explicitly says that he is not offering a proposal for a division hypothesis, and who still defends the unity of 1 Cor 8–16 ("Die Vorgeschichte des sogenannten Zweiten Korintherbriefes," *Geschichte und Glaube*, vol. 2, in his *Gesammelte Aufsätze*, vol. 4, BEvT 53 [Munich: Kaiser, 1971] 162–94, 189 n. 131). For recent analyses of the partition theories with current bibliography, see G. Sellin, "Hauptprobleme des Ersten Korintherbriefes," *ANRW* 2, pt. 25.4 (1987) 2940–3044; 2964–86 (who also proposes his own theory); H. Merklein, "Die Einheitlichkeit des ersten Korintherbriefes," *ZNW* 75 (1984) 153–83; 154–56. See also J. C. Hurd, *The Origin of 1 Corinthians* (London: SPCK, 1965; repr., Macon, GA: Mercer University Press, 1983) 43–47 for the earlier theories (to 1965).

[7] Contents leading up to an epistolary closing have been detected in 4:16–21 (so Schenk, 235; cf. Schmithals, "Korintherbriefe," 266 [but the form itself has been omitted by the redactor!]; Senft, 18) and in 11:34b (Schmithals, "Korintherbriefe," 281). Of overwhelming significance for partition theories (and even unity theories) have been presuppositions about the role of the formula περὶ δέ. See the challenge to those assumptions in M. M. Mitchell, "Concerning ΠΕΡΙ ΔΕ in 1 Corinthians," *NovT* 31 (1989) 229–56 (and discussion in chap. IV below).

[8] Schenk, 242–43; Schenke-Fischer, 94; Suhl, 203–13; R. Jewett, "The Redaction of 1 Corinthians and the Trajectory of the Pauline School," *JAARSup* 46 (1978) 398–444; Pesch, 247–53. Merklein's critique of such attempts (p. 158), that they allow inconsistencies for the redactor's work which they find unacceptable for an author, or vice versa give the redactor

unity of the letter, though more often by allowing the unity rather than actually arguing for it.[9] Where the unity of the letter has been defended it has been mostly on the territorial ground of the partition theories, by attempts to refute their reasonings.[10] Those who hold to the unity of 1 Corinthians have resorted in the main to hypothetical historical reconstructions or psychological explanations of the perceived incongruities and inconsistencies in the text.[11] Still others have

---

credit for the coherence which they deny to the author, remains a trenchant argument which has not been refuted.

[9] J. B. Lightfoot, *Notes on Epistles of St. Paul from Unpublished Commentaries* (London/New York: Macmillan, 1895); K. Lake, *The Earlier Epistles of St. Paul*, (London: Rivington, 1911); A. Robertson and A. Plummer, *A Critical and Exegetical Commentary on the First Epistle of St. Paul to the Corinthians*, ICC (New York: Scribner's, 1925); H. Lietzmann, *An die Korinther I, II*, rev. W. G. Kümmel, HNT 9 (Tübingen: Mohr/Siebeck, 1949⁴); E.-B. Allo, *Saint Paul. Première Epitre aux Corinthiens*, EBib (Paris: LeCoffre, 1956²); F. W. Grosheide, *Commentary on the First Epistle to the Corinthians*, NICNT (Grand Rapids, MI: Eerdmans, 1953); Hurd; Barrett; H. Conzelmann, *I Corinthians*, trans. J. W. Leitch, Hermeneia (Philadelphia: Fortress, 1975); F. F. Bruce, *1 and 2 Corinthians*, NCBC (Grand Rapids, MI: Eerdmans, 1971); E. Fascher, *Der erste Brief des Paulus an die Korinther*, THKNT vol. 7, pt. 1 (Berlin: Evangelische Verlagsanstalt, 1975); C. Wolff, *Der erste Brief des Paulus an die Korinther*, THKNT vol. 7, pt. 2 (Berlin: Evangelische Verlagsanstalt, 1975); F. Lang, *Die Briefe an die Korinther*, NTD 7 (Göttingen: Vandenhoeck & Ruprecht, 1986); Fee; A. Strobel, *Der erste Brief an die Korinther*, Zürcher Bibelkommentare NT, vol. 6, pt. 1 (Zürich: Theologischer Verlag, 1989). To these commentaries we must add the studies by Merklein, D. Lührmann ("Freundschaftsbrief trotz Spannungen. Zu Gattung und Aufbau des Ersten Korintherbriefs," in *Studien zum Text und zur Ethik des Neuen Testaments. Festschrift zum 80. Geburtstag von H. Greeven*, ed. W. Schrage, BZNW 47 [Berlin/New York: de Gruyter, 1986] 298–314), and L. L. Belleville, who has argued for the integrity of 1 Cor on the basis of its epistolary forms ("Continuity or Discontinuity: A Fresh Look at 1 Corinthians in the Light of First-Century Epistolary Forms and Conventions," *EvQ* 59 [1987] 15–37). It is clear that current New Testament scholarship remains divided on the question of the unity of 1 Corinthians.

[10] Perhaps the most vigorous response was that of W. G. Kümmel (*Introduction to the New Testament*, trans. H. C. Kee [Nashville: Abingdon, 1975] 275–78). Merklein's article presents a significant refutation of the arguments upon which the partition theories are founded on the basis of linguistic analysis (see also his judgement against previous attempts to refute partition theories, 154). Nevertheless, though staving off the partition theorists, Merklein does not present a coherent fresh interpretation of 1 Corinthians. Although the unity of 1 Cor cannot be proven by dismantling partition theories alone, one must note, with Lührmann, the extent to which the division hypotheses which have been offered manifest a troubling lack of methodological consensus: "Zwar scheint jeder Teilungsversuch *a priori* diskreditiert durch die ja nicht unerheblichen Differenzen zwischen den einzelnen Hypothesen" (Lührmann, 298; see also Barrett, 17).

[11] Hurd's, the only sustained defense of the unity of 1 Corinthians to date, depends upon both his historical reconstructions of the events between Paul and the Corinthians and the psychological assumption that Paul's tone varied in relation to the source of the topic which he took up. Barrett suggests that pauses in dictation (15; so also Kümmel, 227; cf. Fascher, 44; Conzelmann, 3 n. 20) or the arrival of fresh news (15; Bruce, 24–25) may have caused some of these rough transitions. Despite the inadequacy of prior defenses of the unity of 1 Cor, Sellin's charge against American exegetes deserves a firm rebuttal! "Es ist bemerkenswert, dass in der amerikanischen Exegese . . . kaum Teilungshypothesen aufgestellt wurden . . . was vielleicht

argued for the unity of the letter on the basis of theological coherence.[12] But the issue of the compositional integrity of 1 Corinthians is, first and foremost, a literary question.[13] This work contains a sustained defense of the unity of 1 Corinthians on the basis of a literary rhetorical analysis – the appropriate primary methodology for addressing this question.

Rhetorical analyses of Pauline letters have abounded in recent years, instigated to a large degree by Hans Dieter Betz's work on Galatians and 2 Corinthians.[14] What distinguishes Betz's work from previous examinations of Pauline rhetoric is his focus on the invention and arrangement of arguments in a letter discourse,

seinen Grund in der Vorliebe für eine literaturwissenschaftlich-synchronische Interpretation hat" (p. 2965 n. 135).

[12] The most significant such attempt was made by K. Barth, who centered the unity of the epistle in ch. 15 on the resurrection (*The Resurrection of the Dead*, trans. H.J. Stenning [New York: Revell, 1933; repr., New York: Arno, 1977]), to which R. Bultmann made his famous response arguing for the centrality of ch. 13 (*Faith and Understanding*, trans. L.P. Smith [New York/Evanston: Harper & Row, 1969] 66–94). Prümm argued for unity on the basis of the theological coherence of Paul's response to Corinthian divisions by contesting their conceptions of δύναμις and σοφία; G. Friedrich on the Christocentrism of the letter ("Christus, Einheit und Norm der Christen. Das Grundmotiv des 1. Korintherbriefs," *KD* 9 [1963] 235–58); H. Schlier on "die Erbauung der Kirche" ("Das Hauptanliegen des ersten Korintherbriefes," chap. in *Die Zeit der Kirche: Exegetische Aufsätze und Vorträge* [Freiburg/Basel/Vienna: Herder, 1966⁴] 147–59); Allo on "la communauté de vie avec le Christ" (lxxix-lxxxv); Conzelmann on "faith" (6–7, 9–11) and the theology of the cross (11, 40). An innovative twist on this appeal (with clear literary implications) was provided by K. E. Bailey, who argued for unity on the basis of Paul's consistent theological method in 1 Corinthians ("The Structure of 1 Corinthians and Paul's Theological Method with Special Reference to 4:17," *NovT* 25 [1983] 152–81). J. C. Beker sees two coherent theological poles in 1 Corinthians: "the twin motifs of apocalyptic glory (ch. 15) and church unity" ("Paul's Theology: Consistent or Inconsistent?" *NTS* 34 [1988] 364–77), though he notes that this coherence is not self-evident (371), and does not explicitly argue for literary unity on that basis. Beker's article provides an important reminder that the question of Paul's theological consistency is itself perhaps the greatest debate in Pauline studies. Thus appeals to theological consistency, which can always be claimed "subjective," provide too rickety a foundation for literary conclusions. On the other hand, Paul could have conceivably been theologically consistent over a series of letters or letter fragments. My analysis will demonstrate that I agree with these scholars that there *is* theological consistency and coherence in 1 Corinthians, but ground that view in the historical and rhetorical analysis. Each of these theological motifs is knitted into Paul's deliberative argument for the elimination of factionalism. The result is a coherent and systematic ecclesiology.

[13] As argued also by Merklein, 157 (who responds with a synchronic analysis of its syntactical, semantic and pragmatic *Textkohärenz*). The literary issue of course cannot be completely separated from historical or theological concerns, but I suggest approaching the question from the literary rhetorical point of view. See Barrett's criteria of assessment: "As long, however, as it seems that the epistle as it stands makes reasonably good sense, *historically and theologically*, the balance of probability will remain with the view that we have it substantially as it left the author's hands" (17, emphasis added). To this we shall add and test: *rhetorically*.

[14] H. D. Betz, *Galatians: A Commentary on Paul's Letter to the Churches in Galatia*, Hermeneia (Philadelphia: Fortress, 1979) and *2 Corinthians 8 and 9: A Commentary on Two Administrative Letters of the Apostle Paul*, Hermeneia (Philadelphia: Fortress, 1985). See also his earlier work, *Der Apostel Paulus und die sokratische Tradition: Eine exegetische Untersuchung zu seiner 'Apologie' 2 Kor 10–13*, BHT 45 (Tübingen: Mohr/Siebeck, 1972).

whereas previous studies were mostly confined to style.[15] His approach realizes that Paul's letters undeniably contain argumentation, which can be elucidated by comparison with the conventions for the invention and arrangement of arguments in rhetorical compositions in Greco-Roman antiquity. The present work stands in the tradition of rhetorical criticism as practiced by Betz.

Yet it would be incorrect to suggest that there is at present scholarly consensus about what "rhetorical criticism" is, and upon what particular techniques and resources that methodology draws.[16] This introduction will serve to differentiate the present work from other "rhetorical analyses" of Pauline letters, and of 1 Corinthians in particular, by pointing out some methodological problems which have hampered those works, and by suggesting some specific refinements of the methodology of "rhetorical criticism." This will be accomplished by laying out five mandates for rhetorical criticism of New Testament texts, particularly the Pauline letters, which will be adhered to in this study:

1. *Rhetorical criticism as employed here is an historical undertaking.*
2. *Actual speeches and letters from antiquity must be consulted along with the rhetorical handbooks throughout the investigation.*
3. *The designation of the rhetorical species of a text (as epideictic, deliberative, or forensic) cannot be begged in the analysis.*
4. *The appropriateness of rhetorical form or genre to content must be demonstrated.*
5. *The rhetorical unit to be examined should be a compositional unit, which can be further substantiated by successful rhetorical analysis.*

1. Rhetorical Criticism, as here understood, is one of the panoply of tools which bear the name "historical-critical method."[17] In this exegetical study it will be one method used in concert with the traditional methods of philological, literary and historical analysis. In particular, the rhetoric of 1 Corinthians will be studied in the light of the Greco-Roman rhetorical tradition which was operative and pervasive at the time of the letter's composition. Thus the resources drawn upon in reconstructing this rhetorical tradition are the ancient Greco-Roman handbooks, speeches and letters themselves, not the modern "New Rhetoric,"[18]

[15] See the surveys in H. D. Betz, "The Problem of Rhetoric and Theology According to the Apostle Paul," *L'Apôtre Paul: Personnalité, style et conception du ministère*, ed. A. Vanhoye, BETL 73 (1986) 16–48, 16–21; M. Bünker, *Briefformular und rhetorische Disposition im 1. Korintherbrief*, GTA 28 (Göttingen: Vandenhoeck & Ruprecht, 1984) 13–15; F. Siegert, *Argumentation bei Paulus, gezeigt an Röm 9–11*, WUNT 34 (Tübingen: Mohr/Siebeck, 1985) 5–15 on argumentation in general (in his own study Siegert rejects the emphasis on rhetorical arrangement [see esp. p. 16]), and the works cited there.

[16] For example, the recent programmatic essay "Where is Rhetorical Criticism Taking Us?" (*CBQ* 49 [1987] 448–63) by W. Wuellner, calls for a future of rhetorical criticism diametrically opposed to that here espoused (see below).

[17] See Betz's description of his *Galatians* commentary: "... the work of an historian whose goal is to understand a historical phenomenon with the help of a set of methods called the historical-critical method" (xv).

[18] Ch. Perelman and L. Olbrechts-Tyteca, *The New Rhetoric. A Treatise on Argumentation*,

which, though it draws upon classical sources at times, is an essentially synchronic investigation of human communication and argumentation.[19] Appeals to modern philosophical examinations of the rhetorical force of all texts[20] should not be put at the service of historical arguments. This is not to say that all such investigations are invalid in their own right,[21] but they should not be confused or intertwined with historical arguments about Paul's rhetoric in the light of the Greco-Roman rhetorical tradition,[22] the sources for which are ancient texts.[23]

---

trans. J. Wilkinson and P. Weaver (Notre Dame/London: University of Notre Dame Press, 1969).

[19] Several rhetorical analyses of Paul's letters have depended upon Perelman-Olbrechts-Tyteca: W. Wuellner, "Greek Rhetoric and Pauline Argumentation," in *Early Christian Literature and the Classical Intellectual Tradition:* in honorem *Robert M. Grant*, ed. W. R. Schoedel and R. L. Wilken, Théologie Historique 54 (Paris: Etudes Beauchesne, 1979) 177–88 (a groundbreaking essay in many respects), and "Rhetorical Criticism"; Siegert; R. Jewett, *The Thessalonian Correspondence. Pauline Rhetoric and Millenarian Piety* (Philadelphia: Fortress, 1986) 63–68; E. S. Fiorenza, "Rhetorical Situation and Historical Reconstruction in 1 Cor," *NTS* 33 (1987) 386–403. It is also a resource for G. A. Kennedy's *New Testament Interpretation Through Rhetorical Criticism* (Chapel Hill: University of North Carolina Press, 1984). It must be emphasized that the "New Rhetoric," an important philosophical work (see above, n. 17), does not claim to be a handbook of ancient rhetoric, but rather a revision and reappropriation of it to modern philosophical problems, particularly that of epistemology. Its intention is at basic points contrary to that of these New Testament scholars – it aims at *expanding* the realm of argumentation rather than classifying particular texts according to genre or arrangement (see also below).

[20] See the works cited by Wuellner, "Rhetorical Criticism," 448 n. 1.

[21] K. A. Plank's *Paul and the Irony of Affliction*, SBLSS (Atlanta: Scholars Press, 1987), is an example of a successful synchronic approach to Paul's rhetoric (but he, too, slips over into historical arguments in some places; see my booknote in *JR* 68 [1988] 352).

[22] Jewett's defense of his combination of methods – classical rhetorical analysis, New Rhetoric and linguistic analysis – is in my view unsatisfactory (*Thessalonian Correspondence*, 63–87). In implementation his eclectic methodology has almost nothing to do with classical rhetoric, despite the fact that some of its terms (i. e., epideictic, deliberative) are retained, though from the New Rhetoric. Not one ancient speech or letter is cited, and actual ancient handbooks are only rarely referred to. Where ancient sources are inferred they are second-hand, from G. Kennedy or H. Lausberg (*Handbuch der literarischen Rhetorik* [Munich: Hueber, 1973^{2}]). Jewett's real interest is in the audience-based perspective of the New Rhetoric, which he judges "relevant for historical research," but that leap is made at the sacrifice of appropriate literary analysis.

[23] As an example of how appeals to the New Rhetoric can skew an analysis, Wuellner ("Greek Rhetoric" and "Rhetorical Criticism," 460) argues that 1 Corinthians is epideictic rhetoric on the basis of Perelman and Olbrechts-Tyteca's 1958 *redefinition* of the genre! (see also his "The Function of Rhetorical Questions in First Corinthians," in *L'Apôtre Paul: Personnalité, style et conception du ministère*, ed. A. Vanhoye, BETL 73 [1986] 46–77). This designation tells us nothing about the first century rhetorical genres and conventions, and only confuses because this modern redefinition merely attributes to epideictic rhetoric characteristics and functions which it was not accorded in antiquity; it thus amounts to a mistaken genre classification from an historical perspective. Wuellner does not note that Perelman and Olbrechts-Tyteca's work on epideictic rhetoric is a conscious and deliberate *revision* of the ancient conceptions and uses of the genre which they deem faulty (47–51). In fact, Perelman and Olbrechts-Tyteca openly reject much of the tri-generic classification of epideictic, deliberative and forensic species for their purposes (21; see also Ch. Perelman, *The New Rhetoric and the Humanities. Essays on Rhetoric*

The present study is an historical rhetorical analysis of 1 Corinthians in the light of the literary/rhetorical conventions operative in the first century.[24]

2. In reconstructing the Greco-Roman rhetorical tradition for comparison with New Testament texts it is imperative that the ancient rhetorical handbooks[25] not be the sole source.[26] These handbooks present us with one type of

---

and its Applications [Dordrecht: Reidel, 1979] 5–7). Instead they prefer a general definition of argumentation (see esp. p. 6) which makes all argumentation in some sense what the ancients would term deliberative: "we will consider argumentation above all in its practical effects: oriented toward the future, it sets out to bring about some action or to prepare for it by acting, by discursive methods, on the minds of the hearers" (47). On deliberative rhetoric in antiquity, see ch. II below. The pervasiveness of Wuellner's definition of epideictic rhetoric (with Perelman) is evident throughout works of NT rhetorical criticism, as most recently D. F. Watson, "A Rhetorical Analysis of 3 John: A Study in Epistolary Rhetoric," *CBQ* 51 (1989) 479–501, 484 n. 29. There he defines epideictic rhetoric as producing "adherence to a value already held," citing in support ancient handbook references which do not uphold such a definition.

[24] Wuellner's view of rhetorical criticism is vastly different: "Rhetorical criticism is taking us beyond hermeneutics and structuralism to poststructuralism and posthermeneutics" ("Rhetorical Criticism," 449). See also his description of the "crossroad" at which rhetorical criticism stands between "two competing versions of rhetorical criticism" (453). This study claims the path which Wuellner terms that "in which rhetorical criticism is identical with literary criticism" (although I would quarrel with the designation), which he rejects in favor of "practical criticism." Wuellner's work cannot be considered to define the current consensus, and removes itself from the sphere of this inquiry by its indifference or antagonism to historical issues (see his impatience on p. 457 with the historical questions raised by Bünker). It should also be pointed out that Wuellner's reliance on Kennedy's work proceeds without sufficiently grappling with the fact that Kennedy is interested in authorial intention and the historical reader as integral to his rhetorical criticism (p. 12 and passim), which are antithetical to most of the modern critics Wuellner cites, and his own emphasis on reader-based criticism (463).

[25] The standard handbooks are Aristotle, *The Art of Rhetoric*; [Aristotle], *Rhetorica ad Alexandrum*; Cicero, *de Inventione*; [Cicero], *Rhetorica ad Herennium*; Quintilian, *Institutio Oratoria* (see also his discussion of τέχναι in 3.1). Other τέχναι are collected in L. Spengel, ed., *Rhetores Graeci*, 3 vols., BT (Leipzig: Teubner, 1853–56) and C. Walz, ed., *Rhetores Graeci*, 9 vols. (Stuttgart/Tübingen: Cotta, 1832–36) [these will be cited by volume and page]. For research on the τέχναι, see W. Kroll, "Rhetorik," *PW* Sup 8 (1940) 1039–1138, esp. 1096–1100; F. Solmsen, "Drei Rekonstruktionen zur antiken Rhetorik und Poetik," *Hermes* 67 (1932) 133–54; *idem*, "The Aristotelian Tradition in Ancient Rhetoric," *AJP* 62 (1941) 35–50; 169–90; G. A. Kennedy, "The Earliest Rhetorical Handbooks," *AJP* 80 (1959) 169–78, and the works in note 28 below.

[26] See, e. g., W. A. Meeks's critique of Betz's *Galatians* as "referring almost exclusively to rhetorical and epistolary *theory* rather than to specific examples of real apologies or real letters from antiquity" (*JBL* 100 [1981] 304–307; 306, emphasis original; cf. the comments in reviews of Betz's *Galatians* by P. W. Meyer and D. E. Aune in *RelSRev* 7 [1981] 318–23 and 323–28). But the point Meeks makes of this observation, that the genre of apologetic letter has not been established, can, in this case, be refuted because examples *do* exist (see Betz's response, *2 Corinthians 8 and 9*, 130–31, and his reflections on the debates concerning the *Galatians* commentary in the foreword to the German translation, *Der Galaterbrief. Ein Kommentar zum Brief des Apostels Paulus an die Gemeinden in Galatien*, trans. S. Ann [Munich: Kaiser, 1988] 1–4). But where examples of actual texts cannot be found, I would agree with Meeks and the others that the rhetorical analysis is severely weakened. Recently J. Smit has critiqued Betz's reliance

evidence for what is *prescribed* for rhetorical discourse, and they put forth a far more regular, strict and almost mechanical view of rhetorical composition than actual speeches and letters embody.[27] Using the handbooks alone[28] in doing rhetorical analysis of ancient texts leads to a similarly mechanistic analysis, especially in regard to the arrangement of the argument. The directions which the rhetorical handbooks provide must always be tempered and compared with actual speeches and other rhetorical compositions from the Greco-Roman world,[29] so that the fluidity and variety of possibilities of rhetorical composition in Greco-Roman antiquity can be brought to bear on the analysis. This is especially crucial when one investigates deliberative or epideictic rhetoric, because the handbooks proceed from the point of view of forensic rhetoric as the dominant form.[30] One should not expect a deliberative or epideictic argument to follow the exact same τάξις (arrangement) as the forensic models from the handbooks.[31] The mechanistic approach to rhetorical criticism which results from sole reliance on the handbooks[32] requires one, for example, to hunt down a

---

on Quintilian, but his own solution, to use Cicero's *De inventione* and the *Rhetorica ad Herennium*, in no way solves the problem ("The Letter of Paul to the Galatians: A Deliberative Speech," *NTS* 35 [1989] 1–26, esp. pp. 5–6).

[27] See D. E. Aune, *The New Testament in Its Literary Environment*, Library of Early Christianity 8 (Philadelphia: Westminster, 1987) 199. We should also note that there is more difference of opinion among the handbooks than is always recognized (see Solmsen, "Aristotelian Tradition").

[28] In addition, the ancient handbooks themselves should be consulted, and reliance should not be made on modern compendia of ancient rhetoric as a substitute for the primary texts. This is a limitation of the rhetorical investigations of Wuellner, Jewett and Fiorenza. The standard treatments are: R. Volkmann, *Die Rhetorik der Griechen und Römer in systematischer Übersicht* (Leipzig: Teubner, 1885^2); C. S. Baldwin, *Ancient Rhetoric and Poetic* (New York: Macmillan, 1924; repr. Westport, CT: Greenwood, 1971); Lausberg; G. A. Kennedy, *The Art of Persuasion in Greece* (Princeton: Princeton University Press, 1963); *idem, The Art of Rhetoric in the Roman World* (Princeton: Princeton University Press, 1972); *idem, Classical Rhetoric and its Christian and Secular Tradition from Ancient to Modern Times* (Chapel Hill: University of North Carolina Press, 1980); and J. Martin, *Antike Rhetorik: Technik und Methode*, HAW II, 3 (Munich: Beck, 1974).

[29] Compare Dionysius of Halicarnassus' methodology in his critical essays (e. g., *Lys.* 17, 24; *Isaeus* 14–15).

[30] A particular mark of the Hellenistic rhetorical tradition (D. A. Russell and N. G. Wilson, ed. and trans. *Menander Rhetor* [Oxford: Clarendon, 1981] xxii).

[31] A point which the handbooks themselves make (e. g., Arist. *Rh.* 3.13.1–3; 3.14.12; *Rh.Al.* 28–35; Quint. *Inst.* 3.8.6–11; 4.2.4–5), which often goes neglected. Indeed there is variety in τάξις within all three species of rhetoric – various parts of a speech (the so-called μόρια λόγου) may be omitted to suit the given subject or occasion (Arist. *Rh.* 3.14.8,12; Cic. *Inv.Rhet.* 1.21.30; Quint. *Inst.* 4.1.72). It should also be remembered that the handbooks differ, sometimes quite vigorously, among themselves in regard to the parts of a speech (see Martin, 219–29 for an overview). These differences must be paid attention to; one cannot give allegiance to one handbook but must consult all on each point and explore their variances (contra Smit, 5–6).

[32] Exclusive reliance on handbooks is a drawback of almost all recent "rhetorical criticism," as in Kennedy's *New Testament Interpretation*, which has had much influence. In his methodology section (31–38) and his bibliography (161–62) Kennedy never encourages students to

narratio,[33] despite the lack (or at least rarity) of a *narratio* in epideictic discourses as specified by the handbooks and evident in actual speeches.[34] Such an approach

---

consult actual rhetorical texts. Exclusive dependence on rhetorical handbooks is a problem in Bünker's analysis (48–76), and those of Siegert and G. Lyons, *Pauline Autobiography. Toward a New Understanding*, SBLDS 73 (Atlanta: Scholars Press, 1985). D.F. Watson, *Invention, Arrangement and Style. Rhetorical Criticism of Jude and 2 Peter*, SBLDS 104 (Atlanta: Scholars Press, 1988), and a series of subsequent articles, carries Kennedy's methodology about as far as it can go, but is similarly limited by this sole attention to rhetorical theory.

[33] See Jewett's analysis of 1 Thessalonians as epideictic rhetoric (*Thessalonian Correspondence*, 71–78), which assigns fully half of the letter to "the narratio section" (1:6–3:13; cf. Kennedy, *New Testament Interpretation*, 79, on Jn 13:2–30 as *narratio*, despite his awareness that it is rarely required in epideictic rhetoric). Neither Jewett nor the other rhetorical critics he cites question the appropriateness of *narratio* in epideictic rhetoric or even consider the possibility that there is no *narratio*, because they are following the forensic τάξις. Nor does this overwhelmingly large *narratio* section suggest to him that the argument is thus not epideictic, because there is no interplay between the genre classification and the investigation of the τάξις. There is also no attention given to the different structure and function of "proofs" in epideictic, demonstrative rhetoric, than in forensic discourse (see next note). I would also dispute Jewett's collapsing of epistolary formulae and rhetorical parts (he subsumes the epistolary salutation and thanksgiving formulae under the rhetorical category *exordium* without discussion, 72). This criticism may also be directed to Lyons's analysis of 1 Thess as epideictic: "The fact that thanksgiving, which dominates the first three chapters of the letter, is a definitely epideictic form would seem to tip the scale in the latter direction" (p. 220). But thanksgiving in the Pauline letter is first and foremost an *epistolary* form – not a distinctly epideictic rhetorical form.

[34] Arist. *Rh.* 3.13.3 (cf. *Rhet.Her.* 3.7.13). Even where διήγησις is used in epideictic speeches, according to Aristotle, it should not be consecutive, but disjointed (κατὰ μέρος) (*Rh.* 3.16.1). An analysis of the variety of theoretical statements and actual speeches reveals that the τάξις of epideictic rhetoric is of necessity quite different from that of forensic rhetoric, especially in regard to both *narratio* and *probatio* (Aristotle also says it needs no ἐπίλογος; *Rh.* 3.13.3). This is quite simply because, as Cicero stated: "it does not establish propositions that are doubtful but amplifies statements that are certain" (*Part.Or.* 21.71; cf. Arist. *Rh.* 3.17.3; Martin, 219; Russell-Wilson, 272). Because of this, epideictic argumentation is not singular only because it requires no *narratio* but because the *narratio* and *probatio* collapse into one because they perform the same function – the proof *is* the narration of praiseworthy characteristics and deeds of the subject (see Cic. *Part.Or.* 21.71; cf. Quint. *Inst.* 3.7.4; 4.2.78–79). This is confirmed by T. C. Burgess's standard work on epideictic discourse, which summarized the theoreticians Theon, Menander and Aphthonius on the composition of epideictic arguments as containing the following κεφάλαια or heads: προοίμιον, γένος, γένεσις, ἀνατροφή, ἐπιτηδεύματα, πράξεις, σύγκρισις and ἐπίλογος (*Epideictic Literature*, Ph.D. diss. University of Chicago [Chicago: University of Chicago, 1902], esp. 120–26). Thus the compositional principle in epideictic argument is not so much sectional, like the forensic (i. e., *narratio*, then *probatio*) as chronological and logical, when one praises a person's life (so also *Rh.Al.* 35; *Rhet.Her.* 3.7.13–14; Cic. *Part.Or.* 22; Men. Rh. 2.368–377 [=Russell-Wilson, 76–95, and their discussion on xxii-xxxi], and throughout Treatise II; Hermogenes, *Prog.* 7 [*Hermogenis opera*, ed. H. Rabe, Rhetores Graeci vol. VI, BT (Leipzig: Teubner, 1894) 14–18]; Volkmann, 324; this is so even for praise of gods – see Quint. *Inst.* 3.7.7–8; Alex. *Rh.* 3.4–6 Spengel). But this conclusion must be confirmed by actual speeches, where this is quite clearly the case (see Pl. *Menex.*, esp. 237A; Lys. 2; Dem. *Or.* 60; Thuc. 2.34–46; see also Burgess's rhetorical analysis of Isoc. *Or.* 9 on p. 126 n. 4). For the Greco-Roman period, see Aristid. *Or.* 26, and the compositional analysis by J.H. Oliver, "The Ruling Power," *TAPA* 43 (1953) 871–1003, 878–79 (cf. Quint. *Inst.* 3.7.26).

renders rhetorical criticism a quest for the "divisions" of a text as specified in a frozen model, without attention to the varied requirements of genre, content and rhetorical situation.[35] Throughout this work, deliberative speeches[36] and letters from the Greco-Roman world[37] are analyzed alongside the handbooks to try to achieve a balanced and realistic reconstruction of the characteristics and possibilities of the genre for comparison with Paul's 1 Corinthians.

3. The designation of the rhetorical genre or species of a New Testament text as epideictic, deliberative or forensic[38] cannot be begged in the analysis. It must be demonstrated and supported before the compositional or structural analysis proceeds.[39] Often, when the rhetorical species is designated in rhetorical analy-

---

This is not the place for a thorough examination of the epideictic τάξις, but this brief analysis is intended as an illustration of the point that it is different from the forensic τάξις prescribed in the handbooks, a compilation of which is normally employed by rhetorical critics on all texts. A full understanding of each of the rhetorical species in itself, from a wide variety of primary and secondary sources, is mandatory for rhetorical analysis.

[35] Such criticism of a mechanistic understanding of rhetoric is at least as old as Aristotle, who composed his *Rhetorica* to downplay the μόρια λόγου as much as possible (Solmsen, "Aristotelian Tradition," 37–39); see also Isoc. *Or.* 13.12: "But I marvel when I observe these men setting themselves up as instructors of youth who cannot see that they are applying the analogy of an art with hard and fast rules [τεταγμένη τέχνη] to a creative process."

[36] Deliberative speeches embedded in the historical works of Thucydides, Polybius, Dionysius of Halicarnassus, Josephus, Appian and Cassius Dio are also an important source which will be employed in this investigation (see the defense of this in chap. II, "Excursus: Ancient Deliberative Speeches and Letters").

[37] Also, as much as possible on each point, I shall present evidence for the rhetorical tradition from the classical period down into the Imperial period to demonstrate that such practices and conventions were operative in the time of Paul.

[38] These three categories are found in Aristotle's *Rhetorica* (1.3.3) and throughout the rhetorical tradition (*Rhet.Her.* 1.2.2; Dion. Hal. *Lys.* 16; Cic. *Inv.Rhet.* 1.5.7; *Top.* 23.91; Quint. *Inst.* 2.21.23; 3.3–4; Aristid. *Rh.* 2.502 Spengel; cf. *Rh.Al.* 1.1421a where the three categories are subdivided into seven sub-species). All three categories have at times been applied to 1 Corinthians or parts of it: epideictic (of all of 1 Corinthians: Wuellner, "Greek Rhetoric" and "Rhetorical Criticism"); forensic (of 1 Cor 1–4: N. A. Dahl, "Paul and the Church at Corinth according to 1 Cor 1:10–4:21," in *Christian History and Interpretation: Studies Presented to John Knox*, ed. W. R. Farmer, C. F. D. Moule and R. R. Niebuhr [Cambridge: University Press, 1967] 313–35, reprinted in his *Studies on Paul* [Minneapolis: Augsburg, 1977] 40–61; Plank; of 1 Cor 1–4 and 15: Bünker); and deliberative (of all of 1 Corinthians: Kennedy, *New Testament Interpretation*, 87; Fiorenza; of 1 Cor 1–4: L. L. Welborn, "On the Discord in Corinth. 1 Corinthians 1–4 and Ancient Politics," *JBL* 106 [1987] 83–113, 89; *idem*, "A Conciliatory Principle in 1 Cor 4:6," *NovT* 29 [1987] 320–46, 334–40; of 10:23–11:1 (8:1–11:1): D. F. Watson, "1 Corinthians 10:23–11:1 in the Light of Greco-Roman Rhetoric: The Role of Rhetorical Questions," *JBL* 108 [1989] 301–18, 302).

[39] Here I differ from Betz (in *2 Corinthians 8 and 9* the Literary Genre and Function are treated after the Literary Analysis, as in the *Galatians* commentary). To some degree this represents a difference not so much in the research methodology (where both are of course mutually interdependent) but in the structure of the scholarly argument which reports the results of that research. Making a complete demonstration of the classification of the species of rhetoric employed in a text before the full literary analysis will assist us to minimize the circularity at work in any literary-critical analysis (see Lyons, 115–18). Lyons is correct that the structure of a

sis, it is never proven,[40] or that designation hangs upon single handbook references or singular elements in the text itself.[41] But to demonstrate that any rhetorical categories,[42] and in particular the rhetorical species assigned to a given text,[43] are relevant and useful for an interpretation of a given text is perhaps the heaviest burden of proof upon one employing rhetorical criticism with New Testament texts.

In the present work, two chapters will precede the compositional analysis which will demonstrate why the whole of 1 Corinthians should rightly be

rhetorical text cannot *alone* allow us to determine the rhetorical species (26–27), but because the three species do *not* have the same arrangement, the genre designation must precede the compositional analysis so that the arrangement can be investigated to see if it is appropriate to that species (see above n. 33 for a critique of Jewett on this point). The two investigations must go hand in hand. Lyons makes his determinations of rhetorical species at the end of his exegesis: Gal as deliberative (174–75) and 1 Thess as epideictic (220–21).

[40] Kennedy includes the designation of rhetorical species in his methodology prior to arrangement (*New Testament Interpretation*, 36–37), yet in his rhetorical analyses the classifications are made in a perfunctory way (see, e. g., pp. 87 and 142 on 1 Cor and 1 Thess as deliberative rhetoric, which is correct, but unsubstantiated). Bünker works from a presupposition that 1 Cor 1–4 and 15 are forensic, and provides his structural analyses – based only on forensic models – as proof (despite the fact that he sees 1:18–2:16 as deliberative, and difficult to fit into his scheme, p. 59).

[41] For example, Jewett's support of his designation of 1 Thessalonians as epideictic rhetoric is hardly more than one page. Even the supporting arguments given are not conclusive. He determines that 1 Thessalonians is epideictic because it "concentrates on praise and blame" (71–72, according to Lausberg and Kennedy; the same argument is used by Wuellner on 1 Corinthians, "Rhetorical Criticism," 62–63). However, praise and blame are topics which may be employed in all three rhetorical species, as the handbooks recognize (Arist. *Rh.* 3.16.11; *Rhet.Her.* 3.8.15; Quint. *Inst.* 3.4.11, citing Isocrates; 3.7.2–3; Volkmann, 315; see also chap. IV below). One should not substantiate a genre designation by individual details (in this case the epistolary thanksgiving period/s) – it must correspond with a holistic reading of the text (see the reminder by J. L. White, *Light From Ancient Letters* [Philadelphia: Fortress, 1986] 198). In this case it is hard to see how praise and blame characterize the whole of 1 Thessalonians. Jewett's brief genre designation of 1 Thessalonians does not grapple with two serious objections: 1) epideictic rhetoric is concerned primarily with the present (Arist. *Rh.* 1.3.4, though with exceptions; Alex. *Rh.* 3.1.9–20 Spengel; Cic. *Part.Or.* 20.69), while no one would quarrel with the fact that the chronological emphasis of 1 Thessalonians is future; and 2) epideictic, show rhetoric (*genus demonstrativum*) is for the purpose of the entertainment of the audience (Cic. *Part.Or.* 21.72; Quint. *Inst.* 3.7.3; 3.8.63–64), which seems rather unlike Paul's task in 1 Thessalonians.

[42] A difficulty with Kennedy's *New Testament Interpretation* is that he attempts to push almost all NT texts into some rhetorical category, assuming more than proving that such categories are relevant to them all.

[43] Arguments for a single rhetorical species for all of Paul's letters do not hold (F. F. Church, "Rhetorical Structure and Design in Paul's Letter to Philemon," *HTR* 71 [1978] 17–33, 19; Plank, 12–13). Each letter or letter fragment must be examined on its own terms (see the comment by Aune, Review of Betz, *Galatians*, 326, though I would not characterize the three rhetorical species as three rhetorical "traditions," as he does, but rather as equally parts of one rhetorical tradition; see, e.g, the later comment by Doxopater, *Homil. in Aphth.* 146.26=H. Rabe, ed., *Prolegomenon Sylloge*, BT [Leipzig: Teubner, 1935], cited by page and line).

considered to be deliberative rhetoric,[44] on the basis of several different lines of argument, dealing comprehensively with form, function and content. Specific to this concern, in chapter II deliberative rhetoric as a genre in antiquity will be investigated and defined on the basis of the handbooks and extant speeches and letters. If we go right to the heart of deliberative rhetoric, identify its constitutive features, and demonstrate that 1 Corinthians has all those features, then we have some basis to proceed, albeit still cautiously, with an investigation of 1 Corinthians as deliberative rhetoric.

4. One of the tenets of all literary criticism, including the historical-critical variety, is that form and content are intertwined and must be investigated interdependently.[45] This also conforms with the emphasis in ancient rhetorical handbooks and works of literary criticism on τὸ πρέπον (Latin *decorum*), "what is appropriate."[46] Each of the species of rhetoric deals with particular issues,

---

[44] Of those who have previously identified 1 Corinthians (correctly) as deliberative rhetoric, none has provided a thorough-going proof. Kennedy (*New Testament Interpretation*, 87; followed by Fiorenza, 393) merely remarked in passing that 1 Corinthians is "largely deliberative," without supporting evidence. Fiorenza adds to her case by dismantling the arguments of Wuellner and Bünker for epideictic and forensic genres (390–93), but devotes less than one page to her constructive argument for 1 Corinthians as deliberative (393). Welborn has argued that 1 Cor 1–4 is deliberative rhetoric with supporting evidence from handbooks and actual speeches ("Conciliatory Principle," 334–40) but he quickly moves on to an application of that premise to his subject, the tricky verse 4:6. This work and his "Discord" make important points about 1 Cor 1–4 as deliberative rhetoric with which this study concurs, especially their pointing to other discourses on concord as relevant to 1 Cor (see discussion in chap. II), but they are hampered by the limitation of the rhetorical unit to 1 Cor 1–4, based upon possible partition of the letter, so that the function of those chapters in the larger argument of which they are a part is not fully understood (see below). See also the brief notices of Stowers, 96–97; 108–109 and Aune, *Literary Environment*, 203, identifying 1 Corinthians as a mixed letter combining paraenesis and deliberative rhetoric. Here, too, the shape of the argumentative whole is not sufficiently considered so that parts of the letter are assigned different genres (see also the discussion in chap. II). Kennedy, although seeing 1 Cor as "largely deliberative," considers it to contain "some judicial passages," such as 1:13–17 and ch. 9 (*New Testament Interpretation*, 87), but again, individual passages within a larger work do not have their own *discrete* genre. They must be seen in their relation to the rhetorical whole (see below).

[45] See the statement of the principle by Bünker, 15 (cf. Strobel, 11, on 1 Cor specifically), who also notes the important and parallel concern of the relation of rhetorical and epistolary forms (see H. Hübner, "Der Galaterbrief und das Verhältnis von antiker Rhetorik und Epistolographie," *TLZ* 109 [1984] 242–50). This question will be addressed in the discussion in chap. II of deliberative rhetoric within the epistolary form.

[46] That style should be appropriate to subject matter and genre is the cardinal rule of ancient literary criticism (see Isoc. *Or.* 13.12–13; Arist. *Rh.* 3.2.1; 3.7; Dion. Hal. *Comp.* 20; *Lys.* 9; Demetr. *Eloc.* 2.120; Cic. *Orat.* 21.70; D.L. 7.59; J. F. D'Alton, *Roman Literary Theory and Criticism* [London/New York/Toronto: Longmans, Green, 1931] 104–40; and J. W. H. Atkins, *Literary Criticism in Antiquity* [Gloucester, MA: Peter Smith, 1961] 2.31 and passim). Rhetorical handbooks also extend the principle to the relation of content and rhetorical species (see Arist. *Rh.* 1.4–5; *Rh.Al.* 1.1421b; Cic. *Inv.Rhet.* 2.51.155; Quint. *Inst.* 3.8.51; in ancient criticism in general, see D'Alton, 398–99 and passim). This is rooted in the different issues or ends with which each rhetorical genre is appropriately concerned (Cic. *Inv.Rhet.* 2.4.12–13; see the

questions or ends, and there are material topics appropriate to each.[47] In designating a New Testament text as epideictic, deliberative or forensic rhetoric, the question of whether that rhetorical species is appropriate to the subject matter or issue in the text too often goes completely unaddressed.[48] This criticism, that scholars have not seriously reckoned with the burden of proof that lies upon them in making a rhetorical genre designation to demonstrate that the form and content are indeed compatible, is part and parcel of the second mandate above. If scholars use extant speeches and letters as part of their data base for the ancient rhetorical tradition, then they can determine if indeed such a rhetorical form (epideictic rhetoric, for instance) is used with the same (or similar) content as the New Testament text being investigated.[49] To the extent that such ancient examples are not found, the rhetorical genre designation hangs only upon various interpretations of often single, ambiguous sentences in the handbooks which might conceivably allow for such a composition, but never demonstrate the actuality or even probability of such a literary creation in antiquity.[50]

---

discussion below in chap. II). In addition, ancient theorists required that the subject matter be appropriate to the epistolary genre (Demetr. *Eloc.* 4.230–31).

[47] See Baldwin, 14–17 (in regard to Arist. *Rh.*).

[48] For example, in Jewett's analysis of 1 Thessalonians as epideictic rhetoric, it is never asked if apocalyptic material (1:10; ch. 4 and 5) is indeed compatible with the form of epideictic rhetoric (*Thessalonian Correspondence*, 71–78). This is grounded in the lack of a discussion of what the issue of the (epideictic) argument in 1 Thessalonians is, so the connection or appropriateness of the apocalyptic material to this issue is never demonstrated (so also Lyons, 219–21). For other examples of lack of attention to content, see Wuellner on 1 Corinthians as epideictic rhetoric, where the very specific behavioral issues which call forth a response from the Corinthians are incompatible with display rhetoric ("Greek Rhetoric" and "Rhetorical Criticism," 460); and Bünker on Paul's discussion of the resurrection of Jesus and believers in 1 Cor 15 as forensic rhetoric (59–72). Examples abound in Kennedy's book, for example, Acts 4:24–30 as "a deliberative prayer" (*New Testament Interpretation*, 120), Acts 10:34–43 as epideictic (123), the prophetic oracle in Acts 27:21–26 as epideictic (138); Romans as epideictic despite the paraenesis in ch. 12–15 (154). Rhetorical criticism is not an appropriate methodology for use on all texts (it is simply not relevant, e. g., for study of the genre gospel). Two recent articles have given some attention to this issue (Smit, 23 notes correctly that the handbooks allow for religious subjects to be treated in deliberative rhetoric, though he cites no actual texts; see also D. Zweck, "The *Exordium* of the Areopagus Speech, Acts 17.22, 23," *NTS* 35 [1989] 94–103; 98–100, with some parallel texts).

[49] To demonstrate conclusively that 1 Thessalonians is epideictic rhetoric, it is incumbent upon Jewett to produce ancient epideictic texts which deal with apocalyptic (or similar) material, or at least to justify why the form could be adapted by Paul to treat such a subject. See the similar argument against Malherbe's proposal that 1 Thess is a paraenetic letter by H. Koester, "I Thessalonians – Experiment in Christian Writing," in *Continuity and Discontinuity in Church History. Essays Presented to George Huntston Williams on His 65th Birthday*, ed. F. F. Church and T. George (Leiden: Brill, 1979) 33–44: "but no analogies exist in letters of any kind for the eschatological admonitions which are found in I Thess 4:13–5:11" (39), to which Malherbe has made an apt response ("Exhortation in First Thessalonians," *NovT* 25 [1983] 238–56, 254–56).

[50] This is not to surrender to a completely mechanical understanding of genre. Surely each literary creation is a unique combination of generic traits and authorial adaptations (see Betz,

In this work the question of the relationship between form and content is taken very seriously. Chapter III provides a detailed comparison of 1 Corinthians with ancient political literature to demonstrate that 1 Corinthians is throughout filled with terms and *topoi* derived from politics which are directly related to the issue of factionalism. This provides a second line of proof for why 1 Corinthians is indeed deliberative (=political) rhetoric on the basis of its favorable comparison with other ancient deliberative texts. The content of 1 Corinthians, a series of arguments ultimately rooted by Paul in the subject of factionalism, is appropriate for deliberative rhetoric, as the handbooks state and extant speeches and letters confirm. These two steps, demonstrating that 1 Corinthians shares the essential characteristics of deliberative rhetoric (ch. II), and that its content, a series of arguments which all turn on the appeal for the cessation of community division, is appropriate to and commonly found in deliberative discourse (ch. III), are essential prerequisites to the compositional analysis and exegesis of 1 Corinthians as a unified deliberative letter (ch. IV).

5. The rhetorical unit to be examined should be a compositional unit, which can be further substantiated by successful rhetorical analysis. A preliminary definition of the limits of the literary unit is of course a first step in form criticism, and indeed all literary criticism.[51] In the case of 1 Corinthians, rhetori-

2 Corinthians 8 and 9, 129–31), but if one ventures into genre analysis, one must demonstrate: 1) that the genre did exist and had certain definable characteristics (in ancient terms the *lex operis*); and 2) that the text in question shares them. On this perennial methodological question, see the valuable comments by Aune, Review of Betz, *Galatians*, 323–24. On the first step, we might qualify further that the genre must be at least so specifically defined that it is indeed descriptive of a particular class. Lührmann's designation of 1 Corinthians as a *Freundschaftsbrief* (p. 304) proceeds from so general a description of that genre that all Pauline letters except Galatians fit it (and probably many other ancient letters, though he does not give any non-NT parallels). Lührmann lists as the formulaic characteristics of the *Freundschaftsbrief* the epistolary prescript and thanksgiving, παρακαλῶ formulae, greetings and blessing, but it is not clear that he has established a specific genre *Freundschaftsbrief* so much as a list of universal epistolary formulae and topics which may be employed in a wide variety of ancient letters. Although Lührmann criticizes Bünker for seeing only the *Topoi* of the *Freundschaftsbrief* and missing the significance of these "*Gattungsmerkmale*" (p. 304 n. 31), Bünker's understanding is more correct (note that he deals with friendship *topoi* which are far more specific than the epistolary formulae identified by Lührmann; Bünker follows K. Thraede, *Grundzüge griechisch-römischer Brieftopik*, Zetemata 48 [Munich: Beck, 1970]; cf. H. Koskenniemi, *Studien zur Idee und Phraseologie des griechischen Briefes bis 400 n. Chr.*, Suomalaisen Tiedeakatemian Toimituksia, Annales Academiae Scientiarum Fennicae 102, 2 [Helsinki: Suomalainen Tiedeakatemia, 1956] 60–61). Even leaving aside the debate about distinct ancient epistolary genres (see n. 5 in chap. II), we must note against Lührmann that there is nothing peculiar to the *Freundschaftsbrief* about an epistolary saluation, thanksgiving or final greeting. These are constitutive of the letter genre and provide no indication in themselves of a sub-genre. The same is true, in the Pauline letter, of the greeting formula. On παρακαλῶ in deliberative rhetoric, see n. 114 in chap. III.

[51] E.g., O. Kaiser and W. G. Kümmel, *Exegetical Method*, trans. E. V. N. Goetschius and M. J. O'Connell (New York: Seabury, 1975) 57. Kennedy includes this as the first step in his rhetorical critical methodology (*New Testament Interpretation*, 33), yet he does not provide clear guidelines for that definition, nor does he see the important historical implications here (as

cal analyses which render conclusions about the argumentative structure and rhetorical genre of selected portions of the extant letter are inadequate to the extent that they do not demonstrate why that portion is to be regarded as an independent literary unit with its own genre and structure.[52] The rhetorical genre and function of each part is determined by the compositional whole[53] and cannot be correctly determined apart from it.[54] The contribution which a rhetorical analysis can and must make to investigations of literary composition

---

pointed out by H. D. Betz in his review, *JTS* n. s. 37 [1986] 167). While one can establish arbitrary limits on any text (such as Kennedy's suggestion that "five or six verses" be the minimum), or admit that a text exists in more than one present context (i. e., the *corpus Paulinum*, the New Testament canon; so Wuellner, "Rhetorical Criticism," 455), the original compositional boundaries of a text are of primary importance for an historical rhetorical investigation.

[52] For example, Bünker (48–76) provides rhetorical analyses of 1 Cor 1–4 and 1 Cor 15, each portion containing its own rhetorical genre and argumentative arrangement (*exordium, narratio, peroratio*, etc.). He does not justify why these sections should be regarded as self-contained rhetorical units (curiously, even his unspecific adoption of a partition theory, p. 52, does not substantiate these particular separations). How can 1 Cor 15:1–2 be an *exordium* (Bünker, 62–62) when it occurs in the middle of a larger compositional whole? Even Lührmann's suggestion against Bünker that 1 Cor 9 would have offered a better text for rhetorical analysis (as is done by Pesch, 224–29), would violate this principle (309 n. 51). The work of B. Standaert, despite many good observations, also suffers from this fault ("Analyse rhétorique des chapitres 12 à 14" and "1 Corinthiens 13" in *Charisma und Agape (1 Kor 12–14)*, ed. L. de Lorenzi [Rome, 1983] 23–50; 127–47; "La Rhétorique Ancienne dans Saint Paul" in *L'Apôtre Paul: Personnalité, style et conception du ministère*, ed. A. Vanhoye, BETL 73 [1986] 78–92; esp. 79–82, for example, where he considers 1 Cor 12:1–11 to be *propositio* and *exordium*). Subsections of a larger argument ("proofs") cannot be expected to be composed themselves of the same "parts" as a rhetorical whole, such as an *exordium* (as even the handbooks specify; see, e. g., *Rhet.Her.* 2.18; 3.11.16–17; Quint. *Inst.* 4.1.73–75; and the discussion in ch. IV). Welborn ("Conciliatory Principle," 333–34), in his rhetorical analysis of 1 Cor 1–4 takes up the issue of the place of ch. 1–4 in the composition of 1 Corinthians, but resists a definitive choice, maintaining instead that ch. 1–4 is a rhetorical unit on the basis of the παρακαλῶ periods in 1:10 and 4:16 (of course on those grounds one could substantiate the rhetorical unity of all of 1 Corinthians, as the phrase is repeated in 16:15). But one cannot avoid the compositional issue, because the rhetorical species and arrangement of 1 Cor 1–4 are dependent upon the rhetorical species and arrangement of the literary whole–whatever that is (he intimates that 5:1–6:11 may be part of the same letter, for example [p. 333], but does not include that section in his rhetorical analysis). The same critique must be brought against J. T. Fitzgerald, *Cracks in an Earthen Vessel: An Examination of the Catalogues of Hardships in the Corinthian Correspondence*, SBLDS 99 (Atlanta: Scholars Press, 1988) 117, 128 (an otherwise admirable study), who classes 1 Cor 1:10–4:21 as "a letter of admonition" even while apparently holding to the unity of all of 1 Cor. Part of a letter cannot be generically identified as a sole letter type. Nor does a part have its own rhetorical species which can be determined in isolation from the whole (against Watson, "1 Cor 10:23–11:1").

[53] Which need not be identical with the canonical text (contra Kennedy, *New Testament Interpretation*, 4) and is not necessarily the largest portion of text. By the "compositional whole" I mean the original text as it was created.

[54] This principle is admirably recognized by Dahl in his analysis of 1 Cor 1–4, but I disagree with his results (he takes 1–4 to be an apologetic section which re-establishes Paul's apostolic authority as a necessary prelude to his response to their questions). I do not regard 1 Cor 1–4 as apologetic (see chaps. II and IV).

has been demonstrated by Betz in regard to 2 Corinthians.[55] The present study, in demonstrating that 1 Corinthians as it presently stands is a cohesive deliberative argument, defends the compositional integrity of the letter.

The constructive thesis here presented on the basis of an historical rhetorical analysis, that 1 Corinthians is a unified letter which throughout urges the course of unity on the divided Corinthian church, is a return to the understanding and appreciation of 1 Corinthians held by its earliest readers. *1 Clement* 47.1–3, probably the first reference to 1 Corinthians recorded,[56] says of it: Ἀναλάβετε τὴν ἐπιστολὴν τοῦ μακαρίου Παύλου τοῦ ἀποστόλου. τί πρῶτον ὑμῖν ἐν ἀρχῇ τοῦ εὐαγγελίου ἔγραψεν; ἐπ' ἀληθείας πνευματικῶς ἐπέστειλεν ὑμῖν περὶ ἑαυτοῦ τε καὶ Κηφᾶ τε καὶ Ἀπολλώ, διὰ τὸ καὶ τότε προσκλίσεις ὑμᾶς πεποιῆσθαι. This author knows only one letter (47.1), and surely knows all of 1 Corinthians as he cites it richly and thoroughly.[57] Most importantly, to argue against a later generation of Corinthian factionalists he employs the terms and *topoi* for unity from throughout 1 Corinthians appropriately in his own appeal for cessation of factions, showing how well he understood and appreciated his precursor's argument.[58]

---

[55] By showing that ch. 8 and 9 each have their own rhetorical genre, function and structure, Betz added further substantiation to a five-letter partition theory of 2 Corinthians (*2 Corinthians 8 and 9*, esp. pp. 35–36 on the methodology; see also *Der Apostel Paulus* on 2 Cor 10–13). Rhetorical analysis can also be used to demonstrate the unity of a given text (see D. F. Watson, "A Rhetorical Analysis of Philippians and its Implications for the Unity Question," *NovT* 30 [1988] 57–88, and *idem*, *Invention*, 151–55 on the methodology). The methodology can thus be used to test any hypothesis (unity or partition) of literary boundaries. An argument against the partition theories of 1 Corinthians is that, unlike 2 Corinthians, they do not result in letters which can be understood as rhetorically coherent compositional wholes (but an attempt to analyze the fragments rhetorically should be made in order to test this [see the in my view unsuccessful attempt in a more popular work by Pesch, 73–100, who regards most of the letter fragments as apologetic, which will be discussed in the course of this investigation]).

[56] For possible references to 1 Cor in late NT writings, in the apostolic fathers and early Christian literature, see Bachmann, 19–20 (also 21–25 on writers up to the 5th century).

[57] See Goguel, 141 n. 3.

[58] See W. Jaeger's description of *1 Clement* as the "critical moment [when] the ideals of the political philosophy of the ancient Greek city-state entered the discussion of the new Christian type of human community, now called the church, but in Greek *ekklesia*" (*Early Christianity and Greek Paideia* [Cambridge, MA: Harvard University Press, 1961] 15). That *1 Clement* incorporates political *topoi* was also well appreciated by W. C. van Unnik in his analysis of that letter as a deliberative letter urging concord ("Studies over de zogenaamde eerste brief van Clemens. I. Het Litteraire Genre," *Mededelingen der koninklijke Nederlandse akademie van wetenschappen, afd. letterkunde* 33 [1970] 149–204). Van Unnik's thesis on *1 Clement* has recently been revived in the study by B. E. Bowe (*A Church in Crisis. Ecclesiology and Paraenesis in Clement of Rome*, HDR 23 [Minneapolis, MN: Fortress, 1988], a book which came to my attention after the completion of the present investigation, and with which I have many agreements). As much as these scholars are correct in their analysis of *1 Clement*, they are perhaps too quick to give the credit for the initial application of Greco-Roman political ideals to the Christian church to that author, instead of to Paul, whose 1 Cor perhaps provided both the impetus and the paradigm for that later work. In fact, much of what they say about *1 Clement* is directly applicable to 1 Cor, as we shall see.

The letters of Ignatius of Antioch, who surely knows 1 Corinthians, also apply political terms and *topoi* to situations of factionalism, often referring to 1 Corinthians in a manner fitting to the fractious circumstances which he faced.[59]

The Muratorian Canon regards 1 Corinthians as a letter which combats factionalism: *primum omnium corintheis schismae haereses interdicens.*[60] We shall see throughout this investigation that the early Greek commentators,[61] especially Origen[62] and John Chrysostom,[63] in their exegetical attention to Paul's argumentation,[64] and in particular in their comprehension of the *topoi* and terms

---

59 An important contribution of W. R. Schoedel's commentary (*Ignatius of Antioch. A Commentary on the Letters of Ignatius of Antioch*, Hermeneia [Philadelphia: Fortress, 1985]) is his insistence upon Ignatius' acquaintance with the ὁμόνοια-ideals of the Greek city state: "... the bishop builds on ideas of concord and unity drawn from Greek political thought, but he orients them to a conception of the church as a transcendent reality ... our passage [*Magn.* 7] is another indication that Gnostic parallels are not the decisive ones for our understanding of the theme" (116; see also 51–53). Given Ignatius' sure knowlege of 1 Cor (Schoedel, 9–10; see the list of plentiful citations of 1 Cor in the letters of Ignatius and the letter of Polycarp in Bornkamm, "Vorgeschichte," 188 n. 128; also Goguel, 141–42 and notes), it is most probable that 1 Corinthians provided the model for Ignatius of this kind of rhetorical application of the ideals of political concord to the Christian community.

60 "First of all to the Corinthians (to whom) he forbids the heresy of schism," E. Hennecke, *New Testament Apocrypha*, ed. W. Schneemelcher, trans. R. McL. Wilson (Philadelphia: Westminster, 1963) 1.44, lines 42–43. The Latin text is cited from T. Zahn, *Geschichte des neutestamentlichen Kanons* (Erlangen/Leipzig: Deichert, 1890) vol. 2, pt. 1, 6–7 (with emendation from p. 62). Zahn finds this designation tolerable for both epistles, but especially by reference to 1 Cor 1–4: "Die durch 1. Kor c. 1–4 zunächst veranlasste Angabe passt doch ziemlich gut auch auf den Gesamtinhalt beider Briefe" (p. 63). See also Tertullian, *Baptism*, 14: "But these words [1:17] were written to the Corinthians in regard of the circumstances of that particular time; seeing that schisms and dissensions were agitated among them [*quoniam schismata et dissensiones inter illos movebantur* ...]" [*PL* 1.1324]. Later in the same passage he refers to "the peace-making apostle" [*pacificus Apostolus*].

61 Collections of early exegesis on 1 Cor are cited from J. A. Cramer, *Catenae in Sancti Pauli Epistolas ad Corinthios* (Oxford: University Press, 1841) and K. Staab, *Pauluskommentare aus der griechischen Kirche*, NTAbh 15 (Münster: Aschendorff, 1933).

62 Fragments of a commentary by Origen (cited as *comm. in I Cor.*), found in the catenae, were published by C. Jenkins, "Origen on 1 Corinthians," *JTS* 9 (1907–08) 231–47; 353–72; 500–14; *JTS* 10 (1908–09) 29–51; supplemented by C. H. Turner, "Notes on the Text of Origen's Commentary on 1 Corinthians," *JTS* 10 (1908–09) 270–76.

63 Chrysostom's *hom. I-XLIV in I Cor.* will be cited from Migne, *PG* 61.9–382.

64 The historical rhetorical approach to the letters of Paul is justified in antiquity by the sections on ὑπόθεσις/*argumentum* in the ancient commentators (Chrys. and Theodoret in *PG* 61.9–12; 82.225–28 respectively; in the catenae in Cramer, B-B1), as, for example, in Chrysostom's contemporary and teacher Libanius' discussions of the speeches of Demosthenes, in which the argument line of each speech is briefly sketched (*Argumenta Orationum Demosthenicarum*, in *Libanius. Opera*, ed. R. Foerster, BT [Leipzig: Teubner, 1915; repr. Hildesheim: Olms, 1963] 8.600–81). On the history of these ὑπόθεσις sections, along with the κεφάλαια-lists and other parts in the catenae (the so-called "Euthalian matter"), see C. H. Turner, "Greek Patristic Commentaries on the Pauline Epistles," art. in *A Dictionary of the Bible*, ed. J. Hastings (New York: Scribner's, 1904), Extra Volume, 484–531, particularly 524–29 (on Cramer see 487).

Paul used to combat factionalism in 1 Corinthians, provide even more evidence for this interpretation from readers far closer to the text, the language and the social situation of Paul than we.[65]

In his *Orthodoxy and Heresy in Earliest Christianity* W. Bauer argued that the widespread popularity of 1 Corinthians in the early church was due precisely to the fact that it was so useful as a response to factionalism: "And from that time on [1 Clement], the purpose of 1 Corinthians was firmly established in the church: 'First of all to the Corinthians, censuring the heresies of schism.'"[66] However, Bauer discounted the possibility that 1 Corinthians could have had this meaning and function in its original setting, thus consonant with its later interpretation: "But it is really rather peculiar and in need of an explanation that this extensive and multifaceted epistle is supposed to have had only this purpose."[67] This is precisely what the present study will argue, in line with early exegesis and use: 1 Corinthians is in fact a unified and coherent appeal for unity and cessation of factionalism.

---

[65] This responds to Heinrici's demand (pp. iii–iv) that our interpretations seriously reckon with the ancient readers, whose mother-tongue and cultural situation brought them closer to the text than we are.

[66] W. Bauer, *Orthodoxy and Heresy in Earliest Christianity*, trans. Philadelphia Seminar on Christian Origins (Philadelphia: Fortress, 1971) 220, citing the Muratorian Canon.

[67] Ibid.

Chapter II

1 Corinthians as Deliberative Rhetoric

This chapter contains an examination of deliberative rhetoric, γένος συμβουλευτικόν,[1] in antiquity for the purposes of comparison with 1 Corinthians. Our task is to identify the constituent and characteristic elements of this rhetorical species on the basis of a thorough examination of the extant sources, and then to inquire if those elements are found in 1 Corinthians. We are fortunate to have two kinds of sources on deliberative rhetoric[2] preserved from Greco-Roman antiquity – prescriptive texts (the rhetorical handbooks)[3] and actual rhetorical works, both speeches and letters. It is of particular importance to this study of a text which is quite clearly a letter, 1 Corinthians, that deliberative rhetoric was commonly employed within epistolary frameworks in antiquity. Because deliberative rhetoric is compatible with the letter genre, Paul's use of it in 1 Corinthians is not anomalous in ancient literature, and is fully appropriate to both the epistolary and rhetorical elements which combine in this way.

---

[1] Or δημηγορικόν (*Rh.Al.* 1.1421 b). On the terminology, see Volkmann, 294; Martin, 167.

[2] On deliberative rhetoric in general, see the two approaches of J. Klek, who focuses particularly on actual texts (*Symbuleutici qui dicitur sermonis historia critica*, Rhetorische Studien 8 [Paderborn: Schöningh, 1919]), and I. Beck, who limits his attention to the handbooks and other theoretical statements ("Untersuchungen zur Theorie des Genos Symbuleutikon," Ph.D. diss. Hamburg, 1970; esp. 26–33 on his methodology). The best treatment, notable for its incorporation of both theory and actual texts, remains that of Volkmann, 294–314. See also H. L. Hudson-Williams, "Political Speeches in Athens," *CQ* n. s. 1 (1951) 68–73; Kennedy, *Persuasion in Greece*, 203–206; Lausberg, 123–29; Martin, 167–76.

[3] For the handbooks, see n. 25 in chap. I. The corpus of Cicero's rhetorical writings is far more extensive than his youthful work *de Inventione*. See also his *Topica*, *De Partitione Oratoria*, *De Optimo Genere Oratorum*, *Orator*, *De Oratore* and *Brutus*. Other theoretical works which will be drawn upon, in addition to the works cited in chap I, are: the rhetorical works of Hermogenes (a trans. of one treatise has been done by R. Nadeau, "On *Stases*: A Translation with an Introduction and Notes," *SM* 31 [1964] 361–424); [Longinus], *On the Sublime*; [Demetrius], *On Style*.

Also relevant theoretical works are the epistolary handbooks Ps-Demetrius, Τύποι ἐπιστολικοί, and Ps-Libanius, ἐπιστολιμαῖοι χαρακτῆρες (V. Weichert, ed. *Demetrii et Libanii qui feruntur* ΤΥΠΟΙ ΕΠΙΣΤΟΛΙΚΟΙ *et* ΕΠΙΣΤΟΛΙΜΑΙΟΙ ΧΑΡΑΚΤΗΡΕΣ, BT [Leipzig: Teubner, 1910]; trans. A. J. Malherbe, *Ancient Epistolary Theorists*, SBLSBS 19 [Atlanta: Scholars Press, 1988]; on these see also Koskenniemi, 54–63; Thraede, 17–27 and the discussion in n. 5 below).

Excursus: Ancient Deliberative Speeches and Letters[4]

Deliberative speeches from the orators which have been consulted for this investigation are: Andoc. 3; Isoc. *Or.* 4–8, 14; Dem. *Or.* 1–5, 7–10, 14–17 (F. Blass lists 1–18 as Φιλιππικοί and συμβουλευτικοί [*Die attische Beredsamkeit* (Hildesheim: Olms, 1962³) vol. 3, pt. 1.49–65]; cf. Dion Hal. *Amm.* 1.10 and Lib. *Arg.D.* 1.20–21 [Foerster, 606–607] on Demosthenes' speeches); Lys. 34 (the one extant, which is incomplete; there were more, see Dion. Hal. *Lys.* 1, 3, 16; this is the example he uses of Lysias' συμβουλευτικοί in the critical essay, § 31–34); Thrasym., Περὶ πολιτείας (= Diels, *Vorsokr.* 2.321–24; Dion. Hal. calls this a δημηγορικὸς λόγος [*Dem.* 3]); Herodes Atticus, Περὶ πολιτείας (text [ΗΡΩΔΟΥ] ΠΕΡΙ ΠΟΛΙΤΕΙΑΣ. *Ein politisches Pamphlet aus Athen 404 vor Chr.*, ed. E. Drerup, *Stud. Gesch. Kult. Alt.* vol. 2, pt. 1 [Paderborn: Schöningh, 1908]; on which see Beck 334–41); Dio Chrys. *Or.* 31, 34, 38–41 (although 39 is more epideictic, as we shall see in chap. IV), 48; Aristid. *Or.* 23–24 (text *Aelii Aristidis Smyrnaei quae supersunt omnia*, ed. B. Keil [Berlin: Weidmann, 1898; repr. 1958], vol. II; trans. C. A. Behr, *P. Aelius Aristides. The Complete Works*, vol. II [Leiden: Brill, 1981]). This list (in regard to the Attic Orators) compares favorably with Kennedy, *Persuasion in Greece*, 203–36. In addition, Demosthenes' *Exordia* are mostly deliberative. A fragment of a deliberative speech has been found among the Hibeh papyri (*PHib.* I.15; see the discussion of it by J. A. Goldstein, *The Letters of Demosthenes* [New York: Columbia University Press, 1968] 62, 92, 115). There are also ancient declamations, such as the elder Seneca's *Suasoriae*, in which famous deliberations are recreated (see in general D. A. Russell, *Greek Declamation* [Cambridge: Cambridge University Press, 1983]; on their connection to deliberative rhetoric, see Volkmann, 304–307; 312–14; and Klek, 157–62).

Deliberative speeches embedded in historical works have been recognized by scholars to be an important source for this rhetorical species (Klek 128–54; C. Wooten, "The Speeches in Polybius. An Insight into the Nature of Hellenistic Oratory," *AJP* 95 [1974] 235–51; this was noted already in antiquity – see Dion. Hal. *Lys.* 3; *Thuc.* 2; Quint. *Inst.* 3.8.67). See, for example, Volkmann's comment: "Derartige Reden finden sich nun zahlreich bei den alten Historikern von Thucydides an, und sie sind, wie man bald sieht, nach denselben Kunstregeln gearbeitet, welche für die Anfertigung wirklicher Suasorien in Geltung waren" (312). For such deliberative speeches see, for example: Thuc. 1.86; 2.60–64; 4.17–20; 4.59–64; 6.9–14; 6.82–87; Polyb. 5.58; 5.104; 18.36–37; 21.10; 22.8; 23.11; 23.17; 24.8; 24.12–13; 28.7; Dion. Hal. *Ant.Rom.* 3.7; 3.23; 4.21; 4.23; 5.6; 5.64–65; 5.66–68; 6.19; 6.35–41; 6.43–44; 6.49–56; 6.83; 7.22–24; 7.40–46; 7.48; 8.8; 10.51; 11.7–14; 11.19–20; Joseph. *BJ* 2.345–401; 4.162–92; 4.238–269; 5.362–419; 6.99–110; App. *BCiv.* 4.12.90–100; Cass. Dio 52.1–41 (for commentary on these two speeches as *suasoriae* see M. Reinhold, *From Republic to Principate. An Historical Commentary on Cassius Dio's* Roman History *Books 49–52 (36–29 B.C.)*, American Philological Association Monograph Series 34 [Atlanta: Scholars Press, 1988] 165–210); 56.2–9. See also H. L. Hudson-Williams, "Thucydides, Isocrates, and the Rhetorical Method of Composition," *CQ* 42 (1948) 76–81; and D. R. Runnals, "Hebrew and Greek Sources in the Speeches of

---

[4] Note that the authenticity of several of the speeches and letters named here has been questioned. That does not, however, affect our formal analysis of them. In this work, authors will be named as the person to whom the work is attributed for the sake of clarity without any predisposition to authenticity.

Josephus' Jewish War," Ph.D. diss. University of Toronto, 1971, who gives rhetorical analyses of these six deliberative speeches in the *Bellum*. The present study focuses upon Greek deliberative speeches, but see also Cic. *Leg.Man.* (cf. *Att.* 12.40 for his other attempts at συμβουλευτικά), and the speeches in Livy and Tacitus cited by Klek (135–37).

Ancient Greek letters which I consider to be deliberative[5] are: Isocrates, *Ep.* 1–3, 6, 8–9; Dem. *Ep.* 1 (Περὶ τῆς ὁμονοίας, "On Concord," an especially important text for this inquiry) and 3 (Goldstein, 97–181 argues that these are deliberative, along with *Ep.* 2 and 4); Ps-Aeschin. *Ep.* 11; Pl. *Ep.* 5–8 (cf. Dion. Hal. *Dem.* 23); Ps-Arist., Ἐπιστολαὶ πρὸς Ἀλέξανδρον (*Aristotelis privatorum scriptorum fragmenta*, ed. M. Plezia, BT [Leipzig: Teubner, 1977] 16–18); Socr. *Ep.* 27 (Aristippus to Arete) and 30 (Speusippus to Xenocrates); Cynic *Ep.* 9 (Anacharsis to Croesus) (text and trans. cited from A.J. Malherbe, ed., *The Cynic Epistles. A Study Edition*, SBLSBS 12 [Missoula, MT: Scholars Press, 1977]); Iambl. *Ep.* Περὶ ὁμονοίας(Diels, *Vorsokr.* 2.356=Stob. II,33,15); *1 Clement* (as demonstrated by van Unnik, 149–204; esp. 181–204). These letters explicitly claim to be deliberative letters; note the frequency of the term συμβουλεύειν and cognates (Dem. *Ep.* 1.3, 12; Ps-Aeschin. *Ep.* 11.1, 2, 5, 7; Pl. *Ep.* 5.321C-D; 322B; 6.323A-B; 7.331D; 332C; 334C; 336C; 337E; 351E; 8.352B-E; 354A, D; 355A; 357B; Isoc. *Ep.* 1.2, 4, 7, 9; 2.1, 2, 12; 3.2; 6.6, 11, 14 [7.10 promises a future deliberative letter]; 9.6, 15; Ps-Arist. frag. 658 [=Plut. *Mor.* 329B]; Socr. *Ep.* 27.18; 30.3; Cynic *Ep.* 9.65–70; *1 Clem.* 58:2, and discussion in van Unnik, 181–89). The verb συμβουλεύειν is not used in 1 Cor, but later Greek commentators used it to describe the purpose of the letter (see Chrys. *hom. in I Cor.* 19.1 [*PG* 61.151]; 24.1 [61.199]; 26.1 twice [61.212]; 28.2 noun συμβουλή [61.227]; 35.3 [61.299]). See also the section on ὑπόθεσις in the Catenae: οὐκ ἀποδέχεται δὲ αὐτοὺς ποιοῦντας σχίσματα, ἀλλὰ καὶ συμβουλεύει, μὴ ἐν λόγῳ τὴν ἀρετὴν, ἀλλ' ἐν ἔργῳ καὶ δυνάμει ἡγεῖσθαι (Cramer, p. B lines 17–19; also Theodoret, *1 Cor.*, Argumentum [*PG* 82.228], quoted below in n. 75).

Klek (46–128) cited Cic. *Q.Fr.* 1.1; Pliny *Ep.* 8.24; 9.5; Ps-Sall. *Rep.* (=*ad Caesarem*

---

[5] It is legitimate to ask if "deliberative letter" was indeed a *genre* in antiquity. The epistolary handbook attributed to Demetrius contains a deliberative letter (Ps-Demetr. 11, συμβουλευτικός; see also *P.Bon.* 5, συνβουλευτικαὶ περὶ ἐλαχίστων [Malherbe, *Epistolary Theorists*, 44]); Ps-Lib. 5 differentiates his παραινετική from συμβουλευτική, with which he says some have confused it. But these handbooks do not contain different epistolary genres as such, but rather "a selection of styles appropriate to different circumstances" (Malherbe, *Epistolary Theorists*, 8; White, 202–203; see also Stowers, 51–57, who regards their distinctions to be in the social situation and function of each different type). At this point we are caught between rhetorical and epistolary theory (for discussion see Malherbe, "Epistolary Theorists," Hübner, Stowers, and Aune, *Literary Environment*, 158–74). From what we know of ancient epistolary theory, it is not clear that the ancients divided letters into sub-*genres* (which can be separated on formal grounds) as much as sub-*types* (often on content or functional grounds). It is important to emphasize that the *genre* of 1 Corinthians is the letter, not the speech (see n. 33 in ch. I for a critique of rhetorical analyses which lose sight of that fact). The rhetorical genre, in my view, applies to the argument in the body of the letter; it does not replace the letter as the genre of the text. Thus by my definition a "deliberative letter" is a letter which employs deliberative rhetoric in the letter body, a combination which is common in ancient literature (as demonstrated above; the interplay of rhetorical and epistolary forms is far too simply denied, for example, by Siegert, 16). This does not mean, however, that the epistolary formulae (saluation, thanksgiving) do not play a rhetorical function homogenous with the argument in the body of the letter (see Betz, *Galatians*, 14–15), as we shall demonstrate in ch. IV.

senem de re publica epistula) as Latin *symbuleutici*, along with the Greek letters Pl. *Ep*. 7 and 8; Isocrates' *Ep*. 1–9; Socr. *Ep*. 30 and Ps-Arist. *ad Alexandrum Magnum* (see also his conclusion on p. 154 on deliberative rhetoric in letters). "Letters of advice," or *symbouleutikai*, are discussed by Stowers along with letters of exhortation (91–152; 107–109 on *symbouleutikai*). In his list of letters of advice are: Cic. *Fam*., 110 (= 15.4), NewDocs 1980, 60; *P.Oxy*. 299 (but the citation is incorrect); Socr. *Ep*. 30; Pliny *Ep*. 7.1. His supplementary list on p. 151 includes *P.Oxy*. 531; *P.Bon*. 1, 3, 4, 11, 12; Isoc. only *Ep*. 1; Pl. *Ep*. 6–8; Cic. *Fam*. 15.4; Pliny *Ep*. 1.23; 6.29; 7.9; Crates *Ep*. 12, 22, 25; Socr. *Ep*. 29; Fronto *Ep*. 2.11; *1 Clem*.; August. *Ep*. 228. Noting that the distinction between paraenesis and advice was not always made in antiquity (92–94; 107–108), Stowers differentiates the *symbouleutikai* correctly from paraenesis because: "Advice in the stricter deliberative sense is specific and occasional" and "Letters of advice, above all, contain arguments that move from past experience and precedent to what is advantageous or disadvantageous" (108, see the discussion below). This typology is very useful (and it will be confirmed by this study), but not all of Stowers's examples meet these criteria. The papyrus letters do not fit the deliberative letter category (his "letter of advice") because they simply do not contain argumentation (as Stowers himself notes, 109). This is related to the significant difference in the length of the letter body between the papyrus letters and the "literary letters," as well as those of Paul, except possibly Philemon (this is also a problem with Crates *Ep*. 12, 22, 25; Socr. *Ep*. 29, which should be classed among the letters of exhortation, not of advice). Cic. *Fam*. 15.4 presents us with a more than amply long letter body (cf. *Q.Fr*. 1.1!), but it is actually a letter of request (a classification not included by Stowers), not a deliberative letter (see the explicit language of request: *vehementer te rogo* in 14, *rogatio mea* in 16). Stowers, 108 asserts that this letter contains the parts of a deliberative speech (proem, proposition, proof, epilogue) but this is not at all readily apparent (in fact most of the letter is narration).

Another piece of evidence for deliberative letters is statements about people advising others by letter (e. g., Cic. *Brut*. 3.11; *Att*. 1.5; 12.40; 13.27; Plut. *Cic*. 37.1; App. *BCiv*. 3.11.81; see also Cic. *Att*. 7.12; 8.3, cited by Stowers, 151).

On the basis of these resources, this investigation will demonstrate that deliberative argumentation was characterized by four things: 1) a focus on future time as the subject of deliberation; 2) employment of a determined set of appeals or ends, the most distinctive of which is the advantageous (τὸ συμφέρον); 3) proof by example (παράδειγμα);[6] and 4) appropriate subjects for deliberation, of which factionalism and concord are especially common. Because each of these four elements of deliberative rhetoric is found in 1 Corinthians, this is a clear indication that 1 Corinthians employs that rhetorical species in its argumentation.

[6] See in general G. M. A. Grube on deliberative rhetoric: "concerned with the future, aims to persuade to a certain course of action, and deals with the advantageous or harmful" (*The Greek and Roman Critics* [Toronto: University of Toronto Press, 1965] 93; also, in sum, Kennedy, *New Testament Interpretation*, 36–37; Watson, *Invention*, 32–33).

A. The Time Frame of Deliberative Rhetoric

Deliberative rhetoric is argumentation which urges an audience, either public or private,[7] to pursue a particular course of action in the future.[8] What is at stake in a deliberative argument is the future, because logically one cannot deliberate about how to act in the past.[9] Thus Aristotle distinguished deliberative rhetoric according to time frame: "Further, to each of these a special time is appropriate: to the deliberative the future, for the speaker, whether he exhorts or dissuades (προτρέπων ἢ ἀποτρέπων), always advises about things to come" (*Rh.* 1.3.4).[10] Elsewhere Aristotle admits that deliberative argumentation also deals in some way with the present (*Rh.* 1.8.7), because that is the situation which calls forth some future response.[11] In contrast, forensic rhetoric deals with the past, and epideictic with the present.[12]

If we look at the beginning and end of the letter body in 1 Corinthians[13] we see clearly future-directed statements: παρακαλῶ δὲ ὑμᾶς . . . ἵνα τὸ αὐτὸ λέγητε πάντες καὶ μὴ ᾖ ἐν ὑμῖν σχίσματα . . . ("I urge you . . . to all say the same thing and let there not be factions among you. . . ," 1:10), and the imperatives ἑδραῖοι γίνεσθε, ἀμετακίνητοι, περισσεύοντες ἐν τῷ ἔργῳ τοῦ κυρίου πάντοτε, εἰδότες ὅτι ὁ κόπος ὑμῶν οὐκ ἔστιν κενὸς ἐν κυρίῳ ("be steadfast, immovable and abounding in the work of the Lord always, knowing that your work is not in vain in the Lord") in 15:58.[14] This future time frame was prepared for already in

[7] Arist. *Rh.* 1.3.3; Quint. *Inst.* 3.8.36–39, 70. In the context of Greek politics, the public *Sitz im Leben* of deliberative rhetoric is the assembly (the ἐκκλησία). See Martin, 167 for the various applications of deliberative rhetoric.

[8] Cf. Stowers's identification of one of the fundamental features of letters of advice: "The writer tries to persuade or dissuade the recipient with regard to some particular course of action in the future" (108).

[9] This is so notwithstanding Dio Chrysostom's contorted attempt to argue against this accepted position on the grounds that one cannot deliberate about the future because it is unknown (*Or.* 26; cf. Isoc. *Or.* 8.8, 11).

[10] See also Quint. *Inst.* 3.4.7: *de futuris deliberamus* (and Martin, 167–68). Thus the cause or question answered by a deliberative speech is "what shall we do?" (e. g., Polyb. 4.25.1; see *Rhet. Her.* 3.2.1–2 for a breakdown; for a more complex analysis, which attempts, not with complete success, to apply forensic *status*-theory to deliberative rhetoric, see Quint. *Inst.* 3.8.4–7; cf. Cic. *Top.* 24.93–94). In general deliberative rhetoric treats the στάσις πραγματική (on which see Volkmann, 298, cf. 38–57).

[11] See Quintilian's further distinction: "the deliberative department of oratory (also called the advisory [*suasoria*] department), while it deliberates [*consultare*] about the future, also enquires [*quaerere*] about the past" (*Inst.* 3.8.6). The advice is always directed to the future, but guidance and examples may be drawn from the past to aid in the deliberation (see below).

[12] See n. 41 in ch. I. The other part of Aristotle's famous differentiation of the rhetorical species is the role of the audience: in deliberative rhetoric the audience is a judge (κριτής) of things to come, in forensic a judge of the past, and in epideictic a spectator (θεωρός) (*Rh.* 1.3.1–2).

[13] These two verses are respectively the πρόθεσις and ἐπίλογος of the argument (see the compositional analysis in chap. IV).

[14] See also the imperatives in the recapitulation of the argument of the letter in 16:13–14.

the epistolary thanksgiving, which ends with future hopes and expectations (ὃς καὶ βεβαιώσει ὑμᾶς, 1:8), and of course culminates in chap. 15. The entire intervening section of the letter is concerned with specific actions which the Corinthians should undertake or abstain from in the future. There is also an element of present time here (in line with Aristotle's description): the situation which called forth Paul's response, the factionalism which at present threatens the community, is also described (1:11–13; 3:3–4; 11:18, etc.). Some past time examples are used as appeals to persuade or dissuade them from the same conduct (see the treatment of this below). But the overwhelming future emphasis in the letter, because it is, appropriately, a letter which gives advice about behavioral changes in community life, indicates that of the three rhetorical species, only the deliberative fits 1 Corinthians.

B. The Appeal to Advantage in Deliberative Rhetoric

We shall turn next to an investigation of the appeals or ends of deliberative argumentation. According to the handbooks, deliberative speeches either exhort an audience to or dissuade them from a specific course of action in the future.[15] Deliberative rhetoric may be distinguished from the other two species, according to Aristotle, by its τέλος: "the end of the deliberative speaker is the expedient or harmful" (τῷ μὲν συμβουλεύοντι τὸ συμφέρον καὶ βλαβερόν).[16] In the Latin handbooks *utilitas* corresponds to τὸ συμφέρον, where it is also recommended as a chief argument in deliberative rhetoric.[17] If one wants to convince people to pursue a particular course of action in the future, one must demonstrate that it is to that audience's advantage.[18] Likewise if one wants to dissuade an audience from a course of action one must demonstrate that it is not advantageous. Anaximenes (probably the author of the *Rhetorica ad Alexandrum*) provides a

---

[15] Arist. *Rh.* 1.3.5 (ὁ προτρέπων, ὁ ἀποτρεπων). Two of *Rh.Al.*'s seven sub-species are προτρεπτικόν and ἀποτρεπτικόν (1.1421 b; cf. Quint. *Inst.* 3.8.6; Doxopat. *Homil. in Aphth.* 153.2). The same function, with these rhetorical terms, is given to the συμβουλευτικός epistolary type in Ps-Demetrius 11 (= Malherbe, *Epistolary Theorists*, 36).

[16] *Rh.* 1.3.5. See also Kennedy, *Persuasion in Greece*, 204; *New Testament Interpretation*, 36–37, 46; Goldstein, 106, 108; and Dion. Hal. *Isoc.* 1, on politics and political speeches in general. In distinguishing συμβουλή from παραίνεσις (on which see below), Ammonius says that deliberation, unlike paraenesis, admits of counter-argument. In his example of συμβουλή the question of advantage is central: καὶ γὰρ ἐάν τις συμβουλεύσῃ πόλεμον, ἀμφίβολον εἰ συμφέρει (*Diff.* 455=*Ammonius. De adfinium vocabulorum differentia*, ed. K. Nickau, BT [Leipzig: Teubner, 1966] 119).

[17] *Rhet.Her.* 3.2.3; Cic. *Inv.Rhet.* 2.51.156; 2.56.168–69; cf. Quint. *Inst.* 3.8.34 (see the discussion below), and 3.8.42 (a quotation from a lost letter of Cicero to Brutus: *Suasoris enim finis est utilitas eius, cui quisque suadet*).

[18] This deliberative strategy is known elsewhere in the New Testament, in Jn 18:14, where Caiphas is described as ὁ συμβουλεύσας τοῖς Ἰουδαίοις ὅτι συμφέρει ἕνα ἄνθρωπον ἀποθανεῖν ὑπὲρ τοῦ λαοῦ (cf. Jn 11:47–50).

fuller list of the lines of argumentation or common topics[19] which a deliberative orator must demonstrate, among which συμφέρον holds a chief position[20]: δίκαια, νόμιμα, συμφέροντα, καλά, ἡδέα and ῥᾴδια.

The handbooks besides Aristotle are sometimes ethically uneasy with his description of τὸ συμφέρον as the *only* forceful argument for a deliberative discourse,[21] and wish the orator to point out not only that a course of action is advantageous, but also that it is just,[22] honorable, or praiseworthy. We have noted Anaximenes' list of several possible appeals. But even for him all are not of the same weight. Anaximenes recommends that one should first prove that the

---

[19] He does not use the terms τέλος or τόπος, but describes the elements of each of the rhetorical species under three heads: αἱ δυνάμεις, αἱ χρήσεις and αἱ τάξεις (1.1421 b); from the arrangement of his treatise, this list constitutes the δυνάμεις, or what the deliberative orator must prove (χρὴ δεικνύειν). There was no uniformity among the rhetorical theorists for the name of the category under which these appeals were placed. Later rhetoricians, notably Hermogenes, called them τελικὰ κεφάλαια (Hermog. *Prog.* 1.34; *Stat.* 3.26; also Aps. *Rhet.* 1.380–84 Spengel; Men. Rh. 1.358 [Russell-Wilson, 56]), the "heads or topics of argument" (LSJ, 945; see also Volkmann, 299–307; Martin, 167–76; Beck, 98–104; 156–61). See the discussion of terminology in Cic. *Inv.Rhet.* 2.51.155–57; in *Top.* 24.91 he follows Aristotle (*fines* and *loci*). Alex. *Rh.* 3.1.3 Spengel uses τέλη. Despite the differences in terminology, this list consists of the standard topics or appeals of a deliberative argument. For a good general discussion of deliberative appeals, with an analysis of the proof in the deliberative speech [Herodes Atticus] *Pol.*, see Drerup, 74–82 (who argues that in that speech ἀγαθόν equals συμφέρον).

[20] So Beck, 158–61, who notes that despite this list of six, even in his own exemplary arguments, the author of this rhetorical handbook uses two appeals, τὸ συμφέρον and τὸ δίκαιον, predominantly. This list of deliberative appeals remains throughout the rhetorical tradition, as attested by the rhetorical handbook attributed to Aristides: "One must know that there are these questions for discussion in deliberative inquiries (συμβουλευτικὰ ζητήματα): the just, the advantageous, the possible, the easy, the necessary, the safe, the good, the pious, the natural, the pleasant, and the opposites of these things" (τὸ δίκαιον, τὸ συμφέρον, τὸ δυνατὸν, τὸ ῥᾴδιον, τὸ ἀναγκαῖον, τὸ ἀκίνδυνον, τὸ καλὸν, τὸ εὐσεβὲς, τὸ ὅσιον, τὸ ἡδὺ καὶ τὰ ἐναντία τούτοις) (2.503 Spengel, my trans.; for the commonplace nature of such lists see Plut. *Mor.* 822C). Some narrow the list to four (Longin. *Fr.* 15 [=Spengel 1.327]; Aphth. *Prog.* 2.50 Spengel), or five (Aps. *Rhet.* 1.380–84 Spengel), and Hermogenes' list varies from four to six (*Prog.* 1.34; 11.53; 12.54; *Stat.* 3.26), but συμφέρον is in every collection (Volkmann, 301; Martin, 173). Sopater narrows back to Aristotle's classification which includes one negative and one positive appeal for each species (τὸ συμφέρον for the deliberative), with subdivisions under each (4.713 Walz; Volkmann, 302).

[21] See Volkmann, 300–301; Martin, 169–74.

[22] Aristotle merely calls justice expedient: "Lastly justice, since it is expedient in general for the common weal" (καὶ τὸ δίκαιον. συμφέρον γάρ τι κοινῇ ἐστιν; *Rh.* 1.6.16; see also Quintilian's critique in *Inst.* 3.8.1–3). The dangerous extreme of this position is expressed by Thrasymachus in the *Republic*: "I affirm that the just [τὸ δίκαιον] is nothing else than the advantage of the stronger [τὸ τοῦ κρείττονος ξυμφέρον]" (Pl. *Resp.* 1.338C; see Socrates' reply in 339B). This is of course ultimately a philosophical question; the Stoics held that the morally good must be expedient (Cic. *Off.* 3.3.11). Cf. the saying of Epicurus in D.L. 10.151: "Taken generally, justice (τὸ δίκαιον) is the same for all, to wit, something found expedient (συμφέρον) in mutual intercourse." See Cicero's reflections upon the conflict between *utilitas* and *honestas* throughout Book III of *de Officiis*.

act will be just (he adds: if it is possible to do so), and then that it is expedient, συμφέρον (32.1439 a). Cicero wants to qualify Aristotle: "In the deliberative type (*deliberativum*), however, Aristotle accepts advantage (*utilitas*) as the end, but I prefer both honor (*honestas*) and advantage (*utilitas*)."[23] The *Rhetorica ad Herennium* solves this dilemma by saying that *utilitas* (=συμφέρον) is the total aim (*finis*) of the orator in his speech (3.2.3), and that utilities of security (*tuta*) and honor (*honesta*) are subdivisions of *utilitas*, with justice (*iustitia*) subsumed under the right (*rectum*) as one of the subcategories of honor.[24] This debate was also carried on in the deliberative speeches themselves.[25] Regardless of this discussion over the relative hierarchy of deliberative appeals, all of the handbooks agree that deliberative argumentation chiefly centers on the appeal to τὸ συμφέρον (while there are differing opinions on the standard by which τὸ συμφέρον should be judged).[26] We may expect a deliberative argument to employ many of the appeals we have mentioned, but especially the appeal to advantage, as Aristotle says:

Similarly, the deliberative orator, although he often sacrifices everything else, will never admit that he is recommending what is inexpedient (ἀσύμφορα συμβουλεύουσιν) or is dissuading from what is useful (ὠφέλιμον) (*Rh.* 1.3.6).

---

[23] *Inv.Rhet.* 2.51.156; but cf. *De Or.* 1.141.

[24] See also Cic. *De Or.* 2.82.334–35: "For there is nobody . . . who does not think that moral worth (*dignitas*) is the highest object of ambition, but for the most part expediency (*utilitas*) wins the day when there is a covert fear lest if expediency be neglected worth will also have to be abandoned. But differences of opinion arise either on the question of which of two alternatives is more expedient, or even supposing there is agreement about this, it is disputed whether the chief consideration should be integrity (*honestas*) or expediency (*utilitas*)."

[25] See G. A. Kennedy, "Focusing of Arguments in Greek Deliberative Oratory," *TAPA* 90 (1959) 131–38 (whose attempt to describe a universal change in appeals does not perhaps do justice to the variety we find in the speeches, but draws attention to this issue), and Volkmann, 299–314, in regard to Isoc. *Or.* 6 (cf. Cic. *De Or.* 2.82.335–36). The individual orators are themselves not always consistent in this regard. For example, in Dem. *Or.* 16.10 he argues on the basis that an act is first of all just, and then expedient, whereas in other cases he argues only that the act is expedient (as in the *peroratio* to that same speech in 16.32), and elsewhere argues that the act is both just and expedient (Dem. *Prooem.* 18; 22; 40.1). The rhetorical situation surely influences in each case what kinds of appeals the orator will make. See Kennedy's fascinating discussion of Demosthenes' progressive concessions in his later speeches to the political reality of the need to argue for expediency in his speeches (*Persuasion in Greece*, 223–25). *Rh.Al.* may be taken as a guide here – one always argues for the expediency of the act, and one argues that it is just if one can (see also Cicero's oversimplified "universal rule" in *Inv.Rhet.* 2.58.173–75). One also tempers one's argument to the arguments of others on the same issue. See *Rh.Al.* 34.1440 a: "After the introduction the best plan is to put forward one at a time each of the statements made in the previous speech, and prove that they are not just nor lawful nor expedient (ὡς οὐκ ἔστι δίκαια οὐδὲ νόμιμα οὐδὲ συμφέροντα) nor consistent with the policy advocated by the opponent."

[26] See Quint. *Inst.* 3.8.34–35.

Therefore, by definition, an argument which focuses particularly upon τὸ συμφέρον, the advantageous course to follow in the future, is deliberative.[27]

According to Aristotle, the position which is deemed advantageous (συμφέρον) depends in each case upon the final τέλος of all of one's actions in relation to which one chooses particular acts.[28] Therefore each deliberative argument depends upon stated or unstated assumptions of what is the good (τὸ ἀγαθόν)[29] in relation to which one should choose this course of action. Thus an orator must tailor the proof according to the audience's perception of τὸ ἀγαθόν, or change it, as Aristotle argued in Book One of his *Rhetorica*:

But since the aim before the deliberative orator (ὁ συμβουλεύων) is that which is expedient (τὸ συμφέρον), and men deliberate, not about the end, but about the means to the end, which are the things which are expedient in regard to our actions; and since, further, the expedient is good, we must first grasp the elementary notions of good and expedient in general . . . Lastly and above all, each man thinks those things good which are the object of his special desire, as victory of the man who desires victory, honour of the ambitious man, money of the avaricious, and so on in other instances. These then are the materials from which we must draw our arguments in reference to good and the expedient.[30]

In addition, one must often argue for the greater good or greater expediency of one proposed course of action over another.[31] One common mode of comparison is between a greater future advantage and a present immediate but ultimately lesser advantage.[32] This strategy of appealing to the expedient, which is the

---

[27] Beck, 21; Grube, 93. This is not to deny that appeals to the advantage sometimes appear in forensic speeches, or that there aren't some "mixed types" (see Aristid. *Rh.* 2.503 Spengel where he identifies a deliberative element in a speech on the basis of its appeal to τὸ συμφέρον). Nonetheless, it is unquestionable that the appeal to advantage is particularly distinctive of deliberative argumentation.

[28] So also Seneca: "We must set before our eyes the goal (*fines*) of the Supreme Good, towards which we may strive, and to which all our acts and words may have reference – just as sailors must guide their course according to a certain star" (*Ep.* 95.45).

[29] Cf. Epict. *Diss.* 1.22.1: "For who among us does not assume that the good (τὸ ἀγαθόν) is profitable (συμφέρον) and something to be chosen, and that in every circumstance we ought to seek and pursue it?" (see also 1.22.6–7). Thus the dilemma of deliberation is pessimistically expressed by Isoc.: "It seems to me that, while all men crave their advantage [ἐπιθυμεῖν τοῦ συμφέροντος] and desire to be better off than the rest, they do not all know the kind of conduct which leads to this end but differ from each other in judgement, some possessing a judgement which is sound and capable of hitting the right course of action, others one which completely misses their true advantage [τὸ συμφέρον]" (*Or.* 8.28).

[30] Arist. *Rh.* 1.6.1 and 30. Each place "expedient" is used in this English translation the Greek word is συμφέρον. Not all theorists follow Aristotle's philosophical speculation here. Other handbooks list some absolute expedients (συμφέροντα). See the lists in *Rh.Al.* 1.1422a (among which is ὁμόνοια, concord); *Rhet.Her.* 3.2.3–4.7; Cic. *Inv.Rhet.* 2.56.168–69; Aristid. *Rh.* 2.503–504 Spengel.

[31] Arist. *Rh.* 1.7.1: "But since men often agree that both of two things are useful (συμφέρειν), but dispute which is the more so, we must next speak of the greater good (μεῖζον ἀγαθόν) and the more expedient (μᾶλλον συμφέρον)."

[32] See Volkmann, 311 for a discussion of the time element in determining what is truly

center of deliberative rhetoric, must be kept in mind when we return to Paul's argument in 1 Corinthians.

Thus far we have looked exclusively at theoretical texts to identify for us the classic appeals which are made in deliberative rhetoric. Along with our proposed methodology (set forth in chap. I), this conclusion must be tested in actual rhetorical texts. We shall find that τὸ συμφέρον is not merely a part of theoretical discussion about deliberative rhetoric, but is a part of the technical vocabulary of deliberative arguments themselves.

Isocrates' *Or.* 6, *Archidamus*, is a prototypical deliberative speech.[33] In this speech Archidamus, son of the Spartan king, exhorts the Spartans to fight against Thebes, and reject their offer of peace. Speaking before a congress of allies at Sparta, he says that he has come forth to offer counsel (συμβουλεύω, 6.1) so that they will be able to choose, from all of the positions set forward, the most expedient (τὰ συμφορώτατα,[34] 6.4). Later in the speech he states that judges "at such times seek, not their just rights, but their best interests"[35] (ἀλλὰ τὸ συμφέρον ζητεῖν,[36] 6.34). He further states, "at present we are all agreed as to what is just, while we differ as to what is expedient" (περὶ δὲ τοῦ συμφέροντος ἀντιλέγομεν, 6.37). The neuter participle συμφέρον (or the adjective σύμφορος) is employed three more times in this same deliberative speech.[37] The appeal to advantage, using the term συμφέρον, abounds in the deliberative speeches of Isocrates.[38]

In Demosthenes' *First Philippic Oration*, the term συμφέρειν occurs no less than five times in the *peroratio* of the speech:

For my own part, I have never yet chosen to court your favor by saying anything that I was not quite convinced was to your advantage (συνοίσειν); and today, keeping nothing

advantageous–a comparison of present and future advantages (with Quint. *Inst.* 3.8.34–35; see also Aps. *Rhet.* 1.383 Spengel). In speeches, see, e. g., Dem. *Prooem.* 3 in his discussion of συμφέρον: ἔτι καὶ ἀπὸ τοὺ χρόνου, ὅτι οὐκ εἰς τὸ παρὸν μόνον, ἀλλὰ καὶ εἰς τὸν πάντα χρόνον ἐκ τούτων ἄμεινον οἰκήσομεν.

33 See Volkmann's analysis of it (307–14), and also Dionysius of Halicarnassus' assessment of the speech, which he understands to be deliberative, συμβουλεύειν (*Isoc.* 9).

34 Cf. Aristotle's statement about the comparative element in deliberative argumentation (n. 31 above, and Quint. *Inst.* 3.8.33).

35 Isocrates goes on to refute this position in favor of the appeal to τὸ δίκαιον (*Or.* 6.35–36), but returns to the expedient in 6.37. This is a good example of the varied use of deliberative heads – one can use more than one and play them off of one another.

36 Cf. 1 Cor 10:24, 33! This phrasing is rooted in the very goal of a deliberative argument: *expetenda fugiendaque* (Cic. *Top.* 23.89; Martin, 168). Of many other examples of the phrase ζητεῖν τὸ συμφέρον, see Isoc. *Or.* 8.10 and Dio Chrys. *Or.* 34.16 (and the full discussion in chap. III).

37 6.38, 74, 77. The predominance of this appeal (in addition to the appeals to δίκαιον, δυνατόν and καλόν) was noted by Volkmann, 307–14.

38 *Or.* 4.18; nine times in *Or.* 5 (5.3, 8, 10, 15, 25, 45, 72, 78, 127); three times in *Or.* 7 (7.17, 62, 84); and thirteen times in *Or.* 8 (8.5, 10, 11, 16, 28 twice, 31, 35, 62, 66, 70, 74, 138). See also the discussions of Isocrates' various deliberative appeals in Volkmann, 303–304 and Martin, 170.

back, I have given free utterance to my plain sentiments. Yet, certain as I am that it is to your interest (συμφέρει) to receive the best advice, I could have wished that I were equally certain that to offer such advice is also to the interest (συνοῖσον) of the speaker; for then I should have felt much happier. But, as it is, in the uncertainty of what the result of my proposal may be for myself, yet in the conviction that it will be to your interest (συνοίσειν) to adopt it, I have ventured to address you. Whatever shall be to the advantage (συνοίσειν) of all, may that prevail![39]

The term is common not only in the *perorationes*[40] to Demosthenes' deliberative speeches, but also in their *exordia*.[41] The fact that the term appears abundantly in both the *exordium* and *peroratio* to the speeches clearly shows that τὸ συμφέρον is not a side issue or an ancillary point in these orations – on the contrary it is *the* issue of a deliberative argument. This appeal to τὸ συμφέρον in deliberative speeches is not confined to the classical period, but remains prevalent well into the Greco-Roman period as, for example, in the deliberative speeches of Dio Chrysostom and Aelius Aristides, and the speeches embedded in historical works.[42]

Not surprisingly, the appeal to advantage, using the specific term συμφέρειν, also appears abundantly in deliberative letters.[43] In Demosthenes' *Ep.* 1 he states the intention of his letter as follows:

I think that . . . brief though the writing is, I shall myself be found to be doing my duty by you with all goodwill and that I should demonstrate clearly where your interests [τὰ συμφέρονθ' ὑμῖν] lie.[44]

---

[39] Dem. *Or.* 4.51–55. A major element in this text is the differentiation of to whom advantage would accrue from a given action. I shall discuss this important topic below.

[40] See also *Or.* 3.36; 7.46; 9.76; 14.41; 16.32.

[41] See *Or.* 1.1; 6.1; 7.1; 8.1, 3; 10.1; 17.2. Even more conclusive evidence of this point is provided by the collection of *Exordia* attributed to Demosthenes (whether these are authentic or not is irrelevant to this formal argument; Blass thought they were authentic [3/1.322–29]). These are formulaic, prefabricated *exordia*. A skilled rhetorician or public figure would have a collection of them which could be used in any case which might arise, as they were especially written to be universally applicable. All fifty-six of the *exordia* in this collection are deliberative. The occurrence of the term συμφέρειν is outstanding (Dem. *Prooem.* 3; 4; 5; 6; 10; 18 [2x]; 19; 20 [2x]; 22; 23; 25; 28 [3x]; 31; 32.3; 32.4; 33; 34.3 [2x]; 35.3; 40.1; 40.3; 44; 47.1; 50.1 [2x]; 50.2; 50.3; 51; 52; 56.1; 56.3). This demonstrates that, no matter what topic would arise, the deliberative orator had to be prepared to argue that it was expedient (συμφέρον).

[42] Dio Chrys. *Or.* 31.32; 34.7, 16, 28, 35; 38.6, 49; 39.5, 9; 40.16, 19; 48.6; Aristid. *Or.* 23.7, 32, 46, 65; 24.5, 14. These are all speeches on concord (like 1 Corinthians, I shall argue) which will play a large role in this investigation. The frequency of the appeal to τὸ συμφέρον in deliberative speeches in the historical works adds further confirmation (see, e. g., Polyb. 18.37.2, 8; 21.22.7, 9; 21.23.12; 24.12.2; Dion. Hal. *Ant.Rom.* 4.23; 5.6; 5.65.3; 5.68.3; 7.23.1; 7.42; 7.48.1; 7.53.1; 8.8.1; Joseph. *BJ* 2.346; 4.177 [cf. the reports of deliberative speeches in 1.284; 5.373; *AJ* 13.215–17; *Vit.* 100]; Cass. Dio 52.10.1; 52.13.5; 52.37.8). In regard to Polybius' speeches see Wooten's comment on 5.104: "Agelaus of Naupactus appeals solely to self-interest or expediency (τὸ συμφέρον) which is probably the most popular argument used in the speeches of Polybius" (241).

[43] So also Stowers, 108.

[44] Dem. *Ep.* 1.3–4 (the term appears also in this short letter at 1.5, 9, and 10).

The appeal to advantage is to be expected in deliberative letters,[45] as they offer their recipients what the epistolary author considers to be the most expedient course of action for the future.

Before leaving the term συμφέρειν, so crucial to deliberative rhetoric, we must examine what is often a major issue in deciding what is "the advantageous course to follow" in these deliberative texts. The question is – for whom will the act be advantageous?[46] Often a speaker appeals to the advantage of the city: τὸ μέλλον συνοίσειν τῇ πόλει.[47] Dio Chrysostom says that he wrote many speeches ". . . on behalf of concord, believing that this was advantageous for the city" (ὑπὲρ ὁμονοίας, ἡγούμενος συμφέρειν τῇ πόλει τοῦτο).[48] One of the most frequent appeals orators make is to "the common advantage," τὸ κοινῇ συμφέρον.[49] Often orators appeal directly to the audience's advantage, as Demosthenes does in Or. 15, *On the Liberty of the Rhodians*:

> Moreover, I should never have made this proposal, had I thought that it would benefit (συμφέρειν) the Rhodian democrats alone, for I am not the official patron of that party, nor do I count any of them among my private friends. Yet even if both these motives had not been present, I should not have proposed it, if I had not thought that it would benefit (συμφέρειν) you . . . (*Or*. 15.15).

In many cases the speaker wants to demonstrate that the proposed action will suit the self-interests of everyone involved, as this would ensure widespread support for the measure. Isocrates, in *Ep*. 3, addressed to Philip, tells him that to

---

45 This appeal to τὸ συμφέρον is common in the deliberative epistles of Demosthenes (*Ep*. 3.7, 20, 23, 26, 27 [2x], 35, 36; the deliberative nature of this appeal was noted by Goldstein, 133–35; see previous note for *Ep*. 1), Isocrates (*Ep*. 1.10; 2.5; 3.1; 6.10, 14; 8.4; 9.2, 17, 19) and Plato (*Ep*. 5.322A; 8.352B-C, E; 355D). See also Ps-Aeschin. *Ep*. 11.2, 3, 5 and Socr. *Ep*. 27.18. In Latin letters see Ps-Sall. *Rep*. 2.3; 6.4 (*beneficium*), and *utilissima* in the *peroratio* in 13.8; cf. Ps-Sall. *Caes*. 8.7; Pliny *Ep*. 7.9. Ps-Libanius' ἀναθετική (a letter of consultation, which would occasion an advisory or deliberative letter) also broaches the issue of advantage: "I have decided on the following course of action, and therefore lay it before you. So consider its advantage (τὸ συμφέρον) and write me what I should do. For I am always anxious to receive the opinions of intelligent men, for the excellent advice (συμβουλίαι) contains in itself the most noble service" (84 = Malherbe, *Epistolary Theorists*, 80–81).

46 See Quint. *Inst*. 3.8.35: "A question of expediency may also be concerned . . . with particular persons ('it is expedient, but not for' or 'not as against these')."

47 Dem. *Or*. 1.1 (cf. Polybius' complaint that Demosthenes limited his attention to what would be to the advantage of Athens alone; 18.14.10–12).

48 *Or*. 40.16.

49 E.g., Dem. *Ep*. 1.5, 9, 10; Dio Chrys. *Or*. 34.19, 22; Aristid. *Or*. 24.5; cf. Dion. Hal. *Ant. Rom*. 6.85.1 (in the speech of Menenius Agrippa); 7.39.2. In political theory, see Arist. *Pol*. 3.4.2–5.4. This appeal is especially common in deliberative arguments to cease from factionalism (like the examples listed), because the orator must urge the audience to stop considering their own private interest (which is what factionalism is), and return to a concern for the common advantage (see the full discussion of this in ch. III). This appeal is made by Paul in 1 Cor 10:33 (μὴ ζητῶν τὸ ἐμαυτοῦ σύμφορον ἀλλὰ τὸ τῶν πολλῶν). In ECL (= Early Christian Literature) see especially *Barn*. 4:10: συνζητεῖτε περὶ τοῦ κοινῇ συμφέροντος.

reconcile the Greek states is an act "which concerns both the interest of the city and your interests."[50] In *Ep*. 9, to Archidamus III, the king of Sparta, he counsels "that these things are practicable and expedient for you, for your city, and for all the Hellenes at large."[51] The author of one of the Platonic epistles even goes so far as to state that his advice will be expedient for the enemies![52]

Often an orator must dissolve suspicion that he is acting in his own interests,[53] a tactic recommended by the handbooks,[54] because the good statesman always has the state's interests at heart. Demosthenes makes this argument in his *Ep*. 1:

> I do not think, however, that I have the right while satisfying my private resentment to hurt the public interest (τὸ κοινῇ συμφέρον), nor do I at all mix my private enmity with the general good (εἰς τὰ κοινῇ συμφέροντα). On the contrary, the conduct I urge upon the rest of men I think I ought to be myself the first to practice.[55]

To sum up our investigation thus far, we have found that rhetorical theory considered the appeal to advantage to be the major element of deliberative argumentation. We have confirmed this theoretical viewpoint through an examination of deliberative speeches and letters, where the appeal to advantage (using the same term συμφέρειν) is commonly employed.[56] We have seen that often the deliberative issue involves the question of who will gain advantage from the proposed future action. I conclude that the term συμφέρειν is clearly a part of the technical vocabulary of deliberative rhetorical texts.

---

[50] 3.1. περί τε τῶν τῇ πόλει καὶ τῶν σοὶ συμφερόντων.

[51] 9.19. ὡς δ'ἐστὶ ταῦτα δυνατὰ καὶ συμφέροντα καὶ σοὶ καὶ τῇ πόλει καὶ τοῖς ἄλλοις ἅπασιν.

[52] *Ep*. 8.352B–C, E. See also the ironic appeal in Dem. *Or*. 14.41: "If you act thus, you will be acting for the good (συμφέροντα) both of yourselves and also of those who give you the contrary advice, since you will not have to be angry with them hereafter for errors you have committed now."

[53] See, e. g., the *peroratio* to Cicero's *Leg.Man.*: "But I have made up my mind that, invested as I am with this high office and enjoying the great reward of your goodwill, it is my duty to place your wishes, the honor of the State, and the well-being of our provinces and allies above any advantages and interests of my own" (24.71).

[54] *Rh.Al*. 29.1436b. This strategy was rooted in the political practices of the Athenian democracy, as Goldstein has shown (108–109). This is also a standard piece of political advice (see Arist. *Eth.Nic*. 8.10.2; Dio Chrys. *Or*. 3.39; Plut. *Mor*. 813B). See the full discussion in chap. III.

[55] *Ep*. 1.10; see also Dem. *Or*. 4.51–55 quoted above, and Isoc. *Ep*. 6.14: "but I myself should be ashamed if, while offering counsel (συμβουλεύων) to others, I should be negligent of their interests and look to my own advantage (τὸ ἐμαυτῷ συμφέρον) instead of putting myself altogether beyond the reach of both the personal benefits (αἱ ὠφέλειαι) and all other considerations and advising the best course of action (τὰ βέλτιστα παραινοίην)."

[56] We have focussed on cases where the exact term συμφέρειν appears. Other Greek terms for advantage or gain, such as λυσιτελεῖν or ὠφελεῖν, are also used in such texts, though less commonly.

The Deliberative Appeal to Advantage in 1 Corinthians

This investigation of the appeal to advantage in deliberative rhetoric in antiquity sheds light on 1 Corinthians. Paul uses the verb συμφέρειν in its various parts five times in the letter.[57] The impersonal verb συμφέρει appears in 1 Cor 6:12 and 10:23, the neuter participle συμφέρον in 12:7, and the adjective σύμφορος (in the neuter σύμφορον) in 7:35 and 10:33.[58] In the latter two cases a significant number of manuscripts read the neuter participle συμφέρον.[59] The central role of the appeal to advantage in 1 Corinthians is another strong argument that it is deliberative rhetoric.[60]

The first instance of the appeal to advantage is in 1 Cor 6:12. Paul first quotes the Corinthian slogan πάντα μοι ἔξεστιν ("all things are lawful to me"), and then qualifies it with his own argument, ἀλλ' οὐ πάντα συμφέρει ("but not everything is advantageous").[61] The exegetical tradition has followed Weiss in its understanding of the term συμφέρει in this verse: ". . . ist es ein term. techn. der stoischen Popular-Philosophie."[62] Actually συμφέρειν is a key term used in a wide range of ethical and political discussions in antiquity, one attestation of which is the writings of Stoic philosophy. Discussion of the nature of τὸ συμφέρον in popular philosophy of course affected rhetorical practice (and vice versa), but the term was not restricted to one philosophy or religion.[63] The same

[57] Other terms describing "advantage" or "gain" are also found throughout 1 Corinthians: μισθός in 9:18; κερδαίνειν in 9:20; ὠφελεῖν in 13:3; 14:6; ὄφελος in 15:32; and the litotes οὐκ ἔστιν κενός in 15:58. These are all ways of expressing the deliberative appeal to advantage (see, e. g., Dion.Hal. *Ant.Rom.* 8.44.2, where τὰ συμφέροντα are equated with κέρδος and ὠφέλεια). On this and related appeals in the Pauline corpus see Siegert, 203–206.

[58] "Advantage" is also denoted by the definite article alone in 10:24 and 13:5 (BAGD, 552; Weiss, *Korintherbrief*, 263; Barrett, 238–40, 298; Conzelmann, 175, 217); cf. Phil 2:2, 21. This is commonly found in classical Greek, often where συμφέρον is ellipsed (see, e. g., Arist. *Pol.* 3.5.4). Weiss, *Korintherbrief*, 278, also regards εἰς τὸ κρεῖσσον in 11:17 as equivalent to εἰς τὸ συμφέρον.

[59] The meaning of these two forms, the neuter participle and adjective, is identical (LSJ, 1687–1688). This is a common scribal variation (see Dion. Hal. *Ant.Rom.* 5.12.2; Joseph. *BJ* 4.368; 5.262, 264; *AJ* 5.286).

[60] So also Stowers: "In 6:12–20 he introduces the deliberative argument from expediency, which is recapitulated and amplified in 10:23–11:1 . . . Chapters 7–8 and 10–14 provide advice that is recommended by many different kinds of argumentation. These, however, center on expediency in achieving a high quality of community in the time before the return of Christ" (108–109). However, because of Paul's use of example and the call to imitation, which Stowers considers to be paraenetic, not deliberative (on which see below) he does not conclude that 1 Corinthians is deliberative, but that it is a complex mixture of deliberation and exhortation.

[61] The double refrain is repeated in 10:23. Most commentators agree that πάντα μοι ἔξεστιν is the extent of the slogan, and that ἀλλ' οὐ πάντα συμφέρει is Paul's response to it (Heinrici, 198; Lightfoot, 213; Robertson-Plummer, 121–22; Lietzmann-Kümmel, 27; Barrett, 144; Conzelmann, 109 n. 6).

[62] Weiss, *Korintherbrief*, 158, citing D.L. 7.98; Cic. *Off.* 3.3.11; Epict. *Diss.* 1.18.2; 22.1 (quoted above in n. 29); 27.14; 28.5; 2.22.20 and M.Ant. 3.7.

[63] S. Vollenweider, *Freiheit als neue Schöpfung. Eine Untersuchung zur Eleutheria bei Paulus und*

debate on the nature of τὸ συμφέρον occurs in the deliberative texts themselves (and handbooks), as we have seen. On the basis of the term's widespread use in deliberative rhetoric one must conclude that it was not exclusively a Stoic catchword.[64] συμφέρειν was a term in wide currency; its essential background in deliberative rhetoric and political decision-making (much of which is of course itself influenced by Stoic thought)[65] has not been taken into account in the exegesis of Paul's argument here.

One reason for this oversight is that scholars have seen the slogan πάντα μοι ἔξεστιν to be Stoic in origin (and there are some good parallels to it in Stoic, and popular philosophy generally).[66] But even if the slogan did reflect solely Stoic thought, there is no reason to suppose that Paul's response to that slogan ("not everything is advantageous") must have arisen solely from the same milieu. Another reason is that perhaps scholars prefer to see Paul in dialogue with the Stoic philosophers instead of reflecting more common political insights. Weiss's

---

in seiner Umwelt, FRLANT 147 (Göttingen: Vandenhoeck & Ruprecht, 1989) 61–62 (who rightly emphasizes its Stoic use, and connects it with conceptions of the larger social good and the world organism, as Paul does, especially in 12:7; cf. 6:15).

64 As does Conzelmann, 108–109, following Weiss.

65 In 1 Cor Paul does not merely abstractly discuss what is τὸ συμφέρον, but rather, like his rhetorical counterparts, appeals to his recipients' advantage and must persuade them of what that actually is. This similarity in function between Paul and deliberative texts (and not only the Stoic philosophers) can be most helpful in our interpretation. This also may be suggestive for larger questions of what the conduit was through which Paul encountered and was influenced by Stoic thought and terminology.

66 See the texts cited by Weiss, *Korintherbrief*, 157–58 and Conzelmann, 108–109. In fact even the slogan is political in origin, as also at Corinth (see ch. III on slogans for freedom in political battles). Other parallels to πάντα μοι ἔξεστιν can be found, especially in political texts; see Arist. *Pol.* 6.2.4: "since it is expedient to be in a state of suspense and not to be able to do everything exactly as seems good to one (καὶ μὴ πᾶν ἐξεῖναι ποιεῖν ὅ τι ἂν δόξῃ συμφέρον ἐστίν), for liberty to do whatever one likes (ἡ γὰρ ἐξουσία τοῦ πράττειν ὅ τι ἂν ἐθέλῃς τις) cannot guard against the evil that is in every man's character." Important parallels to the freedom slogans at Corinth are found in the writings of Dio Chrysostom. In his *Or.* 14 *On Slavery and Freedom*, the following dialogue takes place: [Interlocutor to Dio]: "But surely we may put the matter briefly and declare that whoever has the power to do whatever he wishes is free, and that whoever has not that power is a slave" (. . . ὡς ὅτῳ μὲν ἔξεστιν ὃ βούλεται πράττειν, ἐλεύθερός ἐστιν, ὅτῳ δὲ μὴ ἔξεστι, δοῦλος). [Dio]: "If that is so, then men in general are not allowed to do what they wish . . ." (οὐδε τοῖς ἄλλοις ἔξεστιν ἃ ἐθέλουσι ποιεῖν) (*Or.* 14.13; see also 14.17; 34.12; Aristid. *Or.* 24.33). Later in the same treatise he connects τὸ συμφέρον with these definitions of freedom: "Therefore they will not persist in maintaining that rendering obedience to no man or doing whatever one likes constitutes freedom (οὔκουν τὸ μηδενὸς ἀνθρώπων ὑπακούειν οὐδὲ τὸ πράττειν ὅ τι ἂν τις ἐθέλῃ ἐλευθερία ἔτι φήσουσιν εἶναι). But perhaps they will counter by saying that these men obey for their own advantage . . ." ('Αλλ' ἴσως ἐροῦσιν ὅτι οὗτοι μὲν ἐπὶ τῷ αὑτῶν συμφέροντι ὑπακούουσιν . . .) (*Or.* 14.8–9; see also 14.16). The second response Paul makes in 6:12, ἀλλ' οὐκ ἐγὼ ἐξουσιασθήσομαι ὑπὸ τινος is also common: "Now if one were to ask them what the nature of freedom (ἐλεύθερον) is, they would say, perhaps, that it consists in being subject to no one" (τὸ μηδενὸς ὑπήκοον) (Dio Chrys. *Or.* 14.3, and 14.8 previously cited). We shall see in chap. III that the philosophical debate about the nature of true freedom is commonly reflected and drawn upon in deliberative arguments.

argument is based on a presumption that Paul cannot here be doing something as mundane as appealing to the Corinthians' self-interest:

Das im NT nicht seltene συμφέρει bezieht sich hier *natürlich* nicht auf den äusseren Nutzen oder Vorteil (wie Joh 11:50; 18:14; 1 Kor 7:35; 10:33; auch Mt 19:10) oder auch den höheren Nutzen für die Seligkeit (wie Joh 16:17; Mt 5:29f; 18:6), sondern auf die geistige, sittliche Förderung.[67]

It is also interesting that Weiss differentiates the appeals to advantage throughout 1 Corinthians (7:35 and 10:33 refer to external advantages, but 6:12, and presumably 10:23, do not), a distinction which appears arbitrary. This approach does not do justice to the development of Paul's argument about the nature of advantage (τὸ συμφέρον) throughout 1 Corinthians. In his argument, Paul redefines the central term συμφέρειν, which is a common strategy in deliberative rhetoric, as we have seen. It is most important that we do not prematurely interpret the first instance of this term in the letter at 6:12 in the light of the later reformulation of it which Paul will make (particularly in 10:23–11:1). Within Paul's argumentation, when he first introduces the term in 6:12, it carries its usual sense of self-interest until Paul later redefines it within the course of his progressive argument. As we have noted, appealing to the audience's self-interest is perhaps not so base as Weiss thinks; it lies at the heart of deliberative rhetoric, and it is what Paul uses to persuade the Corinthians to work for a new standard of "common advantage," and dissuade them from selfish behavior.[68] We misunderstand the whole argument by redefinition if we presuppose at the beginning of the proof the cumulative argument which is to follow. In 6:12 Paul makes the common deliberative appeal to the interest of the audience as a major ingredient in their decision-making.[69]

In 6:12 Paul seems to grant the Corinthians the freedom slogan,[70] but reminds them of what any person knows, that despite what one *can* do, one doesn't do what isn't to his or her advantage (Arist. *Rh.* 1.5.2). This is the generally accepted assumption upon which all deliberative argumentation is based – that one acts in accordance with one's own best interests.[71] In 6:13–20 Paul begins to

---

67 Weiss, *Korintherbrief*, 158 (emphasis added). The distinction between external and spiritual or moral advantages is also perhaps a false dichotomy. All are utilities to which one can make appeal in a deliberative argument.

68 See Chrysostom's rhetorically appropriate comment on 6:12: Καὶ πρῶτον μὲν ἀπὸ τοῦ ἀσυμφόρου ἀποτρέπει (*hom. in I Cor.* 17.1 [*PG* 61.139]).

69 "The focus of argument in deliberative rhetoric is self-interest and the expedient: not necessarily unenlightened and not dishonorable self-interest, but self-interest" (Kennedy, *New Testament Interpretation*, 46).

70 Heinrici, 198.

71 See Epict. *Diss.* 1.22.1 quoted above in n. 29, and (of many passages) see also 1.19.15; 2.22.15: "It is a general rule – be not deceived – that every living thing is to nothing so devoted as to its own interest [τῷ ἰδίῳ συμφέροντι]." The one who doesn't follow his or her own best interests is the fool (Dio Chrys. *Or.* 38.27; cf. 31.32). This truism is also reflected in Hellenistic

lay the groundwork for his redefinition of τὸ συμφέρον which is at the heart of the entire argument in 1 Corinthians, in his effort to demonstrate to the Corinthians what their true best interests are.[72] As in the deliberative speeches we have considered, here the question revolves around the sphere of advantage. Is what is advantageous to a single person that which is advantageous to her or him alone, or that which benefits the city, the nation, or even its enemies? Whose advantage do we consider when making a decision? These questions are of issue in every deliberative argument. The Corinthian slogan πάντα μοι ἔξεστιν assumes that the answer to these questions is "the individual." Paul counters this assumption by defining the basic sphere of advantage for the Christian not as the individual, but as the entire ἐκκλησία. Rhetorically he presents this as a reminder of something that they already know: οὐκ οἴδατε ὅτι τὰ σώματα ὑμῶν μέλη Χριστοῦ ἐστιν; ("don't you know that your bodies are members of Christ?" [6:15]). This ontological designation had already been prepared for by the discussion of the community as the ναὸς τοῦ θεοῦ ("temple of God") in chapter 3, which is repeated in 6:19 as another reminder. In 6:19 Paul bluntly restates his argument for the community standard of advantage over against the individualistic standard of the Corinthians: οὐκ ἐστὲ ἑαυτῶν ("you do not belong to yourselves"). The higher standard of the community, formed by the choice of the deity, is that to which Paul appeals. Thus in 6:12–20 Paul doesn't just prohibit sex with prostitutes. Instead he reaches behind the particular issue which divides the community to persuade them that it is actually in their self-interests not to do certain things which they now believe to be in their best interests,[73] because they are not realizing the true sphere of advantage – the entire church community – by which they should make decisions. Paul tries to persuade the Corinthians by appealing to their self-interests as he boldly states in 1 Cor 7:35: τοῦτο δὲ πρὸς τὸ ὑμῶν σύμφορον λέγω ("I am saying this for your own advantage").[74] This is exactly what the deliberative speaker or writer must convince his audience, that the course of action he urges is to their advantage.[75]

In 10:23–11:1 Paul overtly and consciously redefines what is τὸ συμφέρον for the Corinthian community. This text provides one of the major clues to Paul's

---

Jewish texts; see Sir 37:26: οὐ γὰρ πάντα πᾶσιν συμφέρει (Heinrici, 200), and *T.Gad* 7.1, on the neighbor's advantage: ἴσως γὰρ ὑμῖν συμφέρει οὕτως (cf. 7.2).

[72] Chrysostom observed Paul's argumentative strategy well: Καὶ τὸ δὴ θαυμαστὸν αὐτοῦ καὶ παράδοξον, ὃ δὴ πολλαχοῦ ποιεῖν εἴωθεν εἰς τὸ ἐναντίον περιτρέπων τὸν λόγον, τοῦτο καὶ ἐνταῦθα κατασκευάζει, καὶ δείκνυσιν ὅτι τὸ ἐν ἐξουσίᾳ ποιεῖν, οὐ μόνον οὐ συμφέρει, ἀλλ' οὐδὲ ἐξουσίας ἐστιν, ἀλλὰ δουλείας (*hom. in I Cor.* 17.1 [*PG* 61.139]).

[73] That unbridled freedom is not in the best interests of a polity is a *topos* in ancient political texts (see, e. g., Pl. *Resp.* 8.557B on democracy; Isoc. *Or.* 7.17–20, 37; Polyb. 6.4.4; Cic. *Rep.* 3.13.23 [*dicitur illa libertas, est vero licentia*]; 1.43.67–68). Compare Barrett's exegesis of 1 Cor 6:12: "Christian liberty is not licence, for licence is not more but less than liberty" (p. 146).

[74] Cf. Mt 19:10: οὐ συμφέρει γαμῆσαι.

[75] See the language of Thdt.'s exegesis on 1 Cor 7: Ἐν δὲ τῷ μεταξὺ [of ch. 6 and 8], καὶ περὶ παρθενίας καὶ χηρείας συμβουλεύει τὰ πρόσφορα (*1. Cor.* Argumentum [*PG* 82.228]).

argumentation in the epistle. Like the argument in chapter 6, it depends upon presuppositions and statements elucidated earlier in the letter, and points ahead to the discussions to follow. The sub-argument opens with the same slogan and response as in 6:12. Then Paul states definitively what he had alluded to in 6:12–20: μηδεὶς τὸ ἑαυτοῦ ζητείτω ἀλλὰ τὸ τοῦ ἑτέρου ("let no one seek his or her own advantage, but that of the other" [10:24]). The same redefinition of proper advantage from individual to community is made in Paul's self-exemplification in 10:33: μὴ ζητῶν τὸ ἐμαυτοῦ σύμφορον ἀλλὰ τὸ τῶν πολλῶν ("not seeking my own advantage, but that of the many").

By the parallel structure of verses 10:23a and 23b, one is led to deduce that the advantageous act is that which builds up the community.[76] Building language, especially the term (ἐπ)οἰκοδομεῖν and cognates, is very important in 1 Corinthians,[77] and is found throughout the letter.[78] Rhetorically, in the argument in 1 Corinthians, the οἰκοδομή is Paul's redefinition of the τέλος in relation to which he urges the Corinthians to choose their actions. Their true interests, he counsels them, are only served when those of the entire community are served (see especially 14:3–5).[79] This whole appeal is substantiated by Paul throughout the epistle by his insistence upon the communal identity of the Corinthians (ναὸς τοῦ θεοῦ in 1 Cor 3:9–17; 6:19; μέλη Χριστοῦ in 6:15–17; the σῶμα Χριστοῦ imagery as fully depicted in ch. 12).[80] Paul's argument is thus consistent with what Aristotle (quoted earlier) stipulated for deliberative discourse – that the orator must draw his arguments on the expedient according to the τέλος or final goal which guides his audience's actions,[81] or modify that τέλος. Paul wisely redefines the Corinthians' assumed goal from self-interest to community inter-

---

[76] See the conclusion of I. Kitzberger on linguistic grounds: "Innerhalb des synonymen Parallelismus ist das Verb [συμφέρειν] Parallelterminus und Synonym zu οἰκοδομεῖν" (*Bau der Gemeinde. Das paulinische Wortfeld* οἰκοδομή/(ἐπ)οικοδομεῖν, Forschung zur Bibel 53 [Würzburg: Echter Verlag, 1986] 159).

[77] In chapter III it will be demonstrated that the image of the building for the stable, non-divided political body is a *topos* in political literature which urges concord on divided groups.

[78] οἰκοδομεῖν in 1 Cor 8:1; 10:23; 14:4 (2x) and 14:7; οἰκοδομή in 3:9; 14:3, 5, 12 and 26; ἐποικοδομεῖν in 3:10 (2x), 12 and 14. The use of the building metaphor goes even beyond the occurrence of these exact terms, as will be demonstrated in chap. III.

[79] Cf. K. Weiss, "συμφέρω," *TDNT* 9.69–78, 77.

[80] Paul talks about the Corinthians' identity frequently in the epistle. The direct address ἐστε is prominently employed: 1 Cor 1:30 (you are God's); 3:3 (fleshly, twice); 3:4 (humanly); 4:8 (satisfied); 5:2 (puffed up); 5:7 (a new lump); 6:2 (judges of the least matters); 6:19 (not your own); 9:1 (my work in the Lord); 9:2 (the seal of my apostolate); 12:27 (the body of Christ); 14:12 (zealous for spirits); 15:17 (still in your sins). Direct address of the audience is another common strategy in deliberative rhetoric (one should make decisions appropriate to one's identity).

[81] See the acute assessment of Paul's rhetorical strategy of dissuasion by Chrys.: Καὶ τοῦτο μάλιστά ἐστιν, ὃ συνεχῶς ἐπιχειρεῖ κατασκευάζειν ὁ Παῦλος, ὅταν τινὸς ἀπάγειν βούληται, εἰς αὐτὰ ἃ ἐπιθυμεῖ δείκνυσιν αὐτὸν παραβλαπτόμενον (*hom. in I Cor.* 36.2 [*PG* 61.308]).

est in order to persuade them to work for the common good.[82] The redefinition of τὸ συμφέρον to mean "the common advantage" is shown to be complete in 12:7, where the spiritual gifts are described: ἑκάστῳ δὲ δίδοται ἡ φανέρωσις τοῦ πνεύματος πρὸς τὸ συμφέρον ("to each the manifestation of the spirit is given for the common advantage").[83] The fact that the deliberative argument in 1 Corinthians is centered, like all such discourses, on the question of advantage, is shown conclusively by 15:58,[84] where Paul concludes that the Corinthians now know that ὁ κόπος ὑμῶν οὐκ ἔστιν κενὸς ἐν κυρίῳ ("your work is not in vain in the Lord"). This is a repetition, in the negative, of the appeal to advantage – the Corinthians are assured that they will get a final reward for choosing the course of action Paul recommends. As is common in deliberative rhetoric,[85] Paul here appeals to future advantage against present, fleeting advantages to urge the Corinthians to adopt the course of action for unity which he proposes.[86]

In our examination of deliberative rhetoric, we saw that some rhetoricians, in addition to τὸ συμφέρον, or as subcategories of it, set forth other appeals by which an orator can convince his audience to follow his proposed course of action: i. e., τὸ δίκαιον, τὸ δυνατὸν, τὸ ῥᾴδιον, τὸ ἀναγκαῖον, τὸ ἀκίνδυνον, τὸ καλὸν, τὸ εὐσεβὲς, τὸ ὅσιον, τὸ ἡδύ.[87] As we have seen, Paul centers his appeal for Corinthian unity on the grounds that it will be expedient (συμφέρον), but, in addition, like most deliberative speakers, he also employs some other appeals to different positive aspects of the specific courses of action which he advises. An important appeal in 1 Corinthians is τὸ καλόν, the good. In 5:6 Paul tells the Corinthians: οὐ καλὸν τὸ καύχημα ὑμῶν ("your boast is not good"). The appeal to the good is also made in regard to the various lifestyles treated in chap. 7:[88] καλὸν αὐτοῖς ἐὰν μείνωσιν ὡς κἀγώ ("it is good for them if they remain as I am").[89] The term ἀγαθός does not appear in 1 Corinthians, but the comparative

---

[82] This is a direct and appropriate response to their factionalism (see the extensive discussion in chap. III).

[83] Commentators widely agree that this refers to the "common advantage" as opposed to individual enrichment. Conzelmann writes on this verse: "we have thus to understand τῇ ἐκκλησίᾳ, 'for the church'" (208 n. 18). So also Heinrici, 365; Weiss, *Korintherbrief*, 298; Robertson-Plummer, 264; Lietzmann-Kümmel, 61; Barrett, 284. As in 6:12 and 10:23, here an individualistic statement (ἑκάστῳ) is tempered with an appeal to the community.

[84] The ἐπίλογος to the argument; see chap. IV.

[85] "A question of expediency may also be concerned with time (for example, 'it is expedient, but not now')" (Quint. *Inst.* 3.8.35; more references in n. 32 above). For a philosophical consideration of συμφέρον in the afterlife, see Pl. *Grg.* 527B.

[86] He will do this throughout the argument (4:1–5; 6:13; 8:3; 9:24–27; 13:8–13; ch. 15). The importance of eschatology in 1 Cor was noted by Bultmann, *Faith and Understanding*, 74: "... Paul is treating every theme from the standpoint of eschatology."

[87] Aristid. *Rh.* 2.503 Spengel.

[88] It is made four times in ch. 7 (7:1, 8, 26, 26), as was pointed out already by Origen (*comm. in I Cor.* 39.26–32 [p. 509]).

[89] The same appeal is made in the slogan of 7:1: καλὸν ἀνθρώπῳ γυναικὸς μὴ ἅπτεσθαι ("it is good for a man not to touch a woman"). Barrett, 155 regards this as an appeal to expediency, as does V.L. Wimbush, *Paul the Worldly Ascetic. Response to the World and Self-Understanding*

adjective κρείσσων is used twice (7:9; 11:17), and μείζων three times (12:31; 13:13; 14:5). Comparative adjectives are common in deliberative discourses because the orator must show that his position is better than those proposed by his opponents.[90] 1 Corinthians abounds in comparative terms, with eighteen instances.[91] An appeal to the just (τὸ δίκαιον) lies behind Paul's outrage in 1 Cor 6:1–11.[92] The question of necessity (τὸ ἀναγκαῖον) is taken up in 1 Cor 7:37; 9:16 (in reference to Paul the example), and 12:22 (in a direct reference to the Corinthians as parts of the body of Christ). Paul also appeals to the natural in 1 Cor 11:14 in regard to proper hairstyle: οὐδὲ ἡ φύσις αὐτὴ διδάσκει . . . ("does not nature herself teach . . ."). Thus, in common with other deliberative speakers, although his main appeal is to τὸ συμφέρον, in places Paul also appeals to other values, as the handbooks dictate. The nature of the appeals which Paul employs in his argument in 1 Corinthians is another indication that the species of rhetoric he employs is the deliberative.

C. The Use and Function of Examples in Deliberative Rhetoric

Having discussed the appeals employed in deliberative argumentation, we shall now turn to its characteristic forms of proof (πίστεις). There is general agreement among the handbooks that "examples (παραδείγματα)[93] are most suitable

---

according to 1 Corinthians 7 (Macon, GA: Mercer University Press, 1987) 15 n. 11 with helpful discussion.

[90] As, e. g., in Isoc. *Or.* 6.4, and recommended by the handbooks (see the discussion above).

[91] 1 Cor 1:25 (2x); 4:3; 6:2; 7:9, 40; 11:17; 12:22, 23 (2x), 24, 31; 13:13; 14:5; 15:9, 10, 19, 52.

[92] Though not a particularly important appeal in 1 Corinthians (probably because it has other meanings for Paul), this is a prevalent appeal in *1 Clement* (see, e.g, 14:1, δίκαιον καὶ ὅσιον, and van Unnik, 188).

[93] On παράδειγμα/*exemplum* in general, see Volkmann, 233–39; K. Alewell, *Über das rhetorische* ΠΑΡΑΔΕΙΓΜΑ. *Theorie, Beispielsammlung, Verwendung in der römischen Literatur der Kaiserzeit* (Leipzig: Hoffmann, 1913); K. Jost, *Das Beispiel und Vorbild der Vorfahren bei den attischen Rednern und Geschichtschreibern bis Demosthenes*, Rhetorische Studien 19 (Paderborn: Schöningh, 1936); S. Perlman, "The Historical Example, Its Use and Importance as Political Propaganda in the Attic Orators," in *Scripta Hierosolymitana VII: Studies in History*, ed. A. Fuks and I. Halpern (Jerusalem: Magnes, 1961) 150–66; A. Lumpe, "Exemplum," *RAC* 6 (1966) 1229–57 (an excellent overview of classical theory and use of *exempla* in all types of literature into the early church fathers); M. H. McCall, *Ancient Rhetorical Theories of Simile and Comparison* (Cambridge, MA: Harvard University Press, 1969); B. J. Price, "Παράδειγμα and *Exemplum* in Ancient Rhetorical Theory," Ph.D. diss. University of California at Berkeley, 1975 (it should be noted that this useful work is not merely a chronicle of theoretical treatments, but also an assessment and often correction of them, which can at several points be disputed); K. Berger, "Hellenistische Gattungen im Neuen Testament," *ANRW* 2, pt. 25.2 (1984) 1031–1432, treats paradeigma and *exemplum* under *genos symbuleutikon* (unfortunately too brief a discussion, pp. 1145–48, but with further bibliography). Two recent NT dissertations have explored the issue of rhetorical personal example: B. Fiore, *The Function of Personal Example in the Socratic and*

for deliberative speakers, for it is by examination of the past that we divine and judge the future."[94] This is borne out by the deliberative speeches and letters themselves,[95] wherein the author brings to mind a past[96] person or situation[97] and either says that the course of action proposed, like the example, will be advantageous, or, in the negative, that the proposed action will, like the example, bring ruin and despair.[98] Often the orator puts forward a person (or persons)

Pastoral Epistles, AnBib 105 (Rome: Biblical Institute, 1986), and G. Lyons, *Pauline Autobiography: Toward a New Understanding*. For definitions of παράδειγμα, see Alewell, 24–28 and Lumpe, 1230–32.

[94] Arist. *Rh.* 1.9.40; 3.17.5 (Price, 48–50 takes this to refer specifically to historical example, but fables may also be used, see below); see also *Rh.Al.* 32.1438b; *Rhet.Her.* 3.5.9; Cic. *De Or.* 2.335; Quint. *Inst.* 3.8.36, 66 (this is something on which "practically all authorities are with good reason agreed"); Volkmann, 298; Kennedy, *Persuasion in Greece*, 204; *New Testament Interpretation*, 36. See Jost, 26: "Das historische Paradeigma ist aber für die Argumentation nur in den symbuleutischen Rede in erster Linie wichtig" (but Jost does not confine his attention to deliberative texts in his investigation). In contrast, forensic proof characteristically employs enthymemes (ἐνθυμήματα), and epideictic amplification (αὔξησις) (Arist. *Rh.* 1.9.40). This is not to deny that examples as a form of proof (or a type of stylistic embellishment to the Roman critics, so Price, 88 and passim) can also be used in forensic rhetoric, but to stress their particular suitability for deliberations (Price, 101, in regard to *Rhet.Her*). It is not merely the *use* of παραδείγματα that sets deliberative rhetoric apart, but the special function which they perform in the argumentation of this rhetorical species (see below).

[95] The use of examples (ὑποδείγματα) is one argument given by van Unnik that *1 Clement* is deliberative rhetoric (191–92; this was argued already by Jaeger: "Clement preaches concord, as he warns of discord and *stasis*, by giving many examples . . . From the rhetorical schools of his own day is derived the extensive use that Clement makes of proof by accumulated examples" [113–14]). Like Paul, that author used examples from both the Hebrew Bible and secular Greek learning (so also Lumpe, 1245–46) to dissuade the Corinthians from their factionalism (surprisingly, neither Jaeger nor van Unnik points to 1 Corinthians in this regard). See below on Paul's use of examples in 1 Corinthians.

[96] All theoreticians agree that the past is suitable for examples; there is debate about present examples (*Rh.Al.* 8.1429a, 1430a; Price, 23–26), especially because of the need for "examples (παραδείγματα) that are akin (τὰ οἰκεῖα) to the case and those that are nearest in time or place to our hearers" (*Rh.Al.* 32.1439a; cf. Price, 27; in later theory see Aps. *Rhet.* 1.373 Spengel). This becomes a *topos* in deliberative speeches themselves: "for you need not look abroad for examples (παραδείγματα) that provide the key to your future prosperity, but at home (οἰκεῖα)" (Dem. *Or.* 3.23; see also Isoc. *Or.* 5.113; Cass. Dio 52.9.4; in letters, e. g., Socr. *Ep.* 5, lines 21–22; discussion in *Ep.* 28.10; for other examples, see Volkmann, 236).

[97] See Andoc. 3.2: χρὴ γάρ, ὦ 'Αθηναῖοι, τεκμηρίοις χρῆσθαι τοῖς πρότερον γενομένοις περὶ τῶν μελλόντων ἔσεσθαι· ("one must use the past as a guide to the future, gentlemen"). See also 3.32 (of the same deliberative speech): "The examples (παραδείγματα) furnished by our past mistakes are enough to prevent men of sense from repeating them" (cf. Dem. *Prooem.* 42.2). For the same commonplace in the Greco-Roman period, see Aristid. *Or.* 24.23: "there is benefit to be gained from the past, the application of well-known examples (παραδείγματα) to the present" (see also 23.41).

[98] This is called a παράδειγμα ἐναντίον (*Rh.Al.* 8.1429a). Of his four examples of these, two are deliberative (Price, 289 n. 61). In regard to Quintilian, Price argues: "we see that for deliberative oratory *exempla similia* alone are recommended" (173 in regard to *Inst.* 5.11.6–8), but this is an argument from silence (because these are the only types Quintilian specifically names for deliberative arguments). In deliberative speeches, both positive and negative παρα-

from the past or present whom the audience respects,[99] and then tells the audience to act as they had. This type of argument is recommended for deliberative discourse[100] because people deliberately choose to do "all things that those whom they admire deliberately choose to do" (Arist. *Rh.* 1.6.29). Examples may be historical or invented.[101] There are also commonly used and even expected examples for certain appeals.[102] While the use of examples *per se* does

δείγματα are used. See also Jost, 19, 32 on "warnende Beispiele" (citing Dem. *Or.* 6.19; 19.232, 263; 23.107, 116; Andoc. 3.32).

99 See the extensive collection of proofs by appeal to personal example in Latin literature by Alewell, 54–118. Jost's work chronicles perhaps the most common and pervasive ancient appeal, to the example of the ancestors as a guide, both positive and negative, for the future (see below). On personal example, see also A.J. Malherbe, *Moral Exhortation, a Greco-Roman Sourcebook*, Library of Early Christianity 4 (Philadelphia: Westminster, 1986) 135–36.

100 This theoretical mandate is very well confirmed by the deliberative texts themselves. Of literally hundreds of examples see, for instance, Dem. *Or.* 3.21–32 (cf. Dion. Hal. *Dem.* 21); *Ep.* 3.31; Isoc. *Or.* 5.113; 6.42 (which Dion. Hal. *Isoc.* 9 calls a παράδειγμα). In speeches in the histories, see, e. g., Polyb. 23.11.6–7; Dion. Hal. *Ant. Rom.* 6.80.1f; 11.13.3; Joseph. *BJ* 2.358–87 (an extensive list of warning examples of the nations which have previously fallen to the power of Rome); 6.103–106 (the καλὸν ὑπόδειγμα of king Jeconiah); Cass. Dio 52.9.4. Historical examples are often presented as reminders (e. g., Isoc. *Or.* 6.99–101; Polyb. 22.8.9). See also Dio Chrys. *Or.* 38.10, 27; Dion. Hal. *Ant. Rom.* 10.51.3; cf. 11.1.4–5 and the texts cited in n. 97 above of many examples where the orators discuss their use of examples explicitly. No statement is more simply put than that of Isocrates: "I believe that I can convince you by many examples (παραδείγματα) that it will be easy for you to do this" (*Or.* 5.57).

101 "There are two kinds of examples (παραδείγματα); namely, one which consists in relating things that have happened before (πράγματα προγεγενημένα), and another in inventing them oneself (τὸ αὐτὸν ποιεῖν)" (Arist. *Rh.* 2.20.2; see Alewell, 15; Lumpe, 1230–31; the overview in Price, 37–39, followed by Fiore, 26–33; on the historical example, see Perlman). This categorization is recognized throughout the rhetorical tradition (Quint. *Inst.* 5.11; cf. Cic. *Top.* 10.44–45; McCall, 188–89; differently Price, 85, 106–19, though he is forced to say that although Quintilian does make this distinction, he didn't himself understand it! [135–47]). Aristotle includes fables (λόγοι) and comparisons (παραβολαί) as sub-categories of invented παραδείγματα (*Rh.* 2.20.3; McCall, 25–30; in later theory see Doxopat. *Homil. in Aphth.* 149.8–14). These distinctions are confirmed for the Imperial period by Plutarch when he describes the various deliberative proofs in *Praecepta gerendae reipublicae*: "And political oratory (ὁ πολιτικὸς λόγος), much more than that used in a court of law (δικανικός), admits maxims, historical and mythical tales, and metaphors (γνωμολογίαι, ἱστορίαι, μῦθοι, μεταφοραί)" (*Mor.* 803A).

102 As we shall see in chap. III, appeals to an audience to cease from factionalism and seek concord use a highly standardized set of παραδείγματα, both historical and invented, many of which are used by Paul in 1 Corinthians. Historical παραδείγματα: Athens and Sparta (Dio Chrys. *Or.* 34. 49–51; 38.24–25; Aristid. *Or.* 23.42–61; 24.24–26); Solon (Aristid. 24.14); the Lesbians and Mytilenaeans (Aristid. 24.54); the ancestors in general (Aristid. 24.49); Homeric times (Aristid. 24.7). Among invented παραδείγματα are common metaphors or analogies: the body (Dio 34.18, 20; 38.11–12; 39.5; 41.9; Aristid. 23.31; 24.16–17); a ship (Dio 34.16, 24, 32–33; 38.14; 39.6; 40.31; 48.7, 14); a household (Dio 38.15; Aristid. 24.7–8, 32–34); a building (Dio 34.24; 48.14; Aristid. 23.31); a chariot (Dio 38.15; 39.6); a chorus (Dio 48.7; Aristid. 24.52); the heavenly bodies (Dio 38.11; 40.35–39; 48.14–15; Aristid. 23.76–77; 24.42; *1 Clem.* 20); various species of the animal kingdom, such as bees, ants and birds (Dio 40.40–41; 48.15–16); an army (Aristid. 23.34; 1 Clem 37); also myths, such as Cleomenes the Laconian

not prove that 1 Corinthians is deliberative, since examples are used throughout a wide variety of literary genres,[103] of the three *rhetorical species*, the deliberative most appropriately employs proof by example. Even more telling than the mere presence of examples, however, for determining the rhetorical species, is the *function* which those examples play in the argument.

1. The Call to Imitation in the Deliberative Use of Example

The deliberative proof by example functions with an implicit or even explicit appeal to imitate the illustrious example (or avoid the negative example). Isocrates puts such an appeal to example in the mouth of Archidamus, where he urges the Spartans to fight Thebes and not sign the peace treaty on the basis of the example of the ancestors:

> We know, moreover, that those who became the founders of this city entered the Peloponnesus with but a small army and yet made themselves masters of many powerful states. It were fitting, then, to imitate (μιμήσασθαι) our forefathers and, by retracing our steps, now that we have stumbled in our course, try to win back the honors and the dominions which were formerly ours (*Or.* 6.82[104]).

The appeal to imitate, as in this text from Isocrates, is common in deliberative discourse, grounded as it is in proof by example.[105] Very often, as here, it is the ancestors who are put forward as the example the audience should imitate.[106]

> Now I have come before you and spoken this discourse, believing that if we will only imitate (μιμησώμεθα) our ancestors we shall both deliver ourselves from our present ills and become the saviours, not of Athens alone, but of all the Hellenes; but it is for you to weigh all that I have said and cast your votes according to your judgement of what is best for Athens (συμφέρειν τῇ πόλει).[107]

(Aristid. 24.38), and the Bacchants tearing up Pentheus (Aristid. 24.39). On exempla-collections in general, see Lumpe, 1234, 1238–40, 1242 and 1253–55; Price, 85–87; for this particular set of appeals, see Plut. *Mor.* 142E-F.

[103] See the overview in Lumpe.

[104] Note also the continuation of this argument in § 83: " . . . when it behooves us to set the example (παράδειγμα) for others in such deeds, even to imitate (μιμήσασθαι) the conduct of the Athenians" (see also [Dio Chrys.] *Or.* 37.23).

[105] Fiore, 37 and passim correctly notes that examples should lead to imitation, but does not connect this with deliberative rhetoric (he focusses on paraenetic or hortatory texts, see below).

[106] See Jost, 149–53; 159–61; 226–31 on the call to imitation as an integral part of arguing by παραδείγματα in Isocrates and Demosthenes. On the ancestors as a commonly used παράδειγμα, see Jost, 126–59; 184–244 and passim. Of many other examples, see the speech of Valerius in Dion. Hal. *Ant. Rom.* 11.20.5: τοῦτο δὴ τὸ παράδειγμα μιμησαμένους ἡμᾶς οἴομαι δεῖν.

[107] Isoc. *Or.* 7.84. This is the *peroratio* to the speech, which accurately sums up what Isocrates had argued all along – that the Athenians should return to the state of limited democracy of the past. In the proof he often compares the auspicious beginnings under the ancestors with the present corrupt political situation (7.72), a common tactic used also by Paul in 1 Cor 3 and 4 (see chap. IV).

Demosthenes[108] eloquently employs proof by example and its corresponding call to imitation in the *peroratio* to his deliberative speech *On the Liberty of the Rhodians*:

My own view is that you ought to grapple with these problems vigorously and act as becomes Athenians, remembering how gladly you hear a speaker praising your ancestors, describing their exploits and enumerating their trophies. Reflect, then, that your ancestors set up those trophies, not that you may gaze at them in wonder, but that you may also imitate (μιμῆσθε) the virtues of the men who set them up (*Or.* 15.35).

The fact that a call to imitation was a common rhetorical technique in deliberative rhetoric[109] is shown by Isocrates' refutation of his opponents' position in *On the Peace*:

For we have been depraved for a long time by men whose only ability is to cheat and delude – men who have held the people in such contempt that whenever they wish to bring about a state of war with any city, these very men who are paid for what they say have the audacity to tell us that we should follow the example of our ancestors (ὡς χρὴ τοὺς προγόνους μιμεῖσθαι) . . . Now I should be glad if they would inform me what ancestors they would have us imitate (τίσιν ἡμᾶς τῶν προγεγενημένων κελεύουσιν ὁμοίους γίγνεσθαι) (*Or.* 8.36–37).

Isocrates then lists various groups of people who (in his opinion) are not worthy of emulation, and proceeds to conclude: "we must emulate (μιμήσασθαι) the position held by the kings of Lacedaemon" (*Or.* 8.143). This demonstrates that Isocrates approves of the tactic of recommending imitation of admirable examples (and indeed assumes that that is the kind of proof required in such a deliberative speech), but he disputes the examples proffered by his opponents and counters with his own, acceptable, παράδειγμα.[110] This form of deliberative proof by example, often combined with a call to imitation,[111] is found in deliberative texts well into the Imperial period. Dio Chrysostom, for example, counsels the citizens of Apameia to act like the Romans, in his speech which urges unity between Apameia and his own city, Prusa:

That city [Rome], while so superior to the rest of mankind in good fortune and power, has proved to be even more superior in fairness and benevolence . . . In emulation (μιμουμέ-

---

108 See Blass's comment on the speeches of Demosthenes: "In den Staatsreden aber, zumal den berathenden, geschieht die Darlegung in grossem Umfange durch Beispiele" (3,1.206).

109 The phrase ὑμῖν δὲ μιμεῖσθαι (reconstructed in part) appears also in Leosthenes' Speech (*PHib.* I.15 line 56). The text is mutilated at that point so we are unable to read who it is that the audience was called upon to imitate.

110 As recommended in theory (see Arist. *Rhet.* 2.15.13–14; Price 50–51; also Aps. *Rh.* 1.375–76 Spengel, on refutation of proof by παραδείγματα). The rhetorical strategy of the call to imitation in this speech was noted by Dion. Hal. (*Isoc.* 7).

111 That is, of course, when what is offered is a positive example. In the case of a negative example, one is warned not to imitate their behavior, so as not to encounter the same disastrous fate.

νους) of that city it is fitting that you should show yourselves gentle and magnanimous toward men who are close to you (*Or.* 41.9–10).[112]

In addition to illustrious figures and ancestors, gods and heroes are used as examples in deliberative rhetoric. Isocrates calls upon Philip to imitate Heracles,[113] who reconciled Greece, which is precisely what Isocrates implores Philip to do. He constructs this proof in his deliberative argument as follows. First he describes Heracles' praiseworthy deeds:

When Heracles saw that Hellas was rife with wars and factions and many other afflictions, he first brought these troubles to an end and reconciled the cities with each other, and then showed by his example (ὑπέδειξε) to coming generations with whom and against whom it was their duty to go to war (*Or.* 5.111).

Then, after a long description of Heracles' behavior, Isocrates tells Philip:

My purpose in relating all this is that you may see that by my words I am exhorting you (παρακαλῶν)[114] to a course of action which, in the light of their deeds, it is manifest that your ancestors chose as the noblest of all. Now, while all who are blessed with understanding ought to set before themselves the greatest of men as their model, and strive to become like him, it behooves you above all to do so. For since you have no need to follow alien examples (ἀλλότρια παραδείγματα) but have before you one from your own house

[112] Of many other examples, see *Or.* 31.129 and 34.42 (on following negative examples); App. *BCiv.* 3.11.81. In *Or.* 23 Aristides presents the emperors as "the greatest example among the humans" (τῶν ἀνθρωπείων παράδειγμα . . . τὸ μέγιστον) of concord. The expectation that an example is presented for imitation lies behind his subsequent argument: "Yet how is it not strange to felicitate ourselves because we are ruled by such men, but to be unwilling to imitate (μιμεῖσθαι) them as far as possible?" (23.78; cf. § 77 on imitation of the gods). See also Aristid. *Or.* 24.11, 32, 54.

[113] Cf. Dion. Hal. *Isoc.* 6: ἔτι δὲ παρακελεύται μιμεῖσθαι τὴν Ἡρακλέους τε προαίρεσιν . . . .

[114] This term is commonly employed in deliberative rhetoric (as in 1 Cor 1:10; 4:16; 16:15). See, e. g., Isoc. *Or.* 5.90, 113, 137; *Ep.* 1.5; 2.14; 3.4; 6.87, 108; 9.1; Dem. *Ep.* 1.10; Polyb. 4.34.7; 36.1 and throughout; 18.37.7; 21.21.5; 22.8.8; 23.17.9; 28.7.2; Dio Chrys. *Or.* 48.10. It is often used of appeals for concord (as in 1 Cor 1:10, as will be shown in chap. III); Polyb. 1.70.3; Joseph. *BJ* 1.465; App. *BCiv.* 4.12.90; Dion. Hal. *Isoc.* 10. In past Pauline scholarship the term has been restrictively regarded as "paraenetic" (see Conzelmann, 31 n. 8; Malherbe, "First Thessalonians," 241 and 245 n. 34; Fiore, 58 n. 33, 68 n. 48 "hortatory language"; Lührmann, 300–305). The work of C. Bjerkelund is often referred to (*Parakalô: Form, Funktion und Sinn der parakalô-Sätze in den paulinischen Briefen*, Bibliotheca theologica Norvegica 1 [Oslo: Universitetsforlaget, 1967]), as by Conzelmann, 31 n. 8, but we must note that Bjerkelund explicitly argues that the term and the exact formula παρακαλῶ οὖν ὑμᾶς are not restricted to paraenesis (58, 87, 189; cf. Lührmann's critique, pp. 300–305). In his comprehensive survey Bjerkelund unfortunately neglects deliberative rhetoric, concentrating mostly on diplomatic speeches and texts, where the term is frequently used. In his only reference to deliberative speeches (pp. 84–85), he concludes prematurely, on the basis of only a few speeches in Dion. Hal. *Ant. Rom.*, that such speeches use παραινεῖν and not παρακαλεῖν. The ancient terminology does not so rigidly separate itself (see "Excursus: Paraenesis and Deliberative Rhetoric" below, and also Fiore, 61 n. 39). The use of παρακαλεῖν in deliberative speeches and letters must be taken into account in analyzing Pauline usage. The variety of use of the term is discussed by Stowers, 24.

(οἰκεῖον), have we not then the right to expect that you will be spurred on by this and inspired by the ambition to make yourself like the ancestor of your race (ὅπως τῷ προγόνῳ σαυτὸν ὅμοιον παρασκευάσεις)? I do not mean that you will be able to imitate (μιμήσασθαι) Heracles in all his exploits; for even among the gods there are some who could not do that; but in the qualities of the spirit, in devotion to humanity, and in the good will which he cherished toward the Hellenes, you can come close (ὁμοιωθῆναι) to his purposes (*Or.* 5.113–114).

In line with rhetorical theory as set forth in the handbooks, Isocrates in his deliberative speeches presents his listener with a παράδειγμα and then exhorts (παρακαλεῖν) the audience to imitate that example in their future actions.[115]

Proof by example and the call to imitation are also common in deliberative letters.[116] Plato, in *Ep.* 7, exhorts the friends of Dion to imitate their dead leader: "I counsel (συμβουλεύω) you, his friends, to imitate (μιμεῖσθαι) Dion in his devotion to his fatherland and in his temperate mode of life" (7.336C). In the same way, Isocrates counsels Philip by letter: "I think that you would profitably (συμφέρειν) imitate (μιμεῖσθαι) the fashion in which our city-states conduct the business of warfare" (*Ep.* 2.5). The very center of deliberative rhetoric is present here – the appeal to example as demonstrative of the advantageous course of action which the audience should follow.[117]

In addition to the common examples of the ancestors, deities, or specific historical persons, an orator can even present himself as the παράδειγμα which his audience should imitate.[118] The role of the person of the orator in any speech is recognized by the handbooks. "Now the proofs furnished by the speech are of three kinds. The first depends upon the moral character (ἦθος) of the speaker."[119] The speaker's personal qualities are essential to the success of any speech, for "moral character, so to say, constitutes the most effective means of proof" (Arist. *Rh.* 1.2.4). Quintilian tells us that this is especially the case in deliberative rhetoric:

115 With nice rhetorical irony, in the *Fourth Philippic*, Demosthenes (or Ps-Demosthenes) suggests that the assembly imitate Philip in their build up of armaments! "Do not vote for war and then fall to disputing among yourselves whether you ought not to have done so, but imitate (μιμεῖσθε) his methods of warfare . . ." (*Or.* 10.19).

116 See also *1 Clem.* 17.1 (cf. 46.1; 62.2–63.1).

117 See Aps. *Rhet.* 1.383 Spengel, in the section subtitled περὶ συμφέροντος: "[One proves τὸ συμφέρον] from example [παράδειγμα], because also formerly it was advantageous to those who did those things; or from the opposite, that it harmed the one who left off doing it" (my trans.).

118 Pliny *Ep.* 7.1: "I mention this, not only in order to enforce my advice [*monere*] by example [*exemplum*] . . . ." See Stowers's analysis of this as an advisory letter: "Pliny explicitly connects his advice with his own example and, in a way common to the hortatory tradition, presents his advice as a project that advisor and advisee have in common" (111). Stowers recognizes the important role of παραδείγματα in deliberative argumentation, but not the call to imitation, which he regards as exclusively paraenetic (108, on which grounds he regards 1 Corinthians to be a mix of exhortation and deliberation). In fact, the call to imitation is also a part of deliberative argumentation.

119 Arist. *Rh.* 1.2.3; the other two are πάθος and λόγος (cf. Plut. *Mor.* 801C).

But what really carries greatest weight in deliberative speeches is the authority of the speaker. For he, who would have all men trust his judgement as to what is expedient and honorable (*de utilibus atque honestis*), should both possess and be regarded as possessing genuine wisdom and excellence of character (*Inst.* 3.8.13).[120]

The character of the speaker is an implicit proof in all argumentation, and especially in deliberations.[121] An orator can even call upon himself explicitly, as Demosthenes does in this deliberative letter: "On the contrary, the conduct I urge (παρακαλῶ) upon the rest of men I think I ought to be myself the first to practice" (*Ep.* 1.10).[122] The practice of using oneself as an example in deliberative oratory is even recognized as rhetorically acceptable (and common) by Plutarch in *De se ipsum citra invidiam laudando*:

It is not enough, however, to praise ourselves without giving offence and arousing envy; there should be some use and advantage in it as well, that we may appear not merely to be intent on praise, but to have some further end in view. Consider first, then, whether a man might praise himself to exhort [προτροπῆς ἕνεκα] his hearers and inspire them with emulation and ambition, as Nestor by recounting his own exploits and battles incited Patroclus and roused the nine champions to offer themselves for the single combat. For exhortation [προτροπή] that includes action as well as argument [ἔργον καὶ λόγος] and presents the speaker's own example [παράδειγμα] and challenge is endued with life: it arouses and spurs the hearer, and not only awakens his ardour and fixes his purpose, but also affords him hope that the end can be attained and is possible . . . Here [at Sparta] the legislator [νομοθέτης] acted well and like a statesman [πολιτικῶς] in proposing to the young examples close at hand and taken from their own people [τὰ πλησίον καὶ οἰκεῖα παραδείγματα], employing as spokesmen the very men whose actions were to be their model (*Mor.* 544D-F).

It is thus clear that deliberative argumentation is characterized by proof from example, and often includes an entreaty that the audience imitate the behavior of the esteemed example (or not imitate a negative example). This function of the παραδείγματα is distinctively to be found in deliberative rhetoric. The orator himself can become a natural παράδειγμα, because the moral character of the orator (ἦθος τοῦ λέγοντος) is an important part of the proof, as the handbooks dictate[123] and as our extant texts demonstrate.

---

[120] See also Cic. *De Or.* 2.333: "To give advice for or against a course of action does seem to me to be a task for a person of the greatest weight of character, for to expound one's advice on matters of high importance calls for both wisdom and ability and eloquence, to enable one to make an intelligent forecast, give an authoritative proof [*auctoritate probare*] and employ persuasive eloquence." Isocrates discusses this at length in the *Antidosis* (see esp. *Or.* 15.278). Cf. Sen. *Ep.* 94.27: "But cannot the influence of the monitor (*monens*) avail even without proofs?"

[121] Martin, 175–76. This may also be rooted in the prevalent educational philosophy of learning by imitation (see Lumpe, 1235–36; Fiore, 33–37 and the works cited there).

[122] Cf. Isoc. *Ep.* 8.10.

[123] Arist. *Rh.* 1.2.3. For the variations on this in the Latin handbooks, see Volkmann, 271–84; Martin, 158–62.

2. *Proof by Example in 1 Corinthians*

In 1 Corinthians, in line with other deliberative arguments, Paul employs proofs by example.[124] In accord with the theory and practice of deliberative rhetoric, he employs several different παραδείγματα throughout his argument. Like the orators we have considered, Paul appeals to the ancestors (οἱ πατέρες ἡμῶν πάντες) from the Hebrew Bible in 10:1–13 as negative examples[125] from whom the Corinthians should learn how *not* to act.[126] His language leaves no doubt that he uses these incidents involving the ancients as examples, τύποι: Ταῦτα δὲ τύποι ἡμῶν ἐγενήθησαν.[127] The negative examples in deliberative argumentation (πα-

[124] Proof by example has been investigated in NT scholarship mostly in regard to paraenesis (Malherbe, "1 Thessalonians" and *Moral Exhortation*; L. G. Perdue, "Paraenesis and the Epistle of James," *ZNW* 72 [1981] 241–56; Fiore; Lyons) and not deliberative rhetoric (see the excursus below).

[125] Klauck, *Herrenmahl*, 256; Malherbe, *Moral Exhortation*, 136 (who also rightly notes the antithesis of this section of 1 Corinthians to the positive example Paul provides in chap. 9); Siegert, 210. Even within the Hebrew Bible itself the ancestors could be used as negative examples, as in Jer 3:25 (Lumpe, 1240). L. Wills has argued that 10:1b–5 "readily qualify as exempla" ("The Form of the Sermon in Hellenistic Judaism and Early Christianity," *HTR* 77 [1984] 277–99, 288), but does so while trying to establish as strict parts of the genre λόγος παρακλήσεως exempla, conclusions or application, and exhortation, a pattern which, however, is in no way restricted to one genre in antiquity.

[126] Each of the Hebrew Bible references to the wilderness period which Paul assembles in 10:1–13 is an example of the factionalist behavior which Paul combats at Corinth (see chap. III). Paul's use of these παραδείγματα thus conforms to Perlman's thesis that the one arguing from historical examples is also an interpreter of that history for a given audience. Here, as in other cases, Paul stands in a tradition of interpretation of that history (see chap. III).

[127] 10:6; cf. 10:11: ταῦτα δὲ τυπικῶς συνέβαινεν ἐκείνοις, ἐγράφη δὲ πρὸς νουθεσίαν ἡμῶν [the majority text reads τύποι συνέβαινον]. The term τύπος means a "prescribed form, model to be imitated" (LSJ s.v. τύπος IX, citing 1 Thess 1:7; see also BAGD s.v. τύπος 5.b). The adverb τυπικῶς similarly means "typologically, as an example or warning" (BAGD, 829). L. Goppelt (*TDNT* 8.246–59) agrees on this meaning for Paul in 1 Thess 1:7 (2 Thess 3:9) and Phil 3:17, where it is clearly connected with imitation (cf. 1 Pet 5:3). In 1 Cor 10:6 and 11, however, he (and others) treats the term as a hermeneutical term denoting specifically *eschatological* interpretation. "Commentators are divided as to whether it is an illustration of wrong conduct taken from history and thus is to be understood as an example in the sense of a warning, or whether it is an instance of Paul's specific 'typological' use of τύπος" (W. P. de Boer, *Imitation of Paul: An Exegetical Study* [Kampen: Kok, 1962] 22, and that page nn. 32–34 for a survey of scholars on both sides). While he defers from deciding on 1 Cor 10:6, in general de Boer concludes: "within the whole complex of ideas expressed by τύπος, that of *personal example* has a natural place" (p. 23, emphasis original; also Klauck, *Herrenmahl*, 256: "... fällt es schwer, in τύποι v.6 und τυπικῶς v.11 etwas anderes angesprochen zusehen als den Vorbildcharakter des alttestamentlichen Geschehens"). Without going into the whole question of the historical origins and emergence of typological interpretation, I would like to suggest that τύπος in 1 Cor 10 means the same as its uses by Paul in Phil and Thess (from which texts we know definitely that Paul was comfortable with this use of the term and the rhetorical principle behind it), an example from which to learn how to act in the future. 1 Cor 10:6 and 11 only differ from those instances in that the call to imitation is lacking, for the simple reason that it is a case of *negative* examples (called "a deterrent example" by E. K. Lee, "Words Denoting 'Pattern' in the

ραδείγματα ἐναντία) contain, of course, not the call to imitation, but its proper converse, a plea not to imitate the example thus introduced. Paul includes this explicitly in his argument in 10:1–13: μηδὲ εἰδωλολάτραι γίνεσθε καθώς τινες αὐτῶν (10:7, and repeated throughout 10:6–10 for each piece of bad behavior which is to be shunned). Other appeals to incidents, people or practices in the Hebrew Bible as examples[128] are found interspersed throughout Paul's argument in 1 Corinthians.[129]

1 Corinthians has long been noted by scholars for its extensive use of examples and images from Hellenistic culture.[130] The analogy which Paul makes in his long list of apostolic sufferings to the περικαθάρματα draws upon the Hellenistic imagery of the scapegoat.[131] In 9:7 the soldier, planter and shepherd are used as παραδείγματα.[132] Paul's use of the example of athletic competition which he applies to a discussion of true Christian freedom in the pursuit of eschatological salvation reflects common rhetorical practice.[133] In 1 Cor 12 (and 6:12–20) Paul makes use of the body of Christ imagery for the church community, which is a clear modification and employment of one of the most common παραδείγματα

New Testament," *NTS* 8 [1962] 166–73, 170). Understanding 1 Cor as deliberative rhetoric offers a solution to this statemate.

In fact, τύπος and (παρὰ)ὑπόδειγμα often alternate in LXX and non-biblical Greek (Goppelt, 249). This usage is also found in deliberative arguments, where τύπος is identical to παράδειγμα, as in Dio Chrys. *Or.* 31.56: "I used this case as an illustration (ὡς τύπῳ)" [but there are variant readings in some mss.]. For the connection of the two terms τύπος and παράδειγμα (not in rhetorical theory, but in architectural terminology), see A. von Blumenthal, "Τύπος und παράδειγμα," *Hermes* 63 (1928) 391–414. For the same kind of argument as in 1 Cor 10:1–13 by appeal to a negative, warning example elsewhere in the NT, see Heb 4:11: Σπουδάσωμεν . . . ἵνα μὴ ἐν τῷ αὐτῷ τις ὑποδείγματι πέσῃ τῆς ἀπειθείας. See also n. 98 above on warning examples in rhetorical texts (and note that this interpretation squares with the description of this passage in the commentaries (Heinrici, 291; Weiss, *Korintherbrief*, 249 ["Das warnende Beispiel der Wüstengeneration"]; Robertson-Plummer, 203; Barrett, 223; Fee, 441 ["The Example of Israel"]). Regarding the argument of 1 Cor 10:1–13 as essentially an appeal to the negative example of the ancestors, so common in deliberative argumentation, also resolves the theological and philosophical problem of whether or not the events of the wilderness generation had any meaning in themselves, or were only prefiguring the church (see Weiss, *Korintherbrief*, 252). From a rhetorical point of view, the past events are in no way deprived of their inherent meaning because they are employed as guides to the future.

[128] Chrys. termed them appropriately παραδείγματα Ἰουδαϊκά (*hom. in I Cor.* 25.1 [*PG* 61.205]) or τὰ παλαιὰ παραδείγματα (24.1 [*PG* 61.197]).

[129] See 5:6–8; 6:16–17; 9:8–10, 13; 10:18; 11:2–16; 14:21; 15:32.

[130] The classic essay is R. M. Grant, "Hellenistic Elements in I Corinthians," *Early Christian Origins. Studies in Honor of Harold R. Willoughby*, ed. A. Wikgren (Chicago: Quadrangle Books, 1961) 60–66. See also Conzelmann, 5.

[131] 4:13. See the parallels in Weiss, *Korintherbrief*, 113–14 and Conzelmann, 90, to which we can add Dio Chrys. *Or.* 8.14 (verb).

[132] Origen, *comm. in I Cor.* 40.17–18 [p. 511]); Chrys. *hom. in I Cor.* 30.1 [*PG* 61.249].

[133] Grant, 63; Conzelmann, 162; V. C. Pfitzner, *Paul and the Agon Motif. Traditional Athletic Imagery in the Pauline Literature*, NovTSup 16 (Leiden: Brill, 1967). Chrys. calls the athlete image in 9:24–27 a κοινὸν παράδειγμα (*hom. in I Cor.* 23.1 [*PG* 61.189]).

for concord and cessation of factionalism[134] in Greek political thought and rhetoric – the body.[135] The personification of ἀγάπη in 1 Cor 13 is another of the examples which Paul employs in this deliberative argument.[136] The *exempla* in 1 Cor 14 on the nature of voice, speech and communication are also common.[137] So also the examples of the seed and the varying illumination of heavenly bodies employed in chapter 15 are common παραδείγματα in Hellenistic thought.[138] In addition, Paul uses Christ as an example, as especially in 11:1.[139]

3. Paul's Use of Himself as an Example for Imitation in 1 Corinthians

But despite this long list of the different examples employed in 1 Corinthians,[140] we still have not discussed what is the single most pervasive deliberative example employed throughout the letter – Paul's use of himself as the example of proper behavior.[141] Twice in the letter Paul explicitly tells the Corinthians to imitate

---

134 This common example is noted here because scholars have long recognized its place in ancient political writings (Grant, 63; see also chap. III n. 554). Other common παραδείγματα for concord which Paul uses in 1 Corinthians (e. g., the building, the ship, common sacrifices) have not been generally recognized, and will be identified in chap. III. Here I shall limit myself to the examples which have previously had some degree of scholarly consensus.

135 The fable of Menenius Agrippa (a μῦθος according to Dion.Hal. *Ant.Rom.* 6.83.2) is the most famous parallel, in which the example of the interdependence of the members of a physical body is used in a deliberative speech urging concord (see the extensive discussion in chap. III). This story (in reference to the version in Livy 2.32) is cited by Quintilian as a use of a fable as a rhetorical παράδειγμα (*Inst.* 5.11.19; see also Price's list of examples, which includes this one, 45; and Bünker, 46–47 on 1 Cor specifically). Heinrici refers to the argumentation in 1 Cor 12:12–31 as "die παραβολή mit einer Anwendung" (358). Chrys. called the body metaphor in 1 Cor a κοινὸν παράδειγμα/ὑπόδειγμα (*hom. in I Cor.* 30.1 [*PG* 61.249–50]).

136 So already Heinrici, 358: "das παράδειγμα in der Darstellung der Liebe als der Führerin zur fruchtbaren Ausnutzung der Gnadengaben."

137 Grant, 63.

138 Ibid., 63–64: "the analogies used to prove the possibility of a resurrection body different from the mortal body are paralleled not in Jewish but in Hellenistic and Greco-Roman thought."

139 Conzelmann, 7; Siegert, 210–11. In other places, see chapters 1–2 (the very important cross imagery); 3:23; 8:11; 11:3; 15:20–22. God is also appealed to as an example in 14:33 (so also Siegert, 213), in a way characteristic of deliberative discourses urging unity (see chap. III).

140 Contra Bünker, 45: "Paulus bringt – im Vergleich zu Seneca – wenig exempla."

141 Wuellner ("Greek Rhetoric," 184) noted the importance of Paul's self references and call to imitation in 1 Corinthians, but concluded that this is a sign of epideictic argumentation. We have seen that the appeal to example and call to imitation are characteristic of the deliberative species. Lyons concludes that Paul's autobiographical remarks in Gal and 1 Thess are exemplary (226–27 and passim), but curiously does not make the connection with deliberative argumentation (he regards Gal as deliberative and 1 Thess as epideictic). For this use throughout the Pauline corpus, see Siegert, 210. Fiorenza, 393, correctly pointed to the appeal to "*ethos* as a reflection of one's own good character" as a way to understand Paul's use of himself as an example.

him.[142] While this call to imitation which Paul employs has been the subject of a great deal of scholarly investigation,[143] the role of example and imitation in deliberative rhetoric has not been considered.[144] New Testament scholarship has of late approached a perhaps premature consensus that appeal to example and call to imitation are to be found only in paraenesis.[145] While the relationship between paraenesis and deliberative rhetoric in antiquity is notoriously difficult to determine with certainty, the demonstrated use of παραδείγματα and the call to imitation in deliberative rhetoric must be factored into the equation. The presence of this type of argumentation is fully consonant with our other arguments that 1 Corinthians is a piece of deliberative argumentation, and not general paraenesis.

Excursus: Paraenesis and Deliberative Rhetoric

The following works have explored paraenesis from various points of view, though none specifically from the perspective of deliberative rhetoric: P. Hartlich, "De exhortationum a Graecis Romanisque scriptarum historia et indole," *Leip. Stud.* 11 (1889) 207–336; Burgess, 229–34; R. Vetschera, *Zur griechischen Paränese* (Smichow/Prague: Rohlicek & Sievers, 1912); K. Gaiser, *Protreptik und Paränese bei Platon. Untersuchungen zur Form des platonischen Dialogs*, Tübinger Beiträge zur Altertumswissenschaft 40 (Stuttgart: Kohl-

---

142 Παρακαλῶ οὖν ὑμᾶς, μιμηταί μου γίνεσθε (4:16); μιμηταί μου γίνεσθε καθὼς κἀγὼ Χριστοῦ (11:1).

143 de Boer; D. Stanley, "Become Imitators of Me: The Pauline Conception of Apostolic Tradition," *Bib* 40 (1959) 859–77; W. Michaelis, "μιμεῖσθαι," *TDNT* 4.659–74; H. D. Betz, *Nachfolge und Nachahmung Jesu Christi im Neuen Testament*, BHT 37 (Tübingen: Mohr/Siebeck, 1967) esp. 153–69; B. Sanders, "Imitating Paul: 1 Cor 4:16," *HTR* 74 (1981) 353–63; Fiore (see also his extensive bibliography, 164 n. 2); Sellin, 3023–25; see also the recent survey (not concerned with the historical/literary background) by O. Merk, "Nachahmung Christi. Zu ethischen Perspektiven in der paulinischen Theologie," *Neues Testament und Ethik. Für Rudolf Schnackenburg*, ed. H. Merklein (Freiburg/Basel/Vienna: Herder, 1989) 172–206.

144 de Boer, 24–28 traces imitation in the Greek world but does not discuss deliberative rhetoric.

145 Conzelmann, 92; Malherbe's work has had a great deal of influence ("First Thessalonians," esp. n. 34 on 1 Corinthians, and *Moral Exhortation*, 135–36); see also Perdue; Fiore, esp. 26–44, 164–84 on 1 Corinthians; and Stowers, 108–109. The important work of Malherbe and Fiore (with H. Cancik, *Untersuchungen zu Senecas epistulae morales*, Spudasmata 18 [Hildesheim: Olms, 1967] 46–113) indeed demonstrates that paraenesis employs examples and calls to imitation, but does not demonstrate that it alone does (see excursus). While Fiore recognizes that 1 Cor 1:10–4:21 is "more than a polite request, friendly exhortation, or moral paraenesis" (168) in his analysis of it he only compares Paul's use of himself as example and the call to imitation with paraenetic models (it is a shortcoming of Fiore's extensive study that deliberative rhetoric is largely passed over, even when he discusses rhetorical theory [pp. 26–44]). This may also be what Malherbe is concerned with when he writes: "examples of both [vice and virtue] were carefully and widely used in protrepsis and paraenesis" (*Moral Exhortation*, 136), but what he considers to be the relationship between protrepsis and deliberative rhetoric is unclear (see excursus).

hammer, 1959). These modern attempts to neatly classify these terms as defined and completely distinct genres (see the surveys in Fiore, 39–42 and Stowers, 91–94) have not received complete consensus because the ancient evidence is ambiguous and contradictory (cf. Malherbe, *Moral Exhortation*, 121; Stowers, 91–94). In antiquity three terms, προτροπή, συμβουλή and παραίνεσις (even a fourth can be added, παράκλησις, cf. Isoc. *Or.* 1.5; Vetschera, 3; Hartlich, 222–23), despite attempts at regularization (see Ps-Lib. 5; Syrian. *in Hermog.* 2.192 [=H. Rabe, ed., *Syriani in Hermogenem commentaria*, Rhetores Graeci 16, BT (Leipzig: Teubner, 1892–93), two vols.]), were used to describe sometimes parallel, sometimes identical and often intersecting literary/rhetorical phenomena (see, e. g., Fiore, 61 n. 39 on Isocratean usage).

Several different criteria of distinction (or at least poles) have been set forth: 1. προτροπή deals with accepted goods, but συμβουλή with things which are debatable (Ps-Lib. 5; Ammon. *Diff.* 132; Syrian. *in Hermog.* 2.192.13–15; Hartlich, 328–329); 2. προτροπή employs exhortation, while παραίνεσις uses precept (Hartlich, 214–19 and passim; Vetschera, 7; Fiore, 40–41; Stowers, 92), to which I would add, with criterion 1, that συμβουλή employs argumentation; 3. προτροπή tries to urge an audience to a new way of life, but παραίνεσις to remain steadfast in their present mode of life (Stowers, 92, based upon a comparison of Aristotle's *Protrepticus* and Isoc. *Or.* 1–3 [and he notes that the terms were not always so differentiated]); similar to this is Syrianus' distinction that συμβουλή deals with one matter and παραίνεσις with many (*in Hermog.* 2.192.5–6); 4. παραίνεσις is more broad than προτρεπτικὸς λόγος, which specifically urges someone on to rhetoric or philosophy, such as Aristotle's *Protrepticus*, while παραίνεσις is concerned with a wide range of life issues (Hartlich, 235–42; Vetschera, 4–7; Malherbe, *Moral Exhortation*, 124–25; but cf. Burgess, 112, 229–34 for extensive documentation for the identification of the two), to which I would add that συμβουλή provides specific advice for a concrete situation which calls forth a response (so also Stowers, 93, 107).

A few observations on these elements of a taxonomy of advisory genres and styles are in order. It is interesting that in the last three criteria the term συμβουλή, the technical term for deliberative rhetoric, has largely fallen out of the scholarly discussion (except where I have added it here). In Fiore's work it (and cognates) is subsumed under the "hortatory terms" (47 n. 9; 57 n. 32). Yet even the term προτροπή [always considered identical to προτρεπτικὸς λόγος in these discussions?] is associated throughout the rhetorical tradition with deliberative rhetoric: Συμβουλῆς δὲ τὸ μὲν προτροπὴ τὸ δὲ ἀποτροπή (Arist. *Rh.* 1.3.3; cf. *Rh.Al.* 34.1440a; Alex. *Rh.* 3.1.10, 22 Spengel). The close connection of these two terms with deliberative rhetoric does not definitely resolve the issue, but should not be overlooked, and some consistency of employment should be sought if one examines this issue from the point of view of rhetorical theory. Malherbe's analysis is confusing on this point. First he describes protrepsis as "designed to win someone over to a particular enterprise or way of life by demonstrating its superiority. First practiced by orators in the political arena and the law courts . . ." (*Moral Exhortation*, 122). Here it sounds as though protrepsis is within the sphere of deliberative rhetoric, perhaps with some relation to forensic. Yet on the same page Malherbe describes the different literary forms in which protrepsis appears, one of which is epideictic discourse. When he later speaks of "paraenetic advice" (125), we see how imprecise the categories remain. Fiore, by limiting his attention to epideictic rhetoric (see 37 and passim, despite the conclusions of Hartlich, 222; Burgess, 112 and Vetschera, 8), presumes that that is the rhetorical species of protreptic pieces. In any case, my point for this particular argument is that even paraenesis is surely to be connected in some way with deliberative rhetoric, so that the observations about the use of example and the call to imitation in paraenesis do not necessarily contradict my thesis that 1 Corinthians is deliberative rhetoric, but may indeed confirm it.

Although this is not the place for a thorough investigation of the connection of paraenesis to the rhetorical species, I must confess that I find Syrianus' classification of συμβουλή as the umbrella category inclusive of προτροπή (I would add παραίνεσις, with Ammon. *Diff.* 132) most reasonable: ὅλον μὲν γάρ τι ἡ συμβουλή, μέρος δὲ ἡ προτροπή (*in Hermog.* 2.192). Others who regard paraenesis as deliberative rhetoric are Hartlich, 222 [but cf. 327–29]; Vetschera, 8; Lyons 175, 220; Burgess regards it as a union of deliberative and epideictic, 112; Berger, 1075–78 treats paraenesis under *genos symbuleutikon*. There is no doubt that the three terms συμβουλή, προτροπή and παραίνεσις in themselves point only to one rhetorical species–the deliberative. Yet one must also admit that the rhetorical categories alone cannot explain the phenomenon of παραίνεσις (see also Burgess, 229 on "προτρεπτικός [as] a union of philosophy and rhetoric" and Gaiser, 33–106 on the sophistic traditions behind it; also Seneca's reflections on advice in *Ep.* 94 proceed not from the point of view of literary genres, but of departments of philosophy). Stowers may go too far in saying that "exhortation transcends the rhetorical categories" (93), but the inadequacy of rhetorical species alone to explain παραίνεσις is well-taken (see also Aune's statement: "paraenesis . . . refers to general moral and religious exhortation that falls between symbouleutic and epideictic rhetoric" [*Literary Environment*, 191; cf. Stowers, 107]).

Thus we have seen that both what are called paraenesis and deliberative rhetoric employ παραδείγματα and the call to imitation (and provide us with an embarrassment of riches for comparison with Pauline usage). The two forms are related in some way, but they are not identical. The difference between paraenesis and deliberative rhetoric was noted even in antiquity (see Isoc. *Or.* 15.68). The standard works of paraenesis treated in the literature are Isoc. *Or.* 1–3, Dio Chrys. *Or.* 1–4,[146] works which *are* different even from the deliberative works by those same authors which are consulted here (see "Excursus: Ancient Deliberative Speeches and Letters" in this chapter), despite some similarities, one of which is the use of examples and the call to imitation. The deliberative speeches and letters are not moral exhortation, but rather specific situation-centered arguments for a person or a group of people to follow a particular course of action (often related to public policy). That is what deliberative rhetoric is.

Complicating the issue further is the fact that the term paraenesis, as used in NT scholarship, goes too often unspecified. Some NT scholars have seen it to be an epistolary formula or style, on the model of the Pauline epistle as made up of dogmatic teaching followed by paraenesis (a model which is based more on theological than literary assumptions [see Conzelmann, 6; also M. Dibelius, *From Tradition to Gospel*, trans. B. L. Woolf (New York: Scribner's Sons, 1935) 238], and which does not fit 1 Corinthians; see also Aune's distinction between *epistolary* paraenesis and *paraenetic styles*, *Literary Environment*, 191). A thorough investigation of paraenesis remains a *desideratum* of NT and classics scholarship (we have noted already some of the complexities involved). A bare bones distinction between paraenesis and deliberative rhetoric which is followed in this study (as stated previously) is that deliberative rhetoric contains advice about specific matters and

[146] But note that Vetschera does not regard Isoc. *Or.* 3 or Dio's kingship discourses as paraenesis.

incidents, whereas paraenesis is more general moral exhortation which is of universal application (see also Stowers, 93; Aune, *Literary Environment*, 191; cf. Syrian. *in Hermog.* 2.192.7–10). This conforms to Vielhauer's differentiation of paraenesis from all ethical teaching; paraenesis is "eine Fülle von Themen, die keinen aktuellen Anlass haben" (50; he follows Dibelius's firm dictum that in paraenesis "their significance is not factual but actual–not the momentary need but the universal principle" [238]). I argue that 1 Corinthians should be understood as the former: an argument which contains specific advice for one particular church situation (see also Lührmann, 305), and not general church teaching unrelated to concrete life-situations in that church.[147] This conclusion is based upon a reading of the whole text, and does not deny that there are individual paraenetic sections within 1 Corinthians (such as the vice-catalogue in 6:9–10), but I maintain that these elements must be examined in regard to their function within an overall deliberative argument. That is the difficulty of Stowers's and Aune's assignment of a mixed genre to 1 Corinthians, part paraenesis and part deliberative argument (see n. 44 in chap. I) – that it does not sufficiently reckon with the generic contours of the whole. 1 Corinthians addresses itself to specific problems within the church community, even though traditional paraenetic forms may be pressed into service as authorities within the larger, concrete concerns which the argument takes up. Again it is Vielhauer who clarifies the issue: "Die Lasterkataloge aus 1 Kor und 2 Kor stehen nicht in eigentlichen Paränesen, sind aber paränetisch gemeint" (52; cf. Vetschera, 9).

This question of the nature of 1 Corinthians not as paraenesis but deliberative argumentation has enormous implications for an examination of the structure and composition of the letter. In terms of paraenesis, as Vielhauer noted: "Das andere Merkmal ist die lose Aneinanderreihung der einzelnen Ermahnungen und Sprüche, ohne Disposition" (51). Thus if 1 Corinthians is understood to be paraenesis, it is not expected to follow any defined or logical structure (see Conzelmann, 6–9, 93 and passim; Lührmann, 304–305; this is confirmed for antiquity by Isocrates' differentiation of his *To Nicocles* from the rest of his deliberative speeches in *Or.* 15.68, and Hartlich 213–24). But if 1 Corinthians is a deliberative *argument*, then it should have a defined structure (τάξις), as we shall see chap. IV.

In his deliberative argument which urges unity on the Corinthian Christians, Paul constantly refers to himself as the example[148] of the non-divisive course of action[149] which he hopes they will imitate. Paul's use of himself as an example is not limited to these two verses where he explicitly urges the Corinthians to imitate him. Those are not isolated statements, but must be seen within the overall argument in 1 Corinthians, in which Paul constantly refers to himself as

[147] Malherbe, *Moral Exhortation*, 125, argued that paraenesis, though of general applicability, can be "related or adapted to the settings in which it is given," but that may be an attempt to stretch the genre of paraenesis to fit actual deliberations.

[148] He is an οἰκεῖον παράδειγμα – well-known and close to his audience (cf. *Rh.Al.* 32.1439a; de Boer, 144–46, 214–16 stresses the father-child relationship as the basis for imitation [4:14–15]).

[149] Many of the epithets which Paul applies to himself (such as "all things to all people," "pleasing to all people in all things," and "not seeking my own advantage") are perfect descriptions of the non-factionalist (see chap. III).

an example,[150] with the purpose in mind that they should imitate him.[151] "In the rest of the letter Paul proposes his example as a norm in each of the problems handled."[152] Because the appeal to himself as example is the unifying rhetorical strategy of the letter, enumerating and describing Paul's self-references in 1 Corinthians almost amounts to a summary of the contents of the letter.[153]

In 1:13 Paul states that he was not crucified for the Corinthians, and proceeds to discuss his limited role in community baptism at Corinth (1:13–17). In 2:1–6 (introduced with κἀγώ) Paul presents himself as the paradigmatic proclaimer of true Christian wisdom by describing his original appearance at Corinth. In 2:6–13 he continues to discuss his manner of speaking and the content of his message, contrasting it with ἡ σοφία τοῦ αἰῶνος τούτου ("the wisdom of this age"). In chapter 3 (also beginning with κἀγώ) Paul gives a narrative of his and Apollos' role at the founding of the church community. He thus sets out his credentials for offering advice and for imitation of him – he is their ancestor/founder (3:6), a servant of Christ and steward of the mysteries of God (4:1), an apostle (4:9) and their father (4:16). Paul's rhetorical method of self-exemplification is deliberate and explicit, as the term μετασχηματίζειν in 4:6 demonstrates.[154] 4:1–15 depicts Paul's role as an apostle and is entirely in the first-person address (although varying from singular to plural). Of special importance are verses 3–5 where Paul discusses earthly judgement (ἀνάκρισις) in terms strictly of himself – ἐμοὶ δὲ εἰς ἐλάχιστόν ἐστιν ("to me it is of the least importance"). This argument in 4:1–5 is not apologetic, as is so often assumed[155] on the

---

[150] The frequency of Paul's self-appeal was noted by Chrys. on 1 Cor 7:7: Τοῦτο πολλαχοῦ ποιεῖ, ὅταν περὶ δυσκόλων παραινεῖ πραγμάτων. ἑαυτὸν ἐν μέσῳ τίθησι, καὶ φησι. Μιμηταί μου γίνεσθε (*hom. in I Cor.* 19.2 [*PG* 61.153]; also 23.1 [61.189]; 35.2 [61.297]).

[151] "The preceding discussion of 1 Corinthians has established that the examples there, Paul's as well as others', do indeed seek to stimulate imitation" (Fiore, 184; see also de Boer, 156).

[152] Fiore, 183 (I agree completely with his analysis on 183–84, as will be seen below, except that Fiore does not connect Paul's use of himself as an example in 1 Cor 5–16 with the problem of factionalism as I do). For another recent treatment see Sellin, 2951–52, who strangely classes Paul's use of self-example as a narrative form, not an argument form.

[153] This section is meant to support the thesis that Paul employs self-exemplification throughout 1 Corinthians. It is not a full argumentative analysis of the interplay between the various sub-sections and their functions, which will follow in chap. IV.

[154] F.H. Colson, "Μετεσχημάτισα in I Cor. iv 6," *JTS* 17 (1915–16) 379–84; Grant, 63; B. Fiore, "'Covert Allusion' in 1 Corinthians 1–4," *CBQ* 47 (1985) 85–102; idem, *Personal Example*, 174–75: "*Mimesis* and *metaschematisis* merge, and the virtuous example that Paul urges the community to imitate emerges as his own."

[155] See Weiss, *Korintherbrief*, 92. Of particular influence in recent years has been the argument of Dahl; see also Barrett, 101; Senft, 64; Bünker, 57–58 (this is the *refutatio*); Pesch, 81–82; Plank, 12–24. One argument for the apologetic content of 4:1–5 (and chap. 9) has been that ἀνακρίνειν and ἡμέρα are judicial terms (Weiss, *Korintherbrief*, 96–97), but the presence of judicial terms alone does not demonstrate that we have a piece of defense rhetoric. One must investigate the *function* of those terms within the overall argument (as also with ἀπολογία and ἀνακρίνειν in 9:3). This language in 4:1–5 is Paul's way of emphasizing the complete unsuitability of Christians judging one another, which is a component of party politics (see chap. III),

basis of a "mirror-reading" of Paul's self-references.[156] It is another instance of Paul's use of himself as an example[157] of proper behavior (in this case, Paul does not prematurely judge, as the Corinthians do in their divisive elitism).[158] The call to imitate follows in 4:16. The reference to Paul's "ways in the Lord" in 4:17 is another self-conscious description of his rhetorical strategy. Paul's behavior,[159] in regard to each of the issues which divide the community which will be discussed in ch. 5–16, will be the model for imitation.[160]

---

by applying these extremes to himself as an example of the proper understanding of Christian judgement (see the exegesis in chap. IV). The other pole of the argument for apologetics here (and in 1 Cor 9) is that the opposition to Paul which is so obvious in 2 Corinthians could not have sprung up without warning (Barrett, 101). Three conclusions are in order: 1. one must distinguish between the historical situation at Corinth, what Paul knew of that situation, and most importantly, what strategy Paul chose in his response to that situation; 2. the role which 1 Corinthians may have played in fanning the flames of opposition to Paul at Corinth should not be overlooked (see below); 3. seeing 1 Cor 9 and 15:9 as genuinely apologetic compels one to argue for the division of the letter (e. g., Schmithals, *Gnosticism*, 92; Héring, xiii; Schenk, 224; vehemently Pesch, 79, 81, 91), but if seen as self-exemplary argumentation, those passages show themselves to be completely harmonious with the rhetorical strategy which Paul employs throughout the letter.

156 Lyons's critique of the assumption behind this methodology (see esp. 96–105), that behind every Pauline denial is an accusation from opponents, is particularly appropriate to 1 Corinthians, where Paul's extensive self-references are a part of his overall deliberative rhetorical strategy, and in no way imply that Paul perceives himself to be under attack. I shall argue that the same is the case for the other two places in 1 Corinthians where scholars have spied out opponents (chap. 9 and 15:9). Would the defendant call upon the judges to imitate him? On the assumptions of "mirror-reading" in practice, see, e. g., Dahl, 48: "From the statement, 'With me it is a very small thing that I should be judged by you or by any human court' (4:3), we may safely infer that some kind of criticism of Paul has been voiced at Corinth." These assumptions govern the study by P. Marshall, *Enmity in Corinth: Social Conventions in Paul's Relations with the Corinthians*, WUNT 2/23 (Tübingen: Mohr/Siebeck, 1987), especially in his treatment of 1 Cor. The assumption that when Paul speaks of himself it is always to ward off charges must, as Lyons has correctly argued, be challenged (however, this does not mean that Paul *never* defends himself by personal reference; see esp. 2 Cor 10–13 and the review of Lyons by R. B. Hays [*JBL* 106 (1987) 723–25]). There is no reason to assume that Paul's self-references all perform the same rhetorical function; each letter (or even sub-argument of a letter) must be examined on its own terms.

157 See Chrys.'s comment on 4:3, applying the appropriate rhetorical term (see n. 96 above): πάλιν ἐπὶ τοῦ οἰκείου προσώπου τὸν λόγον προάγων (*hom. in I Cor.* 11.1 [*PG* 61.88]).

158 Fiore, *Personal Example*, 171. The same use of κρίνειν to refer to inner group scrutinizing of one another's behavior in relation to idol meat consumption is made by Paul in Rom 14 (see also n. 152 in chap. III). See also the verb ἀνακρίνειν in this connection in 1 Cor 10:25 and 27. In fact this verb occurs ten times sprinkled throughout 1 Cor (Allo, lv), and only here in Paul's extant letters (Robertson-Plummer, li), another argument for the unity of this letter in combatting a clearly defined set of problems unique to Corinth.

159 On way as behavior, see Conzelmann, 219; de Boer, 146–52; Fiore *Personal Example*, 179, and below on 1 Cor 12:31. This was noted already by Origen: δδοὺς γὰρ τὰς πράξεις καλεῖ (*comm. in I Cor.* 21.88 [p. 362]).

160 So correctly Fiore, *Personal Example*, 179: "the fatherly example to be imitated is to be found in *hai hodoi* and in the common teaching of Paul . . . which Timothy will recall for the Corinthians" (see also Betz, *Nachfolge*, 155). Bailey pointed to the importance of the verse for

In 5:3 Paul states emphatically his decision on the πορνεία case: ἐγὼ μὲν γάρ.[161] In 5:12, as in 4:3–5, Paul refers to *his* attitudes on judgement (τί γάρ μοι . . .). In 6:15 Paul uses himself as a hypothetical negative example (an appeal he will use particularly in chap. 13): "shall I make the members of Christ members of a prostitute?" Often in 1 Cor 7 Paul appeals to his lifestyle as an example, as in 7:7, where the call to imitation is also in evidence: θέλω δὲ πάντας ἀνθρώπους εἶναι ὡς καὶ ἐμαυτόν ('I wish all people to be like also I am"). This appeal is repeated in the argument in 7:8: καλὸν αὐτοῖς ἐὰν μείνωσιν ὡς κἀγώ ("it is good for them if they remain as I am"). In 7:25 and 40 Paul gives more reasons why his example is worthy of emulation and his advice is to be accepted (he is "one who has been given mercy so as to be trustworthy," and he "has the spirit of God").[162] In 8:13 Paul depicts himself as the example of the one who practices self-sacrifice so as not to jeopardize the brother – οὐ μὴ φάγω κρέα εἰς τὸν αἰῶνα ("no way will I eat meat, forever!"). The whole of chapter 9 is Paul's self-exemplification[163] as the one who has sacrificed himself totally for the gospel (9:23), and who is thus the paradigm of true Christian freedom in action. Paul says of himself that he has "become all things to all people"[164] (τοῖς πᾶσιν γέγονα πάντα). This epithet describes the exact opposite of the factionalists, who seek their own interest with selected people of like mind.[165] In 9:24–27 Paul embraces the athletic imagery within his self-exemplification, and in so doing he describes his struggle to be a

---

Paul's disposition in 1 Corinthians, but instead of emphasizing Paul's self-exemplification stressed the traditions (Paul does appeal to the tradition, alongside these other appeals which we have noted, but I argue for the predominance of self-appeal in 1 Corinthians).

[161] Very often in this epistle Paul pulls the personal pronoun to the front of a sentence for emphasis – "but as for me! . . ." (2:1, 2; 3:1; 4:3; 5:3; 9:26; 11:23; 15:9).

[162] These two enigmatic statements which have troubled exegesis may be best understood as part of the self-exemplification which Paul employs in this deliberative argument.

[163] As noted above, I do not accept that 1 Cor 9 is a defense of Paul's apostleship. The view that 1 Cor 9 is an exemplary argument fully harmonious with chaps. 8 and 10 has been argued before (mostly by those defending the unity of 8–10 and of all of 1 Corinthians). The recent treatment of W. Willis, "An Apostolic Apologia? The Form and Function of 1 Cor 9," *JSNT* 24 (1985) 33–48 presents a viewpoint very close to my own: "Paul gives his self-description, not in defense to objections raised in Corinth, but as a personal example which he wishes the Corinthians to imitate" (p. 38); see also Fiore, *Personal Example*, 183. For the argument that 1 Cor 9 is Paul's personal defense against charges, see, e. g., G. Theissen, *The Social Setting of Pauline Christianity. Essays on Corinth*, ed. and trans. J. H. Schütz (Philadelphia: Fortress, 1982) 40–54; G. Lüdemann, *Paulus, der Heidenapostel. Bd. II. Antipaulinismus im frühen Christentum*, FRLANT 130 (Göttingen: Vandenhoeck & Ruprecht, 1983) 105–13; Marshall, 282–317 (see the tautology this mirror reading methodology inevitably causes: "To his enemies, these assertions would appear to be of the nature of a candid confession" [Marshall, 314]; then how can they be defense?). Even Theissen must ask this searching question: "Why does he pile up arguments on a matter about which he and the Corinthians agree?" (cf. Willis, "Apostolic Apologia," 43 n. 22). The answer to this question is that these arguments establish and amplify Paul as an οἰκεῖον παράδειγμα who is to be imitated (see the full discussion in chap. IV below).

[164] NRSV. For an alternate translation see chap. III n. 412.

[165] See the discussion in chap. III.

good example, and the possible risks[166] which it involves: μή πως ἄλλοις κηρύξας αὐτὸς ἀδόκιμος γένωμαι ("lest, after preaching to others, I myself might be unworthy" [9:27]).[167]

In 10:23–11:1 Paul clearly links his presentation of himself as an example of proper Christian freedom and community participation with the call to imitate: "just as also I am pleasing to all in all things,[168] not seeking my own advantage, but that of the many, so that they might be saved. Be imitators of me, just as also I am of Christ." Here again Paul presents himself as the opposite of a factionalist – he doesn't seek his own advantage, but the common advantage.[169] Alongside these descriptions of himself as the example of proper behavior for community life, Paul repeats the call to imitation from 4:16, this time grounding his ethos as proper example in an even more powerful authority, Christ.[170]

In 11:2 Paul refers to the things which the Corinthians have remembered (or will remember – this remark may well be an anticipation of their being persuaded by his argument) as πάντα μου. These may be the same as αἱ ὁδοί μου in 4:17 of which Timothy is to remind the Corinthians. This would be another refer-

---

166 Using oneself as the example to be imitated is a strategy which is fraught with danger, the most obvious being that it might be read as self-praise, which is rhetorically and socially unacceptable (see chap. III n. 148 on Plutarch's treatise about self-praise). Chrys. combats this possible inference from Paul's argumentation throughout his homilies on 1 Cor. See his reaction to the call to imitation in 4:16: Βαθαί! πόση τοῦ διδασκάλου ἡ παῤῥησία! ... Οὐκ ἐπαίρων δὲ ἑαυτὸν τοῦτο ποιεῖ, ἀλλὰ δεικνὺς εὔκολον οὖσαν τὴν ἀρετήν (*hom. in I Cor.* 13.2 [*PG* 61.110]). From the letters in 2 Cor we learn that 1 Cor did not succeed in reconciling the factions, and perhaps instead intensified opposition to Paul himself. Thus such statements in 2 Cor as "are we beginning to recommend ourselves again?" (3:1; cf. 5:12) may be direct references to a Corinthian evaluation of Paul's rhetorical strategy of self-exemplification in 1 Corinthians. This thesis would have important historical implications for reconstructing Paul's relationships with the Corinthians. Perlman argued that "the historical example is chiefly a means of explanation of the contemporary politics and a method of political propaganda" (152). In choosing to call upon himself as example, is Paul trying simultaneously to win the full allegiance of the church to himself, despite what he says? Or, does his adoption of this rhetorical strategy show that Paul acted from an incorrect assumption that he could command their respect and be a unifying force?

167 Cf. Dem. *Ep.* 1.10: "the conduct I urge upon the rest of men I think I ought to be myself the first to practice" (quoted with the Greek above). This requirement that one who advises be a consistent example of the course of action urged is well-illustrated by this anecdote: "when the orator Gorgias read to the Greeks at Olympia a speech about concord (λόγος περὶ ὁμονοίας), Melanthius said: 'This fellow is giving advice (συμβουλεύειν) about concord, and yet in his own household he has not prevailed upon himself, his wife, and maidservant, three persons only, to live in concord'" (Plut. *Mor.* 144C; see chap. III for the household as a common analogy for the political unit).

168 This is another political *topos* (see chap. III).

169 This is the standard appeal in political literature on factions (see the discussion in chap. III).

170 See Quint. *Inst.* 5.11.42 on *deorum auctoritas*, and Volkmann, 239. I leave aside the much discussed question of whether Paul calls on the example of the earthly or the risen Lord (for a survey of opinions see de Boer, 159–60; Merk, 172–206).

ence, then, to Paul's exemplary behavior.[171] Paul's final appeal in the argument on head-wear is "we do not have such a custom" (11:16). In 11:23 Paul's place in an apostolic succession from the Lord is stressed (Ἐγὼ γάρ).

In 12:31 Paul introduces the famous so-called "Hymn to Love" of chapter 13: ἔτι καθ' ὑπερβολὴν ὁδὸν ὑμῖν δείκνυμι ("I will [or "do"] show you a still more excellent way").[172] In the following Paul will give a demonstration, an exemplification, of the way (= form of behavior) he has been talking about.[173] What has been termed the "Hymn to Love"[174] has been seen by some scholars as a separate composition inserted at this point in the argument.[175] Yet scholars have neglected how much Paul talks about *himself* in this chapter.[176] In fact, much of the chapter is written in the first person. Love is only the subject in six verses (less than half of the chapter). In 13:1–3 Paul becomes the hypothetical example[177] of the "loveless" position against which he argues. His concrete illustrations (speaking in tongues, prophesying, having γνῶσις and boasting) make reference to the precise issues dividing the church at Corinth.[178] Paul says "*if* I did these things without love it wouldn't profit me at all." But, the argument continues, Paul doesn't do these things (v. 11) because he is no longer a child. Paul clearly compares himself with the Corinthians (cf. 3:1–3), urging them to be more like him. He presents himself as a would-be negative example, and then demonstrates that he doesn't fit the conditions and is therefore instead the positive παράδειγμα which they should strive to imitate. Chapter 13 is another instance in the on-going argument of 1 Corinthians where Paul presents himself as an example of the behavior he is urging the Corinthians to adopt.

In 14:6–7 and 11–12, as in 13:1–3, Paul makes himself a hypothetical negative example: "if I came to you speaking in tongues . . ." (14:6); "if, then, I do not

---

171 Betz, *Nachfolge*, 155.

172 Is ὁδός here equivalent to its use in 4:17? I think it is – a fleshing out of Paul's way now defined and specified as the way of love. Paul demonstrates "the more excellent way" through his self-exemplification in the entire letter, as here in chap. 13. For the same use of δείκνυμι (this is a rhetorical term, cf. ἀπόδειξις in 2:4 and Betz, "Rhetoric and Theology," 37; and the verb in 4:9) in a deliberative proof by appeal to a personal example, see Aristid. *Or.* 24.14 who appeals to Solon: "yet this is not only the act of one who exhorts us to concord (οὐ μόνον προτρέποντος εἰς ὁμονοίαν) but also one who shows the way (δεικνύντος) by which concord must be acquired."

173 Betz, *Nachfolge*, 155–56.

174 The genre and composition of 1 Cor 13 will be discussed in chap. IV.

175 Barrett, 297; cf. Conzelmann, 217.

176 But it is correctly emphasized throughout the careful study by O. Wischmeyer (*Der höchste Weg. Das 13. Kapitel des 1.Korintherbriefes*, SNT 13 [Gütersloh: Mohr, 1981] 90–91, 129, 219, 233).

177 Perhaps the use of himself as a hypothetical negative example is an attempt by Paul to avoid the impression that he is praising himself (see also below on chap. 14).

178 In fact all of the examples in the sub-argument that is 12:31b–14:1a are directly pertinent to the situation of factionalism in the church at Corinth. This is strong evidence that the chapter is not a self-contained unit pressed into service here (see the full discussion in chap. IV).

know the meaning of the language . . ." (14:11). That Paul is making himself an example for the Corinthians to imitate is manifested clearly in 14:12 – οὕτως καὶ ὑμεῖς . . . ("thus also you . . ."). The inference is "I don't use my gifts this way, and neither should you."[179] The fact that Paul doesn't misuse his spiritual gifts is plainly stated in 14:19. He becomes once more a paradigm of proper behavior: "I speak in tongues more than all of you, but in the assembly I would rather speak five words in my [right] mind so that I might instruct others, too, than ten thousand words in tongues."

In 15:9–10 Paul describes his role as an apostle, demonstrating in himself the humility to which he has counselled the Corinthians (because all offices are gifts of God [12:28; 15:10; cf. 1:1; 4:1, 9]).[180] In 15:14–15 Paul again presents himself as a hypothetical negative example: εἰ δὲ Χριστὸς οὐκ ἐγήγερται . . . εὑρισκόμεθα δὲ καὶ ψευδομάρτυρες τοῦ θεοῦ ("but if Christ has not been raised . . . then also we are discovered to be false witnesses of God"). But again Paul shows that the conditional negative example has not actually been fulfilled: Νυνὶ δὲ Χριστὸς ἐγήγερται ἐκ νεκρῶν ("But now Christ has been raised from the dead" [15:20]). The understood inference is – therefore, we certainly are not false witnesses[181] (and, your faith is not in vain [15:58]). In 15:30–32 Paul again points to himself as an example of the person who has hope in the resurrection and puts his life on the line for the coming ὄφελος, by alluding once again to his sufferings on behalf of the gospel.

The frequency of the references Paul makes to himself in 1 Corinthians is, as we have seen, outstanding. These self-references are spread consistently throughout the letter;[182] they are not merely clustered in a particular part of it. I take this to be another contributing argument for the unity of the letter,[183] a unity in the rhetorical strategy of (deliberative) argumentation by the example of

179 Still another conditional negative example in the first person is presented in 14:14: ἐὰν γὰρ προσεύχωμαι γλώσσῃ . . . .

180 Again, this is not to be understood as a response to a charge (is admitting a charge apologetic?), but rather an argument from the assumed premise that Paul is an apostle (as in 9:1–3), which demonstrates the proper, non-"puffed up" attitude becoming a Christian. See also the discussion in chap. IV.

181 As the Corinthians themselves are proof (so 9:1–3; 15:1–2, 11).

182 The way in which each self-reference functions within its own sub-argument has only been alluded to here. That is a task of the compositional analysis in chap. IV.

183 The argument of Schenk, 239, followed approvingly by Schmithals, "Korintherbriefe," 267 n. 11 (also Pesch, 82), that 4:16 and 11:1 are "doublets," which on literary critical grounds should not belong to the same letter must be rejected. Should it be a methodological presupposition that Paul can show *no rhetorical consistency* within one letter? (The same argument is made by them in regard to 6:12 and 10:23; see chap. IV n. 225.) Surely the consistency of appeal to Paul's example, both in these important verses and throughout the letter, is an argument for the *unity* of the letter, not its partition. The criterion of doublets in literary criticism cannot be applied to argumentative texts, such as the Pauline epistles, in the same way as we would apply it, for example, to an extended narrative such as a gospel. At this point the methodology upon which the partition theories are based needs to be reexamined (see Merklein, 157–59 for a general critique of their criteria).

Paul himself, and the implicit or explicit call to imitation. The purpose of this self-exemplification is manifestly to get the Corinthians to imitate his example in their behavior. This is precisely the kind of proof employed in deliberative rhetoric. Its employment throughout 1 Corinthians, utilizing a variety of examples alongside his own,[184] constitutes a third proof that the rhetorical species of the argument in this letter is deliberative.

D. Factionalism and Concord in Deliberative Rhetoric

A fourth element of deliberative rhetoric is to be found in the kinds of subjects which it appropriately treats.[185] There is uniformity among the handbooks that deliberative rhetoric, the rhetoric of the assembly, treats such topics as: "religious ritual, or legislation, or the form of the constitution or alliances or treaties with other states, or war, or peace, or finance."[186] Aristotle's list is somewhat shorter than this, but the commonality is apparent:

> The most important subjects about which all men deliberate (βουλεύεσθαι) and deliberative orators (οἱ συμβουλεύοντες) harangue, are five in number, to wit: ways and means, war and peace, the defense of the country, imports and exports, legislation.[187]

This emphasis on the political questions taken up by deliberative rhetoric, particularly war and peace, which are in every such list,[188] is maintained in rhetorical theory down into the Greco-Roman period.[189] Alongside deliberations on war and peace emerges the important and related political topic of ὁμόνοια, "concord,"[190] or unity within the political body. This is not surprising,

---

[184] The variety of examples Paul uses in 1 Cor was well appreciated by Chrys.: Εἶτα ἐφ' ἕτερα ὑποδείγματα ἔρχεται πάλιν. καὶ ὥσπερ ἀνωτέρω τὰ τῶν ἀποστόλων, καὶ τὰ τῆς κοινῆς συνηθείας, καὶ τὰ τῶν ἱερέων καὶ τὰ ἑαυτοῦ τέθεικεν. οὕτω καὶ ἐνταῦθα τὰ τῶν Ὀλυμπιακῶν ἀγώνων. Καὶ τὰ παρ' ἑαυτοῦ θείς, πάλιν ἐπὶ τὰς τῆς Παλαιᾶς πρόεισιν ἱστορίας (*hom. in I Cor.* 23.2 [*PG* 61.190]).

[185] In general, see Volkmann, 294; Martin, 168–69.

[186] *Rh.Al.* 2.1423a (he takes up each one individually throughout the second chapter): ἢ περὶ ἱερῶν ἢ περὶ νόμων ἢ περὶ τῆς πολιτικῆς κατασκευῆς ἢ περὶ τῶν πρὸς ἄλλας πόλεις συμμαχιῶν καὶ συμβολαίων ἢ περὶ πολέμων ἢ περὶ εἰρήνης ἢ περὶ πόρου χρημάτων.

[187] Arist. *Rh.* 1.4.7: περί τε πόρων, καὶ πολέμου καὶ εἰρήνης, ἔτι δὲ περὶ φυλακῆς τῆς χώρας, καὶ τῶν εἰσαγομένων καὶ ἐξαγομένων, καὶ περὶ νομοθεσίας.

[188] See also Isoc. *Or.* 8.2; Polyb. 6.14.10–11.

[189] See Quint. *Inst.* 3.8.14; cf. Cic. *De Or.* 2.82.335. Dion. Hal. confirms the appropriateness of these topics to deliberative rhetoric, with particular emphasis on war and peace, in his critical essays (*Thuc.* 49; *Isoc.* 12). See also Dio Chrys. *Or.* 25.2.

[190] The classic and still valuable study is that of H. Kramer, "Quid valeat ὁμόνοια in litteris Graecis" (Diss. Göttingen, 1915). There is considerable further literature on ὁμόνοια and its Latin counterpart *concordia*: H. Zwicker, "Homonoia," PW 8 pt. 2 (1913) 2265–69; H. Fuchs, "Augustin und der antike Friedensgedanke," *Neue Philologische Untersuchungen* 3, ed. W. Jaeger (Berlin: Weidmann, 1926) esp. 96–138; H. Strasburger, "*Concordia ordinum.* Eine Untersu-

as ὁμόνοια, the opposite of factionalism, is also discussed as a common subject of deliberative rhetoric in the rhetorical handbooks.[191] Thus, according to theoretical statements about the appropriate subjects of deliberative rhetoric, concord and factionalism[192] are commonly treated in that species of rhetoric. Deliberative rhetoric, the rhetoric of the assembly, is often primarily concerned with such matters as political stability and unity.

This theoretical evidence is overwhelmingly confirmed by our extant deliberative texts and testimonia to texts no longer preserved. The most famous discourse Περὶ ὁμονοίας in antiquity was that of Antiphon.[193] Other deliberative speeches on concord[194] no longer preserved are those of Gorgias,[195] Xenocrates,[196] and Demetrius of Magnesia.[197] Isocrates' *Panegyricus*, which despite its

---

chung zur Politik Ciceros" (Diss. Leipzig, 1931); E. Skard, *Zwei religiös-politische Begriffe: euergetes-concordia*, Avhandlinger utgitt av Det Norske Videnskaps-Akademi i Oslo, II. Hist.-Filos. Klasse 1931 no. 2 (Oslo: Dybwad, 1932); W. W. Tarn, "Alexander the Great and the Unity of Mankind," *Proc. Brit. Acad.* 19 (London: Amen, 1933); *idem*, *Alexander the Great* (Cambridge: University Press, 1948) 2.399–449 (app. 25); A. Momigliano, "Camillus and Concord," 36 *CQ* (1942) 111–20; J. Ferguson, *Moral Values in the Ancient World* (London: Methuen, 1958) 118–32; J. de Romilly, "Vocabulaire et propagande, ou les premiers emplois du mot ὁμόνοια," Mélanges de Linguistique et de Philologie Grecques offerts à Pierre Chantraine, *Etudes et commentaires* 79 (Paris: Klincksieck, 1972) 199–209; A. Moulakis, *Homonoia: Eintracht und die Entwicklung eines politischen Bewusstseins* (Munich: List, 1973); C. P. Jones, *The Roman World of Dio Chrysostom* (Cambridge, MA: Harvard University Press, 1978) 83–94; A. R. R. Sheppard, "*HOMONOIA* in the Greek Cities of the Roman Empire," *Ancient Society* 15–17 (1984–86) 229–52; F. Cairns, *Virgil's Augustan Epic* (Cambridge: Cambridge University Press, 1989), ch. 4, "Concord and Discord."

191 *Rh.Al.* 2.1424b: "One who wishes to advocate a law has to prove that it will be equal for the citizens, consistent with the other laws, and advantageous for the state (συμφέροντα τῇ πόλει), best of all as promoting concord (πρὸς ὁμόνοιαν)." Elsewhere he had included ὁμόνοια as something expedient (συμφέροντα) to the state (1.1422a). One of the sample arguments in this handbook on expediency is on the topic of concord: ". . . so also it is expedient (συμφέρον) for states enjoying a period of concord (ὁμονοεῖν) to take precautions against the rise of factionalism" (1.1422b).

192 See Dio Chrys. *Or.* 26.8: περὶ ὁμονοίας καὶ φιλίας οἰκιῶν καὶ πόλεων καὶ περὶ εἰρήνης καὶ πολέμου καὶ περὶ κατοικισμοῦ καὶ περὶ κατοικίσεως, περί τε παίδων καὶ περὶ γυναικῶν (cf. Dion. Hal. *Isoc.* 10 on the subjects and goals of that orator's deliberative speeches).

193 Diels, *Vorsokr.* 2.356–66. See also E. Jacoby, "De Antiphontis Sophistae περὶ ὁμονοίας libro" (Diss. Berlin, 1908), and Kramer, 54–59.

194 See in general Kramer, 38–45. To the speeches listed here we can add the "speech" of Heracleitus as recounted by Plutarch: "So Heracleitus, when his follow citizens asked him to propose some opinion about concord [εἰπεῖν περὶ ὁμονοίας], mounted the platform, took a cup of cold water, sprinkled it with barley-meal, stirred it with penny-royal, drank it up, and departed, thus demonstrating to them that to be satisfied with whatever they happen upon and not to want expensive things is to keep cities in peace and concord [ἐν εἰρήνῃ καὶ ὁμονοίᾳ]" (*Mor.* 511C).

195 See Plut. *Mor.* 144C (and n. 167 above) and Philostr. *VS* 493 (cf. Diels, *Vorsokr.* 2.248–49). This was a deliberative speech, as Plutarch tells us "*he gave advice* concerning concord" (συμβουλεύει περὶ ὁμονοίας). This is confirmed by Philostratus, who describes Gorgias' role in this speech as ὁμονοίας ξύμβουλος.

196 See D.L. 4.12.

title is a deliberative speech, urges the Greek states to unify against the common enemy.[198] His orations *To Philip* and *On the Peace* treat the same topic.[199] There are plenty of examples of deliberative arguments which urge unity on divided factions, or urge one group to be reconciled with another, into the second century C. E., most notably the speeches of Dio Chrysostom and Aelius Aristides[200] to cities throughout Asia Minor, which are thus quite close, both chronologically and geographically, to the cultural milieu inhabited by Paul. A speech on concord to the people of Smyrna is recounted of Apollonius of Tyana.[201] As these examples clearly show, such speeches became extremely common under Roman domination in Asia Minor, as the various inter- and inner-city rivalries were now played out within the larger domain of the Empire.[202] The historians also included speeches on concord in their narratives.[203] Deliberative discourses on concord are also found within the epistolary form, from within a wide

---

197 This was known to Cicero (*Att.* 8.11; cf. *FHG* 4.382), who himself devoted much energy to the cause of the *concordia ordinum* (on which see Strasburger and more recently N. Wood, *Cicero's Social and Political Thought* [Berkeley/Los Angeles/London: University of California Press, 1988] 193–99). Cicero also tells of at least one speech he gave on behalf of concord (*Att.* 1.14).

198 See the πρόθεσις to the speech: "I have come before you to give my counsels [συμβουλεύσων] on the war against barbarians and on concord [ὁμόνοια] among ourselves" (*Or.* 4.3). On Isocrates and the "pan-Hellenic Ideal" of a unified Greece, see W. Jaeger, *Paideia: the Ideals of Greek Culture* (New York: Oxford University Press, 1944) 3.71–83.

199 *Or.* 5.16: "For I am going to advise you [συμβουλεύειν] to champion the cause of concord [ὁμόνοια] among the Hellenes" (cf. *Or.* 8.16; these are the προθέσεις to the respective speeches). Thrasym. Περὶ πολιτείας discusses concord (ἀντὶ δ' ὁμονοίας εἰς ἔχθραν καὶ ταραχὰς πρὸς ἀλλήλους ἀφικέσθαι), but the entire speech is not extant (we have here the prooimion).

200 Dio Chrys. *Or.* 34 (*Second Tarsic Discourse*); 38 (*To the Nicomedians, on Concord with the Nicaeans*); 39 (*On Concord in Nicaea*, but this speech is epideictic in character [see ch. IV n. 165]); 40 (*On Concord with Apameia*); 41 (*To the Apameians, On Concord*); 48 (*A Political Address in Assembly*); Aristid. *Or.* 23 (*Concerning Concord*) and 24 (*To the Rhodians: Concerning Concord*). See also Jones's comment on the representative character of the concord speeches of Dio: "[they] presumably resemble hundreds of addresses on the same topic now lost, or never written down, for every right-thinking politician was expected to strive for harmony within and between cities" (*Dio Chrysostom*, 94). His speeches, and those of Aelius Aristides, are our best examples for comparison with Paul's 1 Cor.

201 See Philostr. *VA* 4.8–9 and Fuchs, 114 n. 3.

202 See Jones, *Dio Chrysostom*, 83–94 and C. A. Behr, trans. and ed., *P. Aelius Aristides. The Complete Works* (Leiden: Brill, 1981) 2.365 n. 1; Sheppard, 230–37 for further literature. This was true also earlier in the Augustan age, for Horace and Virgil and other writers, in whose writings *concordia* was greatly extolled in the aftermath of Actium (Cairns, 85–108).

203 See, e. g., Polyb. 5.104; 23.11; Dion. Hal. *Ant.Rom.* 4.26 (termed a λόγος παρακλητικὸς ὁμονοίας); 5.1.2 (report of a speech); in 6.35–88 is a collection of speeches on factionalism and concord, including one of the most famous in antiquity, the speech of Menenius Agrippa (6.83–88, a speech which Skard, 89 calls "ein echter λόγος προτρεπτικὸς εἰς ὁμόνοιαν"); Joseph. *AJ* 16.133 (=*BJ* 1.457–466); *Vit.* 99–100; 264 (all reports of speeches); App. *BCiv* 4.12.90–100.

chronological spectrum.[204] Arguments to end factionalism (στάσις)[205] and seek concord (ὁμόνοια) were thus, as is well attested, common and appropriate subjects of deliberative discourses,[206] both in speeches and in letters.[207]

One of the universally recognized political values in Greco-Roman antiquity was that of ὁμόνοια,[208] which was discussed in a wide variety of literary genres.[209] But arguments which seek to persuade an audience to end their party

---

[204] Isoc. *Ep.* 1 (this letter is incomplete), 2, 3 and 9 (also incomplete) (see the comment on these letters by L. Van Hook: "Four were written to kings and warlords in furtherance of his long cherished plan, advocated for thirty-four years, that a strong leader should unite the discordant states of Greece in a common cause" LCL ed. vol. 3, 366); Dem. *Ep.* 1 (the title is known in the second century to Aristides, who wrongly quotes *Ep.* 3.45 from it in his *Or.* 23.71 [see Goldstein, 7 n. 6]); Pl. *Ep.* 6, 7 (on which see n. 207 below) and 8; Iamblichus, *Ep.* Περὶ ὁμονοίας (Diels, *Vorsokr.* 2.356). In Latin letters, see Ps-Sall. *Rep. 1 Clement* is also a deliberative letter on concord (as demonstrated by van Unnik; see also Jaeger, *Early Christianity*, 12–26 and notes). Leaving aside the question of rhetorical species, we may note also that Schoedel has demonstrated in his commentary the great significance of the Greek political ideal of ὁμόνοια in the letters of Ignatius of Antioch (8 and passim).

[205] And a host of other terms, see chap. III.

[206] On the commonality of such speeches, see Lys. 18.18.

[207] It was an important contribution of Welborn ("Discord," 89 n. 21 and "Conciliatory Principle," 335) to bring such political texts to bear on part of 1 Cor (chaps. 1–4). As representatives of the "genre" συμβουλευτικὸς λόγος περὶ ὁμονοίας Welborn cites Thrasy., Περὶ πολιτείας; Antiph. Περὶ ὁμονοίας; Isoc. *Or.* 4; *Ep.* 3, 8, 9; Pl. *Ep.* 7; Dem. *Ep.* 1; Socr. *Ep.* 30–32; Ps-Sall. *Ep.* 2 (=*Rep.*); Dio Chrys. *Or.* 38–41; Aristid. *Or.* 23–24; [Herodes Atticus] Περὶ πολιτείας and *1 Clem.* While this list accords with many of the works I consider to be examples of deliberative arguments on the subject of concord, some of those texts do not fit the description. Isoc. *Ep.* 8, despite a reference to factionalism (8.3), is a letter of request for the return of Isocrates' grandsons' music teacher Agenor (see 8.1, 4, 10), not an argument for concord. Socr. *Ep.* 31 and 32 do not discuss concord. Socr. *Ep.* 30 is a deliberative letter to Xenocrates urging him to return to the Academy and keep the School together (lines 26–28). While it may have implications for factionalism and concord, this letter does not explicitly treat those subjects. Of the Platonic Epistles, I have included *Ep.* 7, though I should note that this long and complicated letter, ostensibly advising the friends of Dion to cease from factionalism (330C-337B), is also an ἀπολογία for Plato (see Betz, *Galatians*, 15), through an extensive narration of Plato's part in the political history of Sicily. Pl. *Ep.* 6, which urges Hermeias, Erastus and Coriscus to become unified, and *Ep.* 8, to the confreres of Dion to end their factionalism, provide better examples. [Herodes Atticus] *Pol.*, while it does include some *topoi* about factionalism, which is part of the background to the speech (see Drerup, 90–91), is fundamentally a deliberative speech spurring its audience on to war against the Macedonian king Archelaus and not primarily a speech urging concord (see the πρόθεσις in §4, and Drerup's analysis).

[208] See Lys. 18.17: νυνὶ δὲ πάντες ἂν ὁμολογήσαιτε ὁμόνοιαν (μὲν) μέγιστον ἀγαθὸν εἶναι πόλει, στάσιν δὲ πάντων κακῶν αἰτίαν.

[209] See Dio Chrys. *Or.* 38.10: "concord (ὁμόνοια) has been lauded by all men always in both speeches and writing. Not only are the works of poets and philosophers alike full of its praises, but also all who have published their histories to provide a pattern (παράδειγμα) for practical applications have shown concord to be the greatest of human blessings" (cf. the parody in 38.51). See also Xen. *Mem.* 4.4.16: "And again, agreement (ὁμόνοια) is deemed the greatest blessing (ἀγαθόν) for cities: their senators and their best men constantly exhort (παρακελεύεσθαι) the citizens to agree (ὁμονοεῖν)" (on concord as a commonplace later see also Cic. *De Or.*

strife and live in unity in the future are deliberative. This lofty ideal of ὁμόνοια was not only applied to city-states, but even to smaller, less formal political and social units.[210] Paul's letter to the political body (ἐκκλησία) at Corinth, which urges them to end their factionalism and become reunited, employs the appropriate rhetorical species, deliberative rhetoric, for treating this subject. It has been demonstrated that an appeal to seek ὁμόνοια was an appropriate and frequent topic of deliberative discourse in antiquity. I have yet to demonstrate the other premise of this argument for 1 Corinthians as deliberative rhetoric (alongside the prior arguments from future time-frame, appeal to advantage [τὸ συμφέρον], and proof by appeal to παραδείγματα) – that 1 Corinthians is indeed throughout concerned with the subjects of factionalism and concord. That proof requires the extensive treatment of the whole of 1 Corinthians which will follow in chap. III.

1.13.56). The historian Polybius extolled ὁμόνοια throughout his work (see Skard, 74–75; D. G. Kagan, *The Great Dialogue. History of Greek Political Thought from Homer to Polybius* [New York: Free, 1965] 255). ὁμόνοια is very important also in the writings of Plutarch. In his political advice it plays a major role (*Mor.* 824D; C. P. Jones, *Plutarch and Rome* [Oxford: Clarendon, 1971] 112), as also in his *Lives* (as argued by A. Wardman, *Plutarch's Lives* [Berkeley/Los Angeles: University of California Press, 1974] 57–63, "The 'Politicus' – Harmony and Medicine"). The opposite of concord is therefore also commonly mentioned: "*Stasis* (discord, party strife) is one of the most discussed problems in Greek political thought" (Jaeger, *Early Christianity*, 113 n. 2).

[210] See *SEG* 33 (1983) 1165, where it is applied to two associations of bakers. The term could even be applied to the family, as in *P.Oxy.* 3057 (1st or 2nd century C.E.): παρακαλῶ δέ σε, ἀδελφέ, μηκέτι λόγον ποιεῖσθαι περὶ τῆς κλειδὸς τῆς μονοχώπου. οὐ γὰρ θέλω ὑμᾶς τοὺς ἀδελφοὺς ἕνεκα ἐμοῦ ἢ ἄλλου διαφοράν τινα ἔχειν. ὁμόνοιαν γὰρ καὶ φιλαλληλίαν εὔχομαι ἐν ὑμεῖν διαμένειν ἵν' ἦτε ἀκαταλήρητοι καὶ μὴ ἦτε ὁμοῖοι ἡμεῖν (lines 11–18; note the formal similarity to 1 Cor 1:10). See also the speech of Philip to his sons (Polyb. 23.11; Livy 40.8), which is paralleled in Jewish writings in the speech of Mattathias to his sons (Joseph. *AJ* 12.283, μάλιστα δ' ὑμῖν ὁμονοεῖν παραινῶ). This was also the case in literary works, where the family or household is a common image of ὁμόνοια or στάσις (a good example of the family application of ὁμόνοια is Dio Chrys. *Or.* 38.15 [cf. 38.5]; see also n. 167 above and the full discussion in chap. III). These are just a few examples – see the inscriptional and literary evidence collected by Kramer, 45–49 and his conclusion: "*iam vidimus tres significationes principales voci* ὁμόνοια *attribui: concordiam civilem, concordiam omnium Graecorum, concordiam familiarem*" (p. 49; see also the material collected by Moulakis, 107–10).

In this regard we should mention too the suggestive remarks of W. A. Meeks, *The First Urban Christians. The Social World of the Apostle Paul* (New Haven/London: Yale University Press, 1983) 83–84 on parallels in philosophical schools, where the importance of unity and lack of factionalism is stressed in particular among the Epicureans (in reference to Eus. *p. e.* 14.5). "... Epicurus undertook to maintain that unity among groups of his followers settled in different places, by writing letters 'to the friends' in those places. In a number of ways, then, the groups founded by Paul and his circle and the groups that traced their basis to Epicurus seem to have arrived at similar solutions for a number of parallel goals and practical requirements. The analogies would repay a more careful investigation than the present context permits." In this study we shall pick up on part of this suggestion and investigate in particular Paul's solutions for the parallel goal of unity in the face of factionalism.

Chapter III

Thematic and Rhetorical Unity in 1 Corinthians: The Language of Factionalism and Reconciliation

A. The Questions and the Argument

This chapter, through an analysis of the contents and language of Paul's argument in 1 Corinthians, will perform several functions within the overall argument of this investigation. First of all, this chapter will serve to demonstrate the applicability of the fourth element of deliberative rhetoric identified in chap. III to 1 Corinthians – that the content of 1 Corinthians is a series of arguments ultimately based in the subject of factionalism and concord,[1] political entities appropriately treated by deliberative rhetoric. The second purpose of this chapter is to demonstrate by this coherence in content two other important premises for the compositional analysis of 1 Corinthians which will follow in chap. IV. I shall first demonstrate that 1 Cor 1:10 contains technical language derived from political oratory and treatises concerning political unity. In this verse Paul urges the Corinthians to end their factions and become restored as a unified political[2]

---

[1] This is of course not to deny that many other actual subjects are treated in the various subsections of the argument (idol meats, spiritual gifts, the resurrection, etc.). What I shall show is how Paul's treatment of each of these subjects is rooted *by him* in the overriding concern for concord.

[2] *OED* defines "political" as "of, belonging, or pertaining to the state or body of citizens, its government and policy . . ." (12.32). Paul addresses the Corinthian church as an ἐκκλησία (on this as a political term, see Lightfoot, 32). The church community at Corinth was of course a political body in this wider sense, "a body of citizens." They are a religious association within the polis with its own social structure and membership. That the early churches were political bodies which functioned much as other political/social entities in antiquity (and even modernity) is the presupposition behind the recent works on the sociology of the early church (the most notable being Theissen, and Meeks, esp. 74–110).

In stressing the political nature of the issue of factionalism at Corinth I am not, however, contrasting "political" with "religious" conflict. The problems at Corinth cannot be so neatly separated – they are ecclesiological, and thus simultaneously political and religious. What will be stressed in this chapter is the political nature and background of the terms and arguments which Paul uses in his response to Corinthian problems. In fact, even in "political" rivalries in Greco-Roman literature, "religious" issues often play a role, as we shall see.

community by using stock phrases from Greco-Roman antiquity for dealing with just this issue. In order to demonstrate that this verse (1:10) is the πρόθεσις (thesis statement), the rhetorical part which announces what is to be demonstrated in an argument,[3] I shall then show that the entire letter of 1 Corinthians is indeed consonant with this thesis statement, the appeal to the church at Corinth to be unified and end its factionalism. The evidence which will be produced in support of these two points will also serve to demonstrate the unity of 1 Corinthians, both thematic[4] and rhetorical, as a letter which throughout seeks to persuade the church community to work for unity in all the areas of church life where their divisions are now manifest.

The history of exegesis on 1 Corinthians has predominantly concluded that factionalism and party strife are the topics of consideration only in chapters 1–4, while the rest of the letter (chapters 5–16) takes up other pastoral and theological issues facing the church at Corinth.[5] This point of view has been a contributing factor in various partition theories of 1 Corinthians, as scholars have concluded that 1 Cor 1–4 is so different in content from the rest of 1 Corinthians that it must indeed belong to a separate letter. Hurd summarizes the partition theories[6] of 1 Corinthians with the following statement:

> 1 Cor 1–4, however ('Letter C'), does not concern the Corinthians' letter [7:1], but is solely concerned with the party divisions at Corinth of which Paul had learned from 'Chloe's people' [1:11]. *Paul's indignation over these dissensions appears absent from the rest of 1 Corinthians.*[7]

---

[3] See Arist. *Rh.* 3.13.1, where the prescribed function of the πρόθεσις is to state the subject to be discussed (τὸ πρᾶγμα εἰπεῖν). It should be noted that πρόθεσις is Aristotle's term (who prefers a stream-lined approach to the parts of a speech), which the Latin handbooks discuss under a variety of subcategories (*propositio, expositio, enumeratio, partitio*). See chap. IV for discussion.

[4] Compare Bultmann's approving remarks on Barth's methodology: "The unity to be looked for is therefore a material unity, i. e. one grounded in the subject-matter, not some sort of 'spiritual' unity which would depend on the unity and individuality of the one author's personality. No one will want to deny that this method of inquiry is both appropriate to the content of the Epistle and fruitful for detailed exegesis" (*Faith and Understanding*, 66–67). However, Bultmann goes on to remark that even a letter collection could exhibit such inner unity. But where Barth and Bultmann sought a theological unity (on their own terms) this study seeks evidence of *rhetorical* unity.

[5] P. W. Schmiedel, *Die Briefe an die Thessalonicher und an die Korinther*, HKNT vol. 2, pt. 1 (Tübingen: Mohr/Siebeck, 1892[2]) 58; Weiss, *Korintherbrief*, 123; Conzelmann expresses this representative opinion in his commentary at 4:21: "The discussion of the σχίσματα, 'divisions,' has reached its conclusion. There follows a loosely connected string of topics arising from community life in Corinth" (93; also Heinrici, 169, 186). Welborn's work, while like this study emphasizing the political aspects of the factionalism Paul combatted at Corinth, in common with these other scholars restricts its sphere of reference to 1 Cor 1–4 ("Discord," 89, 93; "Conciliatory Principle," 333–46).

[6] See the discussion and bibliography in chap. I.

[7] Hurd, 45 (emphasis added); see also, e. g., Schmithals, *Gnosticism*, 203. This viewpoint is evident especially in discussion on 11:18, for it is a cornerstone of partition theories that the

The position which will be demonstrated here is that in fact the entire letter of 1 Corinthians is permeated with the vocabulary and *topoi*[8] used in political rhetoric to discuss and combat factionalism;[9] thus dissension is at issue throughout all sixteen chapters of the letter.[10] This demonstration is grounded in a methodological difference from other such attempts. Previously scholars have tried, without success, to line up the sides behind each of the various topics taken up in ch. 5–15 with the three or four parties named in 1:12.[11] They have failed because Paul's rhetorical strategy is to combat the phenomenon of factionalism

---

factions "reappear" there in a context in which discussion of factionalism was absent (see nn. 28 and 513, and full discussion below). But this assumption is not restricted to partition theorists. See Munck's argument: "If the first four chapters of 1 Corinthians really dealt with four different factions, to which the greater number of the church members attached themselves, we should necessarily expect to hear of those factions elsewhere in the letter. But the letter's commentators do not think that any references to factions are to be found outside chs. 1–4" (139). For a lone voice on the other side, see Prümm, whose viewpoint Fee, 5 n. 13a curiously sets up as the "usual understanding" of the letter (in fact Prümm is one of the few who rightly pushes this point of view). Fee argues that "scarcely anything explicit is said in chaps. 5–16 to indicate the existence of actual parties within the church" (47). Against this viewpoint, see the correct statement of Jewett (who himself holds to a partition theory of 1 Cor): "Schenk finds it strange that such a letter included nothing about the schism question proper, overlooking that each of the topics Paul takes up in the answer letter touches on aspects of the controversy" ("Redaction," 398).

[8] A *topos* is literally the "region" from which arguments are drawn (Cic. *Top.* 2.8). Aristotle distinguished universal topics (the more and the less, contraries [*Rh.* 2.18–19]) and specific topics "peculiar to each class of things" (*Rh.* 1.2.22). In this chapter the latter type of *topos* is meant: *topoi* ("commonplaces") specific to deliberative arguments, and especially those which urge concord. For a discussion of meanings of *topos*, and the important reminder that each author uses a *topos* in an individually creative way, see Malherbe, *Moral Exhortation*, 144–45, and p. 147 on *topoi* used to urge civil concord. Methodologically it is necessary to show, not just that parallels to Paul's terminology or arguments exist in Greco-Roman texts, but that these are also paralleled in *function* in both places in order not to treat *topoi* (both Pauline and Greco-Roman) in isolation from their conceptual and rhetorical frameworks. One must also examine the common clusters or combinations of *topoi* which are used in the treatment of specific subjects. In taking up the rhetorical definition of *topos* I am consciously not following those scholars who regard *topos* as an independent *literary form* (D. G. Bradley, "The *Topos* as a Form in the Pauline Paraenesis," *JBL* 72 [1953] 238–46; T. Y. Mullins, "*Topos* as a New Testament Form," *JBL* 99 [1980] 541–47; I agree with the critique of L. T. Johnson, "James 3:13–4:10 and the *Topos* ΠΕΡΙ ΦΘΟΝΟΥ," *NovT* 25 [1983] 327–47; 334 n. 33).

[9] How Paul integrates these terms and *topoi* into his overall argument will be examined in the compositional analysis in chap. IV.

[10] We have noted above in chap. I that this is indeed the interpretation of 1 Cor common in the early church: that the letter as a whole was understood as responding to factionalism (*1 Clem.* 47:1–3; Chrys. *hom. in I Cor.* Argumentum [*PG* 61.9–12]; see also the order in his survey of the letter in 43.1 [61.367]; the Muratorian Canon).

[11] With Welborn, "Discord," 88: "The attempt to identify the parties with the views and practices condemned elsewhere in the epistle, as if the parties represented different positions in a dogmatic controversy, has collapsed under its own weight." See also H. Koester, *Introduction to the New Testament*, 2 vols., *Vol. 2. History and Literature of Early Christianity* (Philadelphia: Fortress, 1982) 121.

itself, not each individual faction directly. This study takes a new approach to this question: we shall investigate how *Paul's argument of response* employs political language and *topoi* to describe the situation at Corinth as factionalism and urge the reunification of the church.[12]

B. Political Terms in 1 Cor 1:10

We shall begin with an analysis of the terms[13] which make up the crucial verse 1:10. In 1:10 Paul uses four phrases (two independent and one double formula), both negative and positive, for the political unity which he urges on the Corinthian Christians.[14] The four phrases used are (ἵνα) τὸ αὐτὸ λέγητε, μὴ ᾖ ἐν ὑμῖν σχίσματα, ἦτε δὲ κατηρτισμένοι ἐν τῷ αὐτῷ νοΐ, ἐν τῇ αὐτῇ γνώμῃ. Each contains a stock phrase in Greek literature for political order and peace; the use of four such phrases gives this πρόθεσις a vehemence and undeniable clarity.[15]

The first phrase in Paul's plea for unity, τὸ αὐτὸ λέγειν is commonly used in ancient Greek[16] literature to describe the opposite of factionalism. Those who "say the same thing" are allies, compatriots, even co-partisans. Simply put, they agree with one another. This has been recognized by scholars since J. J. Wettstein

---

[12] This does not mean that we can draw immediate conclusions about the actual situation at Corinth being "political" (as is done in large measure by Welborn, "Discord"). We begin with Paul's own rhetoric of response (see chap. 1 n. 3).

[13] From a methodological point of view, the terms and phrases which Paul uses in 1 Corinthians must be investigated in order to determine their lexicographical and historical meanings as a background to Paul's usage (the same principle is used with opposite ends and conclusions by Munck, 136–39). An excellent start on the investigation of the political terms in the first four chapters of 1 Corinthians has been made by Welborn, "Discord," 86–88 and "Conciliatory Principle," 331–340. The distinctive positive and negative vocabulary of 1 Cor in itself (among which are terms for unity and division [σχίσμα, αἵρεσις, φυσιοῦν, ἀγάπη, σῶμα]) was presented as an argument for the unity of the letter by G. Segalla, "Struttura filologica e letteraria della prima lettera ai Corinti," *Testimonium Christi. Scritti in onore di Jacques Dupont* (Brescia: Paideia, 1985) 465–80, 465–68.

[14] Paul makes his appeal διὰ τοῦ ὀνόματος τοῦ κυρίου ἡμῶν Ἰησοῦ Χριστοῦ. See Lightfoot's comment: "The exhortation to unity is still furthered. 'I intreat by that one name which we all bear in common, that ye assume not diverse names, as of Paul, and Apollos etc.'" (151; so also Prümm, 206 in regard to both 1:10 and 6:11). The common name plays a unifying role already in the epistolary prescript in 1:2b (see U. Wickert, "Einheit und Eintracht der Kirche im Präskript des ersten Korintherbriefes," *ZNW* 50 [1959] 73–82, esp. 78, and the discussion in chap. IV).

[15] As the handbooks recommend (see Cic. *Inv. Rhet.* 1.22.31–32; Quint. *Inst.* 4.5.26; cf. Arist. *Rh.* 3.13.1–2; Martin, 94–95).

[16] The phrase is clearly Greek (see Lightfoot, 151). The two closest Hebrew analogues are quite different (פה אחד in Josh 9:2; 1 Kgs 22:13/2 Chr 18:12 is rendered into Greek as ἅμα πάντες and ἐν στόματι ἑνί [used by Paul in Rom 15:6 in tandem with ὁμοθυμαδόν; also in *1 Clem.* 34:7], and קול אחד in Exod 24:3; 2 Chr 5:13, translated as μία φωνή [cf. Acts 19:34; *Paraleip. Jer.* 9.14; for further references see BAGD s. v. φωνή 2.a]).

in 1752 cited Polyb. 2.62.4; 5.104.1; Thuc. 5.31.6 (and the scholion to it[17]) as parallels to 1 Cor 1:10.[18] To cite one example, in Polybius 5.104 Agelaus of Naupactus delivers a deliberative speech in favor of unity and peace before King Philip and the Aetolian allies. He begins his deliberative plea for unity with the same phrase with which Paul opens his argument in 1 Corinthians:

It would be best of all if the Greeks never made war on each other, but regarded it as the highest favour in the gift of the gods could *they speak ever with one heart and voice* (εἰ λέγοντες ἓν καὶ ταὐτὸ πάντες).[19]

This stock phrase is also used by the orator Dio Chrysostom, a near contemporary of Paul.[20] Another first century writer, Flavius Josephus, also uses the phrase τὸ αὐτὸ λέγειν in his descriptions of party politics and petty human squabbles.[21] A similar phrase, ταὐτὸ φθέγγεσθαι ("to utter the same thing") is used by Dio Chrysostom and Aelius Aristides in their speeches on concord.[22] Still another variation on this phrase is ταὐτὰ φρονεῖν ("to think the same thing[s]"),[23] which also denotes the state of unity.[24] It is a favorite phrase of Aristides, especially in his deliberative speeches urging concord.[25] That comparable phrase, τὸ αὐτὸ φρονεῖν, is also commonly used by Paul with the same meaning, to be unified.[26] The phrase τὸ αὐτὸ λέγειν (and variations of it) is thus

---

17 The scholion reads τὴν αὐτὴν γνώμην ἔχοντες, thus demonstrating the equivalence of these two phrases for political unity which occur in tandem also in 1 Cor 1:10 (see below).

18 J. J. Wettstein, *Novum Testamentum Graecum* (Amsterdam: Ex officina Dommeriana, 1752) 2.103. These references were picked up by Heinrici, 52, footnote, who also added Thuc. 4.20.4 and Arist. *Pol.* 2.3.3 (from Lightfoot; probably an incorrect citation for *Pol.* 2.1.9), to the known parallels. From Heinrici's commentary these ancient examples of the phrase τὸ αὐτὸ λέγειν entered into the exegetical tradition. What has not been noted is that a number of these ancient occurrences of the phrase occur in *deliberative speeches* embedded in the historical narratives (e. g., Polyb. 5.104.1; Thuc. 4.20.4). See also Lightfoot's important discussion, where he correctly interprets these parallels as all referring to faction-free communities and concludes: "The marked classical colouring of such passages as this leaves a much stronger impression of St. Paul's acquaintance with classical writers than the rare occasional quotations which occur in his writings" (151).

19 More literally translated "if all (were) saying one and the same thing."

20 *Or.* 4.135 (τὸ αὐτὸ εἰπεῖν).

21 *AJ* 10.107; 17.35; 18.375, 378.

22 Dio Chrys. *Or.* 34.17; Aristid. *Or.* 24.52.

23 For the Latin usage *idem sentire*, see J. Hellegouarc'h, *Le vocabulaire Latin des relations et des partis politiques sous la République* (Paris: Société d'Edition les Belles Lettres, 1963) 121 and notes.

24 The two phrases τὸ αὐτὸ λέγειν and τὸ αὐτὸ φρονεῖν are paralleled in a 2nd c. B.C.E. grave inscription from Rhodes, *IG* 12.1.50, no. 149: ταὐτὰ λέγοντες, ταὐτὰ φρονοῦντες, ἤλθομεν τὰν ἀμέτρητον ὁδὸν εἰς 'Αΐδαν ("saying the same things and thinking the same things [i. e., as partners] we came [on] the measureless way into Hades" [first cited by Weiss, *Korintherbrief*, 13; trans. mine]). This demonstrates the appropriate application of these political epithets to personal relationships (here a married couple; on the connection between marriage and concord, see below on 1 Cor 7).

25 *Or.* 23.31, 42, 43; 24.29; cf. 27.43; see also Dio Chrys. *Or.* 34.20.

26 2 Cor 13:11; Phil 2:2; 4:2; Rom 12:16; 15:5 ("think the same thing, i. e. be in agreement,

used in Greek literature to describe persons in a state of political or social unity from the classical period down well into the Greco-Roman era.

The second powerful term used in 1:10 is the noun σχίσμα. In fact, this term plays a central role throughout the letter, as it is repeated again in 11:18 and 12:25.[27] While scholars have continually sought to argue that the term must be used differently in these three instances, or that it must refer to different historical occasions,[28] there is no reason to assume this. It is far more easy and natural to conclude that Paul refers to the same phenomenon using the same specific term. In all three places where the term σχίσμα is used in 1 Corinthians,[29] it means a division or a rift within the social fabric of the community.[30] Throughout the letter the term refers to the phenomenon of factions within the Corinthian church.[31]

---

live in harmony," BAGD, 866). J. P. Sampley (*Pauline Partnership in Christ. Christian Community and Commitment in Light of Roman Law* [Philadelphia: Fortress, 1980] 62–70) rightly noted that τὸ αὐτὸ φρονεῖν is a technical phrase calling for unity, but focused his attention on its use in the formal *societas* relationship (he does, however, recognize that Paul can use the "*societas* terminology" [many of which I would class more broadly as "unity *topoi*"] as sententious epigrams on the Christian life [pp. 94–97]). The phrase is in fact used of all types of interpersonal and political associations (as in Dion. Hal. *Ant.Rom.* 7.59.7, and the texts cited by BAGD s. v. φρονέω, 1).

[27] 12:25 repeats almost the exact same phrase as 1:10: ἵνα μὴ ᾖ σχίσμα ἐν τῷ σώματι (where 1:10 had read ἐν ὑμῖν, because the body imagery has now been fully introduced as equivalent to the church). Note also the phrase τὸ αὐτὸ μεριμνᾶν in 12:25 (cf. τὸ αὐτὸ λέγειν).

[28] This is a foundation of partition theories (see list and quotation below in n. 513), especially those which follow Schmithals. The partition theories of Weiss, *Earliest Christianity* 1.340–41; Schenk, 241; Schmithals, "Korintherbriefe," 282–86; Sellin, "Hauptprobleme," 2968, put the uses of σχίσμα in three different letters. What is surprising is that scholars who argue for the unity of the letter, in combatting Schmithals's objection in regard to 11:18, feel compelled to argue that the σχίσματα in 11:18 are different from those in 1:10 (e. g., Kümmel, 278; Barrett, 260–61; Merklein, 174–75), when in fact the simplest argument for the compositional integrity of the letter is that they are the same! (see correctly Prümm, 211; Allo, 270–71 and surprisingly Munck, 138, who does not consider the term to refer to factionalism; cf. Conzelmann, 193 n. 12). The partition theorists are forced to argue that Paul, who used the term σχίσμα only in the Corinthian correspondence [1 Cor], used it in two or three different letters with different meanings and referents, which is inherently unlikely. See further discussion below on 11:18.

[29] As we shall see, σχίσμα is one of a number of proper political terms which Paul uses to describe the divisions at Corinth.

[30] The term occurs elsewhere in the NT with this meaning at John 7:43; 9:16; 10:19. Cf. the weaker interpretation of σχίσμα by Munck, 137–39. It is hard to see how he knows that the σχίσματα are "temporary" (and why their "temporariness" would make them any less factions – his study suffers from a definitional problem of what "factionalism" is; see excursus). It is often objected to the view that the problem at Corinth was factions, divisions, that Paul addresses them as a whole (Munck; Fee, 31; cf. Conzelmann, 14) but this is of course a central facet of Paul's rhetorical strategy. How else could he urge the church to become reunified than by a communal appeal to the whole? It is the still partial unity of the community (especially in Paul's mind) that determines that their divisions are *factions*. If the divisions were complete, they would not be factions but separate communities! (so correctly Robertson-Plummer, 239: "neither σχίσματα . . . nor αἱρέσεις are separations from the Church, but dissensions within it"; their interpretation squares with that of Chrys. *hom. in I Cor.* 3.1 [*PG* 61.22–23] on this point).

[31] BAGD, 797: "fig. division, dissension, schism."

Excursus: The Descriptive Significance of the Term σχίσμα

When one thinks of the Corinthian σχίσματα, one need not think of "parties" with fixed membership, ideologies and structures, as in the modern sense of the term. Even in ancient Athens a "party" had less strict definitions than today, as classics scholars have noted. "Au lieu du parti, qui propose un idéal et une structure permanents et indépendants des individus qui le composent, l'histoire grecque offre l'image de groupes éphémères, évoluant au gré des circonstances, et totalement tributaires du personnage qui les anime" (O. Aurenche, *Les Groupes d'Alcibiade, de Léogoras et de Teucros* [Paris: Société d'Edition les Belles Lettres, 1974] 9). See also L. R. Taylor, *Party Politics in the Age of Caesar* (Berkeley/ Los Angeles: University of California Press, 1949) 6–24 on the "amorphous character" of the "parties" in Roman politics at the end of the Republic (which she differentiates from the modern point of view). From a totally different perspective, in his sociological analysis of the Corinthian community A. Schreiber argued for the presence of "Untergruppen" even on the basis of the group-dynamic thesis that all groups over twelve to fifteen persons will tend to form sub-groups (*Die Gemeinde in Korinth. Versuch einer gruppendynamischen Betrachtung der Entwicklung der Gemeinde von Korinth auf der Basis des ersten Korintherbriefes*, NTAbh n. s. 12 [Münster: Aschendorff, 1977] 135). But Schreiber differentiates these groups from parties (see p. 136) because he thinks of parties in antiquity as having a much more rigid structure than they actually had. This also does not sufficiently reckon with the fact that *Paul* terms the Corinthian sub-groups "factions" (despite what they might have in fact been on sociological grounds). Schreiber's work, because it focuses on social description, unfortunately does not sufficiently recognize the *prescriptive* nature and function of Paul's arguments in 1 Corinthians.

It is because of too strict and formal an implied definition of factionalism that Munck also can deny that there were factions at Corinth, but admit "disunity" "disputes" and "divisions" (135–39 and passim). Munck also presumes that "factions" would be arranged around specific theological or even doctrinal positions: "It is therefore a question, not of factions, but simply of divisions among church members for non-theological reasons" (138–39). Even if this were true, the lack of theological content to the factions would make them no less factions! (see the language of Chrys.'s exegesis: Οὐδὲ γὰρ ἀπὸ τοῦ διεστάναι κατὰ τὴν πίστιν τὰ σχίσματα ἐγίνετο, ἀλλὰ ἀπὸ τοῦ τὴν γνώμην διῃρῆσθαι κατὰ ἀνθρωπίνην φιλονεικίαν [*hom. in I Cor.* 3.1 (*PG* 61.23)]). It is also methodologically problematic, as Welborn has shown ("Discord," 88–89), to deny the existence of Corinthian factions because scholars cannot reconstruct from 1 Corinthians the coherent and distinct positions of each of the groups named by the slogans in 1:12. The impossibility of that task is due to Paul's rhetorical strategy in the letter – he chooses not to address the factions individually, but instead exhorts all commonly to unity. We cannot conclude from our inability to reconstruct them that there weren't factions.

Two important points need to be made for this study: 1. the *OED* defines "faction" generally as: "a class, sort, or set of persons"; and more specifically, "a party in the state or in any community or association" (5.652). As applied to the Corinthian community, this means simply that it is divided into some number of separate groups. 2. The term "faction," in both antiquity and modernity (ibid.) is *a negative term* (so understood by Chrys.: Τοῦ σχίσματος ἡ ἔμφασις καὶ αὐτὸ τῆς κατηγορίας τὸ ὄνομα ἱκανὰ σφόδρα αὐτῶν καθάψασθαι [*hom. in I Cor.* 3.1 (*PG* 61.22–23; cf. 61.23 comparing σχίσμα and ἔρις)]; see also *OED* 5.652: "always with opprobrious sense, conveying the imputation of selfish or mischievous ends or turbulent or unscrupulous methods"). It is thus not the term which a group would use for itself (Taylor, 13–14). Paul deliberately chooses to describe the divisions within the church as σχίσματα (and a host of other terms which we shall deal with below), as a serious social threat to the life of the church community. We cannot assume from this that the Corinthians would so describe their activity (more likely they would have said that they were "right" and the others were simply "wrong" on the various issues, mostly practical, which cause these divisions). Historical reconstruction of the "factions" at Corinth cannot precede a rhetorical analysis of Paul's argument; indeed it must be dependent upon it. But in order to understand Paul's argument we must take seriously the rhetorical force of the strong terms which he employs, which arise from ancient politics, to describe their behavior which he seeks to change.

In Greek literature, while the verb σχίζειν ("to tear" or "to divide"[32]) is quite common, the concrete neuter noun σχίσμα is actually quite rare and "occurs in connection with divisions in parts of the body or the parts of plants."[33] In fact, prior to the New Testament and early Christian literature,[34] the noun σχίσμα is found with a metaphorical meaning referring to political tears and divisions only in the famous text *PLond.* 2710.13, the injunction against religious factions in the guild of Zeus Hypsistos.[35] Nonetheless, although the noun is rare with the meaning of "faction" prior to Christian texts,[36] the metaphorical use of this linguistic root to refer to divisions of persons into opposing or separate groups is well attested by the verb σχίζειν.[37] To cite one clear example, in Ps-Lucian's

[32] A near synonym, μερίζειν, is used in 1:13 (see below); cf. διακρίνειν in 4:7.

[33] C. Maurer, *TDNT*, "σχίζω," 8.959–65, 963, with references.

[34] The term becomes quite common in ECL (*Did.* 4:3; *1 Clem.* 2:6; 5:9; 46:9; 49:5; 54:2 [clearly in commentary on the use of the term in 1 Cor]; *Barn.* 19.12 [οὐ ποιήσεις σχίσμα, εἰρηνεύσεις δὲ μαχομένους συναγαγών]; *Herm. Sim.* 8.9.4; the agraphon in Just. *Dial.* 35 [BAGD s. v.]). See especially *1 Clem.* 2:6 and 46:9, where σχίσμα is used in parallelism with στάσις, and the inventory of factional terms in *1 Clem.* by J. Rohde, "Häresie und Schisma im ersten Clemensbrief und in den Ignatius-Briefen," *NovT* 10 (1968) 217–33; esp. 224–25. See also Origen's use of διασχίζεσθαι in reference to 1 Cor 4:6 (*comm. in I Cor.* 19.6 [p. 357]), and also the simplex verb in Celsus'charge against the Christians: Ἀρχόμενοι μέν ... ὀλίγοι τε ἦσαν, καὶ ἓν ἐφρόνουν ... αὖθις αὖ τέμνονται καὶ σχίζονται καὶ στάσεις ἰδίας ἔχειν ἕκαστοι θέλουσι (Or. *Cels.* 3.10 [text *Origène. Contre Celse*, ed. M. Borret, SC 136 (Paris: Cerf, 1968) 30]).

[35] C. Roberts, T. C. Skeat and A. D. Nock, "The Gild of Zeus Hypsistos," *HTR* 29 (1936) 39–88. But we must note that the text itself reads σχίματα, which is taken by the authors to be a misspelling (51).

[36] The astrological text cited by BAGD, 797 and Welborn, "Discord," 87 n. 9, in which σχίσματα is paired with πολέμοι, φόνοι, μάχαι and ἀλαζονείαι μεγάλαι in a list of the misfortunes caused by the god Ares, is from the twelfth-century C. E., and thus is not evidence of the pre-Christian use of the term. (The text is *Catalogus Codicum Astrologorum Graecorum*, "Codices Hispanienses" [=vol. 3, pt. 2], ed. C. O. Zuretti [Brussels: Lamertin, 1934] 122, line 24.)

[37] See Hdt. 7.219; 8.34; Xen. *Symp.* 4.59; Dion. Hal. *Ant.Rom.* 7.59.8; Plut. *Mor.* 481C. Most important is Diod. Sic. 12.66.2, where the verb is used explicitly of division into factions, along with another important term which Paul also uses to describe Corinthian divisions in 11:19: τοῦ πλήθους σχιζομένου κατὰ τὴν αἵρεσιν, "while the multitude were divided according to party" (cited by BAGD, 797 "become divided, disunited"; Welborn, "Discord," 86).

Lucius or the Ass, Lucius' transformation at the end of the tale from an ass back into human form creates controversy among the spectators.

All were amazed at this strange, unexpected spectacle and raised a terrible din. The audience were divided into two opinions [τὸ θέατρον εἰς δύο γνώμας[38] ἐσχίζετο]. Some thought [οἱ μὲν] that I should be burnt to death immediately ... the others [οἱ δὲ] advocated waiting and learning what I had to say before deciding on the matter (54).

This metaphorical use of σχίζειν to refer to broken or split communities is grounded in the term's most frequent literal use for divisions of parts of the body and other natural phenomena.[39] As the image of the body is commonly used for the political organism,[40] the transference of σχίζειν and later its noun σχίσμα to human relationships and political communities is easily accomplished.[41] Plutarch, for example, in his treatise *De fraterno amore*, uses the verb σχίζειν and the metaphor of the body[42] together in his discussion of enmity between brothers.

For just as things which have been joined together, even if the glue become loose, may be fastened together again and become united [συνελθεῖν], yet if a body [σῶμα] which has grown together is broken or split [σχισθέντος], it is difficult to find means of welding or joining it; so friendships knitted together through long familiarity, even though the friends part company, can be easily resumed again, but when brothers have once broken the bonds of Nature, they cannot readily come together [συνέρχονται[43]] (*Mor.* 481C).

Elsewhere in the New Testament, the verb σχίζειν is used in Acts 14:4 and 23:7[44] clearly to refer to the division of a political body into factions. Thus the term σχίσμα, especially as attested by the verb σχίζειν, is an appropriate term to use to refer to political or social division and factionalism.[45] Its occurrence in 1:10 and

---

[38] See below on μία γνώμη and synonyms (on the phrase with the verb σχίζειν, see LSJ, s. v. II).

[39] Hdt. 7.31 (a river); Pl. *Ti.* 77D (splitting veins); Arist. *Hist. An.* 1.15.494A (top of foot split into toes); 2.1.499A (the cleft foot of a camel); Polyb. 2.16.11 (a river); Joseph. *AJ* 1.38; 20.97 (a river); 8.207 (a cloth, a kingdom). In the NT see Mark 1:10 (the heavens); Mark 2:21 and par. (cloth); Mark 15:38 and par. (the temple-curtain) and John 19:24 (a garment) (see Maurer, 959, 963). Philo uses σχίζειν for the division of sense perception and functions by eyes, ears, etc. (*Somn.* 1.27; cf. *Agr.* 30; *Fug.* 91).

[40] See the discussion below on 1 Cor 12 (it is important to note here that the image of the body was used in antiquity to promote unity). The connection is made by Paul clearly in 12:25, ἵνα μὴ ᾖ σχίσμα ἐν τῷ σώματι.

[41] See also the Latin *discidium*, "discord, dissension" (OLD, 550, as in Livy 25.18.5; Plautus *Mil.* 654; Cic. *Balb.* 30; Fronto, *Ant.* 1.260), and the verbs *discedere* and *scindere*, as in Lucan, *BCiv.* 10.416–17 of "the body of Rome" by the civil war between Caesar and Pompey (*Latium sic scindere corpus dis placitum*).

[42] As Paul does in 1 Cor 12 (see esp. 12:25). Cf. the use of ἀποσχίζειν and ἀπόσχισμα in Marcus Aurelius' reflections on the body as a metaphor for Nature and the πόλις (M.Ant. 4.29; 8.34), and for human divisions (9.3; 11.8).

[43] On the verb συνέρχεσθαι used to refer to reunification (as twice in this passage), see the discussion below on 1 Cor 11:20.

[44] In this text σχίζειν is identified with στάσις ("faction").

[45] Weiss, *Korintherbrief*, 13 ("Cliquen"); Welborn, "Discord," 86–87.

again in 11:18 and 12:25 (and nowhere else in the Pauline corpus) gives a further indication that factionalism is indeed the topic of this entire letter.[46]

The third and fourth phrases in Paul's call for unity in 1:10 are both governed by the periphrastic construction ἦτε κατηρτισμένοι.[47] Before turning to the two prepositional phrases, ἐν τῷ αὐτῷ νοΐ and ἐν τῇ αὐτῇ γνώμῃ, we shall first examine the verb καταρτίζειν.[48] This verb is also a term used in discussions of political division and unity in antiquity.[49] The basic meaning of the root is to "adjust, put in order, restore."[50] The word is used in a literal sense as a medical term, denoting the knitting together of broken bones or dislocated joints.[51] Perhaps the clearest example of this root meaning is found in the work *Definitiones medicae* by Galen (c. 129–199 C.E.), in which the abstract substantive καταρτισμός[52] is defined. "καταρτισμός is a moving of a bone or bones from (an) unnatural position into the natural position."[53] Both the substantive (4x) and the verb καταρτίζειν are found in a short fragment from another medical writer, Heliodorus (1–2nd c. C.E.), all referring to the process or activity of resetting dislocations.[54] The verb can also refer to restoring or mending a variety of things, for example, nets (Mark 1:19), walls (2 Esd 4:12–16), or a people (2 Esd 6:14).[55] The metaphorical use of καταρτίζειν to describe the "resetting" of broken human relationships and communities is commonly found in Greek

---

[46] But σχίσμα is not the only term by which Paul refers to the Corinthian factions; in line with contemporary practice he employs a host of terms (see below).

[47] Cf. Ign. *Eph.* 2.2: ἵνα ἐν μιᾷ ὑποταγῇ κατηρτισμένοι . . . ἦτε.

[48] A common Pauline word, it appears in Rom 9:22; 2 Cor 13:11; 1 Thess 3:10 and Gal 6:1 (see Betz, *Galatians*, 297). The abstract noun κατάρτισις is used in 2 Cor 13:9. One can argue that with the appearance of both verb and noun in 2 Cor 13:9–11, that the Corinthian correspondence has come full circle from its beginning in 1 Cor 1:10. BAGD's translation of 1:10 as "made complete" (p. 417) is too weak, and will be challenged below.

[49] As noted already by Heinrici, 53 on 1:10: ". . . daher auch bei Griechen καταρτίζειν gebraucht wird, wenn von Herstellung des rechten Verhältnisses durch Entfernung von Uneinigkeit (wie hier)." See also Lightfoot, 47.

[50] LSJ, 910.

[51] See Apollon. Cit. 2 (1st c. B.C.E.): "Dislocations are manifest, some toward the inside, and others toward the outside, both when the joint, being turned, goes in a variety of ways, and when the part bends, sometimes to the outer, and sometimes to the inner part, it is thus prescribed *to set them right* [καταρτίζειν] one after another." The title of the work is "Concerning the Study of Joints" (ed. H. Schöne, *Apollonius von Kitium* [Leipzig: Teubner, 1896], trans. mine).

[52] In the NT this term appears in Eph 4:12, in relation to two other prominent images for unity in 1 Corinthians (εἰς οἰκοδομὴν τοῦ σώματος τοῦ Χριστοῦ) (on which see below).

[53] Galen, *Opera Omnia*, ed. C. G. Kühn (Leipzig: Cnoblochi, 1830) 19.8 (p. 461 line 7, trans. mine).

[54] The title of the fragment is περὶ διαφορᾶς καταρτισμῶν ("Concerning Ways of Setting a Dislocation"), in *Corpus Medicorum Graecorum*, ed. J. Raeder, vol. 6, pt. 2, vol. 2, *Oribasii Collectionum Medicarum Reliquia* [Leipzig: Teubner, 1933] fr. 49.1 (p. 4); cf. Sor. 1.73 (=*Sorani Gynaeciorum*, ed. V. Rose, BT [Leipzig: Teubner, 1882]).

[55] Surprisingly, the term does not occur in either Philo or Josephus.

literature, as in this passage from the treatise on friendship (extant in fragments) of the Neoplatonic philosopher Eusebius Myndius:

May I be no one's enemy, but a friend of an always enduring [friend]. And may I never have a difference with my closest relatives, but, if I have a difference, may I become reconciled as soon as possible ... *May I bring back together* [καταρτίζοιμι] disputing friends.[56]

The term καταρτίζειν was an appropriate choice for Paul to use in parallelism with "let there not be factions among you,"[57] because it is often used exactly to mean to bring warring factions back together again. In the following text from Herodotus, both the verb and agential noun from the same root[58] are used of those who put an end to στάσις ("faction"):

... but for two generations before this she had been very greatly troubled by faction [στάσις], till the Parians made peace [καταρτίζειν] among them, being chosen out of all Greeks by the Milesians to be peace-makers [καταρτιστῆρες] (5.28).

The verb is also used as an antidote to στάσις down well into the Greco-Roman period.[59] The term καταρτίζειν (in the passive "to be reconciled or united"),[60] as used by Paul in 1:10, is thus an exact counterpart to the other political term used, σχίσμα, "faction/division").[61] Paul's meaning is clear: he wants to persuade the Corinthians to end their factionalism and be reconciled as one community.[62]

---

[56] *FPG* 3.7 (trans. mine). Although this text is late (4–5th c. C.E.) I cite it as a good example of the language and process of division and reconciliation.

[57] Bachmann, 55 n. 1. Conzelmann, on the other hand, dismissed the parallelism (both structural and lexical) between the two phrases: "It is mistaken to render σχίσμα as 'breach' and καταρτίζειν as 'repair'" (p. 31 n. 2; he offers no particular supporting evidence).

[58] καταρτιστήρ means "one who restores order, mediator" (LSJ, 910, citing this text, Hdt. 4.161 and Themist. *Or.* 4.61C).

[59] See Dion. Hal. *Ant.Rom.* 3.10.6 (cited as a parallel already by Bachmann, 55 n. 1), referring to the restoration of factions at Alba (this is the reading of a major manuscript B, Urbinas 105; other mss. read καταρτυθῇ, "be regulated"). See also Plut. *Marc.* 10.1: "on entering Nola, he [Marcellus] found a state of discord [στάσις], the senate being unable to regulate and manage [καταρτίζειν] the people, which favoured Hannibal" (this LCL trans. by B. Perrin misses the significance of the term καταρτίζειν and merely applies to it the meaning of μεταχειρίζεσθαι, with which it is in conjunction. The translation should be amended to read "reconcile").

[60] "For the verb καταρτίζεσθαι ... properly means, 'to be joined', and 'to be united', in the same way as the members of the human body are joined together in a very well-balanced arrangement" (J. Calvin, *The First Epistle of Paul the Apostle to the Corinthians*, trans. J. W. Fraser, Calvin's Commentaries [Grand Rapids, MI: Eerdmans, 1960] 25).

[61] Ignatius understands the term as related to factionalism and unity; see *Phld.* 8:1: ὡς ἄνθρωπος εἰς ἕνωσιν κατηρτισμένος. This whole section of the letter describes Ignatius' plea for unity, which is "the main burden of the letter" (Schoedel, 207). Ignatius' plea sounds much like Paul's: παρακαλῶ δὲ ὑμᾶς μηδὲν κατ' ἐρίθειαν πράσσειν (8.2, see below on ἔρις). Note also the use of μερισμός in 8.1 (see the discussion below on 1 Cor 1:13).

[62] Historically, the church at Corinth may actually never have been a unity previously (as noted in chap. I n. 1). That Paul was trying to create a unity from a collection of disparate house

The rhetorical force and sense of the third and fourth segments of the πρόθεσις in 1:10 do not rest, however, solely upon the lexical possibilities of καταρτίζειν, for here the verb is qualified by two prepositional phrases so important in Greek political literature for referring to concord that the meaning of the total phrase is unmistakable.

The first prepositional phrase, ἐν τῷ αὐτῷ νοΐ ("in the same mind"), although not in itself in common use, is synonymous with the technical term ὁμόνοια (literally "sameness of mind"), the most common word for "concord" or political agreement in Greek literature.[63] In Greek and Roman religion, Ὁμόνοια or *Concordia*[64] was worshipped as a goddess.[65] ὁμόνοια, sameness of mind, in the Greco-Roman world means political unity and stability, as contrasted with στάσις, "civil disorder."[66] That Paul's phrase, ἐν τῷ αὐτῷ νοΐ, is equivalent

---

churches has been argued in particular by H.-J. Klauck, *Hausgemeinde und Hauskirche im frühen Christentum*, SBS 103 (Stuttgart: Katholisches Bibelwerk, 1981) 39–40. "Was in Korinth sichtbar wird, ist dies: der schliesslich erreichte Zustand des Nebeneinanders von Ortsgemeinde und Hausgemeinde bringt erste Schwierigkeiten mit sich" (p. 39; also *Herrenmahl*, 290–91; for this point of view see also F. V. Filson, "The Significance of the Early House Churches," *JBL* 58 [1939] 105–12; esp. p. 110: "such a physically divided church tended almost inevitably to become a mentally divided church"; cf. Schreiber, 130–34). The present study may contribute some prerequisites to that historical question. Even if that historical reconstruction is correct, it is extremely important to note that *rhetorically* Paul describes Corinthian unity as the theological and sociological norm from which the Corinthians have fallen short (regardless of whether such unity actually existed in the past). The verb καταρτίζειν is one way in which he emphasizes this.

[63] See the literature cited in chap. II n. 190.

[64] On the identification of the two, see Momigliano; P. Jal, "Pax civilis-concordia," *Rev. Et. Lat.* 39 (1961) 210–31; and Hellegouarc'h, 125–27.

[65] See Skard, 69, 102–105, and the texts cited there. This connection between religious and political dimensions of ὁμόνοια demonstrates again that we cannot separate the two in regard to 1 Corinthians, either by saying that it is religious and not political, or the converse. Because Paul regards (and teaches that) the church is the body of Christ, its rending by factions is both a religious and political offense.

[66] On στάσις see D. Loenen, *Stasis. Enige aspecten van de begrippen partij–en klassenstrijd in oud-Griekenland* (Amsterdam: Noord-Hollandsche Uitgevers Maatschappij, 1953), esp. 4–7 on the term; P. Mikat, *Die Bedeutung der Begriffe Stasis und Aponoia für das Verständnis des 1. Clemensbriefes*, Arbeitsgemeinschaft für Forschung des Landes Nordrhein-Westfalen 155 (Köln/Opladen: Westdeutscher Verlag, 1969) 20–39; A. Lintott, *Violence, Civil Strife and Revolution in the Classical City* (Baltimore: Johns Hopkins, 1982); M. I. Finley, *Politics in the Ancient World* (Cambridge: Cambridge University Press, 1983), 105–21; H.-J. Gehrke, *Stasis. Untersuchungen zu den inneren Kriegen in den griechischen Staaten des 5. und 4. Jahrhunderts v. Chr.*, Vestigia 35 (Munich: Beck, 1985) 1–10 on definitions and terminology (and 357 n. 11 on the opposition of the two terms), and the review by Lintott, *CR* 37 (1987) 108. See also Taylor, 8–14 for the corresponding Latin terminology (*factio* and *pars*).

Paul does not use the term στάσις in 1 Cor, but he uses two cognates, διχοστασία (3:3) and ἀκαταστασία (14:33) (on the connection of these terms with στάσις, see G. Delling, *TDNT*, "στάσις," 7.568–71, 571; see also the discussion below). We might ask why Paul does not use the term στάσις, preferring instead a group of other terms (σχίσμα, ἔρις, διχοστασία, φιλόνεικος, αἵρεσις, ἀκαταστασία [these will be examined, along with other images, below]). Perhaps he doesn't want to reify their conflict by terming it a στάσις (Welborn, "Discord, 110;

to the technical term ὁμόνοια, is demonstrated by this excerpt from Iamblichus' *Epistle Concerning Concord*:

Concord [ὁμόνοια], just as the name itself wishes to show, has brought together a gathering of the same mind [ὁμοίου τοῦ νοῦ] and partnership[67] and unity [ἕνωσις] in itself.[68]

We have already noted in chap. II the frequency of deliberative discourses in antiquity urging concord, ὁμόνοια.[69] In such texts the term would naturally present itself in the πρόθεσις to the argument, since it is the main topic of discussion.[70] See, for example, Dio Chrys. *Or.* 38:

we have noted that σχίσμα, literally "tear" points rather directly to restoration). There are even rhetorical parallels to this; in other speeches on concord στάσις is treated as an unmentionable: "And civil strife [στάσις] does not deserve even to be named among us, and let no man mention it" (Dio Chrys. *Or.* 48.16; cf. Aristid. *Or.* 23.80).

Against the possible objection that στάσις is not the appropriate term for what Paul describes in Corinth, note that, although Paul himself does not employ the term στάσις in 1 Cor, that did not prevent early Greek commentators from using it to describe the situation Paul faced in 1 Cor (Or. *comm. in I Cor.* 89.3: τούτου ('Απολλῶς) περὶ οὗ φησι τοιαύτης στάσεως καὶ ταραχῆς οὔσης ἐν τῇ Κορινθίων ἐκκλησίᾳ [cf. 89.24, 32 twice (p. 50)]; Chrys. *hom. in I Cor.* 44.2, describing the role of the Stephanas delegation: οὗτοι γὰρ οἱ ἐλθόντες εἰσὶ καὶ δηλώσαντες αὐτῷ τὰ κατὰ τὴν στάσιν [*PG* 61.376]; and elsewhere in his homilies, e. g., 11.1 [61.88]; 27.2 [61.226], ἡ στάσις αὕτη καὶ ἡ φιλονεικία; 14.1 [61.113] verb στασιάζειν; Thdr. Mops. uses διαστασιάζειν on 13:3–13 [Staab, 192]; Thdt. uses στασιάζειν *1 Cor.* 1:3 [*PG* 82.229]). To these references we must add the preponderance of use of the terms στάσις and στασιάζειν earlier in *1. Clem.*, where they take their place comfortably alongside the terms Paul uses in 1 Cor (noun 1:1; 2:6; 3:2; 14:2; 46:9; 51:1; 54:2; 57:1; 63:1; verb 4:12; 43:2; 46:7; 47:6; 49:5; 51:3; 55:1 [see BAGD, 764]). In regard to this usage *LPGL*, 1251, lists στάσις with a final gloss "faction; discord," but cites only one text, which might lead one to think that the word is more rare with that meaning in patristic texts than it actually is (as these examples show). Note also that Luke applies the term to inter-Christian disputes (Acts 15:2) and those among Jewish sects (23:7), as Numenius uses the verb στασιάζειν to refer to dissensions among the Stoics (Eus. *p. e.* 14.5, quoted in n. 68 below).

67 κοινωνία, which, along with cognates, plays an important role in 1 Cor also (see the discussion below).

68 Diels, *Vorsokr.* 2.356, trans. mine. Compare also this fragment from Numenius: "Thus the School of Epicurus is like some true republic, perfectly free from sedition [ἀστασιαστοτάτῃ], with one mind in common and one consent [κοινὸν ἕνα νοῦν, μίαν γνώμην ἐχούσῃ] . . . But the Stoic sect is torn by factions [ἐστασίασται]" (Eus. *p. e.* 14.5 [text *Eusebius Werke. Achter Band. Praeparatio Evangelica*, pt. 2, ed. K. Mras, GCS (Berlin: Akademie-Verlag, 1956) 269; trans. E. H. Gifford, *Eusebii Pamphili praeparatio evangelica* (Oxford: Academy, 1903) vol. 3, pt. 2.783–84]). This text uses the similar paraphrase "one mind" [εἷς νοῦς], also in parallel with "one opinion" [μία γνώμη/ἡ αὐτὴ γνώμη] (on which see below). The passage is also important because it shows the natural application of such political phrases to smaller social bodies such as philosophical sects.

69 On ὁμόνοια/concordia as a political slogan, see Skard, 80–82, 92–3; G. Grossmann, *Politische Schlagwörter aus der Zeit des Peloponnesischen Krieges*, Diss. Basel, 1950 (Repr. ed. New York: Arno, 1973) 6, 19–20; and F. W. Walbank, *A Historical Commentary on Polybius*, 3 vols. (Oxford: Clarendon, 1957–79), 1.234–35 (who calls it a slogan of middle class stability against revolution).

70 See nn. 198–99 in chap. II for more examples.

Very well, what is this subject on which I am about to offer advice [συμβουλεύειν], and yet am reluctant to name it? The word, men of Nicomedia, is not distasteful whether in the home or the clan or in friendly circles or nations; for concord [ὁμόνοια] is what I am going to talk about, a fine word and a fine thing (38.6).[71]

The term ὁμόνοια does not appear in the New Testament, but is common in Hellenistic Judaism and early Christian literature.[72] There is no reason to doubt that Paul knew the word (especially because he employs so many terms and *topoi* derived from politics in this argument, as we shall see). Paul's extended literal paraphrase of the term with the prepositional phrase ἐν τῷ αὐτῷ νοΐ in the πρόθεσις to the argument in 1 Corinthians, probably to avoid reference to the pagan goddess and her cult,[73] does not mask the allusion to the realistic need for ὁμόνοια, political or social unity.[74]

Paul's meaning for the phrase ἐν τῷ αὐτῷ νοΐ is further demonstrated by the second prepositional phrase with which it is coordinated in 1:10, ἐν τῇ αὐτῇ γνώμῃ ("in the same opinion"). In fact, elsewhere in Greek literature the two concepts "same mind" and "same opinion" are paired,[75] as in this text from Lysias:

---

[71] See also the πρόθεσις to the argument in the deliberative epistle of Demosthenes on concord: "First of all, men of Athens, it is necessary that you bring about harmony [ὁμόνοια] among yourselves for the common good of the state and drop all contentions [ἀμφισβητήσεις] inherited from previous assemblies and, in the second place, that you all with one mind [ἐκ μιᾶς γνώμης] vigorously support your decisions" (*Ep*. 1.5).

[72] For references see BAGD, 569; see also *LPGL*, 958 (s. v. ὁμόνοια), listing many texts under the gloss "as characteristic of Christian society." Scholars have recognized the political background of the term in Ignatius (Schoedel, 74, 213) and in *1 Clement* (L. Sanders, *L'Hellénisme de Saint Clément de Rome et le Paulinisme*, Studia Hellenistica 2 [Louvain: University of Louvain Press, 1943] 126–30; Jaeger, *Early Christianity*, 13–14 and notes; Mikat, 28; Delling, 571; van Unnik, 177–81; K. Wengst, *Pax Romana and the Peace of Jesus Christ*, trans. J. Bowden [London: SCM, 1987] 105–18). Origen (*comm. in I Cor*. 38.7 [p. 508]) and Chrysostom (*hom. in I Cor*. 1.1 [*PG* 61.13]; 3.1 [61.23]; 24.3 [61.203]; 31.2 [61.260]; 32.1 [61.263]; 36.5 [61.313], etc.) use the term frequently in their exegesis of 1 Cor.

[73] On ὁμόνοια as a part of Hellenistic and then Roman Imperial propaganda, especially on coins, see Kramer, 49–53; Tarn, *Alexander the Great*, 2.416; Zwicker, 2268; on its cultic significance, see Zwicker, 2265–67; Ferguson, 127–32. Because later in the argument (1 Cor 8–10) Paul must deal explicitly with idolatry and pagan gods, it would not do for him to appear to appeal by name to such a deity (he grounds his entire appeal in the Christ). By his paraphrase, he attempts to pick up the clear significance of ὁμόνοια as a cultural value, without bringing in the name of the goddess. That such a paraphrase (which includes the etymology of the term) would not have been misunderstood is demonstrated by the excerpt from Iamblichus quoted above. Does 2:16 contain Paul's Christian counterpart, ἡμεῖς δὲ νοῦν Χριστοῦ ἔχομεν (as suggested by L. T. Johnson, *The Writings of the New Testament. An Interpretation* [Philadelphia: Fortress, 1986] 276)? Cf. in this regard also Phil 2:5–11 and its exegesis by Sampley, 66–67: "Their being in Christ defines what it means to be of the same mind and makes the same-mindedness possible."

[74] This was hinted at by Heinrici, 53, who pointed to the verbs ὁμονοεῖν and ὁμογνωμονεῖν in this regard.

[75] See also Iambl. *Ep. Peri Homonoias*: ὑφ' ἑνὸς μὲν γάρ τις νοήματος καὶ μιᾶς γνώμης

For as often as you heard that the people in the city were all of one mind [τὴν αὐτὴν γνώμην ἔχειν], you had but slight hopes of your return, judging that our concord [ὁμόνοια] was the worst of signs for your exile (25.21).[76]

The parallelism in this text is clear. Those who "have the same opinion" are political allies, which is another way of saying that they are in a state of "common mind" or ὁμόνοια.[77] The phrase ἡ αὐτὴ γνώμη (often as the object of the verb ἔχειν), referring to those in political agreement, is quite common in ancient Greek political texts.[78] A nearly synonymous phrase, μία γνώμη, "of one accord, with one consent,"[79] is likewise commonly used, especially in speeches on concord or texts describing it.[80] The synonymous verb ὁμογνωμονεῖν and the adjective ὁμογνώμων[81] are also commonly used in such texts.[82]

We may conclude from our investigation to this point that 1 Cor 1:10 is filled with terms which have a long history in speeches, political treatises and historical works dealing with political unity and factionalism.[83] In closing off the discussion of this first verse we shall look at one more text which brings together many of the terms and *topoi* used in Greek literature to talk about factionalism and reconciliation. Dio Chrysostom's *Or.* 39, a speech urging concord, has a prayer to the gods as its *peroratio*. Dio invokes a long list of gods, among whom is Ὁμόνοια/Concordia, and then prays:

That from this day forth they may implant in this city a yearning for itself, *a passionate love* [ἔρως], *a singleness of purpose* [μία γνώμη], *a unity of wish and thought* [ταὐτὰ βούλεσθαι καὶ φρονεῖν]; and, on the other hand, that they may cast out *strife* [στάσις] and *contentiousness*

κυβερνώμενος ὁμονοεῖ πρὸς ἑαυτόν (Diels, *Vorsokr.* 2.356), and the Numenius fragment in Eus. *p. e.* 14.5 (quoted above in n. 68). A similar unifying pair is found in Paul's exhortation to unity in Phil 1:27: ἀξίως . . . πολιτεύεσθε ἵνα . . . ἀκούω . . . ὅτι στήκετε ἐν ἑνὶ πνεύματι, μιᾷ ψυχῇ συναθλοῦντες τῇ πίστει τοῦ εὐαγγελίου . . . .

76 On Lys. *Or.* 25 see Kramer, 25–26.

77 In the next paragraph of the same speech Lysias equates στασιάζειν with μὴ τὴν αὐτὴν γνώμην ἔχοντες (25.22; the phrase occurs five more times in the same speech: 25.2, 2, 15, 20, 29). See also Lys. 33.6 and the similar phrase in Apollonius of Tyana's speech on concord to the Smyrnaeans (Philostr. *VA* 4.8).

78 See, e. g., Isoc. *Or.* 5.45; 6.9, 25, 34, 37, 93; Thuc. 1.113.2; 140.1; 2.55.2; Dion. Hal. *Ant. Rom.* 6.23.2; 49.3; Plut. *Mor.* 813B.

79 LSJ, 354.

80 See Thuc. 1.122.2; 6.17.4; Isoc. *Or.* 4.138; Dem. *Ep.* 1.5 (quoted in n. 71 above); 3.36; Polyb. 1.87.6; 3.13.4; Dion. Hal. *Ant. Rom.* 1.85.5; 4.26.1; 8.7.3; 11.4.7; Joseph. *AJ* 7.60, 276; cf. *Ap.* 2.179; Dio Chrys. *Or.* 39.8; Plut. *Arist.* 5.2; *Marc.* 12.3. It is a favorite phrase of Aristides, occurring at least seven times in his two speeches on concord alone (*Or.* 23.31, 34, 42; 24.6, 14, 25, 37; cf. 27.30).

81 "To be of one mind, agree" (LSJ, 1223).

82 E. g., Polyb. 28.6.2; Dio Chrys. *Or.* 48.6. In early Greek writers words from the stem ὁμοφρον- are so used (see Kramer, 8–14, with references).

83 Lack of attention to the kinds of historical and lexical investigations here undertaken can lead one to miss completely the unmistakable clarity of Paul's appeal in 1:10. See Bünker's comment (p. 53) on 1:10: "Die causa bleibt hier noch verborgen."

[ἔρις] and *jealousy*[84] [φιλονικία], so that this city may be numbered among the most prosperous and the noblest for all time to come (*Or*. 39.8).

Each of the terms highlighted in this text from Dio Chrysostom either is employed by Paul in 1 Corinthians or is a counterpart to a term which is used. The counterpart to ἔρως, one of the things in contradistinction to factionalism, in 1 Corinthians is ἀγάπη (8:1; ch. 13; 16:14). The phrase μία γνώμη, synonymous with ἡ αὐτὴ γνώμη in 1 Cor 1:10, has been discussed. The phrases ταὐτὰ βούλεσθαι καὶ φρονεῖν are almost synonymous with Paul's τὸ αὐτὸ λέγειν in 1:10, and our investigation has shown that they are commonly used in Greek political texts. We have noted that Paul does not use the term στάσις,[85] but he does use cognate terms in 3:3 (διχοστασία[86]) and 14:33 (ἀκαταστασία). We have also argued that σχίσμα (1:10; 11:18; 12:25) is a Pauline counterpart to στάσις; among other terms which he uses to refer to the Corinthians' factionalism are ἔρις (1:11; 3:3) and αἵρεσις (11:19). The noun φιλονικία is also matched in 1 Corinthians; the adjective φιλόνεικος is used in 11:16. There is no reason to assume, as scholars have, that when Paul uses different terms he refers to a different situation.[87] Paul's use of a variety of terms to describe Corinthian factionalism is in full conformity with other ancient texts which discuss factionalism and concord.[88] We can even be certain that Paul himself associates these terms with one another, as they appear together elsewhere in his writings.[89]

---

[84] This translation is too weak. φιλονικία is a strong term most frequently associated with party spirit, "contentiousness" (LSJ, 1937; see the full discussion below), as shown clearly in this text.

[85] See the discussion above in n. 66.

[86] The textual evidence will be mentioned below.

[87] See n. 28 above.

[88] In addition to this text cited from Dio Chrys. (and throughout his speeches on concord and those of Aristid.), see the usage in historical works. For example, Dion. Hal. in *Ant. Rom.* uses the terms ἔρις, στάσις and φιλονεικία interchangeably in 1.87 to describe the same situation. In 6.22–34, a continuous narrative, the following terms and phrases are used with no change in historical reference: ἡ πολιτικὴ στάσις; οἱ πολιτικοὶ χειμῶνες; θόρυβος; οὐκ ἔχειν τὴν αὐτὴν γνώμην; στάσις; φιλονεικία; ἀκαταστασίαι; διχοστασία and ἀκοσμία. The same easy variation is found in Appian's *Civil Wars*, where the following terms are used interchangeably: μοῖρα, ἐμφύλια, αἵρεσις, ἔρις, στάσις, ἑταιρεία, φιλονικία (*BCiv*. Books 3–5), as also in Joseph. *BJ* 4.128–132 (στάσις, ταραχή, πόλεμος ἐμφύλιος, ἔρις, τὸ φιλόνεικον). All of these terms which Paul uses are also used, alongside στάσις, throughout *1 Clement* in that discussion of later Corinthian factionalism. See also the analysis of the various terms στάσις, ἑταιρεία and συνωμοσία in Aurenche, 9–41, and the definitions and examples of a collection of terms for factions (στάσις, μερίς, μοῖρα, αἵρεσις, τάξις, ἑταιρεία) by K. D. Stergiopoulos, ΤΑ ΠΟΛΙΤΙΚΑ ΚΟΜΜΑΤΑ ΤΩΝ ΑΡΧΑΙΩΝ ΑΘΗΝΩΝ (Athens: Historike Bibliotheke, 1955), 1.11–23, supplemented by the review by J. de Romilly (*Rev. Et. Grec.* 69 [1956] 459), who insisted on the fluidity and lack of differentiation of this range of terms for describing factionalism in ancient Athens. For later attestation see A. Fuks, "The Jewish Revolt in Egypt (A.D. 115–117)," *Social Conflict in Ancient Greece* (Jerusalem: Magnes; Leiden: Brill, 1984) 322–49, 346–47 on varying terminology. On the variety of terms in 1 Corinthians, see Heinrici, 52–53. This same easy interchange of terms is found in Greek commentaries on the letter; see, e. g.,

C. Political Terms and *Topoi* Introduced in 1 Cor 1:11–4:21

We shall now move on to a survey of the political terminology and *topoi* related to factionalism which are found throughout the rest of 1 Corinthians, beginning with 1:11–4:21. Many of these, as we shall see, are also used by Paul in the rest of the letter (chaps. 5–16). In 1:11 Paul describes the message he has received from Chloe's people: "there are contentions [ἔριδες] among you." This potent term, repeated in 3:3 with ζῆλος,[90] is often translated "quarrels"[91] but that is too weak. It is found in Greek literature "frequently of political or domestic discord."[92] Ἔρις is personified as the Greek goddess of Discord, the opposite of Ὁμόνοια.[93] That the term ἔρις is common in Greek literature to refer to political strife and its causes[94] has long been recognized by the exegetical tradition and needs no further proof.[95] The Corinthian community, as Paul describes it, is experiencing political discord.[96] In the argument of 1 Cor 3:1–4 together the terms ἔρις and

---

Theodoret in his *Argumentum* of *1 Cor.*: Ἐκεῖνοι δὲ τὴν σοφιστικὴν ἔριν καὶ φιλοτιμίαν ἐζήλωσαν. Εἰς πολλὰς γὰρ συμμορίας διῃρέθησαν ... καὶ πρὸς ἀλλήλους περὶ τούτων φιλονεικοῦντες (*PG* 82.228).

89 In the vice-catalogues in Gal 5:20 (ἔχθραι, ἔρις, ζῆλος [cf. 1 Cor 3:3], θυμοί, ἐριθεῖαι, διχοστασίαι, αἱρέσεις, φθόνοι) and 2 Cor 12:20 (ἔρις, ζῆλος, θυμοί, ἐριθεῖαι, καταλαλιαί, ψιθυρισμοί, φυσιώσεις [cf. 1 Cor 4:6, 18; 5:2; 8:1; 13:4] ἀκαταστασίαι). See also the lists in *1 Clem.* 3:2 (including ζῆλος, φθόνος, ἔρις, στάσις, ἀκαταστασία) and 46.5 (ἔρεις, θυμοί, διχοστασίαι, σχίσματα, πόλεμος), and van Unnik, 25 n. 67 on the connection of these terms and "de Griekse HOMONOIA-conceptie." For the traditional nature of these lists in Greek texts, see Soph. *OC* 1234 (φθόνος, στάσις, ἔρις, μάχαι καὶ φόνοι) and Ar. *Thesm.* 788 (ἔριδες, νεῖκη, στάσις, ἀργαλέα, λύπη, πόλεμος); cf. Isoc. *Ep.* 9.8. For similarities elsewhere in the NT, see also Jas 3:13–18.

90 As also in Rom 13:13; *1 Clem.* 5:5; 6:4; 9:1 (and, e. g., Arist. *Rh.* 3.19.3); see also Phil 1:15 where it is paired with φθόνος (cf. Rom 1:29; Plut. *Mor.* 92B).

91 As by Conzelmann-Leitch, 31–32 ("Streitigkeiten"); RSV, "quarrelling." See also Munck, 139, "bickerings."

92 LSJ, 689.

93 The two terms are opposed in Ps.-Phoc. *Sent.* 74–75, in relation to envy, φθόνος. The danger of Ἔρις within any community is severe because she spreads like a cancer. "For this reason it was easy enough for Homer to give the size of Eris by saying, 'With humble crest at first, anon her head, while yet she treads the earth, affronts the skies'" (Dio Chrys. *Or.* 12.72, quoting *Il.* 4.443). See also Ps-Phoc. *Sent.* 78: Ἔρις δ' ἔριν ἀντιφυτεύει (text *Theognis, Ps.-Pythagoras, Ps.-Phocylides, etc.*, ed. D. Young, BT [Leipzig; Teubner, 1961]).

94 See in addition to the texts listed in LSJ, 689 and BAGD, 309, e. g., Hes. *Op.* 11–24; Eur. *Phoen.* 500; Dion. Hal. *Ant. Rom.* 1.87.1; 6.66.1, 4; 7.4.3; 7.16.2; 11.60.3; Joseph. *BJ* 4.132; 5.396; Dio Chrys. *Or.* 34.44; Plut. *Cic.* 46.2; *Ages.* 5.3; App. *BCiv.* 1.2.14; 2.2.10, 11; 2.4.30; 3.12.86. For more insight into the seriousness of the term ἔρις, note the other words with which it is linked: στάσις (Dio Chrys. *Or.* 39.8; App. *BCiv.* 3.12.86); ἔχθρα (Dio Chrys. *Or.* 48.6; cf. Philostr. *VA* 4.8); φιλονεικία (Dio Chrys. *Or.* 39.8; 48.6; 53.2; Aristid. 23.12, 28; 26.20, 97; cf. Plut. *Pomp.* 67.5).

95 BAGD, 309 ("strife, discord, contention"); C. Spicq, *Notes de lexicographie néotestamentaire* (Göttingen: Vandenhoeck & Ruprecht, 1978), 1.290–91. Note how frequently ἔρις appears in *1 Clem.*, and with what other terms (3:2; 5:5; 6:4; 9:1; 14:2; 44:1; 46:5; 54:2; cf. Ign. *Eph.* 8:1).

96 Welborn, "Discord," 87. Heinrici, 52, thought σχίσμα synonymous with ἔρις; Weiss

ζῆλος amount to "walking in a human way" (3:3), i. e. subscribing to earthly and secular values of political glory and strength.[97] In this argument Paul is drawing upon another well-attested *topos* in Greco-Roman literature: that factionalism is a "human" failing,[98] a *topos* to which he will allude throughout the argument in 1 Corinthians (3:1–4; 10:13; 15:32).

In 1:12 Paul qualifies the embassy's report in his own words (λέγω δὲ τοῦτο, "what I mean is this"): ἕκαστος ὑμῶν λέγει ἐγὼ μέν εἰμι Παύλου, ἐγὼ δὲ Ἀπολλῶ, ἐγὼ δὲ Κηφᾶ, ἐγὼ δὲ Χριστοῦ.[99] These have long been identified as political slogans, indicating the nature of the sectarian battles at Corinth.[100] What seems to be described here is that the community is divided into cliques or factions which claim allegiance variously to the three missionaries Paul, Apollos and Cephas.[101] For the purposes of this particular investigation, the "slogans" in 1:12

---

disagreed (*Korintherbrief*, 13), considering ἔρις to be a cause of σχίσμα (both citing *1 Clem.* 46:5; all agree that the two terms refer to the same situation). In fact, ἔρις is used both of the discord itself and of the contentions which give rise to it (as noted by LSJ above n. 92; see, e. g., the progression in App. *BCiv.* 1.7.60). The important point is that both are political terms to describe factionalism which are used by Paul to describe the same situation at Corinth.

97 Other parts of the argument of 1 Corinthians echo this theme (see 2:12–15; 9:24–27; 10:13; 15:32).

98 See Thucydides' famous remark about στάσις being inevitable because of human nature: γιγνόμενα μὲν καὶ αἰεὶ ἐσόμενα, ἕως ἂν ἡ αὐτὴ φύσις ἀνθρώπων ᾖ (3.82.2; cf. 84.2), and F. M. Wassermann, "Thucydides and the Disintegration of the Polis," *TAPA* 85 (1934) 46–54. Compare the same sentiment in Xen. *Hier.* 7.3 on φιλοτιμία (a cause of στάσις, see below n. 151): "But they in whom is implanted a passion for honor and praise [τιμῆς τε καὶ ἐπαίνου ἔρως], these are they who differ most from the beasts of the field, these are accounted men [ἄνδρες] and not mere human beings [ἄνθρωποι]." For the opposite, see Polyb. 6.48.2, where the concordant constitution of Lycurgus is of divine origin, not κατ' ἄνθρωπον. See also Dion. Hal. *Ant. Rom.* 8.52.1 on φθόνος τις ἀνθρώπινος as a cause of στάσις (see also Plut. *Cor.* 31.1, and the discussion below on "jealousy" and party strife), and also the accusation in 6.66.1: "you have fallen into strife [ἔρις], the most baneful of all human maladies [ὀλεθριωτάτη τῶν ἀνθρωπίνων νόσων]." This commonplace is even reflected in Jewish texts, such as the revolt of Korah, which is due to Israel's "fleshly nature" (on which see the discussion below on 1 Cor 10:1–13). Also for Paul factionalism is a work of the flesh (Gal 5:19–21).

The corollary of factionalism being a human failing in Greco-Roman texts is that it is the divine heavenly bodies which provide the best example of concordant behavior (e. g., Dio Chrys. *Or.* 48.14; full references in n. 405 below; cf. the cosmological basis in Ps-Arist. *Mund.* 6.397B). In his argument for concord in *Or.* 38 Dio Chrys. contrasts the divine origin of concord with the human origin of factionalism: "However, the only respect in which we [race of mortals] fall short of the blessedness of the gods and of their indestructible permanence is this – that we are not all sensitive to concord [ὁμόνοια], but, on the contrary, there are those who actually love its opposite, strife [στάσις]" (38.11). Human beings are thus even worse than the animals because of their strife and warfare (Dio Chrys. *Or.* 40.32, 41; 48.16). The same commonplace, that factionalism is a petty, human activity, lies behind Jas 3:13–18 (the comparison of ἡ σοφία ἄνωθεν and ἐπίγειος).

99 "Each one of you says: 'I am of Paul,' 'I am of Apollos,' 'I am of Kephas,' 'I am of Christ.'"

100 Heinrici, 56 called them "Parteiparolen."

101 Scholars remain divided on the last slogan, "I am Christ's," as to whether this represents a

(two repeated in 3:4) point to a common and recognizable aspect of ancient party politics, the dependence of factions upon a leader.[102] The problems at Corinth have to do with selected groups which have galvanized themselves around the three major figures Paul, Apollos and Cephas, as is generally recognized.[103]

We have observed above that it is Paul who describes the Corinthian situation as σχίσματα, which is corroborated by the report of Chloe's people about the presence of ἔριδες. Surely underlying Paul's statements in 1:12 is an historical truth that people at Corinth are lining up behind the various missionaries, such allegiances being a basic component of party-politics. But it is important to ask if the "slogans" in 1:12 are *actual* party-cries from the Corinthians themselves which Paul has quoted, in order to understand the force and logic of Paul's argument against these party allegiances. On the basis of a comparison of these "slogans" in 1:12 and 3:4 with ancient political texts, we must conclude that these are not actual Corinthian political slogans quoted by Paul, but are instead more likely caricatures of the Corinthians' behavior which employ, not a common formula of political sloganeering in antiquity, but instead the language of slave ownership and childish dependence.

Excursus: The Form of the "Slogans" in 1:12

Welborn, "Discord," 90–93, argued that the phrases in 1:12 mirror a common formula of political self-identification in antiquity, concluding: "a declaration of allegiance to a party so personal in organization *could take no other form* than that which is given in 1 Cor 1:12" ("Discord," 91, emph. added). The problem with this conclusion is that in his analysis

---

"Christ-party," whether it is a rhetorical statement (or question) by Paul to demonstrate the absurdity of these petty alliances, or whether it should be considered a scribal interpolation (for a summary of these positions, see Weiss, *Korintherbrief*, 15–19; Hurd, 101–107; Barrett, 43–46; Conzelmann, 33–34; Theissen, 66–67 n. 59; Lang, 23–26). This difficult issue will not be completely resolved here (and is not essential to this particular line of argument), but I can state that I tend to agree with the line of exegesis (which goes back at least to Chrys. *hom. in I Cor.* 3.2 [*PG* 61.24]) which holds that this final exclamation is a Pauline commentary on the previous slogans. Arguments in favor of this view are: 1. that the Christ party is never named again, even where others are (3:4, 22; cf. *1 Clem.* 47.3); 2. the slogan "You are Christ's" is presented as a corrective to the others in 3:23 (see also 15:23; cf. 2 Cor 10:7); 3. the next verse, with its complaint, "has Christ been divided up?" seems to presuppose the unity in Christ and would be inappropriate as a challenging question if it were the case that (only) some claimed Christ (with Vielhauer, 136–37). Theissen's remark on pp. 66–67, "either this is not a party or it is a group which is deliberately opposed to party divisions," is correct except that it perhaps mistakes Paul's *prescription* of what he wants all Christians to be for a *description* of this group.

[102] Welborn, "Discord," 90–92; see also Aurenche, quoted in "Excursus: The Descriptive Significance of the Term σχίσμα" above, and p. 11. See., e.g., Dion. Hal. *Ant. Rom.* 6.59.1.

[103] Ancient exegetes, esp. Chrys., understood μετασχηματίζειν in 4:6 to mean that the names Paul and Apollos were "covers" for other party leaders at Corinth, but that view has not been accepted in most modern exegesis (*hom. in I Cor.* 12.1 [*PG* 61.95–96]; on which see Bachmann, 24, 59–61).

Welborn has not produced one example of an ancient political slogan which has the same formula (personal pronoun + εἰμι [or ellipsed] + genitive of a proper name) (nor has anyone else, to my knowledge). The evidence which he cited is significantly relevant to the background of these slogans, but not to their form. In ancient political parlance one did refer to "the party of someone" [ἡ μερίς τινος] or "the people around someone" [οἱ περί τινα] (Welborn, "Discord, 90–91), but neither of these nominal phrases is a political slogan (on the latter phrase, see BAGD, s. v. περί 2δ; LSJ s. v. περί c.I.2; K.J. Dover, "ΔΕΚΑΤΟΣ 'ΑΥΤΟΣ," *JHS* 80 [1960] 61–77, 69–70, and note its usage in the first century in Joseph. *BJ* 2.440, 443, 445, 453; 3.26, etc. and Acts 13:13; Mark 16:8 *v. l.*; cf. Ign. *Smyrn.* 3.2). As much as these phrases rightly point to the dependence of a faction upon a leader, that is all they can show. They do not supply formal parallels to Paul's statements in 1 Cor 1:12. The same must be said of the Latin wall paintings from Pompeii which Welborn cites as political slogans, as they have a quite different form from Paul's statements in 1:12, described as consisting of: "the name of the candidate and his office, the sponsoring individual or group, and a verb of adherence or support" (92). To say, "I support Marius for aedile" is not the same thing as to say "I belong to Marius." The fact that other types of slogans from ancient politics can be found does not prove that the formulae in 1 Cor 1:12 are in fact slogans created by the Corinthians themselves. The form-critical category "slogan" is a slippery one (look, for example, at the different types of slogans in Arist. *Pol.* 2.1.8 and Thuc. 3.82.8), which needs more study.[104]

The question of the form of the "slogans" in 1 Cor 1:12 requires more investigation. While space precludes a full analysis, let me briefly mention some examples which may open up the question even more. Dem. *Or.* 9.56 is perhaps the best example of a comparable use of the genitive of possession or relation to refer to party membership (Ἦσαν . . . τινὲς μὲν Φιλίππου) (cited by LSJ s. v. εἰμι c.II.d. with the gloss "to express that a thing belongs to another . . . hence to be of the party of"; this is under the sub-category "c. gen., to express descent or extraction"). But even this text is not a slogan, but a description in the third person (it is also plural, not singular). This is not a restrictive formula, as shown later in the same passage, where that party is referred to as οἱ τὰ Φιλίππου φρονοῦντες (for this common phrase, see Joseph. *BJ* 1.140, 326, 358; 2.648; Plut. *Pomp.*6.4; LSJ s. v. φρονέω II.c. and BAGD, 866; Gehrke, 269–70 n. 13, with references). See also Andoc. 1.53 εἶναι τούτων τῶν ἀνδρῶν, which R. C. Jebb considers a use of the genitive meaning "to belong to their party, to be their confederates" (*Selections From the Attic Orators* [London: Macmillan, 1957] 227), but this is probably instead a mere partitive genitive (see LCL trans.). And again, this is not a slogan. Comparable (but not identical) uses of this genitive of the proper name of the leader of a faction are found with the definite article, as in Joseph. *BJ* 1.142; App. *BCiv.* 3.5.34; 3.12.86; 5.6.56, 59; 5.9.86; 5.12.111; Plut. *Cic.* 4.1; *Pomp.* 7.3 (of soldiers); 66.1; 71.5; *Oth.* 12.3 (with ἄνδρες). In all of these cases, because they are embedded in a context, a noun or nouns may be understood by ellipsis, which renders them also somewhat different from the cola in 1:12 (note too the direct parallel to these in 1 Cor 1:11, οἱ Χλόης, and Fiorenza, 394, who concludes that this is the same use of the genitive formula as those which follow in 1:12). None of these phrases is a slogan either, however. An interesting example of the genitive

[104] For a broader treatment of the difficulty of analyzing and interpreting slogans throughout history, see W. Bauer, "Das Schlagwort als sozialpsychische und geistesgeschichtliche Erscheinung," *Historische Zeitschrift* 122 (1920) 189–240.

referring to party affiliation is in Plut. *Pomp.* 61:1: "[he] declared that he would regard as a partisan of Caesar any one who remained behind" [Καίσαρος ἡγήσεται τὸν ἀπολειφθέντα]. The genitive case with a proper name is found in relation to party affiliation (but also even more commonly with other meanings, see below), as these examples show, and LSJ confirms, but no instance has been found of the first person pronoun (with or without εἰμι) plus such a genitive in a slogan or party-cry.

I have also investigated philosophical texts to see if the formulae in 1 Cor 1:12 reflect slogans of adherence to given teachers, but without success. Consistently, a noun is provided (ἀκροατής, μαθητής), as in this direct first person statement: τούτου μαθητής εἰμι (D.L. 2.13; for a factionalist, cf. Antiphon, *Fr.* B.1.1 ὡς στασιώτης ἢ ⟨καὶ⟩ ἐγώ). An exact replica of the formulae in 1 Cor 1:12 from ancient political literature has not yet been adduced in the history of exegesis of 1 Cor. The absence of this formula in our extant historical writings, a considerable corpus of material, is significant, and casts doubt on the view that these share a common *form* of political sloganeering. This means we must look for other possible explanations of these formulae (unless or until new evidence is produced).

The key to these formulae is the proper name in the genitive case (differently, Schmithals, *Gnosticism*, 199–200, takes it, incorrectly in my view, to be equivalent to a predicate nominative in order to equate it with the later Gnostic slogan ἐγὼ εἰμὶ ὁ Χριστός). But this is a "genitive of possession or belonging," defined as follows: "With persons the genitive may denote the relations of child to parent, wife to husband, and of inferior to superior" (H. W. Smyth, *Greek Grammar* [Cambridge, MA: Harvard University Press, 1920, repr. 1980] § 1301). Among the examples cited by Smyth (of literally thousands in Greek literature) are Διὸς Ἄρτεμις, "Artemis, daughter of Zeus" (Soph. *Aj.* 172) and Λυδὸς ὁ Φερεκλέους "Lydus, the slave of Pherecles" (Andoc. 1.17). In analyzing the NT usage of proper names in the genitive BDF 162.7 classifies 1 Cor 1:12 (and 3:4, 21; 6:19; Acts 27:23) as a "genitive of relationship" meaning "I belong to X" (also BAGD, 225). Even LSJ subsumed the genitive of party affiliation under this category. While the genitive case can in some instances be used of party affiliation (which Paul is probably playing off of here), it is most commonly used of parent-child relationships and master-slave relationships. In fact, the most exact formulaic parallel I have found to the phrases in 1 Cor 1:12 is in Is 44:5 LXX, the twice-repeated τοῦ θεοῦ εἰμι (ליהוה אני). This phrase (cf. Acts 27:23 τοῦ θεοῦ, οὗ εἰμι ἐγώ) clearly refers to ownership and possession, as it is to be written on the hand, a mark used to identify slaves as belonging to their master (cf. Rev 13:16).[105] That this practice was applied in the Hebrew Bible to the worshiper's relationship to the deity may be important for Paul's usage. In the argument which follows, Paul seems to regard the worshiper's ownership by the deity or Christ, through his theology and teaching of redemption in Christ, as a premise upon which he can build (3:23; 6:11, 19–20; 7:22–23; 15:23; elsewhere in Paul, see 2 Cor 10:7; Rom 8:9). That Paul interprets to the Corinthians the "slogans" as self-pronunciations, not of self-determined politicos, but of children and slaves, is shown definitively in 3:1–4; 6:19–20, and especially 7:23: μὴ γίνεσθε δοῦλοι ἀνθρώπων. This is indeed Paul's interpretation, and one designed to be particularly nettlesome to the Corinthians who prize freedom, of the very fact that there are factions within the community, and not necessarily of actual Corinthian slogans.

---

105 See E. Henderson, *The Book of the Prophet Isaiah* (London: Hamilton, Adams, 1840) 332; F. Stummer, "Einige Keilschriftliche Parallelen zu Jes. 40–66," *JBL* 45 (1926) 171–89, 187; K. Elliger, *Deuterojesaja*, BKAT 11, 1 (Neukirchen-Vluyn: Neukirchener Verlag, 1978) 393.

But there is also internal evidence that Paul does not quote actual Corinthian slogans in 1:12, because the four phrases there are preceded by λέγω δὲ τοῦτο, which introduces Paul's commentary on the report of Chloe's people. In addition, that these "slogans" are not exact quotations is signaled by the ἕκαστος, which scholars have considered to be exaggeration, and not historical report (e. g., Conzelmann, 33). Thus the "slogans" which follow may also logically be exaggerated caricatures. The rhetorical structure of the deliberative argument in 1 Cor also lends some support to this viewpoint, as these verses are in the narration to the argument. Because one always presents the facts of a case in the light best suited to one's own argument (see ch. IV n. 89), one need not presume that Paul here presents actual party cries. Thus I understand 1:12 as the rhetorical figure προσωποποιΐα, impersonation: "By this means we display the inner thoughts of our adversaries as though they were talking with themselves" (Quint. *Inst.* 9.2.30; on its use in narrative see §37; cf. *Rhet.Her.* 4.53.66; Demetr. *Eloc.* 5.265–66). Paul's impersonation of the Corinthians' "slogans" is vivid and contains within it the seeds of the argument to follow.

While the Corinthians themselves may not have expressed their allegiances in this fashion, Paul interprets their factional activity as indicative, not of political sophistication, but of childishness[106] and renunciation of their precious freedom, through their alignment behind the various missionaries.[107] Paul's response is his replacement slogan which stresses their common allegiance to Christ (ὑμεῖς δὲ Χριστοῦ, 3:23).[108]

In 1:13 Paul asks: "Has Christ been divided up?" The verb μερίζειν is also a part of the political vocabulary used to describe factionalism in antiquity.[109] A denominative verb from μερίς, generally "a part" but often specifically a "party, faction,"[110] in the passive it means "to be split into parties or factions."[111] A good example of the term is in Polyb. 8.21.9:

---

106 See esp. 3:1–4 and the discussion below on how this is a *topos* for factionalists.

107 This activity may well reflect differences (even disputes) between these leaders themselves. Plato observed that governments usually fall because of στάσις among the ruling class (*Resp.* 5.465B; 8.545D; cf. Arist. *Pol.* 5.5).

108 F. Godet, *Commentary on St. Paul's First Epistle to the Corinthians*, 2 vols., trans. A. Cusin (Edinburgh: T & T Clark, 1889) 1.66–67. See Chrys. on 3:23: Εἰ δὲ ἐκεῖνοι ὑμῶν, φησί, τί τοὐναντίον ἐποιήσατε, αὐτοῖς ἐπονομαζόμενοι, ἀλλ' οὐχὶ τῷ Χριστῷ καὶ τῷ θεῷ; (*hom. in I Cor.* 10.4 [*PG* 61.84]).

109 It has been correctly noted that this image depends upon the metaphor of the "body of Christ" (Calvin, 28; Weiss, *Korintherbrief*, 16; Conzelmann, 35 n. 34 with reference esp. to *1 Clem.* 46:7; U. Wilckens, *Weisheit und Torheit*, BHT 26 [Tübingen: Mohr/Siebeck, 1959] 13; Klauck, *Hausgemeinde*, 40; *Herrenmahl*, 289, 333; Welborn, "Discord," 87, who rightly points to the political sense of the term). We may regard this as the first mention of Paul's positive counterpart throughout 1 Corinthians to the factionalism manifest in the community, the body of Christ, which reflects a standard political appeal for the cessation of factionalism (see below). The term σῶμα occurs fully forty-seven times in this letter (Allo, lx), far more than any other NT writing; μέλος occurs fifteen times.

110 LSJ, 1104. μερίς is identical with στάσις, for example, in Joseph. *Vit.* 36. The ancient name for the aristocratic party was ἡ κρείττων μερίς (Dion. Hal. *Ant. Rom.* 6.65.1). The neuter noun μέρος can also mean a "class or party" (LSJ, 1105; BAGD, 506), as in Plut. *Mor.* 805E, and even in the NT in Acts 23:6–9, where it is identified with στάσις and σχίζειν (see also

For they quarrelled among themselves [στασιάσαντες] and divided into two factions [ἐμερίσθησαν], the one placing itself under Aribazus and the other under Laodice.[112]

This usage of μερίζειν to refer to dividing into factions is quite common elsewhere in the New Testament and in early Christian literature.[113] Thus μερίζειν in 1 Cor 1:13 is perfectly synonymous with σχίσματα in 1:10 and ἔριδες in 1:11.[114] All three terms refer to factionalism within the church community at Corinth,[115] and have their background in political terminology.[116]

1:18–31 contains an argument on wisdom and foolishness,[117] in which Paul sets worldly standards on their heads. There are several ways in which this section relates to the issue of factionalism. First of all, the term συζητητής, "disputant,"[118] is used by Paul at 1:20. Certainly the party contenders at Corinth are disputing with one another.[119] This noun remains unattested elsewhere in Greek[120] (with the exception of Ign. *Eph.* 18:1, a quotation of this verse). The

---

J. Schneider, *TDNT*, "μέρος," 4.594–98). This is explicitly connected with the body metaphor, as μέρος often means a body part (see Eph 4:16; Paul prefers the synonym μέλος).

111 LSJ, 1103, citing Polyb. 8.21.9; App. *BCiv.* 1.1; Hdn. 3.104 and our text, 1 Cor 1:13. See also Pl. *Ep.* 9.358A, where it is used of a person being divided up; Dio Chrys. *Or.* 36.30, of the divisions of the unified universe; App. *BCiv.* 4.10.76, of an army; Plut. *Cor.* 32.5, quoting *Il.* 1.188, of one's heart.

112 See also Dion. Hal. *Ant. Rom.* 1.85.4; 2.62.3; Aristid. 24.49 (quoted below in reference to 11:17).

113 Most markedly it is used in the political commonplace of "the house divided against itself" (see Mark 3:24–26; Matt 12:25–26; this is quoted by Chrys. *hom. in I Cor.* Argumentum 2, with his description of the occasion of 1 Cor: ὁ διάβολος . . . διαιρεῖ τοὺς ἀνθρώπους [*PG* 61.11]). For the compound verb διαμερίζειν with the same meaning, see Luke 11:17–18 (par. to Mark 3:24–26); 12:52–53; Joseph. *BJ* 2.458; App. *BCiv.* 1.1.10. Ignatius uses μερίζειν to refer to splitting up into factions in *Magn.* 6:2 (see Schoedel, 114–15), there in opposition to ὁμόνοια and ἀγαπᾶν. See also his use of μερισμός in *Phld.* 2:1; 3:1; 7:2; 8:1; *Smyrn.* 7:2 (and Schoedel, 197). Comparable is the Latin *divido*, as in Caesar, *BCiv.* 1.35: "We understand that the Roman people is divided into two parties [*se divisum esse populum Romanum in duas partes*]."

114 The lexical connection is shown also in an inscription from Mantinea from the end of the 1st c. CE, which praises a married union: ἐζεύγνοντο γὰρ βί[οι βίοι]ς [κ]αὶ σώμασιν ψυχαὶ καὶ παρ' ἀμφοτέροις ἀμέρι[στος ὁ]μόνοια (Ditt. *SIG*[4] 783.33–35; dated by G. Fougères, "Inscriptions de Mantinée," *Bulletin de Correspondence Hellénique* 20 [1896] 119–66, 130; note that Dittenberger's edition changes the reading from Fougères's ἀμερ[ὴς ὁμ]όνοια). That concord is "undivided" (which is virtually a redundancy) is presumed also by Paul in 1 Cor 1:13.

115 See Lightfoot's paraphrase: "Have you by your dissensions rent Christ's body asunder, tearing limb from limb?" (154).

116 Contra Schmithals, *Gnosticism*, 376, who takes μερίζειν to be a *terminus technicus* in Gnosticism.

117 See Betz, "Rhetoric and Theology," 26–34.

118 BAGD, 775 (also "debater"; see also Conzelmann, 43; Barrett, 52–53).

119 The "disputer" is "of this age," just as factionalism and party politics are "human" (see n. 98 above).

120 Heinrici, 69; LSJ, 1670; J. Schneider, "συζητέω, κτλ.," *TDNT* 7.747–48, 748. It is possible that Paul coined the term to describe the unspeakable – Christians viciously disputing with one another.

verb συζητεῖν can mean "to examine together," especially in regard to philosophical speculation, or, more forcefully, "to strive."[121] In the New Testament both the less forceful meaning of the verb, "to discuss"[122] and the stronger, "to dispute"[123] are attested. Commentators often read 1 Cor 1:20 as a paraphrase of LXX Is 19:12 and 33:18.[124] Yet neither quotation contains anything corresponding to the meaning of συζητητής in 1 Cor 1:20.[125] Lightfoot's explanation is the most plausible: σοφός refers to the Greek "wise man," γραμματεύς to the Jewish counterpart, and συζητητής is "a general expression comprehending both."[126] Specifically, the term encompasses all the disputants, whether Greek or Jewish. This is confirmed by the rest of the argument wherein only a two-part distinction is made, between Greek and Jew (1:22–24). Thus the anomalous term συζητητής chosen by Paul in 1:20 may be seen as another reference to the behavior of the factionalists within the community.[127]

As we have noted, the section 1:18–25 is grounded in the antithesis of Jews and Greeks. Though Jews and Greeks differ from one another, the κλητοί, "the called ones"[128] are united in a common perception, a common wisdom (see esp. 1:22–24). Paul attempts to replace old terms of ethnic identification with a single, unified identification for the members of the church community, as κλητοί[129] (as in the address to the letter, 1:2). It is clear that one of the factors responsible for division within the church community[130] at Corinth was this ethnic diversity of Jews and Gentiles.[131] The role of ethnic diversity in causing factionalism in political communities was noted already by Aristotle: "Also a

---

[121] Schneider, *TDNT* 7.747 with references (and LSJ, 1670). See especially *POxy*. 1673, 20: συνεζήτησα πολλὰ καὶ κατέπλεξα ("I had much strife and confusion" [trans. Schneider]).

[122] Mark 1:27; 9:10; Luke 24:15.

[123] Mark 8:11; 9:14, 16; 12:28; Luke 22:23; Acts 6:9; 9:29.

[124] Heinrici, 69; Weiss, *Korintherbrief*, 27–28; Wilckens, 26 n. 1.

[125] Is 33:18 ποῦ εἰσιν οἱ συμβουλεύοντες/איה שקל ("where are the advisors/the ones weighing tribute") is similar only in form.

[126] Lightfoot, 159. It is hard to see how Conzelmann finds this reading (attested already in the church fathers) "too subtle" (43 n. 32).

[127] See Acts 15:2, where ζήτησις is conjoined with στάσις, and also the list of vices in Titus 3:9 containing μωραὶ ζητήσεις alongside γενεαλογίαι, ἔρεις and μάχαι νομικαί. ζητήματα are what keep Prusa and Apameia from concord, according to Dio Chrys. *Or*. 41.8.

[128] To be identified with οἱ σῳζομένοι in 1:18 and οἱ πιστεύοντες in 1:21.

[129] On the place of the κλῆσις in "The Language of Belonging" see Meeks, *Urban Christians*, 85.

[130] This is not to say that it was the only factor. There were probably many contributing factors.

[131] See, in addition to 1:18–31, 7:17–24; 9:20–22; 10:32; 12:13; cf. Acts 18:4, and the recent analysis by P. Richardson, "On the Absence of 'Anti-Judaism' in 1 Corinthians," *Anti-Judaism in Early Christianity. Vol. 1: Paul and the Gospels*, ed. *idem* and D. Granskou, Studies in Christianity and Judaism 2 (Waterloo: Wilfred Laurier University Press, 1986) 59–74. Richardson's conclusion, that there are no anti-Judaistic statements in 1 Cor because Paul is concerned to mediate peacefully between the different groups, is correct, and will be further confirmed by this study.

difference of race (τὸ μὴ ὁμόφυλον) is a cause of faction (στασιωτικόν) until harmony of spirit is reached."[132] This is particularly the case in a new political body, as there is need to establish its identity over and against old forms of self-identification. For example, in unifying ancient Rome, the legendary king Numa faced down the old ethnic and political divisions by stressing the peoples' new common identity:

> And thus, at last, he banished from the city the practice of speaking and thinking of some citizens as Sabines, and of others as Romans, or of some as subjects of Tatius, and others of Romulus, so that his division resulted in a harmonious blending[133] of them all together.[134]

Political realism dictates that a new community formed from members of previously diverse social and ethnic backgrounds must find its common ground.[135] In the case of Numa (as told by Greco-Roman writers), the city of Rome was urged to unite in a new, common name (κοινὴ ὀνομασία), "Latins."[136]

In combatting division in the Corinthian church community caused (at least in part) by ethnic diversity, Paul stresses the Corinthians' unity in Christ through their common identity as κλητοί,[137] thus replacing old ethnic forms of self-identification and allegiance with a new church community identity in Christ.[138] Paul grants the separateness and differentiation of Jews and Greeks (1:22, 23), but he argues that Corinthian Christians, both Jew and Greek in prior background (1:24), no longer partake of this ethnic diversity because both now share

---

132 *Pol.* 5.2.10; Loenen, 16.

133 Greek ἀνάμιξις (see below on the political nature of this term, and the theory of "the mixed constitution" in the discussion of συναναμίγνυσθαι in 5:9, 11).

134 Plut. *Num.* 17.3. See also Dion. Hal. *Ant. Rom.* 2.46.2, where Numa is said to have "attuned the whole body of people, like a musical instrument, to the sole consideration of the common good" (πρὸς ἕνα τὸν τοῦ κοινῇ συμφέροντος λογισμόν). The same strategy is attributed to Alexander the Great (Plut. *Mor.* 329C-D). See also Ps.-Sall. *Rep.* 7.2. Paul uses both of these strategies (on the latter, see below on 10:23–11:1).

135 See Ps-Sall. *Rep.* 7.2 *concordia inter veteres et novos coalescat.*

136 Dion. Hal. *Ant. Rom.* 1.60.2; see also Polyb. 4.1.8; Plut. *Num.* 2.4; *Marc.* 12.3; Cass. Dio 1.5.6.

137 See also 1:2 (in the epistolary salutation only here and in Romans), 9; 7:17–24. The appeal to unity in 1:10 is made διὰ τοῦ ὀνόματος τοῦ κυρίου ἡμῶν Ἰησοῦ Χριστοῦ. This common name is also a response to the names of individual missionaries championed by the Corinthians (see 1:12 and the discussion above). It is interesting that even Celsus acknowledges the importance of the common name for Christian factions! (ἔτι κοινωνοῦντες, εἴ γε κοινωνοῦσιν ἔτι, τοῦ ὀνόματος; Or. *Cels.* 3.12 [Borret, SC 136.34]). For the "name issue" in combatting factionalism see also Apollonius of Tyana *Ep.* 39: "Even the names of your factions are disgraceful – Koddaroi, Xuresitauroi. These are the first names that you give to your children, and you consider yourself fortunate that they are worthy of such names" (text and trans. *The Letters of Apollonius of Tyana. A Critical Text with Prolegomena, Translation and Commentary*, ed. R.J. Penella [Leiden: Brill, 1979]).

138 Heinrici, 33. The definitive statement of this is Paul's "replacement slogan" (so Lightfoot, 195; Lietzmann-Kümmel, 17; Conzelmann, 81) ὑμεῖς δὲ Χριστοῦ in 3:23.

a common κλῆσις,[139] in distinction, no longer from one another, but from those outsiders.[140] This is just the beginning of this type of argument for unity in common bonds among the Corinthian Christians which Paul will make in this letter. Elsewhere in 1 Corinthians Paul will stress Corinthian unity in one God (8:6; 12:6), one spirit (3:16; 6:11, 17; 12:4–11), one Lord Jesus Christ (1:10; 6:11; 8:6; 12:3, 5), and one body (6:16; 10:17; 12:12–27).[141] It is indicative of Paul's

---

[139] *1 Clem.* sums up the argument of 1 Corinthians for use in urging a later generation of Corinthian factionalists to seek unity: ἱνατί ἔρεις καὶ θυμοὶ καὶ διχοστασίαι καὶ σχίσματα πόλεμός τε ἐν ὑμῖν; ἢ οὐχὶ ἕνα θεὸν ἔχομεν καὶ ἕνα Χριστὸν καὶ ἓν πνεῦμα τῆς χάριτος τὸ ἐκχυθὲν ἐφ' ὑμᾶς, καὶ μία κλῆσις ἐν Χριστῷ; (46:6). His last appeal to the one call is the argument which Paul makes here in 1 Cor 1. See also Ign. *Magn.* 7:1–2; *Phld.* 4, and Schoedel, 21–22; 116–17 (but he leaves Paul out of the chain of tradition of these "ones"!). Another step between Paul and *1 Clem* and Ignatius is Eph 4:1–16, which is literally a pastiche of references and metaphors culled from throughout 1 Cor (these are isolated by E.J. Goodspeed, *The Meaning of Ephesians* [Chicago: University of Chicago Press, 1933] esp. 123–31, who calls the passage "a great appeal for Christian unity" [p. 53]). Compare in particular Eph 4:4–6 with Paul's extended argument throughout 1 Cor: Ἓν σῶμα καὶ ἓν πνεῦμα, καθὼς καὶ ἐκλήθητε ἐν μιᾷ ἐλπίδι τῆς κλήσεως ὑμῶν. εἷς κύριος, μία πίστις, ἓν βάπτισμα, εἷς θεὸς καὶ πατὴρ πάντων, ὁ ἐπὶ πάντων καὶ διὰ πάντων καὶ ἐν πᾶσιν.

[140] The insider/outsider distinction is directly related to the issue of factionalism (see below on 1 Cor 5 and 6). Paul's definitions of πνευματικοί, ψυχικοί and σαρκινοί in 2:10–3:3 are also ways of redefining the social situation and church membership along anthropological and theological grounds. For the same argument, see Eph 2:19–22. It is an ancient political commonplace that ὁμόνοια is best maintained when a state faces war with an outside enemy (see Polyb. 6.18.2; Dion. Hal. *Ant. Rom.* 8.83.2; 10.33.2 and throughout; Sall. *Iug.* 41.1–5; see Gehrke, 268–87 for a more complex analysis of the relation of internal and external forces on factionalism), a viewpoint confirmed by sociological analysis (J.H. Elliott, *A Home for the Homeless. A Sociological Exegesis of 1 Peter, Its Situation and Strategy* [Philadelphia: Fortress, 1981] 112–18 and passim, with references to sociological literature). For Paul to stress inner unity in opposition to the outsiders (as especially in 2:6–16; chaps. 5 and 6) draws on this same principle.

[141] 1 Cor contains all the elements of the later compressed expression of this same set of unifying appeals in Eph 4:1–16 (quoted in part above, n. 139) and earlier 2:11–19, a text which includes the two main unifying metaphors of 1 Cor, the body and the building for the church (on which see S. Hanson, *The Unity of the Church in the New Testament, Colossians and Ephesians*, Acta Seminarii Neotestamentici Upsaliensis 14 [Uppsala: Almqvist & Wiksell, 1946] 141–48). On church unity for Paul as grounded in one Lord, one faith, one baptism and one body in brotherly love, see P.I. Bratsiotis, "Paulus und die Einheit der Kirche," *Studia Paulina* in honorem *Johannis de Zwaan* (Haarlem: Bohn, 1953) 28–36. On the εἷς-formulas in 1 Cor see Sellin, 2961–62, and particularly 2998–99, where he argues that Paul applied these teachings and the social practices they imply, which he had learned at Antioch, to the Corinthian situation; on these appeals to "ones" see also Hanson, 73–98. In Greco-Roman texts which appeal for concord we also find appeals to "ones," such as in Dio Chrys. *Or.* 41.10: εἷς ἐστε δῆμος καὶ μία πόλις; Aristid. *Or.* 23.62; 24.31: οὐ κοινὴ μὲν ἅπασα γῆ, βασιλεὺς δὲ εἷς, νόμοι δὲ κοινοὶ πᾶσι; Ps-Sall. *Rep.* 10.8: "For in their day the commonwealth was united [*quippe apud illos una res publica erat*], for its welfare all citizens had regard." For the unifying force of such "ones" in Hellenistic Judaism see Philo, *Virt.* 35: "And the highest and greatest source of this unanimity [ὁμόνοια] is their creed of a single God [ἡ περὶ τοῦ ἑνὸς θεοῦ δόξα], through which, as from a fountain, they feel love [φιλία] for each other, uniting them in an indissoluble bond" (see also below n. 231 on the unifying role of the one temple as expressed in the writings of Philo

thorough-going argument for unity in 1 Corinthians that the word εἷς occurs fully thirty-one times in the letter.[142]

The theme of boasting (καυχᾶσθαι)[143] is prevalent throughout 1 Corinthians.[144] The problem is defined by Paul in 3:21 – "let no one boast in men." "Boasting in men" is another negative description of the Corinthian factionalism[145] parodied in the "slogans" of 1:12 and 3:4, and appropriately rebutted by Paul with the paraphrase from Jer 9:22 in 1 Cor 1:31, "let the one who boasts boast in the Lord."[146] The term καυχᾶσθαι is not common in Greek literature, nor throughout the New Testament, where it is confined to Paul, who uses the verb and nominal cognates frequently.[147] Despite this term's relative rarity, the practice is well understood: boasting means praising oneself.[148] What is preferable to boasting is of course to be praised by others,[149] an insight of which Paul reminds the Corinthians in 1 Cor 4:5, where he counters their boasting with the eschatological reserve: "then the praise shall be to each *from God*."[150] Other results of boasting warned of by Plutarch seem to have surfaced in Corinth – envy (*Mor.* 539D, 546D; 1 Cor 3:3), glory-seeking (540D; 1 Cor 4:10; 12:23),[151]

---

and Josephus). This same appeal to "ones" for unity is found in rabbinic literature, such as *Num.Rab.* 18.8 (on 16:6): "'It is the way of the other nations to have many religious observances and many priests, and they cannot all gather together in one edifice. We, however, have only one God, one Torah, one code of laws, one altar, and one High Priest, and you, two hundred and fifty strong, all seek the High Priesthood!'" For this cultic unity in ECL see again Ign. *Magn.* 7:1–2.

142 Allo, lv. Cf. the logical conclusion of Schoedel, 116 on Ign. *Magn.*: "The word 'one' appears some nine times in this section (7.1–2) and reflects the central concern of Ignatius' letters."

143 See also below on the near synonym περπερεύεσθαι in 13:4.

144 1:29–31; 3:18–23; 4:5–7; 5:6; 9:15–16; 13:3.

145 So Heinrici, 84, 135; Weiss, *Korintherbrief*, 44; Prümm, 202; Barrett, 95; Conzelmann, 80 n. 15. See Chrys. on 1:29: Καὶ ὑμεῖς ἐπὶ τῷ δεῖνι καὶ τῷ δεῖνι ὑμᾶς αὐτοὺς προσενείματε; (*hom. in I Cor.* 5.2 [*PG* 61.41]).

146 Cf. Philo, *Spec.Leg.* 1.311: "Let God alone be thy boast [αὔχημα]."

147 R. Bultmann, "καυχάομαι κτλ.," *TDNT* 3.645–54; BAGD, 425–26.

148 See Plutarch's quotation of Pindar in his treatise on self-praise, where he equates τὸ καυχᾶσθαι with τὸ περὶ ἑαυτοῦ λέγειν (*Mor.* 539C), and discussion in H. D. Betz, "De laude ipsius," ed. *idem, Plutarch's Ethical Writings and Early Christian Literature*, SCHNT 4 (Leiden: Brill, 1978) 367–93, esp. 375–79; *idem, Der Apostel Paulus*, 75–79, and E. A. Judge, "Paul's Boasting in Relation to Contemporary Professional Practice," *AusBR* 16 (1968) 37–50. For a recent general treatment, see C. Forbes, "Comparison, Self-Praise and Irony: Paul's Boasting and the Conventions of Hellenistic Rhetoric," *NTS* 32 (1986) 1–30, 8–10.

149 Plut. *Mor.* 539D; Quint. *Inst.* 11.1.22. In the HB see Prov 27:2.

150 Cf. Rom 2:29. The same argument is used in *1 Clem.* 30:6: ὁ ἔπαινος ἡμῶν ἔστω ἐν θεῷ καὶ μὴ ἐξ αὐτῶν. αὐτεπαινέτους γὰρ μισεῖ ὁ θεός.

151 The one boasting seeks glory, δόξα, and honor, τιμή. Aristotle observed that this can be a common cause of στάσις: "It is clear also what is the power of honor [τιμή] and how it can cause party faction [στάσις]; for men form factions [στασιάζειν] both when they are themselves dishonoured [ἀτιμαζόμενοι] and when they see others honoured [τιμωμένοι]" (*Pol.* 5.2.4; see also 2.4.7: "civil strife [στασιάζειν] is caused not only by inequality of property, but also by

comparative judgements to the diminishment of others (540B; 1 Cor 4:1–5),[152] and, in general, offense (539B; 1 Cor 8:9; 10:32).[153] Boasting is thus a divisive force[154] within the Corinthian community.

We have noted that Paul terms Corinthian factionalism "boasting in men" (3:21; cf. 1:12; 3:4).[155] In particular, boasting in men is a form of ethnic and national self-identification. For example, Josephus refers to "the Carthaginians, who, for all their pride in the great Hannibal [οἱ τὸν μέγαν αὐχοῦντες Ἀννίβαν][156] and in the nobility of their Phoenecian descent..."[157] Josephus differentiates Jews and Greeks by the lawgiver or founder in whom they boast.[158] The Philistines are those who boasted in being descendants of the giants.[159] Ancestry was also the boast of the patriarch Joseph, who "boasted at being a member of the Hebrew race."[160] The connection of this boasting in leaders with factionalism is seen in Aelius Aristides' *Or.* 23, where he attempts to reconcile Ephesus,

---

inequality of honours [τιμαί]"; this is echoed in Philo, *Decal.* 151–53). For concrete examples see, e. g., Dio Chrys. *Or.* 38.29; Sall. *Iug.* 41.2 [*gloria*]; Ps-Sall. *Rep.* 8.4: "it is because sloth and indolence, dullness and torpor, have taken possession of their minds, that they resort to abuse and slander and consider the glory [*fama*] of others a disgrace [*dedecus*] to themselves." For this as a problem at Corinth see esp. 1 Cor 4:10 and 12:22–25 (as later *1 Clem.* 3.3, οὕτως ἐπηγέρθησαν οἱ ἄτιμοι ἐπὶ τοὺς ἐντίμους, οἱ ἄδοξοι ἐπὶ τοὺς ἐνδόξους...). Striving for higher social status is also clearly linked to partisanship at Corinth (see 1:26–29; 4:8–10; 7:17–24; 12:22–26 and Theissen, 54–57).

[152] See Plut. *Mor.* 87B-C, 88A on the judgements and investigations which enemies make of one another's actions. On κρινεῖν as judgement in social ranks (not only as a judicial term), see Plut. *Crass.* 27.4. The term is used by Paul directly in regard to forming negative judgements on others from scrutinizing their eating in Rom 14 (parallel to ἐξουθενεῖν) with the same appeal to the Lord's final judgement (14:4, 10–12). Why not regard 1 Cor 4:1–5 as a reference to the same kind of divisive "judging" among members of the Corinthian church, where we know this was a problem (cf. Jas 4:11)? This is certainly how Chrys. understands it, as he mockingly quotes their "judgements" of one another: Ὁ δεῖνα ἄξιος, ὁ δεῖνα τοῦ δεῖνος ἀμείνων. καὶ οὗτος ἐκείνου καταδεέστερος, κἀκεῖνος τούτου βελτίων. καὶ ἀφέντες τὰ ἑαυτῶν πενθεῖν κακά, ἑτέροις ἐγίνοντο δικασταί, καὶ ταύτῃ πολέμους ἀνῆπτον πάλιν χαλεποὺς ... τοῦτο δὲ τὴν στάσιν ἐπέτριβεν (*hom. in I Cor.* 11.1 [*PG* 61.87–88]; cf. 11.2 [61.90]).

[153] See below on the connection between "offense" and party politics.

[154] καυχᾶσθαι is one of the causes of revolution and στάσις in the examples cited by Arist. *Pol.* 5.8.10. In Greek historical writings boasting is a main ingredient in war rhetoric (see Hdt. 7.103; Thuc. 7.66.3; 75.6; Strab. 13.1.27; Joseph. *BJ* 2.473; 3.333; 7.113; *AJ* 2.252).

[155] This may have been rooted in a misguided affiliation to the person by whom one was baptized (so Chrys. on 1 Cor 1:13–16: Ἐπειδὴ γὰρ καὶ τοῦτο αἴτιον ἐγένετο σχισμάτων, τὸ ἀπὸ τῶν βαπτισάντων καλεῖσθαι [*hom. in I Cor.* 3.2 (*PG* 61.25)]).

[156] Literally translated: "who boast in the great Hannibal."

[157] *BJ* 2.380.

[158] "Such was our legislator [Moses]; no charlatan or imposter, as slanderers unjustly call him, but one such as the Greeks boast [αὐχεῖν] of having had in Minos and later legislators" (*Ap.* 2.161).

[159] Joseph. *AJ* 7.301; cf. 2 Sam 21:20–22.

[160] Philo, *Migr.* 20: τὸ αὐχεῖν ἐπὶ τῷ γένος εἶναι Ἑβραίων. On boasting in one's ancestry, see the section περὶ εὐγενείας in Philo, *Virt.*, esp. 187, 197.

Smyrna and Pergamum from their rivalry for titles and honors.[161] Ephesus and Smyrna, being colonies of Athens, and thus sharing its esteemed ancestry, make boastful claims to more noble descent than Pergamum. Aristides urges unity through a common boast:

[Pergamum] can make a boast [αὐχᾶσθαι] similar to Athens itself in respect to its generation of aboriginal men and heroes. But if not, then a similar boast to these cities. For its colonists are descended from aboriginal Arcadians, so that from this cause it is reasonable for you to have recognized one another as friends and to have paid each other appropriate honors [τιμᾶν].[162]

Using the same strategy to combat factional boasting, Paul calls the Corinthians to unity in the common boast "in the Lord." He reminds them that they are, in fact, ἀγενῆ τοῦ κόσμου, not εὐγενεῖς.[163] The Corinthians, who *each* boast in a different leader/ancestor (as Paul describes it), are urged to unity in their common boast in the Lord (1:31; 3:21–23) and "descent" from *both* himself as founder and Apollos as promoter of the community (3:4–9; 4:15; 15:11). There need be no division by these boasts,[164] according to Paul, as all three men (Paul, Apollos and Cephas) may be claimed by all Corinthians (3:21–23).[165] But most of all, their unity is centered in Christ (3:23).

In addition to boasting in men, some Corinthians are apparently boasting in certain exclusive possessions[166] (see especially 4:7, τί καυχᾶσαι ὡς μὴ λαβών). Group or partisan membership is locked up in these claims to special possessions (e. g. λόγος, γνῶσις, σοφία[167]). Throughout 1 Corinthians Paul counters claims to exclusive possession in two ways. First, he stresses (as already in the epistolary thanksgiving in 1:4–9) the passive nature of these possessions – they are gifts of God, not attained through merit, and therefore not to be boasted in.[168] The

---

161 See R. MacMullen, *Enemies of the Roman Order* (Cambridge, MA: Harvard University Press, 1966) 185–91 and notes on these city rivalries.

162 *Or.* 23.26.

163 1:26–28. On factionalism caused by dispute over lineage (εὐγένεια), see Aristid. *Or.* 24.37.

164 Origen took such boasts to be the content of the Corinthians' ἀνακρίσεις, "comparisons": οἱ ἐν Κορίνθῳ ἀνέκρινον τὸ ὅσον ἐφ' ἑαυτοῖς, οὐκ ἀληθῶς ἀνακρίνοντες. ἀνακρίνοντος γὰρ ἦν τὸ λέγειν ὅτι Κρείττων ἐστὶν ὁ Παῦλος Κηφᾶ καὶ Ἀπολλώ, καὶ ἄλλου τὸ λέγειν Ὁ Πέτρος πολλῷ διαφέρει τοῦ Παύλου (*comm. in I Cor.* 18.30–32 [p. 354]).

165 Cf. Aristid. *Or.* 23.36, where in urging concord he makes an appeal to Homer, "since this poet is our most common possession" (see also 24.7).

166 See Betz, "Rhetoric and Theology," 26–39.

167 The connection between the claim to possess σοφία and factionalism has long been recognized (see C.K. Barrett, "Christianity at Corinth," *Essays on Paul* [Philadelphia: Westminster, 1982] 1–27, p. 6; Theissen, 97–98). Welborn ("Discord," 101–103) argues that this σοφία which is so divisive is rhetoric (cf. Chrys.'s understanding of ὁ λόγος τῶν πεφυσιωμένων in 4:19 [*hom. in I Cor.* 14.2 (*PG* 61.116)]). On religious boasting in exclusive possessions, see Philo, *Mut.* 148: "But in the school of Moses it is not one man who may boast [αὐχῆσαι] that he has learnt the first elements of wisdom [σοφία], but a whole nation, a mighty people."

168 1:5; 3:21–23 (for a well-known formal parallel to the latter text, noted already by Origen

second rebuttal Paul makes to divisive boasts in individual possessions is by stressing throughout 1 Corinthians that *all things belong to all Corinthian Christians,*[169] thus denying any special claims by individuals or splinter groups.[170] These two arguments are combined in 3:18–23, where all objects of Corinthian boasting – men and gifts – are said to belong freely to all (cf. 16:14).[171]

Disputes over unequal distribution of goods within any political or social body can result in factionalism, as Aristotle reported: "the question of property [αἱ οὐσίαι], they say, is universally the cause of party strife [στάσις]."[172] Recent works have argued that economic disparity was responsible for the divisions within the Corinthian community (especially on the basis of 11:17–22).[173] There is no doubt that this was a contributing factor in Corinthian factionalism, yet monetary wealth and propertied status are not the only causes of Corinthian divisions, but are among probably many contributing factors.[174] Not only

---

[*comm. in I Cor.* 17.11 (p. 353)], see the Stoic doctrine τῶν σοφῶν δὲ πάντα εἶναι, as in D.L. 7.125; Plut. *Cic.* 25.3); 4:7–8; 7:17–24; 9:15–16; 12:6–11, 18, 24, 28; 15:57. See chap. IV below on the rhetorical strategy at work here.

169 Cf. Aristides' reconciliatory plea πάντα κοινά in *Or.* 24.42.

170 3:21 [πάντα γὰρ ὑμῶν ἐστιν]; 8:1; 10:17; 12:6, 11–13; 14:5, 26, 40; 15:27–28, 51; 16:14 (this last text is especially important because it is a restatement of the argument of the entire letter; see chap. IV).

171 It is a commonplace in discourses urging concord that united groups get the benefit of both sets of possessions. See, e. g., Dio Chrys. *Or.* 38.44: "Nicaea can be yours and your possessions theirs" (see also 38.41–48; 41.13; Aristid. *Or.* 24.42). See Chrys.'s disquisition on wealth and individual possessions, in which he applies the extended body metaphor to this *topos* (*hom. in I Cor.* 10.3–4 [*PG* 61.86–87]).

172 *Pol.* 2.4.1; cf. Dion. Hal. *Ant. Rom.* 5.53.1; 6.54.1. See the summary statement in Aristid. *Or* 23.65: "Hence faction, battles, disputes. For 'this is not yours, but mine' [οὐ σὸν τοῦτο, ἀλλ' ἐμόν] begins every argument. But where men believe that possessions belong to all in common [κοινά], they also have a common point of view about them." See also Plut. *Mor.* 511C, quoted in chap. II n. 194. Paul's contemporary, the poet Lucan, blames the civil wars in Rome in the previous century on struggles for possessions (*BCiv.* 1.158–82). On socio-economic influences on factionalism earlier, in the 5th and 4th centuries (B.C.E.), see Gehrke, 309–28.

173 The champion of this point of view has been Theissen (69–174); see also the overview of scholarship on the social stature of the Corinthian church in Sellin, 2997–3001. Welborn ("Discord," 93–101) has argued that the terms used in 1:26 are technical terms for socio-economic status which amount to saying "rich and poor" (cf. the examples collected in Gehrke, 309–11). In line with Aristotle's observation, he regards this as the cause of Corinthian factionalism. On the social stratification of the Corinthian church, with particular reference to 1:26, see S.C. Barton, "Paul's Sense of Place: An Anthropological Approach to Community Formation in Corinth," *NTS* 32 (1986) 225–46, 238–39; D. Sänger, "Die δυνατοί in 1 Kor 1, 26," *ZNW* 76 (1985) 285–91; cf. Conzelmann, 50. To these investigations we should also add the connection between being "well-born" and being free: "'But', you will object, 'it is impossible for anyone to be 'noble' [γενναῖος] without being 'well-born' [εὐγενής] at the same time, or for one who is 'well-born' [εὐγενής] not to be free [ἐλεύθερος]" (Dio Chrys. *Or.* 15.31; this may account for the Corinthian objection to compromising their freedom in 10:29; cf. 9:1).

174 It is the complexity of the different lines of influence that makes an assignment of the various positions on issues to specific factions so difficult. Just as not all facets of the Corinthian situation can be completely resolved on the basis of the Jew/Gentile differences, so too the rich/

worldly possessions, but also "spiritual" goods are part of the disputes. The fact that some of the goods that are the object of disputation at Corinth are spiritual does not minimize the divisive effects. In fact, for a religious community it probably exacerbates the problem.[175] Boasting in one's own possessions (spiritual or material) is to be seen as another component of the party conflicts within the Corinthian church.[176]

φυσιοῦσθαι, "being puffed up,"[177] a term found throughout 1 Corinthians,[178] is almost synonymous with καυχᾶσθαι.[179] In fact, the two images, boasting and being puffed up, are often used in tandem in ancient Greek texts,[180] as by Paul in 1 Cor 4:6–7. φυσιοῦσθαι, like its counterpart καυχᾶσθαι, is another component of the Corinthian factionalism[181] which Paul refutes throughout the letter.[182]

---

poor dichotomy cannot explain all the positions. The varieties of factors, social, economic, ethnic, geographical, religious, even gender and marital status, cut across the members of the community. No one factor can account for the spectrum of groupings thus produced, as even Theissen concedes: "thus the bases for the conflict at the Lord's supper are neither purely material nor purely theological. Above all, they are social, the problems of a socially stratified community" (p. 160; cf. Gehrke, 352). While I agree that economic factors fomented the factionalism at Corinth, as so often in history, it is important to note that Paul does not himself explicitly describe the conflict in those terms (as is done, for example, in *1 Clem.* 38:2).

175 See 1:5 for the special content of Corinthian "riches." This is demonstrated quite clearly in the section 11:2–14:40, which deals with manifestations of Corinthian factionalism when they come together in assembly to worship.

176 As Chrys. noted: ἐπὶ τοῖς χαρίσμασι μέγα φρονοῦντες, καὶ πρὸς ἀλλήλους ἐντεῦθεν ζηλοτύπως ἔχοντες, ὅπερ καὶ αὐτὸ μάλιστα διέσπα τὴν Ἐκκλησίαν (*hom. in I Cor.* Argumentum 2 [*PG* 61.12]).

177 φυσιοῦσθαι is Paul's term (cf. Col 2:18; and in *T.Levi* 14.7, 8; φυσίωσις in 2 Cor 12:20). Other Greek writers use φυσάω, from the same root with the same meaning (LSJ, 1964). Both of these denominative verbs from φῦσα ("a pair of bellows") have the literal meaning "to puff or blow" (e. g., Arist. *Metaph.* 2.367B; Philostr. *VS* 483), but often have the metaphorical meaning "to inflate" or in the passive "be conceited." Cf. Chrys.'s literal rendering in ***hom. in I** Cor.* 1.3 [*PG* 61.16].

178 4:6, 18–19; 5:2; 8:1; 13:4 (and only here in the Pauline corpus).

179 The connection was made already by Weiss, *Korintherbrief*, 104.

180 See Philo, *Cong.* 107, 127; *Vit.Mos.* 1.6.30; Plut. *Dem. and Cic.* 2.1–3; *1 Clem.* 21:5; Ign. *Magn.* 12; *Pol.* 4.3; cf. the Latin counterpart *inflatus* in Cic. *Off.* 1.26.91; Suet. *Ner.* 37.3. The Philo text *Vit.Mos.* 1.6.30 is an important parallel to Pauline usage, as the ones who are puffed up and boastful proceed to call their perceived inferiors καθάρματα (cf. 1 Cor 4:13 [cited also by Fitzgerald, 144–45]; *Virt.* 174). Like καυχᾶσθαι, φυσιοῦσθαι is often connected with one's ancestry (Dem. *Or.* 58.5; Herod. 2.32 [ed. Headlam and Knox, note with further references on p. 81]; Plut. *Mor.* 814C) and glory-seeking and wealth (D.L. 6.24). Such behavior is belittled as folly (M. Ant. 5.23; D.L. 6.24).

181 Chrys. takes it that the Corinthians were puffed up by their errant claim of wisdom, which led to their dividing the church (***hom. in I Cor.*** 10.1 [*PG* 61.81]. He later vividly connects their being "puffed up" with the body metaphor for the church, describing it as the literal swelling of a tumor in one member which can destroy the corporate whole (12.1 [61.97]).

182 Heinrici, 166 ("Die ἔριδες und das φυσιοῦσθαι stehen in Wechselwirkung"); Theissen, 55; Welborn, "Discord," 88 and "Conciliatory Principle," 332 (in regard to 4:6, 18–19 only, with supporting texts). See also the extensive parallels in Greek and Latin literature collected by Wettstein, 2.113–14. That Paul connects the term φυσιοῦσθαι with divisiveness is shown also

1 Cor 3 contains many references to Corinthian factions. The "slogans" are repeated in 3:4 (cf. 3:23). Paul compares the factionalists to silly children whose cries for superiority actually demonstrate their infantile dependence on their leaders. This factional behavior is "fleshly" and constitutes "walking in a human way" which is another political *topos.*[183] The image of inner-group contenders as disputing children is another commonplace in literature urging concord on divided groups.[184] Dio Chrys. uses this *topos* in his *Or.* 38:[185]

> . . . and [if] it is not fitting even for private persons to squabble over them [στασιάζειν], much less cities of such importance, then let us not behave at all like foolish children [οἱ ἄφρονες τῶν παίδων] who, ashamed lest they may seem to their fathers or their mothers[186] to be enraged without a cause, do not wish to make it up with one another lightly (*Or.* 38.21).[187]

Paul will return to this *topos* in his exemplary argument for unity in love in 13:11: ὅτι γέγονα ἀνήρ, κατήργηκα τὰ τοῦ νηπίου,[188] and again in 14:20: 'Αδελφοί, μὴ παιδία γίνεσθε ταῖς φρεσὶν ἀλλὰ τῇ κακίᾳ νηπιάζετε.[189]

---

by the terms with which φυσίωσις is associated in 2 Cor 12:20 (see n. 89 above). Synonyms are also used of inflated party politicians (Aristid. uses ἐξοιδεῖν in his vivid depiction of στάσις as a woman in *Or.* 24.44; ἐπαίρεσθαι is also commonly used [see Dion. Hal. *Ant. Rom.* 7.21.3; Dio Chrys. *Or.* 57.6; App. *BCiv.* 2.10.67; 3.4.29]; cf. 2 Cor 10:5; 11:20 [12:7]; *1 Clem.* 21:5; 39:1).

[183] As demonstrated above, n. 98. In patristic exegesis, see esp. Chrys.'s discussion of children's games and τὰ ἀνθρώπινα in his exegesis of 1 Cor 1:1–3 (*hom. in I Cor.* 1.3 [*PG* 61.16]).

[184] As argued by Welborn, "Conciliatory Principle," 337, citing Dio Chrys. *Or.* 38.37 and Aristid. *Or.* 23.62 (but note that the latter text does not say that the factionalists are "like children who fight with their own shadows" [337], but rather that even children know that Rome reigns supreme, so inter-city rivalries are useless, and amount to fighting over a shadow [see n. 320 in this chapter on this separate, well-attested *topos*]).

[185] This argument is combined by Dio with another *topos* on concord: that the things for which the contenders strive are οὐδέν and the issues μικρά and φαῦλα (38.21; see also Aristid. *Or.* 23.63 and the discussion below on 1 Cor 6:4).

[186] The family image is often fleshed out even more in such texts, with parents taking a role vis à vis their disputing children (as in 1 Cor 3:1; 4:14–16, 20 [on the connection with harmony, see Dahl, 46]). See Plut. *Mor.* 480F: "Now, as regards parents, brotherly love is of such sort that to love one's brother is forthwith a proof of love for both mother and father" (see also 480C, E). The political nature of this image is shown by Dion. Hal. in describing the way in which the Romans settled their στάσεις: "but conferring together about what was fair and just, like brothers or children with their parents in a well-governed family [ἐν οἰκίᾳ σώφρονι]" (*Ant. Rom.* 7.66.5). The family image and the building are combined by Paul in ch. 3–4 (see below). This understanding of 1 Cor has been stressed previously by Barton, 239: "First, he appeals for unity between household factions by representing the church to itself as *one household* with Paul himself as its father (4:14–21) and the members as brothers and sisters of one another."

[187] For other examples, see Dion. Hal. *Ant. Rom.* 6.71.3; M. Ant. 5.33.

[188] Compare Eph 4:14 in a section filled with unity *topoi*: ἵνα μηκέτι ὦμεν νήπιοις, κλυδωνιζόμενοι καὶ περιφερόμενοι παντὶ ἀνέμῳ (on wave-tossed as a *topos* for the factionalist, see especially Aristid. *Or.* 24.10, ἀλλ' ὥσπερ εὔριπος ἄνω καὶ κάτω φέρεται, πολεμῶν καὶ στασιάζων αὐτὸς ἑαυτῷ [further references in n. 262 below]).

[189] For the connection with bickerings see Barrett, *First Corinthians*, 322.

The terms ζῆλος and ἔρις make explicit reference to Corinthian factionalism.[190] ζῆλος, "envy" or "rivalry" is an underlying, emotional cause of party strife,[191] and affects all political entities, as Plutarch states:

A government [πολιτεία] which has not had to bear with envy [φθόνος][192] or jealous rivalry [ζῆλος][193] or contention [φιλονεικία][194] – emotions most productive of enmity [ἔχθρα] – has not hitherto existed (*Mor.* 86C).

After rebuking the Corinthians' improper rivalry (ζῆλος) with one another, later on in the argument (12:31; 14:1, 12, 39; cf. 13:4) Paul will present his *positive* version of ζῆλος as he urges the Corinthians to "be zealous [ζηλοῦτε] for the greater gifts." This strategy is paralleled in texts urging concord, where the orator will stress the need for a *positive* form of party-strife and contention which seeks the common and greater good, thus attempting to re-channel the fractious energies in a positive direction.[195]

A third term joins ζῆλος and ἔρις in 1 Cor 3:3 in some manuscripts,[196]

---

[190] For ἔρις see above on 1:11, and BAGD, 337: "ζῆλος seems to be coördinate with ἔρις in the sense of 'rivalry' or 'party-attachment.'" For a similar pair see Jas 3:14, ζῆλος πικρὸς καὶ ἐριθεία, and F. J. A. Hort's extended note (*The Epistle of St. James* [London: Macmillan, 1909] 81–83). On ζῆλος Hort concludes that the term, though it can have a positive sense, in Paul and Jas is exclusively a negative term.

[191] See Mikat, 22 in regard to *1 Clement*: "Wenn Clemens sich jedoch, um die Folgeerscheinungen des ζῆλος zu bezeichnen, der Begriffe στάσις und ἀπόνοια bedient, so ist das gewiss kein Zufall literarischer Topologie." On the relation of ζῆλος to factionalism in 1 Corinthians, see Lightfoot, 186; Heinrici, 117; Welborn, "Discord," 87; and see also the treatment of the comparable φθόνος by Johnson, "James," 327–47, esp. 336–37 on envy destroying ὁμόνοια. On the same role of *invidia* in Latin politics see Hellegouarc'h, 195–98; A. Weische, *Studien zur politischen Sprache der römischen Republik* (Münster: Aschendorff, 1966) 92–104. Compare also Latin *studium*, as in Caes. *BCiv.* 1.8, 30 etc.; Lucan, *BCiv.* 4.348 (with OLD, 1831, "devotion to a person, party, cause, etc. [esp. in a political sense]"). In patristic writings, of special note is Cyprian's treatise *De zelo et livore* 17, in which he aptly describes it as *discordiarum virus* [*PL* 4.675].

[192] On φθόνος as a cause of στάσις, see also Loenen, 16, citing Democr. *Fr.* 245.

[193] The term ζῆλος is commonly used by Plutarch to mean not just simple "jealousy" but more serious "rivalry" (on which see LSJ, 755), as in *Mor.* 796A; *Caes.* 58.2; *Nic.* 20.4; *Crass.* 7.5; *Cor.* 10.4; *Art.* 4.2; *Ages.* 5.4.

[194] See below on 1 Cor 11:16.

[195] This is a *topos* in ancient Greek texts urging concord (see Jones, *Dio Chrysostom*, 92). For examples see Hes. *Op.* 11–24, where two types of ἔρις, one good and one bad, are contrasted (note ζηλοῖ in line 23); Aesch. *Eum.* 974–75; Dem. *Prooem.* 31.1; Isoc. *Or.* 4.79 (and Dion. Hal. *Isoc.* 5); the use of ζηλοῦν in Polyb. 23.11.3; Dion. Hal. *Ant. Rom.* 3.11.8; Plut. *Mor.* 817D; Dio Chrys. *Or.* 34.45; Aristid. *Or.* 23.79 ("let us wish ... to engage in this single struggle against one another [μίαν ταύτην ... φιλονικίαν φιλονικῆσαι πρὸς ἀλλήλους], as to who will first initiate the concord [ὁμόνοια] and as to who will display more and clearer acts of virtue toward the others"); Philostr. *VA* 4.8 ("I think you have a worthy rivalry [ἔρις] and a real contention [στάσις] among youselves in behalf of the common weal [ὑπὲρ τοῦ κοινοῦ]"). *1 Clem.* 45.1 uses the same argument: Φιλόνεικοί ἐστε, ἀδελφοί, καὶ ζηλωταὶ περὶ τῶν ἀνηκόντων εἰς σωτηρίαν (see also 2.4).

[196] P^{46} D F G and the Majority Text as well as some versions. See the arguments for the

διχοστασία. An "explicitly political term"[197] and a cognate of the most common Greek word for factionalism, στάσις,[198] διχοστασία means "dissension"[199] or "sedition"[200] and appears, for example, in Plutarch's list of the perils of the public political life alongside φιλονεικία, φιλοδοξία, ἡ τοῦ πρῶτον εἶναι καὶ μέγιστον ἐπιθυμία and ζηλοτυπία (*Mor.* 788E). διχοστασία is another reference to Corinthian party battles by Paul employing an appropriate Greek political term.[201]

In 3:5–9 Paul appeals for Corinthian concord by stressing the unity of Apollos and himself – they are ἕν (3:7)[202] and συνεργοί. By the term συνεργός Paul demonstrates that he and Apollos do not experience discord, but instead they cooperate,[203] with one another and with God. The noun συνεργός and verbs συνεργεῖν/συνεργάζεσθαι[204] are also used in texts on concord. In discussing concord, Aristides mentions the example of Asclepius and Serapis:

> I am even reminded of the relationship of the two savior gods, who encompass the whole earth and save in common and work together [συνεργάζεσθαι], sending to one another and bestowing benefits in common and sharing the gratitude which they receive from mankind (*Or.* 27.39).[205]

That συνεργεῖν is the opposite of στάσις is demonstrated by Dio Chrys., using the *topos* of the bee hive[206] for ὁμόνοια:

---

term's authenticity in Welborn, "Discord," 88 n. 13, especially the fact that διχοστασία is an established element of Paul's vocabulary (Gal 5:20; Rom 16:17).

197 Ibid., 88.

198 Dion. Hal. uses the two terms interchangeably (*Ant. Rom.* 6.39.2; 38.3; 71.2; 7.42.1; see also Plut. *Alex.* 53.4, and the verbs in Pl. *Resp.* 5.465B). Lightfoot, 152 regards it as even stronger than στάσις (in regard to *1 Clem.* 46:5).

199 BAGD, 200. See esp. *1 Clem.* 46:5; 51:1, and the verb διχοστατέω in 20:4.

200 LSJ, 439, citing Sol. 4.38 (where στάσις and ἔρις occur in the same poem); Theog. 78 and 1 Macc 3.29. See also Ps.-Phoc. *Sent.* 151: Φεῦγε διχοστασίην καὶ ἔριν πολέμου προσιόντος.

201 See the proverb attributed to Callimachus: Ἐν δὲ διχοστασίῃ καὶ ὁ πάγκακος ἔμμορε τιμῆς (Plut. *Nic.* 11.3; cf. *Alex.* 53.4), and also the parallelism in this fragment from one of Solon's *Elegiacs*: παύει δ' ἔργα διχοστασίης, παύει δ' ἀργαλέης ἔριδος χόλον (Dem. *Or.* 19.255.40).

202 Weiss, *Korintherbrief*, 77; Conzelmann, 74; Barrett, *First Corinthians*, 85; Vielhauer, 74; Welborn, "Conciliatory Principle," 338 (see also 1 Cor 12:12; cf. John 17:11, 22–23). See nn. 141–42 above on the frequency of εἷς in 1 Corinthians.

203 See V. P. Furnish, "Fellow Workers in God's Service," *JBL* 80 (1961) 364–70, 368–70 on the role of the term in Paul's treatment of the Corinthian factions; and Welborn, "Conciliatory Principle," 338.

204 See LSJ, 1711.

205 Cf. Plut. *Mor.* 478E where συνεργεῖν is an attribute of brotherly love (as of the body and soul, 491C); Polyb. 6.18.1–3 (of the three parts of a *politeia* united against a common foe); App. *BCiv.* 5.14.144 (of the political partnership of Pompey and Cleopatra); Dio Chrys. *Or.* 41.14.

206 On this as a *topos* in literature on civil concord, see Malherbe, *Moral Exhortation*, 147; Muson. *Diss.* 14, p. 92 (C. E. Lutz, "Musonius Rufus. 'The Roman Socrates,'" *YCIS* 10 [1947] 1–147); Plut. *Lyc.* 26.3.

No one has ever seen a swarm that is factious and fights against itself [στασιάζοντα καὶ μαχόμενον αὑτῷ], but, on the contrary, they both work and live together [συνεργάζονται δὲ καὶ ζῶσιν ἅμα].[207]

The noun συνεργός is also used in Greek texts of a comrade, a co-partisan.[208] If Apollos and Paul are συνεργοί, then so must be the Corinthians who claim allegiance to one or the other.[209] Further, because both Paul and Apollos are subordinate to God (3:6–9), the true head of the community is God,[210] the source of its unity (this is stressed repeatedly throughout 3:10–23). The form of argument Paul employs is paralleled in Cassius' speech to the army to become united[211] under his and Brutus' command:

Let it give no one any concern that he has been one of Caesar's soldiers. We were not his soldiers, then, but our country's. The pay and the rewards given were not Caesar's but the republic's. For the same reason you are not now the soldiers of Cassius, or of Brutus, but of Rome.[212] We, Roman generals, are your fellow-soldiers [συστρατιῶται] (App. *BCiv.* 4.12.98).[213]

To exhort a new political or social body to unity, one must dispense with old or faulty means of self-affiliation through allegiance to individual leaders, as Cassius does in this speech, and as Paul does in 1 Cor 1–4.

The Building Metaphor for Concord in 1 Corinthians

The metaphor of a building (οἰκοδομή) for the community which Paul introduces in 3:9–17, and returns to again and again throughout the epistle,[214] is also a

207 *Or.* 48.15. See also 40.40; Polyb. 6.18.1–3; M. Ant. uses συνεργία of the cooperation of the feet, hands, eyelids and teeth as a metaphor for political unity in 2.1; 7.13 and the substantive συνεργητικόν in 9.42.5; see the same usage of συνεργεῖν in connection with the body metaphor for concord in Xen. *Mem.* 2.3.18 (on the body image for the political unit, see below on 1 Cor 12). Note also the verb συνεργεῖν in 1 Cor 16:16.

208 See Dion. Hal. *Ant. Rom.* 7.7.1 (συνεργοὶ καὶ συναγωνισταί); Polyb. 21.31.12 (βεβαιότατοι συνεργοί); Joseph. *AJ* 6.237 (of Jonathan as David's κοινωνός and συνεργός [see below on the political nature of κοινωνός; for the linkage of the two terms in Paul, see 2 Cor 8:23 and Betz, *2 Corinthians 8 and 9*, 80]); Plut. *Arat.* 33.1 (of a man who helps make peace); Cass. Dio 59.25.7 (parallel with ἑταῖροι, of the companions of Gaius). Furnish, 365 cited Joseph. *BJ* 2.102, translating συνεργός as "accomplice."

209 Furnish, 368–70.

210 As the emphatic genitives show: θεοῦ γεώργιον, θεοῦ οἰκοδομή ἐστε (3:9).

211 See the beginning of the speech: παρακαλεῖν ἐς προθυμίαν τε καὶ ὁμόνοιαν (App. *BCiv.* 4.12.90).

212 ἐπεὶ οὐδὲ νῦν ἐστε Κασσίου στρατὸς οὐδὲ Βρούτου μᾶλλον ἢ Ῥωμαίων.

213 See Aristid. *Or.* 23.34: "but if the masses are going to maintain order, their leaders must first take the lead in this, since it is impossible for the army to be harmonious [μιᾶς γνώμης γενέσθαι] when the generals engage in disruptive faction against one another [στρατηγῶν στασιαζόντων καὶ τεταραγμένων πρὸς ἀλλήλους]; cf. 23.78 (and Welborn, "Conciliatory Principle," 339).

214 See 1:6–8; 6:19; 8:1, 10; 10:23; 14:3–5, 12, 17, 26; 15:58; 16:13, and the discussion below.

topos in literature urging unity on divided groups.[215] In one of his two speeches on concord, Aristides uses the *topos* of the building much as does Paul in 1 Cor 3:

> We do not judge that house [οἰκία] best established [κατασκεύασθαι] which is built of stones which are as beautiful as possible [κάλλιστα λίθων], but which is dwelled in with the greatest harmony [μιᾷ γνώμῃ μάλιστα οἰκῆται], so also it is fitting to believe that those cities are best inhabited [ἄριστα ... οἰκεῖν] who know how to think harmoniously [ταυτὸν φρονεῖν]. Everywhere faction [στάσις] is a terrible, disruptive thing ... (*Or.* 23.31).[216]

---

[215] See Moulakis, 29; Welborn, "Conciliatory Principle," 337, in reference to Paul as an ἀρχιτέκτων, a common metaphor for a politician (citing Plut. *Mor.* 824C-E). This metaphor of the politician as architect is dependent upon the metaphor of the building or household for the state, a most common appeal in discourses urging concord (see n. 219 below). See Malherbe's list of political *topoi*: "... the usual example of a ship, a city, a building, and the body" (*Moral Exhortation*, 149; this is attested by the collection in Plut. *Mor.* 142E-F). One example of the way a building *topos* is applied to community life is provided by Sen. *Ep.* 53: "Our relations with one another (*societas nostra*) are like a stone arch, which would collapse if the stones did not support each other, and which is upheld in this very way." In the NT see also Jude 20 (and Watson, *Invention*, 73).

[216] Aristid. then moves into the *topos* of faction as a disease, which is rooted in the metaphor of the human body, which Paul also uses (see the discussion below on 1 Cor 12).

[217] The research on these terms has been considerable. The standard analysis remains that of P. Vielhauer, *Oikodome. Das Bild vom Bau in der christlichen Literatur vom Neuen Testament bis Clemens Alexandrinus* (Karlsruhe-Durlach: Tron, 1940), repr. in his *Aufsätze zum Neuen Testament*, ed. G. Klein, TBü 65 (Munich: Kaiser, 1979) 2.1–168, who undertook a comprehensive investigation of the metaphor and its terminology throughout Jewish and Greek sources and into ECL. Various theories of the background of the image of the building for Paul have been proposed (biographical, sociological, mythological/cultic, biblical; see pp. 110–15). Vielhauer does not connect the image with the political literature on concord, and generally attributes Paul's usage to the influence of the Hebrew Bible (114–15), although he recognizes some Stoic influence on 1 Cor 3 (115, 144). Vielhauer minimizes the Greek background to the metaphor because it is not used in a religious sense in Greek texts, which is what he looks for (22). But in fact it is precisely the political background of the term upon which Paul draws to counter the problem of factionalism. Vielhauer's work is, I believe, hampered by the fact that he treats Pauline usage in a fragmentary way, assigning three different meanings to the terms in 1 Corinthians alone (in ch. 3 it is mission expansion language; in ch. 14 it is sacral cultic terminology; in ch. 8–10 ethical terminology [see pp. 74–82; 85–93]; the cultic meaning is primary [109–10]). This does not do justice to the cumulative argumentative use of the image in the letter, and seems too easily to equate the *application* of the image with its background. In this study we shall see how Paul draws upon the building image throughout his argument for unity in a consistent and comprehensive manner.

For literature on οἰκοδομή/οἰκοδομεῖν since Vielhauer's important analysis (none of which points to the use of this image as a *topos* for urging concord), see P. Bonnard, *Jésus-Christ édifiant son Eglise. Le concept d'édification dans le Nouveau Testament*, Cahiers Théologiques de l'Actualité Protestante 21 (Neuchâtel/Paris: Delachaux & Niestlé, 1948); J. Pfammatter, *Die Kirche als Bau. Eine exegetisch-theologische Studie zur Ekklesiologie der Paulusbriefe*, Analecta Gregoriana 110 (Rome: Gregorian University Press, 1960); O. Michel, "οἶκος," *TDNT* 5.119–59; Kitzberger. The latter employs a different linguistic approach, and on those grounds connects the οἰκοδομή-Wortfeld ("bei Paulus spezifische Gemeindetermini," 304), with several other equivalent or oppositional referents. What is important to this study is that many of the terms or phrases

Throughout 1 Corinthians Paul uses οἰκοδομή and the verb (ἐπ)οικοδομεῖν[217] to refer to the stable construction, peaceful maintenance[218] and improvement of the Corinthian community, and in so doing applies a political *topos*[219] to their strife-filled situation.

Paul particularizes his application of this *topos* for political and social unification[220] for his addressees through his emphasis on the Christ as the foundation,[221]

---

linguistically defined by Kitzberger as associated with οἰκοδομή (εἰρήνη, ἀγάπη, ἔργον, ἀρέσκειν, [τὸ αὐτὸ] φρονεῖν, ναὸς θεοῦ, συμφέρειν, τὸ ἑαυτοῦ ζητεῖν, πρόσκομμα, φυσιοῦσθαι [pp. 158–305]), will be demonstrated here on historical grounds to be part of the same conceptual and rhetorical cluster of terms related to factionalism and unity in Greco-Roman antiquity.

218 See the parallelism in Rom 14:19: τὰ τῆς εἰρήνης διώκωμεν καὶ τὰ τῆς οἰκοδομῆς τῆς εἰς ἀλλήλους.

219 For other examples of the building metaphor used in discussions of concord and discord, see Soph. *Ant.* 559–662; Xen. *Cyr.* 8.15 (οἰκοδομεῖτε ἄλλα φιλικὰ ἔργα); *Mem.* 4.4.16 (ἄνευ δὲ ὁμονοίας οὔτ' ἂν πόλις εὖ πολιτευθείη οὔτ' οἶκος καλῶς οἰκηθείη); Dio Chrys. *Or.* 38.15; 48.14; Aristid. *Or.* 23.62 (εἷς δ' οἶκος [Rome] ἅπαντα ἐξηγεῖται); 24.8, 32–33 (see note 400 below); cf. 26.102; 27.40; M. Ant. 5.8.1; D.L. 6.6 (ὁμονοούντων ἀδελφῶν συμβίωσιν παντὸς ἔφη τείχους ἰσχυροτέραν). A good example is provided by Cicero: "For what house (*domus*) is so strong, or what state (*civitas*) so enduring that it cannot be utterly overthrown by animosities and division (*odia et discidia*)?" (*Amic.* 7.23). In the first century see also Lucan's images of buildings tottering and shipwrecks for civil war (*BCiv.* 1.493–504). On the background conception of politics as household management, see Arist. *Pol.* Bk. I; Plut. *Crass.* 2.7, and much material collected in D. L. Balch, *Let Wives Be Submissive: The Domestic Code in 1 Peter*, SBLMS 26 (Chico, CA: Scholars Press, 1981) 23–59. One good example of the commonplace and its appropriation in Hellenistic Judaism is Philo, *Jos.* 38: "for a house is a city compressed into small dimensions, and household management may be called a kind of state management, just as a city too is a great house and statesmanship the household management of the general public" [οἰκία τε γάρ πόλις ἐστιν ἐσταλμένη καὶ βραχεῖα καὶ οἰκονομία συνηγμένη τις πολιτεία, ὡς καὶ πόλις μὲν οἶκος μέγας, πολιτεία δὲ κοινή τις οἰκονομία]. We even find evidence for the connection between house and kingdom in the NT. See the easy parallelism of βασιλεία and οἰκία in Mark 3:24–25 and Luke 11:17; in both cases factionalism (δια)μερίζειν is predicated of both house and kingdom. That "a house divided against itself cannot stand" is a piece of common political wisdom (see Michel, *TDNT* 5.132. n.5, with reference to rabbinic, Greek and Latin sources) which lies also behind Paul's argument in 1 Corinthians. Compare these findings with W. Jaeger's description of 1 Corinthians: "The apostle Paul wrote to the Christian community at Corinth, a state within a state, which had to be 'edified,' i. e., literally, constructed like an edifice, so that its members would join together to form an organic whole. There was strife among them . . ." ("Tyrtaeus on True Arete," in *Werner Jaeger. Five Essays*, trans. A. M. Fiske [Montreal: Casalini, 1966] 103–42, p. 140). Elliott, 165–266 has stressed the social/political importance of οἶκος in Greco-Roman antiquity as relevant to 1 Pet. He calls it "a central image of human unification and reunification" (see also D. Lührmann, "Wo man nicht mehr Sklave oder Freier ist. Überlegungen zur Struktur frühchristlicher Gemeinden," *WD* n. s. 13 [1975] 53–83, 76–83).

220 Early commentators understood the unifying force and intention of these metaphors well. See Origen *comm. in I Cor.* 16.7–14 [p. 236]: καὶ παρὰ τῷ ἀποστόλῳ δὲ λέγεται ὅτι ἐσμὲν ναὸς οἱ πάντες εἷς, ἑκάστου ἡμῶν λίθον τινὸς ὄντος ἀπὸ τοῦ ναοῦ . . . [quoting Eph 2:19–22]. Δεῖ οὖν μηδένα λίθον ἀνάρμοστον εἶναι τῇ οἰκοδομῇ. In the rest of the exegesis he ties in the call to unity in 1:10. See also Chrys. on the building and field metaphors in 3:9: Εἰ δὲ οἰκοδομή ἐστε, οὐ χρὴ διεσπάσθαι. ἐπεὶ οὐκ ἂν εἴη τοῦτο οἰκοδομή. Εἰ γεώργιόν ἐστε,

and God as the owner of the edifice.[222] Paul does not merely describe the community as θεοῦ οἰκοδομή, but introduces that designation as a call to the Corinthians to live in the unity which that identity implies.[223] This identity of

---

διαιρεῖσθαι οὐ χρή, ἀλλ' ἑνὶ φραγμῷ τῷ τῆς ὁμονοίας τειχίζεσθαι (*hom. in I Cor.* 8.3 [*PG* 61.72]). On the commonality of these arguments, a few lines later Chrys. remarks: Ἴδε πῶς καὶ ἀπὸ τῶν κοινῶν ἐννοιῶν κατασκευάζει τὸ προκείμενον ἅπαν.

[221] Paul stresses the proper foundation (θεμέλιος) which he has laid, the Christ (on the unifying force of this *one* foundation, see B. Corsani, "L'unità della chiesa nella I. Cor," in *Neues Testament und Geschichte. Historisches Geschehen und Deutung im Neuen Testament. O. Cullmann zum 70. Geburtstag*, ed. H. Baltensweiler and B. Reicke [Zurich: Theologischer Verlag; Tübingen: Mohr/Siebeck, 1972] 219–22), as also Chrys. *hom. in I Cor.* 8.3 [*PG* 61.72]). The common sense fact that one can only build successfully on a strong foundation (cf. Matt 7:24–27 and par.) lies behind his argument (as also, e. g., in Epict. *Diss.* 2.15.8). The same application is also made in literature urging concord, as in Dio Chrys. *Or.* 34.24:

> Take, for example, a house [οἰκία], or a ship or other things like that; this is the way in which I expect men to make appraisal [δοκιμάζειν]. They should not consider merely present conditions, to see if the structure affords shelter *now* or does not let in the sea, but they should consider how as a whole it has been constructed [παρεσκεύασται] and put together [πέπηγεν], to see if there are no open seams or rotten planks (cf. 48.14).

On θεμέλιος and ancient building techniques, see A. Fridrichsen, "Themelios, 1. Kor 3,11," *TZ* 2 (1946) 316–17, who rightly connects the image of the building with the factions and Paul's strategy to stop them. See also recently J. Shanor, "Paul as Master Builder. Construction Terms in First Corinthians," *NTS* 34 (1988) 461–71, whose inattention to the metaphorical sense of Paul's building terminology leads to some problems (he makes no connection with the Corinthian factions).

[222] We should also note that οἰκοδομή is *singular*, which may be a corrective to the divisive force of the various house churches (οἶκοι/οἰκίαι) (see n. 62 in chap. III on this). The one God can only have *one* building (see Thdt. *1 Cor.* 3:9 [*PG* 82.248]: Οὐ τοῦ δεῖνος καὶ τοῦ δεῖνος, ἀλλὰ τοῦ τῶν ὅλων θεοῦ, and further discussion below).

[223] See Kitzberger's conclusion: "Sitz im Leben der Rede vom Aufbauen ist die Paränese" (304; also Vielhauer, *Oikodome*, 110). See also the summary statement on Pauline images for unity by Bratsiotis, 29: "Auch in den anderen von Paulus gebrauchten Bildern von der Kirche als Gottes Pflanzung und Gottes Bau – dessen Hauptfundament Christus ist – sogar als Tempel Gottes und als Braut Christi kommt der Gedanke der Einheit der Kirche zum Ausdruck." Scholars have long understood that the opposite of οἰκοδομή, and indeed what endangers it, is individualism (Vielhauer, *Oikodome*, 108–109; Bonnard, 41–46), an essentially political insight. Yet many scholars have identified what they consider to be various types of individualism throughout 1 Corinthians, restricting chap. 3 alone to party politics (Vielhauer, *Oikodome*, 74–82; Pfammatter, 19), and seeing chaps. 8–10 and 14 to be Paul's response to *different kinds of individualism*, rooted in spiritual or gnostic enthusiasm (Vielhauer, *Oikodome*, 88, 109; G. Bornkamm, "On the Understanding of Worship," *Early Christian Experience*, trans. P. L. Hammer [NY/Evanston: Harper & Row, 1969] 161–79, 161–69). My view is that all the οἰκοδομή/οἰκοδομεῖν uses in 1 Corinthians (and other references to the building metaphor; see below) are part of a coherent response to Corinthian factionalism – which Paul regards as the most serious danger to the church community. Chaps. 8–10 and 14, for example, still employ the building metaphor to respond to factionalism, but in those cases to specific *manifestations* of the divisiveness in ethical decision-making and in assembly behavior in regard to spiritual concerns. The argument, through its continual appeal to the building metaphor, is cohesive. The situation Paul describes in 1 Corinthians is not one of unbridled individualism, but of the most dangerous sort of individualism which seeks its own interests with those like-minded to oneself (e. g.,

the community as God's building is even further particularized in 3:16–17 as the ναὸς τοῦ θεοῦ.[224] Then follows the stern warning: εἴ τις τὸν ναὸν τοῦ θεοῦ φθείρει, φθερεῖ τοῦτον ὁ θεός ("if anyone destroys the temple of God, God will destroy him," 3:17). This sentence is often understood as a reference to temple defilement because of 3:17b[225] (perhaps because of a theological premise of the indestructibility of God's true temple[226]), but instead actual destruction of the Corinthian church community – by factionalism – makes the best sense of the verse.[227] Here too a well-known political axiom lies behind Paul's argument – that factionalism destroys any political body.[228] A remarkable parallel to Paul's argument is provided by Aristides in his speech urging the Rhodians to end their factionalism and seek concord, where this political *topos* and warning are also combined with a theological appeal to a deity as owner of the community:

Although you dwell in a city sacred to the Sun [Ἥλιος] you are as it were corrupted [φθείρεσθε] in darkness. Or do you believe that Odysseus and his Cephallenians will seem to be so cursed by the god as you, if you shall sack his city [διαπορθήσετ' αὐτῷ (sc. Ἥλιος) τὴν πόλιν]? Indeed – if this also must be added – as long as they listened to the best counsel

---

forms factions) to the great detriment of the social whole (see the discussion below on τὸ κοινῇ συμφέρον).

224 Cf. Aristid. *Or.* 27.40–41 on the temple as an image of concord.

225 Weiss, *Korintherbrief*, 85; Vielhauer, *Oikodome*, 81; Welborn, "Conciliatory Principle," 338; differently Conzelmann, 77 sees it as a reference to apocalyptic speculation. On sexual defilement see Chrys. *hom. in I Cor.* 9.3 [*PG* 61.79].

226 See Barrett's treatment of this objection, *First Corinthians*, 91.

227 So Robertson-Plummer, 67 on 3:17: "Here the reference is to unchristian faction, which destroyed, by dividing, the unity of the Church." So also correctly Lightfoot, 194; Barrett, *First Corinthians*, 91; cf. Or. *comm. in I Cor.* 16.30–32 [p. 246].

228 For this piece of political common sense, see Aristid. *Or.* 24.21: στάσει δὲ οἵτινες οὐκ ἐφθάρησαν οὐκ ἂν ἔχοιμεν εὑρεῖν. For other examples, see Aesch. *Eum.* 976–83; Theog. 45, 780; Pl. *Resp.* 7.521A; Polyb. 23.11; Livy 40.8; Dion. Hal. *Ant. Rom.* 2.76.3; 6.86.5; 7.42.1 (φέρε γάρ, εἴ τις ὑμᾶς ἔροιτο, τί μέγιστον οἴεσθε εἶναι τῶν καταλαμβανόντων κακῶν τὰς πόλεις, καὶ τοῦ ταχίστου τῶν ὀλέθρων αἴτιον, ἆρ' οὐχὶ τὴν διχοστασίαν εἴποιτ' ἄν;); 7.60.2; Dio Chrys. *Or.* 32.70; 38.11 (καὶ δι' οὗ σῴζεται πάντα τὰ μέγιστα τοῦτο [ὁμόνοια] ἔστι, καὶ δι' οὗ πάντα ἀπόλλυται τοὐναντίον), 14; 40.26, 32, 37; Aristid. *Or.* 23.54 (βλάπτειν μὲν γὰρ ἀεὶ [ἡ στάσις] πέφυκεν, ἡ δὲ βλάβη πρὸς τοὺς καιροὺς ἀπαντᾷ); Joseph. *Vit.* 264; for the juxtaposition of building and body images, see M. Ant. 5.8.1. See also [Herodes Atticus] *Pol.* 11 [=Drerup, 9]: ἐν μὲν γὰρ τῷ ξενικῷ πολέμῳ τὴν πατρίδα σῴζοντες ἀποθνήσκουσιν, ἐν δὲ τῷ πολιτικῷ [in the context=στάσις, with Drerup, 80] διαφθείροντες ἑαυτούς. On στάσις as πάμφθερσις in early writers, see Gehrke, 1 n. 3 (and the further examples in n. 5 on p. 2). Elsewhere in the NT this is expressed especially in Mk 3:24–25 and pars. This appeal figures prominently in *1 Clement*: ζῆλος καὶ ἔρις πόλεις μεγάλας κατέστρεψεν καὶ ἔθνη μεγάλα ἐξερίζωσιν (6:4; Jaeger characterizes this argument as "the most terrifying *topos* . . . that internal discord had overthrown great kings and destroyed powerful states" [*Early Christianity*, 13; cf. the note on p. 114]). Also in ECL see Ignatius' fusion of Paul's argument in 1 Cor 6:9 and 3:19: οἱ οἰκοφθόροι βασιλείαν θεοῦ οὐ κληρονομήσουσιν (*Eph.* 16:1; to be understood alongside *Phld* 3:3).

and were concordant [ὁμονοεῖν], they abstained from the cows and were saved [σῴζεσθαι]. But when they fell into dissension [διέστησαν], they perished [ἀπολλύσθαι].[229]

That the temple image should be combined by Paul with the *topos* that στάσις destroys[230] is natural, because a temple was a symbol of peace and unity.[231] That is why Aristides, in his vivid personification of στάσις as a woman, says that "she dwells mostly in tombs instead of temples."[232] Thus Paul's warning in 1 Cor 3:17 is to all Corinthian factionalists to cease their community-threatening divisive behavior.[233]

The building metaphor for the undivided, stable church community is (along with the body of Christ imagery)[234] the predominant image of the epistle.[235] Its presence has long been noted, in addition to its introduction in chap. 3, in 6:19; 8:1, 10; 10:23; 14:3–5, 12, 17, 26,[236] that is, in all places where Paul uses the exact

---

229 *Or.* 24.51, in regard to *Od.* 12.260–450. Cf. Dio Chrys. *Or.* 39:2: "But it is fitting that those whose city was founded by gods [ὑπὸ θεῶν ᾠκισμένοις] should maintain peace and concord and friendship [εἰρήνη καὶ ὁμόνοια καὶ φιλία] toward one another."

230 That is the well-attested *topos* at work here (see n. 228 above), not an analogy between factionalists and temple-defilers (Welborn, "Conciliatory Principle," 338, citing Aristid. *Or.* 24.50), which is probably not a *topos*. In the text there cited the prevailing image is that στάσις destroys the polity [λυμαίνεσθαι], which is the god's property.

231 See Aristid. *Or.* 27.40–41. Temples were of course built to the goddess ʽΟμόνοια/*Concordia* to celebrate times of unity and peace (see Plut. *Cam.* 42; *C. Gracch.* 17.6; Aug. *Civ. dei* 3.25, and Skard, 101–105; Zwicker, 2265–67). At Rome the doors of the temple of Janus signified times of peace or war (e. g., Suet. *Aug.* 22; Plut. *Lyc. and Num.* 4.6). The temple in the Hebrew Bible symbolized peace (see 1 Kgs 6:7), and most importantly in Hellenistic and Roman times was a crucial sign of Jewish unity, which Paul would surely have known, as Josephus boasts: Εἷς ναὸς ἑνὸς θεοῦ, φίλον γὰρ ἀεὶ παντὶ τὸ ὅμοιον, κοινὸς κοινοῦ θεοῦ ἁπάντων (*Ap.* 2.193; also Philo *Spec.Leg.* 1.67 ἐπειδὴ εἷς ἐστιν ὁ θεός, καὶ ἱερὸν ἓν εἶναι μόνον; further material in Hanson, 12–13). This emphasis on the temple as a sign and example of unity is retained in ECL (*1 Clem.* 41:2; Ign. *Magn.* 7 [πάντες ὡς εἰς ἕνα ναὸν συντρέχετε θεοῦ]; see the discussion by Schoedel, 116–17).

232 τὰ πολλὰ μνήμασιν ἀνθ' ἱερῶν ἐνδιαιτᾶται (*Or.* 24.44).

233 "Wer Uneinigkeit veranlasst, zerstört den Tempel Gottes (3:16, 17)" (Heinrici, 138). This interpretation solves the question of to which party τις refers. For various hypotheses (Christ, Apollos, Cephas-party), see Weiss, *Korintherbrief*, 86; Vielhauer, *Oikodome*, 80 n. 6; Allo, 64; Barrett, *First Corinthians*, 91. The answer is that all partisans are referred to, for all factionalists risk destroying the church community. As so often in 1 Corinthians, Paul does not take sides against one particular party, but combats the phenomenon of factionalism itself.

234 The two are combined in Eph 4:12 (εἰς οἰκοδομὴν τοῦ σώματος τοῦ Χριστοῦ). See discussion by Hanson, 135–37.

235 "Die verschiedenartigen Bestandtheile des Briefs sind durch den einheitlichen Zweck zusammengehalten, von dem einzig möglichen und zuverlässigen Glaubensgrunde aus (I 3:11) der Gemeinde die Wege zu weisen, sich zu einem Tempel Gottes zu erbauen (I 3:16; 14:26)" (Heinrici, 23). On the frequency of the building metaphor in 1 Cor, see Chrys. on 14:17: Σκόπει πῶς πάλιν ἐνταῦθα πρὸς τὴν σπάρτην τὸν λίθον ἄγει, τὴν οἰκοδομὴν πανταχοῦ ζητῶν τῆς Ἐκκλησίας (*hom. in I Cor.* 35.3 [*PG* 61.300]).

236 Vielhauer, *Oikodome*, 71–115; Pfammatter, 19–61; Kitzberger, 64–116. Michel, *TDNT* 5.140–41 reinterprets Paul's argument, concluding that the term οἰκοδομεῖν has "a more charismatic and spiritual ring than the ecclesiastical word based on it." Actually, as we have

terms οἰκοδομή/(ἐπ)οικοδομεῖν. These later references, grounded in Paul's extended exposition in 3:9–17,[237] apply this ontological designation of the community as θεοῦ οἰκοδομή as a criterion of judgement on particular issues which have divided the community. But even this list does not exhaust the references to the building metaphor throughout 1 Corinthians. The terms οἰκονόμος (4:1) and οἰκονομία (9:17)[238] have been identified as part of the same metaphorical complex of the church as God's building, as has the term ἔργον (9:1).[239] What has not been properly appreciated is the proliferation of building terms and allusions to the building metaphor in the beginning and end[240] of the epistle: βεβαιοῦν (1:6, 8); ἑδραῖος, ἀμετακίνητος (15:58); ἱστάναι, κραταιοῦσθαι (16:13).

The verb βεβαιοῦν in 1 Cor 1:6 and 8 has puzzled scholars.[241] In particular the term has been understood sometimes in its literal sense, as to "make firm, establish"[242] or "confirm,"[243] but at other times is transferred into a more metaphorical, spiritual sense here, such as "was brought home to your deepest conviction."[244] Important studies have assigned the word technical significance

---

seen, the term is explicitly ecclesiological, but has implications for the spiritual life of the community.

237 Only the cumulative effect of Paul's argument from chap. 3 on prepares the reader for these later references to the building metaphor. It is hard to understand why many partition theories separate out instances of the building metaphor into different letters (Schenk; Schmithals, "Korintherbriefe," and *Die Briefe des Paulus*; Senft; Sellin, 2968, all put chap. 3, the introduction of the metaphor, in the *last* piece of correspondence in their reconstruction). The prevalence of this theme and the consistency of its application for community concord is a strong argument for the compositional unity of 1 Corinthians.

238 Pfammatter, 69–71; see also J. Reumann, "OIKONOMIA-Terms in Paul in Comparison with Lucan *Heilsgeschichte*," *NTS* 13 (1966) 147–67; 155–61; cf. Michel, 150–51, who tends too much to downplay the applicability to Pauline usage of the findings of the papyri that these are actual management terms (on which see Theissen, 75–85). I would argue that these words describe Paul's administrative status vis à vis the οἰκοδομή, a ready connection assumed by Philo, *Jos.* 39, δι' ὧν μάλιστα παρίσταται τὸν αὐτὸν οἰκονομικόν τε εἶναι καὶ πολιτικόν ("All this shows clearly that the household manager is identical with the statesman").

239 E. Peterson, "Ἔργον in der Bedeutung 'Bau' bei Paulus," *Bib* 22 (1941) 439–41, with inscriptional evidence, followed by Pfammatter, 28–29, n. 34 and 69. But both miss the best example of this use, in 1 Cor 15:58 (see below, and also Rom 14:20). On the significance of ἔργον in 1 Cor, see Betz, "Rhetoric and Theology," 26–39.

240 In chap. IV I shall structurally identify 1:4–9 as the προοίμιον and 15:58 as the ἐπίλογος of the argument (16:13 is a recapitulation of the argument in the body of the letter).

241 See Weiss's comment on 1:6: "Ein sicheres Verständnis dieses Satzes ist nicht zu erreichen" (*Korintherbrief*, 8).

242 BAGD, 138; C. F. G. Heinrici, *Das erste Sendschreiben des Apostel Paulus an die Korinthier* (Berlin: Hertz, 1880) 79 ("gefestigt wurde"); Weiss, *Korintherbrief*, 8 ("festgeworden [etwa festgewurzelt] sei"); Héring, 3 disputes this rendering.

243 Lightfoot, 148; Heinrici, *Korinther*, 46 (on p. 49 he equates βεβαιοῦν with στηρίζειν); Allo, 5, 8; Barrett, *First Corinthians*, 38–39 ("confirmed", "keep firm"); Senft, 30.

244 Robertson-Plummmer, 6.

as a juridical term[245] or as part of baptismal terminology.[246] The juridical and economic background of the term is significant for Pauline usage, as the prevalence of the term and its cognates in legal texts in the papyri surely demonstrates.[247] Yet, wills and contracts are not the only things which required βεβαίωσις in the Greco-Roman world – βεβαιοῦν and cognates are also a part of diplomatic and political vocabulary to refer to "steadfast allies"[248] and "strong peace treaties."[249] The application of these terms to political bodies may be ultimately rooted in the image of the political unit as a building which is stable, strong and immovable, but which, when affected by στάσις, may totter or

---

245 G. A. Deissmann, *Bible Studies*, trans. A. Grieve (Edinburgh: T & T Clark, 1901) 104–109, on the basis of its use in the papyri and LXX. "By our taking *confirm* and *sure* in the sense of legally guaranteed security, the statements in which [βεβαιοῦν and cognates] occur gain in decisiveness and force" (109).

246 E. Dinkler, "Die Taufterminologie in 2 Kor i.21 f." in *Neotestamentica et Patristica. Eine Festgabe O. Cullmann zum 60. Geburtstag*, NovTSup 6 (Leiden: Brill, 1962) 173–91; esp. 177–80. He connects the juridical meaning of the term (from Deissmann and others following him, see 178 notes) with baptismal conceptions. See also H. Schlier, "βέβαιος κτλ.," *TDNT* 1.600–603.

247 See Deissmann, and the further references compiled in MM, 107–108. To these texts we should add the references to a "confirmed testimony" (βέβαια μαρτυρία) in literary texts as especially relevant to 1 Cor 1:6 (e. g., Dem. *Or.* 47.7 [a διαδικασία]; Polyb. 14.1.1).

248 For the commonplace φίλος βέβαιος see, e. g., Pl. *Ep.* 6.322D; Dion. Hal. *Ant. Rom.* 3.9.5; 5.31.4; 6.6.1; 12.1.12; Plut. *Mor.* 97B; *Crass.* 7.8 (cf. LSJ s. v. βέβαιος, 2). For the opposite, see Theopompus' charge against Demosthenes that he was ἀβέβαιος (Plut. *Dem.* 13.1). On φιλία βέβαιος, see Pl. *Menex.* 244A; Arist. *Eth. Nic.* 8.8.5; *Eth. Eud.* 7.2.21, 49; 7.4.3; Xen. *Hier.* 3.7; the political application of this principle in Thuc. 3.10.1 and Dion. Hal. *Ant. Rom.* 3.29.4. See also βέβαια πίστις, "firm loyalty" in 3 Macc 5:31 (cf. 7:7). The adjective is used in a hard-bitten assessment of political realities in one of the Platonic Epistles: τὸ γὰρ ἀνθρώπινον οὐ παντάπασι βέβαιον (Pl. *Ep.* 6.323B).

249 For steadfast (βεβαιοῦν and cognates) ὁμόνοια, see Polyb. 2.40.2; Dion. Hal. *Ant. Rom.* 2.11.2; Joseph. *BJ* 2.467; Dio Chrys. *Or.* 34.17, 27 (cf. Thuc. 1.24.2 on εἰρήνη . . . βεβαιοῦται). Of a steadfast alliance or allies, see Dem. *Or.* 16.30; Thuc. 6.10.1; 6.78.1; 8.56.2; Isoc. *Or.* 4.173; Polyb. 2.61.11; Dion. Hal. *Ant. Rom.* 6.25.4; 8.37.1; Plut. *Marc.* 10.1; 11.1. That these literary texts reflect actual diplomatic language is shown, for example, by an inscription from Rhodes recording a decree with Rome (καὶ νῦν δὲ βεβαιοῦτες [=βεβαίοντες] τὰν αὐτῶν πίστιν) *SEG* 33 [1983] 637 (on which see Y. Kontorini, "Rome et Rhodes au Tournant du IIIe s. av. J.-c. d'après une Inscription Inédite de Rhodes," *JRS* 73 [1983] 24–32).

250 As in Dio Chrys. *Or.* 48.13, his description of factionalism in Athens: "Is not everything subject to upheaval [κινεῖται] as in an earthquake, everything unsettled [μετέωρα], nothing stable [βέβαιον]?" See also Thuc. 1.2.6: "for the most influential men of the other parts of Hellas, when they were driven out of their own countries by war or sedition [στάσις], resorted to Athens, as being a firmly settled community [ὡς βέβαιον ὄν]." For other instances of βεβαιοῦν and cognates to refer to firmly establishing a political unit, see Thuc. 1.2.1 (βεβαίως οἰκουμένη); 1.8.3 (βεβαιότερον ᾤκουν); 6.10.5 (βεβαιωσώμεθα); Aeschin. 3.8 (βεβαιοῦτε τῇ πόλει τὴν δημοκρατίαν; cf. 2.173); Isoc. *Or.* 7.27 (βεβαιοτέρα . . . δημοκρατία); Philo, *Abr.* 263 (ἀρχὴ . . . βεβαιωθείη) (cf. *Spec.Leg.* 1.138, of marriage as the κοινωνία which is βεβαιοῦσθαι on the truth); of a city, πάγιον καὶ βέβαιον (Hermog. *Inv.* 82 [Rabe, 110]); Artapanus *Fr.* 3.5=Eus. *p.e.* 9.27.5 (ἡ μοναρχία βεβαία [C. R. Holladay, *Fragments from Hellenistic Jewish Authors. Vol. 1: Historians*, Texts and Translations 20, Pseudepigrapha 10 (Chico, CA: Scholars Press, 1983) 210]; Procop. *Aed.* 1.1.9 (ἐν τῷ βεβαίῳ τῆς πίστεως ἐπὶ μιᾶς ἑστάναι κρηπῖδος).

fall.[250] This connection of the verb βεβαιοῦν with the building metaphor[251] is made even in the NT: ἐρριζωμένοι καὶ ἐποικοδομούμενοι ἐν αὐτῷ καὶ βεβαιούμενοι[252] τῇ πίστει (Col 2:7).[253] In the context of Paul's argument in 1 Corinthians, the βεβαίωσις[254] of the Corinthian community is dependent upon its foundation,[255] Christ.[256]

The terms in 1 Cor 15:58 also participate in the building metaphor for political stability and concord.[257] The adjective ἑδραῖος,[258] meaning "steady, steadfast,"[259] is a synonym for βέβαιος. Even more literally, it refers to the steadiness of a foundation,[260] and is thus precisely synonymous with θεμελιοῦσθαι.[261]

See also Aristid. 24.10, his characterization of a man στασιάζων αὐτὸς ἑαυτῷ, "the inconstant, fickle man who never remains firm" (τὸν εἰκῇ καὶ ῥᾳδίως μεταβαλλόμενον καὶ μηδέποτε ἐν ταὐτῷ μένοντα, to which some manuscripts add: ἀντὶ τοῦ διὰ τέλους χρηστοῦ καὶ βεβαίου [Keil puts it in backets]); cf. *Or.* 23.3.

In the NT see also 2 Pet 1:10: σπουδάσατε βεβαίαν ὑμῶν τὴν κλῆσιν καὶ ἐκλογὴν ποιεῖσθαι. ταῦτα γὰρ ποιοῦντες οὐ μὴ πταίσητέ ποτε. In ECL, see *1 Clem.* 47:6, following the reference to 1 Corinthians: τὴν βεβαιοτάτην καὶ ἀρχαίαν Κορινθίων ἐκκλησίαν ... στασιάζειν. Therefore, for a political body, to "be firm" is the opposite of being divided into factions which cause it to totter (an insight known elsewhere in the NT; see Mark 3:24–26 and par. and the discussion below). Note also that Origen uses σείεσθαι, "shaken," as an antonym for βεβαιοῦσθαι (*comm. in I Cor.* 2.34, 39 [p. 233]).

251 Suggested by H. Martin, Jr., "Amatorius," in Betz, ed., *Plutarch's Ethical Writings*, 485 with references. In Plut. *Mor.* 756B, where the building metaphor is applied to religion, the key terms ἕδρα, βέβαιος, and above, the phrase τὰ ἀκίνητα κινεῖν appear (on which see below). This usage is also found in Hellenistic Judaism (see Philo, *Agr.* 160 [of plaster on a house, στηριχθῆναι βεβαίως]; *Conf. ling.* 87, twice, of foundations; *Cherub.* 101–103, of a house). For βέβαιος used in ancient engineering discussions see Procop. *Aed.* 1.1.34; 1.2.3; 4.2.23.

252 Cf. the Ephesians parallel ἐρριζωμένοι καὶ θεμελιωμένοι (3:17).

253 Here, as in 1 Cor 3, the planting and building metaphors are combined (see A. Fridrichsen, "Ackerbau und Hausbau in formelhaften Wendungen in der Bibel und bei Platon," *TSK* Sonderheft [1922] 185–86; Vielhauer, *Oikodome*, 97; Kitzberger, 162).

254 Cf. Phil. 1:7; Heb 6:16.

255 Called by Cyril of Alexandria the θεμέλιος ἀκατάσειστος (*1 Cor.* 3:10 [*PG* 74.865]).

256 That this foundation is rooted in baptism, which resulted from τὸ μαρτύριον τοῦ Χριστοῦ, as Dinkler suggested, is likely (cf. 1:13; 10:2). The tense variation of βεβαιοῦν from past to future (1:6, 8) can also be explained by reference to the building metaphor – the community both is the θεοῦ οἰκοδομή now and is continually being built up for its eschatological climax and judgement (thus Vielhauer refers to οἰκοδομή as a *nomen actionis* [85 and passim; cf. Pfammatter, 36]). Since it is both present reality ("guaranteed as founded" by baptism), and future goal, Paul can both tell them that they *are* θεοῦ οἰκοδομή and exhort them to *be* that (see esp. below on 15:58).

257 Since this verse is the ἐπίλογος of the argument (see chap. IV) the importance of its contents for the rest of the letter cannot be overestimated.

258 Cf. 7:37.

259 LSJ, 478; BAGD, 217.

260 The cognate nouns ἕδρα and ἑδραίωμα mean "foundation" or "base" (LSJ, 478; BAGD, 218).

261 See the triad in Col 1:23: τεθεμελιωμένοι, ἑδραῖοι, μὴ μετακινούμενοι, and Pfammatter's note: "Τεθεμελιωμένοι καὶ ἑδραῖοι sind zwei Synonyme, die die Festigkeit und Unerschütterlichkeit ausdrücken; das folgende καὶ μὴ μετακινούμενοι fügt nichts Neues mehr

Words from this root are attested in political texts, as in App. *BCiv*. 4.3.16, who writes of Octavian as the one "who established the government on a firm foundation" (τὴν ἀρχὴν συστησαμένου τε ἐς ἕδραν ἀσφαλῆ).[262] The connection of ἑδραῖος and cognates with the building metaphor was made throughout the deutero-Pauline literature and in early Christian literature,[263] which adds further support for this understanding of the term in 1 Cor 15:58.[264]

---

hinzu" (118). See below on ἀμετακίνητος in 1 Cor 15:58. The adjective is also used in *Paraleip. Jer.* 1.2: στῦλος ἑδραῖος ... τεῖχος ἀδαμάντινον (text from *Paraleipomena Jeremiou*, ed. and trans. R. A. Kraft and A.-E. Purintun, Texts and Translations 1, Pseudepigrapha Series 1 [Missoula, MT: Society of Biblical Literature, 1972]).

[262] For other examples of metaphorical "foundations" of political bodies and governments, see Dio Chrys. *Or.* 1.78 on tyranny's throne as οὐδὲ ἡδρασμένος ἀλλὰ κινούμενος); Plut. *Lyc. and Num.* 2.6 (ἕδραν καὶ κρηπῖδα τῆς πολιτείας); Dion. Hal. *Ant. Rom.* 8.1.1 (with the synonymous βάθρον); Procop. *Aed.* 1.1.9 (quoted in part in n. 250 above). See also n. 251 above on Plut. *Mor.* 756B. In Latin texts see Cic. *Sest.* 68.143; *Leg.* 1.37 (*stabilis*) and Livy 3.68.4 of *concordia*. The opposite of a firmly grounded polity is metaphorically described as "shaken" (Aristid. *Or.* 24.59 terms the Rhodians' factionalism a σεισμός; cf. 23.74; see also Dion. Hal. *Ant. Rom.* 11.7.2; Lucan *BCiv.* 1.5; 2.290–92; Ps-Sall. *Rep.* 11.1; Dio Chrys. *Or.* 48.13; Amos 9:1; Wis 4:19; cf. Plut. *Mor.* 511D [οὐ μόνιμος]; 756B; Luke 6:48; 2 Thess 2:2); "borne up and down like the tide" (Dion. Hal. *Ant. Rom.* 10.11.1; Aristid. *Or.* 24.10; cf. Eph 4:14; Jas 3:4), or "drifting or veering at sea" (Ps-Sall. *Rep.* 11.1; Dio Chrys. *Or.* 34.19; Plut. *Lyc.* 5.6–7, see below on nautical metaphors for politics). Even the application of "unshaken" to the individual in time of political upheaval is not unparalleled. See Seneca's description of Cato in the time of the civil wars between Caesar and Pompey: "What a pleasure it is to say, in admiration of the unflinching steadiness (*invicta constantia*) of a hero who did not totter when the whole state was in ruins (*viri inter publicas ruinas non labantis*)..." (*Ep.* 95.71; see also his treatise *De constantia sapientis*, where the unshakable man image is explicitly connected with the building metaphor [6.3–8, etc.]). On Cato as "unshaken" see also Lucan *BCiv.* 2.247–48, 268.

[263] Col 1:23 (see n. 261 above), even if not Pauline, points to an early interpretation of Paul's language of 1 Cor 15:58, appropriately connecting ἑδραῖος (and the verbal paraphrase for the adjective ἀμετακίνητος) with an indisputable building term, θεμελιοῦσθαι. The allusion to the building metaphor which these terms make in Col 1:23 is generally recognized (see E. Lohse, *Colossians and Philemon*, trans. W. R. Poehlmann and R. J. Karris, Hermeneia [Philadelphia: Fortress, 1971] 66, who grounds the metaphor in Jewish sources), but strangely is never observed in the use of those same terms in 1 Cor 15:58. But sometimes that the reference has come through can be seen in the exegete's own use of the metaphor, as Calvin, 348 on 15:58: "So he charges them to remain steadfast, because they are resting on an unshakable foundation ... he is pointing out that if the resurrection hope is taken away, the whole structure of religion would collapse in ruins, as if the foundation had been torn out," and also Bruce, 157: "not shifted from this foundation." Elsewhere in the NT, see also 1 Tim 3:15 (ἑδραίωμα), and cf. στερέωμα in Col 2:5. The use of building terminology to refer to the church on the Petrine foundation (Matt 16:18) is of course part of the same idea complex.

The connection of ἑδραῖος and cognates with the building metaphor is common in ECL. See e. g., *1 Clem.* 33:3 (ἥδρασεν ἐπὶ τὸν ἀσφαλῆ τοῦ ἰδίου βουλήματος θεμέλιον) ; Ign. *Pol.* 1:1 (ἡδρασμένην ὡς ἐπὶ πέτραν ἀκίνητον); 3:1 (στῆθι ἑδραῖος ὡς ἄκμων τυπτόμενος) and especially *Phld.* Inscr. (ἡδρασμένῃ ἐν ὁμονοίᾳ θεοῦ). See also Cyril of Alexandria's exegesis of 1 Cor 3:9–17: ὃ γὰρ μὴ ἀνέχῃ Χριστός, τοῦτο δὴ πάντων κινηθήσεται, οὐχ ἑδραίαν ἔχον τὴν στάσιν (*1 Cor.* 3:9–17 [*PG* 74.868]).

[264] One reason scholars have not noted this is that many have regarded 15:58 as solely the conclusion to the argument in 1 Cor 15 on the resurrection (Heinrici, *Korinther*, 509; Allo, 449;

The next adjective in 15:58, ἀμετακίνητος, means "immovable."[265] A *hapax legomenon* in the New Testament,[266] and an uncommon word in Greek texts generally, in usage it is combined with βέβαιος.[267] Both are attributes of a well-grounded, immovable building,[268] metaphorically, a well-established and unchangeable polity[269] which withstands the encroachment of destructive and divisive forces. Metaphorically (and lexically) a "movement" within a political body is a revolution, a faction, στάσις.[270] When Paul urges the Corinthians to

---

Héring, 182; Fee, 807). The verse should rightly be seen as the conclusion to the entire argument in the letter (so Grosheide, 395; see chap. IV).

265 LSJ, 81–82 (also "not to be moved from place to place"); BAGD, 45. See also J. Schneider, "κινέω κτλ.," *TDNT* 3.718–20.

266 But we have noted the paraphrase μὴ μετακινούμενοι in Col 1:23.

267 See Arist. *Eth. Nic.* 2.4.3: βεβαίως καὶ ἀμετακινήτως ἔχειν (used metaphorically of one's disposition of character). See also Dion. Hal. *Ant. Rom.* 8.74.1 in praise of a good politician as βέβαιός τε καὶ ἀμετακίνητος ἐν τοῖς κριθεῖσι. See Ign. *Pol.* 1.1 quoted above for the connection with ἑδραῖος, and also Ps-Arist. *Mund.* 2.391B, of the earth, the center of the cosmos, as ἀκίνητόν τε καὶ ἑδραῖον.

268 See Joseph. *Ap.* 2.254 on temples. The adjective ἀμετακίνητος and verb μετακινεῖν are used of sepulchral mounds or tombstones in an inscription (R. Tonneau, "L'Inscription de Nazareth sur la violation des sépultures," *RB* 40 [1931] 544–64, text 544–5, see lines 5 and 19).

269 μετακινεῖν is frequently used of changing a polity or constitution (Dem. *Or.* 23.205; Xen. *Lac.* 15.1; Joseph. *AJ* 5.179; *Ap.* 2.184; Plut. *Mor.* 152A [adj. μετακινητός]; *Lyc.* 29.2). Likewise agreements and contracts can be said to be "immovable" or "enduring" (Dion. Hal. *Ant. Rom.* 7.44.1 [ἀκίνητος]; cf. Thuc. 5.21.3 [μετακινητός]). A comically literal description of one immovable in the face of enemies is given by Hdt.: "[Sophanes] bore an anchor of iron made fast to the girdle of his cuirass . . . which anchor he would ever cast . . . so that the enemies as they left their ranks might not avail to move him [μετακινῆσαι μὴ δυναίατο]" (9.74). For the political application, see Cic. *Rep.* 1.32.49: "when a sovereign people is pervaded by a spirit of harmony [*concordi populo*] and tests every measure by the standard of their own safety and liberty, no form of government is less subject to change [*inmutabilius*] or more stable [*firmius*]."

270 κίνησις is "movement, in a political sense," as in *OGI* 543.15, ἡ κίνησις ἡ Ἰουδαϊκή, "the Jewish revolt" [Bar Cochba] (LSJ, 952). For this usage see Arist. *Pol.* 2.5.10; Xen. *Ages.* 1.37 (κινεῖν); Thuc. 1.1.2; 3.75.2; Dion. Hal. *Ant. Rom.* 7.1.1; 7.66.3 (who connects it with στάσις); Polyb. 3.4.12 (with ταραχή); 4.32.10 (with μετάστασις); 5.25.7; Joseph. *BJ* 1.218 (κίνημα); Plut. *Pomp.* 20.4; *Pel.* 25.7; *Marc.* 28.1 (κίνημα); Dio Chrys. *Or.* 48.13, quoted in n. 250 above; Aristid. *Or.* 23.74 (verb): "But whenever we are on our own and do what we wish, we become our own earthquakes and we can neither remain quiet nor plan anything for the common good, but just like a balance scale when the load has been removed, we move up and down without purpose [ἄνω καὶ κάτω κινούμεθα τὴν διὰ κενῆς]." Behind this usage (and Paul's) is the conviction that a polity is founded on some unchangeable traditions. See Dion. Hal. *Ant. Rom.* 6.61.1: "not to disturb [συγχεῖν lit. "mix"] the form of government nor to alter the unalterable customs of our ancestors [μηδὲ κινεῖν ἔθη πατέρων ἀκίνητα]." Note also his use of the compound παρακινεῖν (*Ant. Rom.* 6.62.4; 7.13.2; 7.55.6; 8.81.2), and the previous note for the political use of μετακινεῖν. See also Demad. *Twelve Years* 34: "they came to realize clearly the changeability [εὐκίνητον] of the politician's life." Dio Chrys. *Or.* 34.33 describes the waters of the harbor (a metaphor for concord) as ἀκίνητον.

For this usage in the NT see esp. Acts 24:5, κινῶν στάσεις (see BAGD *s. v.* κινέω 4a with references), and note the summary of the divisions causing the Corinthians to write to Paul in the *catenae*: τούτων πάντων ἐν Κορίνθῳ κινουμένων, γράφουσιν οἱ λαοὶ τῷ Ἀποστόλῳ (Cramer, p. B lines 14–15 [ὑπόθεσις]).

remain immovable,[271] he appeals again to the building metaphor to insist on their remaining solidly and unchangeably fixed to their foundation as a unity,[272] as θεοῦ οἰκοδομή[273] on the θεμέλιος which is Christ.[274]

1 Cor 16:13 contains a restatement and final appeal to the argument in the body of the letter.[275] After the typical exhortation to "stay awake," Paul tells the Corinthians to "stand firm in faith"[276] (στήκετε ἐν τῇ πίστει),[277] another reference to their need to be firmly grounded on the foundation of the gospel. The opposite of "to stand" is to fall,[278] which is the fate of the divided house,[279] the house which is not on a firm foundation.[280] The imperative ἀνδρίζεσθε, a term

---

[271] μένειν is another component of the building metaphor (3:14; 13:13), which is the opposite of πίπτειν (see BAGD *s. v.* μένω 1.c.β, with reference to Pl. *Cra.* 440A; see also below on ἵστημι in 16:13). See also n. 262 above on Cato as the exemplary "unshakable" man in time of civil discord. Note also the explicit collection of terms in Thdt.'s exegesis of 1 Cor 13:8: Ἡ ἀγάπη οὐδέποτε ἐκπίπτει. Τουτέστιν, οὐ διασφάλλεται, ἀλλ' ἀεὶ μένει βεβαία, καὶ ἀσάλευτος, καὶ ἀκίνητος, ἐς ἀεὶ διαμένουσα (*1 Cor.* 13:8) [*PG* 82.336].

[272] As we have observed, the building metaphor is a *communal* one (see Sen. *Ep.* 53 quoted in n. 215 above, and other examples throughout the above section using the building as a metaphor for a city or a country).

[273] τὸ ἔργον τοῦ θεοῦ in 15:58 makes explicit this connection (on ἔργον as part of the building metaphor, see n. 239 above). This is observed by Barrett in his exegesis of 15:58: "Compare iii.13ff.; ix.1; xvi.10. In all these passages what is meant is the Christian labour of calling the church into being and building it up" (*First Corinthians*, 385; see also Wolff, 211; Lang, 241).

[274] The Christ and the gospel (15:1–8), single foundations of a single community, are unchangeable, so the edifice constructed on them must be so, too.

[275] See the compositional analysis in chap. IV.

[276] Barrett, *First Corinthians*, 393; Conzelmann, 297; Allo, 464 ("contre les influences de 'libertins'"). Robertson-Plummer stress the military allusions in 16:13 ("there must be no desertion, no λειποταξία," 394). This is not the first place in 1 Corinthians in which Paul writes of the need for the Corinthians to stand. See the ominous warning in 10:12: ὁ δοκῶν ἑστάναι βλεπέτω μὴ πέσῃ, and the conditionally qualified ἐν ᾧ καὶ ἑστήκατε in 15:1 (cf. Rom 14:4; Gal 5:1; Phil 4:1). In his exhortation to unity in Phil Paul urges ὅτι στήκετε ἐν ἑνὶ πνεύματι (1:27).

[277] See Origen's interpretation: Στήκετε. μὴ σαλεύεσθε ἀλλὰ βέβαιοι γίνεσθε (*comm. in I Cor.* 90.6–7 [p. 51]); cf. Chrys.: Στήκετε, ὡς σαλευομένων (*hom. in I Cor.* 44.1 [*PG* 61.375]).

[278] BAGD *s. v.* ἵστημι II.2.c. a.

[279] Luke 11:17 (cf. Mark 3:25 οὐ δυνήσεται . . . σταθῆναι). Its antidote, according to 1 Corinthians, is love, which never falls (13:8; on the connection with factionalism, esp. Dio Chrys. *Or.* 48.14, and next note). On 13:8 see Theodoret's interpretation quoted above, n. 271.

[280] In the NT see esp. Matt 7:24–27 (cf. Luke 6:47–49), and 2 Tim 2:19 (of a foundation). For parallels in literature on concord, see, e. g., the conclusion to the speech of Apollonius of Tyana to the Smyrnaeans to seek concord, where he describes the concordant city: "For a city will recline in peace, nay will rather stand up erect" [ἑστήξει] (Philostr. VA 4.8). Cicero, in a discussion of concord and division, wrote: "But if you should take the bond of goodwill out of the universe no house or city could stand (*stare poterit*)" (*Amic.* 7.23; see also *Rep.* 1.32.49; for this use of *stare* to mean "remain stable, last," see OLD, 1824, definitions 15 and 16, with references). *1 Clem.* 61:1, in a prayer for concord, lists εὐστάθεια, "stability, firmness" (BAGD, 326) alongside ὑγίεια, εἰρήνη and ὁμόνοια (van Unnik, 164–65 n. 43, regards the term as "identiek met εἰρήνη καὶ ὁμόνοια"; see also *1 Clem.* 65:1). The opposite of those who stand is the factionalized community, or person (see Aristid. *Or.* 24.12, who describes the

which appears only here in the Pauline corpus, appeals to another of the great civic virtues in Greek political thought.[281] The verb κραταιοῦσθαι, "be strong," continues the references to the needed stability in the community and its members.[282] This exhortation in 16:13 is thus a final appeal to the Corinthians to end their factionalism for the sake of the survival of the community itself.[283] We conclude that the building metaphor for the concordant, stable community, which Paul adapts from its common use as a political *topos* in discourses urging unity on divided groups, is used repeatedly by Paul throughout 1 Corinthians.

D. References to Corinthian Factionalism in 1 Cor 5–16

Having seen that 1 Cor 1–4 contains language and topics directly related to factionalism (as the exegetical tradition has in a general sense noted[284]), we now turn to an examination of chapters 5–16, to investigate if the material in those chapters relates to this same issue of Corinthian divisions. We shall demonstrate that these chapters too are filled with terms and *topoi* rooted in the issue of political divisiveness; the subject of factionalism is not restricted to 1 Cor 1–4 as has been presumed by scholars.[285]

---

factionalist as οὐχ ἑστώς, and the terms ἀστάθμητος and ἄστατος in Iambl. *Ep. Concerning Concord* [Diels, *Vorsokr.* 2.356]). To stand is thus the opposite of "be moved or shaken," synonymous with Paul's call to be firm (ἑδραῖος) and immovable (ἀμετακίνητος) in 15:58, or not to "fall" (1 Cor 10:12; 13:8; Dio Chrys. *Or.* 34.19; 48.14). With this compare Ps.-Phoc. *Sent.* 74–75: "For if there were strife [ἔρις] among the blessed ones [the heavenly bodies], heaven would not stand firm [οὔκ . . . ἔστη]" (text Young; trans. P. W. van der Horst, *OTP* 2.576). In Philo also εὐστάθεια is contrasted with ταραχαὶ καὶ στάσεις (*Leg. Gai.* 113).

281 Skard observed that ἀνδρεία and ὁμόνοια function as a pair (68, 77, 84–85, 94 and notes): "häufig ist die Verbindung ὁμόνοια-ἀνδρεία, die diejenigen Tugenden bezeichnet, die dem Staat Bestand verleihen" (68; see also Kramer, 33–36 in regard to Sparta). A good example is provided by Polyb. 6.46.7, in reference to Lycurgus: "For, there being two things to which a state owes its preservation [σῴζεσθαι], bravery [ἀνδρεία] against the enemy and concord [ὁμόνοια] among the citizens." Cf. D. S. 7.12.2–4.

282 For the easy connection of this verb with the building (and planting) metaphor, see Eph 3:16–17 (cf. Pfammatter, 116–17). For the *topos*, see Dio Chrys. *Or.* 39.5: "Again what sort of edifices, what size of territory, what magnitude of population render a community stronger (ἰσχυρότερον) than does its domestic concord (ὁμόνοια)?" See also Ps.-Sall. *Rep.* 4.4.

283 See below on 16:14.

284 See the discussion at the beginning of this chapter, esp. n. 5.

285 See above. We have already established that many of the terms or *topoi* introduced in 1 Cor 1–4 run throughout the entire epistle (the building metaphor, being "puffed up," the body metaphor, and the important term σχίσμα).

1. 1 Corinthians 5. The Proper Mix for Unity

In chapters 5 and 6 Paul discusses the relationship between "the insiders" (οἱ ἔσω) and "the outsiders" (οἱ ἔξω).[286] His rhetorical strategy is that before he can fully advise the factions how to unite, he must clarify what membership in the community is.[287] Factionalism is a division of persons within the confines of community ranks. One way to eliminate a cause of division is to remove some persons from membership[288] (in the politics of the πόλις, exiling or expelling them[289]). The man who committed the act of πορνεία in ch. 5 has contributed to community divisiveness (5:2, 6[290]). Paul advises expelling this offender.[291] He is to become an outsider (5:5, 11–13),[292] and is therefore not included in the unity to which Paul calls the Corinthian church.[293]

In 5:6 Paul introduces another community metaphor, the lump of dough, to emphasize the importance of retaining careful boundaries. The φύραμα, "that

---

[286] 5:10, 12–13; 6:2, 6. For the sociological basis of the insider/outsider distinction for group formation see Schreiber, 104–9; Meeks, *Urban Christians*, 94–103. On how both inside and outside forces can endanger ὁμόνοια, see Skard, 78–79, and Plut. *Arat.* 9.3.

[287] Like Paul, Dio Chrys. differentiates internal and external threats to the peace at Tarsus in his *Or.* 34. For the combination of internal and external dangers to a political body as a *topos*, see, e. g., Dion. Hal. *Ant. Rom.* 6.1.1, ἀπὸ τῶν ἔχωθεν πολέμων ... τοὺς ἐντὸς τείχους νεωτερισμούς (cf. 6.23.1), and Polyb. 11.25. The opposite argument is made by Dio Chrys. in his *Or.* 40, where he urges concord on Prusa and Apaemia on the grounds that since they are so close their fighting is like στάσις μιᾶς πόλεως (§ 27; cf. 41.10). In general, see MacMullen for the division of civil dissension in the Roman Empire into internal and external forces.

[288] See Dio Chrys. *Or.* 34.21 (and in general on exiling in party politics see Gehrke, 216–24). The author of *1 Clem.* knows this principle well, as he urges fomenters of στάσις, ἔρις and σχίσματα to voluntarily remove themselves from the community for the sake of the common good (54:2–55:1).

[289] See Finley, 55, 119.

[290] We have established above that φυσιοῦσθαι and καυχᾶσθαι are two of Paul's descriptive terms for Corinthian factionalism. Origen took ὑμεῖς πεφυσιωμένοι ἐστε to be a direct accusation against the party (συμμορία) of the fornicator (*comm. in I Cor.* 23.25 [p. 363]; also Thdt. *1 Cor* 5:2 [*PG* 82.261]). For the consequences generally, see Philo's exhortation on the effects of licentiousness on a *politeia*: εἰ δὲ τὰ ἐξ ἀκρασίας στάσεις ἐμφύλιοι καὶ πόλεμοι καὶ κακὰ ἐπὶ κακοῖς ἀμύθητα, δῆλον ὅτι τὰ ἐκ σωφροσύνης εὐστάθεια καὶ εἰρήνη καὶ τελείων κτῆσις ἀγαθῶν ἀπόλαυσις (*Jos.* 57).

[291] The decision to expel someone from the community is obviously a political decision, with political ramifications, even if made on moral grounds. For the view that Paul expelled this offender for the sake of the entire church community, see A. Y. Collins, "The Function of 'Excommunication' in Paul," *HTR* 73 (1980) 251–63; 259–63.

[292] Meeks, *Urban Christians*, 130: "To shun the offender, especially at common meals–the Lord's Supper and others–would be an effective way of letting him know that he no longer had access to that special fellowship indicated by use of the term *brother.*"

[293] Compare Dio Chrys. *Or.* 34.40, in his argument advising the Tarsans to concord: "When you decide that you are going to remove someone [ὃν ... ἂν κρίνητε ἐξαιρήσεσθαι], and it is thought that he is guilty of such misdeeds [ἀδικεῖν] that it is not expedient [μὴ συμφέρειν] to ignore them, make yourselves ready to convict him [ἐξελέγξοντες] and immediately behave toward him as toward a personal enemy [ἐχθρός], and one who is plotting against you."

which is mixed,"[294] is therefore another symbol of the unified community.[295] But Paul warns that without the proper "mix," the entire community may suffer.[296]

The term which Paul uses in 5:9 and 11, συναναμίγνυσθαι,[297] shows that what is at issue here is political association and membership. This verb with its double prepositional compound meaning literally to "mix up together" and its cognates are used of people "associating."[298] Plutarch uses several μιγνύναι compounds to refer to the blending and mixing of human beings in political associations in general and in factions in particular. See, for example *Phil.* 8.2:

[The Achaeans] by uniting others with themselves [καταμιγνύντες εἰς ἑαυτούς] in a harmonious civil polity [ὁμονοίᾳ καὶ πολιτείᾳ], they purposed to form the Peleponnesus into a single political body [ἓν σῶμα] and power.[299]

Elsewhere Plutarch uses another cognate, ἐμμιγνύναι, to mean "to join a party":

Therefore Solon made a better beginning, when the state was divided into three factions [μέρη] called the Diocrians, the Pedieans and the Paralians; for he entangled himself [ἐμμίξας] with none of them, but acted for all in common and said and did everything to bring about concord [ὁμόνοια] among them.[300]

---

294 BAGD, 869; LSJ, 1962. Its literal connection with συναναμίγνυσθαι in 5:9 and 11 should therefore be noted.

295 "There is only one φύραμα, only one body of Christians, just as there is only one loaf (x.17)" (Robertson-Plummer, 102). See also Klauck, *Herrenmahl*, 333: "Schon die Frage ... in 1,13a hat die Konzeption von der Gemeinde als Leib Christi zur Voraussetzung (vgl. 1 Klem 46,7). In 5,7 weist νέον φύραμα auf den gleichen Gedankenkreis" (see also p. 257 and *1. Korintherbrief*, 43).

296 For more discussion see chap. IV. Note that the *v. l.* in D connects the lump and leaven metaphor with the destruction *topos* (on which see above).

297 Also in 2 Thess 3:14; LXX Hos 7:8.

298 LSJ, 1695; BAGD, 784.

299 See also *Arat.* 11.1; *Publ.* 3.4; *Alc.* 29.1; Aristid. *Or.* 24.14. For συναναμίγνυσθαι in Hellenistic Jewish texts see LXX Hos 7:8; Philo, *Vit. Mos.* 1.278; Joseph. *AJ* 20.164, 165; *Vit.* 242. See also Plut. *Phil.* 21.4 (people mixing together to form a funeral procession), and the interesting metaphorical use of συναναμίγνυσθαι in parallelism with συμπολιτεύεσθαι in Lucian, *Charon* 15.

300 *Mor.* 805E. Of συμμιγνύναι used of groups joining together see Theog. 36, 64, 245, 1165; Arist. *Pol.* 5.7.8; Polyb. 1.19.2, 4; 16.10.1 and Walbank, 2.497; Plut. *Thes. and Rom.* 6.3; App. *BCiv.* 3.14.96 (of mixing two factions). The verb is also used this way in the papyri. See *PEleph.* 29.11 (3rd c. B.C.E.), ἕως τοῦ συμμεῖξαι, "until [they] associate with you", and *PPar.* 49.25 (c. 161 B.C.E.), ἤσχυνται συμμεῖξαι μοι, "he has been ashamed to associate with me" (references from MM, 602; trans. mine). For ἀναμιγνύναι of uniting two factions, see Plut. *Nic.* 11.4; for the political sense see also *Alc.* 29.2; *Num.* 20.4; *Cam.* 33.2; *Cic.* 13.2; *Oth.* 13.7; Dion. Hal. *Ant. Rom.* 1.9.2; 1.18.1; 1.19.3; cf. the metaphorical use in Dio Chrys. *Or.* 40.41. Chrys. uses the verb correctly in his exposition of human ὁμόνοια through natural bonds (*hom. in I Cor.* 34.4 [*PG* 61.291]).

This terminology from the μιγνύναι stem[301] is rooted in one of the most common and enduring political theories in antiquity, that of ἡ μικτὴ πολιτεία, "the mixed constitution."[302] Any political society is made up of some combination of individuals with a variety of backgrounds and particular gifts. The theory of the mixed constitution is directly linked to factionalism and concord, because it holds that the proper mix of citizens is necessary for ὁμόνοια.[303] In writings of the Imperial period, we find Numa and Alexander as the prototypes of the statesman who recognizes and implements this political principle.

Numa [was] aware that hard substances which will not readily mingle [δύσμικτα] may be crushed and pulverized, and then more easily mix and mingle [ἀναμιγνύναι] with each

---

[301] The simplex verb μιγνύναι is also used of persons in community relations and constituencies (e. g., Pl. *Leg.* 12.951D; *Resp.* 8.548C; Eur. *Ion* 399; Plut. *Nic.* 9.5; cf. *Alex.* 9.1).

[302] This title refers in fact to two related political theories, one about the mixed type of governmental philosophy (democracy, monarchy, etc.) and another about the mix of persons which form any body politic (see P. Zillig, "Die Theorie von der gemischten Verfassung," Diss. Würzburg, 1916, 7–69, especially 18, 20, 31 and passim; Kagan, 261; Wood, 159–75, esp. 161, chap. 9, "Essentials of the Mixed Constitution"). See Pl. *Leg.* 6.773D and especially Arist. *Pol.* 2.9.2; 4.6–7 and W. L. Newman, *The Politics of Aristotle*, 4 vols. (Oxford: Clarendon, 1887–1902) 1.264–65, who notes that for Aristotle the theory denotes "rather a combination of social elements – virtue, wealth, free birth, than a combination of constitutions." Zillig, 8 and passim, notes that the theory, though Greek in origin, continues into the period of the Empire; for its prevalence at the end of the Republic, in Cicero's writings, see Wood, 159–75, and later among others see Aristid. *Or.* 26.90 and Men. Rh. 1.360 [Russell-Wilson, 58]. In general see also K. von Fritz, *The Theory of the Mixed Constitution. A Critical Analysis of Polybius' Political Ideas* (New York: Columbia University Press, 1954); G. R. Morrow, *Plato's Cretan City. A Historical Interpretation of the Laws* (Princeton: Princeton University Press, 1960) 521–43 (who argues that in Plato it is not a political doctrine so much as an extension of the universal philosophical principle of τὸ μέτριον), and the bibliography listed in Wood, 249–50 n. 1. For the cosmological analogue to the mixed social constitution see Ps-Arist. *Mund.* 4.396A-5.397A.

[303] See Plut. *Per.* 3: πολιτείαν ἄριστα κεκραμένην πρὸς ὁμόνοιαν καὶ σωτηρίαν κατέστησεν [on (συγ)κεραννύναι see n. 306 and the discussion below on 1 Cor 12:24]. See also Skard, 75–76; Zillig, 66–67, 69 (stability). For the same principle in Roman politics, see Cic. *Rep.* 2.69: "and as this perfect agreement and harmony is produced by the proportionate blending of unlike tones, so also is a State made harmonious by agreement among dissimilar elements, brought about by a fair and reasonable blending together of the upper, middle, and lower classes, just as if they were musical tones. What the musicians call harmony in song is concord in a State, the strongest and best bond of permanent union in any commonwealth" (for this association of the "mixed constitution" and the image of the concordant chorus see also Ps-Arist. *Mund.* 6.399A). The same connection is made by Lucan, *BCiv.* 4.190: "Harmony [*Concordia*], the preserver of the world and the blended universe [*mixtique mundi*]." In Hellenistic Judaism, Philo also connects proper "mixing" with ὁμόνοια (*Mut.* 200; *Rer. div. her.* 183); the same principle is expounded in *Ep. Arist.* 267, where it is maintained that each person taking his or her role is the key to harmony in the "mixed crowds" (παμμιγεῖς ὄχλοι) in the kingdom (cf. 1 Cor 12). See also Wood, 161 on the direct relation of the theory of the mixed constitution and the need for concord: "The ancients sought an immortal form of constitution, one that would be relatively impervious to the passage of time and generate conditions of lasting unity, order, and stability. In the opinion of ancient theorists, the properly mixed constitution was an ingenious contrivance for the political implementation of these principles" (Wood argues throughout that this is a conservative political theory).

other . . . so that his decision resulted in a harmonious blending [ἀνάμιξις] of them all together.[304]

Alexander the Great even went so far as to dramatically symbolize the "mix" of the great society he wished to form in his famous loving cup and libation at Opis.[305]

Paul's understanding of the political reality that a community is formed from a delicate mix of individuals is demonstrated also in 1 Cor 12:24, in his description of the body of Christ, where he depicts the creation of the community at God's hands using the other technical term for the "mixed constitution" in Greek political thought: ὁ θεὸς συνεκέρασεν τὸ σῶμα.[306] Like Numa and Alexander the Great, Paul in 1 Corinthians is attempting to create solidarity within a new political group; that group, too, is a "mix" of what were previously different social communities.[307] But Paul must define the proper boundaries of the new

---

304 Plut. *Num.* 17.1–4, describing his governing of Rome. For a similar sense in Hellenistic Jewish texts see *T. Levi* 14.6 (μεῖξις of intermarriage); 1 Esdr 8:84 (ἐπιμιγνύναι of intermarriage with foreigners) and Conzelmann, 99 n. 56 (but, as this discussion shows, the term is not limited to this use).

305 See Tarn, *Alexander the Great,* 2.439–48 and Plutarch's description: "But, as he believed that he came as a heaven-sent governor to all, and as a mediator for the whole world, those whom he could not persuade to unite with him, he conquered by force of arms, and he brought together into one body all men everywhere, uniting and mixing [μείξας] in one great loving-cup, as it were, men's lives, their characters, their marriages, their very habits of life . . . clothing and food, marriage and manner of life they should regard as common to all, being blended into one [ἀνακεραννυμένοι]" (*Mor.* 329C-D). Note that this list of things which require standardization when a new polity is formed are all issues in the new political body at Corinth (on clothing see 1 Cor 11:2–16; food see ch. 8–10; marriage ch. 7; manner of life covers several of the other controversies).

306 See Dion. Hal. *Ant. Rom.* 2.46.3; 10.60.5; Plut. *Num.* 6.2 (cf. Heb 4:2 and BAGD, 773). The connection was noted by Heinrici, *Sendschreiben,* 405 n. 5: "Συνεκέρασε . . . dient zur Bezeichnung der von Gott gewirkten Harmonie des Leibes," citing usage in Plato (non-political) and Plutarch. Weiss, *Korintherbrief,* 306 n.1 discusses the connection with Stoic writings on the composition of the human body, but does not draw the connection with political theory, in the analogy of the political body to the human body. On the extension of this language and theory to friendships, see Plut. *Mor.* 491A.

1 Clem. 37:4 uses the noun σύγκρασις in its reflection upon 1 Cor 12. The direct relation of that noun to Greek political thought on concord (see, e. g., Thuc. 8.97.2) was pointed out by Jaeger: "Political and social thinkers came to use the word [σύγκρασις] in order to describe their ideal of political unity as a healthy blend of different social elements in the polis" (*Early Christianity,* 21). See also Schoedel's discussion of ἐγκεραννύναι and political harmony in regard to Ign. *Eph.* 5.1 (p. 54–5, with references). Surprisingly, neither discusses the clear antecedent of this usage in *1 Clement* and Ignatius in 1 Cor 12:24. See also the language of Origen's exegesis of 1 Cor 4:7: Χριστὸς γὰρ ἦλθεν τὰ διακεκριμένα ἑνῶσαι, ἵνα μηκέτι ἦμεν διῃρημένοι . . . οὐκέτι ἐσόμεθα ἐν διακρίσει ἀλλ' οἱονεὶ ἐν συγκράσει καὶ τῇ ἐπὶ τὸ αὐτὸ συναγωγῇ ἡμῶν (*comm. in I Cor.* 19.52–56 [p. 358]).

307 "Die Verkündigung des Paulus zielte auf Bildung von Gemeinschaften, die in sich nicht homogen waren. Das Zusammentreffen unterschiedlicher Traditionen, bedingt durch Herkunft und soziale Stellung, führte erst zu den Problemen, die Paulus behandeln muss" (Lührmann, "Freundschaftsbrief," 314).

"mix," as he does in 5:1–13. The wicked [πονηροί] are not included (5:11–13).[308] He does this to ensure the stability of the whole community.[309]

2. 1 Corinthians 6

a) Legal Disputes at Corinth

In 6:1–11 Paul rebukes the Corinthians for taking their "insider" problems to secular "outsider" courts to secure justice. According to Paul, this is a violation of the sanctity of the church community (6:6). As in ch. 5, the underlying principle at work in this argument is the clearly drawn boundary between the insiders, οἱ ἅγιοι,[310] and the outsiders (here called ἄδικοι, "unjust,"[311] or ἄπιστοι, "unbelievers"[312]). Paul stresses in 6:6–8, by the repetition of ἀδελφός,[313] that the Corinthians are defrauding and violating one another and thus their very own selves,[314] making an appeal to a common argument against factionalism.[315]

---

[308] See the exact parallel in Plut. *Mor.* 329C, of Alexander's "mix": "He bade them all consider as their fatherland the whole inhabited earth, as their stronghold and protection his camp, as akin to them [συγγενεῖς] all good men, and as foreigners only the wicked [ἀλλοφύλους δὲ τοὺς πονηρούς]." Cf. also *Mor.* 809E; Philo, *Spec. Leg.* 3.155.

[309] "He does not construe the action primarily as a sanction against the offender, but as a way of purging the community" (Meeks, *Urban Christians*, 130).

[310] This is the term par excellence for an "insider" in the Christian community (see Lightfoot, 145; Meeks, *Urban Christians*, 85). Notice that οἱ ἅγιοι have powers of judgement (5:12; 6:2). For Aristotle the definition of a citizen is one who has the power to judge [κρίσις] and rule (*Pol.* 3.1.4–8).

[311] Plato said that injustice [ἀδικία], hate [μίση] and internecine conflicts [μάχαι ἐν ἀλλήλοις] cause factions [στάσις], while justice [δικαιοσύνη] instead brings ὁμόνοια and φιλία (*Resp.* 1.351D; cf. 1 Cor 6:7–11). Compare Philo, *Rer. div. her.* 163: "So then the God who loves justice [φιλοδίκαιος] hates and abominates injustice [ἀδικία], the source of faction [στάσις], and evil."

[312] 6:1, 6 (also οἱ ἐξουθενημένοι ἐν τῇ ἐκκλησίᾳ in 6:4). On the "Language of Separation" in Paul see W.A. Meeks, "'Since Then You Would Need to Go Out of the World': Group Boundaries in Pauline Christianity," *Critical History and Biblical Faith. New Testament Perspectives*, ed. T.J. Ryan, Annual Publication of the College Theology Society (Villanova, PA: College Theology Society, 1979) 4–29, 8–13; cf. *Urban Christians*, 84–103. The insider/outsider distinction plays a role elsewhere in the argument (1:18–31; 12:1–3; 14:20–25), and is an obvious way to defuse factionalism, by stressing the commonalities of the group in itself over and against the "foreigners."

[313] On this term and ἀδελφή as part of the language of belonging of the early church, see Meeks, *Urban Christians*, 86–87.

[314] Thus Lightfoot, 212, on the emphasis of μεθ' ἑαυτῶν in 6:7.

[315] The same argument is made by Aristid. in one of his speeches on concord: "perhaps there would be some excuse for being hostilely and contentiously disposed toward foreign races [οἱ ἀλλοφύλοι]. But no one would claim that it is either intelligent or fortunate to behave with such distrust and dissension toward one another" (*Or.* 23.41; this is a *topos* in literature urging concord; see *Or.* 24.37–38; Dio Chrys. *Or.* 38.46; [Herodes Atticus] *Pol.* 11 [Drerup, 9, quoted above in n. 228]; Apoll. Ty. *Ep.* 56). In Latin texts, see, e. g., Lucan *BCiv.* 1.682: "what war is

We can see in these legal battles the expression and probably further incitement of the partisan battles at Corinth.[316] Very often in ancient history political divisions and uprisings came to a head in the law courts.[317] Surely court proceedings between members of the Corinthian church community led to divisions within that community, with members forced to choose sides among the combatants.[318] In 6:2–4 Paul claims that all this infighting resulting in court procedures is due, ironically, not to important issues, but to κριτήρια ἐλάχιστα, "trivial cases,"[319] or βιωτικά, "daily life matters." It is a *topos* in literature urging concord to stress how insignificant are the matters about which the various sides contend.[320] This plea is rooted in the reality that dissension in a political body often is a result of squabbles over private and mundane affairs,[321] as Plutarch noted:

But just as a conflagration does not often begin in sacred or public places, but some lamp left neglected in a house or some burnt rubbish causes a great flame and works public destruction, so disorder [στάσις] in a state is not always kindled by contentions about

---

this without a foe?" (this is exemplified in 3.604f. where twin brothers fight in the civil war of Caesar and Pompey; see also 7.464–65, 550), and Seneca, *De ira* 2.31.7, of the parts of a commonwealth, in concert with the body metaphor. For recognition of Paul's use of this *topos*, compare Chrys.'s exegesis in reference to the body metaphor: Οὐδὲ γὰρ ὁμοίως τὰ ἁμαρτήματα κρίνεται, ὅταν εἰς τὸν τυχόντα καὶ εἰς τὸ οἰκεῖον γίνεται μέλος (*hom. in I Cor.* 16.4 [*PG* 61.134]).

316 Theissen, 97.

317 So correctly Welborn ("Discord," 107) in regard to 1 Cor 4:1–5 (without mention of 6:1–11). The standard treatment is G. M. Calhoun, *Athenian Clubs in Politics and Legislation* (Austin: University of Texas Press, 1913). For examples see, e. g., Arist. *Pol.* 5.5.10; Dion. Hal. *Ant. Rom.* 6.22; App. *BCiv.* 1.54. An important parallel is provided by P.Lond. 2710, on the prescriptions of the guild of Zeus Hypsistos, which includes forbidding σχίσματα: "[It shall not be permitted] to indict or accuse another" (μηιδὲ ἐπ[ικα]λήσειν καὶ μὲ κατηιγορή[σ]ειν [[α]] τοῦ ἑτέρου) (text and trans. Roberts-Skeat-Nock, 40–42). See also Dion. Hal. *Ant. Rom.* 6.28.2, where "good faith in the observance of contracts" is called "the preserver of concord [ὁμόνοια] in all states."

318 See the terms Chrys. uses to describe these conflicts: μάχας ἔχοντες καὶ φιλονεικίας ὑπὲρ χρημάτων (*hom. in I Cor.* Argumentum 2 [*PG* 61.11]).

319 BAGD, 248; cf. Dion. Hal. *Ant. Rom.* 10.60.4.

320 See Isoc. *Or.* 4.11: "we risk our lives fighting as we do over trifles [περὶ μικρῶν]." See also later in the speech where he repeats this complaint: "the ones in highest honor are intent on matters of little consequence" (4.171). In *Or.* 34.48 Dio Chrys. tells the Tarsans that the things over which they strive are as "an ass's shadow!" [περὶ ὄνου σκιᾶς] (cf. Aristid. *Or.* 23.63), an insight known also in Hellenistic Judaism, as in Philo, *Post. Cain.* 119: "For it is an invariable rule that broils and factions [ταραχαὶ ἢ στάσεις] arise among men scarcely ever about anything else than what is in reality a shadow." Interestingly, this is the same proverbial appraisal which Celsus made against Christian and Jewish disputes (Or. *Cels.* 3.1, 2, 4 [Borret, SC 136.14, 16, 20]; on the extensive history and attestation of the proverb, with references, see Behr, 1.424 n. 96). For further examples of this commonplace see Dion. Hal. *Ant. Rom.* 3.7.3; 5.65.4; Dio Chrys. *Or.* 34.18, 19; 38.21–23, 38 [deriding the Ἑλληνικὰ ἁμαρτήματα] and n. 184 above.

321 See Arist. *Pol.* 5.3.1 and other references collected by Newman, 4.318–19; Dion. Hal. *Ant. Rom.* 2.24.2; Polyb. 4.53.5; further discussion in Jones, *Plutarch*, 118, and *idem*, *Dio Chrysostom*, 78, 86.

public matters [αἱ περὶ τὰ κοινὰ φιλονεικίαι], but frequently differences arising from private affairs and offences [ἐκ πραγμάτων καὶ προκρουμάτων ἰδίων ... αἱ διαφοραί] pass thence into public life and throw the whole state into confusion.[322]

Plutarch's description applies to the conflict within the Corinthian church as described by Paul in his argument urging unity. The Corinthian divisions have had their genesis in minor matters (6:4). How trivial such cases are is shown by Paul in their paltry comparison with the eschatological judgements which will be entrusted to the saints. Paul's advice to the Corinthians to work toward the end of their factionalism through expelling a vicious offender and settling their legal disputes among themselves is also paralleled among the ancient politicians.[323] All of the issues which Paul treats in 5:1–6:11 (expelling a church member, determining with whom one may associate, adjudicating how the community is to deal with inner-group legal battles, selecting judges) are fundamentally political problems, which Paul addresses using appropriate political terminology and *topoi*. All of these specific issues are facets of the overriding problem of factionalism in the church.

b) Freedom, Individuality and Division

6:12 opens a new sub-argument with the Corinthian slogan πάντα μοι ἔξεστιν. Discussion of what is true freedom was especially common in political discourses and appears throughout 1 Corinthians.[324] Slogans calling for freedom also play a major role in party politics.[325] The issue of freedom is often central in

---

[322] *Mor.* 825A. For the same sentiment see Aristid. *Or.* 23.58, citing Homer as an authority for the commonplace: ὡς ἄρα ἔρις ἄρχεται μὲν ἐξ ὀλιγίστου, προέρχεται δὲ ἐπὶ μήκιστον. For the metaphor of the flame for factionalism see Philo, *Flac.* 17 (cf. Jas 3:6).

[323] See Philostratus' account of the sophist Polemo: "He helped them also in the following manner. The suits [δίκαι] which they brought against one another he did not allow to be carried anywhere abroad, but he would settle them at home [οἴκοι]. I mean the suits about money, for those against adulterers, sacrilegious persons and murderers, the neglect of which breeds polution, he not only urged them to carry them out of Smyrna, but even to drive them out" (*VS* 532). On the similarity in the strategies of the contemporaries Polemo, Plutarch and Dio Chrysostom for urging concord, see Jones, *Plutarch*, 118.

[324] 7:22; 8:9; 9:1–23; 10:23–11:1 (see Strobel, 111 on the universality of calls for freedom in antiquity). See below on 1 Cor 9. For the frequency of ἐξουσία, ἐξουσιάζειν, ἐλευθερία and ἐλευθερός in 1 Cor 5:1–11:1, see Lührmann, "Freundschaftsbrief," 307 nn. 41–42, who rightly concludes that this is the dominant and unifying theme of the section.

[325] See R. Syme, *The Roman Revolution* (Oxford: Clarendon, 1939) 153–56; Hellegouarc'h, 542–59; Weische, 34–38; Reinhold, 108–109, with more bibliography. On freedom in antiquity, especially among the Stoics, see now Vollenweider, 23–104. For freedom calls involved in factionalism see, e. g., Dion. Hal. *Ant. Rom.* 6.86.3, in the depiction of factionalism in the members of the body in the speech of Menenius Agrippa: "Come now, why do we not assert our liberty [ἐλευθερία] and free ourselves from the many troubles we undergo for the sake of this creature?" (cf. 6.82.3; contrast Lys. 2.18: ἡγούμενοι τὴν πάντων ἐλευθερίαν ὁμόνοιαν εἶναι μεγίστην). See also Lucan *BCiv.* 9.28–30, 97.

party and inter-city rivalries. For example, according to Dio Chrysostom the Tarsans complain in regard to their rivalry with the people of Mallus:

'Well, it is a shame, then,' someone will say, 'if they are to be at liberty to do whatever they please [εἰ τούτοις μὲν ἐξέσται ποιεῖν ὅ τι ἂν ἐθέλωσι], and to derive that advantage from their very helplessness, while we are to be in danger if we make a single move.'[326]

Divisions within a social body are usually a result of different types of behavior which clash. As in the above text, both sides of a conflict normally appeal to freedom to justify their particular actions. Like others who urge divided groups to unity, Paul in 1 Corinthians must redefine freedom in order to urge all Corinthians to compromise for the sake of the whole. This argument extends throughout chaps. 6–11, and is centered in the exemplary argument of ch. 9.[327] Paul's response to the Corinthian slogan, ἀλλ' οὐ πάντα συμφέρει, is, as we have seen, the common deliberative appeal, and is the introduction of another line of proof throughout the argument of the letter, redefinition of "the advantageous" course of action to be followed.[328]

The section 6:12–20 explicitly deals with intercourse with prostitutes. Paul appeals to the body of Christ image for the church community (6:15–17) and the complementary temple of God image (6:19; cf. 3:16–17), both ways of stressing the corporate nature of the church.[329] The body as an image for political unity is a *topos* in ancient political literature.[330] It is introduced here (cf. 1:13) and fully depicted in chap. 12. The individualistic consequence of the body metaphor for the community, that a companion is a limb of one's own body, is also common in political texts, as in Plutarch's *De fraterno amore*:

... but the man who quarrels with his brother, and takes as his comrade [ἑταῖρος] a stranger from the market-place or the wrestling floor, appears to be doing nothing but cutting off voluntarily a limb [μέλος] of his own flesh and blood, and taking to himself and joining to his body an extraneous member [μέλος ἀλλότριον] (*Mor.* 479B).

This is the same argument which Paul makes against Corinthian Christians associating with prostitutes: ἄρας οὖν τὰ μέλη τοῦ Χριστοῦ ποιήσω πόρνης μέλη;

In the argument which follows (6:16–17) Paul defines further the consequences of Christian associations, twice using the verb κολλᾶσθαι,[331] which is

---

326 *Or.* 34.12.

327 See below.

328 See the extensive treatment of the relation of this argument to factionalism below in regard to 10:23–11:1.

329 This is not to deny that the focus in 6:12–20 is on individual ethical behavior, but there is no reason to assume that because this is the application of the metaphors they lose this communal thrust (cf. Barrett, *First Corinthians*, 151). See also chap. IV n. 274.

330 See the full treatment below on 1 Cor 12.

331 For the range of uses, see Heinrici, *Sendschreiben*, 181 n. 1 (without enough emphasis on the political uses).

found nowhere else in the Pauline corpus. Just as the image of body members is common in political discourse, so also is κολλᾶσθαι and cognates to refer to "associating" or "joining up" with others.[332] It literally means to "glue together,"[333] but often has this metaphorical application to human relationships.[334] κολλᾶσθαι can also mean "to unite,"[335] even as the opposite of to be factionalized.[336] In 6:17 the proper form of behavior is described in the antithesis: ὁ δὲ κολλώμενος τῷ κυρίῳ ἓν πνεῦμά ἐστιν. Playing off of the sexual associations of the term in its first usage, in repeating it in 6:17 Paul once again appeals for correct forms of association, to the Lord,[337] and thus to the church, his members who share the one spirit (6:19). This argument in 6:12–20, like the rest of chaps. 5 and 6, centers on relations between insiders and outsiders. The insiders are μέλη Χριστοῦ, but the prostitute clearly is not (6:15), and thus should not be mingled with. She is beyond the boundary and is indeed a threat to the health of the whole community.[338] Sex with prostitutes, the sin of πορνεία, is to be avoided on the basis of the principle of communal identity and communal ethical responsibility (6:18–20).

In 6:19 Paul states οὐκ ἐστε ἑαυτῶν, "you do not belong to yourselves."[339] The Christian, having been bought with a price (6:20; 7:23), belongs to the Lord, and thus also to his body, the church.[340] The ethical implication of this principle is

---

[332] BAGD, 441. Acts 5:13; 9:26; 10:28, and often in ECL (*1 Clem.* 15:1; 30:3; 46:2; *Herm. Sim.* 9.20.2; 26.3; *Man.* 11.13; *Barn.* 10:3, 8, 11; 19:2; see *LPGL* s. v.).

[333] See Chrys.'s use of this verb in his interpretation of the building metaphor for unity in 1 Cor 3: ἡ οἰκοδομὴ κατὰ τὸ κεκολλῆσθαι ἕστηκεν. ὡς ἂν διαστῇ, ἀπόλλυται, οὐκ ἔχουσα τοῦ ἐρείσει ἑαυτήν. Μὴ τοίνυν ἁπλῶς ἐχώμεθα τοῦ Χριστοῦ, ἀλλὰ κολληθῶμεν αὐτῷ (*hom. in I Cor.* 8.4 [*PG* 61.72]).

[334] Plutarch uses the abstract noun κόλλησις, for example, in an analogy which compares the process of joining a broken [σχισθείς] body to the restoration of broken friendships (*Mor.* 481C quoted above).

[335] BAGD, 441 citing *1 Clem.* 49:5 (in the ἀγάπη-hymn: ἀγάπη κολλᾷ ἡμᾶς τῷ θεῷ); 56:2. κολλᾶσθαι is commonly employed of sexual associations in Jewish-Christian texts (e. g., Sir 19:2; Philo, *All.Leg.* 2.50; Matt 19:5) because LXX Gen 2:24 translates the Hebrew דבק with προσκολλᾶσθαι, but its double meaning of sexual relations and adherence to the deity was familiar in the LXX (Weiss, *Korintherbrief*, 164).

[336] See esp. *1 Clem.* 46.1–4, in another deliberative letter urging concord.

[337] This usage is also paralleled by דבק in the HB, of paying proper exclusive allegiance to the deity (e. g., Deut 10:20; Jer 13:11; see Heinrici, *Korinther*, 206; BDB, 179).

[338] As the pun on τὸ ἴδιον σῶμα in 6:18, as both one's own body and the body which is the community, shows. Because the body of Christ imagery is a prevailing image of the letter, which is based upon prior instruction which Paul can count on the Corinthians to know (6:15), any time σῶμα is used by Paul in 1 Cor we cannot discount also a communal referent. σῶμα in 6:20 can thus also refer to both the individual body and the communal body of Christ.

[339] Cf. 3:23; Rom 14:7–8. Conzelmann rightly notes that "'you do not belong to yourselves' is the presupposition of the πάντα μοι ἔξεστιν" (p. 113; I presume he means that the non-negated version of the statement is). See already Chrys. *hom. in I Cor.* 18.2 [*PG* 61.146]: Τί γάρ; πράττεις ἃ θέλεις, φησίν. οὐκ εἶ ἑαυτοῦ κύριος.

[340] This being the case, one cannot "give oneself away" to leaders of factions as the caricatures of 1:12 and 3:4 suggest. Paul will make this argument in 7:23 [μὴ γίνεσθε δοῦλοι

that one must make decisions on the basis of the entire church community, for Paul the μέλη Χριστοῦ (or the ναὸς τοῦ ἁγίου πνεύματος), and not merely the self.[341] This political principle was stated already by Aristotle:

We ought not to think that any of the citizens belongs to himself [αὐτὸν αὑτοῦ τινὰ εἶναι], but that all belong to the state [πάντας τῆς πόλεως], for each is a part of the state [μόριον γὰρ ἕκαστος τῆς πόλεως].[342]

For Paul, of course, membership in the Christian community is obtained through baptism into the redemptive death of Christ (6:20; cf. 1:13; 6:11; 12:13), and not ancestral citizenship in the πόλις, as it is for Aristotle. The important similarity between Paul and Greek political thought on this point is the idea[343] that a member of a community cannot live a morally isolated life because of his or her responsibility to the larger community. Significantly, both Aristotle and Paul ground the expression "one does not belong to oneself" in the body metaphor for the community.[344] The metaphor gives expression to the inescapable interdependence of those who live in society with others (see below on 1 Cor 12).

3. 1 Corinthians 7. Domestic Discord

Chapter 7 treats other issues which are dividing the Corinthian church – marital practices and virgins (also circumcision and slavery). How is the institution of marriage related to factionalism? First of all, as all political theorists recognized, the marital relationship is a component of the larger community group.[345] Good marriages contribute to the concord of the political body, and bad marriages lead it into discord, so the marriages within a community must be of concern to the statesman.[346] Marriage is also commonly used as an analogy for the concordant

ἀνθρώπων]. The slave is the one who "is capable of belonging to another [ὁ δυνάμενος ἄλλου εἶναι]" (Arist. *Pol.* 1.2.13).

341 The inverse ethical principle is stated by Marcus Aurelius: "That which is not hurtful to the community cannot hurt the individual" (5.22).

342 *Pol.* 8.1.2 (cited, in part, already by Wettstein, but not taken up by other commentators). For the same formulation, see Plut. *Lyc.* 24.1.

343 And the identical formula with the genitive of possession.

344 For the long history of this concept and references see Newman, 3.501–502. See also Pl. *Ep.* 9.358A. The idea continues from the classical period down well into the Imperial period (as evidenced, e. g., by Plut. *Lyc.* 24.1; 25.3).

345 Arist. *Pol.* 1.1.4 (and throughout Bk. I).

346 See Arist. *Pol.* 5.3; 7.1.4, where marital problems are described as στάσις. A good example of this piece of political realism is this text from Dion. Hal.: "every state [πόλις] since it consists of many families [ἐκ πολλῶν οἴκων] is most likely to enjoy tranquility [ὀρθὴν . . . πλεῖν] when the lives of the individual citizens are untroubled [εὐσταθεῖν], and to have a very tempestuous time when the private affairs of the citizens are in a bad way, and that every prudent statesman, whether he be a lawgiver or a king, ought to introduce such laws as will make the citizens just and temperate . . . For example, in the matter of marriage and commerce

or discordant polity.[347] At Corinth, different opinions and practices in regard to marriage were a further source of contention.[348] In dealing with each of the specific marital (and other) issues he treats in chap. 7, Paul urges a course of action which will promote unification.[349]

Sexual abstinence within marriage can cause alienation and division (7:1–7), as of course does divorce (7:10–11). To prevent these negative outcomes, Paul advises marriage partners not to withhold themselves from one another,[350] he prohibits divorce according to the command of the Lord (7:10), and he urges the married to stay together, and separated partners to become reconciled with their spouses (7:10–11). 7:12–16 treats the issue of church members who are married to unbelievers, a difficult case because it straddles the boundaries of the church body.[351] The unbelievers are outsiders, but they may become insiders,[352] or they

---

with women, from which the lawgiver ought to begin . . . " (*Ant. Rom.* 2.24.2–4; instructions on marriage follow; in the same category of things which can divide a polity, he later turns to τὰ ἀδικήματα εἰς ἀλλήλους [2.29.1, cf. 1 Cor 6:1–11]). See also Dion. Hal. *Ant. Rom.* 10.60.5; Plut. *Mor.* 144B-C, quoted above, where Gorgias is taunted for trying to advise the state to concord when his own marriage is in such a bad state (and see the language used in 140E-F), and Isocrates' exhortation in *Or.* 3.41. On family and social conflicts in general, see H. C. Baldry, *The Unity of Mankind in Greek Thought* (Cambridge: University Press, 1965), 155. Chrys. rightly applies this *topos* to his exegesis of 1 Cor: Ἵνα δὲ μὴ μόνον ἐν ταῖς πόλεσιν, ἀλλὰ ἐν ἑκάστῃ οἰκίᾳ πολλὴ ἡ ὁμόνοια ᾖ, τὸν μὲν ἄνδρα τῇ ἀρχῇ καὶ τῇ ὑπεροχῇ τιμήσας, τὴν δὲ γυναῖκα τῇ ἐπιθυμίᾳ καθοπλίσας (*hom. in I Cor.* 34.4 [*PG* 61.291]).

347 Dio Chrys. *Or.* 38.15: ὁ δὲ γάμος ὁ ἀγαθὸς τί ἄλλο ἐστὶν ἢ ὁμόνοια ἀνδρὸς πρὸς γυναῖκα; καὶ ὁ κακὸς γάμος τί ἄλλο ἐστὶν ἢ ἡ τούτων διχόνοια. See also Aristid. *Or.* 24.7–8 (citing *Od.* 6.182–85): "For there is nothing greater and better than this, than when husband and wife maintain their house with concordant thoughts [ὁμοφρονεῖν]. They are a great grief to their enemies and a joy to their friends . . . Yet do not think that a single house would be properly settled in one way but a whole city in another. Rather if concordant thought [τὸ ταὐτὰ φρονεῖν] is the single means of safety for the individual home, cities must be so much more disposed in this way." Another good example is provided by Muson. *Diss.* 13B: ποῖος μὲν γὰρ γάμος χωρὶς ὁμονοίας καλός; [Lutz, 90], which is paralleled in Hellenistic Judaism in Philo, *Spec. Leg.* 1.138; *Virt.* 119. A similar insight is found in *1 Clem.* 6:3 (ζῆλος ἀπηλλοτρίωσεν γαμετὰς ἀνδρῶν). For further discussion and more references to this *topos* see Kramer, 45–49; Balch, 88–89; and, on household management and social stability, see also D. C. Verner, *The Household of God. The Social World of the Pastoral Epistles*, SBLDS 71 (Chico, CA: Scholars Press, 1983) 27–81.

348 So already Origen: καὶ ἦν ἀκαταστασία ἐν ταῖς οἰκίαις τῶν ἀδελφῶν (*comm. in I Cor.* 33.11–12 [p. 500] quoted fully in ch. IV n. 281). Compare Philo, *Spec. Leg.* 1.108; 3.28.

349 On the importance of family relationships for the church as a whole because of the closeness of the house churches, see Filson, 110; Klauck, *Hausgemeinde*, 39–41.

350 They are to act ἐκ συμφώνου (7:5), "from harmonious agreement" (see Origen's paraphrase: μετὰ πάσης ὁμονοίας [*comm. in I Cor.* 38.7 (p. 508)]; cf. Chrys. *hom. in I Cor.* 19.1 [*PG* 61.153]: Δεῖ δὲ πάντων προτιμᾶν τὴν ὁμόνοιαν).

351 See above on chaps. 5 and 6. On the social implications of this, compare the often cited passage from Plutarch's *Coniugalia praecepta*: "A wife ought not to make friends of her own, but to enjoy her husband's friends in common with him. The gods are the first and most important friends. Wherefore it is becoming for a wife to worship and to know only the gods that her husband believes in, and to shut the front door tight upon all queer rituals and outlandish superstitions" (*Mor.* 140D).

may choose to be separated (7:15). That the marital issue has at its heart the larger issues of community membership and unity is clear also from 7:39, where a widow is allowed to marry, only ἐν κυρίῳ. What is meant by that phrase, here and in 7:22, is "within the community" (cf. 6:17; 11:11; 15:58).[353] At any rate, Paul's overriding concern is peace: ἐν δὲ εἰρήνῃ κέκληκεν ὑμᾶς ὁ θεός.[354]

In 7:17–24 the overarching category under which these marital issues are discussed is unquestionably political in nature – the Corinthians are not to seek to alter their social status.[355] This distinctly conservative political advice,[356] which is a natural and common component of the appeal for concord, is centered in

---

352 Because ἅγιος is the specific term for a Christian insider (see n. 310 above), if an unbeliever becomes "sanctified" [ἁγιάζεσθαι], this means they join the community (see Heb 10:14; Acts 20:32; 26:18; 1 Cor 6:11). Their contact with "the body of Christ" through their spouse may bring sanctification (A. D. Nock, *St. Paul* [New York/London: Harper & Row, 1938] 179–80). When in 7:14 Paul says that the children are ἅγια, it means that they too are members of the comunity (against O. L. Yarbrough, *Not Like the Gentiles. Marriage Rules in the Letters of Paul*, SBLDS 80 [Atlanta: Scholars Press, 1985] 112).

353 Meeks, "Go Out of the World," 17; Yarbrough, 109 with arguments against Lightfoot, 235. See Schoedel, 273 (with references) on "group endogamy" as an instrument of social control.

354 7:15 (cf. 14:33 in relation to community worship). See Barrett's exegesis: "It is the will of God that men and women should live in harmony, and this aim will not be furthered if a Christian partner withdraws from marriage on religious grounds; such a separation could only engender strife" (*First Corinthians*, 166).

355 So correctly Yarbrough, 94 n. 16; see also S. S. Bartchy, Mallon Chresai: *First-Century Slavery and the Interpretation of 1 Corinthians 7:21*, SBLDS 11 (Missoula, MT: Scholars Press, 1973) 161–72 on the considerable exegetical problems. On the connection with the factionalism (of 1 Cor 1–4), see Prümm, 207.

356 R. M. Grant, *Augustus to Constantine* (New York: Harper & Row, 1970) 56: "In many respects the social outlook of the apostle Paul was essentially conservative. His conservatism was partly based on the idea of the church as a body politic, partly on a basically hierarchical picture of the world, and partly on the belief that since the end was at hand no social changes were desirable." See also the discussion in Bartchy, 153 n. 529, and particularly Theissen, 108 on the "moderate social conservatism" of Christian love-patriarchalism. This conservatism is consistent throughout the letter (see also 11:2–16 and 14:33b–36, where it is applied to women), and is to be understood as predictable in the context of *the conservative political appeal* in antiquity, that for concord (see the discussion in ch. IV, esp. nn. 535–38, on the connection between Paul's argument in 1 Cor in this regard and the social conservatism preserved in the early Christian *Haustafeln*). See, for example, the general conclusion of J. E. Crouch: "Ultimately, however, both I Cor. 7 and the *Haustafel* call the believer to an affirmation of his finitude within the social order and, in a larger sense, of his concrete position within the processes of history" (*The Origin and Intention of the Colossian Haustafel*, FRLANT 109 [Göttingen: Vandenhoeck & Ruprecht, 1972] 158 [see also 122–29]). The conservatism inherent in ancient appeals for concord is best displayed in Cicero's political slogan, *concordia ordinum*, "harmony of the orders," a vision which entails keeping concord by retaining the right people in power (see Wood, 193–99). I conclude that Paul's argument in 1 Corinthians, in line with other ancient appeals for concord, is socially conservative in its emphasis on inner-group harmony and preservation over all other considerations. Whether Paul *himself* was a social conservative (both within his own churches and the larger social and political contexts in which he lived) is a larger question best left aside here.

7:17–24. Circumcized or uncircumcized, slave or free, each one is to remain as she or he has been called (7:24 expresses the general principle).[357] It is "to each as the Lord has divided[358] it."

Striving for better or different social status was of course a common cause of political strife and faction throughout antiquity.[359] Platonic *Ep.* 8, a deliberative letter which tries to reconcile the "despotic party" and the "freedom party"[360] in Sicily after the death of Dion, employs an appeal to moderation which is almost identical with Paul's advice in 1 Cor 7:22–23:

For as regards both slavery and freedom [δουλεία καὶ ἐλευθερία], when either is in excess it is wholly evil, but when in moderation consists in being the slave of God, immoderate, in being the slave of men.[361]

But Paul does not merely advise the Corinthians to remain in their present status. He redefines their proper ultimate goal from seeking to alter earthly status (7:8, 17–24, 27, 40) into realizing one's Christian κλῆσις (7:15, 17–24).[362]

---

357 Also 7:17 and 20 (cf. 7:7) contain the general principle (Bartchy, 168–69). Bartchy concluded that 7:21 contains an "exception and explication" (169), and does indeed allow for a slave to be manumitted if the opportunity presents itself. The exegetical problems of that verse (μᾶλλον χρῆσαι) are notorious. I lean in the opposite direction (see below), but leave the question open.

358 The verb μερίζειν harks back to 1:13. The Lord's apportionments in 7:17 are the proper "division" of parts according to function and need (see also 12:24), as opposed to the improper "division" of factionalism (see also 7:34; Rom 12:3).

359 See Newman 4.275–79 on the causes of στάσις (and especially Arist. *Pol.* 5.7.8). Cf. Dion. Hal. *Ant. Rom.* 5.53.3. Bartchy, 85–87 and 130–31 argues that there was no unrest among the slaves at Corinth because general "slave unrest" cannot be documented for the first century. Yet this evidence cannot be conclusive for the members of one small political body in Corinth which prized freedom above all else. Bartchy, too, realizes that one must approach the question from a reading of Paul's argumentation. He concludes that "Paul would not have written 'slaves or free' in 1 Cor 12:13 if there had been any unrest among the slaves in the congregation which was caused by their conversion to Christ" (130), but one could just as easily argue that Paul would not have brought up the status of slave and free if it were not a problem (note that Bartchy does assume [55 and passim] that since Paul uses these categories that there were both slaves and freedpeople in the church at Corinth, a conclusion not necessary if Paul merely uses them as an "illustration of his theology of calling" [131]).

360 8.354C.

361 8.354E. F. S. Jones (*"Freiheit" in den Briefen des Apostels Paulus. Eine historische, exegetische und religionsgeschichtliche Studie*, GTA 34 [Göttingen: Vandenhoeck & Ruprecht, 1987] 29, 36–37) regards ἀπελεύθερος κυρίου in 1 Cor 7:22 as an *ad hoc* Pauline formulation (see also 27–37 on the debate on the juridical background of this concept, and further discussion in Vollenweider, 233–46). The juridical background is relevant to Paul's formulation of this image, but my focus is on the role which that image plays in the overall argument for unity (Jones knows this text from Pl. *Ep.* 8 [p. 175 n. 131], but does not bring it into connection with 1 Cor 7:22). The point to be emphasized is that in both of these texts moderation for the sake of concord is urged by a reformulation of actual freedom. Aristides urges concord with the same argument: "if it is more profitable to be a slave [δουλεύειν] than to use freedom [ἐλευθερία] as a means for evil . . . " (*Or.* 24.58). In ECL see esp. Ign. *Pol.* 4.3 and Schoedel, 270.

362 See Wimbush, 16: "'Remain' was not intended to support the *status quo*; it was designed

As in 1 Cor 1, the κλῆσις is the language of unification despite differentiation,[363] the commonality which binds the community together despite their various statuses in the outside world.[364]

In 7:25–38 Paul treats the issue of virgins. Marriage is a unifying force for those already married, but, if possible, those who are virgins, or widows (7:39–40) or separated (7:11) should remain as they are.[365] The reason for this is that the virgin can have a special calling to be completely "undivided" (7:34) by concentrating on pleasing the Lord and not on earthly concerns. The married person to some degree participates in "the outside world" (7:33–34). The virgin in a special way is devoted to the things of the Lord and the Lord's community, but this call is not for everyone. Paul's advice on the marital issues is given for the Corinthians' advantage (7:35). We may conclude that each of the various subsections of the arguments in chap. 7 takes up another facet of life statuses which was debated at Corinth, and contributed to the divided state of the community in rather concrete ways.[366] In his response Paul does not address specific "parties" as such, but treats all as κλητοί, addressing instead the various states in which people were called, thus assuming the very unity which he urges.[367] There is real advice here on specific concerns which divide the church community, grounded in Paul's overall concern for the preservation of the church body.[368]

---

only to *relativize* the importance of all worldly conditions and relationships." But this is to confuse Paul's motive with his justification. To argue for the *status quo* is a common and direct response to the danger posed by factionalism to the life of a community. Similar arguments of redefinition of the goal toward which the Christian strives are found in 9:24–27 and chap. 15.

363 The repetition of ἕκαστος here plays the same function as in 12:4–11. Differently, Conzelmann on 7:17: "Paul is not advocating a principle of unity in church order" (126).

364 As in 1:18–31, the groups are Jew and Gentile (here by the technical reference to circumcision or uncircumcision, because Paul has already separated the κλητοί from those old names). Slave and free may be implied in the statuses named in 1:26 (Wimbush, 17 sees the strong and weak in this chapter, both of which are ascetics).

365 As the general principle was stated in 7:20, 24 (μενέτω).

366 So rightly Yarbrough: "More to the point here, however, is that the question of marriage and sexual intercourse had created a division *within* the community" (119–20; see also p. 124: "The solidarity of the community, he argues, is more important than the means of distinguishing it. Distinguishing believers, that is, should never result in dividing them").

367 As previously, the only distinction Paul makes is between insiders and outsiders, thus enforcing Corinthian unity through those common boundaries.

368 Seen in this way, Paul is not combatting solely either libertines or ascetics (Weiss, *Korintherbrief*, 169) in 1 Cor 7. The exegetical tradition has too often felt constrained to choose between the two options because it has worked out of a methodological presupposition that one had to reconstruct Paul's "opponents" in every situation, and thus a unified front against which Paul argues (see Bartchy, 26, 127–59 ["pneumatic opponents"]; differently see also Yarbrough, 96, 117–22 for the debate). But Paul describes the Corinthian situation as factionalized, so this approach will not work for 1 Cor (one winds up with one set of opponents who are simultaneously sexual libertines and ascetics [Bartchy, 128]). Most likely both positions were represented in Corinth, although probably not in their extreme forms, hence the conflict (see correctly Conzelmann, 115: "it reflects the discussion between the libertinist and ascetic persuasions within the community"). This position was rightly stressed in the important treatment of Paul's

4. 1 Corinthians 8–10. Factionalism, Freedom and Compromise

a) 1 Corinthians 8

In chaps. 8–10 Paul treats the issue of idol meats, not just as a behavioral issue, but as a case which requires the proper definition of Christian freedom in order to ensure the unity of the church body. Corinthian γνῶσις leads to factionalism (φυσιοῖ).[369] This γνῶσις is one of the precious commodities claimed as an exclusive possession by some,[370] contributing to community division, both in itself and in the justification it provides for certain controversial actions, one of which is eating meats which have been sacrificed to idols.[371] In 8:1 Paul introduces his positive counterpart to both knowledge and freedom which some Corinthians (wrongly) regard as the guiding principles of action.[372] That counterpart is ἀγάπη, love.[373] "Love,"[374] he says, "builds up," referring again to the community as God's unified edifice which should be the theological and behavioral norm.[375] The hymnic fragment in 8:6 stresses Corinthian unity in *one* God and *one* Lord,[376] in common opposition to idolators ("outsiders").[377]

In 8:7–12 Paul describes in more detail the factional consequences of this γνῶσις, despite these many unifying forces. Some Corinthian Christians have been characterized as "weak" and others as "strong," which is yet another indication of the factions within the community.[378] The terms weak and strong are commonly used in literature on factionalism, because they describe concrete-

---

"oscillating" strategy in chap. 7 by H. Chadwick, "'All Things to All Men' (I Cor. IX.22)," *NTS* 1 (1955) 261–75; 264–68 (further discussion on it below in chap. IV n. 282). But in responding to factionalism, Paul treads a fine line between differing groups, treating each with respect and somewhat gingerly (though not holding back his opinion), appealing in particular to the overarching need for community stability (hence the *status quo* conservatism of 7:17–24 [differently Wimbush, 16]). The conservation and building up of the church community is his foremost concern.

369 8:1 (see above on how Paul uses this term to caricature Corinthian factionalism).

370 This is how we must understand the apparent contradiction between 8:1 and 8:7 (as Paul addressing such claims). In 1:5 it is a gift of all.

371 In 8:8 we see the two positions on eating this meat: it will harm you if you eat it; it will benefit you if you eat it. Paul argues in response to this divisive question: no, eating this food *in itself* will neither hurt nor help, but what is important is the effect which the controversy has on the church community.

372 6:12; 10:23, 29.

373 As also in Rom 13–15.

374 For a complete investigation of this term and its role in arguments combatting factionalism, see below on chap. 13.

375 See the discussion of the building metaphor above.

376 See n. 141 above on the frequent appeals to εἷς throughout 1 Corinthians, and Jewish and Greco-Roman parallels.

377 Note the repetition of ἡμεῖς.

378 See the sociological analyses of Theissen, 121–43 and Meeks, *Urban Christians*, 97–100.

ly who has the political advantage and who does not.[379] The whole purpose of a concordant political body is to make all members strong,[380] as Plutarch writes:

The Greek states which were weak [ἀσθενεῖς] would be preserved by mutual support when once they had been bound as it were by the common interest [τῷ κοινῷ συμφέροντι], and that just as the members of the body [τὰ μέρη τοῦ σώματος] have a common life and breath [συμπνεῖν] because they cleave together in a common growth. . . .[381]

To look out for the interests of the weak is an act of political consideration,[382] as Isocrates argues in the *Panegyricus*: "We nevertheless preferred to stand by the weaker even against our interests [ὅμως ᾑρούμεθα τοῖς ἀσθενεστέροις καὶ παρὰ τὸ συμφέρον βοηθεῖν] rather than to unite with the stronger [τοῖς κρείττοσι] in oppressing others for our own advantage."[383] This commonplace is known also in Hellenistic Judaism, as in Philo's praise of Abraham's peace-seeking self-restraint in dealing with Lot: "And yet who else would give way in a single point

379 See Aristid. *Or.* 24.14 on Solon: "he was most of all proud of the fact that he brought the people [δῆμος] together [καταμῖξαι] with the rich [οἱ δυνατοί], so that they might dwell in harmony [ὅπως ἂν μιᾷ γνώμῃ τὴν πόλιν οἰκῶσιν], neither side being stronger [ἰσχύοντες] than was expedient for all in common [κοινῇ συμφέρει]." See also, e. g., Cass. Dio 4.17. For Corinth, Theissen, 124–25 connects the terms with rich and poor (with 1:26 and 4:10).

380 Dion. Hal. *Ant. Rom.* 4.26.1: " . . . and declaring that concord [ὁμοφροσύνη] is a source of strength to weak states [ταῖς ἀσθενέσιν], while mutual slaughter reduces and weakens even the strongest [ταῖς ἰσχυραῖς]." See also Dio Chrys. *Or.* 40.20: "For enmity [ἔχθρα] can not only expose and humiliate the weak [οἱ ἀσθενεῖς], to say nothing of the hardships they have already, but also annoy those who are prosperous [οἱ εὖ πράττοντες] and distress their spirits." Dio throughout this speech on concord deals with competing claims to be "strong": "For while he who is overcome in the one is likely to gain a reputation for mere weakness [δόξα ἀσθενείας], in the other it will be for boorishness and contentiousness [φιλονικία]. Indeed, the better it is to be deemed weak rather than base [ὅσῳ δὴ κρεῖττον ἀσθενῆ δόξαι μᾶλλον ἢ πονηρόν], so much the more preferable is it to be tardy in making war rather than in making peace" (40.24; see also 41.11; Aristid. *Or.* 26.54). See also Ps-Arist. *Mund.* 6.396B on the proper "mix" of even opposites to form a concordant society: "it is as if men should wonder how a city survives, composed as it is of the most opposite classes (I mean poor and rich, young and old, weak and strong [ἀσθενῶν ἰσχυρῶν], bad and good) . . . the most wonderful thing of all about the harmonious working [ὁμόνοια] of a city community is this: that out of plurality and diversity it achieves a homogeneous unity capable of admitting every variation of nature and degree." On weak (οἱ ἀσθενέστεροι) and strong (οἱ ἰσχυροί) to refer to various factions, see [Herodes Atticus] *Pol.* 13 [Drerup, 10, and his commentary on p. 90].

381 *Arat.* 24.5. This text is especially important because the four images of the weak, the common advantage, the body and the breath are linked together (exactly as Paul interweaves them in 1 Cor 12:4–27; see the discussion below). They are all part of the same image-cluster for concord.

382 For Theissen this is "love patriarchalism" (139–40). See, e. g., Dion. Hal. *Ant. Rom.* 10.57.3.

383 *Or.* 4.54. On the connection of advantage [συμφέρον] and strong and weak, see 1 Cor 10:32–33 and the discussion below. In this same speech of Isoc., see also 4.81: "they exulted less in the exercise of power than they gloried in living with self-control, thinking it their duty to feel toward the weaker as they expected the stronger to feel toward themselves."

to the weaker if he were the stronger?"[384] In his own argument Paul urges that the food itself is neither good nor bad, but he makes the divisive effect which the controversy has had on the community (especially its weaker members) the focal point of his response (8:8–13).[385] The specific advice he gives in response to the division between strong and weak is to urge a new consideration for the other as a fellow member of Christ,[386] specifically, not to *offend* one another.[387]

Offense and Factionalism

The antonyms πρόσκομμα and ἀπρόσκοπος which frame Paul's discussion in ch. 8–10 (8:9 and 10:32) are also at home in factional disputes in antiquity.[388] The verb προσκόπτειν is used by Polybius to describe the offense caused by one party against another in peace treaty negotiations.[389] Elsewhere Polybius uses the noun προσκοπή in tandem with μῖσος to describe the result of party politics and divisiveness:

> ... unconcealed indignation and hatred against Callicrates and his party. One can guess from the following circumstance how cordially Callicrates, Andronidas, and the rest of their party were detested ... whenever any of the party of Callicrates and Andronidas went into them [ceremonial baths at the festival of Antigoneia], none of those who were waiting their turn ventured to enter the water after them, before the bathkeeper had let it

---

[384] *Abr.* 216 [καίτοι τίς ἂν ἕτερος ἀσθενεστέρῳ παραχωρήσειεν οὑτινοσοῦν ἰσχυρότερος ὤν;]. The text continues, "who, when he could conquer, would be willing to be defeated [ἡττᾶσθαι] and not avail himself of his power [μὴ συγχρώμενος τῷ δύνασθαι; cf. 1 Cor 9:12, 15, 18!]. He alone took for his ideal not the exercise of strength and self-aggrandizement but a life free of strife [ἐν ἀστασιάστῳ βίῳ] and so far as lay with him of tranquility, and thereby he showed himself the most admirable of men." It is interesting that Chrys. uses the same example of Abraham and Lot in his exhortation against self-seeking in regard to 1 Cor 14 (*hom. in I Cor.* 35.5 [*PG* 61.301]). For the same *topos* elsewhere in Philo, see also *Spec. Leg.* 2.141, where he ties it in with the analogy of the heavenly bodies (on which see n. 405 below)..

[385] So Meeks, *Urban Christians*, 100: "The emphasis in Paul's paraenesis, however, is not upon the maintenance of boundaries, but upon internal cohesion: the mutual responsibility of members, especially that of strong for weak, and the undiluted loyalty of all to the One God and One Lord."

[386] See 8:11–12. To "sin against Christ" implies the metaphor of the σῶμα Χριστοῦ. The brother is a member of one's own body, the body of Christ. The building metaphor is also brought by Paul to bear on this argument: the "building up" or the "destruction" of the brother, and thus the church (note the switch from singular to plural of ἀδελφός in 8:11–12; see Barrett, *First Corinthians*, 196).

[387] Cf. Rom 14:13, and full context.

[388] On the place of Latin *offendere-offensio* in party politics see Hellegouarc'h, 194–95 with references.

[389] 1.31.7; 7.5.6; 6.6.3, 6 (of the inevitable forces at work in forming a *politeia*). In regard to the latter text, on προσκόπτειν in conjunction with δυσαρεστεῖν ("displease") in Polybius, see Walbank, 1.653. The two terms are virtually synonymous; thus Paul's appropriate counterpart to πρόσκομμα is "to be pleasing [ἀρέσκειν] to all" (10:32–33). See also 5.49.5, where a counselor Hermeias causes offense [προσκόπτειν] by praising himself.

run off and poured in fresh . . . So deep was the prevailing *aversion* [προσκοπή] and hatred [μῖσος] of them.[390]

The connection of πρόσκομμα to party politics and battles is relevant to Paul's argument in 1 Cor 8–10. Corinthian factionalists have caused offense to one another, which is wrong in itself, and, even worse, prolongs the conflicts. In 8:9 he urges the "strong" Corinthians not to allow their ἐξουσία to become a πρόσκομμα to the weak. In 8:13 he repeats this advice through his self-exemplification, using a synonym σκανδαλίζειν, which also means "to give offense."[391] In 9:12, in his extended self-exemplification of the proper behavior, Paul characterizes himself using quite similar terms: "But I have not made use of this ἐξουσία, but I have endured all things, so that I might not give any hindrance (ἐγκοπή)[392] to the gospel of Christ." This refrain and self-exemplification are repeated again in 10:32–33: "Be ἀπρόσκοποι ("inoffensive") to both Jews and Greeks and to the church of God, just as I please all in all things . . . ." Once again his focal point is not on the various sides of the dispute, but on the "church of God" which suffers from them. As we have seen, the kind of "offense" Paul is referring to with these terms is a component of party politics and relations – "offense" prohibits peaceful social relations.[393] Paul's urging the Corinthians not to offend one another is certainly germane to the issue of factionalism.[394] In offending others they offend Christ, that is, the body of Christ (cf. 6:18).[395] We shall see that his advice – to yield to the other for the sake of the greater good (8:13; 9:19–23;

---

390 30.29.1–7; see also 5.7.5: ὁ βασιλεὺς καὶ προσκόπτων ἤδη τοῖς περὶ τὸν Λεόντιον, and 6.7.8 on φθόνος and προσκοπή, which spur the overthrow of tyranny and conspiracies against it. That "offense" is part of party politics can also be seen in *1 Clem.* 21:5, where in urging ὁμόνοια that author inverts this principle by arguing that even worse "offense" is caused by the Corinthians' factionalism (μᾶλλον ἀνθρώποις . . . προσκόψωμεν ἢ τῷ θεῷ).

391 G. Stählin, "σκάνδαλον, σκανδαλίζω," *TDNT* 7.339–58, 356 on the two as synonyms; see also BAGD, 752, though they cite 1 Cor 8:13 under the gloss "cause to sin." I argue for the other meaning here on the basis of its proximity to πρόσκομμα, and the conjunction of the two nouns in Rom 14:13. The connection of σκανδαλίζω to factionalism is made also in *1 Clem.* 46.7. See also the parallelism in Rom 16:17 σκοπεῖν τοὺς τὰς διχοστασίας καὶ τὰ σκάνδαλα . . . ποιοῦντας.

392 BAGD, 216. This term, sharing the same root as πρόσκομμα, is found with the meanings "hindrance" (D.S. 1.32.8; cf. the verb in Polyb. 23.1.12; Joseph. *BJ* 1.629; 6.111; 1 Thess 2:18; Rom 15:22; Acts 24:4), or literally "an incision" (Galen 7.38; cf. M. Ant. 11.2.2; LSJ, 473). The lexical and argumentative connection between the terms πρόσκομμα, ἐγκοπή, ἀπρόσκοπος, and σκανδαλίζειν was made by G. Dautzenberg, "Der Verzicht auf das apostolische Unterhaltsrecht. Eine exegetische Untersuchung zu 1 Kor 9," *Bib* 50 (1969) 212–32, 219: "denn ἐγκοπή steht durch den Kontext in Analogie zu den Begriffen πρόσκομμα (8,9), σκανδαλίζω (8,13) und zur Forderung des ἀπρόσκοπον εἶναι (10,32)."

393 In *1 Clem.* 20:10 the adverb ἀπροσκόπως is used in parallel with ἐν εἰρήνῃ (cf. 21:5; 61:1).

394 In Rom 14:13, 21 πρόσκομμα is related to κρίνειν ἀλλήλους, as in 1 Cor (esp. 4:1–5).

395 ἁμαρτάνειν can be used of offending as well as sinning, and is also used in political contexts, as in Polyb. 4.24.6; Dion. Hal. *Ant. Rom.* 5.50.3 (noun); 6.48.1. But the meaning of to sin is of course most common in Paul.

10:32–33) – is consistent with other sagacious political advice in antiquity aiming at establishing and maintaining peace and concord.

b) 1 Corinthians 9. Freedom and Accommodation

In chap. 9, in the form of a mock defense speech (ἀπολογία),[396] Paul presents himself as the example of the proper non-divisive, conciliatory behavior to which he calls the Corinthians. Briefly analyzed for the sake of this part of our investigation, Paul's argument begins from the premise that he is an apostle (9:1), from which he establishes that it is the right of an apostle to live from the gospel (9:3–11, 13–14). The expected logical conclusion is that Paul thus has a right to live from the gospel. But Paul does not conclude as one might expect. After demonstrating the legitimacy of this claim, he states instead that he has never made use of this ἐξουσία (9:12, 18, 23). Paul presents himself as the perfect paradigm of the proper use of Christian freedom[397] – which freely surrenders its right to have its own way for the sake of the entire church community and the gospel.

In times of political strife in antiquity it was common for each side to argue against conciliating the other side because it would entail some loss of their own freedom.[398] Aelius Aristides counters this appeal in one of his speeches on concord:

> You are proud of the fact that you are free [ἐλεύθεροι] . . . Therefore if for no other reason, then for the sake of being free and doing what you wish [ποιεῖν ὅ τι βούλεσθε], abandon this present conduct so that you may not suffer anxieties which will be as great as your present audacity.[399]

Further in the same speech Aristides appeals to the Rhodians for the necessity of the renunciation of some freedoms, for compromise, in order to establish and maintain concord.

> Imitate the form and fashion of a household. What is this? There are rulers in a household, the fathers of the sons and the masters of the slaves. How do these administer their households well? Whenever the rulers do not think that they can do anything, but

---

[396] See chap. IV for a full exegetical treatment.

[397] Two recent works have examined Paul's concept of freedom against its Hellenistic background: Jones, *Freiheit* and Vollenweider (whose extensive treatment of the Stoic background on pp. 23–104 is most valuable).

[398] See Dion. Hal. *Ant. Rom.* 7.59.1: ". . . and to both parties [plebians and patricians] it seemed that their whole claim to life and liberty [ἐλευθερία] was at stake in this trial." See also Dio Chrys. *Or.* 34.12, quoted above, and in general Taylor, 23. Note that loss of freedom is precisely the fear of at least some of the Corinthians: ἱνατί γὰρ ἡ ἐλευθερία μου κρίνεται ὑπὸ ἄλλης συνειδήσεως; (10:29b).

[399] *Or.* 24.22; cf. Dion. Hal. *Ant. Rom.* 4.25.6.

voluntarily give up some of their authority [ὅταν οἱ μὲν ἄρχοντες μὴ πάντ' ἐξεῖναι νομίζωσιν ἑαυτοῖς ἀλλ' ἑκόντες ὑφαιρῶσι τῆς ἐξουσίας].[400]

Political realism dictates that everyone cannot have their way in everything. What is required for concord is a redefinition of freedom from an individualistic to a corporate perspective.[401] Factionalism can be stopped only by compromise, where each side ceases to think only of what it is their right to do,[402] and instead makes concessions to the other side for the sake of the greater good.[403] Plutarch recommends this advice for reuniting factions: "by yielding [ὑφιέμενοι] in a small thing they gain their point in the best and more important matters."[404] This commonplace is also found in Josephus, where Mattathias counsels his sons:

---

400 Or. 24.32–33; see also Fuchs, 119–23. "To think that one can do anything" (also 1 Cor 6:12; 10:23) is an individualistic (wrong) definition of freedom, for both Aristides and Paul. In both cases it is a cause of factionalism which must be responded to with an appeal to a higher standard of freedom. For the same commonplace, attributed to the great lawgiver Lycurgus, see D. S. 7.12.3: "the greatest attention should be devoted to concord [ὁμόνοια] and manly spirit [ἀνδρεία], since it is by these alone that freedom [ἐλευθερία] can be maintained."

401 See n. 73 in chap. II on the "unbridled freedom" not in the best interests of the polity *topos* (and note that Paul uses the correct terminology here). This fact of the relationship of individual and communal freedoms is a microcosm for all political bodies, large and small. See, e. g., J. A. O. Larsen's reflections on Greek notions of freedom enacted in history: "It was this spirit of freedom for oneself but not for others which was largely responsible for the failure of Greek movements for unity" ("Freedom and Its Obstacles in Ancient Greece," *CPhil.* 57 [1962] 230–34; 231; see also Gehrke, 359).

With regard to Paul, Vollenweider's argument (see esp. 58–60, 229–30) that the Stoic concept of freedom was connected with the order of the cosmic body, as Paul's concept of freedom is linked inseparably with the body of Christ, lends important support to this study. He also connects συμφέρον with this same Stoic thought-complex. Vollenweider sees the Corinthian position to be more like the Cynic anarchistic challenge to Stoics, to which Paul like the Stoics responds with an appeal for true freedom grounded in the body metaphor. These insights fit well with Paul's argument for church unity (Vollenweider does not, however, specifically connect Paul's argument with the problem of factionalism, to which even in the Stoics and in other popular political writings it is the perfect antidote [see below on 10:23–11:1]).

402 Cf. Philo, *Abr.* 216, quoted above.

403 A good example is Dio Chrys. *Or.* 40.34: "For the unwillingness ever to yield [εἴκειν] or make concessions [παραχωρεῖν] to our neighbor – that is, without a feeling of humiliation – or while receiving some things ourselves, to concede some to the others, is not manly conduct [ἀνδρεῖον], as some imagine, but, on the contrary, senseless and stupid." See also Dem. *Ep.* 3.45 (quoted also in Aristid. *Or.* 23.71); Dio Chrys. *Or.* 40.20 (and the objection of weakness in concession in § 23 and in *Or.* 34.38). The standard representative of this "no yielding policy" to the demos was Appius Claudius, who opposed all the conciliatory efforts of Menenius Agrippa (Dion. Hal. *Ant. Rom.* 6.38.1; 6.88.3; cf. Cic. *QFr.* 1.1.32, on the dangers of yielding too much to the *publicani*).

404 *Mor.* 824E; cf. *Sol. and Publ.* 4.3. See Sheppard's negative assessment: "Plutarch's political methodology may be summed up as a policy of sweeping all potentially explosive issues under the carpet, in order to avoid aristocratic rivalries getting out of hand and leading to Roman interference" (p. 244).

But most of all I urge you to be of one mind [ὁμονοεῖν], and in whatever respect one of you is superior to the others, in that yield to one another [πρὸς τοῦτ' εἴκοντας], and so make the best use of your several abilities [οἰκείαις χρῆσθαι ταῖς ἀρεταῖς] (*AJ* 12.283).

That compromise is necessary to bring about ὁμόνοια is quite clearly a *topos* in arguments urging concord.[405] Thus Paul's argument in 1 Cor 8–10 in which he redefines freedom[406] and calls for renunciation of the misunderstood right "to do whatever one wants" (6:12; 10:23) is a direct response to the factionalism and divisiveness in the community which he addresses throughout 1 Corinthians. The issue of freedom with which he deals is in fact *the* political issue in antiquity. In response Paul appropriately urges compromise[407] among the factions for the sake of the greater good – the survival of the church body, by defining free-

---

[405] See Dion. Hal. *Ant. Rom.* 6.71.3; Dio Chrys. *Or.* 34.9, 44; 40.34 (quoted above); Aristid. *Or.* 23.70–71; 24.40; Plut. *Lyc.* 7.2. One of the most common *topoi* in literature about concord is the appeal to the κοινωνία of the planets and stars in the orderly running of the cosmos. For the sake of this harmonious unity, the stronger or larger planets freely "submit" to weaker or smaller ones. "Do you not see in the heavens as a whole and in the divine and blessed things that dwell therein an order [τάξις] and concord [ὁμόνοια] and self-control [σωφροσύνη] which is eternal . . . these things . . . are wont to be preserved as a result of their mutual friendship and concord [φιλία καὶ ὁμόνοια] for ever, not only the more powerful and greater [τὰ ἰσχυρότερα καὶ μείζω], but also those reputed to be the weaker [τὰ ἐλάττω δὴ δοκοῦντα]" (Dio Chrys. *Or.* 40.35–36; see the continuation of this argument in 40.36–39; of other examples, see Aristid. *Or.* 27.35; cf. Philo *Jos.* 145; *Cong.* 133; *Spec. Leg.* 2.141; an allusion which may well lie behind 1 Cor 15:27–28; Lucan, *BCiv.* 2.272–73). In ECL this argument for concord is made in *1 Clem.* 20 (for discussion see Jaeger, *Early Christianity*, 14–15 and notes; W. C. van Unnik, "Is 1 Clement 20 Purely Stoic?" *VC* 4 [1950] 181–89, who argues that the Stoic *topos* was already well-attested in Jewish writings; Sanders, *Hellénisme*, 109–30; Wengst, 111 and notes). Throughout *1 Clem.* personal sacrifice for the sake of concord is held up as necessary (chaps. 54–63; cf. Chrys. *hom. in I Cor.* 34.3 [*PG* 61.289–90]).

[406] Jones, *Freiheit*, 53 has rightly argued that Paul's argument about freedom in 1 Cor 9 reflects Hellenistic popular philosophical discussions about freedom (and not specific "Christian" concepts like freedom from the law or death). But his examples from Xenophon on Socrates not taking money in order to remain free, and Euripides on freely giving oneself over to death, take up only two aspects of a much larger question. That Socratic tradition preserved this memory of Socrates teaching without pay elucidates Paul's special application of a larger freedom issue (compromise of self-interest for the interests of the whole) to the example he chooses for his self-exemplification – his renunciation of remuneration. But the larger principle which Paul illustrates by this one example, which he wishes the Corinthians to apply to their strife-filled situation, is the much more universal political need for compromise, which Jones does not specifically discuss (although he comes closest when he touches on the relationship between freedom and duty in Euripides [pp. 48–49]). These ideas were in general commerce in antiquity, as this discussion demonstrates, so no direct singular conduit from Socratic or Euripidean tradition to Paul need be postulated (Jones, 50–51). Jones, it seems to me, too readily identifies the *application* of a freedom concept which Paul makes with its *background*, and thus must propose a rather narrowly defined tradition upon which Paul directly draws (see the summary 143–45; cf. the somewhat similar critiques made by Vollenweider, 21, 209 n. 52).

[407] See Theissen, 139–40 in regard to 1 Cor 8–10 and 11:17 ff. Paul's advice is characteristic of the "love-patriarchalism [which] allows social inequalities to continue but transfuses them with a spirit of concern, of respect, or personal solicitude" (139).

dom[408] not in an individual domain (as the Corinthian contenders do), but in the corporate sphere.[409]

We have seen how in 9:1–18 Paul presents himself as an example of a person who denies himself for the sake of the greater good (here defined as that of the gospel and the church). In 9:19–23 Paul shows how this kind of behavior extends into social relations, which is the application he wishes the Corinthians to make. Paul's goal in 9:1–18 is not to convince the Corinthians likewise to work without pay. It is to show them in very concrete terms how Paul has been true to the counsel he offers – which is to renounce one's "authority" in some matters for the sake of peace in one's relations with others for the sake of the social whole.[410] In 9:19–23 Paul presents himself as a living example of what it means not to be a πρόσκομμα to others, specifically Jews and non-Jews. He has sided with the "weak" members in order to save them for the body.[411] The resounding conclusion is "I have been all things to all people."[412] This is a suitable (and extreme) characterization of a non-factionalist – he is a member of no party, because he

---

[408] Paul redefines freedom paradoxically as slavery to all in 9:19 (cf. 7:22). Likewise Dio Chrys. says of the planets and all the harmonious cosmos that "all things everywhere serve [δουλεύειν] and attend upon the law of reason, obeying and yielding to it" (*Or.* 40.37). For the principle see also Vollenweider, 210 with other references, and his conclusion on 9:19–23: "Paulus spricht ja in diesem Zusammenhang von der kreativen *Oikodome* der Gemeinde, der eine jegliche Exusia zuzuordnen ist." For the same principle in Roman politics see Cic. *QFr.* 1.1.24: "And indeed it is the duty not only of one who governs allies and citizens, but also of one who governs slaves and dumb animals, to be himself a slave to the interests and well-being of those he governs." Differently, Marshall, 70–90, 309–17, has argued that the Corinthians charged Paul with being "servile" (which he then admits in his self-defense!). But Paul is the one who carries his own argument for compromise to this extreme (cf. Rom 14:18).

[409] See also Jones, *Freiheit*, 50 on Eur. *Alc.* 677–90: "... Euripides hier gegen eine populäre Auffassung kämpft, die Freiheit individualistisch verstand" (in relation to freely dying for another, one manifestation of the principle). On individualism as one of the strongest cultural values in Greco-Roman antiquity see P. Wendland, *Die hellenistisch-römische Kultur in ihren Beziehungen zum Judentum und Christentum*, HNT 2 (Tübingen: Mohr/Siebeck, 1972[4]) 45–50.

[410] It is interesting that Paul goes to such lengths to say that he does not do this "voluntarily" (9:17; see also philosophical parallels in Vollenweider, 207 and notes). The appeal to compromise in times of factionalism is rooted in voluntary concessions, as, for example, in the political maxim cited by Dion. Hal.: "a voluntary [ἑκούσιος] agreement between friends is more secure [βεβαιοτέρα] than concessions extorted by necessity [ὑπ' ἀνάγκης]" (*Ant. Rom.* 8.48.4; cf. 1.11.2–3; 6.71.3; Aristid. *Or.* 24.40). Perhaps Paul stresses that he acts under necessity in order to emphasize to the Corinthians that for a Christian to compromise with others is not even a voluntary decision; it is the only way to live out that calling. It may also be a way in which he tries to introduce an element of self-effacement into his use of himself as the example to be imitated ("I do this, but not by my own power–I am not holding up myself for example so much as Christ"). The same type of argument is made in 15:10: ἀλλὰ περισσότερον αὐτῶν πάντων ἐκοπίασα, οὐκ ἐγὼ δὲ ἀλλὰ ἡ χάρις τοῦ θεοῦ (ἡ) σὺν ἐμοί.

[411] Compare Isoc. *Or.* 4.54 and Dio Chrys. *Or.* 40.34 (both quoted above).

[412] But note that πᾶσιν has the definite article, another way of Paul's stressing the corporate body of the church (see Barrett, *First Corinthians*, 215; BDF § 275): "I have been all things *to the whole.*"

shares equally with all and is a partner (συγκοινωνός), not of men or factions, but of the gospel.

To be "all things to all people" is a perfect epithet of a political chameleon. This figure is accurately described by Plutarch:

What man is there, then, so indefatigible, so changeable, so universally adaptable, that he can assimilate and accommodate himself to many persons . . . Such varied adaptation were the task of a Proteus . . . who by magic can change himself often on the very instance from one character to another, reading books with the scholarly, rolling in the dust with wrestlers, following the hunt with sportsmen, getting drunk with topers, and taking part in the canvass of politicians, possessing no firmly founded character of his own.[413]

But Paul is no simple glad-hander. He is not all things to all people to ensure his own popularity,[414] he says, but in order to save them (9:22),[415] and for the sake of the gospel. "All things to all people" thus also defines Paul's role as conciliator of the factions.[416]

Before moving on from 1 Cor 9, we must examine the term συγκοινωνός in 9:23. Words from the κοιν- root play an important role in Paul's argument for unity throughout 1 Corinthians (κοινωνία in 1:9 and 10:16; κοινωνός in 10:20;[417]

---

[413] *Mor.* 96F-97; see also Plutarch's description of Alcibiades' adaptability (*Alc.* 23.4–6). For a similar description of Proteus, see Virg. *G.* 4.407–13. Philo knows this commonplace also: "And so too the politician must needs be a man of many sides and many forms" [καὶ τὸν πολιτικὸν ἀναγκαῖον εἶναί τινα πολυειδῆ καὶ πολύμορφον] (*Jos.* 34). See also further material now collected in Marshall, 70–90, 309–17, who equates Proteus with "the flatterer," and Vollenweider, 216–17 nn. 86–87 (neither of whom connect the image with factionalism). On this theme, see the description of Paul in W. A. Meeks, "The Christian Proteus," *The Writings of St. Paul* (New York: Norton, 1972) 435–44.

[414] Compare this passage from Cassius Dio's encomium of Augustus on the way he dealt with the factions: "He chose, though against his will [ἄκων], to surrender a few to their wrath so that he might save the majority [ὥστε τοὺς πλείους διασῶσαι], and he chose to assume a friendly attitude towards each of them in turn [καθ' ἑκάστους] so as not to have to fight with them all [πᾶσιν] at once. From all this he derived no personal gain [οὐδὲν ἰδίᾳ ἐκέρδανεν], but aided us all [ἡμᾶς . . . πάντας . . . ὠφέλησε] in a signal manner" (56.37.3–4).

[415] See also below on the almost identical statement in 10:33: "I am pleasing to all in all things, not seeking my own advantage but that of the many, so that they might be saved." Chrys. connects the two readily: ἀπέδειξεν, ὅτι οὐδαμοῦ τὸ αὐτοῦ ζητεῖ, ἀλλὰ καὶ Ἰουδαίοις ὡς Ἰουδαῖος ἐγένετο, καὶ ἀνόμοις ὡς ἄνομος, καὶ τῇ ἐλευθερίᾳ τῇ ἑαυτοῦ καὶ τῇ ἐξουσίᾳ οὐκ ἁπλῶς ἐχρήσατο, ἀλλ' εἰς τὸ πᾶσι συμφέρον, δουλεύων ἅπασιν (*hom. in I Cor.* 24.3 [*PG* 61.202]).

[416] As already argued to some degree by Chadwick, 263–70, who linked this verse with the "oscillating character" of Paul's argument in 1 Cor 6 and 7. Compare Dio Chrys. *Or.* 41.5 where he urges concord on Prusa and Apameia by appeal to himself: εἰμὶ μὲν οὖν πολίτης ἑκατέρων (cf. Jones, *Dio Chrysostom*, 94). Thus above the fray, he can call both sides to concord. "All things to all people" is Paul's own self-description, not the Corinthians' charge against him (as argued by Marshall, 309–17). Taking this as the Corinthians' charge produces all kinds of inconsistencies: "Primarily, 'all things to all men' reflects the traditional Greek response to inconstancy" (Marshall, 401). The truth is the other way around – this very claim could *lead to* a charge of inconstancy.

[417] See Betz, *2 Corinthians 8 and 9*, 80 n. 337.

συγκοινωνός in 9:23).[418] The noun συγκοινωνός is rare in Greek literature, occurring mostly in the New Testament.[419] It appears in the papyri referring to business partners.[420] Cassius Dio uses the verb συγκοινωνέω to refer to Lucius Vettius' "taking part" in the Catiline conspiracy.[421] In 9:22 Paul says that his goal has been to be a partner of the gospel (and thus not of human cliques), having previously said that he has been "all things to all people." Similarly, Plutarch describes Solon as being a κοινός to all (κοινὸς ὢν πᾶσι), a member of no faction, who "said and did everything to bring about concord [ὁμόνοια] among them."[422] Later in the same book, *Praecepta gerendae reipublicae*, Plutarch generalizes this advice, calling on his reader not to join any parties or factions, but to be

---

418 Research on κοινωνία and cognates has been considerable, though no investigation has taken into account the relationship of the term to factionalism. A valuable treatment, which rightly stresses the ecclesiological focus of the term for Paul, as against those who prefer the more vague mystical sense of "participation" is J. Hainz, *Koinonia. Kirche als Gemeinschaft bei Paulus*, Biblische Untersuchungen 16 (Regensburg: Pustet, 1982), who refutes in particular the older work of H. Seesemann, *Der Begriff* KOINΩNIA *im Neuen Testament*, BZNW 14 (Giessen: Töpelmann, 1933). Hainz does not, however, bring in Greco-Roman comparative evidence. F. Hauck ("κοινός κτλ.," *TDNT* 3.789–809) collects some political evidence, but disregards its applicability to Paul (see p. 804). J. Y. Campbell, "KOINΩNIA and its Cognates in the New Testament," *JBL* 51 (1932) 352–80 argued that words from the κοιν- root are not used with a genitive of the person with whom one associates. Klauck, *Herrenmahl*, 260–61, introduces Greco-Roman religious parallels of cultic union with a deity, but also does not bring in political texts. A real advance in the study of κοινωνία has been made by Sampley, 29, 44–45 and passim, who has noted the business background to the word group as especially illuminating for Paul's use in Phil and Philem (unfortunately, he never deals with 1 Cor 1:9 and 10:16). In 1 Cor, where the problem is proper community formation and relations, we must take into account the political uses of the word group (I do not presume that all Pauline usages would necessarily be assisted by this insight – it has long been observed that Paul uses this word group in a variety of ways because of its relational character). The social uses of the term are examined and stressed in W. L. Willis, *Idol Meat in Corinth. The Pauline Argument in 1 Corinthians 8 and 10*, SBLDS 68 (Chico, CA: Scholars Press, 1985) 167–81, 215–20, who does not, however, connect the term in 1 Cor with factionalism *per se* (and overstates the case on the social side, though he employs the concept of "covenant" to emphasize this [205–209]). The present study will try to mediate between the ecclesiological and mystical meaning (on the false dichotomy, cf. Conzelmann, 171), by arguing that in fact Paul uses the term κοινωνία in both senses, using the assumed cultic unity as an argument for political/ecclesiological unity.

419 Phil 1:7; Rom 11:17; Rev 1:9 (LSJ, 1666).

420 *P.Bilabel* 19.2 (C.E. 110) and *PMasp.* 2.67158.11 (BAGD, 774). In the latter text the simple adjective κοινός-ή-όν appears eight times in the contract (the text is, however, late [28 April 568 C.E.]).

421 37.41.2; cf. Dem. *Or.* 57.2; Thuc. 8.75.3. Even in the NT the verb can have this meaning (Phil 4:14; Eph 5:11; cf. Rev 18:4, cited by LSJ, 1666 with gloss "take part in, have fellowship with").

422 *Mor.* 805E. See also Plut. *Sol.* 14.1: "[Solon] was neither associated with [κοινωνοῦντα] the rich in their injustice, nor involved in the necessities of the poor" (cf. D. L. 1.58). Yet, elsewhere in his *Solon* Plutarch admits with surprise that one of Solon's own laws prohibited one from remaining neutral in a time of factional strife! (*Sol.* 20.1; cf. Arist. *Ath. Pol.* 8.5).

"a common partisan of all [κοινὸς εἶναι πάντων] by coming to their aid."[423] The simple terms κοινός and κοινωνός are often used in political contexts to refer to allies, partners, co-partisans,[424] as is the verb κοινωνέω.[425] Paul uses the abstract noun κοινωνία to introduce the purpose of 1 Corinthians in the epistolary thanksgiving in 1:9.[426] This term, too, has a long history in political contexts.[427] Paul reminds the Corinthians that God has called them to "partnership"[428] of Jesus Christ, and thus not to their own exclusive sects and associations (as is made even more explicit in 10:16). He provides an example for them, he says, by being a συγκοινωνός of the gospel, not other persons or splinter groups.[429]

In 9:24–27 Paul shifts to an eschatological frame of reference. He compares the corruptible crown for which the athlete strives with the incorruptible crown which the Christian pursues.[430] Using this metaphor of athletic competition[431]

---

[423] *Mor.* 824B. Note the genitive of association here (contra Campbell; also, e. g., in *Mart. Pol.* 17.3).

[424] E. g., Xen. *Hell.* 2.3.17, 19; Polyb. 2.55.8; 5.41.1; 23.17.10; Dion. Hal. *Ant. Rom.* 6.79.3; App. *BCiv.* 1.5.34; cf. Latin *socius*, as in Lucan, *BCiv.* 10.350 (many other references in OLD, 1778–79). Aristid. chides the cities of Asia that by their strife they do not live up to their title τὸ κοινόν (*Or.* 23.40). For further discussion see Sampley, 29 and nn. 25–26, who stresses the business background to the word group.

[425] E. g., Pl. *Resp.* 5.464A and passim; Arist. *Ath. Pol.* 18.3; Isoc. *Or.* 7.31; Polyb. 3.2.4; 4.5.3; 4.22.5; 4.30.5; 4.32.10; 4.33.9; 4.35.10; Dion. Hal. *Ant. Rom.* 1.85.2; 5.12.2; 7.56.1; Plut. *Marc.* 10.3; see also the collection of "common" appeals in Aristid. *Or.* 23.65–67.

[426] 1:4–9, the epistolary thanksgiving formula, functions as the *prooimion* to the argument in the body of the letter (see chap. IV).

[427] See, e. g., Arist. *Pol.* 1.1.1–12; 2.1.2 and passim; *Eth. Nic.* 8.9.1; Polyb. 2.61.11; Philo, *Spec. Leg.* 3.131; Dio Chrys. *Or.* 38.43; 40.27, 36, 39; Aristid. *Or.* 27.35, 44; Plut. *Mor.* 96D; 787E; Iambl. *Ep. Peri Homonoias* (συναγωγὴ ὁμοίου τοῦ νοῦ κοινωνία τε καὶ ἕνωσις [Diels, *Vorsokr.* 2.356]). On the importance of the term κοινωνία in Aristotle, see Newman, 1.41–43; 2.391–3; R. A. Gauthier and J. Y. Jolif, *L'Ethique à Nicomaque* (Louvain: University of Louvain Press, 1959) 2.696–97 and the literature cited there. On the relation of the term to concord, see Kramer, 34–37 and specifically the famous prayer of Alexander for ὁμόνοια, εἰρήνη and κοινωνία (Plut. *Mor.* 330E; Tarn, *Alexander the Great*, 2.443–47). For the generality of the sentiment, see also Plut. *Arat.* 10.2: "loving concord [ὁμόνοια] between nations, community [κοινωνία] of cities, and unanimity [μία φωνή] of council and assembly, beyond all other blessings." See also n. 405 above on the *topos* of the κοινωνία of the planets.

[428] Pl. *Ep.* 6.323C urges Hermeias, Erastus and Coriscus to return to their former state of φιλότης and κοινωνία. See also M. Ant. 11.8, where he argues against human divisions on the grounds that κοινωνία was established by Zeus.

[429] As understood by Chrys. in his exegesis of 1 Cor 9:23: ἵνα δυνηθῶ κοινωνῆσαι τοῖς ἐν τῷ εὐαγγελίου πεπιστευκόσιν (*hom. in I Cor.* 22.3 [*PG* 61.185]). See recently Vollenweider, 221 n. 107: "Zu beachten ist aber die bleibende soziale Dimension, die im συγκοινωνός einbegriffen ist."

[430] Cf. Joseph. *Ap.* 2.217–219. Another aspect of this argument is the logical conclusion that the Christian is not competing against other Christians for the incorruptible crown, unlike the athletes who all compete but only one wins (9:24–25; cf. 15:49–52 "we *all* shall be changed"; for this interpretation, see *2 Clem.* 7:2). In place of striving against others Paul substitutes the practice of competing with oneself for the only important goal – eschatological salvation (9:27). The appeal to divided groups to struggle together for higher goals instead of against one another

Paul urges the Corinthians to revise their priorities – the final goal in relation to which they should make all decisions is not the same as that of the rest of the world.[432] Dio Chrysostom uses this argument in his *Or.* 38, where he belittles the Nicomedians and the Nicaeans for being divided over the prize of which city will be named πρώτη, first.[433]

> But if at best the prize [ἆθλον] for which this evil [their factionalism] is endured is a mere nothing and the supposed issues are both small and trifling [μικρὰ καὶ φαῦλα] and it is not fitting even for private persons to squabble over them, much less cities of such importance . . . .[434]

This argument of stressing the real goal of the Christian and thus trivializing "earthly" and "human" rivalries (3:3; 6:3; 9:24–27) reaches its fullest expression in chap. 15. 9:24–27 is the fitting culmination to Paul's self-exemplification of the proper use of Christian freedom throughout 1 Cor 9, because often in Greek texts the athlete is the paradigm of renunciation of temporary smaller freedoms through ἐγκράτεια (significantly in regard to sex and food) for the sake of the greater goal, the crown of competition.[435] This is what Paul urges the Corin-

---

is a *topos* in literature urging unity (see n. 195 above). Origen comments on εἷς in 9:24: πάντες οἱ σωζόμενοι ἕν εἰσιν καὶ ἓν σῶμα, with appeal to the eucharist (*comm. in I Cor.* 44.4 [p. 514]).

431 Plutarch uses the same metaphor to refer to all kinds of contentiousness and rivalry (*Mor.* 486B). The play between athletic competition and political strife was often made (see the use of ἀγωνίζεσθαι in Thuc. 3.82.8; other examples: Xen. *Lac.* 4; Plut. *Pomp.* 53.6; *Art.* 26.1; *Ages.* 29.1; *Pel.* 4.2; D. L. 6.27). Sociologist A. W. Gouldner has argued that the Greek contest system was a major factor in political instability and factionalism throughout Greek history, because it led to envy and preoccupation with self-interest to the neglect of the larger political community (*The Hellenic World. A Sociological Analysis* [New York/Evanston: Harper & Row, 1965] 41–77, and esp. 52–58).

432 See chap. II on Aristotle's mandate that the deliberative orator must tailor his proof to the audience's final goal of actions, or change it.

433 On these intercity rivalries, see MacMullen, 185–88 and notes, and Jones, *Dio Chrysostom*, 84–89.

434 *Or.* 38.21. In § 23–24 he quoted them as saying "we are contending for primacy!" (cf. Mark 9:33–37; 10:32–45 and par.). In another speech Dio derides the value of a crown, calling it φυλλά, "leaves" (*Or.* 66.5). On the *topos* that factionalists fight over insignificant things, see the discussion above on 1 Cor 6:2–4.

435 This argument is made by K.J. Frantz, "The Function of Paul's Athletic Imagery in 1 Corinthians 9:24–27," M.A.T.S. thesis, McCormick Theological Seminary, 1988 (with references from philosophical texts). An excellent illustration of this is Lucian *Anach.* 15, in which Solon, one of the most famous politicians of all time, speaks of the role of athletics in the πόλις: "And I shall now tell you what we think about our young men, and how we deal with them from the time when they begin to know good from bad, to be physically mature [τῷ σώματι ἀνδρίζεσθαι], and to bear hardships [ὑφίστασθαι τοὺς πόνους], in order that you may learn why we prescribe these exercises for them and compel them to train their bodies [διαπονεῖν τὸ σῶμα]. It is not simply on account of the contests, in order that they may be able to take the prizes–very few out of the entire number have the capacity for that–but because we seek a certain greater good from it for the entire state and for the young men themselves. There is another competition [ἀγών] which is open to all good citizens in common, and a wreath [στέφανος] that is not made of pine or olive or parsley, but contains in itself all human felicity,

thians to do. Instead of using their unbridled freedom to do whatever they want, they should make concessions to one another out of their freedom, for the sake of the entire church community and ultimately their own eschatological salvation.

c) 1 Corinthians 10

(1) The Negative Example of the Wilderness Generation

In 10:1–13 Paul presents a scriptural παράδειγμα which compares the Corinthians with the ancient Israelites. In both cases they were first baptized,[436] and then shared the same sacraments, but despite these unifying factors, they rebelled (through desiring food, idolatry and *porneia*). Paul characterizes the Corinthians' temptation as ἀνθρώπινος in 10:13, which harks back to 3:3 where their factional behavior is termed "walking in a human way" (κατὰ ἄνθρωπον περιπατεῖν). Factionalism is a "human failing," one which results in destruction (10:5, 19).[437] One factor which has not been sufficiently recognized in exegesis is that Israel's behavior in the wilderness consists of a series of "rebellions" – against the deity, against their leaders Moses and Aaron, and against one another – and thus provides a perfect counterexample (τύπος) to the factionalism and uproar in the church at Corinth.[438] In 10:1–13 Paul presents an allegory to the factional strife which has succeeded the founding of the church at Corinth by appropriately choosing several events from Israel's wilderness wanderings which demonstrate the chosen people's destructive divisiveness after its "baptismal" exodus event.

In 10:5 Paul refers to a great killing of many Israelites by God. The event referred to is clearly Num 11:33,[439] where God "struck a very great plague

---

–that is to say, freedom [ἐλευθερία] for each individual singly and for the state in general [αὐτοῦ τε ἑκάστου ἰδίᾳ καὶ κοινῇ τῆς πατρίδος] . . . ."

[436] That party membership is alluded to here is signalled by the formula εἰς τὸν Μωϋσῆν ἐβαπτίσθησαν, which parallels εἰς τὸ ὄνομα Παύλου ἐβαπτίσθητε in 1:13, 15 (which is itself based on the correct formula εἰς Χριστὸν βαπτισθῆναι [Barrett, *First Corinthians*, 221]). We have seen above that Moses is claimed as ancestor/leader in Jewish literature, and is thus an object of Jewish boasts (corresponding to Corinthian factionalists' boasts in their baptizer).

[437] See above on these two themes as *topoi* about factionalism in Greco-Roman texts.

[438] The ecclesiological focus of 1 Cor 10 was correctly pointed out by R. L. Jeske ("The Rock was Christ: The Ecclesiology of 1 Corinthians 10," in *Kirche*, FS G. Bornkamm, ed. D. Lührmann and G. Strecker [Tübingen: Mohr/Siebeck, 1980] 245–55), although he sees Paul's argument as a response to a Corinthian ecclesiology based on an exegesis of Exodus, not to Corinthian factional behavior. I do not agree with him that underlying 1 Cor 10 is a Corinthian exegesis of Exodus, which Paul cites and critiques (p. 251 and passim). Rather, I think Paul introduces these scriptural references himself (his motive is plainly given in 10:6, 11) to respond to Corinthian factionalism and its varied manifestations with warning examples from Israel's past. On the ecclesiological focus of 1 Cor 8–10 see also Merklein, 167.

[439] Num 11 is an etiological narrative built upon word play on the root "to desire" [אוה], as

against the people" for desiring the food they had had in Egypt, as Paul indicates in the next verse (καθὼς κἀκεῖνοι ἐπεθύμησαν).[440] Of special importance to this study is the fact that Josephus, in recounting the events of Num 11, says the people rebelled through factionalism [στασιάζειν].[441] In 10:7 Paul quotes LXX Exod 32:6, referring to the rebellion of the Israelites with the golden calf. Philo uses the political terms ἀναρχία and ταραχή[442] to describe this biblical event.[443] In 1 Cor 10:8 Paul refers to the infamous Baal Peor incident, the revolt of the Israelites with the Midianite women which resulted in 23,000 deaths (actually 24,000, according to Num 25:9). Philo refers to this event as a στάσις, "faction,"[444] as does Josephus.[445] Next in his scriptural allegory, in 10:10 Paul refers to the revolt[446] of Korah (Num 16),[447] termed by Josephus "a sedition [στάσις]

11:34 shows (the city is named קברות התאוה, "graves of desire"). What the Israelites desired was *meat* (Num 11:4, 13). The exegetical tradition has often missed this precise correlation entirely, thinking 1 Cor 10:5–6 to be a reference to Num 14:16 (Heinrici, *Korinther*, 297; Robertson-Plummer, 202; Conzelmann, 167; but correctly Weiss, *Korintherbrief*, 252 n. 2; Barrett, *First Corinthians*, 224; W. A. Meeks, "'And Rose Up to Play': Midrash and Paraenesis in 1 Cor 10:1–22," *JSNT* 16 [1982] 64–78, 68; more hesitantly Willis, *Idol Meat*, 144).

440 Philo (*Spec. Leg*. 4.129) also reads Num 11 as a warning against gluttony and unfounded desire, and draws the same object lesson from it as Paul does in 10:6: "Let no one indulge his lust!" [μηδεὶς τῇ ἐπιθυμίᾳ χαριζέσθω].

441 *AJ* 3.295. His rendition of the plague, in a similar manner to Paul's in 1 Cor 10:5, employs a strange litotes: "in fact no small number of them perished" [ἀπέθανε γὰρ οὐκ ὀλίγον πλῆθος αὐτῶν] (3.299). On political language and rebellion in Josephus in general, see H. W. Attridge, *The Interpretation of Biblical History in the* Antiquitates Judaicae *of Flavius Josephus*, HDR 7 (Missoula, MT: Scholars Press, 1976) 126–40.

442 On the roots of this political usage in classical Athens, see L. Edmunds, *Cleon*, Knights, *and Aristophanes' Politics* (Lanham/New York: University Press of America, 1987) 1–16.

443 *Vit. Mos*. 1.161–64, a rebellion which was caused by οἱ μὴ βέβαιοι τὰς φύσεις, "the men of unstable nature" (1.161). Elsewhere Philo uses the rebellious camp of Exod 32 as an allegory for the human person, using more specific terms for factionalism. "For where else do we find contentions, combats, hostilities [ἔριδες, μάχαι, φιλονεικίαι] and all the works that go with bitter and persistent war, but in the life of the body which in this parable he calls the camp?" (*Ebr*. 99). We cannot know if Josephus too perceived of Exod 32 as a civil rebellion as, for apologetic reasons, he (appropriately?) omits mention of it. *1 Clem*. 53 also uses the golden calf incident in an argument to dissuade later Corinthian church members from factionalism.

444 *Post. Cain*. 182–85. Cf. *Vit. Mos*. 1.305 where these events are summed up as οἱ ἐμφύλιοι κακοί. See also Philo's description of Moses in Egypt as a non-factionalist: "he eschewed all strife and contention and sought only for truth" [ἀφιλονείκως τὰς ἔριδας ὑπέρβας, τὴν ἀλήθειαν ἐζήτει] (*Vit. Mos*. 1.24).

445 *AJ* 4.140. Significantly, Josephus adds that the Israelites "revelled in strange meats" in their consort with the Midianite women (4.139; Num 25:2 "they invited them to the sacrifices of their gods").

446 The Hebrew text itself says this in Num 16:2, ויקמו (LXX translates ἀνέστησαν here, as in Exod 32:6). Could Paul be playing on this term in 10:12 (cf. 10:7)? See above on ἵστημι as a part of the building metaphor for concord.

447 With Heinrici, *Korinther*, 299; Godet, 2.64; Robertson-Plummer, 206; Héring, 91; Meeks, "Rose Up to Play," 68. Note that Joseph. calls their fate an ὄλεθρον (*AJ* 4.50, 61), and stresses that it was a divine and not a human punishment (4.48; cf. Num 16:29). Wisd 18:25, in reference to Num 16:41–50, calls the destructive agent ὁ ὀλεθρεύων (Klauck, *Herrenmahl*, 257).

for which we know of no parallel whether among Greeks or barbarians."[448] Philo also terms Korah's revolt a στάσις.[449]

There is thus a strong connection between the σχίσματα in the church community at Corinth and the scriptural allegories Paul employs in 1 Cor 10:1–13.[450] It is clear from Philo and Josephus (and later rabbinic tradition) that all of the events in Israel's history which Paul draws on in 1 Cor 10:1–13 were regarded as examples of factionalism[451] at the time of Paul, and were thus perfectly appropriate to the divisive situation which he faced at Corinth.[452] This is confirmed by the author of *1 Clement*, who likewise uses the example of Dathan and Abiram (Korah's co-conspirators in Num 16) to exemplify for a later Corinthian generation that ζῆλος causes στασιάζειν, which leads to destruction.[453] The specific examples Paul chooses are relevant to the Corinthian situation both because they are concerned with issues over which the Corinthians were divided (idol meats, *porneia*), and also because each of the events Paul draws on was an acknowledged example of the dangers of factionalism itself.[454] Factionalism, a particularly "human" temptation, can only lead to destruction (10:13; 10:5, 10).[455]

---

[448] *AJ* 4.12; see also 4.13, 32, 36, 59, 66. Josephus tells us how the faction of Korah arose. "Korah, one of the most eminent of the Hebrews, by reason both of his birth and his riches, a capable speaker and very effective in addressing a crowd, seeing Moses established in the highest honors, was sorely envious" (*AJ* 4.14–15). The description of Korah as a factionalist continues in rabbinic literature (see *Num. Rab.* 18.1–23). Also note that Josephus uses appropriate political language to describe these factions, such as οἱ περὶ Δαθάμην, "Dathan's party" (4.38, 39; cf. Sir 45:18; see above, "Excursus: The Form of the 'Slogans' in 1:12," on this formula in political texts), and his general description of Korah's motives: ". . . Korah wished it to appear that he was concerned for the public welfare [τὸ κοινόν]; in reality, he was scheming to have the dignity transferred by the people to himself" (*AJ* 4.20; on this as a description of a factionalist, see below on 10:23ff.). In *AJ* 4.50 Moses asks God to save the people and award ὁμόνοια καὶ εἰρήνη.

[449] *Vit. Mos.* 2.174, 283. The author of *1 Clement* knows this tradition about Korah well, as he too uses the events of Num 16 as a negative example of factional behavior to be avoided at all costs (see στασιάζειν in 4.12 and 51.3). In the NT see also Jude 11; 2 Tim 2:19 (on Korah as a schismatic see also Watson, *Invention*, 60 n. 242).

[450] Differently Meeks, "Rose Up to Play," 99: "the point of the homily remains rather general."

[451] One is reminded in this regard of Celsus' charge about the Exodus event, that it consituted στασιάζειν πρὸς τὸ κοινὸν τῶν Αἰγυπτίων (Or. *Cels.* 3.5 [Borret, SC 136.20], and throughout chaps. 5–8).

[452] These negative examples were collected already in the biblical tradition in Pss 78 and 106 (Klauck, *Herrenmahl*, 252–53). The children of Israel revolted from God because their heart was not firm [εὐθεῖα, LXX Ps 77:37]. Note also that their revolt is due to their "fleshly" nature (ὅτι σάρξ εἰσιν, LXX Ps 77:39; cf. 1 Cor 3:3; 10:13). Cf. the collection of negative examples in Sir 16:5–10 (which Lumpe, 1244 regards as similar to 1 Cor 10:1–11).

[453] *1 Clem.* 4.12. In *1 Clem.* 4 other scriptural allegories are used (different from Paul's in 1 Cor 10) because that author is citing specific cases where ζῆλος and φθόνος resulted in ἀδελφοκτονία (4.7). See also *1 Clem.* 43, where the events of Num 17 are referred to using the verb στασιάζειν and the noun ἀκαταστασία (on this term see below on 1 Cor 14:33).

[454] Even the general "grumbling" (10:10) may be regarded as a manifestation of Corinthian party politics. It is used in regard to the revolt of Korah in LXX Num 14:26–27 of the people

(2) Unity in Sharing the Same Rituals

In 10:14–22 Paul calls the Corinthians to unity and partnership (κοινωνία) in the same cultic rites:[456] εἷς ἄρτος, ἓν σῶμα οἱ πολλοί ἐσμεν.[457] It is a *topos* in ancient literature urging concord to emphasize the cultic ties existing between the now divided groups.[458] For example, Dio Chrysostom calls the Apameians to concord with the people of Prusa:

> since they are men with whom you have common [κοινοί] ties of wedlock, offspring, civic institutions, sacrifices to the gods [θυσίαι θεῶν], festive assemblies, and spectacles.[459]

---

murmuring against their leaders Moses and Aaron (Heinrici, *Korinther*, 299, takes it in 10:10 to refer to murmuring against the Corinthians' leaders Paul and Apollos). Murmuring may refer to the general dispositions behind the Corinthians' contentions (so Lührmann, "Freundschaftsbrief," 310). It may also have an even more direct connection with factionalism (see M.Ant. 9.2, in concert with the body metaphor for unity: "the part [τὸ μέρος] ought not to grumble [μέμφεσθαι] at what is done in the interests of the whole"). The only other place Paul refers to grumbling in his extant letters (γογγυσμός in Phil 2:14) is also in an extended argument contrasting concordant and discordant behavior (cf. Acts 6:1).

455 In the biblical tradition, as in Greco-Roman texts (see n. 228 above), and also in rabbinic exegesis (e. g., *Num.Rab.* 18.12 ["strife brings destruction (כליה)" and 18:4 "come and observe how grievous a thing strife must be, seeing that the Holy One, blessed be He, exterminates all memory of one who foments strife"; cf. 1 Cor 3:17]).

456 Here the eucharist, but elsewhere baptism (12:13; cf. 1:13; 10:2–4).

457 10:17 (see nn. 141–42 above for the frequent appeals to εἷς in 1 Corinthians).

458 One of the ways allies and reunited factions express their unity is through common sacrifice (see Dion. Hal. *Ant. Rom.* 4.25.4–5; 26.3; 6.6.1; 79.2; and meals, see Lucan *BCiv.* 4.196–98; for the 5th and 4th centuries see Gehrke, 261–65). *Ant. Rom.* 4.49.3 describes the "Latin Festivals," which commemorate the alliance of forty-seven cities in peaceful union with Rome under Tarquinius, at which symbolically "one bull is sacrificed in common by all of them, each city receiving its appointed share of the meat" [ἑνὸς δὲ ταύρου κοινῶς ὑπὸ πασῶν θυομένου μέρος ἑκάστη τὸ τεταγμένον λαμβάνει]. See also D. L. 8.34–35 in this regard: "for once friends used to meet over one loaf [εἷς ἄρτος], as the barbarians do even to this day; and you should not divide bread which brings them together [μηδὲ διαιρεῖν, ὃς συνάγει αὐτούς]" (cited as a parallel to 1 Cor 10:17 in BAGD, xxvi). The positive side of this *topos* is expressed by Philo where he describes the effects of pilgrimage festivals: "Friendships [φιλία] are formed between those who hitherto knew not each other, and the sacrifices and libations are the occasion of reciprocity of feeling and constitute the surest pledge that all are of one mind [καὶ κρᾶσιν ἠθῶν ἐπὶ θυσιῶν καὶ σπονδῶν εἰς βεβαιοτάτην πίστιν ὁμονοίας ποιούμενοι]" (*Spec. Leg.* 1.70).

In the same way, enemies may be described οὔτε θυσιῶν οὔτε σπονδῶν οὐθ' ἑστίας ... κοινωνεῖν (Dion. Hal. *Ant. Rom.* 8.28.3). When a new polity is founded, a natural quandary arises about what sacrifices the new group will perform. In ancient Rome both Roman and Sabine rites were continued, and new rites were instituted for their now common history (Plut. *Rom.* 21). In Paul's Christian communities, baptism and the eucharist are unifying rites (10:1–4; 10:17; 12:13; see Meeks, *Urban Christians*, 140–63).

459 *Or.* 41.10. Of this list of appeals to commonalities which Dio makes, common sacrifices are of course the most pertinent to the church at Corinth, a religious community. See also his *Or.* 38.22 where one of his appeals for concord is: "Besides, you worship the same gods as they do, and in most cases you conduct your festivals as they do."

He makes a similar appeal in *Or*. 40:

Consider . . . how much better and more sensible it is at the common religious gatherings and festivals and spectacles to mingle [ἀναμίγνυσθαι] together, joining with one another in common sacrifice and prayer [συνθύειν καὶ συνεύχεσθαι], rather than the opposite, cursing and abusing one another.[460]

Paul's appeal to the Corinthians in 10:14–22 is very similar to this. He urges the Corinthians to be united because their cultic participation in the same rites stresses their fundamental κοινωνία with the same deity and thus with one another as co-worshipers of that deity[461] ("one bread, one body").[462] In 10:16 Paul may be quoting the church's eucharistic liturgy.[463] 10:17 then is Paul's commentary on that traditional authority, by which he applies it directly to the current situation at Corinth.[464] Again, his application of the cultic unity here in the argument is to the social unity which should be its natural consequence: εἷς ἄρτος, ἓν σῶμα οἱ πολλοί ἐσμεν, οἱ γὰρ πάντες ἐκ τοῦ ἑνὸς ἄρτου μετέχομεν. He only then makes the final argument that it is by the extension of this sole relationship that any other allegiances are forbidden (10:19–22).

(3) Factionalism and the Common Advantage

The sub-argument in 1 Cor 10:23–11:1 is an especially significant point in the overall argument of 1 Corinthians. Here Paul redefines τὸ συμφέρον ("the ad-

---

[460] Dio Chrys. *Or*. 40.28. See also Plut. *Mor*. 481D, where enmity between brothers is seen to be so disruptive because brothers must share the same sacrifices (and Betz, *PECL*, 2.245; cf. Arist. *Pol*. 3.5.14 in this regard).

[461] Compare Aristid. *Or*. 23.16 (urging concord): "And neither membership in a chorus, nor the companionship of a voyage, nor having the same teachers is so great a circumstance, as the gain and profit in having been fellow pilgrims at the Temple of Asclepius . . . ."

[462] This has been pointed out recently on sociological grounds. See Theissen, 165–66: "In 1 Cor. 10:17 Paul links a social goal with this notion of numinously charged elements . . . because all have eaten portions of the same element, they have become a unity in which they have come as close to one another as members of the same body, as if the bodily boundaries between and among people had been transcended . . . From a plurality of people emerges a unity." See also his conclusion on p. 167: "Paul moves the sacrament to the center to achieve greater social integration." Meeks reaches the same conclusion: "Paul's social intention in all this is revealed in 10:16; the transformation of a multiplicity of individuals into a unity" (*Urban Christians*, 159). See also Schoedel, 22 n. 106 on Ignatius: "the closely related theme of ὁμόνοια . . . occurs most characteristically in cultic contexts" (see references there).

[463] H.-J. Klauck, "Eucharistie und Kirchengemeinschaft bei Paulus," *Wissenschaft und Weisheit* 49 (1986) 1–14, 3.

[464] Weiss, *Korintherbrief*, 259; Klauck, "Eucharistie," 5: "In v. 17 liegt somit der ekklesiologische Leib-Christi-Begriff vor, mit dem Paulus in Kap. 12 in dem bekannten Leib-Gleichnis weiterarbeiten wird. Der Übergang von v. 16 zu v. 17 beweist, dass Paulus sein Gemeindemodell vom sakramentalen Geschehen aus entwickelt. Er interpretiert die Gemeinde Herrenmahl als ihrem Einheitsprinzip her" (cf. *Herrenmahl*, 262). This may be literally grounded in actual liturgical practice of sharing one loaf and one cup (Hainz, *Koinonia*, 19 with further references in n. 22; Klauck, "Eucharistie," 4).

vantageous") from personal to communal advantage,[465] and on that basis he appeals to the Corinthians to seek, not their own individual advantage, but that of the other, and ultimately the many (10:24, 33).[466] Calling the audience to work for the common advantage is a *topos* in political literature from antiquity urging concord on divided groups because of the very nature of factionalism itself. In describing the effects of the murder of Caesar, Josephus gives a textbook definition of factionalism:

> This murder produced a tremendous upheaval [κίνημα]; leading men split into factions [διαστασιασθῆναι]; *each joined the party which he considered would best serve his personal advantage* [πρὸς ὃ συμφέρειν].[467]

Factionalism is, at its very heart, tied up in the issue of τὸ συμφέρον, "advantage" or "interest."[468] This view is at least as old as Aristotle, who maintained that whereas ἡ πολιτικὴ κοινωνία was formed for τὸ κοινῇ συμφέρον, "other associations aim at some particular advantage."[469] Persons divide into factions to be members of individual groups which serve their own private interests.[470] The

---

465 This redefinition takes place over the course of the whole letter (see chaps. II and IV).

466 See the same sentiment (in concert with many other of the terms and phrases for concord and discord) in Phil 2:1–4, which culminates μὴ τὰ ἑαυτῶν ἕκαστος σκοποῦντες ἀλλὰ [καὶ] τὰ ἑτέρων ἕκαστοι. This is recognized by Sampley, 66: "the reader encounters a veritable handbook [Phil 2:1–5] sketching out what is appropriate to *societas* and what is inappropriate to it."

467 *BJ* 1.218; see also Dion. Hal. *Ant. Rom.* 10.60.2. For the phrase πρὸς τὸ συμφέρον, see 1 Cor 7:35; 12:7 (cf. Plut. *Ages.* 13.4). Elsewhere Josephus connects κοινωνία with "the common good": "At these sacrifices prayers for the welfare of the community [ὑπὲρ τῆς κοινῆς ... σωτηρίας] must take precedence of those for ourselves, for we are born to fellowship [κοινωνία], and he who sets its claims above his private interest [τὸ καθ' αὑτὸν ἴδιον] is especially acceptable to God" (*Ap.* 2.196).

468 See Livy 2.30.2; Cic. *Rep.* 1.32.49: "And they insist that harmony [*concordia*] is very easily obtainable in a state where the interests of all are the same [*idem conducat omnibus*], for discord [*discordia*] arises from conflicting interests [*ex utilitatis varietatibus*], where different measures are advantageous to different citizens [*cum aliis aliud expediat*]." That this was a common principle and reality of Roman politics was noted by Syme, 157: "Roman political factions were welded together, less by unity of principle than by mutual interest and mutual services." Thus "interests" lie at the heart of both Greek and Roman politics (see Finley, 2, 101, 114). In Greek texts, see, for example, Marcus Aurelius' statement of this commonplace with the customary image of the bee hive: "that which is not in the interests [συμφέρον] of the hive, cannot be in the interests [συμφέρειν] of the bee" (M. Ant. 6.54), and more examples below.

469 αἱ μὲν οὖν ἄλλαι κοινωνίαι κατὰ μέρη τοῦ συμφέροντος ἐφίενται (*Eth. Nic.* 8.9.4–5). Thus "justice [δίκαιον] is sometimes defined as that which is to the common advantage [τὸ κοινῇ συμφέρον]" (8.9.4).

470 The factionalist spurns the common good [ξυμφέρον] (Thuc. 3.82.8). The opposite of factionalism is a league, in which one no longer seeks one's own nation's or city's particular advantage [οὐ τὸ τῆς αὑτοῦ πατρίδος συμφέρον] but that of the league (Plut. *Arat.* 24.4). Cf. also Polyb. 2.41.9, where the dissolution of a league results in such διαφορὰ καὶ καχεξία that the cities "began to act against each other's interests" [ἀφ' αὑτῶν ἐναντίως τὸ συμφέρον ἄγειν ἀλλήλαις). In Dion. Hal. *Ant. Rom.* 5.10.2 Brutus charges that Collatinus (who favored tyranny) was "considering his private advantage instead of the public good" [ἀντὶ τῶν κοινῇ συμφερόντων τὸ ἑαυτοῦ σκοπῶν λυσιτελές].

result is, as Josephus bluntly tells us, that "party quarrels are invariably fatal to the common weal,"[471] as everyone concentrates on their own interest to the detriment of the common good.[472] Dio Chrysostom describes the factions at Tarsus in these exact terms:

> . . . each body clearly consulting its own self-interest [ἰδίᾳ τὸ συμφέρον]. It was just as if, when a ship is putting in for shore, the sailors should seek their own advantage [συμφέρον αὐτοῖς ζητοῖεν[473]], the pilot[474] his, and the owner his.[475]

Because factionalism is the problem of self-interest placed above the common interest,[476] in deliberative speeches urging concord[477] it is very common for orators to try to get the divided parties to forsake their individual interests and together strive for the common good (τὸ κοινῇ συμφέρον).[478] Demosthenes in his epistle urging concord advises: "Acquit yourselves, therefore, with magnanimity and statesmanship in the general interests of Greece" [τὰ κοινῇ συμφέρον-

---

[471] στάσιν ὀλέθριον οὖσαν τοῦ κοινῇ συμφέροντος (*Vit.* 264). Of many other examples, see Dion. Hal. *Ant. Rom.* 5.10.2; Cic. *Off.* 1.25.85; Dio Chrys. *Or.* 34.19; Plut. *Thes.* 24.1; *Arist.* 3.3.

[472] The converse of this is that allies are persons who have "the same definition of expediency" [τοὺς αὐτοὺς ὅρους θέμενοι τοῦ συμφέροντος] (Aristid. *Or.* 23.46). This too is linked with possessions (see above on the role they play in party politics and at Corinth): "For where each has separate possessions, what is expedient for each is separate" [οὗ μὲν γὰρ χωρίς τι ἕκαστος κέκτηται, καὶ τὸ συμφέρον χωρὶς ἑκάστου] (Aristid. *Or.* 23.65).

[473] The phrase "seeking the advantage" [ζητεῖν τὸ συμφέρον], as in this text, is extremely common (Pl. *Resp.* 1.341D; 342B; Isoc. *Or.* 6.34; Dem. *Or.* 3.11). It appears twice in Paul's argument in 1 Corinthians (10:24, 33; cf. 13:5; 14:12), and also in ECL (*Barn.* 4.10).

[474] On how this is a *topos* for leadership, along with the physician of the body and the architect of the building, all of whom concentrate upon τὸ συμφέρον, see Pl. *Resp.* 1.341–342E (cf. *Rhet. Her.* 4.44.57 on this common argument from analogy). See also below (in regard to 1 Cor 12:28) on nautical imagery for concord.

[475] *Or.* 34.16. See also Plut. *Lyc. and Num.* 4.3 for the same frequently attested image. The aptness of this parallel to 1 Cor 10:33 is proven definitively by the employment of the exact same *topos* and language in Chrys.'s exegesis of that verse: Διὰ δὴ τοῦτο καὶ ἐν πλοίῳ, εἰ χειμῶνος γενομένου ὁ κυβερνήτης ἀφεὶς τὸ τῶν πολλῶν συμφέρον, τὸ ἑαυτοῦ ζητοίη μόνον, καὶ ἑαυτὸν καὶ ἐκείνους καταδύσει ταχέως (*hom. in I Cor.* 25.4 [*PG* 61.210–11]).

[476] Dividing into "special-interest groups." See, for example, the advice on how to choose political friends in *Rh. Al.* 38.1446b: "We shall establish relations of friendship [φιλία] with people with manners like our own, and those with the same interest [συμφέρει] and those with whom we are compelled to be in partnership [κοινωνεῖν] as to matters of the highest importance." See also Democr. *Fr.* 107 (= Diels, *Vorsokr.* 2.164): φίλοι οὐ πάντες οἱ ξυγγενέες, ἀλλ' οἱ ξυμφωνέοντες περὶ τοῦ ξυμφέροντος.

[477] In chap. II we established that such speeches are deliberative.

[478] See Arist. *Eth. Nic.* 9.6.1, where concord [ὁμόνοια] is said to exist "when the citizens agree as to their interests" [ὅταν περὶ τῶν συμφερόντων ὁμογνωμονῶσι] (cf. 9.6.2, where concord "refers to the interests [τὰ συμφέροντα] and concerns of life"). In the *Politics* Aristotle argued that only constitutions and governments which aim at τὸ κοινῇ συμφέρον are just (3.4.2–5.4; Newman, 2.160–61; cf. *Rh. Al.* 2.1424b). This is also then the goal of deliberation: δίκαιόν τε καὶ συμφέρον (Dion. Hal. *Ant. Rom.* 7.39.2, and the full discussion in chap. II).

τα].[479] In the thesis statement to the argument in the same letter he says, "it is necessary that you bring about harmony [ὁμόνοια] among yourselves for the common good of the state" [εἰς τὸ κοινῇ συμφέρον τῇ πόλει].[480] In order to end factionalism and attain harmony, the factionalists must put the interests of the social whole before their own private interests.[481]

Because the appeal to the common advantage is such a well-attested *topos* for unity, we must conclude that when Paul exhorts the Corinthians to seek, not their own interest but that of "the many," following his example, he is directly addressing their factionalism,[482] and counseling the proper remedy to it: consi-

---

479 *Ep.* 1.9; cf. 1.10.

480 *Ep.* 1.5. See *Rh. Al.* 1.1422a-b where ὁμόνοια is described as συμφέρον πόλει, whereas στασιάζειν is not. See also Dion. Hal. *Ant. Rom.* 7.54.1: "He commended those who held that there was but one advantage to be considered and that the common advantage [ἓν τὸ συμφέρον καὶ κοινόν], and regarded everything else as secondary to harmony [ὁμόνοια]." For other examples of this *topos* in arguments urging concord see Andoc. 1.106; Dion. Hal. *Ant. Rom.* 11.7.3; 11.8.2; 11.9.1, 2, 3 (all in one speech); Dio Chrys. *Or.* 38.49; 39.5; 40.16, 19; 48.6; cf. Aristid. *Or.* 24.30. The same commonplace is also attested in Jewish writings (see Joseph. *Ap.* 2.294: ἢ τί συμφορώτερον τοῦ πρὸς ἀλλήλους ὁμονοεῖν).

In Roman politics we find the analogous and extremely common appeal to the *res publica* (on which see OLD, 1635–36 with full references). For good examples, see e. g., Ps-Sall. *Rep.* 2.4, and Cic. *Off.* 3.6.26: "This, then, ought to be the chief end of all men, to make the interest of each individual and of the whole body politic identical [*ut eadem sit utilitas unius cuiusque et universorum*]. For if the individual appropriates to selfish ends what should be devoted to the common good, all human fellowship will be destroyed [*dissolvetur omnis humana consortio*]." The connection with factionalism is particularly clear in Caes. *BCiv.* 1.8, where Caesar recounts Pompey's reconciliatory appeal to him that he "should not construe as an affront to himself what he had done for the sake of the state [*res publica causa*]. He had always placed the interests of the republic [*rei publicae commoda*] before private claims. Caesar, too, considering his high position, should give up for the benefit of the state [*res publica*] his partisan zeal and passion [*studium et iracundia*], nor be so bitterly angry with his enemies as to injure the commonwealth [*res publica*] in the hope that he is injuring them."

In ECL, see *1 Clem.* 48:6: δοκεῖ μᾶλλον . . . ζητεῖν τὸ κοινωφελὲς πᾶσιν, καὶ μὴ τὸ ἑαυτοῦ (which Jaeger, *Early Christianity*, 117 terms "the much-repeated supreme commandment of classical Greek civic virtue," but does not discuss its conspicuous antecedent in 1 Cor 10:24, 33). Chrys. in fact calls τὸ τὰ κοινῇ συμφέροντα ζητεῖν (in reference to 10:33) the rule of the most perfect Christianity! (*hom. in I Cor.* 25.3 [*PG* 61.208]). See also Ign. *Smyrn.* 7.1 (συνέφερεν δὲ αὐτοῖς ἀγαπᾶν).

481 Aristid. *Or.* 23.7 (φρονεῖν ἃ κοινῇ πᾶσιν ὑμῖν συμφέρει). In the context of Greek politics the appeal to "the common advantage" is often identical with "what is advantageous to the πόλις" (see, e. g., Pl. *Leg.* 9.875A-B; *Ep.* 8.352E; Isoc. *Ep.* 3.1; 9.19; Dem. *Or.* 1.1; 3.36; 15.24; *Prooem.* 50.1; Dion. Hal. *Ant. Rom.* 8.71.4; Dio Chrys. *Or.* 34.35, 40; Plut. *Ages.* 23.4; 37.5–6; *Pomp.* 51.5; Aristid. *Or.* 24.14). For Paul the social context of decision making for the Corinthians should be the ἐκκλησία (see esp. 10:32). Heinrici, *Korinther*, 198–99, is therefore incorrect in arguing that such sentences as οὐ πάντα συμφέρει, οὐ πάντα οἰκοδομεῖ and οὐ ζητῶ τὸ ἐμαυτοῦ σύμφορον "würde der Stoiker als Schwachheit eines unterphilosophischen Standpunkts verurtheilt haben." In fact these sentences comprise good political common sense (Stoic and otherwise) – especially in attempts to combat factionalism which is threatening the very life and stability of a political body.

482 This direct correlation of the argument in 1 Cor 10:23–11:1 with the problem of faction-

deration of τὸ κοινῇ συμφέρον. Paul's language is very clear: μηδεὶς τὸ ἑαυτοῦ ζητείτω ἀλλὰ τὸ τοῦ ἑτέρου (10:24) and μὴ ζητῶν τὸ ἐμαυτοῦ σύμφορον ἀλλὰ τὸ τῶν πολλῶν, ἵνα σωθῶσιν (10:33). The common advantage is defined here, as throughout the letter, as that which "builds up" the community (10:23),[483] specifically love (8:1; 13:5). In 12:7 Paul will connect the appeal to the common advantage with the body metaphor for the political organism, another *topos* which is often combined with this one in ancient texts.[484]

In line with his rhetorical strategy of appeal to himself as the positive example for imitation, Paul presents himself as the one who "doesn't seek his own advantage." This kind of self-representation also has many counterparts in political literature. It is the definition of the sound advisor, the one who is not guided by self or sectarian interest, who thus has the right to call others to do the same.[485]

---

alism has not been recognized by exegetes, who have concentrated solely on the specific application of the principles in 10:24, 33 to the issue of idol meat consumption. But once again, Paul has subordinated the specific issue of controversy to what he considers the most serious overarching problem, divisiveness itself. The closest exegetes have come to this interpretation, that "seeking the advantage of the many" is a common response to factionalism in antiquity, is that the exegetical tradition has picked up one political text from Wettstein (2.144) and carried it along in the notes to commentaries, but without integrating it into the exegesis (Weiss, *Korintherbrief*, 267 n. 4; Conzelmann, 179 n. 40). That text is Arist. *Eth. Nic.* 8.10.2: "A tyrant studies his own advantage, a king that of his subjects" [ὁ μὲν γὰρ τύραννος τὸ ἑαυτῷ συμφέρον σκοπεῖ, ὁ δὲ βασιλεὺς τὸ τῶν ἀρχομένων]. This text (cf. Pl. *Resp.* 1.342E; 347D; for a parallel from the Imperial period see Dio Chrys. *Or.* 3.39) reflects the consequences for political leadership of the commonplace that "the common good" must be the focal point of any concordant community. Robertson-Plummer, 225 cited Joseph. *BJ* 4.320 as a parallel to 10:23, a passage in the encomium on Ananus: πρὸ τῶν ἰδίων λυσιτελῶν τὸ κοινῇ συμφέρον τιθέμενος. But they do not note that Ananus is presented by Joseph. as the very opposite of a factionalist (this line continues καὶ περὶ παντὸς ποιούμενος τὴν εἰρήνην)!

483 See above on the building metaphor for concord.

484 See Dio Chrys. *Or.* 3.106, where he first describes one's friends as extra arms and legs for one's body and then says "he can converse with all the world and accomplish every undertaking, since those who wish him well are saying and doing everything that is in his interest" [συμφέροντα]. For another particularly good example, see Plut. *Arat.* 24.5, quoted above. To substantiate this rhetorical connection, see Vollenweider, 229–30, on the philosophical coherence of Paul's appeals with congruent elements of the Stoic system: "Mit der Stoa rekurriert er auf *Ordnungsstrukturen*, wie sie in Konvention, Gesellschaft und Kosmos zum Ausdruck kommen . . . Zeigt sich Paulus im Bezug auf das *Sympheron* (1 Kor 6,12; 10,23; 12,7) deutlich vom stoischen Ordnungsdenken beeinflusst, so ist dasselbe auch im Bild des *Leibes* für die Gemeindeorganisation (12,12ff; vgl 10,17) handgreiflich zu fassen . . . Wichtiger als die genetische Verbindung ist aber die Paulus und die Stoiker zusammenschliessende strukturelle Analogie, *Freiheit im Kontext eines Ordnungsgefüges zu orten.* Im *Leib Christi* als der Gestalt der neuen Schöpfung gewinnt die *Agape* . . . geschichtliche Konkretion. Freiheit zeichnet sich noch stärker als in der Stoa durch eine gemeinschaftsbezogene, d. h. *ekklesiologische* Signatur aus" (emph. original). Vollenweider regards Paul's argument as a response to a more general "enthusiasm" (similar to the Cynics [pp. 94–95, 229]), where I stress its particular applicability, both in Greco-Roman antiquity generally and in 1 Cor, to the problem of factionalism.

485 The sterotyped nature of this appeal is shown by the sample *prooimion* to a deliberative speech in *Rh. Al.* 29.1436b: "I think it superfluous for me to tell you that I am a loyal citizen, that

. . . but I myself should be ashamed if, while offering counsel to others [συμβουλεύων], I should be negligent of their interests and look to my own advantage [τὸ ἐμαυτῷ συμφέρον] instead of putting myself altogether beyond the reach of both the personal benefits [αἱ ὠφέλειαι] and all other considerations and advising the best course of action.[486]

Therefore, it is clear that in 10:23–11:1 Paul once again shows himself to be a non-factionalist,[487] one who seeks the common interest, and he calls upon the Corinthians to imitate him, as he Christ,[488] and end their divisions. Thus even in taking up the specific problem of idol meats, Paul's overriding concern is once again the unity of the church body. That the terms and images used here essentially counter the problem of factionalism is shown also by the phrase πάντα πᾶσιν ἀρέσκω, "I please all in all things." This is the exact opposite of one who "gives offense" (10:32),[489] which is what the Corinthian partisan contenders do to one another.

(4) "Pleasing Everyone" – the Description of the Non-Factionalist

There was much discussion in Greco-Roman antiquity, especially in political contexts, over whether one could "please everyone."[490] This phrase smacks of the same "political opportunism"[491] as "I have been all things to all people" in

---

you have often been led by my advice to take an advantageous line of action [συμφέρον], and that I show myself true to my public duties [τὰ κοινά] and more ready to sacrifice part of my interests [τὰ ἴδια] than to profit [ὠφελεῖν] at the public expense." See also Dem. *Prooem.* 6; 35.3; 53; Dion. Hal. *Ant. Rom.* 10.51.1, 3; 11.9.3 (a political principle inherited from the ancestors).

486 Isoc. *Ep.* 6.14 (a deliberative letter). Of many other examples, see Pl. *Resp.* 1.342E; Dem. *Or.* 15.15; *Ep.* 1.10; Polyb. 1.70.1; Cic. *Off.* 1.25.85; *Leg. Man.* 24.71; Dio Chrys. *Or.* 34.7; 38.9. Plutarch says that the good statesman must at least "appear to be influenced only by the public advantage" [συμφέρον] (*Mor.* 813B; cf. *Crass.* 15.2; *Cic.* 13.1).

487 On the connection of the common advantage with social relations, see Plutarch's description of Aratus: ". . . ever making a regard for the public weal [τὸ κοινῇ συμφέρον] determine his enmity or his friendship" (*Arat.* 10.1). See also Cicero's exhortation not to be a factionalist but instead to "further the interests of all" (*ut omnibus consultat*) (*Off.* 1.25.86).

488 Who died for the others (8:11). Christ is also presented as the non-fractious example in Phil 2 (Sampley, 66–68; Johnson, *Writings*, 344–45) and *1 Clem.* 16.1–17 (termed a ὑπογραμμός; see also Wengst, 117).

489 The equivalence was noted by Senft, 139. See Cicero's version of this: "In short, I avoid hurting anyone's feelings" (*Att.* 1.19).

490 Dio Chrysostom begins one of his speeches on concord by admitting, "though I am aware that I cannot please even all the citizens of Prusa" [οὐδὲ . . . πολίτας ἅπαντας ἀρέσαι] (*Or.* 41.2). In another speech he admits "it is my desire to please you in every way possible" [ἐγὼ βουλόμενος ὑμῖν ἀρέσκειν πάντα τρόπον] (*Or.* 47.18). In 35.1, with false humility, Dio states: "For I know . . . that I myself am not sufficiently well equipped to satisfy you by my eloquence" [ὑμῖν ἀρέσαι λέγων] (on the false modesty *topos* see Betz, *Der Apostel Paulus*, 64). See also Isoc. *Or.* 8.5 on orators who seek not what will be advantageous to the state, but how to "please" [ἀρέσκειν] the audience.

491 Exegetes have been swift to save Paul from this potential charge. ". . . it is not a case of opportunism, but of devotion and service in terms of his apostleship" (Conzelmann, 179). That is truly Paul's point, but we miss the vehemence of his appeal if we do not recognize precisely

9:22. Many thought that political reality is such that it is downright absurd to even try to please everyone:

Bion believes it impossible to please the crowd [τοῖς πολλοῖς ἀρέσκειν] except by turning into a cake or a jar of Thasian wine – foolishly so believing, in my opinion. For often at a dinner of only ten guests the cake does not please everybody [οὐδὲ ... ἤρεσε πᾶσιν], but, on the contrary, one calls it stale, another hot, and another too sweet.[492]

The connection between "pleasing everyone" and factionalism in Greco-Roman political texts is very clear. One who tries to "please everyone" is the opposite of the factionalist,[493] who pleases only those with whom they have united interests.[494] Isocrates knows this principle well: "For in the absence of a common ground of interest [μὴ κοινοῦ δὲ τοῦ συμφέροντος ὄντος] I do not see how I could please both sides [ἀμφοτέροις ἀρέσκειν]."[495] "Pleasing everyone" was not always negatively perceived (though pleasing "the crowd" was), as long as it is done for good motives.[496] Of great importance to this study is that it is a political

---

how opportunistic this appeal was regarded to be in ancient politics! Paul self-consciously uses these exaggerated phrases to demonstrate again that the Christian has left this-worldly standards behind. Even ancient exegetes saw the danger of this rhetorical strategy. See Theodoret's defense of Paul as a flatterer on πάντα πᾶσιν ἀρέσκω in 10:33: 'Αλλὰ τοῦτο κολάκων ἴδιον. ἀλλὰ τὸ ἑξῆς λεγόμενον οὐ τῶν τοιούτων. Μὴ ζητῶν τὸ ἐμαυτοῦ συμφέρον, ἀλλὰ τὸ τῶν πολλῶν κτλ. Οἱ δὲ κόλακες οὐ τὸ ἀλλότριον συμφέρον, ἀλλὰ τὸ οἰκεῖον ζητοῦσι (*1 Cor.* 10:33 [*PG* 82.309]).

492 Dio Chrys. *Or.* 66.27. In one of his speeches on concord, with apt political realism, Dio urges the leaders not to try to please everyone. "And yet if someone should tell pilots that they should seek in every way to please [ἀρέσκειν] their passengers, and that when applauded by them they should steer the ship in whatever way those passengers desired, it would take no great storm to overturn their ship" (*Or.* 34.32).

493 For example, Theramenes was accused of being a buskin [κόθορνος], a boot which could be worn on either foot. In his reply he acknowledged: "I try to fit both parties [ὡς ἀμφοτέροις πειρώμενον ἁρμόττειν]," and rebutted, "But for the man who *pleases* neither party [ὅστις δὲ μηδετέροις ἀρέσκει], – what in the name of the gods should we call him?" (Xen. *Hell.* 2.3.47; cf. 2.3.15; Plut. *Mor.* 824B; the figure of Theramenes thus becomes proverbial for one who does not join factions, or who tries to join them all). The extreme opposite is "those who cannot even please themselves" [οἵγε οὐδὲ αὐτοὶ ἑαυτοῖς ἀρέσκονται] (M. Ant. 3.4.4).

494 Paul also connects the two, "interests" and "pleasing all" in 10:33.

495 *Ep.* 6.3. See the same sentiment in Dem. *Ep.* 3.27: "For although it is impossible for one who recommends policies [συμβουλεύειν] and administers the commonwealth to please everyone [πᾶσιν ἀρέσκειν], yet if a man, actuated by loyalty, has at heart the same interests as the people [ταὐτὰ τῷ δήμῳ τις φρονῇ], he has a right to security. Otherwise you will teach everyone to serve the interests of others rather than those of the people and to shun recognition for doing any of those things that are to your advantage [συμφέρον]." The first part of this passage (without comment or reference to the connection with συμφέρον below) was cited already by Heinrici, *Korinther*, 320. This passage is especially significant because it is within a deliberative letter.

496 See Demosthenes' extolling of his lover's popularity in the *Erotic Essay*: "While the other lads think it one of the impossible things to please men of every type [τοῖς ἁπάντων τρόποις ἀρέσκειν] you have so surpassed these as to have risen superior to all the difficult and troublesome people ... you succeed in pleasing them all exceedingly [πᾶσι καθ' ὑπερβολὴν

topos that one must please others in order to maintain peace and stability.[497] While Paul's use of this caricatured *topos* of a political conciliator in reference to himself probably enjoys no small dose of self-irony (for the Corinthians knew well what a controversial figure he was in some circles [9:2]), its perfect correspondence with the problem of factionalism is undeniable.

What we have seen is that Paul's juxtaposition of the epithets "not seeking my own advantage" and "being pleasing to all in every way" are rooted in political contexts, and are exact counterparts to the actions of the factionalist.[498] The party member, unlike Paul, seeks his or her own advantage, and pleases his or her own group without concern for the larger social community. Clearly in 10:23–11:1 the factionalism at Corinth is still the main issue with which Paul directly contends.

5. *1 Corinthians 11*

a) Divisive Customs at Corinth

In 11:2–16 Paul presents an argument on the specific topic of hairstyle of men and women in worship. There is division within the community on this issue

---

ἀρέσκειν]. And this is a most unmistakable proof of your goodness" (*Or.* 61.19). See Cass. Dio's description of Maecenas: "This also was a supreme proof of Maecenas' excellence, that he not only made himself liked by Augustus ... but also pleased everybody else" [τοῖς ἄλλοις πᾶσιν ἠρέσκετο] (55.7.4). Thus ἀρέσκειν can be used in the sense of "be popular" (Plut. *Crass.* 3.2; *Alc.* 13.3; cf. App. *BCiv.* 3.8.57 where Julius Caesar is described as μάλιστα ὑπεραρέσκων). But often such "pleasing" is suspect. The adjective ἄρεσκος, "pleasing," mostly means "obsequious" (LSJ, 238), as in Arist. *Eth. Nic.* 9.10.6 (see also Betz, *Galatians*, 55 n. 112). Important in this connection is Theophrastus' description of the character of ἀρέσκεια: "when he is called to help settle a dispute, his desire is to please the opposite party [ἀρέσκειν ἀλλὰ καὶ τῷ ἀντιδίκῳ] as well as the friend he stands for, so that he may be thought impartial [ἵνα κοινός τις εἶναι δοκῇ]" (*Char.* 5).

497 See the political advice of Bias contained in his popular song as recounted by Diogenes Laertius: "Find favor with all the citizens [ἀστοῖσιν ἄρεσκε πᾶσιν] ... in whatever state you dwell" (D. L. 1.85). Platonic *Epistle* 4 contains the same commonplace: "do not forget that successful action depends on pleasing people [διὰ τοῦ ἀρέσκειν τοῖς ἀνθρώποις]" (*Ep.* 4.321B). The connection between pleasing and divisiveness is made concretely also in one of the pieces of Isocrates' political advice: "to be affable, you must not be quarrelsome [δύσερις], nor hard to please [δυσάρεστος], nor always determined to have your own way [φιλόνικος]" (*Or.* 1.31).

498 For another Pauline formulation of the connection between being pleasing to others, advantage and building up the community, see Rom 15:2: ... καὶ μὴ ἑαυτοῖς ἀρέσκειν. ἕκαστος ἡμῶν τῷ πλησίον ἀρεσκέτω εἰς τὸ ἀγαθὸν πρὸς οἰκοδομήν. See also Ign. *Trall.* 2.3 (also in a discussion of unity in the church; Schoedel, 140). It should be noted that the term ἀρέσκειν originally meant "to make peace" or "to reconcile" (W. Foerster, "ἀρέσκω κτλ.," *TDNT* 1.455–57, 455; see also there for the wider use of the term in the NT and ECL).

(termed a συνήθεια, "custom,"[499] by Paul in 11:16), very possibly ethnically based.[500] Perhaps hairstyle was emblematic of one's "party-affiliation" at Corinth, as elsewhere in ancient (and modern) history.[501] Paul himself explicitly links this controversy with the factionalism in the community in 11:16: "and if someone thinks to be contentious[502] [φιλόνεικος] ...." This adjective, and especially its abstract noun φιλονεικία,[503] is one of the most common terms used in Greek literature to refer to party strife.[504] In fact, this is its exact meaning according to the Stoic definition: "Contentiousness [φιλονεικία] is a craving or desire connected with partisanship [αἵρεσις[505]]."[506] Dio Chrysostom says that φθόνος and φιλονικία lead to στάσις.[507] Plutarch associates φιλονεικία with φθόνος and ζῆλος,[508] and elsewhere with ἔρις,[509] both terms which Paul uses to describe the party-strife at Corinth (1:11; 3:3). In a catalogue of "civil ills" Dio Chrysostom lists φθόνος, πλεονεξία, φιλονεικία, τοῦ ζητεῖν ἕκαστον αὔξειν

---

499 Cf. 8:7. On how customs can cause unity or division, see Josephus' boast about the ὁμόνοια of the Jews based upon identity of religious belief and habits and customs [τῷ βίῳ δὲ καὶ τοῖς ἔθεσι μηδὲν ἀλλήλων διαφέρειν] (*Ap.* 2.179, cf. 2.258; and 1 Macc 1:41 f. on Antiochus Epiphanes' strategy to make εἷς λαός through uniformity of customs). In appeals for concord see Dio Chrys. *Or.* 38.22–23: "In fact you have no quarrel as to your customs [τὰ ἔθη] either. Yet, though all these things afford no occasion for hostility, but rather for friendship and concord [φιλία καὶ ὁμόνοια], still we fight."

500 On Jewish and Greek hairstyles, see Conzelmann, 184–86 for bibliography and B. Kötting, "Haar," *RAC* 98 (1984) 176–203, col. 195, who writes that Paul is here adopting the Jewish custom to the new situation (also Grant, "Hellenistic Elements," 61). Note too that style of dress was among the uniformities which Alexander sought for the sake of the unity of his new universal polity (Plut. *Mor.* 329D, quoted in n. 305 above).

501 Hairstyle in antiquity could be a sign of social status, i. e., free, slave, rich, poor (Kötting, 186, 193), of allegiance to particular philosophers (190–91; e. g., D. L. 6.31, 33), and of participation in religious cults (194). See also Dio's description of the Rhodians' tell-tale characteristics which includes the way they trim their hair (*Or.* 31.162). In his *Or.* 39.3, a discourse urging unity, "wearing the same costume" is called a sign of concord.

502 BAGD, 860 (also the weaker "quarrelsome," without justification). LSJ, 1937: "fond of victory, contentious."

503 It can also be spelled φιλονικία, retaining the same meaning (LSJ, 1938). For φιλονεικία in the NT, see Luke 22:24; in ECL see especially *1 Clem.* 45.1.

504 See, e. g., Lys. 33.4; Thuc. 8.76.1; Dem. *Ep.* 3.1; *Prooem.* 31.1, 2; Isoc. *Or.* 4.19; Polyb. 4.36.2; Plut. *Num.* 3.2; *Cam.* 40.1; Cass. Dio 56.40.4. In Hellenistic Judaism see Joseph. *Vit.* 100, 254; and Philo, *Abr.* 210, on Abraham as reconciler of τὰ φιλόνεικα καὶ ταραχώδη καὶ στασιαστικά. Chrys. describes the Corinthian law battles in 6:1–11 as φιλονεικία (*hom. in I Cor.* 16.3 [*PG* 61.134]; cf. Argumentum 2 [61.11]).

505 A term which Paul uses in 11:19 (see the discussion below).

506 D. L. 7.113.

507 *Or.* 38.43; cf. 6.31; Joseph. *Ap.* 2.243; *BJ* 1.460; Plut. *Cam.* 40.1; Aristid. *Or.* 23.60; Julian. *Ep.* 40.425; the verb φιλονεικεῖν in Dion. Hal. *Ant. Rom.* 7.36.1; 38.2; Aristid. *Or.* 23.60.

508 *Mor.* 86C; *Pel. and Marc.* 1.6.

509 *Mor.* 92B. φιλονεικία and ἔρις are commonly used as a pair (see Dio Chrys. *Or.* 39.8; 48.6; Aristid. *Or.* 23.28; 26.97; 27.44; also in exegesis of 1 Cor, Thdt. *1. Cor.* 1:10 [*PG* 82.232]). See also Philo, *Leg. Gai.* 52 on Gaius as φίλερις καὶ φιλόνεικος.

ἑαυτόν, καὶ τὴν πατρίδα καὶ τὸ κοινῇ συμφέρον ἐάσαντα.[510] There is, consequently, a connection between Paul's use of the term φιλόνεικος in 11:16 and ζητεῖν τὸ ἐμαυτοῦ συμφέρον in 10:33 (cf. 10:24).[511] Both are descriptions of the factionalist behavior which Paul combats throughout 1 Corinthians. Whatever the specific issue of hairstyles and headgear involves, 11:16 demonstrates again Paul's focus on the participation of that quarrel in the overall divisiveness affecting the Corinthian community, and reflects once again his rhetorical strategy of response which above all else urges unity and an end to the contentiousness which threatens it.

b) Divisions and "Coming Together"

In 11:17–19 Paul focuses in on a new set of topics related to a particular aspect of the party strife within the community – the ways in which these party battles manifest themselves when the church comes together ἐν ἐκκλησίᾳ. "When you come together in assembly I hear that there are σχίσματα among you" (11:18). As we have noted, these σχίσματα, "factions," are the subject of the πρόθεσις to the argument in 1:10. Because the factions within the church community have been Paul's major concern throughout the letter to this point, there is nothing odd about their "reappearance" here. They have never stopped being of prime importance in the argument.[512] But particularly those who advocate partition theories of 1 Corinthians consider 11:18 to demonstrate Paul ignorant of the very fact he had cited from Chloe's people's report in 1:11, which is judged an impossible occurrence within the same letter.[513] What is often neglected is that in 11:18 the emphasis is not on the fact that σχίσματα exist (i. e., a repeat of the message of 1:11),[514] but on the fact that these σχίσματα are in evidence *when you*

510 *Or.* 34.19 ("envy, greed, contentiousness, the striving in each case to promote one's own welfare at the expense of both one's native land and the commonweal").

511 Cf. Dem. *Prooem.* 12.2: τὰς ἰδίας ἀνελόντας φιλονικίας τὸ κοινῇ βέλτιστον σκοπεῖσθαι (and Dion. Hal. *Ant. Rom.* 11.18.3).

512 Origen's conflation of 11:18 and 1:11 is interesting at this point: Κατὰ τὰς ἀρχὰς τῆς ἐπιστολῆς ἔφασκεν Ἀκούω σχίσματα ἐν ὑμῖν ὑπάρχειν. ἕκαστος γὰρ ὑμῶν, φησί, λέγει Ἐγὼ μέν εἰμι Παύλου, ἐγὼ δὲ Ἀπολλώ . . . (*comm. in I Cor.* 89.1–2 [p. 50]).

513 Weiss, *Korintherbrief*, 278; Héring, 113; Schmithals, *Gnosticism*, 90–91; Schenk, 226–29; Vielhauer, *Geschichte*, 141; Marxsen, 87–88; Schenke-Fischer, 93; Senft, 18; Klauck, *Herrenmahl*, 288–89 (for further references see Hurd, 80 n. 4; this is disputed as grounds for partition by Sellin, "Hauptprobleme," 2974). Schmithals's statement deserves quotation because it has been so influential: "If one compares this passage [11:18ff.] with Paul's statements in 1 Cor 1–4, it is simply inconceivable that both attitudes toward disputes could come from the same epistle. In 1 Cor 11:18–19 it is obviously a case of a *first* reference to disputes within the community" (p. 90, emphasis original).

514 Against the objection that a report of received information (ἀκούω) should not come so late in a letter, see *1 Clem.* 47.7 (αὕτη ἡ ἀκοὴ . . . εἰς ἡμᾶς ἐχώρησεν). For other examples which show that the reason for this reference to oral information later in a discourse is due to rhetorical, not chronological reasons, see Dio Chrys. *Or.* 38.24; Aristid. *Or.* 24.57.

come together in assembly.[515] Thus far in his letter Paul has dealt with manifestations of community disunity and strife which take place in the arena of relations among Christians within the larger social context of the city of Corinth, and specifically in relation to non-believers. He now concentrates on the ways in which the cliques affect community life when these contentious persons come face to face ἐν ἐκκλησίᾳ.[516]

What of Paul's statement "and in part I believe it"? Does this show Paul less informed or less indignant than he had been in 1:11?[517] I argue, no. This is a rhetorical statement.[518] Paul has already demonstrated that factions exist within the church – certainly he believes (knows!) that when all are in the same place this social fragmentation exhibits itself most strongly. Even this type of mock disbelief about political divisiveness is not unparalleled in ancient literature. In one of his two orations on concord Aelius Aristides makes a very similar statement:

> But when the present situation, which is much more terrible, if it is possible to say so, was reported to me, that you distrust one another, have taken sides, and are involved in disturbances unsuited to you, *I did not know whether I should credit it or disbelieve it* [οὔθ' ὅπως χρὴ πιστεύειν οὔθ' ὅπως ἀπιστεῖν εἶχον].[519] For the messengers were your fellow citizens and otherwise trustworthy men, and yet it was impossible to accept easily such accusations against you.[520]

Aristides' disbelief at hearing that factions had resurfaced at Rhodes is no more real than Paul's in 1 Cor 11:18. Both know all too well that contentiousness fills

---

515 So correctly Wolff, 79 (with further references).

516 Cf. Dion. Hal. *Ant. Rom.* 8.73.1, where the factionalism of plebs and patricians is said to manifest itself ἐν ταῖς στασιαζούσαις ἐκκλησίαις. See the conclusion of Hurd, 82: "All that can be said at this point is that 11.18 indicates either that Paul is discussing another facet of the same information which lies behind 1.10–4.21, this time in relation to the conduct of worship (11.1–16; 12.1–14.40), or that Paul discusses here another example of the Corinthians' general tendency toward factiousness."

517 See n. 513 above for the scholars who argue this.

518 Note Allo's suggestion that μέρος τι might be a litotes (270). See also Theissen's reading of it (p. 163): "He carefully puts some distance between himself and his informants, as if only partly willing to credit what he has heard, but perhaps that is mere diplomacy."

519 Compare the exact same formulation in Dem. *Ep.* 4.1: "I am at a loss to know whether I ought to believe or disbelieve the news that Menecrates brings me [Οὔθ' ὅπως χρὴ πιστεύειν οἷς ἀπήγγελλέ μοι Μενεκράτης, οὔθ' ὅπως ἀπιστεῖν ἔχω]." But the letter of course proceeds on the basis that this news (in this instance not about factions) *is* true.

520 *Or.* 24.3. See also Dio Chrys. *Or.* 48.5 (a deliberative speech urging concord): "As for myself, I swear to you by all the gods, I was indeed violently angry when a certain person said to me, 'Bring reconciliation to the city,' and I was vexed at him. For may I never see the day when you need reconciliation." Note also the previous paragraph in the same speech: "For now, in case you have a quarrel with any city – which may none of the gods bring to pass!" (48.4; cf. Polyb. 4.32.9–10). For other examples of such mock disbelief see Dem. *Ep.* 5.1; Dio Chrys. *Or.* 38.24.

the communities which they address, but their mock disbelief[521] is another way of implying that by such divisions these communities have fallen way short of the norm of concord which is to be expected of them. 1 Cor 11:19 may be a further, more honest and weary concession by Paul to the realities of political life – the inevitability of factions.[522]

The term αἵρεσις is used in 11:19, apparently synonymously with σχίσματα.[523] The agraphon in Justin (*Dial.* 35.3) pairs these two terms. In Gal 5:20 Paul puts αἵρεσις alongside other powerful terms for strife: ἔρις, ζῆλος, θυμοί, ἐριθεῖα, διχοστασίαι and φθόνοι. In general usage αἵρεσις means a "sect, party, school";[524] in 1 Cor 11:19 the even stronger sense of "dissension, a faction"[525] is commonly recognized. Regardless of whether or not there is a slight nuance of difference between the terms αἵρεσις and σχίσμα, it is obvious that Paul uses them in tandem in 1 Cor 11:18–19 to refer to the same specific problem of factionalism at Corinth.[526]

In 11:20 Paul uses the phrase συνέρχεσθαι ἐπὶ τὸ αὐτό, which is repeated elsewhere in 1 Corinthians (14:23; cf. 7:5 *v. l.*[527]). This phrase is usually translated "to come together at the same place,"[528] thus synonymous with "to come

[521] This is the rhetorical figure *dissimulation*/εἰρωνεία: "when we say one thing and mean another . . . Hesitation may be expressed between two alternatives" (Quint. *Inst.* 9.1.29–30; see also 6.3.85; Cic. *Orat.* 40.137; *De Or.* 3.203).

[522] See Theissen, 168 (and already Robertson-Plummer, 239–40 who argue that the δόκιμοι are those who "[come] to the front in the interests of unity, or [keep] aloof from all divisions"); also Barth, 63–64; Wolff, 80. See too the later use of this text in Or. *Cels.* 3.12 to justify the existence of factions in Christianity (note his description: ἀναγκαίως ὑπέστησαν οὐ πάντως διὰ τὰς στάσεις καὶ τὸ φιλόνεικον αἱρέσεις ἀλλὰ διὰ τὸ σπουδάζειν συνιέναι τὰ χριστιανισμοῦ καὶ τῶν φιλολόγων πλείονας [Borret, SC 136.36]).

[523] With Barrett, *First Corinthians*, 261; Conzelmann, 194; Wolff, 79; differently Heinrici, *Korinther*, 152. On the different nuances of the two terms, see H. Schlier, "αἱρέομαι κτλ.," *TDNT* 1.180–85, 183 (who still identifies them with the σχίσματα of 1:10) and M. Meinertz, "Σχίσμα und αἵρεσις im Neuen Testament," *BZ* n. s. 1 (1957) 114–18. For early Christian usage see Rohde, 217–33; M. Simon, "From Greek Hairesis to Christian Heresy," in *Early Christian Literature and the Classical Intellectual Tradition:* In honorem *Robert M. Grant*, ed. W. R. Schoedel and R. L. Wilken, Théologie Historique 54 (Paris: Editions Beauchesne, 1979) 101–16; and H. von Staden, "Hairesis and Heresy: The Case of the *haireseis iatrikai*," in *Jewish and Christian Self-Definition*. Vol. 3: *Self-Definition in the Greco-Roman World*, ed. B. F. Meyer and E. P. Sanders (Philadelphia: Fortress, 1982) 76–100.

[524] BAGD, 23–24, as in D. S. 2.29.6; Joseph. *Vit.* 10, 12; *AJ* 13.171 (of the Pharisees and Sadducees). In the NT for the term meaning "party" see Acts 5:17; 15:5; 24:4, 14; 26:5; 28:22 (cf. αἱρετικός in Titus 3:10).

[525] BAGD, 24 (also Gal 5:20). For other ancient uses, see D. S. 12.66.2 (quoted in n. 37 above); Polyb. 4.35.10; D. L. 7.113 (quoted above); App. *BCiv.* 5.1.2; 5.8.70 (see LSJ, 41: "faction, party").

[526] So Merklein, 175 on the grounds of semantic parallelism. For the equation with φιλόνεικος see Thdt. *1 Cor.* 11:19: Αἱρέσεις τὰς φιλονεικίας λέγει [*PG* 82.316].

[527] The verb συνέρχεσθαι alone is used in 1 Cor 11:17, 18, 33, 34 and 14:26, and only here in the Pauline corpus (noted by Wolff, 78; Klauck, *Herrenmahl*, 287, cf. 347, who nonetheless puts them in different letters).

[528] Weiss, *Korintherbrief*, 280; Barrett, *First Corinthians*, 259, 262; Conzelmann, 192.

together in assembly/church" in 11:18. But in fact the entire phrase is a *double entendre*. The prepositional phrase ἐπὶ τὸ αὐτό means literally "to the same place," but also metaphorically "together."[529] The dual meaning of this phrase is used by Paul to stress the irony of the Corinthians' factionalism – when they come together "in the same place" they are not "together" (i. e., united).[530]

The verb συνέρχεσθαι also has both literal and metaphorical meanings applicable to Paul's argument for Corinthian unity. One meaning of συνέρχεσθαι, "to assemble,"[531] has predominated in discussion of 1 Cor 11:20. Surprisingly, the exegetical tradition has not recognized the fact that the verb συνέρχεσθαι can also often mean "to be united or banded together,"[532] and is thus the perfect opposite of σχίσματα, "factions." As with the verb καταρτίζειν in 1:10,[533] συνέρχεσθαι has the literal meaning of re-joining things which belong together,[534] which is then metaphorically applied to human relationships. In fact συνέρχεσθαι is commonly used in Greek literature to refer to the unification of divided persons or groups.[535] Aristotle uses the verb συνέρχεσθαι to refer to the process of

---

529 BAGD s. v. ἐπί III.ζ (as in the same letter at 7:5). See Luke 17:35; Acts 1:15; 2:1, 44 *v. l.* In Acts 4:26 ἐπὶ τὸ αὐτό translates the Hebrew יחד, meaning "unitedness" or adverbially "together" (BDB, 403), as is done in LXX (see, e. g., Ps 132:1). See also Schoedel, 213 on ἐπὶ τὸ αὐτὸ γενομένοι in Ignatius.

530 See Robertson-Plummer, 240: "In any case, ἐπὶ τὸ αὐτό emphasizes the contrast between the external union and the internal dissension."

531 BAGD, 788; LSJ, 1712. The phrase συνέρχεσθαι εἰς τὴν ἐκκλησίαν, "to come together into the assembly" is commonly used, predominantly in political contexts (Dio Chrys. *Or.* 13.19; 50.8; Plut. *Alc.* 33.2; *Ages.* 27.3; 32.4; the verb is also used for cultic assemblies, as in Pl. *Leg.* 6.767C, συνελθεῖν εἰς ἓν ἱερόν; Men. Rh. 1.366 [Russell-Wilson, 72]). The technical meaning of this phrase, now applied to the church at Corinth, was noted by E. Käsemann, "The Pauline Doctrine of the Lord's Supper," *Essays on New Testament Themes*, trans. W.J. Montague, SBT 41 (Naperville, IL: Allenson, 1964) 108–35: "συνέρχεσθαι is the acknowledged term in antiquity for the official assembling of the *demos*, the 'people,' and has obviously been taken over to denote the assembling of the Christian community for worship at the Lord's Supper" (p. 119, who is followed by Klauck, *Herrenmahl*, 287–88, *Hausgemeinde*, 36, who stresses that this is when the smaller housechurches in a city all come together).

532 LSJ, 1712, a lexical possibility not noted in BAGD, *TDNT*, *EWNT* or the commentaries (e. g., Heinrici, *Korinther*, 339; Weiss, *Korintherbrief*, 279; Barrett, *First Corinthians*, 260–61; Conzelmann, 193 n. 10).

533 See the discussion above in this chapter.

534 Dion. Hal. *Ant. Rom.* 14.11.5; Plut. *Mor.* 306E, of a fissure in the earth; the first century medical writer Meges, of a fistula (*Corpus Medicorum Graecorum*, vol. 6, pt. 2, vol. 1, fr. 44.21.10 [LSJ, 1712]).

535 See Hdt. 4.120 (συνελθούσας ἐς τὠυτό); Xen. *Ath.* 2.2 (συνελθοῦσιν εἰς ταὐτό); and very commonly in later writers, sometimes playing off of the two meanings (see Dion. Hal. *Ant. Rom.* 10.60.5; Joseph. *BJ* 5.278 [of two factions]; Plut. *Mor.* 481C [quoted above]; *Publ.* 1.1; *Arat.* 41.1; *Cam.* 40.2; *Galb.* 28.1; *Pomp.* 47.2). It is also used of persons or groups previously separate but now united (e. g., Hdt. 1.202; Pl. *Leg.* 3.680E; *Chrm.* 157E; Dem. *Or.* 18.19; Arist. *Pol.* 1.1.7; Dion. Hal. *Ant. Rom.* 11.47.2; 20.17.1; Philo, *Spec. Leg.* 2.119; Dio Chrys. *Or.* 39.1; Plut. *Caes.* 27.2; *Cic.* 33.3; M. Ant. 8.34, alongside the metaphor of the parts of the body). See especially Arist. *Pol.* 3.4.3, where συνέρχεσθαι is linked with both τὸ κοινῇ

human beings joining together to form a society: "men formed the community and came together [ἐκοινώνησαν καὶ συνῆλθον]."[536] The verb συνέρχεσθαι plays an important role in Aristotle's political theory, as it is the description of the formation of social cohesion which results in the organic unity of the community.

For it is possible that the many, though not individually good men, yet when they come together [συνελθόντας] may be better [βελτίους],[537] not individually but collectively ... for where there are many, each individual, it may be argued, has some portion of virtue and wisdom, and when they have come together [συνελθόντας], just as the multitude becomes a single man with many feet and many hands and many senses, so also it becomes one personality as regards the moral and intellectual faculties.[538]

This passage from Aristotle shows the place which the verb συνέρχεσθαι played in political theory. The following text from Aelius Aristides, an excerpt from one of his two deliberative speeches urging concord, shows that the term (with a very similar prepositional phrase) could also be used to urge unity on divided factions.

Your ancestors, who had formerly been divided [μεμερισμένοι][539] into three parts, united [συνελθεῖν εἰς ταὐτό] because of their trust in one another and settled in one city formed from all the others.[540]

The verb συνέρχεσθαι was therefore commonly used in a wide range of Greek literature[541] to refer to reconciliation of divided persons,[542] just as we speak today of people "coming together again."

συμφέρον and ἡ πολιτικὴ κοινωνία (cf. Aristid. *Or.* 46.11, of things συνελθεῖν εἰς ταὐτόν, and in one of his speeches on concord, εἰς ταὐτὸν ἐλθεῖν, 24.27). The etymology of the *Comitium* in Rome, according to Plutarch, hinges on this word play: "The place where these agreements were made is to this day called *Comitium*, from the Roman word *'conire'* or *'coire', to come together* [συνελθεῖν]" (*Rom.* 19.7; cf. Cass. Dio 1.5.7).

536 *Pol.* 3.5.10; see also 3.6.7; 6.5.2.

537 Cf. 1 Cor 11:17, "not for the better [κρεῖσσον] but for the worse do you come together!" For the common cultic application see Men. Rh. 1.366 [Russell-Wilson, 72–73], on the elements of encomia for assemblies or festivals, the fourth of which is "cause: whether people expect to be happier or better [βελτίοι]."

538 Pol. 3.6.4. Both the theme of "coming together" and the body metaphor for the community, joined here, are used by Paul in his argument in 1 Corinthians (see below on chap. 12).

539 As noted above, the same term, μερίζεσθαι, is used by Paul in 1 Cor 1:13 to describe the Corinthian factionalism.

540 *Or.* 24.49; cf. *Or.* 23.13 (συνελθόντα εἰς ταυτὸν οἰκεῖν). Compare Philo, *Spec. Leg.* 2.119.

541 The Latin equivalent, *uno in loco convenire* "to come together, be united" (OLD, 438), is used metaphorically by Cicero to refer to an alliance between the factions opposed to Caesar (*Div.* 2.24.52). The related phrase *unum in locum congregare* is also used for unification of factions (e. g., Cic. *Inv. Rhet.* 1.2; *De Or.* 1.8.33; *Phil.* 14.15; see OLD, 405). For the Greek equivalent also used in this way, see Dion. Hal. *Ant. Rom.* 6.85.1, the speech of Menenius Agrippa

With this background in mind, the meaning of 1 Cor 11:17 becomes entirely clear. Paul says "you do not come together for the better [i. e., in the good sense of the term!], but for the worse." This statement emphasizes the irony that the Corinthians "come together" but there is no true reunification of their divided cliques (in fact they may be exacerbated in such close quarters). Paul here plays off of the two meanings of the verb συνέρχεσθαι, which can mean simply "to assemble"[543] or, as we have emphasized, also "to be united."[544] Paul chides the Corinthians because they do the former (badly), but not the latter.[545] In the larger compositional unit 11:17–14:40 Paul continues his plea to the Corinthians to "come together" in the positive sense.

Connected with Paul's disappointment about the factionalism manifest in community worship is his presupposition (common in antiquity) that common sacrifices and religious rituals should be unifying forces, as he has already urged in 10:14–22. He continues that line of argument in 11:17–34, here demonstrating in concrete terms the social consequences of the cultic unity argued for in that section.[546] Isocrates makes a similar argument for unity based on common cultic participation in the *Panegyricus*:

> Now the founders of our great festivals are justly praised for handing down [παρέδοσαν] to us a custom by which, having proclaimed a truce and resolved our pending quarrels, we come together in one place [συνελθεῖν εἰς ταὐτόν] where, as we make our prayers and sacrifices in common [εὐχὰς καὶ θυσίας κοινὰς ποιησαμένους], we are reminded of the kinship [συγγενεία] which exists among us.[547]

Like Isocrates, Paul calls the Corinthians to unity in their common παραδόσεις, "traditions."[548] It is a scandal that their fundamental sacrament of unity should be instead a setting for singularity[549] and divisiveness (11:21–22), particularly

---

[συνάγει ἡμᾶς εἰς τὸ αὐτό]; Dio Chrys. *Or.* 40.30; Plut. *Alc.* 13.4; *Arist.* 7.3, and *1 Clem.* 34:7 [ἐν ὁμονοίᾳ ἐπὶ τὸ αὐτὸ συναχθέντες τῇ συνειδήσει, ὡς ἐξ ἑνὸς στόματος βοήσωμεν].

542 In ECL, see *Barn.* 4:10 where this phrase is connected with "seeking the common advantage" [ἐπὶ τὸ αὐτὸ συνερχόμενοι συνζητεῖτε περὶ τοῦ κοινῇ συμφέροντος] and the noun συνέλευσις in *1 Clem.* 20:10 [τά τε ἐλάχιστα τῶν ζώων τὰς συνελεύσεις αὐτῶν ἐν ὁμονοίᾳ καὶ εἰρήνῃ ποιοῦνται]. See also Thdt. *1 Cor.* 14.26 [*PG* 82.345].

543 And, we must stress, even that meaning is itself inherently political, coming as it does from the politics of the πόλις.

544 The same contrast between the literal action of "coming together" and true political unity is made by Aristotle, using the term συνέρχεσθαι (*Pol.* 3.5.13).

545 Cf. 11:34, ἵνα μὴ εἰς κρίμα συνέρχησθε (cf. the warnings in 3:17; 10:12). This must be taken into account everywhere the term is used in 1 Corinthians (see above).

546 See also Prümm, 211.

547 *Or.* 4.43.

548 11:2, 23; 15:1. Even in retelling the traditions Paul stresses and interprets some elements which contribute to a proper understanding of the horizontal dimension of the sacrament – my body *for you*, and the new *covenant* (Klauck, "Eucharistie," 7).

549 See esp. 11:21. ἕκαστος always stresses the individual and not the community (e. g., 1:12; 3:13; 7:2, 24; 12:7; 14:26). It is no coincidence that this term occurs twenty-three times in

between rich and poor,[550] a common cause of factionalism.[551] The problem is "not discerning the body" (11:29), another word play on both the sacramental body of Christ and the ecclesiastical body of Christ, the church.[552] The Corinthian factions, especially as manifested in their cultic assemblies, are an affront to Christ.[553]

6. 1 Corinthians 12. The Body Metaphor for Unity

Chapter 12 contains the full exposition of the famous "Body of Christ" image for the church which was introduced in the argument at 6:15 (cf. 1:13). It has long been acknowledged by New Testament scholars that the metaphor of the body for the society or state was extremely common in ancient political literature, and must have influenced Paul's Christian formulation of it in 1 Cor 12.[554] The well-known fable of Menenius Agrippa,[555] for example, tells of a revolt of

---

1 Corinthians (Allo, lv), more than any other NT book by far. The term ἕτερος is also common (3:4; 4:6; 6:1; 10:24, 29; 12:9, 10; 14:17, 21; 15:40).

550 On drunkenness as a cause of factionalism (cf. 11:21), see N. R. E. Fisher, "Drink, *Hubris* and the Promotion of Harmony in Sparta," *Classical Sparta. Techniques Behind Her Success*, ed. A. Powell (Norman: University of Oklahoma Press, 1988) 26–50. This commonplace is also known in Hellenistic Judaism: καὶ πολέμου δὲ καὶ ταραχῆς αἴτιος γένεται ὁ οἶνος (*T.Jud.* 16.4), as already in the HB (Prov 23:29).

551 Theissen, 69–174; Welborn, "Discord," 93–101 (and the discussion above).

552 So Klauck, "Eucharistie," 7: "v. 29 enthält verdeckt auch einen Fingerzeig auf die Gemeinde als Leib Christi" (also Barton, 241–42).

553 Likewise the revolution of the Gracchi was accused of being not only a crime against the state, but also "ein Verbrechen gegen die Religion, gegen die *dea Concordia*" (Skard, 81, citing Plut. *C. Gracch.* 17.6 and Aug. *Civ. dei* 3.25). For Paul, factions within the Christian community are an offense against Christ (1:13; 8:12; 10:22) and against the God of peace (7:15; 14:33).

554 Many classical references are collected in Heinrici, *Sendschreiben*, 396–97 n. 1; Sanders, *Hellénisme*, 78–93 (who overestimates the difference between 1 Cor 12 and *1 Clem.* 49); Lietzmann-Kümmel, 62–63; E. Best, *One Body in Christ. A Study in the Relationship of the Church to Christ in the Epistles of the Apostle Paul* (London: S.P.C.K., 1955) 83–114, 215–25; Wolff, 110–12; Klauck, *Herrenmahl*, 337–40 (see also his conclusion on p. 339: "Es kann nicht zweifelhaft sein, dass hier ein wichtiger Einflussbereich liegt. Für 1 Kor 12, wo die Parallelen bis ins Detail reichen, liegt das auf der Hand"). For a summary of opinions on the background of the body metaphor (Stoic, gnostic, Hebrew Bible, Christian eucharist, rabbinic speculation on the body of Adam), and references to the extensive bibliography on the subject, see J. Hainz, *Ekklesia. Strukturen paulinischer Gemeinde-Theologie und Gemeinde-Ordnung*, Biblische Untersuchungen 9 (Regensburg: Pustet, 1972), esp. 260 n. 2; Klauck, *Herrenmahl*, 337–43, and the very thorough summation and assessment in Jewett, *Anthropological Terms*, 201–87 (who takes the body image to be Paul's response to "gnostic individualism"). The political background to the image (one attestation of which is in Stoic thought) is most likely here, as we shall see. For Stoic parallels see J. N. Sevenster, *Paul and Seneca* (Leiden: Brill, 1961) 167–74 (who tends to overly stress the dissimilarities between Paul and the Stoics; and more recently Vollenweider, 58–60, who connects the body metaphor with the Stoic concept of true freedom).

555 Livy 2.32.12–33.1; cf. Dion. Hal. *Ant. Rom.* 6.86 (with the appeal to τὸ κοινῇ συμφέρον [6.85.1; cf. 86.2, 4]); 6.54.2; Plut. *Cor.* 6.2–4.

the hands, mouth and teeth against the belly, thus weakening the whole body.[556] This fable[557] is told in a deliberative speech urging the plebs to cease from *seditio* and work for *concordia*. The metaphor of the body for the political organism, both being made up of interdependent μέλη, is very old, going back at least as far as the 5th and 4th centuries B.C.E., as Momigliano has shown.[558] The metaphor is also frequently attested in Greco-Roman literature well into the 2nd century C.E.,[559] as also in Hellenistic Jewish texts.[560] The body metaphor is so often used to combat discord that Aelius Aristides can complain to the divided Rhodians:

> Rather you destroy it [your city] by your actions, while you honor it with your speech, and you await the victory of Cleomenes the Laconian,[561] who chopped up his [own] body,[562] beginning with his feet.

He then moves the analogy forward:

> And how shall you differ from the women who tore Pentheus apart [διασπάσασθαι], when you yourselves have torn apart with your own hands the body of the city which you all share?[563]

The concomitant metaphor of στάσις as a disease in the body (and the statesman as doctor) is also, as is well known, very frequent.[564]

---

556 See the important article by W. Nestle, "Die Fabel des Menenius Agrippa," *Klio* 21 (1927) 350–60. In his discussion of the fable of Menenius Agrippa, Momigliano stated unequivocally: "1 Corinthians 12:12–27 is the striking translation into Christian terms" (117 n. 4). See also Skard, 88–91 on the fable and classical parallels (for his designation of the genre of the speech see ch. II n. 203).

557 Dio Chrysostom records a similar fable of Aesop: "Something must have happened to you like what Aesop says happened to the eyes. They believed themselves to be the most important organs of the body, and yet they observed that it was the mouth that got the benefit of most things and in particular of honey, the sweetest thing of all. So they were angry and even found fault with their owner. But when he placed in them some of the honey, they smarted and wept and thought it a stinging, unpleasant substance" (*Or.* 33.16).

558 Momigliano, 117–19 and notes, with references. For an analysis of Plato's use of the metaphor, see N. R. Murphy, *The Interpretation of Plato's Republic* (Oxford: Clarendon, 1960) 68–86.

559 Dio Chrys. *Or.* 1.32; 3.104–107; 17.19. 50.3; in his speeches on concord see especially 34.23, where he urges the Tarsans to consider the linen workers as μέρος αὐτῶν; 38.12; 39.5; Aristid. *Or.* 17.9; 23.31; 24.18; 26.43; Plut. *Mor.* 426A; *Cic.* 14.4; cf. Lucan, *BCiv.* 5.35–37; 10.416–17 (*Latium sic scindere corpus dis placitum*); Sen. *Ep.* 95.52, (*membra sumus corporis magni*); M. Ant. 8.34; 9.23.

560 Philo, *Spec. Leg.* 3.131; Joseph. *BJ* 1.507; 2.264; 4.406–407; 5.277–79.

561 Hdt. 6.75.3.

562 τὸ αὑτοῦ σῶμα (revising Behr's translation at this point).

563 Aristid. *Or.* 24.38–39, αὐτοὶ τὸ κοινὸν σῶμα τῆς πόλεως ταῖς ὑμετέραις αὐτῶν χερσὶ διασπάσησθε. Compare 1 Cor 1:13; 3:17, and in general the term σχίσματα, "tears." See also Lucan *BCiv.* 1.3: "I tell how an imperial people turned their victorious right hands against their own vitals [*in sua . . . viscera*]."

564 E. g., Pl. *Resp.* 5.470C-D; *Rh.Al.* 1.1422b; Cic. *Phil.* 8.6.15; Joseph. *BJ* 2.11; Dio Chrys. *Or.* 34.17–20, 36; 38.11; 41.9; 48.8–13; 49.13; Plut. *Mor.* 815B; 824A; Aristid. *Or.* 23.31, 58–61;

Paul's uniformity of use of this metaphor with ancient political writers applies even to the details.[565] Many writers who employ the body metaphor for the political unit use the same body parts which Paul uses as examples in 1 Cor 12:14–17 – the hands and feet,[566] and the eyes and ears.[567] Plutarch cites the same four together (adding the nostrils[568]), as does Dio Chrysostom, who also adds the tongue.[569] Even Paul's argument in 12:22 that "the parts of the body thought to be weak are *necessary* [ἀναγκαῖα]" is consistent with other versions of the body metaphor.[570] Paul's rhetorical use of personification of the parts of the body speaking is also paralleled.[571]

This consistency in detail in the body metaphor by Paul is combined with a remarkable correspondence between 1 Cor 12 and ancient political theory in its application. An important component of Paul's argument in 1 Cor 12 is the differentiation of personal gifts and contributions within the community.[572] This is one of the most common applications of the body metaphor for the state in antiquity.[573] The appeal to the apportionment and employment of gifts and

---

24.11, 16. In the NT see esp. Jas 4:1, where πόλεμοι and μάχαι come ἐκ τῶν ἡδονῶν ὑμῶν τῶν στρατευομένων ἐν τοῖς μέλεσιν ὑμῶν (cf. Hort, 89).

565 See Klauck, *Herrenmahl*, 339 (quoted in n. 554 above).

566 Arist. *Pol.* 3.6.4; Xen. *Mem.* 2.3.19 (hands, feet, eyes); Plut. *Mor.* 797E.

567 Dio Chrys. *Or.* 1.32; 39.5.

568 *Mor.* 478D.

569 *Or.* 3.104–107; cf. Jas 3:5f.

570 See Plut. *Mor.* 478D: "And yet the illustration of such common use by brothers Nature has placed at no great distance from us; on the contrary, in the body itself she has contrived to make most of *the necessary parts* [ἀναγκαῖα] double and brothers and twins: hands, feet, ears, nostrils." Paul (and Plutarch) may also be playing on the Latin *necessarius* used of relatives and friends, as in Acts 10:24; Dion. Hal. *Ant. Rom.* 8.47.3; BAGD, 52; or even partisans, as in Caes. *BCiv* 1.3. The "weaker parts" are probably so named by Paul in accordance with his general argument throughout the epistle on the strong and the weak (1:25–27; 8:7–13; 9:22; 15:43 [so also Prümm, 211], but cf. the parallels listed in Klauck, *Herrenmahl*, 339 n. 36 and Plut. *Arat.* 24.5). On honorable/dishonorable members (12:23–24) compare M. Ant. 10.13 and Ps-Sall. *Rep.* 9.2.

571 12:15–16; cf. Dion. Hal. *Ant. Rom.* 6.86.2.

572 12:4–11, 24–30; also Rom 12:3–8. This was well emphasized by Grant, *Augustus to Constantine*, 55. For the sociological need for such role differentiation for community stability, see Schreiber, 77–90; 139–46. In the argument of 1 Cor see previously 3:5, in regard to Paul and Apollos.

573 See Pl. *Resp.* 2.370A-B and note even the similarity in phrasing to 1 Cor 12:4–11: φύσεται ἕκαστος οὐ πάνυ ὅμοιος ἑκάστῳ, ἀλλὰ διφέρων τὴν φύσιν, ἄλλος ἐπ' ἄλλου πρᾶξιν (cf. 1.352E-354). See also Arist. *Pol.* 2.1.4; 3.2.2; *Eth. Nic.* 1.7.11; Dion. Hal. *Ant. Rom.* 6.86.4, the speech of Menenius Agrippa [ὧν ἕκαστον ἰδίαν τινὰ τῷ κοινῷ χρείαν ὥσπερ τὰ μέλη τῷ σώματι παρέχεται]; cf. 86.1; Plut. *Mor.* 812C-E; 819C; M. Ant. 9.42.5; cf. Philostr. *VA* 4.8–9 (a speech on concord, which shows that this appeal to recognize the differentiation of gifts in combatting factionalism can even stand apart from the body metaphor, for there it is combined with the ship analogy). That this is the use which Paul makes of the body metaphor has been recognized by NT scholars, such as Meeks, *Urban Christians*, 90: "Paul uses the image of the body as pagan moralists do, to suggest that differentiation does not compromise but promotes the unity of the group, so long as the interdependence of the members is recognized."

functions for the common advantage [συμφέρον] of the body Paul also shares with ancient political and philosophical writers.[574] The sharing of one spirit or soul is paralleled in ancient political texts as well.[575] The body metaphor as applied by Paul to the factionalism at Corinth is also combined with an awareness of the political theory of the mixed constitution. In the Pauline reformulation of it, it was God who "mixed [συγκεράννυμι] the body"[576] to ensure the proper combination of elements. Just as in Greek political theory the mixed constitution seeks to preserve ὁμόνοια, Paul instructs the Corinthians that the wide individual diversity in the community was carefully blended by God with this very purpose in view: ἵνα μὴ ᾖ σχίσμα ἐν τῷ σώματι (12:25).[577]

We may thus conclude that in 1 Cor 12 Paul is extending a common political metaphor to the Corinthian situation,[578] Christianizing it by transference to "the body of Christ" and the same spirit [πνεῦμα].[579] This conclusion is not in itself

---

[574] 12:7. Compare Epict. *Diss.* 2.10.4–5: "What, then, is the profession of a citizen [πολίτης]? To treat nothing as a matter of private profit [ἰδίᾳ συμφέρον], not to plan about anything as though he were a detached unit, but to act like the foot or the hand [πούς, χείρ], which, if they had the faculty of reason to understand the constitution of nature, would never exercise choice or desire in any other way but by reference to the whole." Of many other examples see Xen. *Mem.* 2.3.19; Plut. *Arat.* 24.5 (a text which combines the body metaphor, its members, the weak members, the same breath shared, and the common advantage); Dio Chrys. *Or.* 39.5 (quoted in next note); Cic. *Off.* 3.5.21–23; Sen. *De ira* 2.31.7; M. Ant. 10.6.1–2; 10.20 (for other references see Klauck, *Herrenmahl*, 339 n. 36). See also the conclusion reached by Jaeger, *Early Christianity*, 115 n. 10: "This distinction between the special virtue or excellence for the common good is also found in Greek political thought from the very beginning; it was natural that this problem should be raised again in the early Christian community as soon as serious differences arose."

[575] 12:4–12. Compare Dio Chrys. *Or.* 39.5: "When a city has concord, as many citizens as there are, so many are the eyes with which to see that city's interest [συμφέρον], so many the ears with which to hear, so many the tongues to give advice, so many minds concerned in its behalf; why it is just as if some god had made a single soul [μία ψυχή] for so great and populous a city." See also Plut. *Mor.* 96E. This concept has parallels in friendship language – friends share one soul (D. L. 5.20, of Aristotle; G. Stählin, "φίλος κτλ.," *TDNT* 9. 146–71; 152). Note also Paul's use of σύμψυχοι in Phil 2:2, in a list of unity *topoi.*

[576] 12:24. On this verb as a technical term, and on the mixed constitution, see the full discussion above on 1 Cor 5. The same connection is made with the noun σύγκρασις in *1 Clem.* 37.4–5, which explicitly cites 1 Cor 12 (on which see Jaeger, *Early Christianity*, 23, quoted in n. 306 above).

[577] Cf. Theodore of Mopsuestia's exegesis of 12:27: . . . ταύτην ἀναγκαίως σώζετε τὴν συμφωνίαν, μηδεμίαν ἀπὸ τῆς διαφορᾶς τῶν χαρισμάτων δεχόμενοι φιλονεικίας παρείσδυσιν (Staab, 191).

[578] As argued especially by Grant, "Hellenistic Elements," 63 and *Augustus to Constantine*, 55–56.

[579] See Meeks, *Urban Christians*, 166: "So, too, when Paul was faced with incipient divisions, jealousies, and spiritual elitism among the charismatics at Corinth, it was to the unity of the Lord (Christ) and the Spirit that he appealed." See the development of this idea in *1 Clem.* 37:5 (πάντα συνπνεῖ) and Jaeger, *Early Christianity*, 22–23: "Both the idea of *synkrasis* and *sympnoia* belong together and reveal their origin from the same philosophical source, which was concerned with the problem of political harmony in human society."

new, but its implications have not always been sufficiently considered. The metaphor of the body for the social organism in ancient political texts, as we have seen, *is used to combat factionalism*,[580] both in Greco-Roman texts and even in Hellenistic Jewish appropriation of it.[581] That is the same application which Paul makes of his transferred metaphor "the body of Christ."[582] There can be no doubt that 1 Cor 12, which employs the most common *topos* in ancient literature for unity,[583] is a straightforward response to the factionalism within the church community,[584] which is the subject of the entire letter.[585] In fact, the body of

---

580 Grant, *Augustus to Constantine*, 56: "The pictures of the church and the state as bodies politic are much the same, as is the goal of unity in such bodies." See also Malherbe, *Moral Exhortation*, 147: "Together with the images of an army, a ship, and the human body, these were the most popular illustrations used in the topos on unity." The connection was made also by Jaeger: "In his first Letter to the Corinthians the apostle told the disunited community the story of the members of the human body which fought against each other, each of them believing itself to be the most honorable and the most essential. The tale is ultimately derived from an old exhortation to unity, λόγος προτρεπτικὸς πρὸς ὁμόνοιαν" ("Tyrtaeus," 140). The connection of the body metaphor with factionalism is surprisingly made only in passing by Klauck, *Herrenmahl*, 334.

581 All the texts in n. 560 above connect the body metaphor with strife and factions.

582 We have pointed to 12:25 as an explicit statement of this intention, to which we should add the statement in 12:12: Καθάπερ γὰρ τὸ σῶμα ἕν ἐστιν καὶ μέλη πολλὰ ἔχει, πάντα δὲ τὰ μέλη τοῦ σώματος πολλὰ ὄντα ἕν ἐστιν σῶμα, οὕτως καὶ ὁ Χριστός (and Rom 12:5, οὕτως οἱ πολλοὶ ἓν σῶμα ἐσμεν ἐν Χριστῷ, τὸ δὲ καθ' εἷς ἀλλήλων μέλη). This has been noted by some NT scholars, not so much on the basis of ancient parallels as on the clear progression of the argument in 1 Corinthians (see Heinrici, *Sendschreiben*, 397–98; Prümm, 211; Barrett, *First Corinthians*, 287–89 [but see p. 23, where Barrett too readily equates this *prescriptive* image with an accurate *description* of the church community]; Belleville, 26–27). For the opposite point of view, see Hurd, 92: "it may well have been part of Paul's purpose in writing 1 Cor. 12 and 13 to encourage the reunion of the Corinthians on the basis of their membership in Christ and in Christian love for one another, but Paul nowhere in this section referred to their dissensions directly." Nothing could be farther from the truth!

583 As a further proof of this, we observe that Paul is followed by the author of *1 Clement*, who shows by his own use of the *topos* (37–38) that this is how he understood 1 Cor. Chrys. also understands 1 Cor 12 to be a direct exhortation to cease from factionalism. In his homily he explicitly takes up the question of the application of the metaphor here, and responds with appropriate political language of description: Ἵνα γὰρ μή τις λέγῃ, Τί πρὸς ἡμᾶς τοῦ σώματος τὸ ὑπόδειγμα; . . . προάγων αὐτὸ τοῖς καθ' ἡμᾶς πράγμασι, καὶ δεικνὺς ὅτι τοσαύτην ἀπὸ γνώμης ὀφείλομεν ἔχειν ὁμόνοιαν, ὅσην ἀπὸ φύσεως ἐκεῖνα . . . Εἰ δὲ τὸ ἡμέτερον οὐ δεῖ στασιάζειν σῶμα, πολλῷ μᾶλλον τὸ τοῦ Χριστοῦ (*hom. in I Cor.* 32.1 [*PG* 61.263]).

584 This conclusion, made here on literary-historical and rhetorical grounds, receives confirmation from recent social scientific studies which point to the unifying force and intention of the body metaphor (see J. H. Neyrey, "Body Language in 1 Corinthians: The Use of Anthropological Models for Understanding Paul and His Opponents," *Semeia* 35 [1986] 129–70: "the body at Corinth, then, is threatened with its most dangerous pollutant, division and disunity" [p. 157]; Schreiber, 19 esp. n. 77; Meeks, *Urban Christians*, 89–90).

585 A very strong argument against most of the major partition theories of 1 Corinthians is that they assign 1 Cor 12 to a different letter from 1:10–4:21, which (alone, they think) discusses the problem of factionalism (J. Weiss's later theory [*Earliest Christianity*, 2.340–41]; Schmithals, "Korintherbriefe," 265–68; Dinkler, "Korintherbriefe," 18; Héring, xiii-iv; Schenk, 223–29;

Christ image runs throughout 1 Corinthians, and is, alongside the metaphor of the building, the predominant image in Paul's extended argument for church unity.[586]

There are two other *topoi* for political unity in antiquity which Paul appropriately weaves into his allegory in 1 Cor 12 – the themes of co-suffering and co-rejoicing. The two parallel cola in 12:26 read: "if one member suffers, all the members co-suffer; if one member is glorified, all the members co-rejoice [συγχαίρειν]." These are standard ancient definitions of political unity and solidarity, rooted, as here by Paul, in the body metaphor for the community.[587] In an encomium on friendship Dio Chrysostom describes the consequences of friendly association in these same terms:

> For is that man not most blessed who has many bodies [σώματα] with which to be happy when he experiences a pleasure, many souls with which to rejoice [χαίρειν] when he is fortunate? And if glory [δόξα][588] be the high goal of the ambitious, he may achieve it through the eulogies of his friends.[589]

In direct contrast to these qualities of friendship and solidarity,[590] Isocrates describes a major symptom of the factionalism among the Greek states:

> . . . they are so far from feeling pity that they even rejoice [χαίρειν] more in each other's sorrows than in their own blessings.[591]

Therefore when Paul likewise argues that the members of the body rejoice and grieve together because they share the same interest (12:7) – the good of the

---

Senft, 17–19; Welborn, "Conciliatory Principle," 333). But 1 Cor 12, containing the stock response to factionalism in antiquity, is surely part of the same argument, the same letter.

[586] 6:12–20; 10:14–22; 11:29; cf. 1:13; see Friedrich, 250, 254 and Klauck, *Herrenmahl*, 333–34 for the extent and application of the references. See also Nock, *St. Paul*, 150–51: "In 1 Corinthians he constantly uses it [the body of Christ image], not as a figure of speech, but as a basis of arguments."

[587] E.g., Pl. *Resp.* 5.462B-E; Plut. *Sol.* 18.5.

[588] Cf. δοξάζεται in 1 Cor 12:26 (and τιμή in 12:23–24). On how the pursuit of glory and honor lead to factionalism, see above, n. 151. See also Paul's response to Corinthian glory-seekers, to seek the δόξα θεοῦ (10:31; cf. 4:10).

[589] *Or.* 3.108–109; cf. Aristid. *Or.* 23.29.

[590] See also the definition of a friend in Arist. *Eth. Nic.* 9.4.1, and the discussion of the related "co-living and co-dying" of friends in antiquity in G. Stählin, "'Um mitzusterben und mitzuleben.' Bemerkungen zu 2 Kor 7,3," *Neues Testament und christliche Existenz*, FS H. Braun, ed. H. D. Betz and L. Schottroff (Tübingen: Mohr/Siebeck, 1973) 503–21, esp. 508–13.

[591] *Or.* 4.168; cf. 1 Cor 13:6. See also the collection of *topoi* including co-suffering and co-rejoicing in Dio Chrys. *Or.* 38.43: ". . . the things which cause you pain – envy [φθόνος] and rivalry [φιλονικία] and the strife [στάσις] which is their outcome, your plotting against one another, your gloating over the misfortunes of your neighbors, your vexation at their good fortune – and, on the other hand, the introduction into your cities of their opposites – sharing [κοινωνία] in things which are good, unity of heart and mind [ὁμοφροσύνη], rejoicing [χαρά] of both peoples in the same things." Another example of this *topos* is provided by Dion. Hal. *Ant. Rom.* 11.22.6: δι' ἣν [στάσιν] ἔχαιρον ἑκάτεροι τοῖς ἀλλήλων κακοῖς.

community and not individual fulfillment – he employs another political *topos* for unity.[592] In chap. 13 Paul argues further that it is love which creates such unity of interest because "love does not seek its own advantage . . . it does not rejoice in injustice, but co-rejoices [συγχαίρειν] in the truth" (13:5–6). Paul was not the first to bring these *topoi* together in a quest for unity. This combination of love, the body metaphor, and co-suffering and co-rejoicing was understood already in Hellenistic Judaism, as evidenced by Philo:

> He commands all members of the nation to love [ἀγαπᾶν] the incomers, not only as friends and kinsfolk but as themselves both in body and soul: in bodily matters, by acting as far as may be for their common interest [ὡς οἷόν τε κοινοπραγοῦντας]; in mental by having the same griefs and joys [τὰ αὐτὰ λυπουμένους τε καὶ χαίροντας], so that they may seem to be the separate parts of a single living being which is compacted and unified by their fellowship in it [ὡς ἐν διαιρετοῖς μέρεσιν ἓν εἶναι ζῷον δοκεῖν, ἁρμοζομένης καὶ συμφυὲς ἀπεργαζομένης τῆς κατ' αὐτὸ κοινωνίας] (*Virt.* 103).

Investigation of the extent to which the argument in 1 Cor 12 employs the language and *topoi* used to describe party strife in antiquity also clarifies the full symbolic meaning of the somewhat unusual term κυβέρνησις in 12:28. This word, literally meaning "steersmanship," is usually translated "administration."[593] It has been correctly recognized that this abstract noun (and more often the corresponding agential noun κυβερνήτης), is a common metaphor for rulership in antiquity.[594] Yet another component of this image has not been sufficiently specified – the central place which the metaphor of the ship captain and his task to keep a ship afloat play in literature on factionalism and concord.[595] Dio Chrysostom uses this *topos*[596] often in his speeches on concord:

---

592 For other examples in speeches urging concord, see Dio Chrys. *Or.* 38.33; 41.13; 48.6; Aristid. *Or.* 23.35. See also Plutarch's definition of the good statesman in *Mor.* 823A: "sharing the griefs [συναλγεῖν] of those who fail and the joys [συγχαίρειν] of those who succeed," and later Lib. *Or.* 20.49. In his other letters Paul makes the same appeal in Rom 12:15–16, in a context in which the body metaphor and love figure predominantly: χαίρειν μετὰ χαιρόντων, κλαίειν μετὰ κλαιόντων. τὸ αὐτὸ εἰς ἀλλήλους φρονοῦντες (see also Phil 2:2, 17–18).

593 BAGD, 456; LSJ, 1004, "steering, pilotage," "metaph., government" (with reference to our text). The word is a *hapax legomenon* in the NT.

594 H. W. Beyer, "κυβέρνησις," *TDNT* 3.1035–37; Conzelmann, 215 n. 49; for the root of the image in classical Athens, see Edmunds, 1–20. For examples, see Pl. *Plt.* 297E; Philo, *Leg. Gai.* 49–50; 149; Plut. *Sol.* 14.4, 14; *Caes.* 28.4; 34.2; *Arat.* 38.3.

595 It was noted by E. Hilgert, *The Ship and Related Symbols in the New Testament* (Assen: van Gorcum, 1962) 25, with references to Greek and Latin sources. A classic formulation is Pl. *Resp.* 6.488A: οἱ ναῦται στασιάζοντες πρὸς ἀλλήλους περὶ τῆς κυβερνήσεως (see also Polyb. 6.44.3–7). In the Imperial period, see Iambl. *Ep. Concerning Concord* (ὑφ' ἑνὸς μὲν γάρ τις νοήματος καὶ μιᾶς γνώμης κυβερνώμενος ὁμονοεῖ πρὸς ἑαυτόν [Diels, *Vorsokr.* 2.356]); Cass. Dio 52.16 (and Reinhold, 186–87); Philostr. *VA* 4.8–9 (and other examples below). In ECL see Ign. *Pol.* 2.3 and Schoedel, 264.

596 On this as a *topos* in literature urging unity see Dio Chrys. *Or.* 34.16 ("For even if this comparison is made repeatedly, still it is your duty not on that account to disregard it"); also Malherbe, *Moral Exhortation*, 149 and Schoedel, 264 and notes.

For if, when a philosopher has taken a government in hand, he proves unable to produce a united city [ὁμονοοῦσα πόλις], this is indeed a shocking state of affairs, one admitting no escape, just as if a shipwright while sailing in a ship should fail to render the ship seaworthy, or as if a man who claimed to be a pilot [κυβερνήτης] should swerve toward the wave itself.[597]

The job of the sea captain is to keep the ship from tipping over and being destroyed by waves, analogous to στάσις demolishing a city.[598] Just as in a polity, on board ship cooperation of passengers and crew is essential to the survival of all.[599] Therefore, in choosing the term κυβέρνησις in 12:28, Paul calls on the "ship of state" image for the polity,[600] which resounds with implications for the unity of the church community. The Corinthians need to be "steered" wisely, and (perhaps more importantly) they must themselves be good, concordant passengers.[601] This is of course consonant with Paul's argument in 12:28–30 – there are different offices and functions within the community (cf. 12:4–11), and these are requisite for order. There cannot be anarchy in the ἐκκλησία (cf. 14:33). In 12:28–30 Paul sets out a hierarchical governance structure as another response to the divisions within the church, especially as manifested when they come together in worship. This governance structure[602] (see also below on 16:15–16) is another way in which Paul tries to insist on some order (cf. 14:40) and unity despite the differentiation of roles within the congregation.[603]

---

[597] *Or.* 48.14. Next in the same speech Dio takes up the *topos* of the builder and his building (see the discussion above).

[598] See above n. 228 on this as a *topos*.

[599] "Any ship which sails the sea with concord [ὁμόνοια] existing between the skipper [κυβερνήτης] and his crew not only is safe itself but also maintains in safety those on board [αὐτή τε σῴζεται καὶ σῴζει τοὺς ἐμπλέοντας]" (Dio Chrys. *Or.* 39.6).

[600] More cautiously, Hilgert, 128–9. This image of the ship for the church is fully understood and taken up in the church fathers (for references see Beyer, Hilgert and *LPGL* s. v. κυβερνάω, κυβέρνησις, κυβερνήτης).

[601] See Dio Chrys. *Or.* 34.22.

[602] Cf. Dion. Hal. *Ant. Rom.* 6.47.3, where in a time of στάσις some patricians argue that "while governing and administering the state was the duty of the patricians, the promoting of friendship and peace [φιλότης καὶ εἰρήνη] was the part of good men."

[603] This is made even more explicit in the Ephesians reformulation: Καὶ αὐτὸς ἔδωκεν τοὺς μὲν ἀποστόλους, τοὺς δὲ προφήτας, τοὺς δὲ εὐαγγελιστάς, τοὺς δὲ ποιμένας καὶ διδασκάλους, πρὸς τὸν καταρτισμὸν τῶν ἁγίων εἰς ἔργον διακονίας, εἰς οἰκοδομὴν τοῦ σώματος τοῦ Χριστοῦ (4:11–12). For this understanding of the argument see also Meeks, *Urban Christians*, 90.

7. 1 Corinthians 13. Love as the Antidote to Factionalism

Chapter 13 contains the famous "Encomium to Love." Indeed, the term ἀγάπη undeniably plays a crucial role throughout the argument of 1 Corinthians.[604] The noun ἀγάπη is rare in Greek literature,[605] but the verb ἀγαπᾶν is quite common. It has long been argued that the New Testament use of ἀγάπη owes much to the Septuagint.[606] We misunderstand the concept of ἀγάπη in 1 Corinthians if we think only of an inner emotion,[607] and do not take into account the political and social nature of ἀγαπᾶν in Greek literature.[608] In Hellenistic Judaism ἀγάπη especially comes to describe brotherly or neighborly love,[609] which in itself would make it an appropriate response to a divided church community. But that love in 1 Corinthians is indeed Paul's positive counterpart to Corinthian factionalism can be even more conclusively demonstrated from two additional lines of argument.

Especially important for our investigation is the connection made throughout Greco-Roman antiquity between love (in all of its various terms) and concord. As far back as Plato ἀγαπᾶν is considered the opposite of στάσις.[610] While praises

---

604 4:21; 8:1; 12:31b–14:1a; 16:14 (a restatement of the purpose of the letter), 24.

605 Lietzmann-Kümmel, 68; E. Stauffer, "ἀγαπάω κτλ.," *TDNT* 1.21–55, 37–38. The available evidence is collected and critiqued in O. Wischmeyer, "Vorkommen und Bedeutung von Agape in der ausserchristlichen Antike," *ZNW* 69 (1978) 212–38.

606 Wischmeyer, "Agape," 229–38; *idem, Weg*, 23–26. Even in the Hebrew Bible love [אהב] is in places a technical term for political allegiance and covenantal partnership (W. L. Moran, "The Ancient Near Eastern Background of the Love of God in Deuteronomy," *CBQ* 23 [1963] 77–87; see also D.J. McCarthy, *Treaty and Covenant*, AnBib 21A [Rome: Biblical Institute, 1981²], 43, 81, 160–61; M. Weinfeld, *Deuteronomy and the Deuteronomic School* [Oxford: Oxford University Press, 1972], 81; J. Bergman, A. D. Haldar and G. Wallis, *TDOT* 1.100–101; 110–16). See already C. Spicq, *Agapè dans le nouveau testament*, 3 vols. (Paris: Gabalda, 1958–59) 2.302: "C'est bien ainsi que les LXX comprenaient l'ἀγαπᾶν, unissant culte, obéissance et fidélité."

607 See, for example, Jaeger's differentiation of the appeals in 1 Cor 13 and *1 Clem.* 49, where he calls 1 Cor 13 an "emotional appeal to the *agapé* or charity" and *1 Clem.* 49 a lesson on "civic order in the Christian *politeia*" (*Early Christianity*, 18; cf. Sanders, *Hellénisme*, 93–108). See also n. 623 below for other reflections of Jaeger on 1 Cor 13 which are more congenial to our line of thought.

608 Investigation of the term ἀγάπη in the NT has been dominated until recently by Spicq, *Agapè* 2.9–305 (on Paul's use), who stressed the uniqueness of both the frequency and semantic meaning of the term in the NT. This perhaps theologically motivated position has been refuted in part by R. Joly, *Le vocabulaire chrétien de l'amour, est-il original?* (Brussells: Universitaires de Bruxelles, 1968), who demonstrated that ἀγαπᾶν was more frequently used than φιλεῖν already in classical writers (pp. 10–29), and that the two terms commonly have the same meaning (pp. 34–47). Joly does not, however, stress the specifically political uses of the term. For the extensive bibliography on ἀγάπη see Spicq, *Notes*, 1.27–30 and G. Schneider, *EWNT* 1.19–20.

609 Wischmeyer, "Agape," 236–37.

610 *Leg.* 3.678E. Aesch. *Eum.* 985 says that the antidote to στάσις is κοινοφιλεῖ (and common hate [καὶ στυγεῖν μιᾷ φρενί in 986]). See also later the Stoic Marcus Aurelius' description

of Ἔρως have been cited as possible formal parallels to 1 Cor 13,[611] it has not been sufficiently recognized that among the traditional characteristics of ἔρως is that it casts out strife and brings concord.[612] For Aristotle it is φιλία which promotes concord and is the proper antidote to factionalism.[613] A fragment of the Stoic Zeno also allies ἔρως with ὁμόνοια.[614] In Polybius' version of Philip's speech to his sons to seek concord with one another, he advises them that the remedy for discord is to love [στέργειν] one another.[615] In the poem *The Civil War* by the first century poet Lucan, a younger contemporary of Paul, the Latin counterpart *amor* is identified with *Concordia*.[616] Dio Chrysostom in his appeals for concord also defines φιλία as ὁμόνοια.[617] Love plays the fundamental role of combatting

---

of the unified associations of the animals (a *topos* for concord) as ἔρωτες, "love-associations" (M. Ant. 9.2).

611 The two texts often cited are Pl. *Symp.* 197C-D and Maximus of Tyre, *Diss.* 20.2 (see Spicq, 2.60–61; Conzelmann, 219–20; and the full discussion in chap. IV on the form of 1 Cor 13).

612 See Pl. *Symp.* 197C-D on Ἔρως as the one "who makes peace [εἰρήνη] among men, and a windless waveless main . . . He it is who casts alienation out, draws intimacy in; he brings us together in all such friendly gatherings as the present . . . kind giver of amity, giving no enmity [φιλόδωρος εὐμενείας, ἄδωρος δυσμενείας]."

613 "Moreover, friendship [φιλία] appears to be the bond of the state; and lawgivers seem to set more store by it than they do justice, for to promote concord, which seems akin to friendship [ἡ γὰρ ὁμόνοια ὅμοιόν τι τῇ φιλίᾳ ἔοικεν εἶναι], is their chief aim, while faction [στάσις], which is enmity [ἔχθρα], is what they are most anxious to banish" (*Eth.Nic.* 8.1.4; see also 9.6.2 [πολιτικὴ δὴ φιλία φαίνεται ἡ ὁμόνοια], and further references and discussion in Moulakis, 99–104; Tarn, *Alexander the Great*, 2.427–33). The same connection is expressed by Aristotle in the *Politics*: "For we think that friendship [φιλία] is the greatest blessing for the state, since it is the best safeguard against revolution [στασιάζειν]" (*Pol.* 2.1.16; see also the full context).

614 "Pontianus said that Zeno of Citium understood that Love [Ἔρως] was a god of friendship and freedom [φιλία καὶ ἐλευθερία], and even more a skilled provider of concord [ὁμόνοια], and of nothing else. Therefore also in the *Politeia* he said, 'Love [Ἔρως] is a god who is a co-worker [συνεργός] for the safety of the city'" (*SVF* 1.263, my trans.). The context of this fragment in Athenaeus, *Deip.* 13.561C continues: "But that others, also, who preceded Zeno in philosophic speculation know Eros as a holy being far removed from anything ignoble is clear from this, that in the public gymnasia he is enshrined along with Hermes and Heracles, the first presiding over eloquence, the second over physical strength; when these are united, friendship and concord [φιλία καὶ ὁμόνοια] are born, which in turn join in enhancing the noblest liberty [ἡ καλλίστη ἐλευθερία] for those who pursue the quest of them."

615 Polyb. 23.11.3; cf. Livy 40.8.

616 "Be present now, thou that embracest all things in an eternal bond, Harmony [*Concordia*], the preserver of the world and the blended universe! Be present, thou hallowed Love [*amor*] that unitests the world!" (*BCiv.* 4.189–91). See also Seneca's depiction of the body metaphor for the society: "As all the members of this body are in harmony with one another (*ut omnia inter se membra consentiunt*) because it is to the advantage (*interest*) of the whole that the individual members be unharmed, so mankind should spare the individual man, because all are born for a life of fellowship, and society can be kept unharmed only by the mutual protection and love (*amor*) of its parts" (*De ira* 2.31.7–8).

617 ἡ δὲ φιλία τί ἄλλο ἢ φίλων ὁμόνοια (Dio Chrys. *Or.* 38.15; cf. 48.2). Note also the union of ὁμόνοια and φιλαλληλία in the letter *P.Oxy.* 3057 (quoted in ch. II n. 210).

factionalism also in the writings of Plutarch.[618] Throughout the Greco-Roman world this commonplace is given expression in the extensive use of terms for love and friendship for political associations and alliances.[619]

Furthermore, we can establish the prevalence of this commonplace association of love and concord even closer to Paul, for it is found also in the writings of Hellenistic Judaism. Ps-Phocylides *Sent.* 219 coordinates love and concord: "Show love to your kinsmen and holy unanimity."[620] In 4 Maccabees the love of the seven brothers for one another issues forth in their archetypical concord:

> The ties of brotherly love [φιλανθρωπία], it is clear, are firmly set and never more firmly than among the seven brothers; for having been trained in the same Law and having disciplined themselves in the same virtues, and having been reared together in the life of righteousness, they loved one another all the more [μᾶλλον ἑαυτοὺς ἠγάπων]. Their common zeal for beauty and goodness strengthened their goodwill and concord for one another [ἡ πρὸς ἀλλήλους εὔνοια καὶ ὁμόνοια], and in conjunction with their piety made their brotherly love [φιλαδελφία] more ardent... How holy and harmonious the concord [συμφωνία] of the seven brothers for piety's sake![621]

---

618 See the conclusion of Wardman, 62–63: "Love, then, is a particular form of the harmony which Plutarch sees as one of the goods of the state... Thus the function of the 'politicus' is seen to depend on his own gentleness of character. His aim is to create a unified state, in which the citizens feel that the state as a whole is more important to them than their individual friends or enemies. An important means of achieving this is by means of *eros* as a social custom, since lovers and loved will act heroically for the good of the whole community." See also his full discussion on pp. 57–63, and the summary statement on p. 60: "[Plutarch] sees love as a force which can unify the state politically."

619 For ἀγάπη/ἀγαπάω see Polyb. 9.29.12; Plut. *Caes.* 5.2; *Pomp.* 65.1; *Dem.* 18.4; *Oth.* 4.1; Joseph. *BJ* 1.171, 172, 211; 2.359; cf. 1.240. For φιλία used of political alliances, see Dion. Hal. *Ant. Rom.* 3.29.4; 3.50.4; 4.49.1; 5.1.1; 5.26.3, 4; Joseph. *Vit.* 30, and also the common treaty formula περὶ τῆς εἰρήνης καὶ φιλίας (*Ant. Rom.* 5.34.4; 5.45.2; 6.95.1, etc.). For the verb φιλεῖν used of political association see, e. g., *Ant. Rom.* 8.32.5; 8.34.1–3; Dio Chrys. *Or.* 38.36. In Latin texts *amare* and *amor* (and *amicitia*) are similarly used to refer to political solidarity and unity. A good example is Cic. *Att.* 2.20.1 (*Pompeius amat nos carosque habet*). For discussion see Hellegouarc'h, 142–43, 146–47 with references. *Amicitia*, "friendship" (noun derived from *amare*, according to Cic. *Amic.* 8.26) is so widely agreed to refer to factional allegiances formed around common interests that P. A. Brunt has had to argue that it can also refer to "non-self-interested" friendships ("'Amicitia' in the Late Roman Republic," *Proceedings of the Cambridge Philological Society* 191 [1965] 1–20). On *amicitia* in Ciceronian party politics see also Taylor, 7–8 and notes with references to the extensive literature, and A. M. Fiske, "Hieronymus Ciceronianus," *TAPA* 96 (1965) 119–38 and the literature cited there, who argues that *amor=amicitia* in Jerome, following Cicero's usage (p. 129). Note also Kramer, 45: *Tertia vis vocis* ὁμόνοια *est haec: concors familiaritas in amore vel amicitia posita.*

620 Συγγενέσιν φιλότητα νέμοις ὁσίην θ' ὁμόνοιαν (trans. van der Horst, *OTP* 2.582).

621 4 Macc 13:23–26; 14:3; trans. H. C. Kee, *OTP* 2.558–59, with one alteration, translating ὁμόνοια in 13:25 with "concord" (cf. RSV, "harmony") for Kee's weaker "fellow feeling." Elsewhere the seven are described as a chorus, the standard Hellenistic *topos* for a concordant group (4 Macc 8:4; 13:8; 14:8; see n. 653 below).

Love and concord are also associated elsewhere in Hellenistic Judaism.[622] For Paul the term ἀγάπη has an important traditional Christian background, but its proper *application* in 1 Corinthians to the problem of factionalism and strife[623] is natural within the Greco-Roman world and Hellenistic Judaism, from which Paul probably made the connection. This interpretation is further confirmed by the earliest readers of 1 Cor 13, who readily understood ἀγάπη there to be a direct response to the Corinthians' factionalism.[624]

However, that concord and love are often paired in Greco-Roman antiquity and even Hellenistic Judaism does not in itself prove that that background is relevant to the interpretation of 1 Corinthians. This can however be demonstrated definitively by the role which ἀγάπη plays in Paul's continuous argument. That love is the principle of social cohesion by which Paul calls the Corinthians to unity[625] is clear from 8:1, "but love builds up."[626] "Building up," as we have seen, is the opposite of factionalism, which destroys. Love as described by Paul

---

[622] See Philo, *Virt.* 35 (quoted above n. 141); 103 (quoted above in the text); *Spec. Leg.* 1.70; cf. 1.52; Sir 25:1 (ὁμόνοια ἀδελφῶν, καὶ φιλία τῶν πλησίον); and *T.Jos.* 17.2–3: καὶ ὑμεῖς οὖν ἀγαπᾶτε ἀλλήλους καὶ ἐν μακροθυμίᾳ συγκρύπτετε ἀλλήλων τὰ ἐλαττώματα. τέρπεται γὰρ ὁ θεὸς ἐπὶ ὁμονοίᾳ ἀδελφῶν καὶ ἐπὶ προαιρέσει καρδίας εὐδοκιμούσης εἰς ἀγάπην (see Wischmeyer, "Agape," 215 n. 8 on the dispute over the date and provenience of this and the other *T. 12 Patr.*). See also *Sib. Or.* 3.373–80 (dated by J.J. Collins to shortly before the battle of Actium in 31 B.C.E; *OTP* 1.358), where ὁμόνοια is paired with στοργή, πίστις and φιλίη, among whose opposites are φθόνος, ὀργή, ἄνοια and ἔριδες. A similar such list is in the later Christian *Herm. Sim.* 9.15.2, in which Ὁμόνοια and Ἀγάπη stand side by side.

[623] In his "Tyrtaeus on True Arete" Jaeger referred to 1 Cor 13 as "the 'Hymn to Love,' which is also [like chap. 12] an answer to the problem raised by the strife in the Corinthian community" (p. 141). G. Bornkamm's debate with Jaeger ("Der köstlichere Weg [1 Kor 13]," *Das Ende des Gesetzes. Paulusstudien*, vol. 1, *Gesammelte Aufsätze* [Munich: Kaiser, 1961] 93–112; the English translation, "The More Excellent Way. 1 Corinthians 13," *Early Christian Experience*, trans. P.L. Hammer [Evanston/New York: Harper & Row, 1969] 180–90, does not contain those parts of the essay) suffers from a lack of attention to this connection of 1 Cor 13 to Corinthian factionalism.

[624] The Apostolic Fathers understood this well. *1 Clem.* 49:5 gives clear expression to the same political ideals already expressed by Paul in 1 Corinthians: ἀγάπη σχίσμα οὐκ ἔχει, ἀγάπη οὐ στασιάζει, ἀγάπη πάντα ποιεῖ ἐν ὁμονοίᾳ (see van Unnik, "Studies," 170, for his comment on this verse: "Zulke uitspraken staan niet in Paulus' 'Hooglied der liefde,' al kunnen ze er wel uit afgeleid worden"). Ignatius also promotes love as a remedy for strife (see *Smyrn.* 7; Schoedel, 241, and his overall comment: "Ignatius' use of the verb 'to love' confirms the fact that for him love is associated primarily with the unity of the group" [p. 26, with many other references]). This is how Chrys. understands love in his list of things which it would eradicate: φόνοι, μάχαι, πόλεμοι, στάσεις, ἁρπαγαί, πλεονεξίαι etc. (*hom. in I Cor.* 32.5 [*PG* 61.271]) (see also n. 631 below on his exegesis of 1 Cor 13). See also Theodore of Mopsuestia on 13:8–13: εἰκότως δὲ τὴν ἀγάπην μείζονά φησι, ἐπειδὴ διεστασίαζον πρὸς ἑαυτοὺς Κορίνθοι καὶ ζῆλον εἶχον καὶ ἔριδας, καὶ κίνδυνος ἦν σχισθῆναι τὴν ἐκκλησίαν [Staab, 192].

[625] Cf. the Pauline argument in Phil 2:2, with the phrase τὴν αὐτὴν ἀγάπην ἔχοντες, reminiscent of the phrases in 1 Cor 1:10, and also the contrast of ἀγάπη and ἐριθεία in Phil 1:16–17 (cf. 1:15; 2:3; on the overriding appeal for fellowship and unity in Phil, see Johnson, *Writings*, 340–48). In Rom 12–15 love plays the same role.

[626] Cf. Eph 4:16.

throughout 1 Corinthians, and notably in chap. 13, is the very specific constructive counterpart to the Corinthians' factionalism.[627] Tongues, prophecy and knowledge can be divisive[628] (13:1–3; cf. 14:2–5, 29–32; 8:1), but love unites.[629] This is shown decisively in the list of things which love is not (13:4–7): "it is not jealous, it does not put itself forward,[630] it is not puffed up,[631] it is not shameful,[632] it does not seek its own advantage,[633] it is not provoked,[634] it does not

---

627 So Calvin, 276: "But the main object is to show how necessary it [love] is for preserving the unity of the Church. And I have no doubt that Paul intended it to reprimand the Corinthians in an indirect way, by confronting them with a situation quite the reverse of their own, so that they might recognize their own faults by their contrast with what they saw."

628 καὶ τοῦτο [τὸ τῶν γλωσσῶν χάρισμα] αἴτιον σχίσματος αὐτοῖς ἐγένετο (Chrys. *hom. in I Cor.* 29.1 [*PG* 61.239]).

629 So Jaeger, "Tyrtaeus," 142: "The elevation of love is a fruit of the struggle for the building of the new Christian society; in the spirit of Tyrtaeus, Xenophanes and Plato, it could be said that it is the highest virtue, because it is a greater κοινὸν ἀγαθόν for the congregation than the gift of tongues and gnosis and even prophecy." This observation has been confirmed especially by our analysis of Paul's argument throughout 1 Corinthians for τὸ κοινῇ συμφέρον, which is explicitly connected with love (8:1; 10:23; 13:5).

630 περπερεύεται. The πέρπερος, "the braggart," causes "offense" (προσκόπτειν; Polyb. 32.2.5; 39.1.1–3; cf. 1 Cor 8:9; 10:32). On this term see also Cic. *Att.* 1.14.4; Epict. *Diss.* 2.1.34; 3.2.14; M. Ant. 5.5.4 (H. Braun, "περπερεύομαι," *TDNT* 6.93–95; BAGD, 653). The verb (or a compound) may be present (reconstructed) in the injunctions on assembly behavior in the text from the guild of Zeus Hypsistos (P.Lond. 2710, line 19; Roberts-Skeat-Nock, 54). Conzelmann, 224 n. 59 connects it with ζηλοῦν and φυσιοῦσθαι, to which we should add καυχᾶσθαι, and repeat that all three are manifestations of Corinthian party strife, with Braun, 94: "What Hellenism repudiates in περπερεύεσθαι from Polybius to Marcus Aurelius Antoninus is in essentials opposed in the NT too, namely, the aesthetic, rhetorical form of boasting which wounds others, causes unrest and discord, and represents unfounded presumption."

631 Ἡ γὰρ ἀγάπη οὐ ζηλοῖ, οὐ φυσιοῦται. Ὥστε πανταχόθεν τεῖχος αὐτοῖς ἀῤῥαγὲς περιέβαλε, καὶ πολύπλοκον ὁμόνοιαν ἀναιροῦσάν τε τὰ νοσήματα ἅπαντα, καὶ ἐντεῦθεν πάλιν ἰσχυροτέραν γινομένην (Chrys. *hom. in I Cor.* 34.1 [*PG* 61.285]). See his whole exegesis of 1 Cor 13, which regards each clause as a direct antidote, or proper medicine, for healing the Corinthians' disease, their factionalism (see 34.1 [61.286] and the summary statement: Ὁ γὰρ ἁλοὺς ἅπαξ ὑπὸ τῆς ἀγάπης, φιλονεικίας ἀπήλλακται, 34.1 [61.286]). Then follows in this homily a long description of all the factors which should contribute to ὁμόνοια (see esp. § 3-7). This is an important text which combines Hellenistic and Christian *topoi* for unity.

632 See Weiss's comment on 13:5: "Das folgende Doppelpar von Sätzen mag sich ebenfalls auf das Parteiwesen beziehen" (*Korintherbrief*, 316). For Paul ἔρις καὶ ζῆλος are the opposite of εὐσχημόνως περιπατεῖν (Rom 13:13).

633 This reading is to be preferred over τὸ μὴ ἑαυτῆς (A. Harnack, "Das hohe Lied des Apostels Paulus von der Liebe (I Kor. 13) und seine religionsgeschichtliche Bedeutung," *Sitzungsberichte der königlich preussischen Akademie der Wissenschaften* [Berlin: Königliche Akademie der Wissenschaften, 1911] 132–63, 145–46, who points to *1 Clem.* 48.6, καὶ ζητεῖν τὸ κοινωφελὲς πᾶσιν, καὶ μὴ τὸ ἑαυτοῦ). This reading receives further confirmation from our findings that indeed this is the very definition of the factionalist – the one who seeks his or her own advantage. See also Chrys. *hom. in I Cor.* 33.3 [*PG* 61.280] on 13:5: οὕτω καὶ ἐνταῦθα τὸ ἑκάστῳ συμφέρον τῷ πλησίον ἔδωκεν, ἵνα ἀλλήλων ἐντεῦθεν κατατρέχωμεν, καὶ μὴ ὦμεν διεσπασμένοι.

634 The verb παροξύνεται in 13:5 is usually translated "to be irritable" (RSV; Senft, 168), "embittered" (Heinrici, *Sendschreiben*, 418) or even "touchy" (Barrett, *First Corinthians*, 303).

account the evil, it does not rejoice in injustice but co-rejoices with the truth [and] endures all things."[635] This list bears a one-to-one precise correspondence with Paul's description of Corinthian factional behavior[636] – they are jealous (3:3)[637] and provoked to factional tumult, they offensively put themselves forward by boasting and "being puffed up,"[638] they do account evil,[639] they are childish.[640] So too, conversely, love's positive characteristics in this list replicate the content of Paul's advice for unity: be patient and kind;[641] do not seek your own advantage (10:23–11:1; 12:7);[642] rejoice and grieve together like members of

---

LSJ, 1342–43 gives the possibilities "urge on, spur on, stimulate" or "provoke, irritate," in the passive "to be provoked." Sometimes the term can mean "to become intensely angry," but it is often found in a more particular context than the above translations would suggest – that of wars and factions. The significance of this verb in 1 Cor 13:5 has largely been overlooked by scholars, even though Weiss pinpointed its connection with Corinthian factionalism: "οὐ παροξύνεται (vgl. Apg. 15:39!) wird sich auf die ἔριδες beziehen" (*Korintherbrief*, 316; see also H. Seesemann, "παροξύνω, παροξυσμός," *TDNT* 5.857: "Paul uses this expression with a conscious eye on the tensions in the church at Corinth, where there has been a good deal of provocation"). In Acts 15:39 the substantive παροξυσμός is the descriptive term for the bitter division between Paul and Barnabas (see also the verb in Heb 10:24 and substantive in Ign. *Pol.* 1.2 [a letter which urges church unity, according to Schoedel, 259]). Of course even if the term means only "to be bitterly angry" it would be a component of party divisions. But the link between παροξύνεσθαι and political dissension is even more direct. See Arist. *Pol.* 5.3.5 [Δόξανδρος ἦρξε τῆς στάσεως καὶ τοὺς Ἀθηναίους παρώξυνε]; Dem. *Or.* 45.14 [παροξυσμὸς καὶ φιλονικία]; Isoc. *Or.* 5.114. In the first century see Joseph. *BJ* 2.489 [ἡ στάσις μᾶλλον παρωξύνετο]; 2.269 [ἔτι μᾶλλον παρωξύνοντο πρὸς τὴν στάσιν]; *AJ* 4.24, 63 [of Korah's revolt]; 7.17 [ἄνδρας ὁμοφύλους εἰς ἔριδα καὶ μάχην παροξύνειν]; Dio Chrys. *Or.* 34.44 urging concord [μηδὲ τοὺς παροξυνοῦντας ὑμᾶς ἀποδέξασθε]. Hence the anomalous term παροξύνεσθαι in 1 Cor 13:5, found only here in Paul's extant letters, is easily understood as yet another clear reference to Corinthian factional behavior.

[635] Cf. 9:12 of Paul as the example (πάντα στέγομεν). This argumentative connection was pointed out by Dautzenberg, 219–20.

[636] The connections between 1 Cor 13 and the rest of the letter are elucidated by Wischmeyer, *Weg*, 39–162 throughout her exegesis of the chapter. She concludes: "1 Kor 13 ist keine systematische Lehre über die ἀγάπη . . . Auch die breite Entfaltung der Wirkungen der ἀγάπη hat nicht gänzlich allgemeinen Charakter, sondern formuliert möglichst umfassend bei genauer Zielrichtung auf die spezifische Situation in Korinth im besonderen und die πνευματικά-Problematik, besonders die γνῶσις, im ganzen" (p. 228). But Wischmeyer, like all exegetes who do regard 1 Cor 13 as related specifically to the Corinthian situation, takes it to be a response to Corinthian "enthusiasm" and not their factionalism, as here argued.

[637] See above on ζῆλος/ζηλοῦν and Corinthian factionalism.

[638] See above on the connection of these two terms with factionalism.

[639] See 6:1–11 and the common "judging" motif (in particular 4:1–5).

[640] 3:1–4; cf. 13:11. On this as a *topos* for factionalism, see above n. 184.

[641] The opposite of "provoked" and "jealous," and of ἔρις and στάσις in *1 Clem.* 14.3. Compare Dio Chrys. *Or.* 41.10 urging the Apamaeans to concord through being "gentle and magnanimous" [πρᾷος καὶ μεγαλόφρων], and his *Or.* 38.35 [πρᾴως δὲ καὶ μετρίως]. Calvin wrote on 13:4: "The first description of love is that by patiently enduring many things it strengthens the harmony of the Church. Love's second quality is very similar" (p. 276).

[642] *The* definition of non-factional behavior, as was demonstrated above.

a body (12:26; cf. Rom 12:15, also after the body metaphor).[643] Love, which builds a strong structure, never falls (8:6).[644] It is the mortar between the bricks of the Christian building, the ἐκκλησία. The one who acts in love is mature, one who has set apart τὰ τοῦ νηπίου (13:10–11).[645] Love remains, and is the greatest of gifts, the gift which unites rather than divides the church. The centrality of the appeal to love as the proper antidote to factionalism[646] throughout 1 Corinthians is further verified by the summary of the letter in 16:14: "let all things be yours ἐν ἀγάπῃ."[647]

8. *1 Corinthians 14. Disunity at Worship*

In chapter 14 Paul deals with divisive manifestations of the spirit in worship, urging throughout those spiritual expressions which promote unity. Paul calls on the Corinthians to "be zealous" (ζηλοῦτε) for the better spiritual gifts, instead of being zealous for their own advantage which sets them apart from others.[648] Speaking in tongues is divisive, but interpreting tongues is edifying (14:2–27).

---

643 Cf. Dio Chrys. *Or.* 48.6: "For truly it is a fine thing and profitable [καλὸν καὶ συμφέρον] for one and all alike to have a city show itself of one mind [ὁμογνώμων], on terms of friendship [φίλη] with itself and one in feeling [συμπαθής], united in conferring both censure and praise, bearing for both classes, the good and the bad, a testimony in which each can have confidence" (here too this follows a list of the "bad things" now happening: ἔχθρα, ἔρις, φιλονεικία ἄλογος κὰι ἀνόητος).

644 See above nn. 278–80 on "standing" and "falling" as components of the building metaphor for concord. See also Chrys. on 13:8: Τί γάρ ἐστιν, Οὐκ ἐκπίπτει; Οὐ διακόπτεται, οὐ διαλύεται τῷ φέρειν (*hom. in I Cor.* 33.4 [*PG* 61.281]), and also Thdt. *1 Cor.* 13:8 (quoted in n. 271 above).

645 The connection between this part of ch. 13 and the factional children in 3:1–4 is not made in modern commentaries, but see Theodoret on 13:11: διδάσκων πάλιν διὰ τούτων, μὴ μέγα φρονεῖν ἐπὶ τῇ γνώσει τοὺς κατατέμνοντας τῆς Ἐκκλησίας τὸ σῶμα (*1 Cor.* 13:11 [*PG* 82.336]).

646 See Theissen, 107–10, on "love-patriarchalism" which creates social solidarity in a stratified community. In the introduction to that volume J. H. Schütz summarizes Theissen's viewpoint thusly: "Love-patriarchalism is a fundamental Pauline ethical stance which seeks integration at the level of the religious sphere when the apostle faces divisions arising from the social order" (p. 15). Elsewhere Theissen refers to it as a "radicalization of ancient democratic traditions" (p. 110). E. S. Fiorenza's critique of Theissen (*In Memory of Her. A Feminist Theological Reconstruction of Christian Origins* [New York: Crossroad, 1983] 79), that he superimposes this model on 1 Cor, overstates the case. As this investigation wishes to show, Theissen's thesis can be demonstrated exegetically throughout 1 Cor. Love is the unifying, concordant power which Paul urges on his divided church.

647 This is synonymous with the parallel statement in 14:26: "let everything be for building up" (see also 16:22). 16:14 also points to the *topos* that in concord all parties get the benefit of all the shared possessions (see n. 171 above).

648 See 12:31; 14:1; cf. 3:3. For demonstration that urging new, edifying "rivalries" for the benefit of the whole social body is a *topos* in texts urging concord, see above n. 195.

The language controversy at Corinth is a spiritual version of a prevalent political problem[649] – common language is needed for concord.[650] Paul exhorts the Corinthians to "build up the church" (14:4–5, 12, 26)[651] and stop their partisanship and separation from one another which manifests itself in this way. The matrix of decision-making and value, he appeals once again, must be the insiders, and not the outsiders (14:22–25). That the community is divided in worship is shown in 14:26: *each one*[652] has his or her own kind of speech, his or her own way of doing things. All speaking at the same time and not listening to one another is a sure sign of discord, a *topos* for divided groups,[653] a *topos* often combined, as here, with a parallel discussion of musical instruments.[654] What is required is a proper and orderly exercise of this spiritual differentiation within the community.

Several of the terms which Paul uses as counterparts to the dissensions in community worship also point to factionalism. In 14:33 Paul grounds his argument for unity in an appeal to the nature of the deity who is to be imitated: "for God is not of anarchy [ἀκαταστασία] but of peace." This term means

---

[649] Notice that Paul himself even phrases it this way – see the double use of βάρβαρος in 14:11 – a clear reference to social alienation and diffusion. See also Philo, *Conf. ling.* 6–7, where the primordial common language meant that all mourned and rejoiced in common (cf. § 12 on the advantages of a common language).

[650] On common language and ὁμόνοια, see Tarn, *Alexander the Great*, 2.431 and Moulakis, 33–37, esp. 36: "die zugleich Zerstörung der Sprache wie Zerstörung der Politik ist." Good examples are found in Dion. Hal. *Ant. Rom.* 1.29.3–4 (kinship shown by common language); 1.90.1 (Romans intermingling with others has affected the proper pronunciation of the language). Aristid. *Or.* 24.56–57 complains to the Rhodians that their lack of adherence to a strictly Dorian dialect is a sign of their discord. In the NT see the graphic example of common language in Acts 2:5–11.

[651] See the extensive discussion above on the building metaphor for concord, which is also connected with seeking the common good, as we have seen (10:23). This is how Origen understood ch. 14 in his paraphrase of 14:12: ὡς ὅτι οὐ περισσεύει ἐν τοῖς χαρίσμασιν ὁ μὴ ζητῶν τὸ κοιν(ω)φ(ε)λές (*comm. in I Cor.* 60.4 [p. 37]; cf. 62.1, καὶ διὰ τούτων τὸ κοινωφελὲς τῆς ἐκκλησίας διδασκόμεθα ζητεῖν [p. 38]).

[652] See above n. 549 on ἕκαστος.

[653] Welborn, "Discord," 93, "Conciliatory Principle," 336–37 (but without reference to 1 Cor 14!), citing Dio Chrys. *Or.* 39.4; 40.28–29 and Aristid. *Or.* 24.56 (all good examples). See also Dio Chrys. *Or.* 38.46; 39.3: "Even as I myself rejoice at the present moment to find you wearing the same costume, speaking the same language [μίαν δὲ φωνὴν ἀφιέντας] . . . indeed what spectacle is more enchanting than a city with singleness of purpose [ὁμοφρονεῖν], and what sound is more awe-inspiring than its harmonious voice." It is important to note that these examples have to do also with *behavior in the assembly* which manifests unity (concordant speaking) or factionalism (saying different things and not listening to others), and are thus directly applicable to Corinthian worship when they come together. The positive counterpart is the image of the chorus of united voices (cf. τὸ αὐτὸ λέγειν in 1 Cor 1:10), which is used in ECL especially by Ignatius (see *Eph.* 4:1–2; *Rom.* 2:2 and the fine analysis of this *topos* by Schoedel, 51–53).

[654] Dio Chrys. *Or.* 34.18; 48.7; see also Grant, "Hellenistic Elements," 63.

"instability, anarchy, confusion."[655] The noun is used in Greek writers to refer to political upheaval and civil strife.[656] The political context of ἀκαταστασία is also shown by the cognate verb καταστασιάζειν, to "overpower by forming a counter-party."[657] That Paul himself regards ἀκαταστασία as "party strife," and not merely general confusion, is shown in 2 Cor 12:20 where it is associated with other terms for political rivalry, instability and in-fighting.[658] Elsewhere in the New Testament, the Epistle of James too associates ἀκαταστασία with ζῆλος and ἐριθεία (3:16), and there, as here, its opposite is εἰρήνη, peace (3:17–18).[659] Therefore, when Paul says in 14:33 that God is not of ἀκαταστασία but of peace, this key term clearly refers not to some general undefined unruliness, but to the specific manifestation of Corinthian partisanship[660] and divisiveness in the worship of the community. Even regarded as "instability," ἀκαταστασία can be seen as the perfect negative counterpart to Paul's positive image of the unified community, the οἰκοδομή, which is especially prominent in chap. 14 (14:3–5, 12, 17, 26).[661]

---

655 LSJ, 48 (it is morphologically related to στάσις, "party strife"). For references see also BAGD, 30. Robertson-Plummer, 324 observed how strong a term ἀκαταστασία is, translated *dissensio* in the Vulgate and *seditio* by Calvin.

656 For example, Dion. Hal. *Ant. Rom.* 6.31.1: "While the commonwealth was in such an unsettled condition [ἀκαταστασία] a kind of truce that intervened on account of the traditional sacrifices, and the ensuing festivals, which were celebrated at lavish expense, restrained the sedition [διχοστασία; see discussion above on 1 Cor 3:3] of the populace for the moment." See also Polyb. 1.70.1; 14.9.6 and 32.5.5, where it is paired with ταραχή; 31.8.6 [ἡ ἀκαταστασία τῆς βασιλείας]. Nicolaus of Damascus uses the term ἀκαταστασία to refer to the tumult between Antony and Octavian after the death of Julius Caesar (*Vit. Caes.* 28.110 [*FGrH* 2A.413]). In the LXX ἀκαταστασία is said to arise from "an uncovered mouth" (Prov 26:28) and "arrogance" [ὑπερηφανία, surely a problem at Corinth!] (Tob 4:13; see also the quotation in *2 Clem.* 11:4). In the writings of the second century (C.E.) astrologer Vettius Valens (*Vettii Valentis anthologiarum libri*, ed. G. Kroll [Berlin: Weidmann, 1908]) ἀκαταστασία appears ten times in lists of misfortunes meted out by the various planets and stars, often accompanied by other terms for social and political upheaval: στάσις (190.33; 191.25; 230.34), ταραχή (190.33; 191.25), ἔχθρα (191.3, 26; 193.14; 197.4), and ζηλοτυπία (191.25).

657 LSJ, 913. See the fragment of Theopompus found at Oxyrhynchus (*Hist.* 233 in *Hellenica Oxyrhynchia*, ed. B. P. Grenfell and A. S. Hunt [Oxford: Clarendon, 1909]). The text says that Lysander's mother was killed when Agesilaus the king politically overpowered [καταστασιάσας] Lysander. Xenophon uses the same verb: "but when he found out that Lysander's friends were intriguing against him [καταστασιαζόμενος] . . ." (*Hell.* 1.6.4). It is also used with the meaning "to rebel by forming a party" into the second century (see D. S. 19.36.4; Joseph. *BJ* 1.20; Plut. *Per.* 9.4; *Them.* 5.5).

658 See above n. 89. The author of *1 Clem.* also associates ἀκαταστασία with factionalism (see 3:2; 14:1; 43:6).

659 Hort, 85–86. Cf. Luke 21:9, where ἀκαταστασία is set alongside πόλεμος.

660 Delling, *TDNT* 7.571 says that ἀκαταστασία is the Pauline counterpart to στάσις. See Origen's use of the term to describe the marriage controversies at Corinth (*comm. in I Cor.* 33.11 [p. 500], quoted above in n. 348; also 34.42 [503]).

661 It is also the opposite of βεβαίωσις (cf. 1:6, 8), and the adjectives ἑδραῖος and ἀμετακίνητος in 15:58 (on these terms as a part of the building metaphor see above). Compare the ἀκατάστατος, "unstable" one in Jas 1:8 (on which see Hort, 13).

That peace [εἰρήνη, 14:33; cf. 7:15] is the opposite of factionalism is so obvious as to hardly need comment.[662] Ares, the god of war, causes σχίσματα,[663] but the God of the Christians, on the contrary, causes peace. There should be agreement between the god and its worshippers in this regard.[664] Dio Chrysostom extolls Zeus in much the same language: "But our god is peaceful [εἰρηνικός] and altogether gentle, such as befits the guardian of a faction-free [ἀστασίαστος] and concordant [ὁμονοεῖν] Hellas."[665] The connection between faction and peace could not be more straightforward; as Aristides says, "faction destroys peace."[666] 14:33 contains an implicit appeal by Paul to the Corinthians to turn from faction and instability towards peace and unity, in imitation of the deity (cf. 11:1).[667] Concrete advice in 14:34–35 once again appeals to the *status quo* social conservatism which accompanies the appeal for unity as the primary goal, where Paul urges submission and silence of women for the sake of peace.[668]

In 14:40 Paul concludes this entire section (11:2–14:40) on manifestations of divisiveness in worship with the words "let everything be seemly[669] and orderly [κατὰ τάξιν]." The opposite of κατὰ τάξιν, ἀταξία, is another synonym for

---

[662] See Jal, 231: "Pour Rome comme pour nous, la vraie *pax* était surtout la concordia." On εἰρήνη and ὁμόνοια paired in political terminology, see Kramer, 52–53; Skard, 93; van Unnik, "Studies," 162–81; Jones, *Plutarch*, 115 and notes; Wengst, 21–22, 105–18 on *1 Clem* (see also p. 88 on 1 Cor 14, which he doesn't connect with factionalism). On *otium* as a code-word for political concord in Cicero see Wood, 193–99.

[663] *Catalogus Codicum Astrologorum Graecorum* 122 (cited in n. 36 above). Closer to Paul's time and milieu see Philo, *Leg. Gai.* 113: "This other [Ares/Gaius] was the foe of peace, the friend of wars, the converter of stability into turmoil and faction [ἧς (εἰρήνης) ἐχθρὸς μὲν ἦν ἕτερος, ἑταῖρος δὲ πολέμων, τὴν εὐστάθειαν εἰς ταραχὰς καὶ στάσεις μεθαρμοζόμενος]."

[664] See, e. g., Plut. *Nic. and Crass.* 3.2 (cf. 7.15), and the religious appeal of Aristides: "If you are beloved by the gods, do you think that you should be involved in faction [στασιάζειν] and unrest . . . since faction [στάσις] is both foreign to you and hateful to the gods" (*Or.* 24.48).

[665] *Or.* 12.74. Later in the same discourse Dio describes Zeus as "God of Friendship" [Φίλιος] and "God of Comradeship" ['Εταιρεῖος], because "he brings all men together and wills that they be friends of one another and never enemy or foe" (12.76). This appeal surfaces also in his speeches on concord. In 39.4 he claims that the gods pay heed to those who live in ὁμόνοια, and elsewhere that concord is "godlike" [θεῖον] (41.13).

[666] *Or.* 23.55 [στάσις . . . εἰρήνην λύει]. See also the inscription dedicated to Octavian at Rome: τὴν εἰρήνην ἐστασιασμένην ἐκ πολλοῦ συνέστησε κατά τε γῆν καὶ θάλασσαν (App. *BCiv*. 5.13.130).

[667] "Als Vorbild der Einheit ist Gott auch ein 'Gott des Friedens': 1 Kor 14,33 (implizit 1,13 und 3,3); Phil 4,9" (Siegert, 213; cf. p. 200 where he classes it, along with τάξις in 14:40, among the *Ordnungstopoi*). Cf. Rom 14:19, where τὰ τῆς εἰρήνης are paralled by τὰ τῆς οἰκοδομῆς τῆς ἀλλήλους, and 2 Cor 13:11 (καταρτίζεσθε, παρακαλεῖσθε, τὸ αὐτὸ φρονεῖτε, εἰρηνεύετε, καὶ ὁ θεὸς τῆς ἀγάπης καὶ εἰρήνης ἔσται μεθ' ὑμῶν).

[668] See the discussion in chap. IV.

[669] On εὐσχημόνως in parallel with εὐτάκτως (and πάντα γίνηται) see Dittenberger, *SIG*³ 736.42 (first cited by Weiss, *Korintherbrief*, 343 n. 2). The text prescribes proper liturgical behavior for ῥαβδοφόροι. Weiss defines εὐσχημοσύνη as "das wohlgesittete, nicht eifersüchtig-egoistische Verhalten" (cf. love in 13:5, οὐκ ἀσχημονεῖ). In Paul, see Rom 13:13, where two of the things "not seemly" are ἔρις καὶ ζῆλος.

στάσις in ancient literature.[670] Aristides uses the term in the *Roman Oration* in praising the *pax Romana* which put an end to all strife:

Before the rule of Zeus, as the poets say, the universe was full of strife [στάσις], confusion [θόρυβος] and disorder [ἀταξία] . . . before your empire there had been confusion [συνταράσσεσθαι] everywhere and things were taking a random course, but when you assumed the presidency, confusion and strife [ταραχαὶ καὶ στάσεις] ceased, and universal order [τάξις πάντων] entered as a brilliant light over the private and public affairs of man.[671]

Thus the concluding phrase in 1 Cor 14:40 must be seen as another reference to the Corinthian factions,[672] and an appeal for their cessation.[673]

9. 1 Corinthians 15. Controversy over the Resurrection

The relationship of chap. 15 to Paul's overall argument against factionalism is to be seen in his overarching strategy of redefining the standards and goals in relation to which the Corinthians should make their daily life decisions. He appeals to the resurrected life to minimize the importance of the present striving to supremacy within the community, holding those insignificant gains and losses up against the great eschatological victory which all will share (culmi-

670 See Arist. *Pol.* 2.2.11; 5.2.6; Philo, *Jos.* 143, 145; Dio Chrys. *Or.* 34.21; Plut. *Mor.* 304F; Philostr. *VS* 488; App. *BCiv.* 4.12.94; see also the cessation of factionalism described as the return of κόσμος (Dion. Hal. *Ant. Rom.* 6.91.1; 7.33.1; cf. ἀκοσμία in 8.15.2). In ECL see εὐταξία in Ign. *Eph.* 6.2, and εὐτάκτως in *1 Clem.* 6.2; 37.2; 42.2. Robertson-Plummer are close to this connection in concluding that in κατὰ τάξιν we probably have a military metaphor (p. 328). The military use is a specific application within the phrase's larger, political sphere of reference. See also Origen on 1 Cor 14:36: Ὡς τῆς ἀταξίας ταύτης οὔσης ἐν Κορίνθῳ . . . (*comm. in I Cor.* 74.40 [p. 42]), and Chrys. *hom. in I Cor.* 34.3, ἐν ὁμόνοια . . . καὶ εὐταξίᾳ [*PG* 61.290]). In *hom. in I Cor.* 37.2, Chrys. introduces the common examples of a dance, a ship, a chariot and a camp to show that without τάξις all are destroyed [*PG* 61.318].

671 *Or.* 26.103 (trans. Oliver). The same terms, τάξις and ἀταξία, are used also in discourses urging concord (see Dio Chrys. *Or.* 34.21; 40.35; Aristid. *Or.* 23.9). This language of political propaganda in the Roman Empire is also well known to Philo, who describes Augustus as ὁ τὴν ἀταξίαν εἰς τάξιν ἀγαγών (*Leg. Gai.* 147). Lietzmann-Kümmel, 191 pointed to the remarkably secular nature of Paul's expression here in 14:40. In ECL see especially *1 Clem.* 40.1.

672 We have seen in this chapter that many terms used for factions and reconciliations of the political body were used literally by medical writers of the human body. See Gal. *Definitiones medicae* 19.407 Kühn, where ἀταξία is defined as ἀκαταστασία in a discussion of pulse rate.

673 See Kitzberger, 161 on the linguistic connection of εὐσχημόνως and κατὰ τάξιν with the building metaphor ("Beide Begriffe stehen kontextbezogen in positiver Relation zu οἰκοδομή"). The terms ἀκαταστασία and τάξις are discussed by G. Dautzenberg, *Urchristliche Prophetie. Ihre Erforschung, ihre Voraussetzung im Judentum und ihre Struktur im ersten Korintherbrief*, BWANT 104 (Stuttgart: Kohlhammer, 1975) 278–84, with comparative materials mostly in cultic settings. Though he does not examine the more general political meaning of the terms, he does connect the meaning "good order," on the basis of his reading of Paul's argument, with the σχίσματα and αἱρέσεις in 11:18–19. This function of Paul's argument in 1 Cor 14 was also noted by Conzelmann, 245 n. 50: "τάξις, 'order,' and οἰκοδομή, 'edification,' are *ecclesiastical* criteria" (emph. original).

nating in 15:54–55). Paul calls them to unity in their common traditions (15:1; cf. 11:2, 23), and in their future eschatological destiny (a further extension of the σῶμα argument; 15:35–49). Even this appeal to future life to urge concord in the present is not unparalleled in deliberative discourses for unity from antiquity. In *Or.* 23, also near the end of the argument, Aristides uses the same appeal.

Shall you not stop this, dear sirs, and shall you not realize that these things to which we are devoted, even if they have some value, are nonetheless mortal [θνητά] and of the second rank, but that good sense is the closest thing of all to the gods, and not the least part of it in a disposition towards friendship?[674]

Within the context of the entire letter 1 Cor 15 stresses the ultimate goal in relation to which the Corinthians should make all decisions.

The argument in 15:25–28 stresses the mutual subjugation of all cosmic elements to the Christ and to God. We have seen above (n. 405) that this is a *topos* in Greco-Roman literature urging concord. Another specific reference in this chapter to factionalism is in 15:30–33: "If I fought the beasts in Ephesus κατὰ ἄνθρωπον."[675] The phrase is thus clearly linked with the "humanly strivings" of the factionalists (3:3; cf. 10:13), which Paul contrasts with the genuine, non-this-worldly apocalyptic sufferings which he endures. The maxim in 15:33 also refers to relationships: "bad associations [ὁμιλίαι] corrupt morals." Could this not be another reference to Corinthian party politics?[676]

But the major factional element in 1 Cor 15 is that here Paul must respond to different views on the resurrection which various groups within the church hold, another facet of the church's dissension.[677] This is said plainly in 15:12 (cf. 15:35): "some among you say that there is no resurrection of the dead."[678]

---

[674] *Or.* 23.75. The same appeal is made by Dio Chrysostom in a speech against greed: "As for me, I wonder greatly how we should have acted if we had not received the shortest span of life from the gods. However, just as if we were making our plans for an endless life, we strive earnestly each to have more than his neighbor" (*Or.* 17.20; cf. *Cynic Ep.* 9). See also Dio's *Or.* 34. 51, at the very end of a speech urging concord: "What then? Is there nothing noble in this our day to merit one's serious pursuit? The greatest things, yes the only things worthy of serious pursuit, were present then, are present now, and always will be; and over these no man, surely, has control." For the appeal to immortality in another deliberative speech (not on concord), see Isoc. *Or.* 5.134.

[675] Regarded as a *crux interpretum* by Weiss (*Korintherbrief*, 365).

[676] Cf. Plut. *Mor.* 491E: so that they may not "enter into association [ὁμιλία] with knaves or sluggards."

[677] G. Sellin has argued that the Corinthian resurrection controversy resulted from Hellenistic-Jewish wisdom theology which came from Apollos (*Der Streit um die Auferstehung der Toten*, FRLANT 138 [Göttingen: Vandenhoeck & Ruprecht, 1986] 65–69, 290–94), although he puts chap. 15 in a different letter from 1 Cor 1–4 (p. 51 n. 55; 65).

[678] On the various interpretations of this statement see the summaries of scholarship in J. H. Wilson, "The Corinthians Who Say There is No Resurrection of the Dead," *ZNW* 59 (1968) 90–107; A. J. H. Wedderburn, "The Problem of the Denial of the Resurrection in 1 Corinthians XV," *NovT* 23 (1981) 229–41; Sellin, *Streit*, 17–37.

This dispute has contributed to Corinthian factionalism,[679] just as it had in first century Judaism.[680] The denial of the resurrection by some members of the church community may have led to exclusive claims on the resurrection by other members.[681] This can be seen in 15:23, where the resurrected ones are οἱ Χριστοῦ, Paul's correction for Corinthian factions (3:23). Throughout 1 Cor 15 Paul stresses that *all* shall share in the resurrection, not a select few (15:22, 51), thus combatting factionalists' claims.[682] The argument properly concludes with a final reminder that *it is God* who has given the gift of the resurrection (15:57) in which all Christians will partake. It is not earned by individuals or groups, and is thus not to be boasted in or disputed about (cf. 1:4–5; 4:7 and the discussion above).

In 1 Cor 15:58, the conclusion to the argument in the body of the letter,[683] Paul turns once again to the building metaphor for the community which is his positive counterpart to factionalism throughout the letter, as we have seen.[684] The Corinthians, as God's building, are urged to be firm and immovable, abounding in the work of the Lord (the upbuilding of the church) always. Such a course of action will be to their ultimate advantage (ὁ κόπος ὑμῶν οὐκ ἔστιν κενὸς ἐν κυρίῳ).

10. 1 Corinthians 16. Final Matters of Concern

Chap. 16 contains news and closing epistolary formulae, but the issue of factionalism is still very much present. A possible future visit of Apollos, one of the men to whom party allegiance was claimed (1:12; 3:4), is discussed,[685] once again with Paul emphasizing the comfortable relationship between Apollos and himself.[686] Perhaps another of the strategies for keeping the peace is for Apollos (and

---

679 This is certainly how the earliest readers understood it. Origen's defense of the charge brought by Celsus, that Christians were at the beginning unified [ἓν φρονεῖν], and only later became divided [σχίζεσθαι], is to argue that divisions existed from the very beginning, pointing to the dispute over the resurrection at Corinth and elsewhere (*Cels.* 3.11 [Borret, SC 136.32]). See also Chrys. *hom. in I Cor.* Argumentum 2 [*PG* 61.12]: ἐντεῦθεν διῄρηντο (he argues that this is just like heathen philosophies) and 38.1: περὶ γὰρ τὴν ἀνάστασιν αὐτὴν ἐστασίαζον [61.321].

680 See the same formulation in Acts 23:7–8, where the στάσις between Pharisees and Sadducees is the result of their "saying" different things in regard to resurrection.

681 See above on the divisiveness of the claim to the special possessions γνῶσις, λόγος and σοφία.

682 See also the statement ἵνα ᾖ ὁ θεὸς τὰ πάντα ἐν πᾶσιν in 15:28 (cf. 3:21; 9:22; 12:6).

683 See chap. IV.

684 See the discussion above.

685 A visit of one of the other such men, Paul, is also mentioned (16:5–9). Schreiber, 117–22 regards Paul's having left the community after its founding as being of prime importance for the strife which followed, so a future visit of Paul could also be related to this.

686 This is no indication of a change in Paul's knowledge of the situation or his strategy in

Paul?) to remain separated from the community for some time.[687] Paul also sends Timothy, who "does the work of the Lord" (cf. 15:58). Timothy surely plays a role in Paul's reconciliatory strategy.[688] Sending him on back to Paul ἐν εἰρήνῃ will demonstrate the success of his mission and Paul's letter – that the Corinthian church is reunified.[689]

16:13–14 summarizes the argument for unity in the body of the letter. The imperatives in 16:13 include "stand firm" and "be strong," a final call to the Corinthians to be concordant as God's building.[690] Even the imperative ἀνδρίζεσθε, "be courageous," may be a part of the ὁμόνοια-complex,[691] as ἀνδρεία is one of the cardinal civic virtues in Greek political thought.[692] In 16:14 Paul's reconciliatory strategy is summed up: "let all things be yours in love."[693] He did not take anything away from any of the combatants (as in 3:22, "all things are yours"), but urged that they all enjoy these many gifts in love, thus rejecting factionalist claims to exclusive possession. Paul concludes with a reference to love, ἀγάπη, the principle of social cohesion he has urged on the Corinthians throughout his argument for unity (cf. 16:24).

Paul's final advice to the Corinthians to end their factionalism is contained in 16:15–16, beginning with the παρακαλῶ δὲ ὑμᾶς formula (cf. 1:10; 4:16). He

---

response. Likewise, it is not necessarily indicative of the exact nature of Paul's relationship with Apollos, either.

687 Barrett, *First Corinthians*, 392: "It is a reasonable guess that Paul and Apollos had decided that the interest of Christian unity would be better served by Apollos' absence." Apollos' εὐκαιρεία will be ὅταν μηκέτι ᾖ ἐν ὑμῖν σχίσματα (Didymus of Alex., *Comm.* 1 Cor 16:12 [Staab, 13]; also Or. *comm. in I Cor.* 89.39 [p. 51], ἐὰν ὑμεῖς εἰρηνεύητε).

688 4:17 (see ch. IV for discussion of division hypotheses on the basis of perceived incongruities between these two references). On Timothy's reconciliatory role, see Origen, *comm. in I Cor.* 89.23–24: νῦν μὲν ἔρχεται πρὸς ὑμᾶς εἰρήνην ποιήσων. στάσιν γὰρ ὑμῶν εὑρίσκει ἐν τῇ ἐκκλησίᾳ [p. 50]. Note that Timothy is to perform the same reconciliatory function at Philippi (Phil 2:19–24; F. W. Beare, *A Commentary on the Epistle to the Philippians* [San Francisco: Harper & Row, 1959] 96).

689 ἀλλ' ὁμονοήσαντες καὶ διορθωθέντες ἐκ τῶν λεγομένων ὑπ' αὐτοῦ (καὶ) εἰρήνην ἀναλαβόντες, προπέμψατε αὐτὸν ἐν τῇ ὑμετέρᾳ ὁμονοίᾳ καὶ εἰρήνῃ (Or., *comm. in I Cor.* 89.25–26 [p. 50], consecutive to the passage in the previous note). Observe his addition of ὁμόνοια! See also Chrys. on Timothy's purpose: ὥστε τὰς αἱρέσεις ἀνελεῖν (*hom. in I Cor.* 14.1 [*PG* 61.115]). Notice too that the same convention about the envoy is at work in the reconciliation to be effected by *1 Clem.*: ἐν εἰρήνῃ ἀναπέμψατε (65.1).

690 See the full discussion above.

691 See above n. 281.

692 See Lucian *Anach.* 15 quoted in n. 435 above, and the parallels in H. D. Betz, *Lukian von Samosata und das Neue Testament*, TU 76 (Berlin: Akademie, 1961), 208 n. 9.

693 Robertson-Plummer, 394: "He is glancing back at the party-divisions, at the selfish disorder at the Lord's Supper, and at their jealousy in the possession of special charismata, and is recalling xiii." The early commentators also understand this as a final appeal to the factionalists to cease: τὸ δὲ πρὸς τοὺς στασιάζοντας καὶ διασπᾶν ἐπιχειροῦντας, τὸ Πάντα ὑμῶν ἐν ἀγάπῃ γινέσθω (Chrys. *hom. in I Cor.* 44.1 [*PG* 61.375]); also Thdt. *1 Cor.* 16:14: πρὸς τοὺς διελόντας τῆς 'Εκκλησίας τὸ σῶμα [*PG* 82.372].

urges the Corinthians to be unified in their submission[694] to the authority of the house of Stephanas.[695] Paul's overall advice to the Corinthians, to build up their community through love, is here supplemented by a concrete political dictum[696] – these are your leaders, obey them![697] The holy kiss greeting may also be a reconciliatory gesture.[698] Even the curse in 16:22 may be a last threat to the factionalists to desist: "if anyone does not love [φιλεῖν] the Lord, let him or her be anathema."[699] Loving the Lord, according to the argument throughout 1 Corinthians, means building up the church for common strength and unification. Paul closes this letter, appropriately,[700] with a final appeal to both ἀγάπη and to himself as its exemplar after his customary Christological blessing (16:24). 1 Corinthians is the only Pauline (or deutero-Pauline) letter to bear such an addition. The unifying force of the plea is made once again with πάντες – my love is with *all of you*, and is grounded in a final appeal to Christ Jesus, the one Lord shared by all, by the unifying force of whose name Paul had introduced this letter appealing for unity (1:10).[701]

---

694 The political nature of ὑποτάσσεσθαι is shown in Rom 13:1, where it is used of subjection to secular authorities. There is no reason to see in 1 Cor 16:16 a completely different, non-political sense just because here it is used with respect to Christian leaders (contra BAGD, 848). That ὁμόνοια results from submission is a *topos* in ancient literature (see M.Ant. 5.30, and n. 405 above on the ὁμόνοια of the heavenly bodies through submission). See also the reconciliatory plea in Ign. *Eph.* 2:2: ἵνα ἐν μιᾷ ὑποταγῇ κατηρτισμένοι . . . ἦτε, and *1 Clem.* 20:1 (heavenly bodies); 37:1–5 (with the human body metaphor); 57:1–2: Ὑμεῖς οὖν οἱ τὴν καταβολὴν τῆς στάσεως ποιήσαντες ὑποτάγητε τοῖς πρεσβυτέροις . . . μάθετε ὑποτάσσεσθαι. In the NT see also Jas 4:7.

695 See also Filson, 112 on the connection between house-owner and house-church: "It was not merely an inherited theory of polity but in part at least the actual leadership provided by the hosts of the house churches which determined the form of church life." Yet Filson does not for his purposes reckon with the prescriptive nature of Paul's advice in 16:15–16.

696 16:15–18 does not constitute a letter of recommendation for Stephanas *et al.* (contra Belleville, 33–34; Marshall, 264). They are already known to the church (neither οἴδατε nor ἐπιγινώσκετε here is equivalent to συνιστάναι). Belleville does, however, correctly stress the unifying force of 16:19–24.

697 The factionalism at Corinth may well be due to conflicting claims to leadership (see n. 695 above). As Aristotle said: "When each of two persons wishes himself to rule, like the rivals in the *Phoenissae*, there is discord [στασιάζειν]" (*Eth. Nic.* 9.6.2). In Dem. *Ep.* 1.14–16, at the end of this deliberative epistle urging concord, the author also turns to the issue of proper leaders for the best interests of the Athenian assembly.

698 Chrys. *hom. in I Cor.* 44.2 [*PG* 61.376]).

699 So Prümm, 214: "ein letztes Wetterleuchten der Entrüstung des Apostels gegen die Quertreiber, die Christus zerreissen"; similarly Barrett, *First Corinthians*, 397: "The party-spirit and moral laxity of the Corinthian church would be remedied by devotion to Jesus." Pl. *Ep.* 6, an appeal for concord, ends with a command to the disputants to swear by a common oath (323D).

700 See Barrett, *First Corinthians*, 399: "It would not be wrong to say that, in sense, not construction, they [the last three words] cover the whole epistle."

701 See also 2:2; 3:23; 6:11; 8:6; 12:3. Weiss's comment on 16:24 is apt: "mit dem Namen Christus Jesus schliesst der Brief, weniger weil es nötig gewesen wäre, seine Liebe zu ihnen als

E. Summation of Terms and Topoi Related to Factionalism in 1 Corinthians

This chapter has contained a survey of the terms and commonplaces for factionalism and concord which Paul weaves into his argument in 1 Corinthians. A summary of the most important points is in order:

1. The following terms and phrases in 1 Corinthians have been demonstrated to be particularly appropriate to an ancient discussion of factionalism and concord: τὸ αὐτὸ λέγειν, σχίσμα, καταρτίζειν, ὁ αὐτὸς νοῦς, ἡ αὐτὴ γνώμη, ἔρις, μερίζειν, συζητητής, καυχᾶσθαι, φυσιοῦσθαι, ζῆλος/ζηλοῦν, διχοστασία, συνεργός, συναναμίγνυσθαι, συγκεραννύναι, κολλᾶσθαι, πρόσκομμα/ἀπρόσκοπος/ἐγκοπή, συγκοινωνός/κοινωνός/κοινωνία, ζητεῖν τὸ συμφέρον, ἀρέσκειν πᾶσιν, φιλόνεικος, αἵρεσις, συνέρχεσθαι ἐπὶ τὸ αὐτό, σῶμα, συγχαίρειν/συμπάσχειν, κυβέρνησις, ἀγάπη, παροξύνεσθαι, ἀκαταστασία, κατὰ τάξιν, εἰρήνη. These terms and phrases are found well-distributed throughout the sixteen chapters of the letter.

2. The following *topoi* or common appeals for concord are used by Paul as also by other ancient writers urging unity on divided groups:

a) Appealing to "ones," things which the group has in common (in this argument one κλῆσις, one God, one Lord Jesus Christ, one Spirit, one confession of faith, one baptism, one eucharistic celebration of one bread and one body, one body of Christ, one common language, one set of common traditions). The term εἷς is used a remarkable thirty-one times in the letter.

b) Appealing to the need to seek "the common advantage," which is the direct response to factionalism, in which one seeks one's own advantage. Appealing for voluntary compromise of one's right to do things which one can do for the sake of the common good and thus true freedom.

c) Appealing to the building as an example of concord, here particularized as "God's building" which is also "the temple of the Holy Spirit." The consequences of this metaphor are that the members of the building must be strong, unwavering and unchanging, in order to build up the building instead of allowing it to totter and fall, and ultimately be destroyed by inner division.

d) Appealing to the political or social unit as a body, here specified theologically as "the body of Christ." The body metaphor for concord entails customary political consequences (distribution of gifts and functions, sharing of a common "advantage," proper "mix" of elements for unity, co-suffering and co-rejoicing of the members, exclusive allegiance of the members).

e) Appealing to the commonplace that factionalism is "human," while concord and peace are divine. Calling factionalism a childish failing, and concomi-

---

eine speziell christliche, im Herrn begründete zu bestimmen, als um zum Schluss noch einmal zu nennen, was sie alle eint" (*Korintherbrief*, 387).

tantly arguing that the things over which the factionalists strive are trivial and silly. Urging the audience to divert their fractious energies into positive strivings for the important things which deserve such energy and attention (for Paul, eschatological salvation).

f) Appealing to the unity of the leaders to whom the factionalists claim varied allegiance.

g) Appealing to the commonplace that factionalism destroys any political body infected with it.

h) Appealing to past examples of people and nations who suffered because of their factionalism.

i) Stressing the distinction between the political body itself and the "outsiders" to emphasize and consolidate group loyalty.

j) Urging people to maintain the *status quo* in order to preserve group stability.

These are all arguments for unity which Paul uses throughout 1 Corinthians which have direct parallels in other ancient texts which urge concord and, significantly, are found in those texts also in combination with one another. They are part of a common conceptual and linguistic body of *topoi* used to promote social and political unity in Greco-Roman antiquity. This similarity in appeals shows definitively that Paul is calling on political principles of universal commerce which he assumes the Corinthians will understand and share.[702] Neither Paul nor the Corinthian parishioners were political philosophers. These stock terms and images of political realism were generally employed and recognized in first century antiquity.[703] Especially important for understanding Paul is the fact that the same images and pleas for unity in a state were also used for families and other smaller social groups.[704] Thus Paul's transference of these insights to the church (which he can describe more formally as an ἐκκλησία or intimately as a household family) is quite in keeping with others who draw upon teachings about concord.

However, this does not mean that 1 Corinthians is merely a pile of political commonplaces strung together, nor is it to imply that political *topoi* are the only sources of Paul's arguments.[705] But these findings do indicate that we must take

702 That Paul uses such political language to describe the problems at Corinth also does not mean that that is an accurate description of the actual situation. The question of the impact of these findings for historical reconstruction will be taken up in the Conclusion in chap. V.

703 See F.G. Downing, "*A bas les aristos*. The Relevance of Higher Literature for the Understanding of the Earliest Christian Writings," *NovT* 30 (1988) 212–30, whose thesis is: "There is no sign of a culture-gap between the highly literate aristocracy and the masses . . . we are therefore fully justified in taking the surviving writings of aristocratic writers of around the first century . . . as indicating at least elements in the popular oral urban culture of the day" (229–30).

704 See ch. II n. 210; ch. III nn. 346–47.

705 Throughout 1 Cor Paul draws heavily upon traditional Christian material, as is well recognized (for catalogues see E. E. Ellis, "Traditions in 1 Corinthians," *NTS* 32 [1986]

into account the proper cultural understandings which lie within and behind Paul's appeal to this particular religious community to live together without strife. It is important to stress here that the "political" significance of Paul's arguments in 1 Corinthians does not mean that it is not also a "religious" document. The ways in which Paul adapts these political and social commonplaces (some of which have been suggested above) and integrates them into his overall argument, with its distinctly Christian presuppositions and insights, will be discussed in the compositional analysis in the next chapter.

F. Conclusions

This chapter has demonstrated that the issue of factionalism, set out by Paul in 1 Cor 1:10 with appropriate political vocabulary, runs throughout all sixteen chapters of 1 Corinthians. Paul's argument in the entire letter is permeated with terms, *topoi* and subjects relating to *his* central topic of discussion – the divisiveness within the community. This letter throughout urges all Corinthian factionalists to unite by using common terms and metaphors derived from ancient politics for this problem which can affect any social group, from a city to a family.

We may draw several conclusions from this weight of evidence:

1. The content of 1 Corinthians, a series of arguments rooted by Paul in the issue of factionalism and concord, is appropriate for the rhetorical species of deliberative rhetoric. This completes the argument of chap. II that 1 Corinthians is rightly understood to be deliberative rhetoric.

2. 1 Cor 1:10 is the πρόθεσις of the argument in the letter because it introduces the appeal for concord and cessation of factionalism which is the topic of consideration throughout the letter. This conclusion will be a cornerstone of the compositional analysis to follow in chap. IV.

3. This chapter has provided strong evidence for the compositional integrity of 1 Corinthians against partition theories which see the canonical letter as made up of several individual letters on different topics. One of the pillars of such partition theories, that chapters 5–16 are lacking in reference to factionalism, the topic of (only) chapters 1–4, is clearly untenable. The appeal for concord and an end to factionalism unites all sixteen chapters. We have also observed that many of the specific appeals, terms and images for concord or factionalism run throughout the entire letter (such as the body metaphor, the image of the building for concord, boasting, being puffed up, love). To this body of evidence for the unity of the letter we can add the conclusion of chap. II, that 1 Corinthians

481–502 [though I don't agree with all of his exegesis]; Sellin, "Hauptprobleme," 2942–64). See the conclusion of Grant, "Hellenistic Elements," 61: "Paul can build his arguments on data both Christian and non-Christian."

employs a unified and coherent rhetorical strategy as well – Paul's appeal to himself as the example to be imitated. 1 Corinthians shows both thematic and rhetorical unity when seen as a deliberative letter urging the Corinthians to come together in unity.

This final conclusion leads us on to the compositional analysis of 1 Corinthians as a deliberative letter urging concord (chap. IV), and provides further justification that the entire letter is the compositional unit to be examined.[706]

---

706 In line with the methodological mandates set out in chap. I.

Chapter IV

Compositional Analysis: 1 Corinthians as a Unified Deliberative Letter Urging Concord

Ten subjects, more or less extended and very heterogeneous, were present to the apostle's mind, when he set himself to compose this letter; and the question which arises is this: Will he confine himself to passing from the one to the other by way of juxtaposition, or will he find the means of binding them to one another by a logical or moral gradation, so as to leave an impression of order and unity on the mind of the reader. In other words, will the First Epistle to the Corinthians be a heap or a building? In this very letter St. Paul compares himself to an architect who has wisely laid the foundation of the Church. We shall immediately see that . . . he has shown himself such also in the composition of the letter which he has addressed to it.[1]

A. Outline of Epistolary and Rhetorical Structure of 1 Corinthians

The compositional epistolary and rhetorical structure of the deliberative letter 1 Corinthians may be outlined as follows:

1. 1:1–3 *Epistolary Prescript*
2. 1:4–9 *Epistolary Thanksgiving* which forms the προοίμιον (*Introduction*) to the argument in the body of the letter
3. 1:10–15:58 *Epistolary Body* containing a Deliberative Argument.
   a) 1:10 πρόθεσις (*Thesis Statement*) to the argument: The Call for Unity and an End to Factionalism.
   b) 1:11–17 διήγησις (*Statement of Facts*): Description of the present situation and correction of a possible misunderstanding.
   c) 1:18–15:57 πίστεις (*Proofs*): Advice for Seeking and Maintaining Concord in the Church, in 4 subsections.
      (1) 1:18–4:21 *First Section of Proof*: Censure of Corinthian Factionalism

[1] Godet, 1.27.

and the Need for Paul's Advice. Introduction of key rhetorical *topoi* (the Building Metaphor for Concord) and Paul's Rhetorical Strategy (Appeal to Imitate Him as the Example of Proper Behavior, 4:16).

(2) 5:1–11:1 *Second Section of Proof*: The Integrity of the Corinthian Community Against Outside Defilement. Advice on Divisive Issues within the Group (under subheads).

(a) 5:1–7:40 Πορνεία and Group Solidarity

(i) 5:1–13 A Case of πορνεία.

(ii) 6:1–11 Court Battles

(iii) 6:12–20 A Second Case of πορνεία with treatment by general principles.

(iv) 7:1–40 Marriage and Status

(b) 8:1–11:1 Idol Meats, Freedom and Group Unity

(i) 8:1–13 Idol Meats and Division, First Treatment.

(ii) 9:1–27 Exemplary Argument: The Proper Use of Freedom for the Common Good

(iii) 10:1–13 The Negative Example of the Wilderness Generation

(iv) 10:14–22 Idolatry, Second Treatment. Cultic Unity as Norm and Standard.

(v) 10:23–11:1 Final Appeal to the Common Advantage as Opposed to Factionalism. Conclusion to the Second Proof Section.

(3) 11:2–14:40 *Third Section of Proof*: Manifestations of Corinthian Factionalism when "Coming Together"

(a) 11:2–16 Divisive Customs in Worship

(b) 11:17–34 Divisions at the Lord's Supper

(c) 12:1–14:40 Spiritual Gifts and Unity

(i) 12:1–31a First Treatment. The Body of Christ: Corinthian Unity in Diversity

(ii) 12:31b–14:1a Exemplary Argument: The Gift of Love as the Antidote to Factionalism

(iii) 14:1b–40 Second Treatment. Unity in Diversity of Language

(4) 15:1–57 *Fourth Section of Proof*: The Resurrection and the Final Goal. Unity in the παραδόσεις.

d) 15:58 ἐπίλογος (*Conclusion/Summation*) to the Argument in the Body of the Letter. Summary Appeal to the Building Metaphor for Concord.

4. 16:1–24 *Epistolary Closing* with customary business, travel plans, final admonitions and greetings.

a) 16:1–4 Instructions on the Collection

b) 16:5–12 Visit plans (Paul, Apollos, Timothy)

c) 16:13–18 Recapitulation of the Argument. Final Concrete Advice for Unity.
d) 16:19–21 Epistolary Greetings
e) 16:22–24 Final Curse and Prayer calling for Unity in Love and in Jesus Christ

B. Preliminary Remarks on the Composition of 1 Corinthians

Because 1 Corinthians is a deliberative letter, a hybrid category in which the epistolary body contains a deliberative argument,[2] both epistolary and rhetorical forms are present.[3] 1 Corinthians is quite clearly and indisputably a letter, because it contains the appropriate parts of the Greek letter[4]: epistolary prescript (1:1–3),[5] thanksgiving formula (1:4–9),[6] letter body (1:10–15:58),[7] and closing

---

[2] For the frequency and attestation of this combination in antiquity, see chap. II, "Excursus: Ancient Deliberative Speeches and Letters."

[3] "Although an epistle requires a salutation and a complimentary close, its body can take the form of a deliberative, epideictic, or judicial speech with the traditional parts and all the inventional and stylistic features of an oration" (Kennedy, *New Testament Interpretation*, 86–87).

[4] On Greek epistolography see F. J. Exler, *The Form of the Ancient Greek Letter of the Epistolary Papyri (3rd c. B.C. – 3rd c. A.D.): A Study in Greek Epistolography* (Washington: Catholic University of America Press, 1923; Repr. Chicago: Ares, 1976); J. Schneider, "Brief," *RAC* 2 (1954) 563–85; I. Sykutris, "Epistolographie," PWSup 5 (1931) 185–220; O. Roller, *Das Formular der paulinischen Briefe. Ein Beitrag zur Lehre vom antiken Briefe*, BWANT 58 (Stuttgart: Kohlhammer, 1933); Koskenniemi; Thraede; Vielhauer, *Geschichte*, 58–70; N. A. Dahl, "Letter," *IDBSup* (1976) 538–41; W. G. Doty, "The Classification of Epistolary Literature," *CBQ* 31 (1969) 183–99; *idem*, *Letters in Primitive Christianity* (Philadelphia: Fortress, 1973); J. L. White, *The Form and Function of the Body of the Greek Letter. A Study of the Letter-Body in Non-Literary Papyri and in Paul the Apostle*, SBLDS 2 (Missoula, MT: Society of Biblical Literature, 1972); Malherbe, *Epistolary Theorists*; Berger, 1326–40 (though it is not clear why the letter should be classed under "vorliterarische Gattungen"). See also the recent summaries of the debates and analyses (many still correcting the influential earlier work of G. A. Deissmann, *Light From the Ancient East*, tr. L. R. M. Strachan [London: Hodder & Stoughton, 1927] 143–246; *idem*, *Bible Studies*, 3–59), with full bibliography, by White, *Light From Ancient Letters*; Stowers; and Aune, *Literary Environment*, 158–82. Conzelmann's emphasis on the "oriental epistolary formula" (p. 19) can be disputed.

[5] With A to B χαίρειν epistolary formula (see the standard treatment by Exler, 23–68), with the customary adaptation of the greeting by Paul to χάρις ὑμῖν καὶ εἰρήνη (observed, interestingly, already by Tertullian, *Marc.* 5.5).

[6] The pioneering work was P. Schubert, *Form and Function of the Pauline Thanksgivings*, BZNW 20 (Berlin: Töpelmann, 1939).

[7] So already Lightfoot, 139–51 on the structure of 1 Corinthians: 1:1–3 Salutation; 1:4–9 Thanksgiving; 1:10–15:58 Body of the Letter; 16:1–24 Conclusion. On the letter body in general see White, *Form and Function* (a study not without some difficulties, in my view; see n. 70 below).

formulae consisting of news and farewell greetings[8] (16:1–24). This letter also contains a deliberative argument (as argued in chaps. II-III), which permits analysis in regard to the so-called μόρια λόγου, or "parts of a speech/argument."[9] We shall see that the epistolary framing is homogeneous with the function and rhetorical stance of the argument in the body of the letter.

Past compositional analyses of the whole of 1 Corinthians have proceeded mostly from the point of view of content analysis. The present historical rhetorical study, which dovetails with some such analyses,[10] is meant to provide further substantiation for the comprehensive structure of the whole letter by examining it as a deliberative letter.[11] However, unlike previous analyses, this study argues that 1 Corinthians is not merely a list of loosely connected topics[12] which one might conceivably grant to have been a part of the same original letter, but indeed constitutes a thoroughgoing argument for church unity,

---

[8] Exler, 69–77, 113–16; Koskenniemi, 148–54; T. Y. Mullins, "Greeting as a New Testament Form," *JBL* 87 (1968) 418–26; Aune, *Literary Environment*, 186–87.

[9] For an overview see Volkmann, 123–27; Martin, 52–166.

[10] The content analysis and interpretation of 1 Corinthians by Godet, 1.28–31 (1:10–4:21 *ecclesiastical* question of parties; 5:1–11:1 *moral* questions; 11:2–14:40 *liturgical* questions; 15:1–58 *doctrinal* question) and Johnson, *Writings*, 276–90 (1 Cor 1–4 The Church of God, 5–10 The Church in the World, 11–14 The World in the Church, 15 The Church and the Kingdom) are especially on target (but they do not emphasize the unity of the letter in the appeal to unity and an end to factionalism as I do) and will be further confirmed by this study. See also the valuable recent analysis of Strobel, 5–8, which resists classification by the distinction of oral and written information (on which see below). The topical changes and transitions in the letter from 1:9–10; 4:21–5:1; 6:20–7:1; 7:40–8:1; 9:27–10:1; 11:1–2; 11:34–12:1; 12:31–13:1; 14:40–15:1; 15:58–16:1 are generally accepted by both division and unity theorists, although they differ in regard to whether these transitions are to be understood as movements into a new argument or sub-argument, or whether they betray full compositional breaks (see, e. g., Robertson-Plummer, xxv-xxviii; Allo, xxv-xxviii; Lietzmann-Kümmel, 1–2; Schmithals, *Gnosticism*, 90; Vielhauer, *Geschichte*, 127–28).

Even Weiss's analysis of the unified letter is close to our view of the structure: "Lassen wir den 1. Korintherbrief als eine Einheit gelten, so ist nicht zu verkennen, dass über dem Ganzen eine geschickt disponierende Hand gewaltet hat. Im grossen und ganzen sind die Massen schön verteilt: A 1:10–4:21 Über die Parteien; B 5–6 Über sittliche Missstände in der Gemeinde; C 7:1–11:1 Über sittliche Zweifelfragen; D 11:2–14:40 Über Missstände in den Gemeindeversammlungen; E Kap. 15 Über die Auferstehung; Schluss: Kap. 16" (*Korintherbrief*, xliii). Compare Barrett's analyis (*First Corinthians*, 28–29), and even the analysis of the (for him redacted) whole by Sellin, "Hauptprobleme," 2942.

[11] That the rhetorical structure has been visible to some prior readers and exegetes of the letter must be seen as an argument in its favor. Depictions of a structure of a text which has never before been observed (in a long history of close scrutiny of those texts!) render themselves somewhat suspect. If an argument "works," readers should be able to understand it even if not able to define exactly how it does so. In fact, the content analysis of 1 Cor works because deliberative proofs are often topically arranged (see below).

[12] So, e. g., Heinrici, *Korinther*, 31; Vielhauer, *Geschichte*, 141; Conzelmann, 6, 8. See also chap. II, "Excursus: Paraenesis and Deliberative Rhetoric," on the presupposition that 1 Cor, as paraenesis, should not be expected to follow any logical or rhetorical arrangement.

centered in the πρόθεσις in 1:10. It has been established in chap. III that 1 Corinthians is filled with terms and *topoi* rooted in political discussions of factionalism, and thus there is a significant correspondence between the call for unity in 1:10 and the rest of 1 Corinthians. The purpose of this chapter is to examine in more depth the way in which Paul has arranged his many arguments and sub-arguments for unity throughout 1 Corinthians to form a rhetorical whole in support of the thesis statement in 1:10. By comparing the arrangement of the argument in 1 Corinthians with other deliberative arguments from antiquity, with emphasis on similar arguments to end factionalism, we shall see that it manifests, in addition to the previously demonstrated thematic unity, rhetorical and compositional unity.

Of primary importance to any discussion of the composition of 1 Corinthians is the connection between what have been regarded as two large sections in the letter: 1 Cor 1–4 and 5–16 (or for some exegetes 1–6 and 7–16). A successful compositional analysis of the unified letter must account for the relationship between these sections.[13] As we have observed above in chap. I, often historical reasons have been promulgated as explanations for the composition of 1 Corinthians.[14] According to many commentators, 1 Cor 7–16 is a distinct section (or set of letter fragments) because it (alone) responds to a written inquiry from Corinth.[15] The numerous possible historical occasions of the letter (the news from Chloe's people in 1:11, unnamed, presumably oral reports in 5:1 and 11:18, the Corinthian letter to Paul mentioned in 7:1, the visit from the Stephanas delegation in 16:17), it is thought, bear primary responsibility for the variation

---

[13] Dahl's attempt to account for the rhetorical force of 1 Cor 1–4 in the entire letter has been noted (see chap. I n. 54).

[14] As representative statements see, e. g., Heinrici, *Korinther*, 23: "Die Anordnung des Ganzen aber ist durch die äusseren Veranlassungen bestimmt, denen P. Schritt vor Schritt nachgeht"; cf. Vielhauer, *Geschichte*, 128: "Inhalt und Aufbau des 1Kor sind ganz von der 'Korrespondenz' bestimmt"; and Johnson, *Writings*, 275: "The outline of the letter corresponds to the sequence of events." This assumption is also held by Merklein, 183 in his defense of the unity of 1 Cor.

[15] Among those arguing for unity, see Robertson-Plummer, xxvi (7:1–11:1 "Reply to the Corinthian Letter"); Allo, xxvi (7–14 "Réponses de Paul aux demandes formulées dans une lettre des Corinthiens"); Barrett, *First Corinthians*, 28–29 (7:1–16:4 "A Letter From Corinth"); Conzelmann, vii, 114 (7–15 "Answers to Questions"); Bruce, 26 (7:1–16:4 "Paul Answers the Letter from Corinth"); Fee, 22–23 (7:1–16:12 "In Response to the Corinthian Letter"). Among partition theorists, see in particular the proponents of the so-called *Antwortbrief* which is excerpted from 7:1–16:24, in which Paul is thought to have responded point by point to the Corinthians' letter (Schenk, 224–25, 241; Schmithals, *Gnosticism*, 90–96; *idem*, "Korintherbriefe," 268–73; Senft, 17–19; Pesch, 88–92, 191–246; cf. the simpler theory of Marxsen, 86–95, which identifies two letters, 5:1–16:24 [the "Themen"-Brief] and 1:1–4:21). See also Sellin's argument against partition theories which do not rigidly enough adhere to this questionable assumption: "Aber auch bei den Teilungen im Gefolge von J. Weiss ist es ein Schönheitsfehler, dass der Antwortbrief sowohl auf schriftliche (7,1) wie auf mündliche (5,1) Nachrichten antwortet" ("Hauptprobleme", 2971 n. 164).

between 1 Cor 1–4 (or 6) and 7–16.[16] This kind of reasoning is shared by partition theorists and unity theorists alike.[17] But while historical causes may have affected the composition of 1 Corinthians, research along those lines remains speculative and unable to produce certainty because of our paucity of information about precisely who visited Paul in Ephesus, who wrote to him, and what the timing was of each contact. Yet for many scholars in their analysis of 1 Corinthians the reverse problem seems to be in effect – there are simply *too many* epistolary occasions, it is thought, to account for only one letter. But there is nothing in ancient epistolary practice to demand that one letter must correspond with only one contact, and there is in fact much counterevidence.[18]

The most important issue at stake here is, who or what is responsible for the arrangement of 1 Corinthians? Analyses which have depended with too much

---

[16] That is why the reference to an oral report in 11:18 is so puzzling to both unity and partition theorists. They presume that Paul would single-mindedly respond to a written inquiry without "interrupting" himself with topics he learned of orally (see, e. g., Schmithals, *Gnosticism*, 91; Sellin, "Hauptprobleme," 2974). But this distinction is an unreal one. There is no reason to assume (as especially Hurd does [p. 62 and passim]) that an ancient letter writer must isolate responses or frame them according to the way in which she or he had learned of the information. Especially since many ancient letters respond to *both* oral and written information, this rigid separation made in regard to 1 Corinthians must be challenged. We should also note with Bachmann, 17 that many contacts could have been simultaneously underway because of the closeness and geographical accessibility of Ephesus to Corinth.

[17] For unity theorists, more news must have come while Paul was in the act of composing this long letter of response (Barrett, *First Corinthians*, 15), whereas for partition theorists, each possible epistolary occasion must be lined up with a separate letter or letter fragment (as especially Schenk, 237: "die drei im I Cor genannten Informanden auch die Veranlassung für drei verschiedene Schreiben des Pl gewesen sind"; and Senft, 18: "Ce sont là autant d'indices d'une diversité de situations et par conséquent d'une pluralité de documents en 1 Cor"; also Sellin, "Hauptprobleme," 2968, who includes this in his list of mandates for partition theories). This last argument is especially weak, simply because of our lack of historical information – presumably someone delivered the Corinthian letter to Paul, but we do not know who! Thus, instead of three contacts, there may only have been two, if Chloe's people or the Stephanas group brought the letter. Or, there could have been four or more: if yet another party brought the letter, they could have brought even more reports which could lie behind the anonymous oral news mentioned by Paul in 5:1 and 11:18. Even Apollos, who is with Paul in Ephesus (16:12), could have given him oral reports (on the multiplicity of contacts, see Strobel, 11–12). And what of Sosthenes, who is the co-sender of the letter (1:1; cf. Acts 18:17)? We simply do not know, so that literary reconstructions which demand such a one-to-one correspondence with reconstructions from admittedly limited (and numerically uncertain!) historical data must be questioned.

[18] See the many examples of both literary and documentary letters in Mitchell, 239–50 (another good example is Cic. *Att.* 12.40). A letter is a form of communication between two parties who share many common experiences and events (to which the modern scholar is an outsider, in most cases). Many ancient Greek letters respond to and make reference to many different contacts between sender and recipient (visits from friends, a previous letter or letters, previous conversations, events shared, etc.). The presupposition that each letter must correspond to a single isolated "epistolary occasion" remains unproven for other ancient letters, and thus should not be used as a dictum in Pauline scholarship (cf. also Merklein, 157).

certainty on presumed "historical" factors[19] have tended to downplay Paul's own creative role in fashioning his letter of response. In fact, a large body of scholarly opinion has held that, at least for part of the letter, the composition of 1 Corinthians is actually not a Pauline creation at all, but Paul merely follows the Corinthians' letter to him, in its order.[20] But we have seen in the previous chapter that 1 Corinthians is not a loosely connected, disharmonious set of replies to a variety of posed questions on their own terms. Instead the argument focuses deliberately on a single appeal: the call for church unity and an end to factionalism. There is no reason to assume that Paul merely followed the Corinthians' letter.[21] I shall argue that 1 Corinthians is Paul's own creation,[22] reflecting his own *inventio* and *dispositio*,[23] which responds to the varied and contentious situation in the Corinthian church of which he had been informed by several different parties. It is his awareness of the situation from various points of view which enables him to diagnose the problem, not merely as the different Corinthian groups themselves might have described it, but in more overarching terms which indicate that the individual quarrels have higher stakes: the very unity and stability of the church.

Arguments that the structure of 1 Corinthians simply mirrors that of the

---

[19] One does not want to stray into an antihistorical bias, however. Surely Paul's letter responds to a very specific set of historical circumstances. But here I challenge the absolute validity of such presuppositions by asking if we can understand the letter's composition as Paul's own creation, by seeing how its composition is appropriate to the genre deliberative letter, and the subject matter, an appeal to seek concord. The assumption that an ancient letter writer would indeed *as a matter of course* follow the sequence of the varied correspondence which she or he has received has never been documented, and must be questioned, both in itself and in its applicability to this particular letter.

[20] See Conzelmann, 6: "Plainly, he simply follows the order of the Corinthians' letter." Of many others, see also Hurd, 64, and his partial list of scholars who hold this view on p. 65 n. 1. This is also the logic behind the theory of the excerpted *Antwortbrief* (see n. 15 above).

[21] "Sind Paulus damit zwar Themen für seinen Brief vorgegeben, so doch nicht unmittelbar auch die Reihenfolge, in der er sie behandelt . . . Der Aufbau des 1 Kor ist also nicht vorgegeben, sondern muss einer von Paulus selber intendierten Ordnung folgen" (Lührmann, "Freundschaftsbrief," 305). The same conclusion is reached by Standaert, "Analyse Rhétorique," 25: "Paul distribue les différentes questions à traiter selon un ordre sans doute réfléchi."

[22] There is an inherent contradiction in the scholarship on 1 Cor in that even those who argue that the composition of 1 Cor was *determined* by outside events nonetheless note with approval the theological and even rhetorical consistency of Paul's continuous argument in 1 Cor (e. g., Heinrici, *Korinther*, 23; Vielhauer, *Geschichte*, 128). The same inconsistency can be observed in partition theories which praise the final composition of the redactor, which they deemed unacceptable as the author's final work (e. g., Weiss, *Korintherbrief*, xliii; critique with Merklein, 158).

[23] The terms refer to the "invention" and "arrangement" of arguments (the Greek counterparts are εὕρεσις and τάξις). Along with style, delivery and memory, these constitute the works (ἔργα) of the rhetorician (for discussion and references see Volkmann, 26–32; Martin, 11–12 and passim; Solmsen, "Aristotelian Tradition," 46–50; the note by H. Caplan, LCL vol. *[Cicero] ad C. Herennium* [Cambridge, MA: Harvard University Press, 1954] 6–7).

Corinthians' letter to Paul rest upon widely held assumptions, in particular about the περὶ δέ formula which is repeated in 1 Cor 7:1, 25; 8:1; 12:1; 16:1, 12:

1. the assumption that each περὶ δέ in 7:25 ff. refers back to 7:1 (Περὶ δὲ ὧν ἐγράψατε), and thus must introduce a topic contained in the Corinthians' letter.[24]

2. the inverse assumption that Paul would *only* introduce a topic broached by the Corinthians in their letter to him with περὶ δέ.[25]

3. the further assumption that Paul responds with περὶ δέ point by point, in its order, to the Corinthians' letter.[26]

In a separate study I have investigated the use and function of the formula περὶ δέ throughout ancient Greek texts (literary and rhetorical works, literary letters, private documentary letters and the New Testament).[27] From this body of comparative evidence the conclusion emerges that the formula περὶ δέ is simply a topic marker, a shorthand way of introducing the next topic of discussion, *the only requirement of which is that it is readily known to both author and reader.* Consequently, Paul's repeated use of περὶ δέ in 1 Corinthians, while it does indicate to us that Paul is moving on to another topic, a topic which he assumes the Corinthians will immediately recognize, does not in itself give us any clues as to: a) the source of that topic between the epistolary partners; b) the literary integrity of the work; or c) the rationale for the order of presentation of the topics thus introduced. The three assumptions about περὶ δέ listed above, which have

---

24 See n. 15 above.

25 See Conzelmann, 182: "There is a certain tension between the outward and inward plan of chaps. 11–14. A new topic is introduced only in 12:1, once again with περί, 'concerning,' and thus apparently once again on the basis of an inquiry from Corinth." On this assumption Hurd becomes puzzled at 11:2 because "this allusion immediately suggests that Paul is still dealing with the Corinthians' letter although the introductory περὶ δέ is absent" (p. 90; also p. 69 on 9:1). For the partition theorists, this assumption demands that all material in chapters 7–16 *not* introduced by περὶ δέ must belong to another letter. Pesch's argument from this presupposition is typical: "Da weder in 1 Kor 10,1 noch in 1 Kor 10,23 eine *Überschrift* (mit 'über . . . aber') zu finden ist, die auf die Beantwortung einer brieflichen Anfrage aus Korinth durch Paulus schliessen liesse . . . wird man nicht alle Abschnitte von Kapitel 8–10 dem Antwortbrief zuschreiben können" (p. 89; see also Schmithals, *Gnosticism*, 85–89; Schenk, 225; Suhl, 206). See J. Murphy-O'Connor's vehement rejection of this assumption ("outside the bounds of rational discussion") in his review of Pesch (*RB* 95 [1988] 149).

26 See n. 20 above.

27 What follows is a brief summary of the arguments and conclusions of Mitchell, "Concerning ΠΕΡΙ ΔΕ in 1 Corinthians." Since my article was completed another study has appeared which touches on some of these same issues: E. Baasland, "Die περί–Formel und die Argumentation(ssituation) des Paulus," *ST* 42 (1988) 69–87. In the course of his study Baasland reaches the same conclusion as I do, that περί is not solely a formula for answering questions (81–82). While this conclusion is surely correct, Baasland's analysis suffers, in my view, from a lack of definition of the formula, so that he investigates the realms of "περί-Sätze" and "περί-Literatur" (most of what he describes are titles and subtitles) which are too broad to be actual categories. That is why his case for the "school discussion" as the *Sitz im Leben* is not convincing, since a preposition does not have a *Sitz*! In fact, the formula περὶ δέ is found in a wide variety of genres in ancient Greek literature (Mitchell, 223–54).

had such an enormous influence on scholarship on 1 Corinthians (both for those who argue for unity and those who argue for partition), are therefore without substantiation, and cannot be the foundation of an investigation of the composition of the letter.[28] So, on both historical and literary grounds, there is no reason to assume, as so many scholars have, that in 1 Cor 7–16 Paul slavishly follows the Corinthians' letter to him.[29] Instead, in his argument for unity which responds to the Corinthian situation, Paul arranges his topics of discussion, which have emerged from his varied contacts with the church at Corinth,[30] in the way which best suits his rhetorical purpose. He is responsible for the *inventio* and *dispositio* of the argument. An investigation of the structure and composition of 1 Corinthians as Paul's deliberative argument for church unity is the subject of this chapter.[31]

C. Compositional Analysis

1. 1:1–3 Epistolary Prescript

Paul[32] addresses his letter "to the church of God which is in Corinth" [τῇ ἐκκλησίᾳ τοῦ θεοῦ τῇ οὔσῃ ἐν Κορίνθῳ] (1:2). The singular ἐκκλησία indicates already Paul's intention to call them to unity – they are one church,[33] God's

[28] Mitchell, 254–56; also Baasland, 82.

[29] So correctly also Bailey, 154 (without reference to the περὶ δέ formula): "Some of the Corinthians' questions (oral and written) are worked into Paul's outline, rather than the other way around. *He* sets the agenda, not the Corinthians" (emph. original). I do not, however, agree with all parts of Bailey's own constructive analysis (Paul is not writing "essays" but arguments).

[30] The assumptions of the earliest exegetes on this question are very important. See Chrys.'s view of the composition of 1 Cor: Ἔγραψαν μὲν οὖν αὐτῷ διὰ Φορτουνάτου καὶ Στεφανᾶ καὶ Ἀχαϊκοῦ . . . οὐ μὴν περὶ πάντων, ἀλλὰ περὶ γάμου καὶ παρθενίας. διὸ καὶ ἔλεγε. Περὶ δὲ ὧν ἐγράψατέ μοι. Αὐτὸς μέντοι, καὶ ὑπὲρ ὧν ἔγραψαν, καὶ ὑπὲρ ὧν οὐκ ἔγραψαν, ἐπιστέλλει (*hom. in I Cor.* Argumentum 2–3 [*PG* 61.12]; cf. 44.2 [61.376]). He is followed by Thdt. *1 Cor* 16:17: Διὰ τούτων ἔγραψαν οἱ Κορίνθιοι, καὶ τὸν Ἀπόστολον ἐπηρώτησαν περὶ τῶν γεγαμηκότων [*PG* 82.372].

[31] Of course a verse-by-verse commentary of 1 Corinthians is well beyond the scope of this inquiry. We shall concentrate on the rhetorical structure and function of each of the epistolary and rhetorical forms, and the sub-arguments within the proof section. The outcome of the exegetical investigations in chaps. II and III is here presumed.

[32] His self-address as κλητὸς ἀπόστολος Χριστοῦ Ἰησοῦ does not indicate an apologia (so Lightfoot, 142–43; Weiss, *Korintherbrief*, 1). Chrys. takes it as an immediate rebuke of Corinthian pride (*hom. in I Cor.* 1.1 [*PG* 61.11--12]). Χριστοῦ Ἰησοῦ he also regards as a pointed reference to their factions: ὁ διδάσκαλος ὑμῶν Χριστός. καὶ ὑμεῖς ἀνθρώποις ἐπιγράφεσθε τῆς διδασκαλίας προστάτας; (1.1 [61.12]).

[33] Paul may be responding to the reality of house churches (see chap. III n. 62). Despite the variety of house churches there is, for Paul, one church of God in Corinth.

church.[34] But, like any social or political body, the church at Corinth is composed of a variety of individuals. Paul points this out in the dual plural appositives[35] ἡγιασμένοις ἐν Χριστῷ Ἰησοῦ and κλητοῖς ἁγίοις. The plurality of individuals which comprises the church is named here in its commonality – all are sanctified in Christ Jesus, all are called, all are saints.[36] Already in the epistolary prescript Paul begins to lay the groundwork for his argument[37] for unity in the "ones," the common things shared by all Corinthian Christians despite their differences.[38] This dual form of identification of the epistolary addressee – first to the church named as a singular body and then named twice again as a composite of individuals,[39] unparalleled in Paul's extant letters,[40] is significant. The problem faced by this church and by Paul in his letter – ecclesial formation, the attempt to unite diverse individuals into a cohesive community – is thus alluded to already in the prescript.[41] This is the case even before we get to the controversial section of this expanded address formula in 1:2b, σὺν πᾶσιν τοῖς ἐπικαλουμέ-

---

[34] The addition τοῦ θεοῦ (here and in 2 Cor) is not found in Paul's other letters which address an ἐκκλησία (1 Thess, [2 Thess], Gal). See Chrys.'s exegesis: Τῇ Ἐκκλησίᾳ τοῦ θεοῦ. Οὐ τοῦδε καὶ τοῦδε, ἀλλὰ τοῦ θεοῦ ... Ἐκκλησίαν δὲ θεοῦ καλεῖ, δεικνὺς ὅτι ἡνῶσθαι αὐτὴν χρή. Εἰ γὰρ θεοῦ ἐστιν, ἥνωται. καὶ μία ἐστὶν, οὐκ ἐν Κορίνθῳ μόνον, ἀλλὰ καὶ ἐν πάσῃ τῇ οἰκουμένῃ. Τὸ γὰρ τῆς Ἐκκλησίας ὄνομα οὐ χωρισμοῦ, ἀλλὰ ἑνώσεώς ἐστε καὶ συμφωνίας ὄνομα (*hom. in I Cor.* 1.1 [*PG* 61.13]; followed by Robertson-Plummer, 2; cf. Grosheide, 23; note especially the development of this argument in 1 Cor 3:9).

[35] "The plural in apposition to the collective singular throws a passing emphasis upon the individual responsibility of those who had been consecrated in baptism (vi. 11) as members of Christ" (Robertson-Plummer, 2). See also Heinrici, *Korinther*, 41: "Sie [die Adressaten] sind charakterisirt mit Rücksicht auf die Einheit (ἐκκλησία) und mit Rücksicht auf jeden einzelnen, der als Glied der Gemeinschaft Gottes Eigentum ist (κλητοὶ ἅγιοι u. s. w.). Die starke Betonung der Zusammengehörigkeit ist durch die sogleich zu rügenden Streitigkeiten (1:10f.) veranlasst" (see also Allo, 2; differently Fee, 32 n. 19).

[36] Καλεῖ δὲ αὐτοὺς καὶ κλητοὺς καὶ ἁγίους, καὶ συνάπτει τοῖς κατὰ τὴν οἰκουμένην πεπιστευκόσι, διδάσκων ὡς οὐκ αὐτοὺς μόνον ὁμονοεῖν προσήκει, ἀλλὰ καὶ πάντας τοὺς τῷ σωτηρίῳ πεπιστευκότας κηρύγματι ἓν ἔχειν φρόνημα (Thdt. *1 Cor.* 1:2 [*PG* 82.229]).

[37] On this as Pauline practice, see Betz, *Galatians*, 37. On 1 Cor in particular see Belleville, 16–18. Customizing the greeting (though not always as extensively as this) to express the relationship between writer and sender is also attested of course in a variety of Greek letters (see Exler, 133).

[38] See chap. III nn. 141–42. The abundance and repetition of Christological referents in 1:1–9 is a part of this unifying appeal (with Friedrich, 240).

[39] Some ancient witnesses (P^{46}, B, D, etc.) interlace ἡγιασμένοις ἐν Χριστῷ Ἰησοῦ between τῇ ἐκκλησίᾳ τοῦ θεοῦ and τῇ οὔσῃ ἐν Κορίνθῳ, a word order which would emphasize even more the dual nature and mutual interdependence of the church as a body both communal and individual.

[40] 1 Thess (2 Thess) and importantly 2 Cor have only the church address (τῇ ἐκκλησίᾳ Θεσσαλονικέων, τῇ ἐκκλησίᾳ ... τῇ οὔσῃ ἐν Κορίνθῳ), as does Gal, though plural (ταῖς ἐκκλησίαις τῆς Γαλατίας). The plural saints address is used by Paul in Rom (πᾶσιν τοῖς οὖσιν ἐν Ῥώμῃ ἀγαπητοῖς θεοῦ, κλητοῖς ἁγίοις) and Phil (πᾶσιν τοῖς ἁγίοις ἐν Χριστῷ Ἰησοῦ τοῖς οὖσιν ἐν Φιλίπποις (cf. Col and Eph). Only 1 Cor has both.

[41] "A formal salutation, which is amplified with topics important for the ethos and logos of the letter ..." (Kennedy, *New Testament Interpretation*, 24).

νοις τὸ ὄνομα τοῦ κυρίου ἡμῶν Ἰησοῦ Χριστοῦ ἐν παντὶ τόπῳ αὐτῶν καὶ ἡμῶν. This anomalous phrase, taken by Weiss to be a later editor's addition to "catholicize" the letter,[42] is another introductory argument for the unity of the Corinthian Christians (and even those in all of the world[43]), because all call upon the name of the same Lord (cf. 1:10; 6:11; 8:6; 12:3).[44]

2. 1:4–9 *Epistolary Thanksgiving/Rhetorical* προοίμιον

These verses comprise the epistolary thanksgiving formula,[45] which doubles as the προοίμιον,[46] or introduction to the deliberative argument in the body of the letter. Just as in the epistolary opening formulas, here Paul weaves into the formulaic thanksgiving period/προοίμιον key terms for the argument to follow[47] – λόγος, γνῶσις, καλεῖν/κλῆσις, βεβαιοῦσθαι, κοινωνία.[48] As Paul thanks

---

[42] Weiss, *Korintherbrief*, xli, 4 (it serves to introduce the *corpus*); Sellin, "Hauptprobleme," 2983, with further references. I take it to be original, because it so well suits Paul's rhetorical purpose, and because ἐν παντὶ τόπῳ is a well-attested Pauline phrase which refers to the worldwide mission and extent of the church (1 Thess 1:8; 2 Cor 2:14).

[43] The enigmatic αὐτῶν καὶ ἡμῶν may refer to τόπῳ, so that Paul is uniting his greeting of the Corinthians with all Christians (Chrys. *hom. in I Cor.* 1.1 [*PG* 61.13–14]; Weiss, *Korintherbrief*, 3). Differently, Lightfoot argues that those words construe with τοῦ κυρίου: "'Our Lord, did I say – their Lord and ours alike.' There is a covert allusion to the divisions in the Corinthian Church, and an implied exhortation to unity" (p. 146; Lietzmann-Kümmel, 5; Barrett, *First Corinthians*, 34; Allo, 3, "c'est encore un rappel à l'unité"). The emphasis on unity is there in the phrase τὸ ὄνομα τοῦ κυρίου ἡμῶν Ἰησοῦ Χριστοῦ, regardless of how one interprets the latter construction (see Chrys. *hom. in I Cor.* 1.1 [*PG* 61.13], Οὐ τοῦ δεῖνος καὶ τοῦ δεῖνος, ἀλλὰ Τὸ ὄνομα τοῦ Κυρίου; also Thdt. *1 Cor.* 1:2 [*PG* 82.229]).

[44] As argued by Wickert: "Vielmehr ruft er sie zu derjenigen Einheit zurück, in welcher sie als Christen immer schon stehen, im Sinne der für ihn so charakteristischen Verknüpfung von Indikativ und Imperativ: zur Einheit hat uns Christus befreit, so besteht nun in der Einheit" (p. 79). See also Lightfoot's exegesis: "It perhaps arose out of the idea of unity prominent in the Apostle's mind, and was suggested by the dissensions which divided the Corinthian church" (p. 146), and more recently Belleville, 16–18.

[45] Paul follows conventional epistolary practice, as the προσκύνημα formula in the papyrus letters shows (Koskenniemi, 139–45), but customizes this part to his special purposes (Schubert, 4; Stowers, 21–22; Aune, *Literary Environment*, 163–64, 185–86).

[46] Dinkler, "Korintherbriefe," 19; Vielhauer, *Geschichte*, 127; Conzelmann, 25; Lührmann, "Freundschaftsbrief," 300 (though this is the only rhetorical term they employ in their analysis of the letter); Kennedy, *New Testament Interpretation*, 24; Betz, "Rhetoric and Theology," 33 n. 89. Aune describes this dual function: "The thanksgiving period is not just ornamental. It often praises the recipients, functioning as an exordium aimed at securing their goodwill . . . Pauline thanksgivings usually encapsulate the main themes of letters, like the thanksgiving periods in papyrus letters and introductions of speeches" (*Literary Environment*, 186). See already Heinrici, *Korinther*, 44: "In den Briefen des P. ein ebenso feststehendes Stück [das Dankgebet], wie die captatio benevolentiae in der antiken Rede."

[47] See Friedrich, 240; Allo, 5; Grosheide, 26; Doty, *Letters*, 32–33; Betz, "Rhetoric and Theology," 24–39 (esp. 33); Belleville, 18–21 (the passage functions as the table of contents to 1 Cor); Stowers, 22: "In 1 Corinthians (1:4–9), he gives thanks for the speech, knowledge, and

God for the Corinthians' gifts, certain themes emerge which will also play a role in the argument to follow:[49] the passive nature of the Christian call and charismatic powers,[50] Christocentric emphasis,[51] and an eschatological reserve as a corrective to overly enthusiastic reception of the spiritual "riches" which has had divisive consequences in the church.[52] Yet other key terms, such as ἀγάπη and ἔργον, are conspicuously absent from Paul's list of Corinthian accomplishments.[53] The work of building up the church[54] through the unifying power of love is what the Corinthians lack, and is the course of action for church unity which Paul will urge on the Corinthians throughout this letter. Thus the thanksgiving prayer in 1:4–9 forms an appropriate προοίμιον which fulfills the rhetorical requirement that it make the hearers attentive, receptive, and well-disposed,[55] and orient them to the argument to follow. Even the use of a prayer in the προοίμιον to a deliberative speech is paralleled in actual texts,[56] so the marriage of epistolary and rhetorical forms in this way is a comfortable one.

---

spiritual gifts of the Corinthians. In chapters 1–4, 8, and 12–14 the reader learns that the improper uses of wisdom, knowledge, charismatic speech, and spiritual gifts are, according to Paul, central problems for the Corinthian church." We have seen in chap. III that exclusive claims to possess these gifts played a role in Corinthian factionalism (see 4:8 on "wealth" and chaps. 12–14 on χαρίσματα), as did γνῶσις (see ch. 8; cf. 13:2).

48 See ch. III for the importance of the latter two terms in discussions of concord.

49 See Strobel, 29–32, for a summary.

50 Chrys. *hom. in I Cor.* 2.1 [*PG* 61.17].

51 Robertson-Plummer observed that Christ is named ten times in the first ten verses of 1 Corinthians (p. 7).

52 Notice that all Corinthian Christians ("you") are said to suffer no lack of riches, with no distinctions.

53 Weiss, *Korintherbrief*, 6, noticed the lack of reference to works of love, as in the epistolary thanksgivings of 1 Thess and Col; on ἔργον as missing here, but present in the conclusion to the argument in 15:58, see Betz, "Rhetoric and Theology," 33: "Paul's letter with its advice on the practical matters in the church is designed to bring the Corinthians' praxis (ἔργον) up to the same standards as their 'eloquence and knowledge.'" See also Barrett. *First Corinthians*, 36 on faith, hope and love missing here (but cf. 13:13).

54 The building metaphor is already alluded to in the double use of βεβαιοῦν in 1:6 and 8 (see the full discussion in chap. III). See Weiss's comment: "dafür deutet er an (v. 8) dass die Gemeinde der Befestigung bedarf" (*Korintherbrief*, 6).

55 *Rh.Al.* 29.1436a–1438a; *Rhet.Her.* 1.4.6–8; Cic. *Inv.Rhet.* 1.15.20; Quint. *Inst.* 4.1.5; Doxopat. *Homil. in Aphth.* 131.12–16. On the προοίμιον in general see Volkmann, 127–48, 295–97; Martin, 60–75. On 1 Cor 1:4–9, see Kennedy's description: "Paul begins with a proem (1:4–9) revealing none of his anxiety about the Corinthians and aiming to secure their goodwill" (*New Testament Interpretation*, 24). See below on the role of praise in effecting this.

56 "Introductory prayers were common, too, in *demegoriae*" (Goldstein, 177, citing Dem. *Prooem.* 25.3; 50; *Or.* 3.18; Ar. *Eccl.* 171–72; *Eq.* 763–72; *Thesm.* 295–310, and Plutarch's report that Pericles always prayed to the gods before delivering a speech [*Per.* 8.43]; see also Cic. *Inv.Rhet.* 1.16.22 and Dem. *Prooem.* 54 where the gifts of the gods to the city are noted). For prayers at the beginning of deliberative discourses urging concord see Dio Chrys. *Or.* 38.8–9 (a speech which also ends with a prayer in §51, as in *Or.* 39.8 and the Latin Ps-Sall. *Rep.* 13.8); 40.19 (in the middle of the speech); Pl. *Ep.* 8.352E and especially Dem. *Ep.* 1, which has a prayer placed before the epistolary salutation (on which see Goldstein, 176–77). Forensic and epideictic

Paul begins his argument for Corinthian unity in 1:4–9 by praising all Corinthian Christians[57] in apparently glowing terms: ἐπλουτίσθητε ... ὥστε ὑμᾶς μὴ ὑστερεῖσθαι ἐν μηδενὶ χαρίσματι.[58] It is clear that Paul's praise is accompanied by an eschatological reserve (which is also consistent with his stance throughout 1 Corinthians[59]), but it is nonetheless praise. In fact, Paul's praise of his addressees in this προοίμιον to his deliberative argument for concord reflects common practice,[60] as Aelius Aristides argues explicitly in the προοίμιον to his *Or.* 23, *Concerning Concord:*

I believe that it is incumbent upon whoever wishes to create a common friendship [φιλία κοινή] for the cities with one another, not to laud some of them and slander others, but to mention them all with praise, so that, to begin with [πρῶτον], by being pleased you may all more eagerly accept his advice [συμβουλή], and one part of concordant [ὁμόνοια] behavior may already be accomplished. For if you accept being praised in common and none of you regards the praise of the others as an act of dishonor toward himself, but each of you is delighted by the attributes of one another as if they were your own, first of all right from the start you shall give a demonstration of concord, and next you will gradually become accustomed also to praise one another and to have thoughts which are expedient for all of you in common [φρονεῖν ἃ κοινῇ πᾶσιν ὑμῖν συμφέρει]. But to come to advise concord [συμβουλεύσων ὁμονοεῖν] and at the same time to hesitate to praise you, seems to me to be a kind of cowardice, and even the act of one who is destroying his argument [ὑπόθεσις], and either has badly attempted it, or does not know in what way it is proper to deal with it (23.6–7).[61]

Like Aristides, Paul begins his argument for unity by preparing his hearers to accept his advice through his common praise of them all.[62] It is most character-

---

speeches may also contain prayers (e. g., Dem. *De Cor.* 1, 8; Aristid. *Or.* 26.3; Goldstein, 177). Note also Aune, *Literary Environment,* 186 on thanksgiving in speeches (citing Dio Chrys. *Or.* 48.1, a deliberative speech urging concord).

57 Lietzmann-Kümmel, 1 refers to 1:4–9 as "Lob der Korinther."

58 Compare the litotes in this line from the exordium of a speech urging concord on the Nicaeans: ὥσπερ ἡ ὑμετέρα πόλις, κατά τε ἰσχὺν καὶ μέγεθος οὐδεμιᾶς ἡττωμένη ... τὸ δὲ μέγιστον ἥρωάς τε καὶ θεοὺς οἰκιστὰς λαβοῦσα (Dio Chrys. *Or.* 39.1; see also 34.7).

59 See especially 4:1–5; 9:24–27; 13:8–13; ch. 15.

60 And theory; see *Rh.Al.* 29.1436b; Arist. *Rh.* 3.14.7; *Rhet.Her.* 1.5.8; Cic. *Inv.Rhet.* 1.16.22; Quint. *Inst.* 4.1.16: "We shall win the good-will of the judge not merely by praising [*laudando*] him, which must be done with tact and is an artifice common to both parties, but by linking his praise to the furtherance of our own case." Rhetorical theory also customarily held that the προοίμιον could be derived from the speaker, the opponent, the hearer, or the subject (Arist. *Rh.* 3.14.7; *Rhet.Her.* 1.4.8; Cic. *Inv.Rhet.* 1.16.22; Quint. *Inst.* 4.1.6–22). In 1 Cor 1:4–9 it is clearly concentrated on the hearers.

61 Cf. Dio Chrys. *Or.* 40.22.

62 This is well understood (expressed in proper rhetorical terms) by Chrys.: Ἄλλως δὲ, κἂν μὴ σφόδρα τῆς ἀληθείας ἔχωνται οἱ ἔπαινοι, ἀλλ' ὅμως οἰκονομικῶς ἔγκεινται προοδοποιοῦντες τῷ λόγῳ. Ὁ μὲν γὰρ ἐκ προοιμίων εὐθέως φορτικὰ φθεγγόμενος ... Ἵν' οὖν μὴ ἀπὸ ἐγκωμίων δοκούντων εἶναι ποιεῖται τὴν ἀρχήν. Οὐδὲ γὰρ ἐγκώμιον τοῦτο ἦν αὐτῶν, ἀλλὰ τῆς τοῦ Θεοῦ χάριτας (... ἵνα ἐπιπλεῖον αὐτῶν ἐκκαθάρῃ τὸ νόσημα) (*hom. in I Cor.* 2.1 [*PG* 61.18]).

istic of Paul's argument throughout 1 Corinthians that he always addresses the church *as a whole*, and will not reify their factions by naming them in specifics. Instead he combats, not individual factionalists or factions, but the very phenomenon of factionalism itself.[63] In this he conforms with other discourses which urge unity on divided factions.[64]

Thus we see that Paul's praise of the Corinthians in 1:4–9 serves the rhetorical function of any προοίμιον, and in particular those in deliberative discourses urging concord: to unify the recipients in their common praise in order to prepare them to receive the at times stern advice to follow.[65] This commendation of the Corinthians will also later serve to highlight the severity of their shortcomings as demonstrated in their factions, especially in the section 1:18–4:21.[66] This προοίμιον ends with the important reminder to the Corinthians that they were called by God (the passive is pointed)[67] not to their own factions and in-groups, but to κοινωνία τοῦ υἱοῦ αὐτοῦ 'Ιησοῦ Χριστοῦ τοῦ κυρίου ἡμῶν.[68] The unifying appeal to the Corinthians has already begun. This provides a transition into the proposition of the argument.[69]

3. 1:10–15:58 Epistolary Body

With 1:10 Paul makes a transition into the body of his letter to the Corinthians.[70] This letter body contains an argument, a deliberative argument, for church

---

[63] "Die Schwierigkeit, sie historisch zu erfassen, besteht darin, dass Paulus die Parteien nicht einzeln nach ihren Anschauungen, sondern das Parteitreiben grundsätzlich kritisiert und dabei immer die Gemeinde als ganze anspricht" (Vielhauer, *Geschichte*, 134). See also, e. g., Heinrici, *Sendschreiben*, 153–54; Schmiedel, 115 (who thinks that arguments against specific parties are mixed in with censure against factionalism in general); Lang, 24.

[64] See below on 1 Cor 1:18–4:21.

[65] Μέλλων κατηγορεῖν προθεραπεύει τὴν ἀκοὴν, ὥστε δεκτὴν γενέσθαι τὴν ἰατρείαν (Thdt. *1 Cor.* 1:4 [*PG* 82.229]).

[66] See the discussion below on the σύγκρισις motif in 1 Cor 3–4.

[67] Hainz, *Koinonia*, 16.

[68] For the connection with factionalism, see Photius on 1:9: εἰς κοινωνίαν ἐκλήθητε Χριστοῦ. τί ἄλλους καὶ ἄλλοὺς ἐφιστῶντες ἑαυτοῖς προστάτας καὶ διδασκάλους, τῆς θαυμασίας ἐκείνης καὶ σωτηρίου κοινωνίας ἑαυτοὺς φιλονεικεῖτε διασχίζειν καὶ ἀποτέμνεσθαι; [Staab, 545]. Modern commentators point to the connection with the body of Christ: ". . . Paul parle à ses lecteurs de la part qu'ils ont au Christ en vertu de la vocation qu'ils ont reçue et de leur statut de membres de son corps" (Senft, 31; see also Friedrich, 239). The body of Christ image is one of the predominant images for unity found in 1 Cor (as we have seen in chap. III).

[69] Cf. Quint. *Inst.* 4.1.76. Schenk's argument (240–41) that 1:1–9 belongs to a different letter from 1:10–4:21 has received no support because of this clear and smooth transition from 1:9 to 1:10 (Schmithals, "Korintherbriefe," 267).

[70] On the transition from 1:9 to 1:10 see J. T. Sanders, "The Transition from Opening Epistolary Thanksgiving to Body in the Letters of the Pauline Corpus," *JBL* 81 (1962) 348–62. With Lightfoot, 139; Godet, 1.vii, 61; Segalla, 468, the letter body extends from 1:10–15:58. White argued that the letter body extends only from 1:10–4:21 (*Form and Function*, 73 and passim, followed by Belleville, 21–23, as also Doty, *Letters*, 43), which leaves ch. 5–15 out of

unity.[71] We have already noted that the argument has been well prepared for in the epistolary prescript and the epistolary thanksgiving formula, and thus forms a continuum with them. This letter body, because it contains a rhetorical composition, can be analyzed (along with its epistolary frame, as we have seen) according to the rules and conventions for rhetorical composition in the Greco-Roman world. We shall do so, paying special heed to the methodological principles delineated and defended in chap. I, especially the mandate that one must examine actual rhetorical compositions alongside and in comparison with the rules of the rhetorical handbooks in order to achieve a balanced understanding of the realities as well as the ideals of rhetorical composition in the first century.[72] It is especially important that we do so in this case, as we are investigating a piece of deliberative rhetoric, while the handbooks describe primarily forensic rhetoric, and then treat deliberative and epideictic by (sometimes forced) analogy to it.[73]

a) 1:10 πρόθεσις/Thesis Statement to the Deliberative Argument

The beauty and simplicity of Aristotle's bare bones description of the τάξις of a rhetorical composition serves well in analyzing deliberative arguments. Aristotle asserted that arguments contain essentially two parts: the πρόθεσις (statement of what is to be proven) and the πίστις (proof) for it.[74] In deliberative arguments the πρόθεσις states in brief the advice which the orator urges his audience to accept. While narrative may not be required in a deliberative argument, a statement of the course of action that is recommended to the audience is always

---

the letter body, but this is incorrect, and results from a too rigid application of the argument of R. W. Funk that discussion of "the apostolic *parousia*" appears at the end of the letter body ("The Apostolic Parousia: Form and Significance," in *Christian History and Interpretation: Studies Presented to John Knox*, ed. W. R. Farmer, C. F. D. Moule and R. R. Niebuhr [Cambridge: University Press, 1967] 249–69). Instead the apostolic parousia is better understood as a *topos* or theme than as an epistolary formula (T. Y. Mullins, "Visit Talk in New Testament Letters," *CBQ* 35 [1973] 350–58; Aune, *Literary Environment*, 190), which need not appear at the end of the letter body. White's view also holds to the now questioned assumption (see Stowers, 23; Aune, *Literary Environment*, 191; and further discussion in chap. II, "Excursus: Paraenesis and Deliberative Rhetoric") that the compositional model of the Pauline letter is ordinarily a dogma section followed by a section of paraenesis (see p. 71), which is how he would apparently characterize 1 Cor 5–15. There is no reason to truncate the letter body to end at 4:21.

[71] See the proof of this in chaps. II and III.

[72] Compare Burgess's methodology (p. 91) in his study on epideictic rhetoric, and also that of van Unnik, "Studies," 181–94.

[73] An exception to this is the early work *Rhetorica ad Alexandrum*, which provides the most thorough treatment of deliberative speeches on their own terms (1.1421b–2.1425b; 29.1436a–34.1440a).

[74] *Rh.* 3.13.1, 4: Ἔστι δὲ τοῦ λόγου δύο μέρη. ἀναγκαῖον γὰρ τό τε πρᾶγμα εἰπεῖν περὶ οὗ, καὶ τότ' ἀποδεῖξαι. Aristotle here is consciously combatting traditional τέχναι, with their emphasis on multiple parts of a speech, preferring a functional to a mere structural approach (Solmsen, "Aristotelian Tradition," 35–39).

required.[75] Greek and especially later Latin handbooks become more and more atomistic in regard to the introductory parts of speeches,[76] differentiating *propositio/expositio, partitio/divisio, enumeratio* and *distributio*,[77] but Aristotle's simplified description well fits the extant deliberative texts. It is also well suited to the argument in 1 Corinthians because it contains only a single proposition, the call for unity. Thus *partitio* or *enumeratio* is not required. Paul does not lay out at the beginning a plan for the succession of arguments he will make in the proof to come, because all the topics he will take up are well known to his readers. Instead, he prefers to state simply and openly the overall course of action for the church to pursue.[78]

1 Cor 1:10 is exactly this: a statement of the advice which Paul urges (παρακαλεῖν)[79] on the Corinthians. In chap. III we have demonstrated that this verse does indeed correspond with the argument to follow which throughout, in its treatment of a variety of topics, urges concord on the divided church. Both from the point of view of composition and content, therefore, 1:10 is quite clearly the πρόθεσις to the argument in 1 Corinthians.[80] This receives even more confirma-

[75] On προθέσεις in deliberative discourses see Dion. Hal.'s description of those of Isocrates: ἃ δεῖ πράττειν ἕκαστον ὑποτιθέμενοι (*Isoc.* 10).

[76] For an overview see Volkmann, 124, 167–75; Martin, 91–95.

[77] *Rhet.Her.* 1.10.17 lists *divisio, distributio, enumeratio, expositio* (which corresponds to πρόθεσις: "the exposition consists in setting forth, briefly and completely, the points we intend to discuss"); Cic. *Inv.Rhet.* 1.22.31–33 gives types of *partitio*; Quint. *Inst.* 3.9.1–9 discusses the various positions on *propositio* and *partitio* (which he does not consider to be a separate part of a speech). Generally *partitio* or *enumeratio* is required when there is more than one proposition. Hermogenes uses the inclusive term προκατασκευή to refer to the functions of *propositio* and *divisio*: ἔργον δὲ αὐτῆς τὸ προεκτίθεσθαι τὰ κεφάλαια καὶ τὰ ζητήματα, οἷς περιπλακεὶς ὁ λόγος συμπληρώσει τὴν ὑπόθεσιν (*Inv.* 99 [p. 126]; cf. Aps. *Rhet.* 1.348–53 Spengel on προκατάστασις). *Rh. Al.* 29.1436a included the function of a πρόθεσις in the προοίμιον to a deliberative speech (29.1436a: τὸ μὲν οὖν προεκτιθέναι τὸ πράγμα τοῖς ἀκούουσι). Although not including the πρόθεσις as a part of a speech, this earlier handbook does use the term to refer to the subject of deliberations (προθέσεις περὶ ὧν δημηγορήσομεν, 2.1423a; cf. 35.1440b). See also 29.1437b: "If no prejudice attaches either to our speech or to our subject, we shall set out our proposal [πρόθεσις] straight away at the beginning."

[78] By focussing his appeal on unity Paul is able to exhort all to a common course of action without risking the alienation of diverse portions of the church at the outset by naming his points of disagreement with them. Those will come in the course of his proofs.

[79] On this term as common in deliberative arguments, see ch. II n. 114. Dahl, 46 noted that παρακαλῶ is "a formal pattern which Paul uses when he sets forth what is a main purpose of his letters." He is followed by Fitzgerald, 149 n. 106, who rightly appreciates the implications of this conclusion for the analysis of the whole letter: "... the opening parakalô-section [1:10], which urges the unity of the Corinthians. Unity is the concern especially of 1:10–4:21 and continues to be of importance in other parts of the letter (cf. esp. chapters 6, 8, 10–12, 14)."

[80] Wuellner, "Greek Rhetoric," 182–83: "[1:10], which expresses the main theme of the whole of 1 Cor." The same conclusion is reached by Kennedy, *New Testament Interpretation*, 24: "He follows this [the proem in 1:4–9] with the proposition of the entire letter, summarized in a single sentence." Fiorenza, 393 also takes 1:10 to point to the main goal of 1 Cor (she does not use the term proposition). Despite their correct assessment of 1:10 as the proposition, none of these scholars has gone on to examine the important implications of that determination for the

tion from the striking similarity which the verse bears to other προθέσεις to deliberative discourses which urge unity on divided groups, in terms of both language and form.[81] This insight, that 1:10 is the πρόθεσις to the argument *in the entire letter*, is a major building block in our compositional analysis. Having established that this is the πρόθεσις from several converging lines of argument, this exegetical conclusion becomes a major tool for our understanding of the structure of the entire composition.[82] Paul's appeal for unity is made διὰ τοῦ ὀνόματος τοῦ κυρίου ἡμῶν Ἰησοῦ Χριστοῦ, as throughout 1:1–10, centering the unity in Christ.[83]

b) 1:11–17 διήγησις/*Statement of Facts*

Although narrative is not always required in deliberative argumentation,[84] we do find it to set the stage for the situation which calls forth the advice,[85] and

---

exegesis of the entire letter (Wuellner does not see that it is incompatible with the epideictic species to which he assigns the letter, and Fiorenza's determination of the *status* of the argument as a *status translationis* [p. 394] also cannot tie it in with the proposition of 1:10).

Paul employs a rhetorical πρόθεσις also in other letters, as here placed directly after the epistolary thanksgiving. The most conspicuous example is Rom 1:16–17 (E. Käsemann, *Commentary on Romans*, trans. G. W. Bromiley [Grand Rapids, MI: Eerdmans, 1980], and most commentators); cf. 2 Cor 1:12; Gal 1:11–12.

[81] A good example is provided by Dem. *Ep.* 1.5: Δεῖ δ' ὑμᾶς, ὦ ἄνδρες Ἀθηναῖοι, πρῶτον μὲν ἁπάντων πρὸς ὑμᾶς αὐτοὺς ὁμόνοιαν εἰς τὸ κοινῇ συμφέρον τῇ πόλει παρασχέσθαι, καὶ τὰς ἐκ τῶν προτέρων ἐκκλησιῶν ἀμφισβητήσεις ἐᾶσαι, δεύτερον δὲ πάντας ἐκ μιᾶς γνώμης τοῖς δόξασι προθύμως συναγωνίζεσθαι. See also Dio Chrys. *Or.* 39.2: Πρέπει δὲ τοῖς ὑπὸ θεῶν ᾠκισμένοις εἰρήνη καὶ ὁμόνοια καὶ φιλία πρὸς αὑτούς; or *Or.* 38.7: Φημὶ δεῖν ὑμᾶς, ἄνδρες Νικομηδεῖς, ὁμονοῆσαι πρὸς Νικαεῖς; other examples are Isoc. *Or.* 4.3; 5.16; 8.16; Polyb. 5.104.1–2; Dion. Hal. *Ant. Rom.* 6.83.3; Dio Chrys. *Or.* 40.22; 41.8; 48.2; Aristid. *Or.* 23.3; 24.6. See also the remarkable parallel in the documentary papyrus letter *P.Oxy.* 3057, lines 11–18 (quoted in chap. II n. 210), which conclusively shows the ready commerce of such terms and appeals for concord in everyday epistolary practice.

[82] It is perhaps the failure to recognize the compositional function of 1:10 that has led so many scholars to disregard or overlook the explicit references to Corinthian factionalism throughout the entire letter (see chap. III). The dovetailing of the historical and rhetorical investigations at this point provides even more confirmation for this reading.

[83] Weiss, *Korintherbrief*, 12; Klauck, *1. Korintherbrief*, 20; succinctly put by Robertson-Plummer, 10: "This appeal to the one Name is an indirect condemnation of the various party-names."

[84] Arist. *Rh.* 3.13.2; 3.16.11; *Rhet.Her.* 3.4.7; Quint. *Inst.* 3.8.10–11; Volkmann, 297; Martin, 227. The later rhetorician Doxopater presumes that διήγησις belongs in a deliberative speech, and includes the function of a πρόθεσις [ἔκθεσις] within it (*Homil. in Aphth.* 131.17–20). The same is true of the early handbook *Rh. Al.*, which connects διήγησις with the προοίμιον (30.1438a–31.1438b). "Occasionally [in deliberative rhetoric] a narration is employed; when it does occur, it is often after rather than before the proposition" (Kennedy, *New Testament Interpretation*, 24; cf. Volkmann, 167).

[85] "Then comes a brief narration (11–12) explaining the background event which has prompted him to write" (Kennedy, *New Testament Interpretation*, 24–25; he takes 1:12–17 as a

sometimes to correct mistaken impressions.[86] In 1:11–17 Paul does both of these things. 1:11–13a describes the present situation[87] which demands corrective advice on the basis of the report of the envoys, Chloe's people: "there are contentions (ἔριδες) among you." In other deliberative arguments the διήγησις is formed by the announcement that a delegation has been received, or some other type of announcement of received or acknowledged information about the present difficult circumstances which pose some dilemma.[88] Here the deliberative situation (ἔριδες) corresponds perfectly with the advice (μὴ ᾖ ἐν ὑμῖν σχίσματα κτλ.), as it should. In 1:12–13 Paul proceeds to amplify the description from the envoys in his own words (λέγω δὲ τοῦτο) in such a way that the severity and ludicrousness of the present situation are heightened. In any narration the orator should present the facts in the light which will best serve his case.[89] Paul is setting out to demonstrate the great shortcoming which the Corinthians have displayed by their factions, and he makes this plain already here in the way in which he caricatures their behavior by impersonation in 1:12 as childishness and self-imposed slavery.[90] 1:14–17 presents a brief narration which serves to refute Paul's own rhetorical question[91] which combats their factionalism directly: μὴ . . . εἰς τὸ ὄνομα Παύλου ἐβαπτίσθητε; He dismisses this possible false impression[92] immediately by a brief narration of his baptismal activities in Corinth in the past (the proper time frame for narration).[93] But this is not a major concern.

---

defensive sort of argument). Welborn, "Conciliatory Principle," 334, considers 1:11–16 to be the narration of the deliberative argument in 1 Cor 1–4.

86 See Dio Chrys. *Or.* 40.8–19; 41.1–6.

87 As Aristotle noted (*Rh.* 3.16.11), one cannot narrate about the future! This philosophical theme arises also in deliberative speeches (Isoc. *Or.* 8.8; Dio Chrys. *Or.* 26).

88 Compare Aristid. *Or.* 24.3 (quoted in chap. III), an exact parallel to 1:11 – the report of envoys who tell that the city is in factions is narrated because it forms the occasion of the speech of advice. This conforms to rhetorical theory, as in *Rh. Al.* 30.1437b: "After this we must either report or remind our hearers of events that have occurred before, or arrange in groups and exhibit the facts of the present, or forecast what is going to occur. So when we are reporting an embassy, we should give a clear account of everything that was said . . . ." For other examples of deliberative narrations to set the rhetorical situation, see Isoc. *Or.* 8.2; *Ep.* 1.5; 3.2–3; Dion. Hal. *Ant. Rom.* 6.83.3.

89 Arist. *Rh.* 3.16.1–7; *Rhet.Her.* 1.8.12; Cic. *Inv.Rhet.* 1.30; Quint. *Inst.* 4.2.31. Paul does so with almost mock disbelief (cf. 11:18): μεμέρισται ὁ Χριστός;

90 See chap. III, "Excursus: The Form of the 'Slogans' in 1:12."

91 This function of proof within the *narratio* is allowed by Quint. *Inst.* 4.2.54: "Sometimes, however, one must also support our assertions by a certain amount of argument" (cf. 4.2.79, 82). See also Arist. *Rh.* 3.15.1 on removing prejudice (in regard to the προοίμιον).

92 Paul's true teaching of baptism emphasizes the unity of all in the same baptism (12:13), not their divisions (Wilckens, 13–16). On rhetorical anticipation see *Rh.Al.* 33.1439b (treated in regard to the proof section).

93 "But if there is narrative [in deliberative rhetoric], it will be of things past, in order that, being reminded of them, the hearers may take better counsel about the future. This may be done in a spirit of blame or of praise" (Arist. *Rh.* 3.16.11). In 1 Cor 1:11–17 the narrative is about the present time and the past time, and is surely cast in a spirit of blame.

After this brief treatment, v. 17 provides a smooth transition into the *Proof* section, and introduces the first two topics, wisdom and the cross. This too conforms to rhetorical practice.

c) 1:18–15:57 πίστεις/Proofs

Almost all of the letter body of 1 Corinthians constitutes the proof for the πρόθεσις in 1:10, the call for Corinthian unity. An accurate understanding of the nature of proofs in deliberative rhetoric as opposed to forensic rhetoric is crucial to an analysis of the composition of 1 Corinthians. Whereas in forensic rhetoric the proof concerns a fact which will be proven true or false, deliberative proofs are meant to provide advice for the future, together with justification of why the audience should take up that course (or courses) of action in the future. Deliberative proofs as discussed in rhetorical theory focus on a specific set of κεφάλαια or "heads," chief among which is the appeal to advantage, τὸ συμφέρον, as we have argued in chap. II. Mostly the handbooks discuss the *kinds* of proofs in deliberative rhetoric, not the arrangement of individual arguments within the proof section of the discourse. The only sustained discussion of the arrangement of deliberative proofs is in the *Rhetorica ad Alexandrum*, which recommends that the proof be arranged according to those varied appeals:

> Then you must treat the subject of expediency [τὸ συμφέρον] in a manner similar to what you have said already in the case of justice [τὸ δίκαιον], and at the end of this division add either a recapitulation or a definition, and then put forward any other subject that you have available. This is the way in which you must join one division to another, and link your speech together (*Rh.Al.* 32.1439a).

In line with this theoretical prescription,[94] the proof sections of some deliberative arguments are indeed arranged according to the various appeals: first one argues that a proposed act is just, and then expedient, etc.[95] In this way the proof

---

[94] See also *Rhet.Her.* 3.4.8. Since proof is usually treated in the handbooks under forensic rhetoric, besides these prescriptions we have little discussion in rhetorical theory of the arrangements of the various proofs in deliberative arguments, but we do have many actual speeches to make up for this lack.

[95] See, e. g., Isoc. *Or.* 5 and Volkmann's analysis (p. 304) of the proof by appeals: Part I, 36–38 συμφέρον, 39–56 δυνατόν, 57–65 ῥᾴδιον, 68–80 ἔνδοξον; Part II, 89–105 ῥᾴδιον, 105–15 ἔνδοξον. The two major subsections of the proof (Parts I and II) are topically arranged (see 5.16), first regarding the concord of the Hellenes, and then regarding war with the barbarians. It is clear from Volkmann's analysis of the appeals that the proof of this deliberative argument is organized first topically and then by appeals within certain subsections (notice the repetition of appeals). Another example is provided by Isoc. *Or.* 6 (analysis by Volkmann, 307–11), where the appeals form the sub-arguments within the larger wholes. But there too this is not the only organizational principle (see the summary of the argument in the critical essay of Dion. Hal., *Isoc.* 9 which is entirely subject-based; note also that Dion. Hal. highly esteems the invention and arrangement of proofs in Isocrates' speeches [*Isoc.* 4, 12; cf. Philostr. *VS* 505, on the *Archidamus* as one of his most skillfully composed speeches]). For another example, see the

is formed of subsections of which the organizational principle is the succession of given appeals to justify the advice. Yet even this straightforward arrangement becomes much more fluid in actual rhetorical pieces,[96] which are not nearly so rigidly organized.[97]

But the arrangement of proofs by successive deliberative appeals is not the only option, as sole reliance upon the handbooks might lead one erroneously to conclude. Many actual deliberative texts, both letters and speeches, contain a proof section which is organized *topically*,[98] because the advice given often relates to a variety of subjects affecting the audience's decision for future action. These too are called rhetorical κεφάλαια, or "heads."[99] In such cases the different deliberative appeals are contained within the various subsections of proof, which are thus logically and topically arranged.[100]

---

speech of Decius in Dion. Hal. *Ant. Rom.* 7.40–46: πρόθεσις laid out in 7.40.2; proofs: 7.41 δίκαιον, 7.42.1–4 συμφέρον, 7.42.5–43.2 ἀναγκαῖον, followed by a completely new section with an address to an opponent (7.44–46).

[96] For one thing, many deliberative speeches only focus on one type of appeal; see Wooten's comment on the speeches in Polybius: "The tendency to concentrate on a single argument is seen even better in these speeches, and by far the most popular argument is that of expediency" (p. 245; see also above, chap. II).

[97] As the examples in n. 95 demonstrate.

[98] This possibility is allowed by *Rhet.Her.* 3.2.2: "In causes in which the subject itself engenders the deliberation, the entire discourse will be devoted to the subject itself."

[99] For the term κεφάλαιον, see LSJ, 945: "Rhet., head, topic of argument," as in Dion. Hal. *Comp.* 1, and in particular in the scholia to Ps-Dem. *Or.* 7, to describe the sections of proof introduced by Περὶ δέ (*Scholia Demosthenica*, ed. M. R. Dilts, BT [Leipzig: Teubner, 1983], vol. 1, lines 5a, 12, 14, 37, 39). For the term in rhetorical theory, see chap. II n. 19, and Hermog. *Inv.* 106–111 [Rabe, 132–36]. See Kennedy's description of these heads: "The proof [of a deliberative argument] is divided up into a series of headings, treating the various material topics. The term 'heading' (*kephalaion*) came into regular use among Greek rhetoricians of the Roman Empire. Though not commonly used by modern rhetorical critics, it is a convenient label for this kind of division of the subject" (*New Testament Interpretation*, 24; see also Burgess, 120 n. 1 on the term in epideictic rhetoric).

[100] Dio Chrys. announces his deliberative proof for concord in *Or.* 38.3 in the following way: "Well now, there are indeed some things in your city which deserve correction, and one after the other I shall apply my treatment to them [κατὰ μέρος αὐτῶν ποιήσομαι τὴν θεραπείαν]." See also the πρόθεσις to Isoc. *Or.* 8 (§ 15): "I have come before you . . . to make known the views I hold, first, regarding the proposals which have been put before you by the Prytaneis, and, second, regarding the other interests of the state." Ps-Dem. *Or.* 7 promises advice in the proof section arranged by subjects (πρῶτον μὲν περὶ ὧν Φίλιππος ἐπέσταλκε . . . ὕστερον δέ, περὶ ὧν οἱ πρέσβεις λέγουσι, 7.1). In the proof new subsections, which are the next topics of consideration, known both from oral and written communication (the neat structure promised in the πρόθεσις breaks down at points), are introduced with περὶ δέ (7.14, 18, 30, 33, 36, 39). For other examples of deliberative proofs arranged by the various subjects of consideration, see the speeches in Dion. Hal. *Ant.Rom.* 3.7–8; 4.26.1–4; 6.35–36; 6.49.3–56.5; 6.83.4–5; cf. the speeches promised in Dem. *Prooem.* 29.3; 37.2. These elements of deliberative proof are clearly manifested in Dion. Hal.'s praise for Isocrates in his critical essay: "And the arrangement [τάξις] and division of topics [μερισμοὶ τῶν πραγμάτων], their development by means of argumentation [ἡ κατ' ἐπιχείρημα ἐξεργασία], the relief of monotony by varying the treatment of the

This type of structure is precisely what we find in the Proof Section of the deliberative argument in 1 Corinthians, which is composed of many sub-arguments under a variety of heads.[101] In these sub-arguments Paul arranges his proofs logically and topically, as he takes up the assorted subjects of Corinthian contention one by one,[102] in each case urging the course of unity and compromise he proposed in 1:10. New topics or subtopics, which are thus correspondingly new sub-arguments in the deliberative proof, are introduced by a variety of introductory formulas: περὶ δέ (the most frequent formula used, in 7:1, 25; 8:1; 12:1; in the epistolary closing in 16:1, 12),[103] οὐ θέλω γὰρ ὑμᾶς ἀγνοεῖν (10:1), ἐπαινῶ δὲ ὑμᾶς (11:2), ὑμῖν δείκνυμι (12:31); γνωρίζω δὲ ὑμῖν (15:1).[104] In some cases the transition to a new topic is made in other ways, by an introduction of a slogan (6:12; 10:23), or by a reference to Paul's learning of the topic orally or by letter (5:1; 7:1; 11:18). This conforms with what we find in actual deliberative speeches and letters, where a variety of introductory formulas

---

different elements of the subject itself and by introducing digressions from external sources [ξένα ἐπεισόδια], and all other techniques concerned with the disposition of subject-matter [ἡ πραγματικὴ οἰκονομία], are found to a greater degree and to greater effect in Isocrates" (*Isoc.* 4).

[101] Compare the list of the ΚΕΦΑΛΑΙΑ of 1 Corinthians in the *Catenae* (Cramer, B2), which divides the letter under nine heads: ά. Περὶ τοῦ μὴ διχονοεῖν πρὸς ἀλλήλους ἐκ φιλοδοξίας τῆς ἐπὶ σοφίᾳ ἀνθρωπίνῃ; β́. Κατὰ πορνῶν καὶ πορνείας, καὶ τῶν τούτοις κοινωνούντων; γ́. Περὶ τοῦ μὴ δεῖσθαι δικῶν, καὶ ταῦτα ἐπὶ ἀπίστων; δ́. Περὶ γάμου καὶ χηρείας καὶ ἀγαμίας; έ. Περὶ διαφορᾶς ἐδεσμάτων, καὶ ἀποχῆς δαιμονικοῦ σεβάσματος; ς́. Περὶ σχήματος ἀνδρῶν καὶ γυναικῶν, ἐν εὐχαῖς καὶ προφητείας; ζ́. Περὶ κοινωνίας θεοπρεποῦς, οὐ πλησμονικῆς; ή. Περὶ διαφορᾶς χαρισμάτων, καὶ οἰκονομίας αὐτῶν; θ́. Περὶ ἀναστάσεως σωμάτων καθολικῆς (on the history of these κεφάλαια lists in patristic exegesis see Turner, 524–29). For the term κεφάλαιον used in patristic exegesis see *LPGL*, 748, "as subst., *topic, subject*," (though at times not easy to differentiate from its meaning as a "*section* of a written work [which may be the same thing], or a chapter").

[102] See Strobel's compositional analysis (tabulated on pp. 3–8), which treats 1 Cor as broken up into eight sections, each termed a "Stellungnahme zu einem [numbered] Gemeindeproblem."

[103] We may attribute Paul's preference for this phrase to the intersection of rhetorical and epistolary employment of the formula (the best rhetorical style would be more varied). Paul uses it in 1 Cor and 1 Thess because both are deliberative letters.

On the basis of περὶ δέ Berger concluded: "Die informativen Briefe sind allgemein auf die vorangehende Korrespondenz bezogen, und so gehört 1 Kor sicher in diese Gattung" (p. 1329). Several counterarguments may be offered: 1. As we have demonstrated, the formula περὶ δέ is not limited to any one genre (see Mitchell, 236–54), so no genre classification can be made solely on the basis of its use; 2. many letters are occasioned by other letters, but that does not in itself specify *their own genres*; 3. the genre informative private letter surely fits many short papyrus letters, but it cannot account for the long and developed *argumentation* (not merely information passing) found in 1 Cor.

[104] On introductory formulas see T. Y. Mullins, "Disclosure. A Literary Form in the New Testament," *NovT* 7 (1964) 44–50; *idem*, "Formulas in New Testament Epistles," *JBL* 91 (1972) 380–90; J. L. White, "Introductory Formulae in the Body of the Pauline Letter," *JBL* 90 (1971) 91–97.

introduces the next topic for consideration. Περὶ δέ, and even more commonly the contrastive pair Περὶ μέν ... Περὶ δέ are often so used in deliberative arguments, to summarize the topic just discussed and/or to move on to the next.[105]

We have already observed that Paul employs characteristic deliberative appeals (τὸ συμφέρον, τὸ καλὸν, τὸ ἀναγκαῖον, τὸ δίκαιον) within the various sub-arguments, and that the characteristic type of deliberative proof, proof by example, is consistently employed by Paul throughout these sub-arguments, using a variety of examples, the most common of which is himself.[106] He also incorporates and builds upon a variety of *topoi* for factionalism and concord derived from ancient politics throughout the argument which he can count on his Corinthian audience to recognize. Understanding 1 Corinthians as deliberative rhetoric can be a key to a proper understanding of the compositional integrity of the letter. What many scholars have termed the "loosely connected string of topics" which we find in 1 Corinthians is no more loosely connected than other deliberative arguments which enter into complicated and multi-dimensional life situations which require advice. Each of the sub-arguments in 1:18–15:57, then, participates in the overall argument for church unity, and in its own way incorporates the overall rhetorical strategies of deliberative appeals and employment of examples. Long proofs will also contain varied approaches and appeals to the audience in order to convince them to follow a given course of action. Isocrates' description of the spectrum of deliberative proofs is illustrative of this point:

> But anyone who attempts to discourse on a subject out of the common [δημηγορεῖν] and who desires to bring about a change in your opinions must needs touch upon many matters [πολλῶν πραγμάτων ἅψασθαι] and speak somewhat at length [διὰ μακροτέρων τοὺς λόγους ποιήσασθαι], now reminding [ἀναμνῆσαι], now rebuking [κατηγορῆσαι], now commending [ἐπαινέσαι], and again counselling you [περὶ δὲ τῶν συμβουλεῦσαι].[107]

---

105 Of hundreds of examples, see particularly the deliberative speech Ps-Dem. *Or.* 7.14, 18, 30, 33, 36, 39 (the authenticity of this speech was doubted already in antiquity because of its rigid style [Lib. *Arg.D.* 7.3 (p. 619): ὁ δὲ λόγος οὐ δοκεῖ μοι Δημοσθένους εἶναι. δηλοῖ δὲ ἡ φράσις καὶ ἡ τῆς συνθέσεως ἁρμονία πολὺ τὸν Δημοσθενικὸν πεφευγυῖα τύπον]). Like 1 Cor this speech responds to a letter and the oral report of envoys. Περὶ δέ is used for both types of topics, and there is topical overlap between the letter and oral reports. See also Dem. *Ep.* 1.2; 3.1, 36; Isoc. *Or.* 4.15, 34; 5.30, 83, 95, 98, 105, 109; 6.24; (6.97, the synonymous preposition ὑπέρ); 8.15, 18, 25, 26, 73 (ὑπέρ); *Ep.* 9.5, 7, 11 (ὑπέρ), 14, 19; Dion. Hal. *Ant. Rom.* 6.83.5; 85.3; App. *BCiv.* 4.12.90; Dio Chrys. *Or.* 34.38, 40; 38.14; *1 Clem.* 62.1. Other transitional formulas, such as πρῶτον μὲν οὖν (1 Cor 11:18), and τὰ δὲ λοιπά (11:34) are also commonly used in deliberative speeches (see, e. g., Isoc. *Or.* 6.16 πρῶτον μὲν οὖν; 5.154 λοιπὸν οὖν; Dio Chrys. *Or.* 38.21 τὸ μὲν οὖν πρῶτον [of a subhead]; *Or.* 38.49 λοιπὸν δέ).

106 See chap. II.

107 Isoc. *Or.* 8.27. The distance from Isocrates to Paul is bridged by Philo: "If I act as a councillor [βουλεύω] I will introduce such proposals as are for the common good [τὰς κοινωφελεῖς], even if they be not agreeable. If I speak in the general assembly [ἐκκλησιάζων] I

In fact, this is a most accurate description of the variety of approaches Paul uses throughout the proof section of the deliberative argument in 1 Corinthians to persuade his readers to follow his advice for unity.[108]

Our next step is to investigate the arrangement of the various sub-arguments within the proof section. I propose that the varied topic heads in the proof section of the argument in 1 Corinthians form four larger sub-sections:

1:18–4:21, Censure of Corinthian Factionalism and the Need for Paul's Advice
5:1–11:1, The Integrity of the Corinthian Community Against Outside Defilement
11:2–14:40, Manifestations of Corinthian Factionalism When "Coming Together"
15:1–57, The Resurrection and the Final Goal.

Even in putting forth this schema[109] I must admit to some hesitation about dividing up Paul's arguments in too mechanical a fashion, since there are several appeals, arguments and themes which appear throughout the four sections of continuous argument.[110] As is well known, Paul often doubles back in his argumentation and builds upon points already proven.[111] These four proof sections do not stand independently of one another, but rather form four subsections of the same overall proof. Within each of the four major sections of proof are other smaller subsections. Actual deliberative speeches and letters show great elasticity in the arrangement of the proof sections too, as we have seen, but they also exhibit certain tendencies which illuminate Paul's arrangement. The following analysis of the arrangement of the proof section is intended to be exegetically fruitful, and tries to work closely from the text, not from an

will leave all talk of flattery to others and resort only to such as is salutary and beneficial [συμφέρουσιν], reproving [ἐπιτιμῶν], warning [νουθετῶν], correcting in words studied to show a sober frankness [σωφρονίζων] without foolish and frantic arrogance" (*Jos.* 73).

[108] The number of matters taken up in 1 Corinthians goes without saying ("[1 Cor] trägt darum den Charakter eines Briefes, den man schreibt, wenn eine Summe von Angelegenheiten sich aufgehäuft hat, die nun endlich erledigt werden müssen" [Bachmann, 30; more recently Strobel, 95]). Reminding is also the purpose of the letter, according to 4:17. Paul accuses and rebukes throughout 1:18–4:21, but especially in 3–4 (see 4:14; also chapters 5–6; 15:34; full discussion below). Paul praises the Corinthians in 11:2 (and in 1:4–9, as we have seen), but withholds his praise in 11:17 and 22. He gives counsel on a variety of topics (περὶ δέ in 7:1, 25; 8:1; 12:1; 16:1, 12, and on topics introduced in other ways). Compare the language of Chrys.'s description of Paul's rhetoric in 1 Cor 14: Ἐπειδὴ γὰρ ἐνεκάλεσε καὶ ἐπετίμησε καὶ τὸ ἀνωφελὲς ἔδειξε, καὶ συμβουλεύει λοιπὸν λέγων ... (*hom. in I Cor.* 35.3 [*PG* 61.299]).

[109] One not unlike some other investigations of the contents of 1 Cor (see above n. 10).

[110] As documented in chap. III.

[111] See Weiss, *Korintherbrief*, xliii on "aba" argumentation in 1 Cor (though he attributes it to the redactor); J. Jeremias, "Chiasmus in den Paulusbriefen," *ZNW* 49 (1958) 145–56; Chadwick; J. J. Collins, "Chiasmus, the 'ABA' Pattern and the Text of Paul," *Studiorum Paulinorum Congressus Internationalis Catholicus 1961* (Rome: Pontifical Biblical Institute, 1963) 2.575–83, with more bibliography; Kümmel, 278 on excursus; Conzelmann, 39 on "ring composition"; Fee, 16 (following Collins). In this investigation we shall concur with the view that the ABA structure is commonly used by Paul in 1 Cor (observed in the early church by Chrys. *hom. in I Cor.* 23.3 [*PG* 61.192–93]).

outside model which is imposed on the text. Other analyses of the relationship of the various subheads to one another might also be possible; one cannot be absolutely certain because Paul himself is not explicit about this arrangement (we have observed that he provides no *partitio*[112]). But he does provide many clues in the transitional formulas and logic of the argument itself, which must be our first set of evidence for the arrangement. When we examine the text our analysis receives further confirmation from other ancient texts which urge concord on divided groups in a similar fashion.

(1) 1:18–4:21. *First Section of Proof:*
Censure of Corinthian Factionalism and the Need for Paul's Advice

While scholars are virtually unanimous in regarding 1:18 (or 1:10) – 4:21 as a discrete section of the letter, a section which treats the problem of Corinthian factions,[113] there is debate about the function and purpose of this section within the whole composition.[114] We have demonstrated in chap. III that this is not the only part of 1 Corinthians which deals directly with the problem of factionalism. But, as a discrete proof section, what is its function? Again comparison with other deliberative discourses urging concord can assist our inquiry.

In *Or.* 34 Dio Chrysostom uses a *partitio* to introduce the logical movement of his deliberative proof under three heads:

First of all I wish to point out to you one thing, in case you are not fully aware of it – that you need good judgement in the present emergency, and that your problems are such as to

[112] "Zu fragen ist also nach möglicherweise erkennbaren Hinweisen auf diese Intention; leider hat Paulus uns hier so wenig wie in anderen Briefen eine Disposition hinterlassen" (Lührmann, "Freundschaftsbrief," 305). Here we are proposing the thesis that Paul's intention is contained in the πρόθεσις in 1:10, the call for unity.

[113] The παρακαλῶ sentences in 1:10 and 4:16 are regarded as forming an *inclusio* (I would agree, pointing also to 16:15 as delineating the rhetorical whole, with Dahl, 51). For this as a subsection of the argument see Lightfoot, 139 ("Divisions"); Weiss, *Korintherbrief*, 12 ("Über die Parteien in der Gemeinde"); Robertson-Plummer, xxv ("The Dissensions"); Lietzmann-Kümmel, 1 ("Warnung vor Parteiwesen"); Allo, 6 ("Contre des factions"); Dahl; Barrett, *First Corinthians*, 28 ("Wisdom and Division at Corinth"); Fascher, 87 ("Die Parteiungen in Korinth"); Senft, 32 ("L'Evangile de la Croix, Fondement de l'Eglise"); Merklein, 159; Fee, 21 ("A Church Divided – Internally and Against Paul"); Lang, 19 ("Die Spaltungen in der Gemeinde"); Strobel, 5 ("Spaltungen in der Gemeinde"). Schenk, 229, 241–42, followed by Schmithals, "Korintherbriefe," 267 and Senft, 17–19, takes 1:10–4:21 to be a separate letter (the others include 1:1–9), as does Marxsen, 86–95, and along with 5:1–6:11 possibly Welborn, "Conciliatory Principle," 333. A lone dissenter is Bailey, 160–65, who has argued that this section ends in 4:16, not 4:21 (he takes 4:17–7:40 to be a new subsection of the argument; a similar argument was made by Bachmann, 204). Bailey is right in seeing 4:17–21 as pointing ahead, but that does not mean that these verses must belong to the next subsection (they also appropriately conclude this section; see below). Bailey generally downplays the role of factionalism in the argument.

[114] "No clarity has been reached with regard to the relation between Chapters 1–4 and the rest of the epistle" (Dahl, 43).

merit counsel and much foresight; secondly, that no man in this company can readily advise you as to the proper course of action . . . Next I shall indicate my own opinion with reference to these affairs and suggest by what course of action on your part at the moment and by what general policy in your leadership of the city, things will, as I believe, work out in all respects to your advantage.[115]

Before he can offer specific advice to the Tarsans, Dio must first demonstrate that they are in fact in trouble. What he demonstrates (34.7–26) is that they are experiencing στάσις, political discord, which has manifested itself in both external and internal affairs. In *Or.* 38 Dio uses a similar arrangement in another deliberative argument for concord.[116] This same pattern is found again in Demosthenes' *Ep.* 1 *On Concord*, where first the need for reunification is demonstrated (1.5–10), and then the specific actions required in the present instance are advised (1.11–16). Still more deliberative speeches on concord also follow this plan of proof[117] because it is logical – first one demonstrates the *need* for concord,

[115] 34.6–7. The proof section follows this plan carefully: Section I (7–26), Section II (27–38), Section III (38–51). He slips out of his plan once, in § 23, where he begins to give concrete advice too soon, but he calls himself back to his order in § 24. On the arrangement of this speech see also Jones, *Dio Chrysostom*, 76–82.

[116] See the *partitio* in 38.8: "But I want to break up my address, and first of all to speak about concord itself in general, telling both whence it comes and what it achieves, and then over against that to set off strife and hatred in contradistinction to friendship. For when concord has been proved to be beneficial to all mankind, the proof will naturally follow that this particular concord between these particular cities is both quite indispensable for you and quite profitable as well. I shall not, however, refrain from telling also how concord may endure when once achieved." The proof follows this scheme: Section I (10–20, Concord is Good and Factionalism Bad), Section II (21–49, Concord between Nicomedia and Nicaea will be Advantageous), Section III (49–51, How Concord will Endure). See Jones, *Dio Chrysostom*, 85–89 on this speech, who also observes: "Dio follows the destructive part of his speech with more positive advice" (p. 87). Compare also Dio's *Or.* 41.9–14, a proof section on the need to eradicate strife.

[117] See the speech of Tullius reported in Dion. Hal. *Ant. Rom.* 4.26, where first concord is proven to be a fine thing, and the audience is exhorted to it (4.26.1), after which specific advice follows about their relations to outsiders, about building a temple and convening a general council (4.26.2–4). See also the speech of Titus Laucius in 6.35–36, where first it is demonstrated that the present state of στάσις is bad and concord much more desirable (6.35–36.2), and then particular advice on the Volscians and the Latins follows (6.36.2: "As to the answers to be now given to them, this is the advice I have to offer . . ."), arguing for the courses which are best and most just (6.36.2–3). The speech of Menenius Agrippa to the Senate also has this rough plan (6.49.3–55.3 on the dangers of the present στάσις; 6.56.1–5 on precisely how to appease the sedition). See also Behr's analysis (2.369) of Aristid. *Or.* 24: 1–3 Proem; 4–21 Concord an indisputable good: traditional evidence; 22 Faction injurious to Rhodes' freedom; 23–27 Examples from history; 28–40 Appeal for settlement of present dispute [see the transition in § 32: "It is not very hard to prove that faction is the most extreme of evils, but perhaps it is difficult to find how you shall be rid of it"]; 41–44 Praise of concord; 45–57 Rhodes' glorious tradition opposes faction; 58–59 Peroration. The proof in the deliberative letter Platonic *Ep.* 8 first contains the call for concord and moderation (354A-355B), followed by concrete advice to the Syracusans (355B-356E, put in the mouth of Dion). Compare the analysis of Klek, 72 (352E-353B Prooem; 353A-E Proposition/Narration; 354A-355B Consilium Universum; 355B-356E Praecepta; 357A-D Epilogos).

and then one gives concrete advice for its enactment.[118] How does this apply to Paul's argument? In 1 Cor 1:18–4:21 Paul illustrates through his censuring of the Corinthians that they are indeed engaging in factional behavior (named in various ways) which is unacceptable for a Christian community, and argues that they must cease from it through following his advice. The proof section 1:18–4:21 does not itself contain the specific advice,[119] as much as the necessary prelude to it – the demonstration of the foolishness of the Corinthians' factional behavior, and their need for Paul's advice. In establishing his *ethos* as their proper adviser and good *exemplum* to imitate (especially in 4:6, 16), Paul also introduces the deliberative proof by appeal to the example of himself which he will use throughout the succeeding subsections of proof. After thus setting up his proof in this first section (1:18–4:21), in the later three proof sections in 5:1–11:1: 11:2–14:40; and 15:1–57 Paul will give his specific advice for church unity in relation to each of the topics which currently divide them.[120]

Therefore, like the other arguments for concord we have examined, this first proof section in 1 Cor 1:18–4:21 forms a unified subsection of deliberative proof[121] which has as its purpose the censuring[122] of the Corinthians for their

---

118 Cf. Dio Chrys. *Or.* 38.3: "Well now, there are indeed some other things in your city which deserve correction, and one after the other [κατὰ μέρος] I shall apply my treatment to them, provided I win your confidence by speaking the truth about the greater matters [περὶ τῶν μειζόνων]. But for what strange reason or with what purpose do I not first give advice about the smaller matters [οὐχ ὑπὲρ τῶν μικροτέρων συμβουλεύω πρότερον] and in those matters test the willingness of the people to be persuaded, instead of choosing to jeopardize my reputation at the start by offering advice on the weightiest matter of all [περὶ τοῦ μεγίστου συμβουλεύων πράγματος]? It is because it seems to me far easier to persuade men concerning the weightiest matters than concerning those which are slighter or trivial."

119 This is the difficulty of Welborn's argument for 1 Cor 1–4 as the deliberative argument for unity ("Conciliatory Principle," 334–40). Chaps. 1–4 do not contain so much advice as censure of improper behavior. Censure indeed plays a role in deliberative discourses, to prepare the hearer to accept the advice, once admitting that they need it. Censure alone, however, does not constitute advice, or full deliberative proof.

120 Commentators have observed this function of 1:18–4:21 even without the comparative rhetorical evidence given here. "The flock once gathered under the shepherd's crook, he may with hope of success attack the particular vices which had crept into it. These first four chapters are thus the foundation of the whole Epistle" (Godet, 1.238). "Now of course the whole letter is concerned with topical subjects which had arisen in Corinth or been put to Paul in the form of inquiries. Compared to these, however, the first part [1:10–4:21] again forms an exception, because Paul must first of all make the Corinthians aware of pertinent questions that are posed by their party system" (Conzelmann, 30). This same viewpoint is embedded in Jewett's apt critique of Schenk's deleting 1:10–4:21 from the *Antwortbrief*: "To separate the *peri de* sections from 1 Cor 1:11 ff. is to assume an unwarranted omniscience on the part of scholarship about precisely what Chloe's people reported *and why Paul chose to answer the basic question of divisions before coming to the specific questions posed by the Corinthian factions*" ("Redaction," 399 emph. added). See also already Chrys. *hom. in I Cor.* 15.1 [*PG* 61.122].

121 "Die Funktion von 1 Kor 1–4 innerhalb des 1 Kor ist (leider) keine 'Apologie des paulinischen Apostolates'" (Lüdemann, 122 n. 61). For contrary opinions see Dahl and especially the recent attempts by Bünker, 52–59 and Pesch, 79–82 (who appears to follow him) to

factionalism. This functions as a preparation for Paul's later treatment of the specific issues upon which the church is divided.[123] It is significant that in 1:18–4:21 Paul treats the *symptoms and manifestations* of Corinthian factionalism – boasting, being puffed up, allegiances to leaders, judgmentalism, claims to be wise and enriched – not the specific causes of the factionalism, or the issues on which the church is pulled apart.[124] Correspondingly, he offers no concrete advice in this section except that, through his clear disapproval of the divisive behavior, he overtly attempts to dissuade them from it and turn instead to unity. This is clear from the imperatives in this section, which all call for an end to factionalism and the general dispositions from which it arises, calling on several *topoi* about factionalism in Greco-Roman antiquity.[125]

Commentators have long noted the importance of wisdom and the cross in 1 Cor 1–4. These twin themes of the section, introduced in the transition verse 1:17, are both correctives to Corinthian factionalism.[126] Throughout 1:18–4:21 Paul refutes the false wisdom of the Corinthians which is, unfortunately, more like "the wisdom of the world" (1:20; 2:6, 13; 3:3, 19; 4:10) than God's wisdom,

---

analyze the disposition of this "Gerichtsrede." Both are unsuccessful, in my view, for two reasons: 1. They have incorrectly named the rhetorical species because of their presupposition of Paul's need for defense; and 2. these works are methodologically hampered by their limitation to rhetorical theory, which they impose on the text too mechanically. How, for instance, is 1 Cor 1:18–2:16 a forensic *narratio*? (even Bünker admits its deliberative character [p. 55]; what crime or alibi does it relate?). How does the report of factions in 1:10–12 function as an *exordium* to Paul's self-defense?

[122] On the use of epideictic elements in deliberative rhetoric see Stowers's conclusion: "Admonition plays an important role in the paraenesis of 1:10–4:20. Paul admonishes the Corinthians because of strife and exhorts them to unity" (p. 128; see also Welborn, "Conciliatory Principle," 334, and the discussion below). Robertson-Plummer, xxv, entitle the section 1:10–6:20 "Urgent Matters for Blame."

[123] Dahl rightly held that 1:10–4:21 in some way prepares for the advice to follow (p. 60 and passim), but these chapters do not do so by providing a defense of Paul. This section censures the Corinthians' behavior (as Paul himself is acutely aware in 4:14!), as a part of a larger deliberative argument for church unity. The section is a sustained argument (1:19–3:21 is not a digression, as Wuellner, "Greek Rhetoric," 185–86, argued).

[124] "In his observations upon this fact, Paul makes hardly more than a few allusions to the actual character of the ideas represented by these movements" (Barth, 14). This is why commentators have had such a difficult time reconstructing the Corinthian parties and their beliefs and practices (see chap. III n. 11 and chap. IV n. 63). We have seen in chap. III that all of these symptoms are also attested in other Greco-Roman texts discussing factionalism, and that several of them are common and severe caricatures of contentious behavior.

[125] 1:31 ἐν κυρίῳ καυχάσθω. 3:10 βλεπέτω πῶς ἐποικοδομεῖ. 3:18 Μηδεὶς ἑαυτὸν ἐξαπατάτω . . . μωρὸς γενέσθω. 3:21 μηδεὶς καυχάσθω ἐν ἀνθρώποις. 4:1 ἡμᾶς λογιζέσθω ἄνθρωπος ὡς ὑπηρέτας Χριστοῦ κτλ. 4:5 μὴ πρὸ καιροῦ τι κρίνετε; cf. the ἵνα clauses in 1:10 and 4:6. The importance of the imperatives in 1 Cor 1–4 was rightly pointed out by Welborn, "Conciliatory Principle," 334 n. 73.

[126] "Dass das Thema der Verkündigung des Kreuzes und der Ablehnung jeglicher Menschenweisheit wesenhaft und unmittelbar mit dem Problem der Gruppenbildung in Korinth zusammenhängt, ist nun deutlich geworden" (Wilckens, 21).

the wisdom of the cross.[127] Scholarship has long debated what the Corinthians' wisdom was, trying especially to find history of religions parallels in Hellenistic Judaism, mystery religions, or gnosticism.[128] But the wisdom of the world as defined by Paul in 1 Cor 1:18–4:21 refers not merely to any of these specific religious speculations, though clearly some Corinthians made exclusive claims to some kind of wisdom,[129] but rather to the norms and values of human politics which the Corinthians are mirroring by their factionalism. In particular, in 1:18–4:21 Paul draws upon the political *topos* that factionalism is a "human" failing (κατὰ ἄνθρωπον περιπατεῖν in 3:3) which is unworthy of the spiritual, unworldly calling which the Corinthians have received.[130] That factionalism was widely considered to be a human failing in Greco-Roman antiquity allows us to fill in the unstated premise behind Paul's argument, to which he alludes frequently.[131] The wisdom of the world is the set of values and norms which divide persons of higher and lower status into separate groups, a wisdom which prefers dissension to unity, superiority to cooperation.[132] This wisdom is, paradoxically, foolishness.[133] The cross, the symbol of the humility and lowli-

---

127 Ibid., 16: "Die Einheit der Gemeinde ist für Paulus im Geschehen der Kreuzigung Christi begründet; und darum kann allein der λόγος τοῦ σταυροῦ die gespaltene Gemeinde 'wieder zurechtbringen'" (see esp. 1:13). Paul turns to the cross to combat divisions also in Phil 2.

128 For summaries of the spectrum see ibid., 97–213; Sellin, "Hauptprobleme," 3020–22; R. A. Horsley, "Wisdom of Word and Words of Wisdom in Corinth," *CBQ* 39 (1977) 224–39; and especially B. A. Pearson, *The Pneumatikos-Psychikos Terminology in 1 Corinthians. A Study in the Theology of the Corinthian Opponents of Paul and its Relation to Gnosticism*, SBLDS 12 (Missoula, MT: Society of Biblical Literature, 1973) 27–43. The latter important study effectively refutes those who argue for "Gnostic" opponents of Paul, but in my view does not deal with Paul's *own* description of what he combats at Corinth, factions, by attempting instead to uncover a unified opposition which Paul uniformly combats (see chap. III, "Excursus: The Descriptive Significance of the Term σχίσμα"). R. M. Grant's connection of the Corinthians' wisdom claims with the Stoics remains significant ("The Wisdom of the Corinthians," in *The Joy of Study: Papers on New Testament and Related Subjects Presented to Honor F. C. Grant*, ed. S. E. Johnson [New York: Macmillan, 1951], 51–55).

129 1:26; 3:18; 12:8. This is Paul's starting point for his redefinition here.

130 The same argument, contrasting ἡ σοφία ἐπίγειος and ἄνωθεν, is made in Jas 3:13–4:12 (called by M. Dibelius "A Group of Sayings Against Contentiousness" in *James. A Commentary on the Epistle of James*, rev. H. Greeven, trans. M. A. Williams, Hermeneia [Philadelphia: Fortress, 1976], 207–29). His exegesis of Jas 3:13–17 could easily apply to 1 Cor 1 and 2: "our author executes his arguments against contentiousness by using the concept of wisdom. He has in mind the possibility that disputes could be carried on in the name of and for the sake of wisdom, and he wishes to prove the fallacy of using such an excuse for strife" (p. 208).

131 See chap. III n. 98. Note that Dio Chrys. calls it a specifically Greek failing! (*Or.* 38.38; cf. 1:22).

132 Betz, "Rhetoric and Theology," 36–38, followed by Welborn, "Discord," 101–103, has pointed to rhetoric as the human wisdom, which is correct in that rhetoric is the form by which these human values are given expression. Paul clearly connects wisdom with rhetoric in 2:4 and 13.

133 It is another *topos* in arguments urging concord that factionalism is foolishness, even madness. See, e. g., Dio Chrys. *Or.* 48.6: "having constantly engaged with you in discussions

ness of the Christ, is the true Christian wisdom, God's wisdom. It is characteristic of Paul's adept argumentation that he can draw simultaneously on the Christian kerygma and common political lore – and that he contrasts the two as he does. Paul grounds this exhortation by appeal to his own example: he did not teach the Corinthians human wisdom, but God's wisdom (2:1–7). God's wisdom has the power to unite all those who are called, both Jew and Greek (1:24; cf. 12:13), thus ending ethnic separation[134] in the common acceptance of the scandal of the cross (1:23–24).

Human wisdom also finds its expression in "boasting in men" (1:29–31; cf. 1:12; 3:4), which is another way in which Paul characterizes the Corinthians' factionalism. He returns to this theme, and its counterpart "being puffed up," throughout 1:18–4:21, urging, with appeal to Jer 9:22–23, the unification of the church in a common boast in a common Lord.[135] The difference between human wisdom and divine wisdom (1:18–2:8) can also be described in terms of the closely synonymous contrasting pair τὸ πνεῦμα τοῦ κόσμου[136] and τὸ πνεῦμα τὸ ἐκ τοῦ θεοῦ, to which Paul turns in 2:10–16. Human wisdom is opposed to God's wisdom, which is spiritual wisdom (2:13) for the mature (2:6). Thus one can similarly differentiate the πνευματικοί, who are filled with God's spirit, God's wisdom, from the ψυχικοί, who are not. The ψυχικός, the unspiritual person, is the one who subscribes to earthly wisdom, which upholds the earthly values of superiority and competition which result in factionalism.[137]

The explicit application[138] of these antitheses of 1:18–2:16 to the current Corinthian situation in 3:1–4 is severe. The Corinthians are not πνευματικοί, but

---

conducive to concord and amity [ὁμόνοια καὶ φιλία], so far as I am able, and trying in every way to eradicate unreasonable and foolish enmity and strife and contention [ἔχθρα δὲ καὶ ἔρις καὶ φιλονεικία ἄλογος καὶ ἀνόητος]." For other examples see Lucan, *BCiv.* 1.8, 106, 681–82; 5.262; 6.63; Dio Chrys. *Or.* 32.5; 41.12; Aristid. *Or.* 23.29, 40, 51, 59, 60, 73; 24.4, 12, 31 (also Sheppard, 243 on Aristid.); *1 Clem.* 63.1; cf. Dion. Hal. *Ant. Rom.* 7.42.4–5. This also may partake of another *topos* in all kinds of deliberative arguments in which the orator urges the audience to "do the intelligent thing" and not the stupid or foolish thing (as in Dio Chrys. *Or.* 46.14; Aristid. *Or.* 24.36).

[134] Cf. Eph 2:11–22.

[135] 1:31; 3:21; 4:7; elsewhere see especially 8:6; 12:3. We have noted the Christocentrism of 1:1–10. The same argument is made in *1 Clem.* 13.1 (34.5).

[136] This is a contrast retained in the rest of the argument (for κόσμος see 3:19, 22; 4:9; 5:10; 6:2; 7:31, 33–34; 8:4; 11:32; 14:10; cf. already in 1:20, 21, 27–28 and αἰών in 2:6–8).

[137] For such a rare NT word, it is significant that in two other uses ψυχικός is found also in a discussion of factionalism; see Jud 19: Οὗτοι εἰσιν οἱ ἀποδιορίζοντες, ψυχικοί, πνεῦμα μὴ ἔχοντες, and Jas 3:15, as an epithet of divisive σοφία. This similarity is such that Pearson, 14 posits literary dependence of Jas on 1 Cor, a judgement with which I tend to concur (differently Hort, 84). If this is correct, then we have another piece of early evidence for this reading of 1 Cor. The term as used by Paul and these authors is not part of a gnostic system, though later it would be taken up into them (Dibelius, *James*, 211–12; Conzelmann, 71 n. 23; for the opposite point of view, see Schmithals, *Gnosticism*, 169; Wilckens, 89–91).

[138] Klauck, *1. Korintherbrief*, 31, subtitles the section 3:1–23 "Andwendung auf das Parteienwesen."

they are σάρκινοι/σαρκικοί, "fleshly." This is neatly defined by Paul as such a commonplace that he can make it in the form of a rhetorical question: ὅπου γὰρ ἐν ὑμῖν ζῆλος καὶ ἔρις [καὶ διχοστασίαι], οὐχὶ σαρκικοί ἐστε καὶ κατὰ ἄνθρωπον περιπατεῖτε; (3:3).[139] Party strife is a human, earthly failing. Those who engage in it act like little children crying over silly squabbles who are unable to see what is truly important (3:2).[140] In 3:5–17 Paul demonstrates the need and possibility for Corinthian unity by appealing to the concord which exists between himself and Apollos, one of the leaders to whom some kind of allegiance was also paid. He uses their relationship as a paradigm for Corinthian unity rather than a cause for division (1:12; 3:4, 22; 4:6; 16:12): ὁ φυτεύων δὲ καὶ ὁ ποτίζων ἕν εἰσιν (3:8).[141]

With 3:9 Paul begins his extended introduction of the building metaphor for church unity which will predominate in this epistle. In doing so he calls upon another political *topos*, which he skillfully particularizes for application to the Corinthian Christian community: they are θεοῦ οἰκοδομή, which has Jesus Christ as its firm and unitary θεμέλιος, forming the ναὸς τοῦ θεοῦ in which the holy spirit dwells. The Corinthian church is theoretically united in all these elements, but its members must pay careful attention to how they build upon this structure. We have already seen in 1:8 that the stability of the Corinthian church is in question. Paul threatens that God will not tolerate anyone who destroys the church through factionalism (3:17). Underlying this argument is an unstated premise, one well known to anyone in Greco-Roman antiquity: factionalism destroys any political or social body that it infects.[142] The positive metaphor of the concordant building will be drawn upon by Paul throughout the specific advice sections (6:19; 8:1, 10; 10:23; 14:3–5, 12, 17, 26; cf. 15:58; 16:13), where he will differentiate unifying activity (that which builds up) from divisive activity, always advising the former.

Epideictic Elements in 1:18–4:21

The argument throughout 1:18–4:21, particularly in ch. 3–4, contains epideictic elements of censure,[143] which amount to a diagnosis of the problem before the advice for resolution is offered. The rhetorical handbooks in a few places allow for epideictic elements of blame or praise in deliberative rhetoric.[144] These

---

139 ζῆλος and ἔρις are "works of the flesh" for Paul (Gal 5:20).

140 See the treatment in chap. III.

141 Cf. Dio Chrys. *Or.* 38.46 on the appeal to concord in the same ancestors, and further examples in chap. III.

142 See chap. III.

143 On the theory and practice of epideictic rhetoric see Volkmann, 314–61; Burgess's standard treatment; Martin, 177–210; and now Russell-Wilson, xi-xxxiv (for other resources see also chap. I n. 34).

144 The most important text is *Rhet.Her.* 3.8.15: "And if epideictic is only seldom employed by itself independently, still in judicial and deliberative causes extensive sections are often devoted to praise or censure" (see also Arist. *Rh.* 3.16.11; Quint. *Inst.* 3.4.11, citing Isocrates as his authority; 3.7.2–4, and further references and discussion in Burgess, 95, who concludes:

allowances in rhetorical theory are overwhelmingly confirmed by actual deliberative texts which very consciously use blame and praise in their argumentation.[145] Isocrates is explicit about this strategy in his *Or.* 4, *Panegyricus*:

It is not, however, possible to turn men from their errors [ἀποτρέπειν τῶν ἁμαρτημάτων], or to inspire in them the desire for a different course of action without first roundly condemning [ἐπιτιμᾶν] their present conduct; and a distinction must be made between accusation [κατηγορεῖν], when one denounces with intent to injure, and admonition [νουθετεῖν], when one uses like words with intent to benefit.[146]

The same strategy, using even the same language distinctions, is employed explicitly by Paul in 1 Cor 1:18–4:21, as he says in his summary statement in 4:14 (Οὐκ ἐντρέπων ... ἀλλὰ ... νουθετῶν).[147] For what does Paul admonish the Corinthians in 1:18–4:13? For their factionalism and all its petty manifestations. The proposition[148] of this entire proof section is boldly stated in 3:2–3: οὐδὲ ἔτι νῦν δύνασθε, ἔτι γὰρ σαρκικοί ἐστε.[149] It is this blameworthy fact, that the

---

"the propriety of introducing epideictic features in other forms was generally recognized"). This is particularly important because the rhetorical species of the text remains *deliberative*, even though it contains epideictic elements. That is why the entire compositional unit must be examined in a rhetorical analysis (as argued in chap. I). That censure is allowed in the handbooks on deliberative rhetoric was noted by Welborn, "Conciliatory Principle," 334 n. 76, citing Arist. *Rh.* 1.9.28–37 and Quint. *Inst.* 3.7.28. On praise and blame in letters see Stowers, 77: "Praise and/or blame is used in virtually every type of letter that the theorists isolated."

[145] For examples of blame in deliberative arguments see, e. g., Dem. *Ep.* 1.5; 3.11, 21; Isoc. *Ep.* 8.4; 9.8, 17; Dio Chrys. *Or.* 34.37; 38.23–31; 40.24, 29; 48.5, 16; Aristid. 23.66; 24.50, 55, 59. In ECL see especially *1 Clem.* 47:6: αἰσχρά, ἀγαπητοί, καὶ λίαν αἰσχρὰ καὶ ἀνάξια τῆς ἐν Χριστῷ ἀγωγῆς ἀκούεσθαι, τὴν βεβαιοτάτην καὶ ἀρχαίαν Κορινθίων ἐκκλησίαν δι' ἓν ἢ δύο πρόσωπα στασιάζειν πρὸς τοὺς πρεσβυτέρους. One of the ways in which this custom is given expression is in the *topos* of the deliberative orator as the physician who cannot give a "painless cure" (Pl. *Ep.* 7.330C-D; Dio Chrys. *Or.* 40.9; Aristid. *Or.* 23.61). It is so common for the deliberative orator to blame that Aristides can say in one speech: "And do not be surprised that although I have nothing to censure, I think that I should offer some advice. And do not think that advice is the act of only those who come to speak in criticism. But it is also the business of those who bestow praise" (*Or.* 27.42).

[146] 4.130 (a passage noted by Arist. *Rh.* 3.17.10); see the same distinction in his *Or.* 8.72 (also §27, quoted above). In the first century the relationship between censure and advice was maintained also by Seneca, *Ep.* 94.39: "On this ground, you ought to say that consolation does not avail, and warning, and exhortation, and scolding, and praising; since they are all varieties of advice."

[147] On this verse see Stowers, 128. The importance of these terminological distinctions into the Imperial period is shown in the later epistolary handbooks, which (somewhat artificially) differentiate the following letter types: μεμπτικός, ὀνειδιστικός, ἐπιτιμητικός, νουθετητικός, ψεκτικός, κατηγορικός (Ps-Demetr. Prologue=Malherbe, *Epistolary Theorists*, 30; cf. Ps-Lib. 4=Malherbe, *Epistolary Theorists*, 66; on which see also Stowers, 85–86, 125–41).

[148] Individual proofs or proof sections often focus on their own propositions. On proposition with proof appended see Quint. *Inst.* 4.4.7. See also Cicero's description of inductive and deductive proofs (*Inv.Rhet.* 1.31.51–42.77; cf. *Rhet.Her.* 2.18.28 and the context, mostly on forensic proofs).

[149] This proposition is amplified by the two synonymous descriptions in verses 3–4: κατὰ

Corinthians are immature and fleshly because they engage in partisan rivalries, which this section proves. This proof is appropriately epideictic in character because the issue in this section revolves around *the present time.*[150]

Epideictic proof consists of blame or censure of a person, or a city, or a thing. It is fascinating to see how Paul's censure of the Corinthian church here proceeds along the lines which Quintilian recommended for praising or blaming a city:

> Cities are praised [substitute blamed] after the same fashion as men. The founder takes the place of the parent, and antiquity carries great authority, as for instance in the case of those whose inhabitants are said to be sprung from the soil. The virtues and vices revealed by their deeds are the same as in private individuals. The advantages arising from site or fortifications are however peculiar to cities. Their citizens enhance their fame just as children bring honour to their parents. Praise too may be awarded to public works, in connexion with which their magnificence, utility, beauty and the architect or artist must be given due consideration. Temples for instance will be praised for their magnificence, walls for their utility, and both for their beauty or the skill of the architect (*Inst.* 3.7.26–27).

Paul's censure of the church at Corinth for its factionalism in 1:18–4:21, in addition to metaphorically employing several of the topics named by Quintilian, bears a remarkable similarity to this rhetorical strategy recommended for epideictic praise or blame. In antiquity epideictic proof of praise or blame[151] for persons or cities[152] followed a regular plan of common topics treating successively γένος, ἀνατροφή, πράξεις and σύγκρισις.[153] While 1:18–4:21 does not

ἄνθρωπον περιπατεῖτε, and ἄνθρωποί ἐστε. The repetition of two of the caricatured slogans in 3:4 makes the same point (the connection between all of these epithets and factionalism in antiquity was demonstrated in chap. III). That 3:2–4 is the proposition which Paul proves here gives further confirmation that the function of this proof section 1:18–4:21 is the same as in other deliberative discourses which urge concord: to demonstrate to the hearers that factionalism is a foolish, self-destructive form of behavior, and that they should turn from it to concord to save themselves.

150 Note, in addition to the present tense verbs, the repetition of ἔτι, the νῦν in 3:2–3, and the repeated ἄρτι in 4:11 and 13 (on epideictic proof as dealing with the present see chap. I n. 41). The overall deliberative proof in 1 Cor 1:18–15:57 appropriately points to *future* actions (chap. II n. 10) to remedy this present bad situation, as especially the πρόθεσις in 1:10 shows. This can be seen already in the imperatives in 1:18–4:21 (see above n. 125).

151 The handbooks agree that the same topics for praise are used in reverse fashion for blame (*Rh.Al.* 3.1426a; 35.1441b; *Rhet.Her.* 3.6.10; Cic. *De Or.* 2.85.349; Quint. *Inst.* 3.7.19).

152 Praise or censure of cities is regularly treated in rhetorical theory on epideictic rhetoric; see Dion. Hal. *Rhet.* 3.228 and 5.256–58; Men. Rh. 1.346–367 [Russell-Wilson, 32–75 (the most extensive treatment)]; Hermog. *Prog.* 7.41–42 [Rabe, 18]; and in general Russell-Wilson, 250.

153 This analysis follows Burgess, 120–26 (see the discussion in chap. I n. 34), who observes: "The ideal for the encomium of a person, both in theory and practice, was remarkably uniform. It agrees in general conception, and even largely in details, from almost the earliest to the latest period of Greek literature" (pp. 119–20). The theorists agree that an encomium or vituperation of a city follows the same plan as for a person. "And indeed you may handle an encomium of a

strictly adhere to a chronological scheme,[154] nonetheless all of these vituperative topics are plainly handled, as Paul treats the Corinthian church much as one would a city.[155] The γένος of the Corinthians is a central topic in 1:18–4:21, especially because the problem is the Corinthians' boasting in their missionaries, their spiritual ancestors.[156] The encomiastic topic of γένος[157] deals with several things: founders, settlers, date, changes, causes of foundation.[158] In 1:18–31, in particular in 1:26–28, Paul rebukes any Corinthian claims to exalted *individual* γένη.[159] In 2:1–5 he refers to the foundation of the church and his role as founder at his initial visit, as he will again later with the customary foundation metaphors of planter and architect in 3:6 and 10. Paul's role as founder/progenitor is definitively expressed in the summation to the argument in 4:15, ἐν γὰρ Χριστῷ

---

city from these [topics] without difficulty. For you will speak about birth [γένος], that it was the original race, and about nursing [τροφή], that they were nursed by gods, and about education [παιδεία], that they were educated by gods. And you will prove it clearly as [for an encomium] on a person: From where did the city's customs arise? From where its constitution? What practices did it engage in? What did it accomplish?" (Hermog. *Prog.* 7.41–42 [Rabe, 18], my trans.). See also Men. Rh. 1.346 [Russell-Wilson, 32], and Menander's whole treatment, in addition to references in the other handbooks on epideictic topics (e. g., Arist. *Rh.* 1.9.3–13; *Rhet.Her.* 3.6.10; 7.13; Cic. *Inv.Rhet.* 2.59.177; *De Or.* 2.84.342–44; Quint. *Inst.* 3.7.10). In actual texts, see Burgess's analysis of Isoc. *Or.* 9 on p. 126 n. 4 and also the general outline of Aristid. *Or.* 26, *The Roman Oration*, one of the most famous encomia of a city in later antiquity, in which σύγκρισις predominates (see Oliver, 878–79 for an analysis). On encomium and synkrisis see also Berger, 1173–1191, who does not mention 1 Cor 1–4 (but see 1178–89 where he describes Phil 2:6–11 as an encomium within a deliberative argument).

[154] Because of the particulars of this rhetorical situation. Since Paul wants to demonstrate that the Corinthians are not yet adult, for that reason and because of his apocalyptic perspective he cannot move the proof chronologically into their adult behavior.

[155] For a similar use of epideictic topics in a deliberative speech for concord (here praising), see the speech of Menenius Agrippa: "As for us of the senate, plebeians, one assurance suffices, that you will never, if you return, behave yourselves badly toward us, and that is the knowledge we have of your excellent rearing [τροφαί], of your law-abiding habits [ἐπιτηδεύματα], and of all your virtues [ἀρετή] of which you have given many proofs both in peace and in war" (Dion. Hal. *Ant. Rom.* 6.85.2).

[156] As argued in chap. III, the caricatured slogans and boasting amount to claims to a high pedigree or descent.

[157] "We shall place first the introduction of the genealogy of the person we are speaking of, as that is the fundamental ground of reputation or discredit [ἔνδοξον ἢ ἄδοξον]" (*Rh.Al.* 35.1440b; compare 1 Cor 4:10c). For an actual example, see Aristid. *Or.* 27, *Panegyric in Cyzicus*, especially § 13 and 18 (cited as an example in Men. Rh. 1.345 [Russell-Wilson, 30; see also their note on p. 247]).

[158] Men. Rh. 1.353 [Russell-Wilson, 46–47]. See also Aphthonius' schema taken up by Burgess, 12–22, which includes ἔθνος, πατρίς, πρόγονοι, πατέρες.

[159] οὐ πολλοὶ εὐγενεῖς ... καὶ τὰ ἀγενῆ τοῦ κόσμου καὶ τὰ ἐξουθενημένα ἐξελέξατο ὁ θεός. Paul argues that Christians have no pedigree and thus no boast apart from that of the community (hence the new name, κλητοί, over and against other forms of self-identification). It is the wisdom of the world which regards such matters as wisdom, power and noble birth as praiseworthy attributes of the individual (thus the very structure of epideictic praise and blame of individuals). See also the insightful comparison of 4:10 and 1:26–28 in Plank, 47.

Ἰησοῦ διὰ τοῦ εὐαγγελίου ἐγὼ ὑμᾶς ἐγέννησα. Not content with pointing to the human agency of the church foundation (himself and Apollos), throughout 3:7–17 (cf. 1:9) Paul names the true founder and owner of the church, God,[160] and its divine foundation stone, Jesus Christ. In direct contrast with their lowly individual γένη, the *community* shares an esteemed birth and implied destiny. Even the early growth of the community under divine agency boded well for their future.[161] The Corinthians' pedigree is secure in their proper illustrious church founding (as already stated in 1:6), so that their status appears to be extraordinarily praiseworthy in itself: θεοῦ γεώργιον,[162] θεοῦ οἰοδομή ἐστε (3:9).[163] There is nothing to blame in the γένος of the Corinthian church – the reason for their present shortcomings must lie in their πράξεις,[164] in what they have done with the considerable advantages afforded by their esteemed community foundation. Paul's rhetorical strategy of censure of the church is paralleled in other discourses on concord from antiquity which contrast a city's auspicious founding by the gods with its present divisive behavior.[165]

---

160 Compare Men. Rh. 1.353 [Russell-Wilson, 46–47]: "if we inquire who the founder was, we say whether he was a god, hero, or man, and then, according to status, whether he was a general, a king or a private individual. If a god, the encomium is the grandest."

161 3:6, ἀλλὰ ὁ θεὸς ηὔξανεν. Growth [ἐπαυξάνειν], is one of the categories under "change" as a subcategory of the topic γένος in an encomium of a city (Men. Rh. 1.355–56 [Russell-Wilson, 50–51]).

162 The field metaphor may also be connected with the appeal for peace: "[Numa] wished . . . to turn the people to agriculture [ἐπὶ γεωργίαν], that they might be subdued and softened along with the soil they tilled. For there is no other occupation which produces so keen and quick a relish for peace [εἰρήνη] as that of a farmer's life" (Plut. *Num.* 16.3–4; cf. *Cam.* 38.3).

163 One should also show that a city is θεοφιλότης, "a god-loved one" (Men. Rh. 1.361–62, who uses among his examples that Helios and Poseidon competed for Corinth [cf. Dio Chrys. *Or.* 37.11–12]). This argument is used by Aristid. to the Rhodians: "Well! If you are beloved of the gods [θεοφιλής], do you think that you should be involved in faction and unrest and live to suit the curses of your enemies or rather on the contrary act in accordance with the prayers of men of moderation, honoring the gods, accepting one another, thriving in every way?" (*Or.* 24.48)

164 This is consistent with the absence of ἔργον in the list of Corinthian gifts in 1:4–9, and its presence in the conclusion to the argument in 15:58 (see n. 53 above).

165 "But it is fitting that those whose city was founded by gods should maintain peace and concord and friendship toward one another. For it is disgraceful [αἰσχρόν] if they do not prove to be extremely lucky and blessed of heaven and to some extent superior to the others in good fortune, desiring, as they must, to show birth [τὸ τοῦ γένους] to be something real and not merely a sham and empty term. For founders, kinsmen, and progenitors who are gods desire their own people to possess nothing . . . so much as sobriety, virtue, orderly government, honour for the good citizens and dishonour for the base" (Dio Chrys. *Or.* 39.2, a speech which is entirely censure and never moves to specific advice before breaking off, and thus is an epideictic argument [on which see Jones, *Dio Chrysostom*, 89]). See also Dio's *Or.* 34.7f.; 40.9f.; 41.9; 48.8; the first proof section in Aristid. *Or.* 23.12–26, which provides an encomium of each of the three cities which follows the course of epideictic topics [with Behr, 2.365, "Praise of province. Three chief cities"]; and his *Or.* 24.5, and 45–57: "Indeed, it does not even make sense that your ancestors, who had formerly been divided into three parts, united because of their trust in one another and settled in one city formed from all the others, while you by your

The encomium topic of ἀνατροφή is broken down by the rhetorical theorists into such subcategories as ἔργα, τροφή and ἐπιτηδεύματα.[166] Paul gives a very literal rendering of the Corinthians' τροφή in 3:2: γάλα ὑμᾶς ἐπότισα, οὐ βρῶμα. The ἔργα of the Corinthian church, which Paul describes as the "building onto" [ἐποικοδομεῖν] the foundation of Christ, are still going on, and still await final judgement and assessment (3:12–15 [ἑκάστου τὸ ἔργον]; 4:1–5).

The actions, πράξεις, of the person or city being blamed form the most important part of an encomium.[167] One's gifts of soul, body and fortune form subcategories of this division.[168] The handbooks recommend discussion of such virtues as justice, courage, temperance and wisdom,[169] along with such external gifts as strength and wealth.[170] The Corinthians' gift of wisdom is a predominant topic, especially in 3:18–23; 4:10. As with their founding, the gifts of the Corinthians are abundant and praiseworthy in themselves.[171] It is in what they have done with their considerable gifts[172] that the Corinthians are to be censured.[173] The blameworthy acts of the Corinthians are the basis for Paul's

---

divisiveness have made many cities out of one ... Do you not feel a sense of shame [οὐκ αἰσχύνεσθε] before the sun who ... is the founder of your race?" (24.49–50). Cf. also the "then and now" argument in *1 Clem.* 1–2; 47:6.

[166] For variety here see Burgess, 120–23.

[167] "It is universally agreed that this is the chief topic" (Burgess, 123). Deeds are classed sometimes among the ἀνατροφή, but in most theorists comprise a separate topic, πράξεις (see Burgess, 120–25). In actual texts see Dio Chrys. *Or.* 48.9: "Do you imagine there is any advantage in market or theatre or gymnasia or colonnades or wealth for men who are at variance [στασιάζειν]? These are not the things which make a city beautiful, but rather self-control, friendship, mutual trust" (see also Aristid. *Or.* 27.40–41 on harmony as the best adornment of a city). Aristotle is adamant that praise [ὁ ἔπαινος] should be founded on actions and achievements (*Rh.* 1.9.32–33; cf. *Rh.Al.* 3.1426a; Quint. *Inst.* 3.7.13, "moreover the praise awarded to external and accidental advantages is given, not to their possession, but to their honourable employment").

[168] Burgess, 120–25.

[169] *Rhet.Her.* 3.8.15; *Rh.Al.* 35.1441b (δικαιοσύνη, σοφία, ἀνδρεία).

[170] See the lists in *Rh.Al.* 35.1440b (εὐγένεια, ῥωμή, κάλλος, πλοῦτος); Arist. *Rh.* 1.9.3–13; *Rhet.Her.* 3.7.14; 3.4.8; Cic. *Inv.Rhet.* 2.59.177; *De Or.* 2.84.344 (one distinguishes goods of nature and of fortune).

[171] πάντα γὰρ ὑμῶν ἐστιν in 3:21; cf. 1:5, ἐπλουτίσθητε, and 4:8, ἤδη ἐπλουτήσατε. The Corinthians are also strong (4:10b).

[172] "Moreover, in praise and censure it will be necessary to observe not so much what the subject of the speech possessed in bodily endowment or in extraneous goods as what use he made of them" (Cic. *Inv.Rhet.* 2.59.178). "In censure, if the subject has these physical advantages, we shall declare that he has abused what, like the meanest gladiator, he has had by chance and nature" (*Rhet.Her.* 3.7.14).

[173] Compare Aristid. *Or.* 23.30, after praising the gifts possessed by the three cities: "But the choice of concord and proper behavior toward one another is the act of those who will so. Therefore it is reasonable that they who excel in fortune not feel as much pride as they who are superior in their behavior" (see also 23.66, 68, 76). This commonplace comparison of a city's goods with its actions is used also by Dio Chrys.: "And it becomes you, since you excel in cultivation [παιδεία] and in natural gifts [φύσις] and are in fact pure Hellenes, to display your nobility in this very thing (concord)" (48.8, see also § 4). "Again what sort of edifices, what size

admonition: they boast (1:29–31; 3:21; 4:7), they are puffed up and give themselves airs (4:6, 8),[174] they claim allegiances (1:12; 3:4), they judge others as inferior to themselves (4:1–5), all of which add up to a single picture, that they engage in factional behavior.[175] That one has abused one's gifts is a stock argument in epideictic vituperation, one which Paul uses explicitly in 4:7: τί δὲ ἔχεις ὃ οὐκ ἔλαβες; εἰ δὲ καὶ ἔλαβες, τί καυχᾶσαι ὡς μὴ λαβών;[176] Yet precisely because the Corinthians remain in adolescence (3:1–4), their πράξεις can still be described in terms of future hopes (3:12–15; 4:1–5). This censure has as its purpose above all changed behavior in the future. That is why Paul cannot follow the encomiastic or vituperative pattern into the Corinthians' adulthood – it has not been reached, and no definitive judgement, of praise or blame, can be given until the eschaton: καὶ τότε ἔπαινος[177] γενήσεται ἑκάστῳ ἀπὸ τοῦ θεοῦ.

The final section of epideictic proof, a very important part; is the σύγκρισις or comparison.[178] It is standard rhetorical practice in an encomium or vituperation to compare the person or city under discussion with illustrious examples.[179] In

---

of territory, what magnitude of population renders a community stronger than domestic concord?" (*Or.* 39.5).

174 That this is a fitting epideictic topic of censure is clear from Cic. *De Or.* 2.84.342: "a panegyric must also treat of these goods of nature and of fortune in which the highest praise is not to have been puffed up [*non extulisse se*] in office or insolent in wealth, or to have put oneself in front of others because of fortune's bounty – so that wealth and riches may seem to have provided opportunity and occasion not for pride and license but for beneficence and temperance."

175 They risk destroying the church through their factionalism (3:17).

176 "One ought not to pride oneself on goods which are due to fortune, but on those which are due to oneself alone" (Arist. *Rh.* 1.9.36). Cf. *Rh.Al.* 35.1441 b: "In vituperations also you should employ irony, and ridicule your opponent for the things on which he prides himself." For the use of this *topos* in another argument on concord, see Dio Chrys. *Or.* 38.38: "In truth such marks of distinction, on which you plume yourselves, not only are objects of utter contempt in the eyes of all persons of discernment, but especially in Rome they excite laughter and, what is still more humiliating [ὑβριστικώτερον], are called 'Greek failings!'" On irony in 4:9–13 see Plank, 33–69 (though he takes the irony to be in service of Paul's defense, not the Corinthians' censure). What Paul is using in this argument are stock epideictic *topoi* of censure (one need not postulate a specific "ὕβρις-tradition" to account for them, nor can one perform social reconstruction of the Corinthians by reading these *topoi* as social or class-determined descriptions [as is done by Marshall, 182–218]).

177 This is of course the proper term for an encomium (see also Conzelmann, 84 n. 27).

178 Burgess, 125–26, with many references (see also Hermog. *Prog.* 8.42–44 [Rabe, 18–20]). "The rhetoricians indicate two distinct kinds of comparison. There is the minor or incidental σύγκρισις . . . , where some one phase of a subject or a single quality is likened to some other, and the final or general σύγκρισις (τελειοτάτη, or περὶ ὅλης τῆς ὑποθέσεως), where a more comprehensive comparison is made" (Burgess, 125).

179 "And you must compare him with illustrious personages, for it affords grounds for amplification . . . and amplification is most suitable for epideictic speakers" (Arist. *Rh.* 1.9.39). "Moreover a splendid line to take in a panegyric is to compare the subject with all other men of high distinction" (Cic. *De Or.* 2.85.348; see also *Rh.Al.* 35.1441 a; Quint. *Inst.* 2.4.21). In actual texts, of many examples see Burgess, 126 n. 4 on Isoc. *Or.* 9, and Aristid. *Or.* 26.14–70, where Rome is compared with a variety of examples (for analysis see Oliver, 878–79).

4:1–13 Paul sets up and executes a comparison between the Corinthians and the apostles,[180] the most illustrious Christian examples.[181] In 4:6 Paul explicitly tells what he is doing – μετεσχημάτισα[182] – he is making an example of himself and Apollos to set forth this comparison with the Corinthians.[183] In 4:9 another rhetorical term, ἀπέδειξεν,[184] is used of the apostles, to explain their God-given role as exemplars or living metaphors for the community.[185] In careful argumentative style Paul holds his strongest argument until the last. Using the rhetorical figure of concentration of examples, in 4:10–13 Paul contrasts the Corinthians'

---

[180] On "the synkrisis of the Corinthians and the Apostles" in 4:8–13, see now the detailed comparative analysis of Fitzgerald, 132–48. Fitzgerald does not discuss the role of σύγκρισις in an encomium or vituperation (but he does refer in passing to the "specific epideictic function" of the peristasis catalogue in 4:8–13 [p. 147]).

[181] This section is not a defense of Paul's conduct (so Dahl, 47–49; Welborn, "Discord," 107; Plank, 12–24; a position correctly rejected by Fitzgerald, 128). The rhetorical σύγκρισις *depends* upon Paul's assumed stature as an illustrious person worthy of comparison and emulation (along with all the apostles). Would a defense plea end in a call for imitation, or a disclaimer of censure? Paul may well have wrongly estimated the extent to which he could assume that the Corinthians held him in esteem (as the letters in 2 Cor doubtless show), but his rhetorical strategy of self appeal throughout 1 Cor assumes that regard, to which he adds his humility and self-effacement as a corrective to their arrogance. See Plank's attempt to deal with the rhetorical inconsistency between what Paul does here and the function or strategy of an apology for which he argues: "Given the Corinthian rationality, Paul's marriage of apostleship and weakness *could only seem to be at odds with his intent to defend his authority. The surprising strategy risks the readers' rejection of Paul's case* but, at the same time, begins to set weakness apart from what it had been assumed to be" (p. 88, emph. added).

[182] For literature on this term see chap. II n. 154. See the remarkable parallel in Plut. *Num.* 20.8: "For possibly there is no need of any compulsion or menace in dealing with the multitude, but when they see with their own eyes a conspicuous and shining example [παράδειγμα] of virtue in the life of their ruler, they will of their own accord walk in wisdom's ways [σωφρονοῦσι], and unite with him in conforming themselves [συμμετασχηματίζονται] to a blameless and blessed life of friendship and mutual concord [ἐν φιλίᾳ καὶ ὁμονοίᾳ τῇ πρὸς αὐτούς]."

[183] Recently two inventive solutions have been offered for the exegetical crux of 4:6. Welborn, "Conciliatory Principle," 341–46 has argued that it is a conciliatory principle reflecting peace treaty formulae, but his study has not established that such a convention was indeed formulaic, or how 4:6 fits that form (and not just its possible function). None of the examples cited mirrors the ὑπὲρ ἃ part of 4:6 which is, after all, the most difficult part (parallels to γράφειν are given). Fitzgerald's hypothesis, that it refers to the ancient mode of tracing letters for learning the alphabet is ingenious but not readily anchored in this particular context in 1 Cor 1–4. Nor is it clear how this domestic image fits with the conflict expressed in the parallel clause ἵνα μὴ εἷς ὑπὲρ τοῦ ἑνὸς φυσιοῦσθε κατὰ τοῦ ἑτέρου. I take the phrase as a reference back to the scripture quote (3:21; cf. 1:31), an interpretation which receives further support by the already established parallelism of καυχᾶσθαι and φυσιοῦσθαι as Paul's caricatured description of Corinthian factionalism. For the extensive literature on this verse, see Welborn and Fitzgerald.

[184] Weiss, *Korintherbrief*, 109; Conzelmann, 55 n. 26; Betz, "Rhetoric and Theology," 37; cf. the noun in 2:4, and δεικνύναι in 12:31 b.

[185] The comparison with "the apostles" also serves to show Paul's unity with his coworkers (3:8, 22; 4:1; 9:1–6; 15:11; 16:12), as well as showing the ridiculousness of the Corinthians' misunderstanding of the proper role of the apostles (as people to whom party allegiance is due).

blameworthy behavior with the apostles' behavior by a devastating set of ironic antitheses.[186] Each of the examples given is a variation on the theme of boasting and humility, wisdom and foolishness, each with its own twist, with v. 13 as the resounding culmination.[187] In a kind of chiastic construction these comparisons reverse the order of the epideictic topics of this demonstration: Paul begins with the gifts of fortune, wisdom and strength, and then moves to physical advantages (or discomforts), and then to personal identity and descent. The description of the apostles' behavior thus forms a paradoxical encomium.[188] The inclusio of vv. 11–13 with ἄρτι points once again to the second comparison going on here – the temporal one. The apostles *now* act this way, but, despite all of the advantages given to them at their founding, the Corinthians do not. This in turn points back to 3:2–3, οὐδὲ ἔτι νῦν δύνασθε, ἔτι γὰρ σαρκικοί ἐστε. The censure of the Corinthians' behavior is definitively proven.[189]

4:14–21 summarizes the proof section 1:18–4:21 and elucidates the purpose of this section within the argument of the whole letter.[190] Paul is careful to state that his severe admonishment is not gratuitous[191] – it is to bring about a change in the Corinthians' behavior.[192] It is also rooted in his familial relationship with the

---

186 Especially 4:10c: ὑμεῖς ἔνδοξοι, ἡμεῖς δὲ ἄτιμοι (on the reverse order as chiastic, see Jeremias, 146). The purpose of an encomium is to demonstrate that the person or city being praised is ἔνδοξος. When the standards have been set on their head in this paradoxical encomium, this "praise" of the Corinthians becomes full vituperation. "Paul's argument and admonition thus rest on the paradox that he creates of the exalted Corinthians and the abased apostles" (Fitzgerald, 148; cf. Conzelmann, 89: "the representation of the opponents' position is essentially accurate; what makes it ironical is the criterion, the *theologia crucis*"). On irony in 4:9–13 see Plank, 33–69, and especially pages 51–62 on paradoxical irony.

187 περίψημα reaches the depths of humility.

188 In its reverse logic, not the unimportance of the theme. On the paradoxical encomium see Men. Rh. 1.346 [Russell-Wilson, 31–32]; Burgess, 158–66. The paradox will be resolved eschatologically (cf. the same paired contrasts in 15:42–43).

189 Many commentators on this section blush for the Corinthians' shame in hearing this argument! Heinrici, *Korinther*, 169 referred to "Die Rüge des Parteiwesens" (also *Sendschreiben*, 146: "das Gesagte musste sie beschämen"; Allo, 77; Barrett, *First Corinthians*, 114). Its censorious nature is also noted: "Die Wendung für die persönliche Haltung des Briefes bezeichnend: denn 4:7–13 sind doch wahrhaftig nach Absicht und Wirkung 'beschämend' für die Korinther" (Lietzmann-Kümmel, 21). Berger, 1345 classed 3:4–13 as a *Scheltrede* (but 3:18–4:6 as an *Apologie* [p. 1347]).

190 So Heinrici, *Korinther*, 159–60: "Der Abschnitt [4:14–21] ist sowohl Abschluss des Vorhergehenden, als auch Vorbereitung der folgenden Erörterungen über Fragen des sittlichen Lebens und der Organisation der Gemeinde."

191 Nor is it dissimulation (Welborn, "Discord," 108) when seen within the entire rhetorical composition. It is only when one restricts the argument to ch. 1–4 that one is forced to conclude thus, because in that hypothetical construction the actual advice never follows (cf. Isoc. *Or.* 4.130, quoted above).

192 Schmithals, "Korintherbriefe," 266 argued for partition on the grounds that 4:14 was the beginning of a *Briefschluss*, but the Pauline examples he cites are similar in neither form nor content (he offers no non-NT evidence). There is no proof that the denial of shaming is at all formulaic in a letter closing.

Corinthians,[193] and perhaps in Paul's disappointed expectation that the Corinthian Christians would have concord like a family.[194] The call for imitation in 4:16 points both backward and forward.[195] For each of the comparisons in 4:1–13 by which the Corinthians fared so badly, they are to seek to emulate Paul's behavior. Each type of behavior there, we noted, is an example of humility and self-effacement as opposed to fractious boasting and self-interest seeking. Throughout 1 Corinthians Paul will present himself as the opposite of a factionalist,[196] in regard to each of the contested issues championing in himself the conciliatory position. 4:16 thus serves to introduce the predominant rhetorical strategy of the proof sections to follow, a strategy already explicitly used in the first proof section.

The sending of Timothy and Paul's reference to some future visit (4:17–21) have puzzled scholars. Why should Paul discuss these matters in the middle of the letter body? Partition theorists regard this (and the apparent inconsistency with the call to receive Timothy in 16:10–11) as evidence that this is the end of a letter fragment.[197] Instead, the introduction of Timothy here, the envoy who either brings 1 Corinthians or will arrive soon after the letter,[198] has the rhetori-

---

[193] Those who make deliberative appeals often call on the father image for the counselor who has the audience's best interests at heart, even if he must be stern like a father (Philo, *Jos.* 73, quoted above; Joseph. *BJ* 1.481 of Herod to his sons, ἐνουθέτησεν ὡς πατήρ [Conzelmann, 91 n. 6]; Dio Chrys. *Or.* 39.8; 50.10; 77.38–39 [cf. 77.42 where the one who gives νουθεσία is said to be even kinder than a father]; Plut. *Mor.* 802F, on παρρησία πατρική; 810B-C on the difference between νουθετεῖν and λοιδορεῖν; *1 Clem.* 7.1 and the nouns in 56.2 and 6). The verb νουθετεῖν is also used for the task of advisors (Dio Chrys. *Or.* 32.27; Aristid. *Or.* 24.55).

[194] On these as *topoi* in Greco-Roman literature, see chap. III.

[195] This call to imitation of Paul, made explicitly in 4:16 and 11:1, and implicitly throughout the letter, because it is a consistent rhetorical strategy, is another argument for the unity of the letter (see chap. II).

[196] See esp. 8:13; all of ch. 9, particularly 9:22; 10:33; 13:11; 14:18–19, with documentation in chap. III.

[197] Schenk, 235–37; Schmithals, "Korintherbriefe," 265–68; Pesch, 78, 82–85; Sellin, "Hauptprobleme," 2977–78.

[198] The question revolves around two issues. First, is the ἔπεμψα in 4:17 an epistolary aorist, or a genuine preterite? Secondly, and of greater difficulty, what should be made of the conditional 'Ἐὰν ἔλθῃ in 16:10? It is interesting that two early commentators, Origen and Chrysostom, thought that Timothy *was* the bearer of the letter. ἀλλ' ἀνθ' ἑαυτοῦ ἐξελέξατο Τιμόθεον καὶ ἔπεμψεν αὐτὸν διορθωσόμενον τὰ ἐν Κορίνθῳ καὶ ἀναγκαίως μετὰ τῆς ἐπιστολῆς πέμπων αὐτὸν παρακατατιθέναι τῇ ἐκκλησίᾳ (Or., *comm. in I Cor.* 89.8–10 [p. 50]; cf. Chrys. *hom. in I Cor.* Argumentum 3 [*PG* 61.12] cited below n. 207; but Thdt. on the basis of 16:10 says that Timothy did not bring the letter [*1 Cor.* Argumentum D (*PG* 82.228)]). Most modern commentators take 4:17 as a genuine aorist, and think that Timothy had been sent already before the composition of 1 Corinthians by the land route (Lightfoot, 201; Heinrici, *Korinther*, 516; Weiss, *Korintherbrief*, 384; Robertson-Plummer, 90; Lietzmann-Kümmel, 89; Hurd, 138; Barrett, *First Corinthians*, 116; Strobel, 93). Then we must ask, does 16:10 contain a *genuine* conditional? Certainly in the rest of 16:10–11 Timothy's eventual arrival is expected. It has been noted that ἐάν can sometimes have the meaning of ὅταν, "when" or "whenever"

cal purpose of introducing the next three sections of proof (to be supplemented by Timothy's oral report), which will contain and confirm Paul's specific teachings and advice for unifying and conciliating behavior.[199] 4:18–21 is not the only place in 1 Corinthians (besides 16:5–8) where Paul makes mention of his travel plans or shows himself acutely aware of his absence from the church (5:3–4, 11; 9:15; 11:2, 33; 14:37).[200] In 16:5–8 Paul promises a long visit in the future. Rather than immediately assuming that this extensive "presence" and "visit-talk" is a sign of the edges of letter fragments,[201] we should first ask if these constant references to Paul's distance from the church could not play a *rhetorical* role in the argument in the letter. Even though a letter in antiquity was regarded as a substitute for one's personal presence,[202] those who advise by letter realize that they are at a decided disadvantage. It is far better to advise someone in person. A deliberative letter is a necessity in some circumstances, but it is still a *temporary* substitute for advice given in person.

I know, to be sure, that when men essay to give advice [συμβουλεύειν], it is far preferable that they should come in person [αὐτοὺς πλησιάσαντας] rather than send a letter, not only because it is easier to discuss the same matters [περὶ τῶν αὐτῶν πραγμάτων] face to face

---

(BAGD, 211, but not citing this text; J. H. Moulton, *A Grammar of NT Greek. Vol. 3: Syntax*, ed. N. Turner [Edinburgh, T & T Clark, 1963] 114; Conzelmann, 297). While the question of whether Timothy actually brought 1 Corinthians or was to interpret and supplement it upon his later arrival is not crucial to our argument here, I would like to suggest that it is possible that the conditional ἐάν may be an epistolary commonplace for referring to the arrival of the letter itself and/or envoys. The conjunction ἐάν then functions in a proleptic way (from the point of view of the writer) to refer to the fact that the writer does not know exactly when the arrival will be, rather than in a fully conditional sense of doubting the certainty of the arrival itself. For possible parallels see, for example, Pl. *Ep.* 2.312D and 313D, where Archedemus, who is clearly the bearer of this letter, is twice referred to in the following way: ἐπειδὰν ἔλθῃ, even though the fact of his arrival is not in doubt. In papyrus letters, see Sb 9252 lines 3 and 8–9 ('Εὰν ἔλθῃ, which may or may not be conditional; the letter does not give definitive proof); *PTeb.* 1.12 line 9 and *POsl.* 1460 lines 2 and 9, about the receipt of the letter itself (ἐάν σοι ἔλθῃ ἡ ἐπιστολή [on which see White, *Light From Ancient Letters*, 144 n. 2]); cf. the optative in Socr. *Ep.* 2, and in the NT perhaps Col 4:10 and 3 Jn 10. In his important discussion of verbal tenses in letters, unfortunately Koskenniemi did not investigate the tenses used to describe the *receipt* of the letter or envoys (pp. 189–200). This matter requires further study.

199 Note the repetition in the rest of the argument of Paul's teaching "in all the churches," as promised here in 4:17 (7:17; 11:16; 14:33).

200 With Belleville, 25 (also Bünker, 31–33 on the epistolary *topos*).

201 This argument rests upon far too mechanical expectations of epistolary forms and conventions than actual texts embody. Here Schenk appeals to a *Briefeschatokoll* which he must admit is no longer there (it must have followed on these verses, which lead up to it). On visit or presence talk in the middle of letters, Schenk assumes: "Reise- und Sendungspläne erwartet man aber gegen Briefende" (p. 235). But he cites as examples two Pauline letters where it appears in the middle! (Phil 2:19 ff. [his epistle B] and 1 Thess 1:31 ff. [his epistle D]; with Jewett, "Redaction," 398). This assumption has never been thoroughly tested against extant letters, which it must be, before it can hold such weight in literary operations.

202 Koskenniemi, 38–42, 172–80; Thraede, 95–106, 146–61; Funk, 249–69; Bünker, 22–31; White, *Light From Ancient Letters*, 190–92, 218–20.

[παρὼν πρὸς παρόντα] than to give their views by letter [δι' ἐπιστολῆς δηλώσειεν], nor yet because all men give greater credence to the spoken rather than to the written word, since they listen to the former as practical advice and to the latter as to an artistic composition; but also, in addition to these reasons, in personal converse, if anything that is said is either not understood or not believed, the one who is presenting the arguments, being present [παρών], can come to the rescue in either case; but when written missives are used and any such misconception arises, there is no one to correct it, for since the writer is not at hand [ἀπόντος γὰρ τοῦ γράψαντος], the defender is lacking.[203]

That Paul should refer to his personal presence[204] in 4:18–21, in a stern, almost threatening way, is rhetorically quite understandable after his censure of the Corinthians. They must hear the whole letter through, to move from censure to advice for unity.[205] Censure was necessary to move the Corinthians to change, but censure is hard to get away with, even if done in person,[206] a difficulty for which Paul compensates in two ways. First, he sends his envoy Timothy with (or before) the letter "to remind them of Paul's ways in Christ Jesus," and thus to strengthen the epistolary appeal by one who represents Paul.[207] The Corinthians will demonstrate their reception of Paul's letter by the way they receive his envoy. If they accept Paul's argument for concord they will send Timothy on ἐν εἰρήνῃ.[208] Second, throughout the argument in 1 Corinthians Paul refers to his

[203] Isoc. *Ep.* 1.2–3; for this common complaint see also Dem. *Ep.* 1.3: "It is a difficult thing, I know, for advice conveyed by letter to hold its ground, because you Athenians have a way of opposing many suggestions without waiting to understand them. In the case of a speaker, of course, it is possible to perceive what you want and easy to correct your misapprehensions; but the written page possesses no such aid against those who raise a clamour." Other examples are Isoc. *Ep.* 2.12; 3.4; Dem. *Ep.* 3.35, which is particularly important since it is in the *middle* of the letter: "If I were present in person [παρῆν] I should be trying to explain [ἐδίδασκον] these matters to you by word of mouth, but since I am in such a plight as I pray may be the lot of anyone who has uttered falsehoods against me to my ruin, I have sent my message in the form of a letter . . . ."

[204] Merklein, 160 rightly notes that 4:18–21 is not an announcement of visit plans.

[205] 4:14 deals explicitly with the possible objection which one could make at this point in hearing the letter, that Paul's censure is merely gratuitous.

[206] "Furthermore, while those who admonish [νουθετεῖν], even if only verbally, are hated by most men, but those who delight with flattery are approved to a surprising degree. . ." (Dio Chrys. *Or.* 51.4; see also § 52). Deliberative orators frequently feel the need to explain why they are hard on their audience. "Not by way of censure [ἐπιτιμᾶν] have I cited these examples, for so far am I from censuring as to declare it my belief that such repayments are in the highest degree in the interest [συμφέρειν] of the state" (Dem. *Ep.* 3.19–20). Isocrates makes the same plea: "and I should prefer to be disliked for having justly censured [ἐπιτιμήσας] than to win favour through having given unmerited praise [ἐπαινέσας]" (*Ep.* 9.12).

[207] This is so understood by Chrysostom: Καὶ τὸν Τιμόθεον δὲ ἀποστέλλει μετὰ τῶν γραμμάτων, εἰδὼς ὅτι πολλὴν μὲν ἰσχὺν ἔχει καὶ τὰ γράμματα, οὐ μικρὰν δὲ αὐτοῖς οἴσει προσθήκην καὶ ἡ παρουσία τοῦ μαθητοῦ (*hom. in I Cor.* Argumentum 3 [*PG* 61.12]).

[208] This is how patristic exegesis understood Timothy's role (see chap. III nn. 688–89; recall Origen's addition ἐν ὑμετέρᾳ ὁμονοίᾳ). For the practice, compare Isoc. *Ep.* 7.13: "And you yourself will soon make it clear if you reciprocate my regard [τὴν αὐτὴν γνώμην ἔχεις ἡμῖν]; for you will be considerate of Autocrator, and send me a letter renewing our former friendship

coming visit with the Corinthians to substantiate the authority of his letter of advice, and to warn them that he will soon have personal contact with them to check on whether or not they have heeded his advice. The apparent inconsistency between 4:18–21 and 16:5–11 may therefore be resolved when understood in regard to the rhetorical strategies and places within the argument of the two texts.[209]

(2) 5:1–11:1. *Second Section of Proof:*
The Integrity of the Corinthian Community Against Outside Defilement

In this section of proof, itself composed of many sub-arguments under topical heads, Paul begins to give advice on the specific behavioral and social issues which divide the Corinthian church.[210] Most commentators in their analysis of 1 Corinthians, because they presume that Paul's letter follows the course of events, think that ch. 5–6 are a separate section from ch. 7–11, as the former treats questions posed orally (see 5:1), whereas 7:1 f. refers to written questions.[211] We have already noted the limitations of this approach, and the extent to which it rests on assumptions unproven for ancient epistolary practice.[212] We are thus free to understand the logic of Paul's argument on its own terms. 5:1–11:1 is a distinct section of proof because it manifests rhetorical unity and coherence.[213] In

---

and hospitality." The same convention is at work in Titus' role in 2 Cor (esp. 7:15, ὡς μετὰ φόβου καὶ τρόμου ἐδέξασθε αὐτόν); on which see V. P. Furnish, *II Corinthians*, AB 32A (Garden City, NY: Doubleday, 1984) 398.

209 "Die scheinbare Spannung zwischen den beiden Stellen erklärt sich hinlänglich aus der unterschiedlichen Textstrategie" (Merklein, 160). Even many of the partition theories do not find this prohibitive, as they put the two Timothy passages in the same letter (Weiss, *Korintherbrief*, xlii; *Earliest Christianity* 1.341; Goguel, 75–76; Schmithals, *Gnosticism*, 95; Jewett, "Redaction," 398 [see his argument against other partition theories there]).

210 "The exhortations of the body of the letter (chapters 5–15) are intended to facilitate a growing abundance in what Paul calls 'practice' (ἔργον). As these chapters show, in the area of practice the Corinthians have great deficiencies to make up" (Betz, "Rhetoric and Theology," 39).

211 Among those who take 5:1–6:20 as a discrete argument section are Lightfoot, 139–40; Weiss, *Korintherbrief*, xliii, 123–267 (of the redacted whole); Allo, xxvi-vii; Fascher, 155; Conzelmann, 94. Others take 1:10–6:20 to be a larger section with two subsections, 1:10–4:21 and 5–6 (Robertson-Plummer, xxv; Barrett, *First Corinthians*, 28; Fee, 21).

212 For instance, did the Corinthians' reaction to Paul's first letter (5:9) reach Paul orally or in written form? Most scholars think by letter (Heinrici, *Korinther*, 181; Weiss, *Earliest Christianity*, 1.326–27; Allo, 128; Conzelmann, 99–100; Fee, 221 n. 9; differently Senft, 75 and Lang, 74, say it could be either; for a summary of positions see Hurd, 83, who himself resists a definitive choice, but later puts the section with the written questions, p. 93). Even if it did come by letter (we simply don't know), must it have been the letter of 7:1? Since the ἀκούεται in 5:1 is usually understood as referring to oral news, once again we see that Paul's letter or even its individual sub-arguments do not easily divide along the lines of oral and written reports.

213 This is the important contribution of Lührmann, "Freundschaftsbrief," 306–14, whose argument will in large measure be followed here (though he does not see factionalism and church unity to still be the central concern here, as this study argues). Godet, 1.28–31 took

this section Paul treats two very sensitive issues over which the church is divided: πορνεία and εἰδωλόθυτα, which he develops under the overarching theme *of his own choice*: ἐξουσία/ἐλευθερία,[214] which constitutes an important argument for the unity of the section. In both cases Paul must define what these actions are for the Christian community.[215] Because the topical coherence of πορνεία and εἰδωλολατρία is traditional in Judaism and early Christianity, we have further external justification for this analysis of Paul's argument in 1 Cor 5:1–11:1.[216] These two central topic heads form two subsections of the argument, in 5:1–7:40 under the category of πορνεία, and 8:1–11:1 on εἰδωλόθυτα. But the two sections are not isolated and discrete treatments. The unity of treatment of sexual immorality and idol meat is seen particularly in the cross-references throughout 5:1–11:1, such as the reference to idolatry in the vice-catalogues in 5:11 and 6:9,[217] to food already in 6:13,[218] and to sexual immorality in the exemplary argument in 10:8.[219] Even in Paul's self-exemplification in chap. 9, the issues of marriage and eating and drinking are combined (9:4–5),[220] along with instruction on real freedom as a corrective to the Corinthians' individualistic mind-set. The refrain ἠγοράσθητε τιμῆς is repeated in 6:20 and 7:23,[221] as is the ultimate goal of God's glory in 6:20 and 10:31.[222] The section

---

5:1–11:1 to be a section on "moral questions," as does Johnson, *Writings*, 277–83 ("The Church in the World"), but he still regards the composition as tailored to the contacts from Corinth (5–6 from oral reports, 7–10 from the Corinthian letter).

[214] "ἐξουσία ist aber nicht nur auch das Thema von Kap. 9, sondern die Wortgruppe begegnet in den Kapiteln 6–10 in auffälliger Häufung gegenüber nur vereinzelten Belegen in anderen Paulusbriefen" (Lührmann, "Freundschaftsbrief," 307; also Godet, 1.303).

[215] "Was πορνεία ist und was εἰδωλολατρία, entscheidet sich nicht in den autoritativen Bestimmungen des Gesetzes; dem Evangelium entsprechende Normen müssen erst gefunden werden" (Lührmann, "Freundschaftsbrief," 313).

[216] C. K. Barrett, "Things Sacrificed to Idols," *Essays on Paul* (Philadelphia: Westminster, 1982) 40–59, with rich documentation; see also Lührmann, "Freundschaftsbrief," 310, 313, who refers to the vice-catalogues in 1 Cor 5:10 and 6:9. In the HB, see especially the Baal Peor incident (Num 25), to which Paul aptly refers in 10:8. Note also that the command "to cast the evil one from your midst," quoted in 1 Cor 5:13, in Deut 17:7 is directed against an idolator, and in 22:24 against an adulterer (with Lightfoot, 209; Bruce, 59).

[217] See Lightfoot on εἰδωλολάτρης in 5:11: "We have a prospective reference here to the discussion which is introduced subsequently (ch. viii) upon εἰδωλόθυτα" (p. 208; also Barrett, "Things Sacrificed," 43).

[218] Noted by Goguel, 73, but he thought it meant that 10:1–22, on idol meats, must *directly* follow (see Lührmann, "Freundschaftsbrief," 308). However, there is no reason to suppose such a rigid rhetorical arrangement.

[219] The example of Israel in the wilderness (10:1–13) incorporates several of the evils named in the vice-catalogues in 5:10 and 6:9 (Lührmann, "Freundschaftsbrief," 310).

[220] With Merklein, 171 n. 73; cf. Lührmann, "Freundschaftsbrief," 309.

[221] Most partition theories of 1 Cor put the two verses in different letters, again denying Paul any rhetorical consistency (e.g, Weiss, *Korintherbrief*, 167, who recognizes the problem with this and proposes that perhaps 6:20a was a later interpolation as a "prelude" to 7:23; also Schmithals, *Gnosticism*, 93 [with hesitation about its placement]; Pesch, 75–100).

[222] "But Paul did not write either chapters v.–vii. or chapters viii.–x. for the sake of these

5:1–11:1 is also unified in that all of the subjects raised center on the proper relations between Corinthians and outsiders.[223] There is further unity in rhetorical stance in this section in Paul's use of himself as an example (5:12; 6:15; 7:7, 8, [25, 40]; 8:13; 9:1–27; 10:33–11:1), and in the stark imperatives about these two divisive issues: Φεύγετε τὴν πορνείαν (6:18) and Φεύγετε ἀπὸ τῆς εἰδωλολατρίας (10:14).[224] Most important in this rhetorical consistency is the summary argument of 10:23–11:1, which clearly ties in with 6:12–20[225] and brings the whole section to a resounding conclusion in the call for renunciation of one's own advantage for the sake of the common good, for the glory of God (cf. 6:20).[226]

Beginning with 5:1 the uniqueness of Paul's argument for concord becomes most apparent in the topics which divide this community,[227] such as sexual

---

practical injunctions . . . 'do all to the glory of *God.*' That is the goal of this section" (Barth, 38). Cf. Rom. 15:6, also urging unity.

223 Hence the aptness of Johnson's title for this section, "The Church in the World" (*Writings*, 277).

224 Weiss, *Korintherbrief*, 157, 165, 256 (he puts them in the same letter [p. xli]); Barrett, *First Corinthians*, 230; Lührmann, "Freundschaftsbrief," 311.

225 Strangely, almost all partition theories of 1 Cor put 6:12–20 in a different letter from 10:23–11:1 despite or even *because of* the shared refrain Πάντα [μοι] ἔξεστιν ἀλλ' οὐ πάντα συμφέρει in 6:12 and 10:23 (noted by Merklein, 163; Belleville, 28 n. 27). The partition theories seem to predicate against *any* rhetorical consistency on Paul's part, regarding any repetition with suspicion as being a doublet (Weiss, *Korintherbrief*, xli, 263, puts 10:23 in parentheses in his analysis, taking it to be a doublet left over from the redactor's detachment of 6:12–20 from 10:22; cf. Schmithals, *Gnosticism*, 93: "The doubled reference to the catch phrase 'Πάντα μοι ἔξεστιν' in the same letter, especially on different themes [cf. 6:12 with 10:23], would moreover be not exactly apt" [also Klauck, *Herrenmahl*, 272; Pesch, 78]; critiqued by Suhl, 206–207). How else does one build an argument than by stating and restating premises (see Quint. *Inst.* 9.1.28)? This becomes especially important when one recognizes that the argument for advantage, used by Paul throughout 1 Cor (see chap. II), is particularly appropriate and frequently found in appeals for an end to factionalism in antiquity. Deliberative appeals are frequently repeated in arguments! On the criterion of doublet for literary criticism on rhetorical texts see chap. II n. 183, and further discussion in chap. V.

226 The generality of application of this section is shown in 10:31: Εἴτε οὖν ἐσθίετε εἴτε πίνετε εἴτε τι ποιεῖτε (cf. Rom 14:21). On the glory of God in 11:2–14:40 see also Wolff, 65. On the glory or honor of God as a unifying force, see also Philo, *Spec. Leg.* 1.52: "For the most effectual love-charm, the chain which binds indissolubly the goodwill which makes us one is to honor the one God [ἡ τοῦ ἑνὸς θεοῦ τιμή]" (cf. 1.317).

227 In Greco-Roman discourses on concord we find (among others) the following subjects of contention: relations with outsiders (Dio Chrys. *Or.* 34.14–15, 38–51; 38.36–38; Dion. Hal. *Ant. Rom.* 6.36.2–3); assembly and council disputes (Dio Chrys. *Or.* 34.16–20); disputes over citizenship (Dio Chrys. *Or.* 34.21–23); rivalries for honors, primacy and superiority (Dio Chrys. *Or.* 38.21–40; Aristid. *Or.* 23.32 and throughout); financial matters and disputes over possessions (Ps-Sall. *Rep.* 5.4–7.12; Dion. Hal. *Ant. Rom.* 6.83.4–5; Dio Chrys. *Or.* 48.11; Aristid. *Or.* 23.69); and refusals to conciliate (Dio Chrys. *Or.* 34.38–42; 40.20–39; Aristid. *Or.* 24.32–36; cf. Joseph. *AJ* 12.283). More general manifestations of factionalism named are insults or slanders (App. *BCiv.* 4.12.90; Dio Chrys. *Or.* 48.4–5); contempt (Aristid. *Or.* 23.69); boasts (Aristid. *Or.* 23.26; 24.37); grudges (Dem. *Ep.* 1.6); and envy and greed (Aristid. *Or.* 24.32). In these works, as in 1 Cor, there are difficulties in reconstructing the actual situation of dispute from the orator's argument for reconciliation, which tends to focus on the general manifesta-

behavior and idol meats, and in the next sections, comportment in community worship and the resurrection from the dead. Yet what appears at first so different from other discourses on concord actually still bears a great deal of similarity to them. The issues of customs, social behaviors and group membership are of importance in any political or social body. Court battles, marital problems and striving for better social status are causes of factionalism in any social group, as is the name-calling of "strong" and "weak," and the appeal to freedom to justify one's own behavior and to counter calls for concession and compromise.[228] Within the whole proof section 1:18–15:57, the function of this second subsection of proof is first to move from the censure of the Corinthians' factionalism (1:18–4:21) into specific advice on the divisive issues. In particular, this first set of contested issues is entirely concerned with the integrity of the social/political boundaries of the church. The call to unity must be grounded in unambiguous definitions of who is in and who is out of the group.[229] This rhetorical strategy, including the need to expel dangerous elements from the membership is, as we have seen, paralleled in other ancient texts which urge concord.[230] Group unity must be created through a heightened group consciousness which regards the social unit (here named variously as the lump of dough, the body of Christ and the temple of the holy spirit) as the fundamental context of decision making, not the individual or any factions which serve the needs and interests of only some members to the detriment of the social whole.

(a) 5:1–7:40 Πορνεία *and Group Solidarity*

(i) *5:1–13. A Case of* πορνεία

First a notorious community problem must be dealt with, the case of a man who is having sexual relations with his father's wife.[231] The connection of this problem with the Corinthian factions is made by Paul in 5:2 and 6.[232] Paul revises his old advice from a past letter,[233] here concerned to draw the social boundaries of the Corinthian community with heavy strokes, separating insiders from outsiders.[234] Before he can call all to a course of unity, Paul must first expel an

---

tions of factionalism rather than getting into too many particulars about who argues what position.

[228] For documentation see chap. III.

[229] The sociological effect of Paul's argument in 1 Cor 5–6 was recognized by Meeks, *Urban Christians*, 127–131. See also Heinrici, *Sendschreiben*, 177 on 6:12–20: "Handelte es sich nämlich vorher um Erhaltung der Integrität der Gemeinde und um die gegenseitigen Pflichten der Gemeindeglieder . . . ."

[230] See chap. III.

[231] See Allo, 117–20 and Conzelmann, 95–96 for the possibilities. It is important to note (with Schmiedel, 117; Heinrici, *Korinther*, 170) that Paul terms the act πορνεία, not μοιχεία.

[232] See chap. II for the role of φυσιοῦσθαι and καύχημα in the factions.

[233] Cf. Isoc. *Ep*. 3.2–3.

[234] Compare Dio Chrys. *Or*. 34, where the problems between Tarsus and outsiders (the

offender to whom he denies group membership. Paul executes an epistolary legal decision (5:3–5, 13[235]), while also extending a general principle for *all* the Corinthians. His interest is not merely juridical; it is also explicitly ecclesiological. The issue at stake here is with whom one can associate or mix [συναναμίγνυσθαι]. The proper mix of the society for concord is an assumed premise here.[236] Paul advises a new standard: Corinthian Christians are to refrain from association with fornicators, the avaricious, idolators, revilers, drunks or thieves within their own community.[237] Like the orators who describe factionalism as a disease which attacks one member and then spreads like an inflammation throughout the body,[238] Paul draws upon the traditional image of the lump of dough[239] and the leaven to warn of the consequences of such behavior for the whole community.[240] Immoral behavior is not only dangerous to the individual

---

Roman general, the people of Mallus) are treated separately from inner-city disputes (34.14–15, 38–51 on outsiders; 34.16–23 on inside factions).

235 V. 13 is the appropriate conclusion to the case (cf. 5:2). The arguments of Suhl, 206–10; Pesch, 79–80, 85–87 and Sellin, "Hauptprobleme," 2968–72, to put 5:9–13 in a different letter from 5:1–8, in their search for the *Vorbrief*, disregard this fact (for refutation on other grounds, see also Merklein, 179–83).

236 As in 1 Cor 12:24 (see discussion of the mixed constitution, with references, in chap. III).

237 See Sellin, "Hauptprobleme," 2970 on the correspondence between this vice catalogue and parts of (the for him redacted) 1 Cor.

238 Older commentators cited Roman political proverbs as analogues, such as Calvin, 109–10: "But he makes use of a proverbial saying to the effect that a whole society is infected by one person's disease. For in this context this proverb has the same meaning as these words of Juvenal (*Sat.* 2.79ff.): 'A whole herd in the fields is laid low by the mange in one pig; and one choice grape becomes tainted by another.'" Robertson-Plummer, 101 cited Tac. *Ann.* 1.43: "stand clear of the infection [*contactus*] and set the malignants apart" (they do not note that this injunction is a direct response to *discordia*). Bruce, 56 takes the proverb later in the argument in 1 Cor 15:33 about wicked companions to inculcate "much the same lesson."

Especially pertinent examples are also provided by Joseph. *BJ* 1.507; 2.264; 4.406–407: "And as in the body [σῶμα] when inflammation [φλεγμαίνοντος] attacks the principle member all the members catch the infection [πάντα τὰ μέλη συνενόσει], so the sedition and disorder [στάσις και ταραχή] in the capital gave the scoundrels in the country free licence to plunder." Chrys. regards "being puffed up" in 1 Cor as being like a swollen member of a body which, like a tumor, sucks away the body's nourishment (*hom. in I Cor.* 12.1 [*PG* 61.97]). In his homily on 1 Cor 5, Chrys. draws the connection between the lump metaphor and the body: Εἰ γὰρ καὶ ἐκείνου τὸ ἁμάρτημα, φησὶν, ἀλλ' ἀμελούμενον δύναται καὶ τὸ λοιπὸν τῆς 'Εκκλησίας σῶμα λυμήνασθαι . . . Ταῦτα δὲ λέγει, δεικνὺς ὅτι ὑπὲρ ὅλης τῆς 'Εκκλησίας, οὐχ ὑπὲρ ἑνὸς αὐτοῖς ἐστιν ὁ ἀγὼν καὶ ὁ κίνδυνος (15.3 [61.124]). Compare Lightfoot, 203: "'you are puffed up'; while this plague-spot is eating like a canker at the vitals of the church." Conzelmann sees Paul's other community metaphor, the temple of God, to lie behind this argument also (p. 96).

239 On the lump, or mix, as a unifying community metaphor see chap. III. As with the body and the building metaphors (Body of Christ, Temple of God), Paul Christianizes the lump and leaven metaphor by a switch to a Christianized Passover tradition. The ecclesiological focus is clear: "the cultic command has now become a moral injunction" (H. Windisch, "ζύμη κτλ.," *TDNT* 2.902–906, 903).

240 That leaven can destroy the dough is sufficiently demonstrated by Plut. *Mor.* 289E (cited by Wettstein, 2.118; against Lietzmann-Kümmel, 24, and with Weiss, *Korintherbrief*, 134,

perpetrator, but even more importantly endangers the whole society,[241] both in itself, and in the effects it has on the concord of that body (cf. 3:17). The proper "mix" of the Christian society, varied though it may be on demographic grounds, cannot include those who perform immoral acts.[242] They are excluded from table fellowship, and therefore from unity with the group. Here again Paul centers Christian unity in the Christ, "our passover sacrifice." Paul's advice in this case is very specific: the offender is to be expelled. He is not included in the unity to which Paul calls the Corinthian church.

(ii) *6:1–11. Court Battles*

In the next subsection of this proof[243] Paul turns to another practice which endangers the unity of the church: court proceedings between members undertaken in secular jurisdictions.[244] The connection of this section to 5:1–13 has been debated,[245] but commentators have rightly proposed several connections. First, the terms κρίνειν and πλεονέκτης are repeated in the two passages.[246] Another possibility for traditional arrangement which has not been noticed is that the quotation from Deut 17:7 in 1 Cor 5:13 in its original context was followed immediately by a discussion of proper court procedures within Isra-

---

especially his note on the possible authenticity of the variant δολοῖ): "Yeast [ζύμη] is itself also the product of corruption [φθορά], and produces corruption in the dough with which it is mixed [καὶ φθείρει τὸ φύραμα μειγνυμένη]." This text also shows clearly the connection between φύραμα and μείγνυναι, found also in Paul's text between the φύραμα and the social συναναμίγνυσθαι (a connection which has surprisingly not been made in the commentaries).

241 As commentators have noted; see Barrett, *First Corinthians*, 27: "one corrupt member is sufficient to corrupt a whole church"; and Senft, 74: "la faute d'un seul de ses membres est une atteinte à l'intégrité de la communauté entière."

242 Cf. Alexander's political strategy in Plut. *Mor.* 329C (quoted in chap. III n. 305).

243 No information is given about how Paul learned of this object of dispute (for a summary of positions see Hurd, 84–85, who on the basis of style takes it to have been occasioned by oral information; cf. Fee, 228).

244 "Wenn man gar vor Ungläubigen den Streit austrägt, dann ist dies ein Beweis innerer Zerrissenheit. Parteisucht und Gruppenbildung sind somit Ausdruck einer tieferen Unordnung" (Strobel, 108; see also Pesch, 141).

245 The older partition theories (e. g., Weiss, *Korintherbrief*, 145; Goguel, 76; Schmithals, *Gnosticism*, 93) kept 5:1–6:11 as an indivisible unity. The more recent theories of Schenk, 229–30; Schmithals, "Korintherbriefe," 279–80 and Senft, 19, have put 5:1–13 and 6:1–11 in different letters (cf. the very tentative suggestion in Bornkamm, "Vorgeschichte," 189 n. 131). The furthest extreme has now been reached in Schmithals's *Briefe*, 55–56, where 5:1–13 is the sole remnant of his letter G, with no apparent connections to any other part of the extant Pauline corpus.

246 κρίνειν in 5:12–13; 6:1–3, 6 [7] (Godet, 1.284; Lightfoot, 210; Weiss, *Korintherbrief*, 145, who regards 6:1–11 as "fest verklammert" with the preceding; Robertson-Plummer, 109; Allo, 132; Schmithals, *Gnosticism*, 93; Conzelmann, 104 n. 9; Barrett, *First Corinthians*, 134); πλεονέκτης in 5:10; 6:10, in a context which suggests financial improprieties, esp. in 6:7–8 (Robertson-Plummer, 109; Allo, 132). That the vice-catalogue could be the clue to Paul's arrangement also for 6:1–11 is tentatively proposed by Lührmann, "Freundschaftsbrief," 310 n. 52: "In 5,10f. folgt auf die πορνεία die πλεονεξία – ein Vorblick auf 6,1–11?"

el.[247] But most importantly, the argument in 6:1–11 continues to refine and argue for the proper relationship between those in the community and those outside of it.[248] Going to court against fellow Christians at Corinth must have been both cause and further incitement for the factionalism in the community,[249] with church members forced to take sides. Like others who urge unity on divided groups, Paul expresses his consternation over the paltry things which have caused these fights; they are κριτήρια ἐλάχιστα and βιωτικά.[250] This is especially true of the Corinthian Christians because of their eschatological destiny as judges of the world and of angels. Paul shames their behavior (6:5)[251] to dissuade them from it,[252] and with irony expresses his surprise that among the Corinthians who boast in their wisdom there is no one wise enough to judge.[253]

Once again Paul argues for church unity and integrity on Christological grounds: since all share the same sanctification in Christ, all now share a common identity (notice the repetition of the name of the Lord in 6:11; cf. 1:10, and the spirit of God, cf. 2:12), over and against their past sinful identities. By carrying out lawsuits in civil courts, Paul argues, the Corinthians are retaining old understandings of their community allegiances which are no longer appropriate. The Corinthians have not fully understood that their identity as *Christians* should now be their primary frame of social and even civil reference.[254] The inclusion of the second vice-catalogue in 6:9–10 is fully consonant with the argument in 5:10–11.[255] In both cases the application of the paraenesis in the argument is the same: the emphasis is not merely upon the immorality of these acts in themselves, but on *the social implications of those acts* vis à vis membership in

---

247 Deut 17:8–13 (LXX), which itself culminates in the injunction ἐξαρεῖς τὸν πονηρὸν ἐξ Ισραηλ. Significantly, the phrase ἀνὰ μέσον occurs four times in Deut 17:8 (as in 1 Cor 6:5).

248 "Then he turns to the question of lawsuits, not just because the topic of judgment has come up but because again it illustrates their confusion about the lines dividing 'inside' from 'outside'" (Meeks, *Urban Christians*, 129).

249 Chrys. refers to these court cases as φιλονεικίαι (*hom. in I Cor.* Argumentum 2; 16.3 [*PG* 61.11, 134]; see 1 Cor 11:16 and the full discussion of this term in chap. III). See also the descriptive terms used by the later writer Photius of Constantinople in reference to 6:3: πόσῳ μᾶλλόν ἐσμεν ἱκανοὶ τὰ βιωτικὰ διαλύειν φιλονεικήματα καὶ τὰς πρὸς ἀλλήλους δίκας καὶ ἔριδας; (Staab, 555).

250 See chap. III.

251 Cf. 15:35; 4:14.

252 ἀποτρέπειν (Chrys. *hom. in I Cor.* 16.2 [*PG* 61.132]).

253 The connection with the argument in 1:18–4:21 is clear (Weiss, *Korintherbrief*, 149; Conzelmann, 105; on irony here see Strobel, 106).

254 Having been sanctified and made righteous, they are ἅγιοι and δίκαιοι, insiders with powers of judgement and full community responsibility (on this language of insiders, and the important term ἀδελφός, which features so prominently in this argument, see Meeks, *Urban Christians*, 85–96).

255 Partition theorists presume that one would not repeat two catalogues so closely together in the same letter (e. g., Schenk, 230; Klauck, *1. Korintherbrief*, 49; Pesch, 76–77), but they ignore the argumentative coherence of the employment of the two sets here.

the church community. Those who perform the forbidden acts are no longer members of the group.[256] The fellow Christian is a "brother" who is to be treated like a true brother (6:6, 8),[257] and for whose interests each one is responsible.[258] As so often in 1 Corinthians, here Paul argues for personal compromise for the sake of concord: "Why not suffer wrong yourselves? Why not rather be yourselves defrauded?" (6:7).

(iii) *6:12–20. A Second Case of* Πορνεία, *with Treatment by General Principles*
This sub-argument begins with the asyndetic quotation[259] of a slogan (which will be similarly reintroduced in 10:23[260]). The slogan[261] is here used by Paul to continue his argument of dissuasion from πορνεία[262] with an anticipated Corinthian objection: Πάντα μοι ἔξεστιν. Paul's response is his introduction of the deliberative argument by appeal to advantage: ἀλλ' οὐ πάντα συμφέρει. He does not need to state the well-known premise upon which all deliberative arguments are based: that one does not do what is not to one's advantage.[263] In this

256 Note the role which ἄδικοι plays in the argument (6:1, 9). This opens up a problem that the later church had to deal with – Paul has no room for "de-Christianized persons" in his concept of the church.

257 For the emphasis see Lightfoot, 212.

258 See chap. III for the *topos* that factionalism is insane because by fighting one's brother one hurts one's own self. In this context, see Lightfoot, 212, on μεθ' ἑαυτῶν in 6:7: "The Apostle does not say μετ' ἀλλήλων, for though the pronouns are often interchanged, the reciprocal ἑαυτῶν differs from the reciprocal ἀλλήλων in emphasizing the idea of corporate unity ... 'Αλλήλων here would bring out the idea of diversity of interest, ἑαυτῶν emphasizes that of identity of interest: 'you are tearing yourselves to pieces!'" (also Godet, 1.293; Schmiedel, 122; compare Chrys. on ἁμαρτήματα ... εἰς τὸ οἰκεῖον μέλος [*hom. in I Cor.* 16.4 (*PG* 61.134)]).

259 Heinrici, *Korinther*, 200. Weiss, *Korintherbrief*, 156 admits that its introduction is no more abrupt than other turns of thought in Paul's letters, yet he argues for the separation of 6:12–20 from 6:1–11. His arguments for this separation are not based so much on this section's incongruity with its placement as on its definite congruence with 10:1–22 (p. 157). He is surely correct on the congruence of the two sections, but that coherence is not lost if the two sections are not immediately adjacent. They are a part of the same developed argument, the same letter.

260 "Thus this slogan spans the whole content of chaps. 6–10" (Conzelmann, 109; also Lührmann, "Freundschaftsbrief," 312).

261 The context from which Paul quotes the slogan (written, oral, in person) cannot be reconstructed. The lack of περὶ δέ is not definitive proof that the slogan was not in the Corinthians' letter (against Bachmann, 246; Weiss, *Korintherbrief*, 157; differently Allo, 142, thinks it may have been in their letter; Schmiedel, 123 thinks 6:12 was probably not, but the next verse probably was). The slogan may well have originally come from Paul himself! But that does not mean that the slogan did not appear in other contexts also. This shows again the difficulty of using such distinctions of oral and written topics as the basis for Paul's argumentation.

262 Allo, 141; Barrett, *First Corinthians*, 144. Paul uses the ABA structure of arrangement here, too (on which see n. 111 above). R. Kempthorne argued that 6:12–20 treats the same case as 5:1–3 ("Incest and the Body of Christ: A Study of 1 Corinthians VI.12–20," *NTS* 14 [1967/68] 568–74).

263 See chap. II nn. 29 and 71.

argument, as again at the end of this section in 10:23–11:1, Paul redefines the Corinthians' understanding of advantage from an individualistic sphere of reference to the community in Christ.[264] This is standard practice in deliberative arguments, as we have seen in chap. II, and it is especially common in arguments urging an end to factionalism in Greco-Roman literature, because factionalism is, after all, placing one's own interests above those of the community. The syllogisms in 6:12 also serve to link Paul's argument on the nature of true advantage with the definition of true freedom, thus introducing his second theme of consideration in this argument. Both advantage and freedom, Paul will argue throughout this proof section down to its resounding conclusion in 10:23–11:1, cannot be defined or determined apart from the community as a whole.

The subsection 6:12–20, in addition to carrying on the discussion of πορνεία begun in 5:1–13 and continued in ch. 7,[265] makes proleptic reference to other topics of Corinthian debate which Paul will take up later in his argument.[266] 6:13 shows again that Paul considers the issues of food (idol meats) and πορνεία indivisibly linked. 6:14 also contains within it the proposition which Paul will defend in chap. 15, that the resurrection of the Lord and that of the believer stand together.[267] Introducing it here as a commonplace without need of supporting

---

264 Calvin, 128: ". . . each one has freedom within himself, on this condition, that all ought to limit the use of their liberty in the interests of each other's well-being" (also Lightfoot, 214).

265 Heinrici (citing Zwingli) takes 6:12–20 to be "eine παρασκευὴ *ad sequentia*" (*Sendschreiben*, 178 n. 1; *Korinther*, 198). On the connection of 6:12–20 and 7:1–7, especially on the theme of ἐξουσιάζεσθαι, see C. Maurer, "Ehe und Unzucht nach 1. Korinther 6,12 – 7,7," *WD* n. s. 6 (1959) 159–69. In a contrary way of assessing these overt connections between 6:12–20 and ch. 7, Weiss argues that ch. 7 is another letter which answers questions which were raised by 6:12–20 (*Korintherbrief*, xlii; also Klauck, *1. Korintherbrief*, 48), but it is not at all clear why this particular argument on sexual intercourse with prostitutes would occasion the questions on marriage, divorce and virgins treated by Paul in ch. 7. Sellin's attempt to improve on this argument by equating the very different words κολλᾶσθαι and ἅπτεσθαι is unsuccessful ("Hauptprobleme," 2970). This is best understood as advance reference to the next proofs, standard practice in argumentation.

266 Lightfoot, 215: "it is noticeable that these three verses [6:12–14] contain the germ of very much which follows in the Epistle." See the thorough analysis of these connections in Hurd, 87–89, who concludes: "It would be exceedingly improbable to expect that such an appropriate fragment could have been found in Paul's Previous Letter" (88; also Grosheide, 153).

267 Prümm, 206; Allo, 144; Fee, 256 (with arguments against those who take it as a gloss); Lührmann, "Freundschaftsbrief," 306. Note also that this appeal to the resurrection indicates that the true sphere of advantage is not the present but the future, when God will destroy belly and food, but raise those in the Lord. This appeal to future advantage, common in deliberative rhetoric (see chap. II), is used consistently by Paul throughout 1 Cor (4:1–5; 9:24–27; 13:10–12; ch. 15; and especially in the final appeal in 15:58). This consistency of Paul's appeal to final eschatological advantage (see previous note), as well as Paul's argumentative coherence, militates against some partition theorists' argument that ch. 15 is a later response to questions raised by a reading of 6:14: "Nach 1 Kor 15 weiss Paulus aber, dass der Satz von der leiblichen Auferweckung der Christen in Korinth bestritten wird. Die Folgerung ist unausweichlich, dass

argumentation prepares the reader/listener for its acceptance when that part of the argument is reached. The body of Christ image for the church, which will be given its full expression in chap. 12, is also introduced here,[268] with the particular application, not to spiritual gifts as there, but to the implications of that designation for one's sexual behavior.[269] One's body does not belong to oneself, but to the Lord,[270] and thus to the Lord's body, the church,[271] of which one is only one member. As with the lump and the leaven, one does not have the right to endanger the whole body by abusing one's own body[272] which is but one member of the larger whole. With a nice *double entendre* Paul exhorts the Corinthians to cleave to the Lord (and thus *his* body, the church), instead of cleaving (sexually) with prostitutes.[273] Because the Christian belongs not to her or himself (6:19), but rather to the Lord and thus to his body, the church, the claim that "one can do anything" cannot be the sole standard of conduct. In this short passage Paul draws on still another image of the church, the building image, which was prepared for already in chap. 3. Here its application is simultaneously individualistic and corporate ("your body is the temple of the holy spirit in you").[274] Not individual advantage but God's glory should be the measuring-rod for Christian decision-making.[275]

6,14 und Kap. 15 nicht im selben Brief gestanden haben können" (Sellin, "Hauptprobleme," 2971, with Weiss, *Korintherbrief*, xlii). But this is to underestimate Paul's rhetorical proficiency.

[268] Prümm, 206; see also Allo, 141 on "l'union au Christ" as "l'idée centrale de toute cette épître"; differently Fee, 258 rejects interpreting this in the light of 12:12–26 (incorrectly, in my view). That the metaphor is here applied from the perspective of the individual member does not mean that the metaphor itself is a substantially different one.

[269] As in 12:12–13, the σῶμα, μέλη and πνεῦμα are combined in the thought complex. In 10:16–17 the body of Christ image will be applied to the problem of idol meats and cultic participation.

[270] Because one belongs to Christ (3:23, in direct opposition to the factional claims of 1:12 and 3:4). Here the exact nature of that relationship is spelled out even more clearly: one has been bought with a price (6:20). 7:23 will carry this argument one step further to its logical conclusion: τιμῆς ἠγοράσθητε. μὴ γίνεσθε δοῦλοι ἀνθρώπων.

[271] The corporate nature of σῶμα in this passage was rightly stressed by Kempthorne, 572–74. He cites *1 Clem.* 46:7 as an excellent example of ἴδιον σῶμα with a corporate meaning (ἱνατί . . . διασπῶμεν τὰ μέλη τοῦ Χριστοῦ καὶ στασιάζομεν πρὸς τὸ σῶμα τὸ ἴδιον).

[272] Because one is a member of the body of Christ, one destroys it when one harms oneself or a brother or sister (τὸ ἴδιον σῶμα in 6:18; cf. μεθ' ἑαυτῶν in 6:7 [and n. 258 above]). This is pointed out in the catenae. On 6:18c Photius of Constantinople writes: αὐτὸς μερίζει τὸ ἴδιον σῶμα (Cramer, 116). Isidore of Pelusium is explicit: ἐπειδὴ σῶμα ἕν ἐστιν ἡ ἐκκλησία. ὁ δεκαθεὶς [leg. δίχα θείς] ἀλλήλων μέλη, ὁ πορνεύων, εἰς πάντας ἁμαρτάνει (Cramer, 118).

[273] The flesh/spirit dualism operative in the argument in 1:18–4:21 is here employed to differentiate the quality of spiritual association with the Lord from "fleshly" associations.

[274] For the corporate sense in this image here, thus identical with 1 Cor 3, see Kempthorne, 572–73. Klauck, *1. Korintherbrief*, 49, argued that 6:12–20 should be part of the *Vorbrief* because of "die eigentümliche Verwendung der Leib-Christi-Vorstellung und die unterschiedliche Tempelmetaphorik" in 6:19 and 3:16 (of course if this truly were a problem, putting the passages in two different letters doesn't completely resolve it). Even though the *application* of these metaphors here is tailored to the specific case at hand in this sub-argument (both move to

(iv) *7:1–40. Marriage and Status*

Still under the overarching category of πορνεία,[276] Paul gives advice[277] on specific cases of marriage and sexual behavior about which the Corinthians have written him. The introductory formula Περὶ δὲ ὧν ἐγράψατε served more specifically to define the sphere of reference of the next topic for the Corinthians (who wrote that letter), than it does for us who stand apart from that extended conversation. Because the subject introduced in 7:25 (Περὶ δὲ τῶν παρθένων) is topically so closely related to the subjects of sexual immorality and marriage, we can regard it as a subsection of the larger treatment.[278] It may be surprising to modern readers that Paul treats marriage under the topic of πορνεία, but that is the case.[279] The argument in ch. 7 contains Paul's specific advice for the Corinthians on proper marital relations, with an inserted exemplary argument devaluing earthly status, κλῆσις, in general.[280] As in so many arguments for concord, here Paul is socially conservative in the interests of the survival of the church. As elsewhere in ancient history, in the Corinthian church divisions and conflicts within individual households contributed to factionalism in the entire group,[281] as did the variety of opinions on the lifestyles themselves, which caused sufficient controversy that the Corinthians wrote to Paul for advice. Paul's argumentation here is adept. He will not address the various factions directly (those with ascetic or libertinistic tendencies), but instead addresses, one by one, each of the marital (and later other) statuses which have come under question (7:8, 10, 12). In each case his oscillating argument,[282] in which he shows a preference but will

---

the individual consequences of the corporate realities), we should not conclude that it has no coherence with ch. 3 and 12 (for the connections, see E. Käsemann, "1. Korinther 6,19–20," *Exegetische Versuche und Besinnungen* [Göttingen: Vandenhoeck & Ruprecht, 1960²] 1.276–79).

275 For the unifying force of this appeal, see Rom 15:5–6 (and of course 1 Cor 10:31). This is how Paul redefines the τέλος in relation to which the Corinthian Christians should make their decisions.

276 It is possible, as e. g., Weiss, *Korintherbrief*, 169, Chadwick, 264 have argued, that Paul in ch. 5–6 took on the more libertinist partisans, where in ch. 7 he turns to the more ascetic elements of the church, but if he does so, it is under cover of topical arrangement.

277 Chrys. refers to ch. 7 as παραίνεσις καὶ συμβουλὴ ἡ περὶ τοῦ γάμου καὶ τῆς παρθενίας (*hom. in I Cor.* 19.1 [*PG* 61.151]). This is of course an exact description of deliberative proofs (as argued above). See Heinrici, *Korinther*, 210: "Die Inhaltsübersicht zeigt, dass Paulus Rathschläge giebt."

278 The formula περὶ δέ can introduce a new argument or a sub-argument. It can also serve to refocus the topic at hand (see 8:4; 1 Thess 5:1; Mitchell, 253 n. 109).

279 Exegetes have been forced to admit that Paul does not provide a *positive* rationale for marriage in this chapter. It is acceptable διὰ τὰς πορνείας.

280 Once again we see the ABA pattern (with Hurd, 178; Bartchy, 161–72).

281 See the explicit language of Origen's exegesis: καὶ ἦν ἀκαταστασία ἐν ταῖς οἰκίαις τῶν ἀδελφῶν, πὴ μὲν ἀνδρῶν πὴ δὲ γυναικῶν ἐγκρατεύεσθαι πειρωμένων καὶ ἀλλήλων κατεξανισταμένων (*comm. in I Cor.* 33.11–13 [p. 500]), and that of Chrys. : Ὅταν γὰρ ἐν οἰκίᾳ ἀνὴρ καὶ γυνὴ διεστηκότες ὦσιν, οὐδὲν νηὸς χειμαζομένης ἄμεινον ἡ οἰκία διακείσεται, τοῦ κυβερνήτου πρὸς τὸν πρωρέα διαστασιάζοντος (*hom. in I Cor.* 19.2 [*PG* 61.153]).

282 Chadwick's article remains very important in pointing to this character of Paul's argu-

not demand it, serves his overall intention of conciliation. In fact, what many scholars have regarded as hopeless inconsistency by Paul in chapters 5–7 (and 8–10) of 1 Corinthians may very well be understood when all of 1 Corinthians is regarded as Paul's argument for Corinthian unity. His "inconsistency" lies in his *rhetorical* strategy by which he agrees, as far as he possibly can, with the positions on both sides of the issues,[283] so as to appease both and alienate neither, while at the same time calling all to reconciliation.[284]

The organization of this sub-argument in 7:1–40 is once again topical. First Paul expounds the general principle of 7:1 b, and positive exceptions to it which allow for sexual behavior within marriage. Paul urges concordant behavior (ἐκ συμφώνου) between the two partners, as he will later in 7:15 in regard to marriage and separation from unbelievers (ἐν εἰρήνῃ κέκληκεν ὑμᾶς ὁ θεός).[285]

---

mentation in 1 Corinthians. "The seventh chapter makes admirable sense if it is boldly interpreted as apostolic opportunism. The result is that the chapter oscillates between statements which surrender virtually everything to the ascetics, and qualifications which Paul subtly insinuates, which tell for the opposite standpoint. The consequence is without doubt a masterpiece of ingenuity" (pp. 264–65). Chadwick does not, however, fully appreciate how Paul's argument is the necessary response to factionalism, instead calling it "apologetic" and, rather than examining it as a *rhetorical* strategy, regarding it as more of a psychological phenomenon (p. 269). The same is true of Weiss's interpretation: "It is very easy to imagine that this variety of mood and behavior existed together in his personality, it is very hard to conceive of them from a literary point of view as occurring in a single letter" (*Earliest Christianity*, 1.329; see also Collins, "Chiasmus," 579–80 who also seeks "the psychological basis" of Paul's oscillation). But in fact it is primarily from a *rhetorical* point of view that this oscillation makes sense, and should be investigated.

283 "Paul adopts his regular procedure in waging war on two fronts, with the libertines on the one hand and the ascetics on the other: he goes along with each party as far as he can, agreeing with its contention but adding something which neutralizes its excesses" (Bruce, 62). "Independent, wilful, and regardless of the reproach of inconsistency, he plunges with his opinion, straight through the various camps into which the Church was split up, indifferent whether he appears now as an ascetic, now as a man of the world" (Barth, 39; see also Richardson, 60, 73 on "accommodation and deliberate compromise as fundamental aspects of the interpretation of 1 Corinthians").

Paul's reconciliatory strategy here can be compared with other Greco-Roman texts. See, for example, the explicit strategy of conciliation in the deliberative epistle Pl. *Ep.* 8.354A: "For indeed I am speaking somewhat like an arbitrator [διαιτητής], and addressing to the two parties, the former despot and his subjects, as though each were a single person [ὡς ἑνὶ ἑκατέρῳ], the counsel I gave of old." In the argument which follows he first addresses one group ("those of you who are rushing after despotic power I exhort to change their course . . ." [354C]), and then the other ("and I should counsel those who follow after the ways of freedom . . . to beware lest . . ." [354D]). Then comes the relativizing summary plea about both freedom and slavery (354E, quoted in chap. III), and finally an appeal to both sides to follow a middle, unifying course (355D). In Pl. *Ep.* 6 we see the same strategy on a smaller, personal level, where in urging three persons to unity the author first addresses Hermeias (323A), and then Coriscus and Erastus (323A-B), and finally all three in common (323C).

284 He is explicit about his method in 9:22 and 10:33 (as we have seen in chap. III, by calling upon political *topoi*).

285 See Chrys. on 7:16: Εἰ γὰρ μὴ στασιάζει, μένε (*hom. in I Cor.* 19.3 [*PG* 61.155]).

He then turns to the unmarried and widows (7:8–9), and to the married (7:10–11), to whom he urges no separations, and reconciliation where separation has taken place. Next he turns "to the rest," who apparently are synonymous with or are at least inclusive of those who have married outside of the Christian community, both men and women (7:12–15). Virgins are advised in 7:25–28, and those who might marry them in 7:36–38. Within these topical treatments are two more general arguments, in 7:17–24 on the κλῆσις in general,[286] and 7:29–35 on the apocalyptic justification for all of Paul's advice (which is given πρὸς τὸ ὑμῶν αὐτῶν σύμφορον). Throughout this chapter Paul appeals to his own example (7:7, 8, 25, 40), but not in an absolute way. With all of his advice in ch. 7 Paul is careful to provide allowances for alternative positions,[287] and also to show that he has the Corinthians' advantage in view. In this way he does not repudiate out of hand the marital practices of any, though he absolutely rejects πορνεία in all cases, as in 5:1–6:20. His advice in each case stresses reunification and integrity.

(b) 8:1–11:1. Idol Meats, Freedom and Group Unity

The second topic in this larger subsection of 5:1–11:1, following traditional arrangement, is εἰδωλολατρία. Using the introductory formula περὶ δέ Paul moves into his next argument.[288] The variability and awkwardness of terminology in this section[289] demonstrates that the issue upon which Paul is to give advice is at heart a definitional one: who is an idolator?[290] But Paul's own larger consideration is how the Christian community can retain its internal unity when faced with pressures from the outside culture which pull the community apart. The community is divided on this particular issue, with some saying that there is nothing wrong with eating meats which have been sacrificed to idols, and others

---

286 The conservative principle is named twice and several times elucidated: μενέτω, "stay the way you are" (7:20, 24). On 7:17–24 as containing and exemplifying this general principle see Weiss, *Korintherbrief*, 183 (the passage is an "Einlage" like ch. 9 and 13); Hurd, 178; Bartchy, 168–69; N. Baumert, *Ehelosigkeit und Ehe im Herrn. Eine Neuinterpretation von 1 Kor 7*, Forschung zur Bibel 47 (Würzburg: Echter Verlag, 1984) 99–160, with references to the considerable literature on the passage; Wimbush, 14–22.

287 Paul is content to name certain behaviors as "better" (7:9, 40). On comparatives in deliberative appeals, see chap. II.

288 We note that Περὶ δὲ τῶν εἰδωλοθύτων is the way in which *Paul* chooses to introduce this first treatment of the subject. We cannot infer from this means of introduction that this is the exact phrasing which the Corinthians used (or that it was their exact question; rightly Baasland, 80), but only that it is a term which he expects them to understand. This is an important point, because, by the way in which he names the disputed matter, Paul already enters into the debate on someone's terms.

289 εἰδωλόθυτον (8:1, 7, 10; 10:19); ἡ βρῶσις τῶν εἰδωλοθύτων (8:4), εἴδωλον (8:4, 7; 10:19), βρῶμα (8:8, 13), εἰδωλεῖον (8:10), κρέα (8:13), εἰδωλολάτρης (10:7), εἰδωλολατρία (10:14), ἱερόθυτον (10:28).

290 With whom one must not associate, according to 5:10–11.

arguing against that practice on the grounds of the prohibition of idolatry.[291] Paul is well acquainted with the arguments on both sides, and grants concessions to each side as far as he is able;[292] hence the different points of view which scholars have long recognized in 8:1–13 and 10:1–22. The difference in treatment can be attributed once again to Paul's reconciliatory strategy (and his corresponding rhetorical strategy of ABA), and not to literary partition.[293] Paul tried (perhaps unsuccessfully) to hold two balls in the air by allowing the eating of idol meats (unless in a particular situation it hurts the fellow Christian) but condemning idolatry. This is because Paul's overriding concern here is not merely idol meats in themselves, but the impact of conflicts over idol meats on the concord of the church community.[294]

The literary integrity of the section 1 Cor 8–10 has been the locus of all partition theories of the letter.[295] Although Paul delivers an admittedly convoluted argument here (much of the reasons for which are inaccessible to us),[296] significant exegetical challenges have already been made by scholars to the

---

[291] J. Murphy-O'Connor, "Freedom or the Ghetto (1 Cor 8:1–13; 10:23–11:1)," *RB* 85 (1978) 543–74, 544–56, against Hurd, 117–25 (who argues for a unified Corinthian position). See also Barrett, "Things Sacrificed," 56. Theissen, 121–43 provides an important analysis of the socioeconomic factors in this dissension in the community ranks.

[292] Even Weiss must grant that for Paul "there is truth in both positions: the rigorous and the one which allows compromise" (but he cannot allow that Paul expressed both truths in the same letter; *Earliest Christianity*, 1.329).

[293] Hurd's argument, that if indeed these parts of 1 Cor are fully contradictory to put them in different letters doesn't resolve the problem, has not been refuted: "Concerning all these differences it should be noted first of all that the scholars who divide 1 Corinthians consider the discrepancies between 'AC' [8:1–13; 10:23–33] and 'B' [10:1–22] great enough to show that 'B' was not written by the same author, to the same group, and on the same topic as 'AC'. These scholars allow Paul to be inconsistent with himself concerning the Corinthians' use of idol meat from one letter to the next, but they do not allow this inconsistency in the course of a single letter" (p. 132; cf. before him H. von Soden, "Sakrament und Ethik bei Paulus. Zur Frage der literarischen und theologischen Einheitlichkeit von 1 Kor. 8–10," *Urchristentum und Geschichte. Gesammelte Aufsätze und Vorträge*, ed. H. von Campenhausen [Tübingen: Mohr/Siebeck, 1951] 1.239–75, 257; also Wolff, 36). In addition, this variance is not due to Paul's adherence to the Corinthians' arguments in their letter in 8:1–13 and to his own formulations in ch. 10 (so Willis, *Idol Meat*, 270–71, depending too much on the περὶ δέ; Jones, *Freiheit*, 169–70 n. 80 refutes Willis, but on the wrong grounds. However the ecclesiological focus throughout 8–10 was correctly emphasized by Willis, and can be concretely demonstrated in the relation of the entire argument to the problem of factionalism [as I shall argue below]).

[294] With Meeks, *Urban Christians*, 160 on 1 Cor 8–10: "[Paul is] confirming the right and freedom of Christians to participate in the macrosociety so long as that participation does not upset the internal harmony and development of the Christian community."

[295] Weiss, *Korintherbrief*, xli–ii, 211–13; Schmithals, *Gnosticism*, 92–93; *idem*, "Korintherbriefe," 263–88; Schenk, 237–40; Suhl, 204; Schenke-Fischer, 93; Klauck, *Herrenmahl*, 241–85; for summaries of the arguments see Merklein, 162–73; Sellin, "Hauptprobleme," 2972–74.

[296] The exegetical problems posed by this section are notorious and considerable, and I have no illusions about dealing with all of them here. I shall present a suggestive reading of the section out of the emphases of this particular study.

arguments of the partition theorists to separate out ch. 9[297] or 10:1–22 from their present context. In particular the following arguments[298] are most damaging to those partition theories: the connection between ch. 9 and 8:1–13 is clearly made by Paul's first person reference at the end of that argument in 8:13.[299] The section 8:1–11:1 is unified lexically by the repetition of several key terms or word groups: ἐξουσία/ἐλεύθερος/ἐλευθερία,[300] πρόσκομμα/ἐγκοπή/ἀπρόσκοπος,[301] συνείδησις, ἀσθενής, μετέχειν[302] and οἰκοδομεῖν, and topically of course by discussion of εἰδωλόθυτα/εἰδωλολατρία. In addition, a comprehensive parallel to the overall argument and its structure is provided in Rom 14–15.[303] Lastly it

---

297 The integrity of chap. 9 itself has also been questioned, with compositional breaks detected at 9:19 and 24 (Schmithals, *Gnosticism*, 92–93, separated 9:24–27 from 9:1–23; in "Korintherbriefe," 271 he put 9:24–10:22 in Letter B, 9:19–22 in Letter C, and 9:1–18 in Letter F, with 9:23 taken as a redactor's insertion; Klauck, *Herrenmahl*, 249–52, takes 9:19–23 out of its present context in chap. 9 and into the *Antwortbrief*). It is interesting that most of these theories proceed as much or more from correct observations of the *connections* between various parts of the argument than from disruptions. For example, Schmithals's assertion that 9:24–27 goes well with what follows is correct, as is the observation (already by Weiss, *Korintherbrief*, 242) that 9:19–23 fits very well with the argument for accommodation in ch. 8 (*Gnosticism*, 92). But to argue for literary partition on these grounds is perhaps based more on impatience with the way in which Paul develops his arguments than anything else, and presupposes a too rigid type of rhetorical arrangement. On what grounds can we dictate that all argumentative connections which we perceive in the text must have originally been *adjacent* (cf. Allo, 208: "Tous ces professeurs exigent d'un écrivan comme Paul une logique pareille à celle d'un candidat aux examens")? See the early observation of Chrys.: Ὅτι ἔθος αὐτῷ διὰ πλειόνων ἃ βούλεται κατασκευάζειν, καὶ τὰ ἰσχυρότερα ὕστερον τιθέναι, καὶ ἐκ περιουσίας νικᾶν (*hom. in I Cor.* 24.3 [61.202], on 10:22).

298 The classic essay is that of von Soden. See also the more recent exegetical treatments of Hurd, 131–42; G. Bornkamm, "Lord's Supper and Church in Paul," *Early Christian Experience*, trans. P. L. Hammer (New York/Evanston: Harper & Row, 1969) 123–60, esp. the excursus 152–54; Merklein, 163–73; Willis, *Idol Meat*, 267–75; *idem*, "Apostolic Apologia"; Jones, *Freiheit*, 38–42. Their arguments are summarized below.

299 See also below on ch. 9.

300 Dautzenberg, "Verzicht," 212–15; Willis, *Idol Meat*, 273; Merklein, 171–72 (who demonstrates the extent to which this exhibits *argumentative* and not merely lexical coherence); Jones, *Freiheit*, 39 (along with the term ἐσθίειν); Lührmann, "Freundschaftsbrief," 307. Of course those who argue for division can ascribe these connections to the redactor (e. g., Klauck, *Herrenmahl*, 249).

301 As argued especially by Dautzenberg, "Verzicht," 218–19.

302 Willis, "Apostolic Apologia," 39, who also adds the references to Jews and Greeks in 9:19–23 and 10:32.

303 See von Soden, 257; Hurd, 133–34; Willis, *Idol Meat*, 274–75. Klauck, *Herrenmahl*, 281–83, points out that connections have not been so much demonstrated with 10:1–22, the most difficult section. Jones, *Freiheit*, 39–40 buttresses von Soden's analysis of the parallels in response to this same objection by pointing to the formal similarity in use of Scripture warnings in 1 Cor 10:11 and Rom 15:4, and the warning about standing and falling in 1 Cor 10:12 and Rom 14:4 (along with 10:13 and 14:4c). To this we can add that Rom 14–15 is similar to 1 Cor 8–10 also in its rhetorical strategy of conciliation (many of the same *topoi* for concord are also used in Rom 14–15 and its larger context).

can be exegetically understood that Paul does not contradict himself in 8:1–13; 10:23–11:1 and 10:1–22[304] because in those treatments Paul distinguishes between idolatry (cult meal participation) and the eating of idol meats. He prohibits the first (8:10–13; 10:7, 14, 20–22), but not the second (unless it harms other Christians).[305] To these arguments we shall add several more out of the particular focus of this study.

A major building block of theories which doubt the unity of 1 Cor 8–10, unquestioned assumptions about the formula περὶ δέ, has been rebutted, so that this "formal argument" must be dismissed.[306] There is no reason to doubt the compositional unity of various parts of this argument because they do not begin with this formula. Furthermore, the ecclesiological emphasis on unity within the church, which is Paul's concern throughout 1 Corinthians, gives another insight into the coherence of this section. Of particular importance are the connections of every subsection of this entire argument with Corinthian factionalism which have been demonstrated in chap. III, such as the role of "weak" and "strong" in political arguments, the appeal to freedom to countermand calls for compromise, the role of "offense" in factionalism, the traditional understanding of Israel's wilderness rebellions upon which Paul draws in 10:1–13 as paradigms of factionalism, the commonplace of appealing to cultic unity in arguments for social unity, and above all, that the appeal to forsake one's own advantage (συμφέρον) for the sake of the common good is *the standard appeal for concord in antiquity*. The original and logical placement of Paul's self-exemplification in ch. 9 receives further confirmation from our study in chap. II of the frequency of examples and calls to imitation in deliberative appeals in antiquity, which are thus appropriately recurrent in the argument in 1 Corinthians. Paul's frequent pattern in this overarching argument of treating first one side of an issue, then giving an appeal for compromise with general principles or an exemplary argument (7:17–24; ch. 9; ch. 13), followed by treatment of a second side of the controversy, is found here also.

---

[304] As argued especially by Weiss, *Korintherbrief*, xli, 210–13; *Earliest Christianity*, 1.325–29 (the difference in tone is also important in his consideration); Héring, xiii, 100; Senft, 18, 127–28, 136. It is particularly surprising that arguments in partition theories have been made for the partition of this section on the grounds that 10:1–22 *contradicts* 8:1–13; 10:23–11:1 (the above listed scholars), and on the grounds that it is a *repetition* of that discussion (Schenk, 237–38 terms it a doublet; see the critique of Merklein, 163–64). It surely cannot be both! Schmithals, *Gnosticism* 92, took only 10:1–22 to be dealing with cult meals, and thus on thematic grounds regarded it as a different consideration from 8:1–13 and 10:23–11:1, which must therefore belong to a different letter. The extent of this confusion in the partition theories can be seen where Jewett assesses Schmithals's argument and concludes: "his division hypothesis is correct at this point, though for the wrong reasons" (*Anthropological Terms*, 24)!

[305] Following G. D. Fee, "Εἰδωλόθυτα Once Again: An Interpretation of 1 Cor 8–10," *Bib* 61 (1980) 172–97; Wolff, 36–37, 58; Merklein, 163–70; see also earlier Robertson-Plummer, 219; Barrett, *First Corinthians*, 16, 225.

[306] See Mitchell, 229–56 (and the discussion above, esp. n. 25).

(i) *8:1–13. Idol Meats and Division. First Treatment*

In this subsection of the argument, introduced with the topic marker περὶ δέ, Paul begins his discussion of idol meats from the point of view of "the strong,"[307] those who recognize that since there is no such thing as an idol, then there can be nothing wrong with eating meats sacrificed to idols. While *all* Christians have knowledge of this, not all agree on the particular behavioral consequences of it (hence the contradiction between 8:1 and 7).[308] In the two syllogisms of 8:1 Paul bridges his argument in 1 Cor 1:18–4:21 and his forthcoming advice for unity on this and other issues: ἡ γνῶσις φυσιοῖ, ἡ δὲ ἀγάπη οἰκοδομεῖ.[309] Being "puffed up" is engaging in divisive, separatist behavior, which is directly opposed to unifying behavior, that which "builds up" the church community (as proven in 1:18–4:21).[310] Thus right from the beginning, although accepting the knowledge of the strong, he advises the best practice of all, building up the church community in harmony[311] through love. Paul's overriding concern throughout this proof section 8:1–11:1 is *ecclesiological.*[312] In 8:4–5 he affirms the theological principles of "the strong" unconditionally, just as in 10:7 and 14 he will uncompromisingly urge all the Corinthians to flee from idolatry (not idol meats).[313] He agrees with the fundamental principles *of both sides*, to which he adds a proper reminder of their theological unity[314] in the common baptismal acclamation of one God and one Lord in 8:6.[315] His compro-

---

[307] See Chrys. *hom. in I Cor.* 20.1 (on 8:1): Τοὺς ἀσθενεῖς ἀφεὶς, ὅπερ ἀεὶ ποιεῖ, τοῖς ἰσχύουσι διαλέγεται πρώτοις [*PG* 61.160].

[308] In the face of this unambiguous contradiction, it is interesting that no partition theorists, on the basis of their methodological principle of resolving contradictions, put these two verses in different letters!

[309] "The commentary on ἀγάπη is supplied by chap. 13, that on οἰκοδομεῖ, 'builds up,' by chaps. 12 and 14 (cf. especially 10:23)" (Conzelmann, 141). See also Chrys. on 8:1: Ὁρᾷς ὅπως ἤδη προανακρούεται τὸν περὶ ἀγάπης λόγον; He goes on to say that from their not loving one another comes τὸ διασπασθῆναι αὐτούς (*hom. in I Cor.* 20.2 [*PG* 61.161]).

[310] This is *Paul's* own argument, his constructive image for the church (cf. already 1 Thess 5:11), not a reformulation of the Corinthians' position (as has been argued by Weiss, *Korintherbrief*, 230; von Soden, 243 [taken as a possibility]; Murphy-O'Connor, "Freedom," 548; Willis, *Idol Meat*, 268).

[311] In chap. III we established that the building metaphor as used by Paul throughout 1 Cor is his positive image for a concordant community.

[312] Also Merklein, 166–67; Willis, *Idol Meat*, 280–86.

[313] With Barrett, "Things Sacrificed," 46, Paul never in 1 Cor prohibits eating meat which has been sacrificed to an idol; he does, however, reject participation in temple cult meals (Merklein, 169).

[314] He emphasizes that these theological principles are held by all Christians in common, as opposed to outsiders, and should therefore be a unifying point (signified by the repetition of εἷς and ἡμεῖς).

[315] J. Murphy-O'Connor, "1 Cor. viii, 6 – Cosmology or Soteriology?" *RB* 85 (1978) 253–67, who also points to its unifying function in the argument. Even if this text formally resembles a Greek philosophical doxology (good examples are Ps-Arist. *Mund.* 6.397B, 399B) and not a baptismal acclamation, those forms also focus on the unity of all created things (R. A.

mise position on idol meats is clearly stated in 8:8: οὔτε ἐὰν μὴ φάγωμεν ὑστερούμεθα, οὔτε ἐὰν φάγωμεν περισσεύομεν.[316] What this means is that there is no *personal* advantage to be gained from either point of view (this must fly in the face of those who argued these two positions at Corinth).[317] Instead, Paul argues (8:9–13; 9:19, 22; 10:33–11:1; cf. 6:12–20), one must consult the *community* advantage (that which builds up the church) in deciding about one's eating habits.[318]

Like the previous arguments on πορνεία, this argument on idol meats is linked by Paul with freedom, ἐξουσία. As in other factional disputes in antiquity, at least one side of the controversies at Corinth appealed to their freedom to justify their behavior,[319] and their refusal to compromise with the other side. Here Paul argues that the nature of true freedom lies even in renunciation of one's liberty for the sake of the other, the brother (8:10–13), on behalf of whom Christ made the ultimate self-sacrifice.[320] The correct index of abused freedom is its impact on others – if it causes offense (8:9, 13), which divides the community,[321] then it is wrong and must be redirected. The true community member, the true brother, consults not her or his own interests, but rather that of the brother (especially the weak one), through love.[322] This does involve one's curtailing

---

Horsley, "The Background of the Confessional Formula in 1 Kor 8,6," *ZNW* 69 [1978] 130–35, 131).

316 "But we have here a positive declaration on Paul's part . . . The neutrality of food does *not* mean neutrality of *conduct*" (Conzelmann, 148; emph. original; also Hurd, 123; against those who have ascribed this verse to the Corinthians [Barrett, *First Corinthians*, 195; J. Murphy-O'Connor, "Food and Spiritual Gifts in 1 Cor 8:8," *CBQ* 41 (1979) 292–98; Willis, *Idol Meat*, 96–98, 268 (Paul added the οὔτε . . . οὔτε); for earlier exegetes see the table in Hurd, 68]).

317 Chrys. *hom. in I Cor.* 20.4 [*PG* 61.166].

318 As Conzelmann noted (147–48), here Paul neither commands the "weak" to strengthen their conscience, nor does he forbid the "strong" to go to the εἰδωλεῖον. But, with Merklein, 165, the rhetorical force of 8:10, to urge renunciation of that right, is very strong (strong enough not to contradict 10:1–22).

319 This is not to deny that it may also refer to freedom from Torah observance. ἔξεστιν in 6:12 and 10:23, probably in an original context (Paul's own teaching?), did.

320 Ὅτι Χριστὸς μὲν οὐδὲ ἀποθανεῖν παρῃτήσατο ὑπὲρ αὐτοῦ, σὺ δὲ αὐτῷ οὐδὲ συγκαταβαίνειν ἀνέχῃ (Chrys. *hom. in I Cor.* 20.5 [*PG* 61.167]).

321 See chap. III on the role of "offense" in factionalism in antiquity. εἰς Χριστὸν ἁμαρτάνετε in 8:12, which is parallel to ἁμαρτάνοντες εἰς τοὺς ἀδελφούς [notice the plural here and the same locution as εἰς τὸ ἴδιον σῶμα ἁμαρτάνει in 6:18] means hurting the body of Christ, the church (cf. 1:13), by dividing it over this issue. This was understood by Chrysostom, who also connected it with the building metaphor: Καὶ πῶς εἰς Χριστὸν ἁμαρτάνουσιν; Ἑνὶ μὲν τρόπῳ, ὅτι τὰ τῶν οἰκετῶν αὐτὸς οἰκειοῦται. δευτέρῳ δὲ, ὅτι εἰς τὸ σῶμα αὐτοῦ καὶ εἰς τὸ μέλος τελοῦσιν οἱ τυπτόμενοι. τρίτῳ δὲ, ὅτι τὸ ἔργον αὐτοῦ, ὃ διὰ τῆς οἰκείας ᾠκοδόμησε σφαγῆς, τοῦτο οὗτοι καθαιροῦσι διὰ τὴν οἰκείαν φιλοτιμίαν (*hom. in I Cor.* 20.5 [*PG* 61.167]). Among modern exegetes see Murphy-O'Connor, "Freedom," 564: "'Christ' is interchangeable with 'Body of Christ' . . . To destroy a brother is to destroy the community" (followed approvingly by Willis, *Idol Meat*, 107).

322 With 10:24, 33; 13:5. "Es handelt sich um den Konflikt zwischen der ἐξουσία und der ἀγάπη oder besser das richtige Verständnis der ersteren aus der letzteren" (von Soden, 244).

activities which in principle are allowed, but for the sake of the church one should gladly do so. In 8:13 Paul turns once again to his own example of this type of self-renunciation for the sake of the common good: "but if food offends my brother, no way will I eat meat [of any kind!] forever, lest I cause offense to my brother." This generalizing verse introduces the full exemplary argument of ch. 9, that having ἐξουσία does not mean that one automatically exercises it without regard for the consequences it has for others.

(ii) *9:1–27. Exemplary Argument: The Proper Use of Freedom for the Common Good*
In the argument in 1 Cor 9, in continuity with his rhetorical strategy throughout 1 Corinthians, Paul presents himself as the example to be imitated. In 1 Cor 9 Paul shows himself to be a person of accommodation through self-renunciation, one who does all that he can to avoid offending others and thus causing and perpetuating divisions in the church.[323] One's understanding of the progression of this argument directly affects (and is affected by) one's view of the overall composition of 1 Corinthians.[324] Many of those who argue for the compositional unity of 1 Cor 8–10 take this chapter to be an exemplary argument[325] on the nature of true Christian freedom (ἐξουσία/ἐλεύθερος/ἐλευθερία).[326] Those who deny its original placement, and even some who begrudgingly accept its position here, focus on the forensic term ἀπολογία in 9:3,[327] and attempt to read this

[323] "Dann allerdings steht der Hinweis des Paulus auf sein eigenes apostolisches Beispiel im Mittelpunkt einer der brennendsten Fragen der korinthischen Gemeinde" (C. Maurer, "Grund und Grenze apostolischer Freiheit. Exegetisch-theologische Studie zu 1. Korinther 9," *Antwort. Karl Barth zum siebzigsten Geburtstag am 10. Mai 1956* [Zollikon-Zurich: Evangelischer Verlag, 1956] 630–41, 630 [but Maurer offers a theological justification of the suitability of 1 Cor 9 in its present position, not an argumentative analysis]).

[324] Correctly understood by Willis, *Idol Meat*, 271–72: "[1 Cor 9] has been viewed as an aside on Paul's apostleship which interrupts the topic of idol meat. This is almost inevitable when the subject of chapter 9 is regarded as Paul's defense of his apostleship against attacks by the Corinthians." This is an important illustration of the methodological mandate I argued for in chap. I, that a rhetorical analysis must come to terms with the full compositional unit, and cannot be applied in isolation to subunits of a given text.

[325] We shall take up the issue of whether this is a "digression" or an "excursus" only after we have given an analysis of the argument.

[326] As recognized by Jones, *Freiheit*, 42: "Gemäss der obigen Gliederung ist Kap. 9 als Explikation des 8,13 aufgestellten neuen Prinzips aufzufassen. Darüber besteht ein Konsens unter den Forschern, die an der Einheitlichkeit von 8,1–11,1 festhalten." See, e. g., Lake, 229; von Soden, 244–45; Allo, 208; the convincing case assembled by Willis, "Apostolic Apologia"; Vollenweider, 200: "Zwar lässt sich noch nicht von einer *ausdrücklichen* Bestreitung des paulinischen Apostolats wie im 2 Kor sprechen, aber Paulus wird doch zu einer *'Apologie'* für den Unterhaltsverzicht gedrängt." Cf. Robertson-Plummer, 179 on Paul's "spurious defense."

[327] "This interpretation of ch. 9 as a personal defense relies on the presence of the word *apologia*" (Willis, "Apostolic Apologia," 34; for an example of this reasoning see Lührmann, "Freundschaftsbrief," 309 n. 51). There is no doubt that ἀπολογία and ἀνακρίνειν are forensic terms (Heinrici, *Korinther*, 269; Robertson-Plummer, 179), but that does not immediately determine whether or not the following argument is genuinely apologetic in structure or

argument as Paul's self-defense.[328] But even many who argue for the unity of this section have propounded the dubious "kill two birds with one stone" position: that Paul here defends himself against serious charges while simultaneously presenting that very disputed behavior as an example to be imitated.[329] However, all attempts to analyze 1 Cor 9 as a true defense against actual charges have failed.[330] Any rhetorical analysis of 1 Cor 9 as an actual ἀπολογία must

---

function (I take 9:3 to refer to what follows). That depends on an analysis of the argument itself, and of its place within the whole of 1 Corinthians. One cannot determine a separate genre for one chapter of a larger literary whole, however tempting the term ἀπολογία may be.

[328] This is done by many scholars, such as Barrett, *First Corinthians*, 200–202; Conzelmann, 153; Schmithals, "Korintherbriefe," 270; *idem*, *Briefe*, 57–60; Schenk, 238–39; Theissen, 40–54; Lüdemann, 105–15; Klauck, *1. Korintherbrief*, 63–70; Lührmann, "Freundschaftsbrief," 309–10; Pesch, 224–29; Marshall, 282–317; Fee, *First Corinthians*, 392–441, for whom this interpretation is a central argument of his entire commentary. See p. 392 n. 4 where he tries to refute Willis, "Apostolic Apologia," on the basis of "the decidedly defensive nature of most of 1 Corinthians, especially chaps. 1–4" (which we have already shown to be an incorrect understanding of those chapters), and Paul's defense in 2 Cor 10–13. But that later situation should not be read back onto 1 Cor (rightly Merklein, 173). Fee himself recognizes the difficulty of his position: "That is unusual argumentation under any circumstances" (*First Corinthians*, 392); "although Paul calls this his 'defense', the issue is hardly what we might expect in such" (398).

[329] This is a very common position, sometimes stated overtly and often merely by juxtaposition or alternation of the two points of view in the exegesis: Calvin, 182–84; Lietzmann-Kümmel, 89; Grosheide, 202; Barrett, *First Corinthians*, 199–202; Conzelmann, 153; Theissen, 48; R. F. Hock, *The Social Context of Paul's Ministry: Tentmaking and Apostleship* (Philadelphia: Fortress, 1980) 60–61 (despite his correct insistence on Paul's positive paradigmatic use of his work already in 1 Thess [p. 47]); Wolff, 17; Lüdemann, compare pages 109 and 110; Jones, *Freiheit*, 38 and n. 65: "die beiden Funktionen schliessen sich nicht gegenseitig aus"; Lührmann, "Freundschaftsbrief," 309; Pesch, 224. This contradiction was noted correctly by Schenk, 238 against Schmithals, *Gnosticism*, 92 (he himself takes it as a defense argument), and was aptly named as the "two birds" argument by Merklein, 173: "Man könnte Paulus allenfalls vorwerfen, dass er zwei Fliegen mit einer Klappe schlägt, wenn er die Exemplifikation des in Kap. 8 angemahnten ἐξουσία-Verzichts im Sinne christlicher Freiheit mit einer 'Apologie' (9,3) seines Apostolates verquickt." But this position is clearly rhetorically untenable. The two birds are not only separate but *contradictory* (see below). Is it not naive (and rather more than coincidental) to think that the Corinthians' "charge" played so completely into Paul's hand? For a good example of the inconsistency caused by these assumptions see Marshall, 304–305, where the Corinthians' "charge" is also Paul's own "radical self-description."

[330] So rightly Willis, "Apostolic Apologia" (see before him Maurer, "Grund und Grenze," 632; Dautzenberg, "Verzicht," 213 n. 2). The rhetorical analysis of Pesch, 224–29 seems arbitrary and in places contradictory. He identifies the following τάξις: 9:1–2 *exordium*; 9:3 *transitus*; 9:4–14 *narratio*; 9:15–18 *propositio*; 9:19–23 *probatio*; 9:24–27 *peroratio*. He analyzes this as an apologia but intersperses interpretations of it as an exemplum, and never discusses the relationship between the two (see previous note). This analysis is hampered by methodological problems. Even though he takes ch. 9 to be in the middle of a letter (his *Antwortbrief*) he analyzes it with its own *exordium* and *peroratio* as though it were a separate composition. Pesch also does not demonstrate what the charges were (except to name the rhetorical questions in 9:1), or particularly how the *narratio* and *proof* sections he identifies indeed do line up with those charges (how does Paul's claim that he has a right to pay like the other apostles prove that he is an apostle?). It has also not been demonstrated how 9:24–27 functions in any way as a *peroratio* to a defense argument.

In my own attempts to analyze 1 Cor 9 rhetorically as an ἀπολογία, I have been continually confronted with the fact that the charge and issue of the case tend to disappear, no matter which starting point one takes. For example, if the charge is that Paul did not take their money (granting for argument's sake the historical likelihood of this charge), then his "defense" seems to be that he admits having done the charged act (9:12, 15), but disputes its illegality (taking the case as a juridical issue [*Rhet.Her.* 1.14.24]). But in 9:4–11, 13–14, Paul seems to be proving not that the act of which he is accused (not taking their money) was legal, but rather the converse: that *if* he had taken their money, it would have been legal. The "proof" against the charge of not taking their money thus proves only its opposite! (the difficulty of 9:4–13 as an apology was noted by Schmiedel: "Allein 4–12b 13f bringt Ansprüche, keine Vertheidigung ... Sie hätte aber in 4–12b 13f eine unvorsichtig lange und unvorsichtig behauptende Einleitung *e contrario*" [p. 140; also Heinrici, *Korinther*, 269; this argument leads them both to take αὕτη to refer to what precedes it]). The only logical conclusion one can reach at the end of v. 15 is that if Paul had taken their money, it would not have been a crime since he had the ἐξουσία to do so, but that no crime has indeed taken place (so why a defense?).

Neither is this the proof of a conjectural issue ("I didn't do it" [*Rhet.Her.* 1.2.18]) since the claims in 9:12 and 15 *stand without supporting proof.* They cannot thus be the charge. This difficulty is also recognized by Theissen: "What is remarkable is that Paul feels he must justify in such detail his right to support, even though he came under attack in Corinth precisely because he renounced it." Another way to defend oneself against a charge is by shifting responsibility for the act (*Rhet.Her.* 1.15.25). Is this what Paul does in 9:16, that he acted not freely but from ἀνάγκη? Or in vv. 17–18 where he discusses the reward, μίσθος, which he gained from not having done this crime (compare *Rhet.Her.* 2.2.3–3.4, where the exact opposite course is advised)? No, these verses cannot be taken on any logical forensic grounds as a defense against the charge that Paul did not take their money.

Could these verses be a defense against the charge that Paul is not an apostle (Lüdemann, 105–15)? No, because none of the expected arguments are there (cf. 2 Cor 11:1–12:13). The proofs of his apostolate are in fact presented bluntly and explicitly as common principles in 1 Cor 9:1–3, as already Weiss recognized: "v. 1.2 sind eine Einleitung, in der zunächst einmal festgestellt wird, dass P. das Recht hat, sich Apostel zu nennen. Der Apostolat selber kann also nicht Gegenstand der ἀπολογία sein" (*Korintherbrief*, 232). Clearly in 1 Cor 9 the fact that Paul is an apostle is something upon which he builds in the argument (9:5), not the conclusion towards which he argues (see Lüdemann's note on M. Smith's corrective to his position on p. 110 n. 23). Neither can ch. 9 "seem intended by Paul as a defence against the charge of inconsistency" (Hurd, 128; Marshall, 233–58; 282–317), for free admission of a charge is no defense!

One may also refute the view that this is a piece of forensic rhetoric from the point of view of rhetorical τάξις. There is apparently no *narratio* (against Pesch, 9:4–14, whatever it is, contains arguments and illustrations, not narration), which is normally required in forensic proof, and, more damaging, there is no *peroratio* to the argument which is at all suitably apologetic. 9:19–27 are so patently hortatory in character that one is forced to conclude that this argument in which Paul talks about his own behavior functions in an exemplary fashion (that is why at that point in the exegesis scholars have been forced into the "two birds" position). On a different tack, Marshall, 306–17, takes 9:19–23 to be invective, presuming that Paul merely takes up his opponents' descriptions of him, but he does not indicate how such an acceptance and restatement of invective can serve in any way suitably in an argument of self-defense.

As a final counterargument, we may ask if there are any comparable examples from ancient literature where a defense speech is simultaneously an appeal to one's own example (none has been produced in the history of exegesis to back up this contradictory claim for 1 Cor 9). The example of Isocrates (see n. 335 below) shows that the use of a *fictional defense* for rhetorical purposes *is* paralleled in ancient rhetorical texts (in line with our methodological mandate set forth in chap. I).

reconstruct the charge against which Paul defends himself here. But given the line of this argument, the only possible charge which one can unearth[331] is an historically implausible one: *that Paul did not take the Corinthians' money*![332] That such an accusation would ever have been made is, in my view, scarcely possible,[333] yet it persists in scholarship on 1 Corinthians. But even if that unlikely charge were historically feasible, the argument in 1 Cor 9 does not constitute an appropriate rhetorical defense against it. 1 Cor 9 is no defense speech by Paul. Instead, Paul calls it "defense"[334] to justify rhetorically his use of himself as the example for imitation, a rhetorical stance paralleled in antiquity,[335] because he is

---

[331] As admitted by Lüdemann: "Abgesehen von dem Angriff gegen den paulinischen Apostolat under Hinweis auf seinen Unterhaltsverzicht ist kein weiterer Angriff in 1 Kor 9 zu verifizieren" (p. 115).

[332] And therefore is not an apostle. But this does not reckon with the form of the rhetorical questions in 9:1 (with Willis, "Apostolic Apologia," 34; BDF 472.2), or with the way in which these sentences function as *premises* (not conclusions) in the argument which follows. "Paul is not really *defending* his conduct, but is arguing from it" (Willis, "Apostolic Apologia," 40; already Godet, 2.2, 5–6; cf. Quint. *Inst.* 5.10.12–14 on arguing from accepted principles).

Recently Marshall has argued that Paul's not taking the Corinthians' money, while he took that of other churches, led to the charge of inconsistency, and enmity in his relations with them. However, Marshall is not able to document this in 1 Cor 9 (only by "implication"), but argues by reading 2 Cor 11:7–15 and 12:11–15 back onto it. "Paul's refusal . . . is implied in his statement to the effect that he did not make use of his right (vv. 12b, 15, 18)" (Marshall, 174; cf. p. 242: "It is true that Paul never says in 1 Cor 9, 'I refused your offer' . . . "). In my opinion Marshall's reconstruction does not sufficiently grapple with Paul's own rhetorical strategy throughout 1 Cor (he only deals with 4:6–13 and ch. 9), and with the extent to which *he* is in control of the rhetoric (Marshall regards Paul's constructive argumentation by reference to his own example as his unlikely acceptance and rhetorically inexplicable repetition of their invective against him). See the similar critique in the review of Marshall's work by D. B. Martin, *JBL* 108 (1989) 542–44: "Marshall claims that it is the Corinthians, not Paul, who first introduce a charge that he is changeable . . . But the first reference to Paul's 'inconstancy' is in 1 Cor 9:19–23, and Paul is not here countering accusations that he is changeable; rather, he is volunteering the image of himself as the changeable, opportunistic, indeed 'enslaved' leader" (p. 543).

[333] "1 Corinthians, however, reveals a Paul on the defensive precisely because he would not accept payment from the Corinthians; i. e., would not put himself in the posture of a beggar. This passage has always puzzled exegetes. Why would not the Corinthians be happy not to have to pay their minister?" R. Scroggs, "The Sociological Interpretation of the New Testament: The Present State of Research," *NTS* 26 (1980) 164–79, 175. Scroggs takes Theissen's historical reconstruction to resolve the problem, but even Theissen must admit that Paul's argument is rather strange (see quotation and discussion in chap. II n. 163).

[334] See the suggestion of Weiss, *Korintherbrief*, 233: "Aber ernstlich kann ihm sein Recht nicht bestritten worden sein . . . Dann aber kann die ausführliche Begründung seines Rechtes *nur eine Form sein*; er will zeigen, wie klar er sich über sein Recht ist, wie fest es begründet ist, wie gross daher sein Verzicht" (emph. added).

[335] Isoc. *Or.* 15.8: "I saw, however, that if I were to attempt a eulogy of myself [ἐπαινεῖν ἐμαυτόν], I should not be able to cover all the points which I proposed to discuss, nor should I succeed in treating them without arousing the displeasure or even the envy of my hearers. But it occurred to me that if I were to adopt the fiction of a trial [ἀγών] and of a suit brought against me

well aware of the risks he takes in using himself as the example for imitation.[336] That 1 Cor 9 is a self-exemplary argument receives further confirmation by the argument of this study that indeed the appeal to example, and especially that of Paul himself, is the unifying deliberative appeal found throughout 1 Corinthians (see chap. II).

In 9:1 Paul begins to answer a possible objection[337] to his self-sacrificing behavior named in 8:13: οὐκ εἰμὶ ἐλεύθερος;[338] His answer to the question which lies underneath this – "if I am free, then why do I have to curtail my freedom from doing things which I am admittedly free to do?" – follows in his "defense" against this objection. Paul's argument progresses in the following way.[339] In 9:1–3 he lays out the fundamental premises upon which his argument will build[340] – that he is free, and that he is an apostle (because he has seen the Lord, and because he has founded churches such as the Corinthian church itself). In 9:4–12a, 13–14 Paul presents a series of consequent arguments for his rightful ἐξουσία since he *is* an apostle. In doing so he draws richly upon a variety of exempla: the behavior of the other apostles (9:4–6), common human wisdom (9:7),[341] Scriptural proofs (9:8–11), common practice once more (9:12a), cultic norms (9:13), and finally a word of the Lord (9:14). All of these proofs demonstrate without a doubt that, since Paul is an apostle, he has certain ἐξουσίαι: to eat and drink, to marry, and particularly to receive support from his churches for his

– if I were to suppose that a sycophant had brought an indictment and was threatening me with trouble and that he was using the calumnies which had been urged against me in the suit about the exchange of property, while I, for my part, cast my speech in the form of a defence in court [ἐμαυτὸν δ' ἐν ἀπολογίας σχήματι τοὺς λόγους ποιούμενον] – in this way it would be possible to discuss to the best advantage all the points which I wanted to make." Compare this with Chrys. *hom. in I Cor.* 21.1: Καὶ ὁρῶν ἀνάγκην οὖσαν ἑαυτὸν ἐγκωμιάσαι (οὕτω γὰρ Κορίνθιοι διωρθοῦντο), καὶ μηδὲν βουλόμενος μέγα περὶ ἑαυτοῦ εἰπεῖν, ὅρα πῶς ἀμφοτέροις εἰς δέον κέχρηται (*PG* 61.170).

336 Von Soden, 250, 253; Dautzenberg, "Verzicht," 225; Merklein, 172 rightly note that 11:1 refers back also to ch. 9.

337 Paul responds to much the same objection as in 10:29: ἱνατί γὰρ ἡ ἐλευθερία μου κρίνεται ὑπὸ ἄλλης συνειδήσεως; For the same form of argument responding to an objection to a deliberative appeal for compromise see Dio Chrys. *Or.* 48.9: "ἡμεῖς ἄρα τὰ αὑτῶν ἀπολέσωμεν;" οὐθείς φησιν.

338 That chap. 9 exemplifies 8:13 has been argued by many scholars since Chrys. (Heinrici, *Korinther*, 265; Jeremias, 156; the list of scholars in Hurd, 127 n. 5; more recently Willis, "Apostolic Apologia," 34; *Idol Meat*, 273; Jones, *Freiheit*, 38; differently Vollenweider, 199 n. 2). Chrys. took it to be a defense against the objection that Paul doesn't behave in the way he promised in 8:13: ἵνα μή τις λέγῃ, ὅτι Κομπάζεις εἰκῆ, καὶ φιλοσοφεῖς ἐν λόγοις ... εἰ γὰρ ἀπὸ ψυχῆς ταῦτα λέγεις, δεῖξον διὰ τῶν ἔργων τίνος κατεφρόνησας ὑπὲρ τοῦ μὴ σκανδαλίσαι τὸν ἀδελφόν. διὰ τοῦτο ἀναγκάζεται λοιπὸν εἰς τὴν ἀπόδειξιν τούτων καθεῖναι, καὶ δεῖξαι πῶς καὶ τῶν συγκεχωρημένων ἀπείχετο ὑπὲρ τοῦ μὴ σκανδαλίσαι (*hom. in I Cor.* 21.1 [*PG* 61.169]). On Paul as a ὑπόδειγμα in 8–10 see also Clem. Alex. *Str.* 4.15 [*PG* 8.1305].

339 See Jones, *Freiheit*, 42–44 for an overview of previous analyses of the disposition of 1 Cor 9.

340 As he does, e. g., in 6:12; 8:1; 10:23–24; 12:3; 14:1; 15:1–8.

341 Defined in 9:8 as κατὰ ἄνθρωπον λαλεῖν.

labors. The heart of Paul's argument is to be found in 12b, 15a and 18b, all three of which sentences say the exact same thing: ἀλλ' οὐκ ἐχρησάμεθα τῇ ἐξουσίᾳ ταύτῃ ... 'Εγὼ δὲ οὐ κέχρημαι οὐδενὶ τούτων ... εἰς τὸ μὴ καταχρήσασθαι[342] τῇ ἐξουσίᾳ μου ἐν τῷ εὐαγγέλιον.[343] Paul has not exercised his ἐξουσία, though he surely had the right to. He has curtailed his use of it in order not to abuse this right, so that he might give no hindrance [ἐγκοπή] to the gospel of Christ. This is the same piece of advice which Paul urges on the Corinthians in ch. 8 (μή πως ἡ ἐξουσία ὑμῶν αὕτη πρόσκομμα γένηται τοῖς ἀσθενέσιν), so that the function of this argument as exemplary of that piece of advice is rhetorically very clear. In 9:15–23 Paul expounds upon the advantage to be gained from this kind of self-renunciation, and in so doing redefines the μισθός and the κέρδος. This argument is consequently another progression within his whole argument in this proof for redefinition of τὸ συμφέρον, the advantageous course of action to follow. The common advantage (that of "the all," "the many" and "the all" [9:19, 22]) is that which one should pursue with one's ἐξουσία, not merely one's own advantage. 9:19–23 gives the specific application of the exemplary argument to the Corinthian situation. Paul is not concerned for the Corinthians likewise to work for their living, but rather to be accommodating[344] of one another in all things, but especially in regard to meat-eating practices. Thus it is no surprise that the groups which he names in 9:20–22 are Jews, Greeks (under cover as the "lawless ones") and "the weak." That self-abnegation for the sake of the greater good (compromise for the sake of concord!) does not mean that one entirely forsakes one's own advantage is demonstrated by Paul again in the summary argument of 9:24–27, where he points once more to the eschatological advantage (the final μισθός, the ἄφθαρτος στέφανος).[345] As throughout the entire section 5:1–11:1, the emphasis in this passage is on the ultimate advantages to be gained from compromise of immediate liberties in the present. Paul handles the problem by redefining freedom. The analogy of the athlete's ἐγκράτεια is

---

342 The wordplay here serves again to highlight what is at issue: the difference between use and abuse of freedom. The same wordplay and principle are evident in 7:31 (cf. Dautzenberg, "Verzicht," 221).

343 Also Chrys. *hom. in I Cor.* 22.1 [*PG* 61.182]. On χρᾶσθαι and compounds in relation to freedom and compromise, see Joseph. *AJ* 12.283 and Philo, *Abr.* 216, quoted in chap. III.

344 On Paul's ethic of accommodation see P. Richardson and P. W. Gooch, "Accommodation Ethics," *TynBul* 29 (1978) 89–142, who correctly call attention to this piece of Paul's thought (especially important is their pointing to the use of συγκαταβαίνειν in early exegesis of Paul's letters, on pp. 91–93). In their analysis, however, Richardson and Gooch treat this accommodation in terms of Paul's *behavior*, without attention to the *rhetorical strategy* involved in Paul's call for accommodation here in 1 Cor. Richardson also grounds Paul's accommodation principle in rabbinic teaching (following Daube) and the Jesus tradition, without reference to Greco-Roman materials on freedom and compromise, or noting the connection between this call for accommodation and the problem of factionalism.

345 This is equivalent to the eschatological verdict δόκιμος (9:27). The same point is made in 9:26 with οὐκ ἀδήλως and οὐκ ἀέρα δέρων – i. e., not without profit (as in 14:9, of ineffectual speech).

particularly apt for Paul's conclusion to this self-exemplary argument on the nature of true freedom because the athlete's self-renunciation is precisely in those areas of Corinthian dispute: sexual behavior and diet.[346] The athlete forgoes present pleasures for the sake of a later ultimate good, which is the advice which Paul urges on the Corinthians.

Having analyzed this argument and demonstrated its place within the argument subsection 5:1–11:1, we are now in a position to evaluate the various descriptions of 1 Cor 9 by commentators as a "digression,"[347] or "excursus."[348] The *function* of this chapter is that it is an exemplary argument,[349] as we have seen. Whether it is indeed a "digression" or not, we must conclude, is in the final analysis entirely a definitional question.[350] Even ancient rhetorical theory on the subject of digressions was itself concerned to define what is and what is not a digression, amidst differences of opinion on the same questions as the debate among New Testament scholars on Paul's "digressions."[351] Quintilian is ada-

---

346 πᾶς δὲ ὁ ἀγωνιζόμενος πάντα ἐγκρατεύεται, 9:25 (see Bachmann, 335 n. 1; Weiss, *Korintherbrief*, 247 [he does not draw the same connection]; and especially Chrys. *hom. in I Cor.* 23.1 : Οὐδὲ γὰρ μεθύειν ἔξεστι τοῖς ἀγωνιζομένοις ... οὐδὲ πορνεύειν [*PG* 61.189]). Chrys. also takes the phrases ὑπωπιάζειν τὸ σῶμα καὶ δουλαγωγεῖν to mean controlling the body's appetites for meat and sex (23.1 [61.190]). Compare also Clem. Alex.'s expansion of the metaphor on the proper diet and training of the athelte in *Quis dives salvetur*, 3.

347 Weiss, *Korintherbrief*, xliii (along with 2:6–16; 6:1–11 and ch. 13) and 231 (eine μετάβασις εἰς ἄλλο γένος); Robertson-Plummer, xxiv; Barrett, *First Corinthians*, 219; the important treatment by Wuellner, "Greek Rhetoric" (who takes the extent of the digression to be longer than most, from 9:1–10:13 [pp. 186–87]). Wuellner's conclusion that 1 Cor is epideictic rhetoric because digressions are fitting to that species (p. 184) can be refuted because digressions in fact can be found in all three species (note, for example, that the rhetorical handbooks treat digression in regard to the forensic species [see Martin, 89–91, who follows them in his treatment]). For rejections of 1 Cor 9 as a digression, see, e. g., Heinrici, *Korinther*, 265; Dautzenberg, "Verzicht," 213.

348 Lietzmann-Kümmel, 43; Kümmel, 278; Senft, 87; Merklein, 171 ("dessen Exkurscharakter kaum zu bestreiten ist"); Pesch, 224. Bornkamm, "Lord's Supper," 154 talks of an "interruption."

349 As noted in the section titles in the commentaries: Godet, 2.1 ("The example of abnegation given by Paul"); Bachmann, 316 ("Die Berufsübung des Pl als Vorbild selbstverleugnender Liebe"); Weiss, *Korintherbrief*, 231 ("Das Beispiel des Apostels"); Robertson-Plummer, 174 ("The Great Principle of Forbearance"); Grosheide, 199 ("Paul's Example of Self-Sacrifice"); Senft, 116 ("L'Exemple de l'Apôtre"); Lang, 113 ("Das Beispiel des Apostels"); Strobel, 6, 141 ("Beispielhafte Vertiefung"); cf. in studies Jeremias, 156 ("Erläuterung"); Horsley, "Consciousness," 587 ("autobiographical illustration").

350 As Wuellner has well seen: "... digressions in Paul's letters are illustrative of his rhetorical sophistication and ... they serve to support his argumentation. This view runs counter to the current scholarly opinion that Paul's digressions are interruptions in his arguments and often carry him off into irrelevant material" ("Greek Rhetoric," 177). Wuellner thus keeps the term digression, but redefines it with the help of modern scholars of rhetoric Lausberg and Perelman (see next note).

351 There is variation in regard to whether or not it is a distinct part of a speech, on where in a speech it may occur, on its acceptable length, and on how it should or should not be related to its context (see Volkmann, 164–67, with many actual examples, and Martin, 89–91). It is on this

mant that a digression (*digressio*, *egressio*) must be connected with the case at hand.[352] Among its functions a digression may make a comparison[353] or often amplify a given point in the argument.[354] It is in the latter category that 1 Cor 9 would fit, an amplification of the παράδειγμα (Paul) introduced in 8:13.[355] If a digression is so broadly understood as being able to include such amplification of an example which is well suited to the case at hand, then 1 Cor 9 can be called a digression, but since that term has also been used to connote the lack of connection between a passage and its context, we shall instead term it an exemplary argument.

(iii) *10:1–13. The Negative Example of the Wilderness Generation*

After presenting his positive example of the proper use of freedom for the common good, Paul turns to a series of negative examples[356] to warn the

---

point that Wuellner's redefinition of the digression is on too shaky ground (he does not sufficiently reckon with the conflicting nature of the ancient evidence on the question).

[352] ". . . this form of digression can be advantageously appended . . . but only if the digression fits in well with the rest of the speech and follows naturally on what has preceded, not if it is thrust in like a wedge parting what should naturally come together" (Quint. *Inst.* 4.3.4; see also 4.3.14).

[353] Cic. *Inv. Rhet.* 1.19.27.

[354] Cic. *Inv. Rhet.* 1.19.27; *De Or.* 2.19.80; Quint. *Inst.* 4.3.15.

[355] For digression used to introduce an extended παράδειγμα, see the discussion in Dio Chrys. *Or.* 7.128–31: "The hearer should therefore not be annoyed at digressions [ἐκτροπαί] even if they do seem excessively long, if only they are not about trivial or unworthy or irrelevant things, since the speaker has not abandoned the real theme of the whole [ὑπόθεσις] provided he treats of the matters that are essential and pertinent to philosophy. Probably if we imitated the hunter in this we should not go far astray. When he picks up his first trail and, following it, all at once comes upon another that is clearer and fresher, he does not hesitate to follow up this latter and then, after bagging his game, goes back to the first trail. Neither should we, perhaps, find fault with a man [Plato in the *Republic*] who set out to discuss the just man and justice and then, having mentioned a city for the sake of illustration [παράδειγμα], expatiated at much greater length on the constitution of a state and did not grow weary until he had enumerated all the variations and the kinds of such organizations, setting forth very clearly and magnificently the features characteristic of each; even though he does find critics here and there who take him to task for the length of his discussion and the time spent upon 'the illustration [παράδειγμα], forsooth!'"

The handbooks do not discuss digression in deliberative rhetoric. Actual deliberative discourses do contain extended treatments to introduce or amplify on a given παράδειγμα (Isoc. *Or.* 5.109–14, narration and praise of Heracles' behavior leading up to a call for imitation [see Isocrates' justification of this treatment in 5.110 as προσήκουσα, πρέπουσα, and not too long!]; 6.16–25 on the ancestors; Dem. *Or.* 3.23–26, the ancestors; Dion. Hal, *Ant. Rom.* 6.80.1–3 discussion of historical examples; Joseph. *BJ* 2.358–87 with its list of short narrations on all the nations which have fallen to Rome; for many other examples see the documentation in chap. II on παραδείγματα in deliberative rhetoric). Again, whether such background information or reminders about an example being introduced constitutes a digression is a question on which one could find both supporters and opponents in antiquity as among modern scholars, but this is the phenomenon we see in 1 Cor 9, as in these texts.

[356] Εἶτα ἐφ' ἕτερα ὑποδείγματα ἔρχεται πάλιν . . . Καὶ τὰ παρ' ἑαυτοῦ θεὶς, πάλιν ἐπὶ τὰς

Corinthians away from the specific behaviors which divide them: idolatry, sexual immorality, testing the Lord and grumbling. In this respect this section resumes previous treatments within the overarching section 5:1–11:1.[357] Also here in 10:1–13 Paul names the issue as not merely such actions in themselves, but the community consequences of them.

In this argument Paul constructs an analogy between ancient Israel and the church at Corinth (an analogy which will be fully carried out in 10:14–22). 10:1–4 does not contain sophisticated reflection on whether or not Israel had "sacraments" *per se*.[358] Paul is concerned merely to sketch out the analogy with the Corinthians.[359] The most difficult exegetical task posed by this text is therefore to isolate correctly the direct application of the analogy which Paul is making from those elements which are merely incidental, forming the analogical framework.[360] Most scholarship on this text has supplied its own suppressed premise to explain Paul's argument – the Corinthians' incorrect belief that the sacraments have the magical power to protect one from any pollution or punishment for sins.[361] But that viewpoint finds little support in the text itself.[362] Nowhere is it said that the Corinthians (or the Israelites!) engaged in the eating of idol meats or in sexual immorality because they believed that the magical powers

τῆς Παλαιᾶς πρόεισιν ἱστορίας (Chrys. *hom. in I Cor.* 23.2 [*PG* 61.190]). See further discussion of this use of examples in chap. II (with treatment of τύπος/τυπικῶς).

357 Lührmann, "Freundschaftsbrief," 310–11. See also Strobel, 153 (on 10:1–13): "In gewisser Hinsicht werden sogar alle Themen der vorausgehenden Abschnitte mit dieser schriftgelehrten Reflexion noch einmal beleuchtet und einer Antwort zugeführt." Meeks, "Rose up to Play," 74 regards the issue of group boundaries to be "the policy question behind the immediate concern about eating meat." We saw above how important this was in Paul's argument in 5:1–7:40.

358 The exegetical tradition has often, in my view, asked the wrong questions of this passage.

359 Conzelmann, 166; Willis, *Idol Meat*, 127–32.

360 Willis, *Idol Meat*, 123.

361 The argument of von Soden, 259–61 has been influential. Among others who argue this position are Lietzmann-Kümmel, 46–47; Héring, 84; Käsemann, "Lord's Supper," 113–19; Barrett, *First Corinthians*, 220–29; Conzelmann, 167; Bornkamm, "Lord's Supper," 127–30; Klauck, *Herrenmahl*, 257; Merklein, 167; Pesch, 159–62.

362 So correctly Willis, *Idol Meat*, 138–42, 154, 159–60, but in favor of too general a reading himself: "The history of Israel was recounted to show that God's people may not sin safely, presuming upon their election" (p. 155). The more specific intent is that the church (like Israel) must live out the implications and realities of her cultic unity, or else perish. Willis is correct in insisting that the central subject of the passage is idolatry, but it is not the only subject.

The evidence cited for this premise is Plut. *Mor.* 21F, on the power of initiation into the mysteries (von Soden, 259, followed by many). One then jumps to Ignatius, *Eph.* 20.2, where the eucharist is described as φάρμακον ἀθανασίας. In fact, even in that text the emphasis is not only magical, but on the unity of the church in its cultic participation (Schoedel, 95–98). But even if Ignatius understands the sacrament as in some way protective (as do later gnostics, who are also cited in support of this view), one still needs to demonstrate the relevance of this viewpoint for (at least some of) the Corinthians. It is at this point that this argument appears to me to be weakest.

of the eucharist would protect them from harm.[363] We can suggest another possibility for understanding the application of this analogy in 10:1–13 out of the particular findings of this study.

In chap. III we demonstrated that each of the events of the wilderness generation drawn upon by Paul in 10:6–11 (Exod 32; Num 11, 14, 25) was considered an example of rebellion through factionalism in the first century, as evidenced by Philo and Josephus. Therefore, in 10:1–13 Paul continues to treat, not merely the divisive issue of idol meat in itself, but retains his own chosen focus on the unity of the church in the face of controversies surrounding such practices.[364] The emphasis in the verses which set up the analogy, 10:1–4, is most pronounced: *all* Israel was unified at the beginning in *common* baptism,[365] *common* experiences and *common* spiritual food and drink.[366] But despite this auspicious beginning, tragedy befell the community when factions appeared[367] and sought their own advantage over that of all Israel. Their rebellions through sinful acts brought harm to almost all the people Israel.[368] This is consequently an argument of the form "then and now," a comparison of fortuitous, divinely assisted beginnings with later misfortunes.[369] The application to the Corinthians will be made explicit in 10:14–17 (it is, however, already very present in this passage in 10:6, 11). Like Israel, despite common founding experiences, common baptism (8:6; later 12:13) and unifying cultic practices of one shared food and drink, the Corinthians too are in danger of being divided by factions on these same issues

363 The only motive which Paul combats in 1 Cor 6–11 is quite clear: that some Corinthians perform these acts because they are free to do so (6:12; 10:23; esp. the objection in 10:29b).

364 This would tend to militate against the view that he is taking up wholesale a preexistent Jewish or Christian midrash (a viewpoint entertained by Conzelmann, 165; Barrett, *First Corinthians*, 220; Klauck, *Herrenmahl*, 253; Meeks, "Rose Up to Play"; Strobel, 153 [a passover haggadah]; debated by Willis, *Idol Meat*, 127). The fit is too perfect to imagine a pre-Pauline source incorporated wholesale here.

365 The formula εἰς τὸν Μωϋσῆν ἐβαπτίσθησαν is an ad hoc formulation to parallel εἰς τὸν Χριστὸν βαπτισθῆναι, which is Paul's correct (and unifying) point of view on baptism, in distinction from factionalists' boasts (see discussion on 1:12–18).

366 πάντες is repeated five times (emphasis noted by Weiss, *Korintherbrief*, 250; Conzelmann, 165–66; Klauck, *Herrenmahl*, 252; Willis, *Idol Meat*, 125), forming an anaphora in vv. 2–4 (cf. 10:17, of the church, οἱ πάντες). The food shared is "the same" (vv. 3–4; though some early manuscripts delete this [see Weiss, *Korintherbrief*, 251]).

367 Note the repetition of τινες αὐτῶν in vv. 7, 8, 9 and 10, in direct contrast to πάντες in 10:1–4.

368 ἐν τοῖς πλείοσιν αὐτῶν, "the majority of them" (10:5).

369 This is very similar to the kind of arguments we get in vituperations, where the auspicious childhood and gifts of a person or city are then compared with their adulthood (or what they have done with those gifts). See the full treatment of this above on 1:18–4:21, with examples of the then and now *topos* in other discourses on concord. Note also that this function squares with Paul's overt description of νουθεσία in 10:11, as in 4:14 where Paul summed up his previous contrast of Corinthian beginnings with their present strife. (Incidentally, compare νουθεσία in 10:11 with Wisd 16:6, in reference to the attack of snakes in Num 21:5–9 which is mentioned in 10:9.)

and thus risking the very survival of the community.[370] On this reading, the assumed premise of the argument is not that sacraments make one immune to defilement, but instead the premise that cultic unity should as a natural consequence issue forth in social unity (and vice versa).[371]

As he had in 3:17, in 10:1–13 Paul once again warns the Corinthians that their choice is not simply between "right" and "wrong" theological positions or behaviors, or even only unity and disunity, but is truly between survival and destruction. In this section of the argument Paul gives Scriptural proofs for the *topos* on which he had relied in ch. 3: that factionalism destroys any community infected with it. Here the destruction is more than the political inevitability of such behavior (as also in 3:17)[372] – God will bring destruction as God did to the wilderness generation if this disobedience continues, and all will be harmed.[373]

As with ancient Israel, one clear limit of behavior can be set: no Christian is an idolator (10:7, 14).[374] Paul can state this position without reservation (it is particularly the argument pushed absolutely by the "weak"). Likewise, as he had stated unequivocally in 6:18, Christians should flee from πορνεία (10:8). Both positions are consistent with the social norms prohibiting mixing with a brother who is a πόρνος or εἰδωλολάτρης (5:9–10). He agrees with the theological principles of "the weak," but the last two irregularities of ancient Israel (10:9–10), which stand fully parallel to the first two, generalize once again to Paul's central concern: all Christians should not tempt the Lord and should not grumble.[375] The Corinthian Christians should put group unity above specific quarrels. The general conclusion to this sub-argument, introduced with ὥστε,[376]

---

370 This is a well attested *topos* in ancient literature urging concord (see chap. III nn. 458–61), one which is relevant to the situation of factionalism faced in 1 Cor. This may also be what Paul is getting at in 10:18.

371 A very graphic Christian depiction of this is Acts 2:42–47.

372 And in other texts urging concord; see chap. III n. 228.

373 Threats are also used in deliberative arguments "since a common fear is wont to reconcile all differences [πάντα γὰρ ὑπὸ δέους κοινοῦ συνίστασθαι φιλεῖ τὰ διάφορα]" (Dion. Hal. *Ant. Rom.* 8.26.2).

374 Klauck, *Herrenmahl*, 256 and Willis, *Idol Meat*, 160–61, rightly have pointed to these two texts as the focal point. Merklein's argument that both 8:10–13 and 10:1–22 prohibit participation in temple cult meals (thus idolatry) is attractive, and might resolve the apparent contradiction. 10:25–30 then deals with sacrificial meat outside of the cultic context, which is acceptable for eating unless it harms the brother, a position also compatible with 8:1–13 (p. 167; before him Fee, "Εἰδωλόθυτα," 172–97, and now his *First Corinthians*, 357–491, but he doubts that Paul is giving advice which straddles two different Corinthian viewpoints).

375 The Corinthians also grumble, as did the Israelites, because they had to endure deprivations in the present for the sake of future advantages, as Chrys. understood it: ... καὶ τῶν πειρασμῶν δὲ ἕνεκεν ἐγόγγυζον λέγοντες, Πότε ἥξει τὰ ἀγαθὰ, πότε τὰ ἔπαθλα; (*hom. in I Cor.* 23.4 [*PG* 61.193]). Differently Barrett, *First Corinthians*, 226: "there is nothing to suggest that *complaining* was a special failing of the Corinthians." See also ch. III n. 454 on grumbling and divisions.

376 Barrett, *First Corinthians*, 228; Willis, *Idol Meat*, 155.

is in 10:12: Ὥστε ὁ δοκῶν ἑστάναι βλεπέτω μὴ πέσῃ. This concluding phrase may be another reference to the building metaphor for concord so prominent in this epistle: even if you think you yourself stand, you will indeed fall if others do.[377] All stand or fall together as one building. The temptation to seek one's own way and disregard one's community is the ultimate human temptation, which endangers the social whole – in this instance, the church. This warning is therefore applicable to both sides of the controversy over idol meats and idolatry. That Paul is still dealing with the Corinthian factions is evident from the verse which has been so troubling to exegesis, 10:13: πειρασμὸς ὑμᾶς οὐκ εἴληφεν εἰ μὴ ἀνθρώπινος. Factionalism is the quintessential "human" affliction which now threatens the Corinthian community.[378]

(iv) *10:14–22. Idolatry, Second Treatment: Cultic Unity as Norm and Standard*
In 10:14–22 Paul extends the analogy of the wilderness generation to the Corinthians by filling in the complementary primary cultic unity shared by them in the body and blood of Christ. The common baptism of the Corinthians, analogous to that of Israel, has already been introduced in the argument (1:12–18; cf. 8:6), as it will be later in 12:13,[379] so it stands as a premise in Paul's argumentation here as well. The cultic κοινωνία is introduced by Paul[380] as an argument to advise social unity (ὅτι εἷς ἄρτος, ἓν σῶμα οἱ πολλοί ἐσμεν, οἱ γὰρ πάντες ἐκ τοῦ ἑνὸς ἄρτου μετέχομεν),[381] particularly through exclusion of outside cultic associations.[382] As we have seen in chap. III, such an appeal is common in arguments urging unity in antiquity. Cultic ties are commonly appealed to in attempts to get divided groups back together again.[383]

---

[377] Note the similar phrasing in 3:18. See also the language of Chrys.'s exegesis: Τὸ γὰρ ἐνταῦθα στῆναι οὐκ ἔστιν ἑστάναι βεβαίως (*hom. in I Cor.* 23.4 [*PG* 61.194]), and full discussion in chap. III.

[378] On this as a *topos* see chap. III n. 98, and especially 1 Cor 3:3. For much more vague renderings of this phrase, see Conzelmann, 169; Willis, *Idol Meat*, 158.

[379] καὶ γὰρ ἐν ἑνὶ πνεύματι ἡμεῖς πάντες εἰς ἓν σῶμα ἐβαπτίσθημεν ... καὶ πάντες ἓν πνεῦμα ἐποτίσθημεν. Baptism is linked in Paul's thought to the one body image (emphasized correctly by Käsemann, "Lord's Supper," 111, 113, who however connects it with the body of the Archetypal Man, emphasizing the mythic over the ecclesiological/sociological meaning).

[380] Κρίνατε ὑμεῖς ὅ φημι. There is no evidence that it was part of the Corinthians' own argument. The emphasis on unity in the body of Christ (cf. 6:12–20; 12:12–27) and in the one loaf (5:6–8) is Paul's own. It is interesting that Chrys. brings in the leaven and the lump also in his exegesis of this text, saying that Christ brought in a new lump of dough and leaven ἵνα ... εἰς τὴν ζωὴν τὴν ἀθάνατον διὰ τῆς τραπέζης ἀνακερασθῶμεν ταύτης (*hom. in I Cor.* 24.2 [*PG* 61.201]). We should also note, as commentators have recognized, that this is not an argument on the nature of the eucharist itself. Here the eucharist is employed as an argument within another context (Barrett, *First Corinthians*, 231; Willis, *Idol Meat*, 192).

[381] "Der Aufruf zur Einheit richtet gegen die differierenden Verhaltensweisen in Korinth" (Strobel, 78; see also Jewett, *Anthropological Terms*, 256–59, on the importance of 10:17 for corporate horizontal unity, against those who take it as an aside in the argument).

[382] Paul makes the same argument by appeal to the body of Christ in regard to πορνεία in 6:12–20 (Meeks, *Urban Christians*, 159; Neyrey, 143).

[383] This may be a way to resolve the dichotomy in scholarship on the meaning of κοινωνία in

But also here, as elsewhere throughout his proof in 1 Corinthians, Paul does not argue for Corinthian unity in the abstract, but in regard to the very specific practices and beliefs which divide them. In this case his concern is still with defining what constitutes εἰδωλολατρία for this Christian community, which means simultaneously defining what are the boundaries of this social body.[384] In adjudicating between competing Corinthian points of view, in 8:1–8 Paul made it clear that the eating of εἰδωλόθυτα in itself does not constitute idolatry, and therefore cannot be condemned on those grounds, but nevertheless it should still be avoided if necessary for the sake of the harmonious upbuilding of the church community. Via the example of the wilderness generation, Paul argued the other side of the question by stressing that, even if the act of eating εἰδωλόθυτα *per se* is not idolatry, that does not mean that there is no such thing as εἰδωλολατρία, for there is, and it is to be condemned categorically (10:7, 14), as the golden calf incident is a permanent reminder. The next difficult argument in 10:14–22 first reminds the Corinthians that the mandate of their concord is rooted in their authentic and unifying participation in the eucharistic rites. That fundamental value should be held up against any behaviors which fragment the church. Yet precisely because cultic and social unity bear a one-to-one correspondence with each other, Paul brings up a second ominous consequence of cult meal participation:[385] that it makes the participants κοινωνοὶ τῶν δαιμονίων. This is in direct contrast to Paul's own behavior which he has held up for emulation, that the Christian should be a συγκοινωνὸς τοῦ εὐαγγελίου (9:23), a member of the κοινωνία τοῦ σώματος τοῦ Χριστοῦ (10:16; 1:9). Countering the possible objection of self-contradiction in his treatment of idolatry,[386] Paul remains consistent

---

this passage – is it sacramental or social? (see chap. III n. 418). The sacramental κοινωνία is here presumed (as in 11:23–34), as is the social, but most crucial of all is *the assumption of their interrelationship*, which is the operative feature of Paul's argument. Willis, *Idol Meat*, 168–212 has rightly stressed the social dimension of Paul's argument here, but he feels compelled to deny any sacramental meaning in order to justify his argument, because he rightly rejects the "hyper-sacramentalism" hypothesis. But the two meanings are not at odds with one another, especially in this text.

384 "For Paul and his co-workers, the corollary of unity in the body of Christ is strict exclusion from all other religious connections. That is, group solidarity entails strong boundaries" (Meeks, *Urban Christians*, 159).

385 Not εἰδωλόθυτα (as he is quick to affirm in 10:19). That cult meal participation is what he discusses is clear from 10:21, where in the parallelism of Christian and "demon" cults Paul uses not the expected ἄρτος but switches to the τράπεζα, denying power to the meat *per se* (again consistent with 8:1–13), but reckoning with the power of the cultic participation. Klauck, *Herrenmahl*, 269 accounts the switch to the fact that Paul could not find a pagan counterpart, but the mention of the cult place θυσιαστήριον in Paul's first analogy of Israelite priests suggests that Paul himself is already moving his argument in that direction.

386 With 8:4. This can be taken as an argument for the unity of the letter, since Paul shows himself aware of what a line he is treading with what he has argued above (with Bornkamm, "Lord's Supper," 125). This verse can be used against claims that Paul "changed his mind" between two different letters. Rather here he shows himself well aware of his delicate mediating position.

in his denial of the existence of idols, but shows the danger of cult meal participation by recourse to "demons." This compromise position allows Paul to urge the Corinthians to avoid any other cultic associations[387] without theologically having to encroach upon his radical monotheism. By reference to the demons (in whom he no doubt believed) Paul can warn the Corinthians against cult meal participation, which divides the church by luring some Corinthians into competing κοινωνίαι, without giving an outright prohibition.

(v) *10:23–11:1. Final Appeal to the Common Advantage as Opposed to Factionalism. Conclusion to the Second Section of Proof*

The subsection 10:23–11:1 is the summary of the second section of continuous proof in 5:1–11:1.[388] Such recapitulation within arguments is recommended in rhetorical theory.[389] It is in this concluding section of proof that the oscillating character of Paul's argument about idol meats and idolatry (and sex and marriage) is fully understood. His primary concern throughout this argument has been, not the practice of eating this meat itself, but the consequences of both eating and disapproving of others who eat on the unity of the church. He is willing to compromise on the issue of eating this meat, though not on idolatry, as in 5:1–7:40 he compromised on various marital statuses but not on sexual immorality. In both cases he subordinates the specific controversy to the more important concern of the concord of the church community.

The section 10:23–11:1, beginning with the repetition of the slogan in 6:12,[390] makes continual reference to significant *topoi* about factionalism and concord, as we have demonstrated in chap. III. Paul's advice is the standard advice to factionalists in Greco-Roman antiquity, especially in deliberative arguments seeking unity: stop seeking your own advantage and instead seek the advantage

---

[387] Again he does not command. The phrasing of 10:20b is the same (negated) as his compromise position in 7:7.

[388] The summary character of this section has been noted by commentators, though it is mostly taken to refer only to 8–10: "Closer comparison reveals that the whole of 1 Cor. 10.23–11.1 is a point by point restatement and summary of the argument of 1 Cor. 8 and 9" (Hurd, 125, with a table of the points of contact on pp. 129–30; also Barrett, *First Corinthians*, 239, "it is time to sum up in terms of practical advice and precept"; Willis, *Idol Meat*, 223, 262–63; Watson, "1 Cor 10:23–11:1," 310–12, who investigates the role of the rhetorical questions in 10:29b–30 in effecting this rhetorical recapitulation).

[389] "It is however admitted by all that recapitulation [ἀνακεφαλαίωσις] may be profitably employed in the other portions of the speech as well" (Quint. *Inst.* 6.1.8; see also *Rh. Al.* 20.1433b; 32.1439a; *Rhet. Her.* 2.18.28, where *complexio* [the résumé] is named as a part of each argument; 2.30.47; cf. 3.9.16; Cic. *Inv. Rhet.* 1.37.67–40.74; Anon. *Rh.* 1.454 Spengel).

[390] "Paulus macht dieses Stichwort [ἐξουσία] zum übergreifenden Thema des ganzen Abschnitts, und πάντα (μοι) ἔξεστιν markiert dessen Beginn (6,12) wie Abschluss (10,23)" (Lührmann, "Freundschaftsbrief," 312). The lack of μοι in the oldest manuscripts is significant. Throughout this argument Paul has demonstrated that true "advantage" is not that of the individual, as he will in a summary fashion argue here.

of the other (10:24),[391] which works ultimately for the common advantage (10:33). This general principle is applicable throughout the argument in relation to each specific subject of dispute (hence 10:31, with the behaviors stated εἴτε ... εἴτε[392]). Here he also links it with his particular appeal for Corinthian unity in this letter, the building metaphor for concord (10:23). The syllogism fits both logically and contextually: that which is advantageous (τὸ συμφέρον) is what builds up (οἰκοδομεῖ).[393] Therefore, 10:23–24 applies to all Corinthian factionalists in the interests of unity.[394] This reading of Paul's argument receives external confirmation from the abundant evidence that these principles were commonly used in Greco-Roman texts to combat factionalism.[395] This conclusion consequently adds further justification to our reading of this entire section 5:1–11:1 as still overtly combatting the phenomenon of Corinthian factionalism in its varied manifestations.

In the middle of his exposition of general principles in 10:23–24, and his self-exemplification of those principles in 10:31–11:1, Paul inserts two last concrete examples of how one should go about seeking the advantage of the other and the many in deciding whether or not to consume εἰδωλόθυτα (not whether one can practice idolatry, for on that there can be no compromise). This guide is, not coincidentally, another example of Paul's reconciliatory strategy: he grants the freedom to eat the meat itself (10:25–27), but still argues for the need to compromise one's own ἐλευθερία when it might offend the other (10:28–29). Decision making[396] is again subjected to new τέλη by a defined negative consideration (offense to other individuals and thus the church) and a positive consideration: the glory of God (10:31; cf. 6:20).[397] Conciliatory, harmonious behavior is termed yet again (8:9; 9:12) being "without offense," ἀπρόσκοπος, to

---

391 "This is the man – for example, the man who disagrees with me about food sacrificed to idols – whose interests I must consider rather than my own" (Barrett, *First Corinthians*, 240).

392 And in particular the last one, εἴτε τι ποιεῖτε. This same conciliating construction is found throughout 1 Cor (3:22; 12:26; 13:8; 15:11, with the objects of dispute; on the style of εἴτε ... εἴτε clauses in Paul's writings see J. Weiss, "Beiträge zur paulinischen Rhetorik," FS B. Weiss, *Theologische Studien* [Göttingen: Vandenhoeck & Ruprecht, 1897] 165–247, 179–80). Dio Chrys. uses the same construction in *Or.* 34.48 to describe the possibilities of dispute and stress their unimportance in relation to unity: καὶ εἴτε Αἰγαῖοι πρὸς ὑμᾶς εἴτε 'Απαμεῖς πρὸς 'Αντιοχεῖς εἴτε ἐπὶ τῶν πορρωτέρω Σμυρναῖοι πρὸς 'Εφεσίους ἐρίζουσι, περὶ ὄνου σκιᾶς, φασί, διαφέρονται.

393 The logic of a cumulative reading from 6:12 to 8:1 to here leads to this conclusion.

394 Also Murphy-O'Connor, "Freedom," 568: "[10:24] was applicable to both strong and weak whose behavior betrayed self-centered superiority and fear respectively." On the unifying force of the principle (as documented extensively in chap. III), see Chrys.'s exegesis: Ταῦτ' οὖν καὶ ἡμεῖς εἰδότες, ἀγαπητοί, προνοῶμεν τῶν ἀδελφῶν, καὶ τὴν ἑνότητα τὴν πρὸς αὐτοὺς διατηρῶμεν (*hom. in I Cor.* 24.3 [*PG* 61.203]).

395 See chap. III.

396 The goal of a deliberative argument.

397 Barrett, *First Corinthians*, 244.

Jews and Greeks (as Paul the example is in 9:20–23)[398] and to "the church of God." This is a not so subtle reminder that God will not leave unpunished those who threaten God's church with destruction through their self-seeking divisiveness (3:17; 10:1–13). As in 1:18–31, Jews and Greeks should be understood as separate from the church – which is now the primary identity of all Christians.[399] That is why one must seek the advantage of the many (the body of Christ)[400] by pleasing all in everything, that is, being a non-factionalist. The reason for doing this is so that they might be saved, which is the ultimate κέρδος (9:19–22), the ultimate advantage which is to be sought in all decision making. Paul ends this second proof section with a resumptive call to imitate him (the call which was first stated at the end of the first proof section). This time Paul strengthens his appeal for the Corinthians to emulate him by reference to Christ whom he himself imitates, Christ who made the most complete self-sacrifice for the many.[401]

(3) 11:2–14:40. *Third Section of Proof:* Manifestations of Corinthian Factionalism When "Coming Together"

In this third section of deliberative proof urging unity, in 11:2–14:40[402] Paul[403] turns to the specific manifestations of Corinthian factionalism when the church comes together[404] in one place for worship. The divisions and contentions which exist in general, and in the relationships between church members themselves and with the outside world, would have another set of specific appearances when the contending persons (perhaps different house churches with different affilia-

---

398 "Beide Parteien – Juden und Heiden – mussten gewisse Konzessionen abverlangt werden" (Strobel, 163).

399 See Weiss, *Korintherbrief*, 267 on the church as the *tertium genus*.

400 Strobel, 163.

401 Cf. the collection of unity appeals from the spirit (clearly dependent upon 1 Cor) in Ign. *Phld.* 7:2: . . . τὴν σάρκα ὑμῶν ὡς ναὸν θεοῦ τηρεῖτε, τὴν ἕνωσιν ἀγαπᾶτε, τοὺς μερισμοὺς φεύγετε, μιμηταὶ γίνεσθε Ἰησοῦ Χριστοῦ.

402 11:2–14:40 has been recognized as a coherent argumentative section by many scholars, such as Lightfoot, 141 ["Regulations affecting Christian assemblies"]; Heinrici, *Korinther*, 321; Godet, 1.28–29 ["three questions which are *liturgical* or relative to public worship"], 2.103–104; Bachmann, 369 ["Über Misstände in den gemeindlichen Zusammenkünften," without 11:2–16]; Weiss, *Korintherbrief*, 268, of the redacted whole ["Über einige Misstände in den Gemeinde-Versammlungen"]; Robertson-Plummer, xxvi, 226 ["Disorders in Connexion with Public Worship"]; Allo, 253 ["Questions concernant les assemblées du culte"]; Conzelmann, 181 ["Questions of Divine Worship"]; Wolff, 65 ["Gottesdienstprobleme in der korinthischen Gemeinde"]; Johnson, *Writings*, 283–89 ["The World in the Church"]; Fiorenza, *In Memory of Her*, 226; *idem*, "Rhetorical Situation," 393; Lührmann, "Freundschaftsbrief," 305.

403 It is Paul who is responsible for this logical arrangement, not the Corinthians' correspondence (oral or written).

404 See chap. III for the dual signification of the phrase: literally "coming together" in one place, and "becoming unified." The lexical coherence of this section is thus evident: συνέρχεσθαι is used in 11:17, 18, 20, 33, 34; 14:23, 26, and only here in the Pauline corpus (cf. 7:5 *v. l.*).

tions and customs) are forced to be together in one assembly.[405] We can expect on sociological grounds that the Corinthian divisions would naturally exert great influence on whole church gatherings. This conclusion is further supported by the important role played in factional rivalries and appeals for concord in antiquity of any assembly situations where the tumultuous groups meet face to face.[406] For a religious community like the Corinthian church this must have been most acutely a problem. Corinthian factions have been disputing with one another over proper hairstyles in worship, the manner of celebrating the Lord's supper, and the exercise of spiritual gifts. In this third subsection of proof Paul censures Corinthian factionalism once again, and appeals for unity and loving compromise on all sides. Throughout 11:2–14:40 Paul continues to appeal to the building and body images for concord which have played such an important role in the first two proof sections. His own example continues to be the basis for his deliberative argumentation, as is his sustained appeal to the community advantage as the basis for all decision-making. The purpose of the section 11:2–14:40, to persuade the Corinthians to be united rather than divided in their common worship ("to come together for the better rather than for the worse"),[407] is definitively expressed summarily in its conclusion in 14:40: πάντα δὲ εὐσχημόνως καὶ κατὰ τάξιν γινέσθω (cf. 16:14).

---

[405] So correctly Allo, 270–271, on σχίσματα in 11:18: "On pense naturellement d'abord à un effet de ces disputes dont il a été parlé au premier chapitre, lequel aurait pu être dénoncé aussi par les gens de Chloé; l'effet de ces divisions serait apparu jusque dans le banquet eucharistique (20–22), et, à plus forte raison, dans les rivalités entre 'inspirés' (voir ch. xiv)."

[406] In discourses urging concord see Dio Chrys. *Or.* 38.46; 40.28–30; 48.3; Aristid. *Or.* 24.56, a description of concordant behavior (οὓς ... τότε ἑωρῶμεν κἂν ταῖς ἐκκλησίαις οὐ μόνον μιᾷ φωνῇ χρωμένους, ἀλλ' εἰ οἷόν τ' εἰπεῖν καὶ ἑνὶ ῥήματι ὡς τὸ πολύ), and Philostr. *VA* 6.38, "the ruler of Syria had plunged Antioch into a feud [στασιάζειν], by disseminating among the citizens suspicions such that when they met in assembly they all quarrelled with one another [διειστήκεσαν ἐκκλησιαζομένη πόλις]." In the early Principate factionalism often manifested itself in public assemblies and meetings, including the theater, sporting events and other public occasions (see MacMullen, 163–91 and Jones, *Dio Chrysostom*, 41–44, 92–93 for references and discussion). This phenomenon is recognized also in the NT (see Mark 14:2 and pars.; the accounts of the crowd in the passion narratives; unruly crowds in Acts [e. g., 17:5f.; 24:18]; a particularly good example is provided by the parody of communal assembly behavior in Acts 19:32). The great extremes to which combatting among spectators at the theater and amphitheaters went is well captured by Dio Chyrs. in his *Or.* 32 (note also that drunkenness is one of the "unruly crowd" behaviors he censures, as does Paul in 11:21). This social reality, that factions are made acutely manifest in assemblies, is also attested on a smaller social level where, in the list of proscriptions for the guild of Zeus Hypsistos, after forbidding σχίσματα, proper banquet behavior is commanded: "[It shall not be permitted] to abuse one another at the banquet [μηδὲ κακολογ[ήσειν] ἕτερος [τὸν] ἕτερον ἐν τῶι συμποσίωι]" (P.Lond. 2710, line 15 [text and translation Roberts-Skeat-Nock, 40, 42]). See also their conclusion about this papyrus text on p. 87: "The prohibitions in this as in other texts relating to ancient clubs indicate the perils which threatened table-fellowship and illustrate the disorders of the Corinthian Eucharist" (cf. Klauck, *Herrenmahl*, 289 n. 22). See also the bylaws of a funeral association quoted by MacMullen, 176. In ECL compare *Did.* 14.2.

[407] See also Weiss, *Korintherbrief*, 277–78.

(a) 11:2–16. Divisive Customs in Worship

In 11:2, beginning with ἐπαινῶ δὲ ὑμᾶς, Paul makes a transition from his second call for the Corinthians to imitate him into the next subsections of proof.[408] As we have seen, praise is commonly used in deliberative argumentation, as is blame,[409] to move the audience to proper behavior in the future and to placate them so that they will be receptive to critical advice.[410] This lends even more support to the interpretation of 11:2 by several scholars as a *captatio benevolentiae*,[411] and undermines the argument that it is impossibly inconsistent with its prior context or inappropriate in the middle of a letter.[412] In this long proof section in 1 Corinthians Paul varies his approaches, here with praise, in order to break up the arguments.[413] Paul's praise in 11:2 stands in direct contrast to 11:17 and 22, where he withholds his praise in regard to divisive behavior at the Lord's supper.[414] Thus the subsection 11:2–34 is united rhetorically.

---

408 The topic of the παραδόσεις hangs over 11:2–14:40 and 15:1–57 (11:2, 23; 15:3; with Allo, 253).

409 See the discussion above on 1:4–9 and 1:18–4:21.

410 See Isoc. *Or.* 8.27 quoted above on variety within deliberative proofs. For actual examples, see Isoc. *Or.* 4.51, 73 (ἀλλὰ διὰ τοῦτο καὶ μᾶλλον ἐπαινεῖν ἔχω τὴν πόλιν), and throughout the speech; Dio Chrys. *Or.* 40.20 (καὶ νῦν ὑπὲρ τούτου ἐπαινῶ τόν τε ἄρχοντα καὶ τὸν εἰσηγησάμενον); cf. 40.19, 22; in deliberative speeches in the histories see Dion. Hal. *Ant. Rom.* 7.54.1 (contrast of ἐπιτιμῶν and ἐπαινῶν); 7.60.2; Polyb. 18.36.6. For withholding praise, as in 1 Cor 11:17, 22, see Andoc. 3.34 (Τὸν λόγον οὖν τοῦτον οὐκ ἐπαινῶ). On the connection of praise and blame with statescraft see Plut. *Mor.* 810C: "For blame which is mingled with praise [ὁ γὰρ μεμιγμένος ἐπαίνῳ ψόγος] and contains nothing insulting but merely frankness of speech, and arouses not anger but a pricking of the conscience and repentance, appears both kindly and healing." Seneca also classed praise among types of advice (*Ep.* 94.39).

411 Barrett, *First Corinthians*, 247; Conzelmann, 182 (who attributes it to epistolary rather than to rhetorical style [n. 13]); Fiorenza, "Rhetorical Situation," 395; Fee, *First Corinthians*, 500; Strobel, 165. See also Merklein, 174: "Das Lob, das Paulus dafür spendet, hat primär rhetorische Funktion."

412 This is the argument on which several partition theories are based (Weiss, *Korintherbrief*, 268; followed by Schmithals, "Korintherbriefe," 281; *Briefe*, 21; Sellin, "Hauptprobleme," 2974–75, presume that such praise would only be found at the beginning of a letter, but this is unfounded, from the point of view of both epistolary and rhetorical style). The other argument behind such partition theories, that 11:2–34 must belong to a different letter because it does not begin with περὶ δέ (Schmithals, *Gnosticism*, 91; Suhl, 206; Sellin, "Hauptprobleme," 2974; Pesch, 89), has already been refuted above. The fate of 11:2–16 in the hands of partition theorists also primarily rests on its connection with the disputed 11:18 (e. g., Schenk, 229; Vielhauer, *Geschichte*, 141, on which see below). The integrity of 11:2–34 itself has been disputed only by Schmithals, *Briefe*, 21, 34, who puts 11:3–16 at the beginning of the *Antwortbrief*, but he has left off the *captatio benevolentiae* of 11:2 which is the very argument for this section being at the beginning of a letter! See below on other arguments which consider the passage to be an interpolation.

413 Chrys. *hom. in I Cor.* 26.1 [*PG* 61.211]).

414 "In 1 Corinthians 11, Paul balances praise and blame in the service of giving advice (cf. 11:2, 17, 22)" (Stowers, 80). In this instance the partition theorists correctly take the "contradiction" to be rhetorically appropriate (cf. Conzelmann, 182 n. 12).

The sub-argument proper is introduced with the disclosure formula θέλω δὲ ὑμᾶς εἰδέναι, and the topic is appropriate adornment of the κεφαλή,[415] specifically when praying and prophesying in public worship (11:4–5). From the entire argument it is evident that there is disagreement in the church at Corinth about the various customs of head attire. Such differences of opinion on custom would be very publicly asserted in worship, with those on different sides clearly so marked, and the community unquestionably divided.[416] This passage has received a great deal of attention, especially recently, in regard to exactly what kind of head attire is under discussion (veils, haircuts, hairstyles), what the meaning is of several key phrases, how Paul's argument can or cannot be harmonized with 14:33b–36, whether men are a genuine part of the controversy or are introduced here so Paul can argue to proper women's behavior by analogy, how this argument fits into its present context, and whether or not the passage is original here or even genuine to Paul.[417]

---

415 Scholars have argued both that hair attire was mentioned in the Corinthians' letter (Lietzmann-Kümmel, 53; Hurd, 90–91; Lang, 137; Fee, *First Corinthians*, 491–92) and that it was not (J. Murphy-O'Connor, "Sex and Logic in 1 Corinthians 11:2–16," *CBQ* 42 [1980] 482–500, 491; Klauck, *1. Korintherbrief*, 77–78; Wolff, 65; Pesch, 89). But in fact it is not possible to determine how Paul learned of the head attire controversy (correctly Barrett, *First Corinthians*, 245–46). He may indeed have learned of it from several different sources. The absence of περὶ δέ provides no information for the question, as we have seen. This is another instance of the problem of analyzing the composition of 1 Cor as determined by a strict separation of "oral" and "written" topics.

416 Whatever the motivation for these differences (realized eschatology, the influence of Paul's baptismal teaching of Gal 3:28, cultural differences), we can see how they would have had this effect. No woman in the community participating in worship could avoid making a choice! See also chap. III for the self-identifying role of hairstyles in antiquity.

417 The authenticity of 11:2–16 (or 3–16) has been questioned by those who otherwise do not think that 1 Cor is a letter collection (W. O. Walker, "1 Corinthians 11:2–16 and Paul's Views Regarding Women," *JBL* 94 [1975] 94–110; *idem*, "The 'Theology of Women's Place' and the 'Paulinist Tradition,'" *Semeia* 28 [1983] 101–12; L. Cope, "1 Cor 11:2–16: One Step Further," *JBL* 97 [1978] 435–36; G. W. Trompf, "On Attitudes Toward Women in Paul and Paulinist Literature: 1 Corinthians 11:3–16 and its Context," *CBQ* 42 [1980] 196–215). The arguments given by these scholars are in my view unconvincing (with J. Murphy-O'Connor, "The Non-Pauline Character of 1 Corinthians 11:2–16?" *JBL* 95 [1976] 615–21; *idem*, "Sex and Logic"; *idem*, "1 Corinthians 11:2–16 Once Again," *CBQ* 50 [1988] 265–74 and A. Padgett, "Paul on Women in the Church: The Contradictions of Coiffure in 1 Cor 11:2–16," *JSNT* 23 [1984] 69–86). The present study emphasizes the appropriateness and rhetorical acceptability of 11:2–16 in its present position, and provides a way to account for the contradictory nature of the argument (see below). Arguments for the inauthenticity of 11:2–16 rest upon a compositional assumption which is questioned here: that 11:17–34 belongs rightly to the argumentative subsection of 8–10 on the subjects of eating and drinking (Walker, "1 Corinthians 11:2–16"; Trompf, 198–201) which is "interrupted" by 11:2–16. This problem is alleviated when 11:2–14:40 is understood to be a coherent argument section on behavior in the worship assembly. On the various questions posed by this text see, in addition to the works already cited, J. A. Fitzmyer, "A Feature of Qumran Angelology and the Angels of 1 Cor xi. 10," *NTS* 4 (1957/58) 48–58; M. Hooker, "Authority on Her Head: An Examination of 1 Cor xi, 10," *NTS* 10 (1963/64) 410–16; A. Jaubert, "Le Voile des Femmes (I Cor. XI. 2–16)," *NTS* 18 (1971/72)

While these questions cannot be fully taken up here, the emphasis of this study on Paul's rhetorical strategy of focussing on factionalism itself (and not just individual factions or sides of the controversies) can contribute to these discussions the largely overlooked significance of the term φιλόνεικος in 11:16, a very strong term which undeniably refers to factionalism in antiquity.[418] Whatever the specific controversy which Paul tries to adjudicate in 11:2–16, we must conclude that he again subordinates the issue itself to his overall concern for the unity of the church. That is not to say, however, that in 11:2–16 Paul does not express a point of view. In an effort to compromise, though his own preference is for women to remain covered at prayer,[419] he softens this position by arguing for the mutual interdependence of women and men in the church (11:11–12) and for the common divine origin of all (11:12; cf. 3:21–23; 8:6).[420] If some recent interpretations are correct, in a direct reversal[421] of 11:4–9, in 11:10 Paul argues that women have the ἐξουσία to do what they want with their heads.[422] Yet he seems to uphold the bases of the more conservative position in 11:3–9 and 13–16. If this is true, then the best parallel for this argument may be 1 Cor 8–9, where Paul establishes his ἐξουσία but then calls for its renunciation for the sake of the greater good.[423] Once again we see in Paul's reconciliatory argument the conservative leanings typical of arguments for concord:[424] women are to remain

419–430; R. Scroggs, "Paul and the Eschatological Woman," *JAAR* 40 (1972) 283–303 and *idem*, "Paul and the Eschatological Woman: Revisited," *JAAR* 42 (1974) 532–49; W. A. Meeks, "The Image of the Androgyne: Some Uses of a Symbol in Earliest Christianity," *HR* 13 (1974) 165–208; Fiorenza, *In Memory of Her*, 226–30; a fair and clear discussion of the issues is given by Fee, *First Corinthians*, 491–530.

[418] Conzelmann, 191 rightly noted the importance of v. 16 to the argument, but not the term φιλόνεικος. The emphasis I am making, however, is that the contentiousness of which Paul writes is not that of the Corinthians against his teaching, but the Corinthians against one another. This then frees one to recognize more than one Corinthian position on head wear in 11:2–16, and not a uniform "Corinthian position" which Paul combats (as in particular argues Padgett, 76, who considers 1 Cor "apologetic").

[419] But "Paul nowhere denies women the right to engage in charismatic leadership of worship" (Meeks, "Androgyne," 201; also Scroggs, "Revisited," 534).

[420] Meeks calls this a "tortuous theological compromise" (*Urban Christians*, 71) and elsewhere "rhetorical balance" ("Androgyne," 199). He points to 4:21b–23 (*sic*) and 15:23–29 as other places in 1 Cor where he does this. Scroggs also sees Paul's difficult position here: "But in and of itself it [11:2–16] is a dispassionate attempt to square the distinction in habits of dress with the equality of man/woman in the community" ("Eschatological Woman," 302).

[421] Exegetes are forced to conclude that Paul is contradictory here (Meeks, "Androgyne," 200–201; Fee, *First Corinthians*, 520–24; Padgett, 69 and passim). Our study would suggest that he is trying to argue both sides of the question towards conciliation.

[422] 11:10 (Hooker; Jaubert; Padgett, 71–72).

[423] Padgett, 75–76 sets up "Cultural Accommodation" as the most likely interpretation of 11:2–16 before his own (he attributes it to Jaubert, who does not really argue for that position).

[424] "Among those who advocated preservation of the status quo, the constantly salient concern is a sense of order: everything must be in its place, and the differentiation and ranking of women and men became a potent symbol for the stability of the world order. That concern comes through clearly, for example, in the protestations by moralists about the 'natural'

with head covered when prophesying and praying in worship to avoid φιλονειϰία in the church,[425] in union with the custom[426] of the church universal.[427]

(b) 11:17–34. Divisions in the Lord's Supper

After a more conciliatory argument in 11:2–16, Paul next turns to admonish the Corinthians for behavior in community worship which is even more divisive than the head wear disagreements. He begins this argument with his censure of their improper behavior (οὐϰ ἐπαινῶ) first named in general terms, and then he describes specifically the abuse which he will treat, σχίσματα/αἱρέσεις in the assembly (11:20–22). Because he returns to this ecclesiological concern in 11:33–34, we conclude that the disunity of the church is *the* main topic of this argument, to which the tradition (11:23–26) is a response. Paul begins with great irony in 11:17–18, expressing his profound disappointment that the Corinthian worship assemblies for common rites do not unite the church (a cultural assumption held throughout Greco-Roman antiquity and argued by Paul above in 10:16–17), but have on the contrary become showcases for the factions within the church community.[428]

11:18 has been the locus of virtually all partition theories of the letter, which maintain that here Paul seems unaware of the factions which so preoccupied him in 1 Cor 1–4.[429] This argument has been refuted in this study on three grounds. First, these arguments are based on the assumption that only 1 Cor 1–4 dealt with Corinthian factions, but this presupposition has been refuted in chap. III. Since Paul has directly addressed Corinthian factionalism throughout all of 1 Corinthians to this point, it is incorrect to think that the factions magically "reappear" here. Secondly, mock disbelief at the presence of factions in political

difference in hair styles of men and women" (Meeks, "Androgyne," 179–80, citing 1 Cor 11:2–16, alongside other texts). On the conservatism of Paul's stance here see also Barth, 58–59; Bultmann, "Faith and Understanding," 77; Hurd, 184, with other references; Fiorenza, *In Memory of Her*, 236. See also below on 14:33b–36 on the relation between Paul's social conservatism and the *Haustafeln*.

425 See the language of Chrys.'s exegesis: Παρ' ἡμῖν μὲν γὰρ εἰϰότως ὑποτέταϰται τῷ ἀνδρὶ ἡ γυνή. ἡ γὰρ ἰσοτιμία μάχην ποιεῖ (*hom. in I Cor.* 26.2 [*PG* 61.215]; see also his later exhortation in this homily: ϰαὶ πάντων ἡμῖν προτιμότερον ἔστω τὸ τὴν μεθ' ἡμῶν ἐπὶ τῶν οἴϰων ϰαθημένην μὴ στασιάζειν μηδὲ διχοστατεῖν πρὸς ἡμᾶς (26.8 [61.224]).

426 See chap. III n. 499 on how customs can play a unifying or a divisive role in a society. See also the conclusion of Padgett, 77: "Alternatively, one might understand that the great plethora of social groups united by the church (rich and poor, Jew and Gentile, slave and free, male and female) has resulted in the fact that not all people dress the same, or wear the same kind of hairstyle." But in his exegesis Padgett does not fully reckon with the implications of this inference, because he reconstructs a single "Corinthian point of view."

427 Conzelmann, 191. Cf. 1:2 and the discussion above. "Paulus appelliert hier am Schluss an die Einheit der christlichen Kirche, die er als die Einheit das Leibes Christi versteht" (Lang, 144).

428 "But when a church is in the moral state in which that of Corinth is, it must inevitably become a theatre of discord" (Godet, 2.139).

429 See chap. III n. 513.

bodies is found in other discourses which urge concord, even later on in the speech or letter.[430] Thirdly, the grammar of this text provides yet another clue to its emphasis. The repeated genitive absolutes in 11:18 and 20 emphasize that Paul is dealing here with the very specific manifestations of the Corinthian divisions *when they come together for worship.*[431]

In particular, the celebration of the Lord's supper has occasioned and reinforced separations within the community on economic and social grounds.[432] The statement that "one is hungry, but another is drunk" may be a hyperbolic way of depicting the discord and division in the meal,[433] but clearly all food was not shared by all because of the different social norms operative in the setting of a meal in a private home.[434] Even the architectural limitations of early Christian house churches would have contributed to the manifestations of factions at the meal.[435] Paul's compromising response is to make a separation between private and public eating habits,[436] as he had in ch. 8–10, and, as there, to remonstrate them for the offense to the church community which ostentatious consumption causes.[437] Next in his argument he calls the church to unity in the παράδοσις of

[430] See chap. III. Counterexamples are given there also for the announcement of receipt of information towards the end of long arguments.

[431] Also Klauck, *Herrenmahl*, 288 (with different conclusions); see also chap. III n. 515.

[432] Theissen, 69–174; Meeks, *Urban Christians*, 67–68.

[433] ἕκαστος also plays this role (as elsewhere in the argument; see chap. III n. 549). Cf. in particular 14:26. On drunkenness cf. 5:11; 6:10.

[434] Theissen, 145–74.

[435] See Heinrici, *Korinther*, 341–42; Weiss, *Korintherbrief*, 280, 293; cf. Robertson-Plummer, 239, on how the need for different tables to accommodate the large group may have aided the divisions. The use of separate tables seating nine to twelve persons, though caused by space limitations, would have led to further complications of who should sit where, always potentially a socially fragmenting decision, as is well-known in the NT (see Luke 14:7–11 and Jas 2:1–4, where it results in διακρίνειν) as elsewhere in Greco-Roman antiquity (a good example is provided by Dio Chrys. *Or.* 30.29–32; note that in that text the different portions of food are directly linked with where one sits). Further support for the forces endemic to Corinthian factionalism in assembly meetings has been given by J. Murphy-O'Connor, who has argued that the architecture of a typical Corinthian house would have required using the *atrium* as well as the dining-room (*triclinium*) to accommodate even a fifty-person meal (*St. Paul's Corinth. Texts and Archaeology*, GNS 6 [Wilmington, DE: Glazier, 1983] 153–61). Murphy-O'Connor regards the role of house churches, which on some occasions assembled together for worship, to be an important factor in the Corinthian divisions (see also chap. III n. 62), a judgement with which I concur. This conclusion is also reached by Barton, 238–39, who in his anthropological analysis also discusses the significance of the "symbolic geography of a meal" operative there (p. 236).

[436] Theissen, 164: "Within their own four walls they are to behave according to the norms of their social class, while at the Lord's Supper the norms of the congregation have absolute priority. Clearly this is a compromise." Confirmation for this on anthropological grounds comes from Barton, who has argued that in 11:17–34 (as in 14:33b–36) Paul is concerned to differentiate the norms pertaining to the different spatial realms of the οἶκος and the ἐκκλησία (234–42).

[437] Their behavior amounts to "despising the church of God" (11:22), thus emphatically contradicting Paul's general rule for conciliatory behavior (10:32).

the institution of the Lord's Supper, in the sharing of the one loaf and one cup by all in the new covenant which is the solemn memorial of the death of Christ.[438] Possibly to counter the προλαμβάνειν of 11:21 Paul urges the order of bread, meal and cup with μετὰ τὸ δειπνῆσαι in the tradition (11:25) to end the separatism caused by a preliminary (not so)common meal.[439] He also urges them not to minimize the sacral power of the eucharist by their inappropriate, separatist behavior,[440] which may lead to severe punishment from the Lord.[441] The Corinthians must correctly discern the body, which means simultaneously the eucharistic body and the ecclesiological body of Christ.[442] In 11:27–34 it appears that Corinthian divisiveness has expressed itself in negative judgements of the worthiness of others to participate (δόκιμος, δοκιμάζειν, 11:19, 28).[443] In a two-pronged argument, as in 4:1–5 when dealing with such Corinthian judgements of others and also in 8–10 on the idol meat controversy,[444] Paul affirms the importance of each individual's *self* judgement (as against others' judgement), but again he relativizes even that by reference to the Lord's eschatological judgement which alone is important. The goal that the Corinthians not "come together for judgement" (11:34) is a *double entendre*: don't come together to judge and rank one another disparagingly, because a far more serious (eschatological)

---

438 As in 1:18–4:21, here too the death of Jesus is emphasized as a corrective to Corinthian self-aggrandizement (Klauck, *Herrenmahl*, 304, 317).

439 "Paul wanted the meal to enhance the solidarity of the community by encouraging them to begin and end together" (Barton, 241). This is consistent with the conclusion in 11:33: Ὥστε . . . ἀλλήλους ἐκδέχεσθε. For this position see, e. g., Weiss, *Earliest Christianity*, 1.333; 2.648–49; Conzelmann, 199; differently Bornkamm, "Lord's Supper," 137–38.

440 "What Paul means by *unworthily* is explained by verses 21 f.; he is thinking of the moral failings of factiousness and greed which marked the Christian assembly" (Barrett, *First Corinthians*, 272). Cf. *Did.* 14.2, where individual quarrels can defile the eucharistic sacrifice.

441 3:17; 10:1–13; and the full discussion in chap. III of the *topos* that factionalism destroys. In fact the punishment has already begun (11:30). Trompf, 198–201 correctly points to the connections between 10:1–11:2 and 11:17–34, but this should not be taken as an argument against the authenticity of 11:3–16, or for partition (so Klauck, *Herrenmahl*, 286, with further references).

442 "To discern the body, to esteem Christ's body in its peculiarity, means to understand that the body of Christ given for us and received in the sacrament unites the recipients in the 'body' of the congregation and makes them responsible for one another in love" (Bornkamm, "Lord's Supper," 149, see also p. 152 on the connection with ch. 12–14, and "Understanding of Worship," 168–69). For the same viewpoint see Conzelmann, 202 n. 104: "We offend against the Lord because we offend against his body, the community" (among other scholars who hold this position are Klauck, "Eucharistie," 7; Barton, 241–42). This argument works rhetorically because in 10:16–17 Paul laid down the premises which also function in this later argument.

443 On the proliferation of judgement terminology here (and in Rom 14–15), see Conzelmann, 203; Klauck, *Herrenmahl*, 323–24; on the theme see Bornkamm, "Lord's Supper," 150. Could this be related to the different kinds of food which they ate in the meal proper, thus related to the idol meat controversy in some way? (see possibly Barrett, *First Corinthians*, 261; cf. Theissen, 159).

444 Prümm, 211.

judgement awaits.[445] Some elements of Paul's advice on community worship will have to wait until he is with them (11:34).[446] They may simply not be pertinent to the present argument for church unity.[447]

(c) 12:1–14:40. Spiritual Gifts and Unity

Still under the third section of proof which deals with manifestations of Corinthian factionalism during worship assemblies, Paul turns to a third, most divisive issue: the importance and proper employment of spiritual gifts.[448] We have seen already in 1:18–4:21, and elsewhere in the argument, that there are disputes in the church community in Corinth over the possession of such gifts as wisdom and knowledge. 12:1–14:40 deals in particular with such debated gifts, and notably with the gift of speaking in tongues.[449] As in any social body, members of the church possess different talents, different outward and public manifestations of their worthiness and importance for the social whole. As might be expected on purely sociological grounds, this has resulted in divisiveness in the church at Corinth,[450] to which Paul responds with arguments for unity and concord which appropriately mirror and address the underlying political nature and consequences of this set of problems. His argument begins with a first treatment of spiritual gifts, followed by an exemplary argument (in this case of love as the most valuable gift of all for the church) and again a return to the specific use of spiritual gifts within the context of community worship in chap. 14. Throughout this subsection of proof Paul once again urges the church to pursue concord, in this instance in regard to their worship assemblies. Though the unity of this section has been questioned by some partition theorists,[451] this

---

445 Cf. *1 Clem.* 21.1.

446 This is not an announcement of visit plans which should come at the end of a letter (Schmithals, "Korintherbriefe," 281). It is understandable that he needs to be present to deal with some of these issues (with Merklein, 175–76; see also above on the perils of advising by letter).

447 The inverse is also true. The topics which Paul chose to deal with in 1 Cor are those which constitute manifestations of Corinthian factionalism.

448 Περὶ δὲ τῶν πνευματικῶν introduces the topic for the whole subsection 12:1–14:40. The adjective could be neuter or masculine, in which case the topic is "spiritual people." Both are equally possible since in this section Paul's whole point is that gifts are incarnated in individuals and cannot be evaluated apart from their value for the social whole.

449 See Chrys.'s description of this argument: οὕτω καὶ εἰς τὸν περὶ τῶν χαρισμάτων ἐκβαίνει λόγον, καὶ τὴν φιλονεικίαν διορθοῦται τὴν καὶ ἐντεῦθεν γινομένην (*hom. in I Cor.* 29.1 [*PG* 61.241]; and also on 12:4ff., ὥστε τὴν ἐντεῦθεν γενομένην διάστασιν ἀνελεῖν [29.2 (61.245)]).

450 Neyrey, 149–51. See also Meeks, *Urban Christians*, 119–22 on spiritual gifts as a "currency of social power." Meeks also hints at the possible implications of this social reality: "Tantalizing, too, is the question whether the factions addressed in the first four chapters of 1 Corinthians had anything to do with the problem of 'spiritual gifts' discussed in chapters 12–14" (p. 121).

451 The major issue in the discussions of the unity of this section is the placement of ch. 13 (actually 12:31b–13:13). Several partition theorists keep 12:1–31a; 12:31b–13:13 and 14:1–40 in

study will lend support to the many who argue for its integrity with new arguments on the basis of its unified and coherent response to the phenomenon of Corinthian divisions, and its rhetorical strategy which is paralleled in other texts which urge concord on divided groups.

(i) *12:1–31a. Spiritual Gifts, First Treatment. The Body of Christ: Corinthian Unity in Diversity*

Paul counters Corinthian division surrounding spiritual gifts and status by appealing to unity most explicitly in the argument in chap. 12. In 12:3 Paul relativizes all claims to greater or lesser spiritual attainment because of ecstatic gifts by saying that every Christian is indeed a spiritual person,[452] because every Christian who makes the common acclamation Κύριος Ἰησοῦς (cf. 8:6) shows

---

the same letter (the *Antwortbrief*), but rearrange the order (Weiss argues for it to follow ch. 8 [*Korintherbrief*, 309–11], which ignores the fact that 13:1–2, 8 deals with tongues and prophecy, the topic of chaps. 12 and 14 [with Harnack, 135 n. 2], while Schmithals, *Gnosticism*, 95 n. 23; *idem*, "Korintherbriefe," 268–69; and Schenk, 226–229 break with him and take 12:31b–13:13 to have originally followed ch. 14). Against these arguments in themselves, we must note several counterarguments (other positive arguments for the unity of the section will be offered below). First of all, the subjective element involved in making these decisions of literary integrity must be recognized. See, for example, Schmithals's argument: "thus chap. 13, which clearly represents a climax, has *a proper place* in conjunction with the statements περὶ δὲ τῶν πνευματικῶν, which now [when he moves chap. 13 to follow chap. 14] move in a *sensible progression*" (*Gnosticism*, 95 n. 23, emphasis added; note that he refers next to the "senseless rearrangement" created by the editor). The attempt to buttress this impressionistic argument on "formal" grounds is also unsuccessful. Schenk's application of the observation about the presence and absence of περὶ δέ for making literary-critical decisions ultimately involves him in a contradiction when it contravenes against where he wants to put chap. 13: "I Cor 15 unterbricht die Beantwortung der brieflichen Anfragen wirklich, während Kap. 13 das nur scheinbar tut" (p. 225). In addition, the same argument which Schmithals uses again Weiss's transposition of chap. 13 after chap. 8 can be used against him and others who wish to move chap. 13 from its present position (as we have argued often in this study): "Er konstatiert 'ausserordentlich nahe Beziehungen' von Kap. 13 zu Kap. 8, eine richtige Beobachtung, die aber nur die gleiche Situation, das heisst denselben Brief, nicht aber eine *direkte* literarische Verbindung anzeigt" ("Korintherbriefe," 268, emphasis original).

Besides these partition theories, Schenke-Fischer alone have put ch. 13 in the *Vorbrief*, thus apart from chaps. 12 and 14 entirely (93–94; see also their n. 3 on p. 106, where they are attracted to the hypothesis of a non-Pauline origin of the passage). However, many scholars who divide 1 Cor into a set of letters do not contest the unity of chaps. 12–14 but instead consider those chapters to constitute a coherent argument (Goguel, 72–86; Héring, xiv [but see also p. 134]; Dinkler, "Korintherbriefe," 18 [following Bultmann]; Suhl, 208; Senft, 19, 165–66; Klauck, *1. Korintherbrief*, 93; Pesch, 92, 234–36; Sellin, "Hauptprobleme," 2984, 3010). For summaries of the partition arguments on 1 Cor 12–14 see Wischmeyer, *Weg*, 16–22, 27–38 (whose study is a comprehensive defense of the unity of this section and of its Pauline origin); Merklein, 176–77; Sellin, "Hauptprobleme," 2984, 3008–10.

452 Standaert, "Analyse Rhétorique," 31, takes 12:3 to be the proposition of ch. 12–14, which is a compelling suggestion. The rest of his disposition must, however, be questioned. 12:1–11 is no exordium, nor is 12:12–27 a narration. This is an argument within a larger composition, so it cannot be analyzed as a separate speech (see the critique in chap. I n. 52).

that she or he is possessed by the holy spirit.[453] In 12:4–11 Paul presents his Christian version of a most common appeal to counter factionalism: the argument that each person has his or her own individual gifts and roles to play, each of which in its own way benefits the community.[454] Paul even uses the proper technical language for this argument for political unity despite differentiation: ἑκάστῳ δὲ δίδοται . . . πρὸς τὸ συμφέρον. As throughout the deliberative proof in the letter body of 1 Corinthians, Paul continues to urge the Corinthians to seek the common good – in this instance in regard to their exercise of spiritual gifts in the worship assembly. The different personal gifts and roles here named are distinctly Christian: a word of wisdom, a word of knowledge, faith, gifts of healing, works of miracles, prophecy, discerning of spiritual gifts, types of tongues and interpretation of tongues. They are also, not coincidentally, the very gifts which are at the center of Corinthian controversy.[455] The parallelism of 12:4–6 reverberates back to 8:6 in its emphasis on Corinthian unity in the same spirit, the same Lord, and the same God. How can there be discord in the church when there is unity in these strongest of forces?[456] Paul repeats this refrain in a doubly emphatic way in 12:11: if it is *one and the same spirit* who apportions the gifts to each, then how can there possibly be divisions among the church members about what are, in fact, only manifestations (φανερώσεις) of the same spiritual status which all share as members of Christ? The differences between members are not only natural, but have in fact been divinely ordained and sanctioned.[457]

From the unity in the same spirit Paul turns next to the complementary image[458] of the body of Christ to continue his argument for the mutual interdependence of all Corinthian Christians. We have demonstrated in chap. III that Paul's Christian version of the body image, the body of Christ, is an exact correlative of its Greco-Roman counterparts not only in its details, but especially in its application: to demonstrate the interrelatedness of all members in one body

---

453 With Pearson, 47–50, against Schmithals, *Gnosticism*, 124–30. We also note, with Meeks, *Urban Christians*, 166, that in 12:1–3 Paul argues (again) for Christian unity in separation from outsiders.

454 See the documentation for this in chap. III. Paul makes the same argument in Rom 12:3–8.

455 See chap. III on the divisive impact of exclusive claims to possess σοφία and γνῶσις, and of exhibitions of γλῶσσαι.

456 Chrys. describes this unifying argument as τὸ φάρμακον τὸ καθολικὸν τῆς παραμυθίας (*hom. in I Cor.* 29.3 [*PG* 61.244]).

457 διαιροῦν ἰδίᾳ ἑκάστῳ καθὼς βούλεται (12:11). This argument is found frequently in 1 Cor. The same sentiment is expressed in 7:17 (ἑκάστῳ ὡς ἐμέρισεν ὁ κύριος) and 12:18 (ὁ θεὸς ἔθετο τὰ μέλη, ἓν ἕκαστον αὐτῶν ἐν τῷ σώματι καθὼς ἠθέλησεν); cf. 15:38. Even the mix of the individuals which results (12:24) was God's choice. One should therefore accept one's lot.

458 The connection is made in 12:13.

politic in order to urge concord and end factionalism.[459] Paul places his full exposition of this image for unity here because this proof section (11:2–14:40) deals with relations within the group at worship where the resulting mutual interdependence despite differentiation is so appropriate.[460] In 12:12–27 Paul sets up and executes this full exemplification of the church as the body of Christ.[461] His exposition evidences the same reconciliatory strategy we have seen before, as first in his personification of the strife between the members he counsels the "unglorious members" that they are not any less part of the body than the "glorious" (12:15–17), and then he turns and counsels the "glorious members" that they cannot do without the "unglorious" who are necessary for their very livelihood (12:22–24).[462] The source of this necessary interdependence for concord is God, who correctly "mixed" the very constitution of the church body with the purpose in mind that there should be no factionalism (ἵνα μὴ ᾖ σχίσμα ἐν τῷ σώματι, 12:25).[463] In 12:26, once again with εἴτε . . . εἴτε[464] the two sides of this Corinthian contention over spiritual gifts are urged to reconciliation. The pain of the "unglorious" at feeling inferior to the "glorious" should in fact be shared by the glorious, not inflicted upon them or rejoiced over. Likewise, the glory of the "glorious" should also be shared by the "unglorious," for as members of the same body they too should rejoice because they are honored by the honor given to a fellow member. The members of the concordant body are united in both grief and joy, which is another *topos* in texts urging concord, often in conjunction with the body metaphor, as here in Paul's argument.

With v. 27 as a transition, in 12:28–31a Paul presents even more concrete consequences of this teaching for ecclesial unity. For the sake of concord and order in the church, God has ordained a limited hierarchy of roles and functions,

---

459 See the full treatment in chap. III. Barth called 1 Cor 12 Paul's "urgent exhortation to *unity*" (p. 69).

460 But Paul had alluded to the body image in 6:15–16 in regard to the relations between insiders and outsiders to urge exclusiveness for harmony, another application of this image to a different facet of the same problem. We have also noticed that Paul's description of Corinthian σχίσματα, μεμέρισται ὁ Χριστός, is predicated on the presupposition of Christian unity in the body of Christ (see chap. III n. 109).

461 As with Menenius Agrippa, Paul's adaptation of the fable "bore a close resemblance to the situation of the moment" (Dion. Hal. *Ant. Rom.* 6.83.2).

462 For this interpretation see throughout Chrys. *hom. in I Cor.* 29–31 [*PG* 61.239–64].

463 The connection between the mixed constitution and ὁμόνοια has been demonstrated in chap. III. The opposite of factionalism is the general principle in 12:25: τὸ αὐτὸ ὑπὲρ ἀλλήλων μεριμνῶσιν τὰ μέλη, which is exemplified twice in the next verse. This description is identical with "not seeking one's own advantage." See Chrys.'s comment on the verse: Οὐ γὰρ ἵνα μὴ ἀποσχίζηται μόνον ἀλλήλων, οὕτως ᾠκονόμησεν ὁ Θεός, ἀλλ' ἵνα καὶ ἀγάπη ᾖ καὶ ὁμόνοια (*hom. in I Cor.* 31.2 [*PG* 61.260]). The same connection with concord in 12:25 is made by Photius: εἶτα ταῦτα εἰπὼν πάλιν συμβιβάζει αὐτοὺς εἰς τὴν ὁμοτιμίαν καὶ ὁμόνοιαν, ἵνα μὴ ᾖ, φησί, σχίσμα ἐν τῷ σώματι κτλ. [Staab, 572].

464 See n. 392 above.

corresponding to the distribution of gifts argued for in 12:4–12.[465] It is no accident that here the gift of tongues comes last (12:28; cf. 12:10), for it is the spiritual gift which has caused the most friction in the group, due to its public and separatist nature.[466] Just as at the beginning of this argument Paul urged that each Christian is a spiritual person because her or his confession that Jesus is Lord must be fueled by the one same spirit, Paul now turns to another argument for the democratization of spiritual gifts against those who see a pecking order of spiritual social status. The most important spiritual gift is not the divisive tongues, but a gift which all can possess, love. Love is the spiritual gift[467] which unifies the body. Thus, if you are going to be zealous or contentious, Paul counsels the Corinthians, be so in your attempt to manifest even more than the others this concordant behavior which is in reality the greatest spiritual gift: love.[468]

(ii) 12:31b–14:1a. *Exemplary Argument: The Gift of Love as the Antidote to Factionalism*

In this sub-argument Paul presents ἀγάπη as the highest gift which he urges the Corinthians to pursue, as is clear from its full conclusion in 14:1a: διώκετε τὴν ἀγάπην. Those who have sought to defend the unity of 1 Cor 12–14 have rightly pointed to the fact that throughout chap. 13 Paul's focus remains on the competing spiritual gifts of γνῶσις, γλῶσσαι and προφητεῖαι which are the subject of chaps. 12 and 14.[469] Further demonstration of the argumentative coherence of 1 Cor 12–13 is provided by Rom 12, where Paul again turns from the body image directly to love. The objection that 1 Cor 14 does not fit with chap. 13 because the word ἀγάπη is not used there[470] is easily refuted because in the syllogism of 8:1 Paul had already explicitly equated ἀγάπη with the οἰκοδομή, which figures prominently in the argument in chap. 14.[471] Other elements of Paul's description of love in chap. 13, such as its not seeking its own advantage, and its not rejoicing in wickedness but co-rejoicing in the truth, echo parts of

---

465 Notice that only the first three are numbered, and thus stand apart from the others in importance.

466 It will be further devalued in chaps. 13 and 14.

467 12:9; Gal 5:22.

468 This is the force of ζηλοῦτε in 12:31 and 14:1. We have demonstrated in chap. III that the call to the audience to rechannel their fractious energies in a positive direction for the sake of the greater social good is a *topos* in arguments which urge concord. This interpretation allows us to see much more clearly (*pace* the partition theorists) the smooth and natural rhetorical connection between 12:31 a and 14:1, which enclose the exemplification of love (for scholarly discussion on the exegesis and function of these verses see Wischmeyer, *Weg*, 31–38). Chrys. makes the same argument for positive ζῆλος in his exegesis of 1 Cor 12 (*hom. in I Cor.* 31.4 [*PG* 61.263–64]).

469 Allo, 341; Grosheide, 303; Hurd, 112–13, 189–90; Bruce, 124; Standaert, "1 Corinthiens 13"; Wolff, 118; Merklein, 176–77; Fee, *First Corinthians*, 626–28.

470 Weiss, *Korintherbrief*, 310; Senft, 165–66 (of course, this is outside of 14:1!).

471 Also Bornkamm, "Understanding of Worship," 165.

Paul's advice in chap. 12 (12:7, 26). It has furthermore been correctly observed how much 1 Cor 13 ties in with the whole of 1 Corinthians.[472]

Even though several scholars have understood 1 Cor 13 as intimately connected with the specific situation which Paul was combatting at Corinth, the full force of this argument has not been illuminated because they have presumed that Paul was combatting merely "Corinthian enthusiasm" or "gnosticism."[473] In chap. III we have presented evidence for two important conclusions relative to the interpretation of 1 Cor 13. First of all, there it was demonstrated that throughout Greco-Roman antiquity love was considered to be the opposite of and indeed the antidote to factionalism. Therefore, even though Paul's own teaching on love was surely founded on particular Jewish and Christian grounds, its application by him here to the specific problem of inner-group contention (as also in other Hellenistic Jewish writers) is fully understandable and appropriate. Nevertheless, this argument alone is not conclusive unless it can be documented for this particular text. But we have demonstrated exegetically in chap. III that in fact each one of the epithets of love in 1 Cor 13:4–7 (8a), from both a lexical and a rhetorical point of view, constitutes a direct response to Corinthian factionalism as described by Paul throughout this letter (and factionalism as described and caricatured in other ancient writings). This means that 1 Cor 13 is a logical and coherent piece of Paul's argument for church unity. Our purpose now is to turn from these prior exegetical conclusions to enter into the discussion of the formal composition of 1 Cor 13.

The genre and composition of 1 Cor 13 have been the subject of intense study and debate.[474] The chapter has been called variously a hymn,[475] a speech,[476] a paraenetic exhortation,[477] an encomium,[478] a digression,[479] a *Wertepriamel* ("ex-

---

[472] Hurd, 112–13; Klauck, *1. Korintherbrief*, 93, 95; Wischmeyer, *Weg*, 228 and passim; and my full exegetical treatment above in chap. III.

[473] Spicq, 2.53–120; Wolff, 118; Wischmeyer, *Weg*, 228, 233.

[474] For overviews see Spicq, 2.59–63; Conzelmann, 217–31; Wischmeyer, *Weg*, 191–223. The survey by J. T. Sanders, "First Corinthians 13, Its Interpretation Since the First World War," *Int* 20 (1966) 159–87 is marred by the author's apologetics and his neglect of Catholic scholarship.

[475] Robertson-Plummer, xxiv, 285 ("A Psalm in Praise of Love"); Godet, 2.234; Héring, 135; Allo, 340 ("une sorte de poème, d'hymne, de psaume"). This view was contested influentially by Weiss, *Korintherbrief*, 311.

[476] Often quoted is Harnack's observation that 1 Cor is not poetry or a hymn, but "Rede" (153 n. 4).

[477] Spicq, 2.59–63. See also Johnson, *Writings*, 288: "Chapter 13 is not a digression but serves the paraenetic function of presenting Paul as a model of 'seeking the higher gifts' (12:31; cf. 9:1–27)"; cf. Jeremias, 156 ("Erläuterung").

[478] See Spicq, 2.62 on ἐγκώμιον συγκριτκόν (he connects it with the priamel), and his general conclusion on p. 63: "On peut conclure, par conséquent, que s'il est vain de dépister dans I Cor. XIII un emprunt direct à une source littéraire juive ou profane, il est assuré que saint Paul, pour mettre en valeur l'excellence de la charité, s'est conformé à l'usage de la rhétorique classique, rédigeant sa composition sur le type traditionnel des éloges de vertus." Other scholars

emplary discourse on the highest values"),[480] didactic wisdom teaching,[481] and most recently a "religiös-ethischer λόγος."[482] The question of the genre of this text, which is entirely interconnected with its originality of composition, placement and even authenticity,[483] has been advanced in recent years by Conzelmann's insistence that the chapter is itself not a unity, but is made up of three subsections or sub-forms, vv. 1–3, 4–7 and 8–13.[484] This observation became an important methodological mandate in Wischmeyer's recent detailed analysis of 1 Cor 13, whose survey of the debate on the genre of 1 Cor 13 correctly concludes that while each of the theories proposed may account for one or two of the subsections, they flounder when they try to account for the whole of the chapter.[485] Her solution, which may be the best to date, understands the two subsections 13:1–3 and 8–13 as each a *Wertepriamel*, but takes 13:4–7 to be a *Bekenntnisreihe* ("a succession of confessions") on the abstract ethical good, love.[486] To the whole final composition she then applies the compositional

promoting this view include Hurd, 189 ("panegyric on love"); Vielhauer, *Geschichte*, 70 ("der Preis der Liebe"), as earlier Schmiedel, 170 and Heinrici, *Korinther*, 396 (alongside other designations, among which is *exemplum* [358, 396]); Kennedy, *New Testament Interpretation*, 18, 156 ("an encomium of charity/love"); Lang, 181; and Strobel, 200.

479 Weiss, *Korintherbrief*, 311 (that is, in its present position); Kümmel, 278; Wuellner, "Greek Rhetoric," 187–88; Standaert, "1 Corinthiens 13"; *idem*, "Analyse Rhétorique," 29–30; Fee, *First Corinthians*, 626.

480 Jaeger, "Tyrtaeus"; U. Schmid, *Die Priamel der Werte im Griechischen von Homer bis Paulus* (Wiesbaden: Harrassowitz, 1964) 118–38; his definition of this form is on pp. ix-xi (see also Wischmeyer, *Weg*, 196). But note that Schmid does not oppose this view to the description of 1 Cor 13 as a "hymn," but sees it as compatible (118–19, 138).

481 Conzelmann, 217–31.

482 Wischmeyer, *Weg*, 217–223 (she admits that this is a rather broad designation [p. 222], but finds it more helpful than other rigidly defined categories).

483 Some have argued that 1 Cor 13 is a separate Pauline composition which he incorporated here (Schmid, 136, who claims consensus for this point of view; Barrett, *First Corinthians*, 297, 299; correctly rejected by Wolff, 118; Wischmeyer, *Weg*, 224, among others). A few scholars have thought that it is non-Pauline (E. Lehmann and A. Fridrichsen, "1 Kor. 13. Eine christlich-stoische Diatribe," *TSK* Sonderheft [1922] 55–95; E. L. Titus, "Did Paul Write I Corinthians 13?" *JBR* 27 [1959] 299–302).

484 Conzelmann, 218. Where he errs, in my judgement, is in thinking that 1 Cor 13 can be understood apart from its context.

485 *Weg*, 205–207. She sums up her judgement and method thusly: "Denn die Teile des Kapitels ... haben auch ihre eigenen Formen. Diese kleineren Formen müssen zunächst bestimmt werden. Diese Differenz zwischen den Teilformen und der Gesamtform ist in der Forschung nicht hinreichend klar beobachtet worden" (207).

486 Ibid., 207–217 (following G. von Rad, "Die Vorgeschichte der Gattung von 1. Kor. 13,4–7," *Geschichte und Altes Testament*, FS A. Alt, ed. W. F. Albright, *et al.*, BHT 16 [Tübingen: Mohr/Siebeck, 1953] 153–68). The best part of von Rad's analysis is his pointing to passages from *T. 12 Patr.* as good parallels to 1 Cor 13:4–7 (pp. 153–58), where he speaks of the *Aussagenreihe*. Where he later connects this genre with the earlier *Bekenntnisreihe* of the Israelite cult his argument is less convincing. Though the stylistic parallels between *T. 12 Patr.* and 1 Cor 13 are surely significant (a row of asyndetic short sentences with indicative verbs and the same subject), the genre *Bekenntnisreihe* does not solve the larger question of the composition of 1 Cor

designation "religös-ethischer λόγος."[487] While founded on many good observations, Wischmeyer's thesis inevitably becomes too complicated, when fully *four different genre designations* are required to account for only these thirteen verses! Although she correctly regards 1 Cor 13 as an integral part of all of 1 Corinthians, her overall view of the whole composition as merely a "letter"[488] perhaps obscures the extent to which the argumentative structure of this chapter can be understood in a way more coherent with not only the content, but also the rhetorical strategy of the whole.[489]

The present study has argued that 1 Corinthians is throughout a deliberative argument. The very purpose of a deliberative argument, as we have demonstrated in chap. II, is to persuade its listeners to undertake a particular course of action in the future on the grounds that it is the most advantageous course (among various options) to follow. Significantly, this is the exact same definition which Wischmeyer gives to the sub-genre *Wertepriamel*, to which she assigns 13:1–3 and 8–13: "Antwort auf die Frage: 'was nützt jetzt wirklich dem Menschen.'"[490] But since Paul has argued for the advantageous course of action throughout 1 Corinthians,[491] when he does so explicitly in 13:1–3 (οὐδὲν ὠφελοῦμαι), and in 13:8–13, where he appeals to the eschatological advantage over present transitory goods,[492] we can see that this is fully consonant with the rhetorical species and strategy of the whole argument.[493] This receives further confirmation from the fact that, as so often throughout the proof of 1 Corinthians, Paul here appeals to *himself* as the example to be imitated (13:1–3, but here he is a hypothetical negative example to be rejected;[494] 13:10–11). Consequently the exemplary function of these verses, which has also been attributed to the specific *Wertepriamel* form,[495] is more easily understood as yet another deliberative argument by

---

13 because it fits neither 1 Cor 13 nor the passages from *T. 12 Patr.* in their present form. Note also that von Rad proceeds *from the assumption* that 13:4–7 is not a free composition by Paul (p. 153).

487 *Weg*, 217–223.

488 Ibid., 222–23.

489 Although Wischmeyer rightly considers the place of chap. 13 within chaps. 12–14, in my view her study does not sufficiently reckon also with the generic contours of the rhetorical whole (as argued on methodological grounds above in chap. I).

490 Ibid., 213 (see also 208).

491 See chap. II. In this connection Chrys.'s discussion of the different reading at 12:31 is interesting: Καὶ οὐκ εἶπε, Τὰ μείζονα, ἀλλὰ, Τὰ κρείττονα, τουτέστι, τὰ χρησιμώτερα, τὰ συμφέροντα (*hom. in I Cor.* 32.3 [*PG* 61.267]).

492 Wischmeyer, *Weg*, 213–17, 226–27, as before her Schmid, 127–33.

493 Thus the argument of Lehmann-Fridrichsen, 72–73 that this is an imported Stoic argument (cf. Spicq, 2. 114 n. 2), and therefore non-Pauline, is refuted.

494 This is a rhetorical strategy used repeatedly throughout 1 Cor (6:15b; 9:16–17; 14:6, 11, 14; 15:14–15, 20, 32). One should look at Pauline parallels first; the conditionals in LXX Ps 138:8 (or those in the Tyrtaeus fragment) cited by Schmid, 120–22 are not really parallel to 1 Cor 13:1–3.

495 Schmid, 118–19, 126 and passim; Wischmeyer, *Weg*, 208–209, 213–17.

appeal to example. Seen in this way there is no need to postulate separate individual genres for 13:1–3 and 8–13. These two subsections continue the deliberative argument of the letter,[496] providing another instance of an exemplary argument in which Paul sets forth the general principles by which in the surrounding sections of advice he urges church unity.[497]

This leaves us with the most singular part of the argument in chap. 13, 13:4–7, in which love is the subject. These verses comprise a very brief encomium on love,[498] as many commentators have noted.[499] Love is the subject of a succession of positive and negative epithets. We have noted already the precise correspondence between love's characteristics in 13:4–7 and Paul's description of Corinthian factionalists and the content of his advice for unity.[500] Love is the principle of Christian social unity which Paul urges on the Corinthians.[501] We have also

---

496 This is of course not incompatible with the high style of these verses (note that even Schmid, 130, regards vv. 8–13 to be in the same style as the rest of the letter [cf. Conzelmann, 225 on the style change in vv. 8–13]). With this conclusion we thus return to Harnack on 1 Cor 13 as *Rede* (though he himself favored a Jewish provenance). That 1 Cor 13 is *deliberative argumentation* is a more accurate designation than Wischmeyer's more vague "religiös-ethischer λόγος" (naturally depending upon what one means by λόγος/*Rede*).

497 I thus concur with those (e. g., Jeremias, 156; Kümmel, 278), who point to the similarity with 7:17–24 and ch. 9.

498 This alternative is too quickly rejected by Wischmeyer, *Weg*, 205, 210, by assertion more than argument. See also the false distinctions on which Sanders argues: "Nor is the passage a praise of anything. If it were a praise of *agape*, this alone would be most unusual, since praise is normally given only to God, occasionally and only very rarely to Christ in primitive Christianity. But I Corinthians 13 is far more description than praise" ("1 Cor 13," 160). See the discussion above on the role of "description" and "narration" in praise. Note also that in fact Paul often praises things other than God – like the Corinthians (11:2; 1:4–9)!

499 See n. 478 above (but note that we are referring not to the whole chapter, but to 13:4–7). This interpretation is confirmed by the text's earliest readers. See Origen, *comm. in I Cor.* 51.2: Τὰ ἐγκώμια τῆς ἀγάπης τῆς ὑπερεχούσης τὰ χαρίσματα διεξέρχεται. ἔδει γὰρ αὐτὸν διδάξαι καὶ τί ἐστιν ἀγάπη καὶ πῶς ἐστιν ὁ ἔχων τὴν ἀγάπην [p. 34]. Chrys.'s analysis of the argument from 13:1–7 is precisely what is argued here: Εἶτα μέλλων ἐμβαίνειν εἰς τὸν περὶ αὐτῆς [ἀγάπῆς] λόγον καὶ τὸ ἐγκώμιον τοῦ κατορθώματος τούτου, πρῶτον καθαιρεῖ ταῦτα τῇ πρὸς ἐκείνην συγκρίσει, οὐδὲν ὄντα δεικνὺς ταύτης χωρίς, σφόδρα συνετῶς (*hom. in I Cor.* 32.3 [*PG* 61.267]; cf. 34.3, on 13:13, Ἕτερον πάλιν ἐγκώμιον τῆς ἀγάπης [61.289]).

500 See chap. III. On these grounds I do not think that ch. 13 was an originally separate composition (see n. 483 above). It is hard to see why in an abstract or generalist praise of love one would naturally introduce a contrast with knowledge, prophecy and tongues. This is an argument with the express purpose of demonstrating that love is a higher and more valued spiritual gift than those others, which fits completely with Paul's rhetorical purpose in chaps. 12–14. It is possible that 13:4–7 goes back to some originally separate composition, but even this section's point-by-point correspondence with Paul's argument against factionalism and for unity throughout the letter casts doubt on this hypothesis also. Because of its rhetorical appropriateness and continuity here (and because of the definitional problems as discussed above on 1 Cor 9), I do not take 1 Cor 13 to be a digression, but instead an exemplary argument.

501 Ὥστε καὶ κατὰ τοῦτο εἰκότως ἂν μεγάλη φανείη, εἴ γε τὰ μὲν χαρίσματα οὐ μόνον αὐτοὺς οὐ συνήγαγεν, ἀλλὰ καὶ ἡνωμένους διέστησαν. αὕτη δὲ τοὺς δι' ἐκείνων διαστάντας δι' ἑαυτῆς μέλλοι συνάγειν καὶ ποιεῖν σῶμα ἕν (Chrys., *hom. in I Cor.* 32.3 [*PG* 61.268]). The

previously observed the extent to which deliberative arguments employ praise and blame. In 1 Cor 13:4–7, unlike 1:18–4:21 or 11:2, 17, 22, the subject of the praise or blame is not the Corinthians, but the particular course of action which Paul urges the Corinthians to undertake, love. Here love is personified as Paul names its positive behaviors and outcomes, and implicitly extols the values of unity and peace it preserves.[502] Our conclusion, that 13:4–7 contains a small encomium[503] within the deliberative argument for unity which appeals to love as the principle by which concord will be achieved, receives further confirmation when we turn to other discourses on concord. There we see that in fact small encomia on the highest abstract good are often found within deliberative discourses[504] to illustrate in general terms the impulse for unity which the orator persuades the audience to follow in a given situation.[505] In particular in the Greco-Roman speeches and letters which urge concord we find encomia to ὁμόνοια (and their opposite, vituperations of στάσις). For example, Aristides' *Or.* 24 contains a proof section devoted to "Praise of Concord."[506]

Concord alone preserves the order of the seasons which are given by Zeus, alone confirms all things, adorning the countryside with farming and granting profit from one's property along with additional possessions, while in the city it conducts affairs as one would pray for, for through it there are seasonable offers of marriage to be given and received, to

---

argument of Lehmann-Fridrichsen, 60–65, that love in 1 Cor 13 is not "social-active" as it is in Paul's genuine writings, but is "an individual moral self-affirmation," misses the entirely ecclesiological, corporate focus of this argument.

502 Love has the same power in the more general paraenesis of Rom 12:9–21.

503 It does not contain the whole chronological scheme of an encomium (on which see above on 1:18–4:21), but is a terse, abbreviated list of what is especially relevant to this argument. There is no need to think that Paul said all that he could have about love here, which is the difficulty of commentators who fear, *ex silentio*, that Paul may not be talking about love for God here. That is correct, he isn't (but he does discuss it elsewhere, where relevant).

504 The common use of praise and blame in deliberative rhetoric has been demonstrated above in this chapter.

505 And to dissuade them from the other possible courses of action. It is on this point that Spicq's mention of the ἐγκώμιον συγκριτικόν is attractive: "l'éloge de la plus grande vertu ou du bien suprême est un lieu commun des discussions entre sages et de la prédication philosophique populaire. D'une part, on se demande quelle est la plus grande, ou la plus puissante, ou la plus advantageuse, ou la meilleure chose du monde, et c'est spécialement au cours des banquets que l'on se pose de semblables apories" (2.62). The difficulty with this parallel is of course the change of *Sitz im Leben*. Surely 1 Cor 13 is not an idle speculation on the highest value at a banquet or other such conversational or school setting, so one must presuppose that that genre could be transformed into other settings in order to make it relevant for 1 Cor 13 (it seems to me that the *Wertepriamel* is also open to this critique). But if one looks at the list of "standards" Spicq names for these debates in popular philosophy, they are of course our list of standard deliberative appeals (see chap. II). Thus in deliberative rhetoric we have the conduit which we seek between the noted parallels in philosophical speculation on the highest good and their concrete application to human decision making in argumentation, which is what we find in 1 Cor 13.

506 24.41–44 (following the analysis of Behr, 2.369). This same speech also has an extended section "Concord an indisputable good: traditional evidence" in § 4-21.

whom and from whom one wishes, and the raising of children, and education according to ancestral custom, and for women there is security, and there is faith in keeping contracts, and the reception of guests, and the worship of the gods, and processions, and choruses and pleasures . . . (24.42).[507]

After a call to seek these advantages which concord brings, Aristides gives a full and vivid personification of both ὁμόνοια and στάσις in terms of their appearance (not their behavior, as above):

Then as if some painter had set forth pictures of both, you must gaze at each in turn: the one shapely, compact, with good complexion, charming, throughout harmonious in every detail, and come from the gods to earth; but the other the bitterest of all sights, with head flung back, livid lips, cross-eyed, puffy, ever encompassed with new shed tears, with palsied hands, carrying in concealment a sword at her breast, raised up on thin, bandy legs, with gloom and darkness surrounding her, like a net, because she dwells mostly in tombs instead of temples – gazing at these images, it is fitting thus to make your choice, by examining at leisure with which of the two it is better to live. Indeed, it is worth everything for all mankind to work seriously for concord [καὶ μὴν ἅπασι μὲν ἀνθρώποις τοῦ παντὸς ἄξιον σπουδάζειν ὑπὲρ τῆς ὁμονοίας], but it needs not much argument to show how worthwhile it is for you beyond all the others . . . (24.44–45).

Aristides' deliberative argument incorporates an encomium to concord alongside a vituperation of discord, followed by an exhortation to his audience to seek earnestly the object of the praise, not the blame.[508] This rhetorical strategy is also used by Dio Chrysostom in his *Or.* 38, *To the Nicomedians on Concord with the Nicaeans*:

But I want to break up my address, and first of all to speak about concord itself in general [ὑπὲρ αὐτῆς εἰπεῖν τῆς ὁμονοίας τῆς καθόλου], telling both whence it comes and what it achieves, and then over against that to set off strife and hatred [στάσις καὶ ἔχθρα] in contradistinction to friendship [φιλία]. For when concord has been proved to be beneficial [ὠφέλιμος] to all mankind, the proof will naturally follow that this particular concord between these particular cities is both quite indispensable for you and quite profitable [λυσιτελεστάτη] as well (38.8).

In the proof section which follows (38.10–20), Dio introduces what he will do as praise,[509] and follows with a (rather convoluted) discussion of the praises of concord and the damage done by discord.[510]

---

507 This passage had the typical epideictic opening: "The arguments which one could make on behalf of the other side, concord [ὁμόνοια], already are found in innumerable writers. . . ."

508 Similar arguments are also used in his *Or.* 23.27–40 "Exhortation. Advantages of concord. Disadvantages of faction" (analysis Behr, 2.365).

509 See the terms ἐπαινεῖν and ἐγκωμιάζειν in 38.10.

510 See also his *Or.* 41.13–14, which begins a praise of concord (φιλίας δὲ καὶ ὁμονοίας οὐδὲν κάλλιον οὐδὲ θειότερον), but the speech breaks off soon thereafter. For another example, see the speech of Tullius recounted in Dion. Hal. *Ant. Rom.* 4.26.2: "[he] made a long speech exhorting them to concord [λόγον διεξῆλθε παρακλητικὸν ὁμονοίας], pointing out

Paul's argument for church concord uses the same rhetorical strategy as these authors, but with its distinctly Christian accent on ἀγάπη as the very source of ecclesial social unity. In his argument in 13:4–7 he presents an abbreviated encomium to personified ἀγάπη which in its positive statements praises its unmatchable force for unity, and in its negated statements contains an implicit vituperation of discord, the behavior of the Corinthians.[511] Once again this understanding of Paul's rhetorical strategy in 1 Cor 13 receives further confirmation from the way in which it was interpreted in the early church. The author of *1 Clement*, who himself constructs a deliberative argument for concord, imitates Paul in incorporating an encomium to love in his argument (ch. 49),[512] and makes even more explicit in his terminology what is already there in the work of his predecessor:

ἀγάπη κολλᾷ ἡμᾶς τῷ θεῷ, ἀγάπη καλύπτει πλῆθος ἁμαρτιῶν, ἀγάπη πάντα ἀνέχεται, πάντα μακροθυμεῖ. οὐδὲν βάναυσον ἐν ἀγάπῃ, οὐδὲν ὑπερήφανον. ἀγάπη σχίσμα οὐκ ἔχει, ἀγάπη οὐ στασιάζει, ἀγάπη πάντα ποιεῖ ἐν ὁμονοίᾳ (49.5).[513]

This investigation therefore renders the following (briefly expounded) interpretation of 12:31b–14:1a. The exemplary sub-argument is introduced in 12:31.[514] The "most excellent way" which Paul will demonstrate in the person of himself is love, the highest spiritual gift, the highest Christian good. In 13:1–3 Paul presents a series of three parallel sentences in which he is the hypothetical negative example of one who acts without love. In each case the result of these conditionals points directly to "non-advantage." The one who speaks in tongues without love (the example is not general but very particular to the argument in chaps. 12–14) is like a musical instrument which is out of tune, which emits senseless and irritating noises.[515] For those who prize speaking in tongues as a

---

what a fine thing it is [καλόν] when a number of states agree together [μιᾷ γνώμῃ χρώμεναι] and what a disgraceful sight [αἰσχρά] when kinsmen are at variance."

[511] None of the Greco-Roman examples given above is a stylistic parallel to 1 Cor 13. They are, however, parallel in content (praise of an abstract), in conception (concord and love are respectively the general courses of action named and urged), and in rhetorical function (praise for the course of action which the deliberative argument urges on a specific audience). However, none of the examples which are currently drawn upon in the debate on the composition of 1 Cor 13 is parallel in all three – function, content and style – either (though such identical parallels to singular literary creations are hardly to be routinely expected).

[512] See 49.2–3, where he begins with a standard epideictic opening to this encomiastic sub-argument (and Sanders, "Hellénisme," 93–94): τὸν δεσμὸν τῆς ἀγάπῆς τοῦ θεοῦ τίς δύναται ἐξηγήσασθαι; τὸ μεγαλεῖον τῆς καλλονῆς αὐτοῦ τίς ἀρκετὸς ἐξειπεῖν; τὸ ὕψος, εἰς ὃ ἀνάγει ἡ ἀγάπη, ἀνεκδιήγητόν ἐστιν.

[513] See also the equation in 50.2; 62.2. I thus disagree with Wischmeyer, *Weg*, 213, who states that the author of *1 Clem.* transformed Paul's argument into an encomium. It was an encomium already! Early patristic exegesis also understood love in 1 Cor 13 to be the antidote to factionalism, as we have seen (in chap. III, and in the notes above in this chapter).

[514] Called by Origen τὸ προοίμιον τῶν λόγων (*comm. in I Cor.* 49.10 [p. 32]).

[515] Notice the parallel language in which this argument is taken up again in 14:6–12 (τί ὑμᾶς ὠφελήσω;).

way of displaying their personal talent and glory, this argument is a sharp corrective. In 13:2 the gifts of prophecy, knowledge and faith are also shown to be without advantage to the individual if not accompanied by love (οὐθέν εἰμι). The last example, which may or may not be hyperbolic, as so often in 1 Corinthians again censures boasting,[516] arguing that even such praiseworthy actions as giving away all one's possessions and handing over one's body will bring one no advantage if they are not done in love. The deliberative argument by appeal to advantage is thus fully operative in 13:1–3, in each case stressing that tongues, prophecy, knowledge, faith and heroic acts are not *the most advantageous* thing the Christian should seek.[517] That is love.

In 13:4–7 love is described as the opposite of contentious and discordant behavior. Instead, it is all of the things which will work to promote concord in the community. In particular, love does not seek its own advantage, which is the exact definition of a non-factionalist. In the argument at hand on the meaning and use of spiritual gifts, this means that the one who acts in love takes into account the needs of the other when giving expression to one's spiritual gifts in the worship assembly (as will be illustrated further in chap. 14). This means, as it did in regard to idol meats, both personal compromise (πάντα στέγει, as in 9:12) and endurance of others. 13:8a by style continues the argument in 13:4–7, concluding that love, which builds up the concordant edifice, never falls.[518]

In 13:8–13 Paul turns to arguing the deliberative question of best advantage for the community from a different perspective – that of eschatology. The role which time plays in many arguments for advantage in Greco-Roman antiquity has been noted.[519] For a Christian community such as the Corinthians it is an especially pertinent argument to convince them to forsake present, temporary pleasures for the sake of the greater eschatological good. Paul demonstrates the transitory nature of prophecy and knowledge, as he urges the Corinthians not to be contentious over that which is of lesser importance. In 13:11 he calls upon his personal example once again to urge the Corinthians to put aside, as he has, the things of childhood (τὰ τοῦ νηπίου). Those things are the strife and contentiousness of the Corinthians in their desire to be more prominent spiritual experts than one another (3:1–4). The greatest advantage, however, is to be sought in love (13:13).[520] The argument ends with the call to action, διώκετε τὴν ἀγάπην,

---

[516] On the textual evidence see Harnack, 139–45; B. M. Metzger, *A Textual Commentary on the Greek New Testament* (London/New York: United Bible Societies, 1971) 563–64.

[517] On the common argument that praiseworthy attributes are counted as nothing if not accompanied by concord, see the examples cited in the discussion above on 1 Cor 1:18–4:21.

[518] Surely Chrys. has well understood Paul's continuous use of the building metaphor when he writes of ἀγάπη: Αὕτη τείχους ἰσχυροτέρα, αὕτη ἀδάμαντος στεῤῥοτέρα. κἂν ἑτέραν ταύτης ἰσχυροτέραν εἴπῃς ὕλην, πάντα ὑπερβάλλει τῆς ἀγάπης ἡ στεῤῥότης (*hom. in I Cor.* 32.6 [*PG* 61.272]; see also 33.4 [61.281], ἰσχυρὰ γὰρ ἦν ἡ τῆς ἀγάπης κρηπίς. Διὸ καὶ πάντα στέγει).

[519] See chap. II nn. 32 and 85.

[520] See chap. II n. 31 on the role of comparative adjectives in deliberative arguments.

and a transition in 14:1b to the next sub-argument on the relative advantage of prophecy over speaking in tongues (ζηλοῦτε δὲ τὰ πνευματικά, μᾶλλον δὲ ἵνα προφητεύητε). Even though I have shown that all other gifts are inferior to love, Paul continues, you can still, if you must, "be contentious for spiritual gifts" as long as it is for that which promotes unity, prophecy.[521]

(iii) 14:1b–40. *Spiritual Gifts, Second Treatment. Unity in Diversity of Language*
This argument unit combines the argument of ch. 12 on the unity of the church despite diversity of spiritual gifts with the call in ch. 13 to pursue the greatest gift of love. Next Paul gives a concrete explication of this Christian standard of love as applied to community worship. The concord of the church community at Corinth ironically is threatened in its common worship, which should bring it together, but there instead different languages divide those who should be united. The picture Paul paints of present Corinthian worship in this second treatment of spiritual gifts is of a virtual cacophony of individual expressions which sunder the unity of the body.

Paul's argument in 14:1b–40 is a logical progression of the argument in ch. 12–13, and of his strategy of reconciliation throughout 1 Corinthians. He concedes to the Corinthians their "contentiousness" [ζηλοῦτε/ζηλωταί] for spiritual gifts (14:1, 12, 39; cf. 12:31 a), but attempts to redirect those energies for the sake of the concordant building up of the whole church. His advice is repeated several times in the argument: tongues are acceptable, but not the *best* course of action church members should seek. Best of all is to prophesy,[522] because prophecy unifies the church while tongues divide it (14:6–17). The predominant appeal by which Paul argues for this course of action is thus the appeal to the common advantage,[523] here again named as that which builds up the church (ἡ οἰκοδομὴ

---

[521] In chap. 13 Paul stressed the relative inferiority of even prophecy to love, but he never told them that prophecy should not be exercised or even striven for, just that it should be done with love. The force of the deliberative argument, in which one often argues for one course of action as "more advantageous" than another, lends a helpful insight into this question. One can argue for one course of action as better than another without repudiating that other course of action. "Nor is expediency [*utilia*] compared merely with inexpediency. At times we have to choose between two advantageous courses after comparison of their respective advantages" (Quint. *Inst.* 3.8.33). Paul's allowance of prophecy (and even tongues) in chap. 14, though he has subordinated them to love, does not contradict chap. 13, but is quite clearly a part of his conciliatory strategy.

[522] 14:1, 5 (μᾶλλον δὲ ἵνα προφητεύητε), 5 (μείζων δὲ ὁ προφητεύων ἢ ὁ λαλῶν γλώσσαις), 39 (ζηλοῦτε τὸ προφητεύειν καὶ τὸ λαλεῖν μὴ κωλύετε γλώσσαις). The role of comparative adjectives in deliberative appeals was noted in chap. II n. 31 (see also n. 91 on comparatives in 1 Cor).

[523] Εἶδες πόθεν τὸ ἐξαίρετον δείκνυσι τοῦ χαρίσματος τούτου, ἀπὸ τοῦ κοινῇ συμφέροντος, καὶ πῶς πανταχοῦ τοῦτο προτιμᾷ τὸ εἰς τὴν τῶν πολλῶν ὠφέλειαν γινόμενον; (Chrys. *hom. in I Cor.* 35.1 [*PG* 61.296]; for the commonality of the appeal see also 35.3, 4 [61.299–301], and throughout this homily).

τῆς ἐκκλησίας; 14:3, 4, 5, 12, 17, 26),[524] synonymous with love. The general principle is repeated summarily in 14:26, πάντα πρὸς οἰκοδομὴν γινέσθω (cf. 14:12).[525] The common advantage in liturgical speech (τί ὑμᾶς ὠφελήσω), Paul advises, is measured by its intelligibility, not its dramatic expression (14:6–12). Language which no one can understand is not advantageous but rather fruitless,[526] and causes fellow church members, one's brothers and sisters, to be actually estranged from one another.[527] The other appeal which Paul makes in this argument is once again to his own example,[528] both the hypothetically negative (14:6, 11, 14–15) and his actual self-renunciatory behavior which is to be imitated (14:18–19). Just as he had argued in ch. 8–10, here in ch. 14 Paul urges the Corinthians to curtail the exercise of their own spiritual prowess if it is not to the advantage of the whole church.[529] The issue of spiritual gifts, like those of sexual immorality and idol meat, is severe because it risks dissolving the boundaries of the church community. Paul argues yet again for the inner cohesion of the church by contrast with the outsiders (14:20–25), and for a third time in his argument chides the Corinthians' disputatiousness for spiritual superiority as childishness (14:20).

Very specific advice for unity in the assemblies for worship (ὅταν συνέρχεσθε)[530] follows in 14:26–36. As in ch. 12, Paul admits the inevitable differentiation and distribution of spiritual gifts among the members of the church (14:26), but gives advice for their orderly expression. This advice is for each to give way to the other (personal compromise for the sake of harmony) and to remain silent

---

524 The premise was established in the syllogism of 10:23 (cf. 8:1).

525 See Dautzenberg, *Prophetie*, 254 on this as a general principle. The parallelism with 16:14 is significant also (πάντα ὑμῶν ἐν ἀγάπῃ γινέσθω).

526 Literally so in regard to the mind in 14:14, ἄκαρπος. Note also that Paul's use of the common Hellenistic image of the musical instruments in 14:6–12 parallels his own appropriation of the athletic imagery in 9:24–27 precisely on the point of their usefulness. Compare εἰς ἀέρα λαλοῦντες in 14:9 and ἀέρα δέρων in 9:26; the ἄδηλος φωνή in 14:8 with τρέχω ... ἀδήλως in 9:26. Both are graphic illustrations of actions which are without advantage (see Chrys. on 14:9: Καὶ πανταχοῦ τὸ ἀνωφελὲς δείκνυσι [*hom. in I Cor.* 35.2 (*PG* 61.298)]). For this argument compare Dio Chrys. *Or.* 38.27–28 and the full context (οὗ τί τὸ ὄφελός ἐστιν; 38.29).

527 They become βάρβαροι to one another (on sociological grounds see Neyrey, 151). Common language has immediate and serious consequences for group unity (see discussion and documentation in chap. III).

528 See Chrys. on 14:6: Ταῦτα δὲ λέγει, δεικνὺς ὅτι τὸ ἐκείνοις συμφέρον ζητεῖ ... καὶ ἀεὶ δὲ τὰ φορτικὰ ἐπὶ τοῦ οἰκείου προσώπου γυμνάζει (*hom. in I Cor.* 35.2 [61.297]).

529 Just like the eating of idol meat in ch. 8–10, the exercise of glossolalia is not forbidden in itself, but an even better conciliating course of action is urged. In both cases the rights of an individual to certain behaviors are to be voluntarily compromised for the sake of unity in the social whole.

530 See the exegesis of Thdt.: Πάλιν ἔδειξε τὸ σῶμα καὶ τὰ μέλη τοῦ σώματος. Διὰ γὰρ τοῦ, συνέρχησθε, τὸ ἓν ἔδειξε τὸ σῶμα. διὰ δὲ τοῦ, ἕκαστος ὑμῶν τόδε ἔχει καὶ τόδε, τὴν τῶν μελῶν διαφοράν (*1. Cor.* 14:26 [*PG* 82.344–45]).

while it is others' turn to speak.[531] Because of the nature of ecstatic speech, the Corinthians cannot be a choir of harmonious voices in their common worship. Instead Paul counsels that each should take their turn ἀνὰ μέρος, καθ' ἕνα so that *all* will mutually benefit.[532] Concord results from such concessions and from submission[533] – the submission of the spiritual power to the prophet and the submission of women to the church as a whole and to their husbands.[534] The sudden surprising conservatism[535] of Paul's appeal here, which has led some scholars to question its authenticity,[536] may perhaps be understood when we

---

531 14:30, 34.

532 14:31, the thrice-repeated πάντες is very emphatic.

533 "... but in the interests of peace and good order he could command the women to be silent, precisely as he could give orders for a male prophet to be silent if his continued speech was likely to prove unedifying" (Barrett, *First Corinthians*, 332). The connection between the subjugation of the spirit and Corinthian partisan strife is demonstrated also by Chrys.: Ἵνα γὰρ μὴ φιλονεικῇ, μηδὲ στασιάζῃ ὁ ἄνθρωπος, αὐτὸ τὸ χάρισμα δείκνυσιν ὑποτασσόμενον ... Εἰ δὲ τὸ πνεῦμα ὑποτάσσεται, πολλῷ μᾶλλον σὺ ὁ κεκτημένος οὐκ ἂν εἴης δίκαιος φιλονεικεῖν (Chrys. *hom. in I Cor.* 36.4 [*PG* 61.312]).

534 For the relationship between concord and ὑποταγή in Greco-Roman antiquity see chap. III nn. 405 and 694. One further example is Ps-Sall. *Rep.* 10.6, a letter urging concord: "Therefore, since the commons submit [*oboedire*] to the senate as the body does to the soul, and carry out its decrees, the fathers ought to be strong in counsel, but for the people cleverness is superfluous." We should also note some further parallel elements in the speech of Marcus Porcius Cato in Livy 34.2–4 on the submission of Roman women, a text often cited in relation to 1 Cor 14:34–35. There the speaker wants the women to remain under the Oppian law because he fears their *seditio* (34.1.7–8; 3.8, as also pointed out by his opponent in 34.5.5), and by appeal to the common good, even if it is not for the women's good (34.3.5).

535 "Die von der Gemeinderegel vertretene Gottesdienstordnung hat konservativen Charakter" (Dautzenberg, *Prophetie*, 261, who himself attributes it to the influence of the hellenistic synagogue). See also Barton, 232: "This conformity argues in favor of the interpretation of Paul as a *social conservative*, at least at this point; for he appears here as strongly resistant to a gender-related redefinition of traditional categories of public and private" (emph. original).

536 Several scholars regard 14:33b–36 (or 14:34–35) as a post-Pauline interpolation (Schmiedel, 181–82; Weiss, *Korintherbrief*, xli, 342; Conzelmann, 246; Klauck, *1. Korintherbrief*, 105–106; G. Fitzer, "'Das Weib schweige in der Gemeinde.' Über den unpaulinischen Charakter der mulier-taceat-Verse in 1. Korinther 14," *Theologische Existenz Heute* n. s. 110 [Munich: Kaiser, 1963], of only vv. 34–35; Strobel, 222–25, of 33b–35; Dautzenberg, *Prophetie*, 253–300, who also includes vv. 37–38 in the interpolation [pp. 297–98]; Sellin, "Hauptprobleme," 2984–85; Fee, *First Corinthians*, 699–708, of vv. 34–35; for an intelligent and balanced discussion of the arguments see Barrett, *First Corinthians*, 330–34). Not only the conservatism here, but also its apparent contradiction with Paul's presumption that women pray and prophesy in 11:2–16 is important to these scholars, along with the text-critical observation that in the Western text vv. 34–35 are transposed after v. 40. The similarity with 1 Tim 2:11 f. is taken as evidence that the interpolation must also have come from a deutero-Pauline hand. This is an instance in which the methodology of partition theories breaks down and is supplanted by interpolation theories because (as elsewhere, in my view) to put the two passages 11:2–16 and 14:33b–36 in different letters does not resolve the problem (with Wolff, 141 and Klauck, *1. Korintherbrief*, 105, against Schmithals, *Gnosticism*, 243–44; Schenke-Fischer, 93–94).

I regard the passage as probably authentic because it fits well the argument for concord throughout 1 Corinthians (see next note). It also contains the very same advice for order and

observe that, as far as the subject of this investigation is concerned, the call to submission and silence is fully consonant and rhetorically consistent with the argument for inner-group concord,[537] with its conservative tendencies.[538]

---

peace in the assembly as is found in its context: silence (14:28, 30, 34), and it assumes the same purpose for this worship assembly, learning (14:31, 35). The appeal to shame when dealing with more extreme behavior by women was also made by Paul in 11:5–6. But these arguments will not be convincing to those who take this passage to be an interpolation because they account for the same observations by arguing that those were the grounds for the redactor's placement of the piece. Even the scholars who argue for some form of interpolation here are inconsistent with one another because they vary on the extent of the interpolation, and not all arguments work equally well to support all interpolation theories. The text-critical argument actually works for neither side of the debate because the manuscript variations deal with the placement of only verses 34–35 (something with which those who argue for the interpolation to be 33b–36 do not sufficiently contend), and on the other side because the redaction would presumably have preceded the circulation of the corpus and would not be reflected in any manuscripts. The strongest argument for the interpolation of 14:33b–36 is that in its absolute rejection of women's speaking in worship it stands in apparent contradiction with 11:2–16, where Paul seems to assume that women pray and prophesy in church. Several hypotheses have been advanced to resolve this contradiction by those who guard the authenticity of the text: that in 11:2–16 Paul does not condone women's praying and prophesying in church but only passes over it until he takes it up later (Crouch, 133–35), that 14:33b–36 refers only to married women where 11:2–16 refers to all women (Fiorenza, *In Memory of Her*, 230–31), or that 14:33b–36 does not refer to liturgical speech but rather to more general chatter or questions from non-officiants in the ceremony (Heinrici, *Korinther*, 436; Héring, 154; Wolff, 142; further scholars listed in Crouch, 134 n. 61 and Dautzenberg, *Prophetie*, 266 n. 38). I regard the latter hypothesis as the most likely of the three, though it is not without its difficulties. Even if the passage is an interpolation, however, that would not interfere directly with the conclusions of this study.

537 Notice that the same strategy of calling women to silence to end factionalism is used in *1 Clem*. 21.6–7: τὰς γυναῖκας ἡμῶν ἐπὶ τὸ ἀγαθὸν διορθωσώμεθα. τὸ ἀξιαγάπητον τῆς ἁγνείας ἦθος ἐνδειξάσθωσαν, τὸ ἀκέραιον τῆς πραΰτητος αὐτῶν βούλημα ἀποδειξάτωσαν, τὸ ἐπιεικὲς τῆς γλώσσης αὐτῶν διὰ τῆς σιγῆς φανερὸν ποιησάτωσαν, τὴν ἀγάπην αὐτῶν μὴ κατὰ προσκλίσεις, ἀλλὰ πᾶσιν τοῖς φοβουμένοις τὸν θεὸν ὁσίως ἴσην παρεχέτωσαν.

538 The position Paul ultimately espouses here (and in ch. 7; 11:2–16; 16:16) clearly bears a resemblance to the later *Haustafeln* (on the continuity, see Theissen, 164; Lührmann, "Sklave," 82–83), though different in form (Crouch, 131–45; Walker, "Woman's Place," 103), because the *function* here is to foster concord and stability *within* the church, as is also likely with the later *Haustafeln* (Elliott, 165–266, esp. 110–12, 213–18 with arguments against Balch, 65–116, on the function of the *Haustafel* in 1 Pet as apologetic; note that Balch himself fully recognizes that the goal of submission in the *Haustafeln* is ὁμόνοια [88–90], but takes it to refer to non-Christian households; on the Colossians *Haustafel* see W. A. Meeks, "In One Body: The Unity of Humankind in Colossians and Ephesians," *God's Christ and His People: Studies in Honour of Nils Alstrup Dahl*, ed. J. Jervell and W. A. Meeks [Oslo/Bergen/Tromsö: Universitetsforlaget, 1977] 209–21, 214: "[it] serves here to reinforce the same emphasis on internal order and harmony"). Elliott stresses the relationship of the *Haustafel* in 1 Pet to the image of the οἶκος (which is of course related to Paul's οἰκοδομή/ναὸς τοῦ θεοῦ in 1 Cor): "Since the believers constitute the household of God, they are to live and behave as the distinctive *oikos tou theou*. Subordination to the will of God is outlined according to the pattern of the household code" (p. 229). The literature on the *Haustafeln* is considerable; see the survey of the discussions with bibliography in P. Fiedler, "Haustafel," *RAC* 103 (1986) 1063–73. For good Greco-Roman parallels see Dio Chrys. *Or*. 38.15; Aristid. *Or*. 24.32–33. The very same principles and

In general, Paul counsels, worshippers should exhibit not wild, inharmonious behavior, but behavior which suits the very nature of the God worshipped[539] and honors the full distribution of the spirit to all members of the community.[540] God is not of partisan strife but of peace.[541] The proof section 11:2–14:40 concludes[542] with Paul's overall advice: orderly and concordant behavior[543] is to be sought in worship, where at present instead, shockingly, the Corinthian factions manifest themselves when "coming together." The general sense of the argument sub-section 11:2–14:40 is well captured by Chrysostom's comment on 14:40: Οὐδὲν γὰρ οὕτως οἰκοδομεῖ, ὡς εὐταξία, ὡς εἰρήνη, ὡς ἀγάπη, ὥσπερ οὖν καὶ τὰ ἐναντία διαλύει.[544]

(4) 15:1–57. *Fourth Section of Proof:*
The Resurrection and the Final Goal. Unity in the Παραδόσεις

It is especially appropriate for Paul's Christian argument for social concord in the Corinthian church that he ends with a discussion of the resurrection. As throughout this proof section in 1:18–15:57, Paul takes up another subject of controversy which has played a role in the Corinthian divisions, and in his treatment stresses the unity of the church and calls all to return to it. In the case of the resurrection Paul transforms a subject of dispute into the very τέλος or goal which should govern all Christian decision making, and against which all feeble and insignificant struggles are to be compared and belittled.[545] For the Christian there can be only one final goal of one's actions: the ultimate victory in the

---

language are evident in Chrys.'s exegesis of Paul's argument in 1 Cor 13, a very important text in this connection: Εἶτα ἵνα τὸ μὲν ὑποτάττηται, τὸ δὲ ἄρχῃ τὸ γὰρ ὁμότιμον οἶδε πολλάκις μάχην εἰσάγειν. οὐκ ἀφῆκε δημοκρατίαν εἶναι, ἀλλὰ βασιλείαν, καὶ καθάπερ ἐν στρατοπέδῳ, ταύτην ἄν τις ἴδοι τὴν διάταξιν καθ' ἑκάστην οἰκίαν. Ἔστι γοῦν ἐν τάξει μὲν βασιλέως ὁ ἀνήρ, ἐν τάξει δὲ ὑπάρχου ἡ γυνὴ καὶ στρατηγοῦ. καὶ οἱ παῖδες δὲ ἀρχὴν κεκλήρωνται τρίτην. εἶτα μετὰ ταῦτα ἀρχὴ τετάρτη ἡ τῶν οἰκετῶν . . . Καὶ πανταχοῦ δι' ὀλίγου καὶ πυκνὰς ἐποίησε τὰς ἀρχὰς ὁ Θεός, ἵνα πάντα ἐν ὁμονοίᾳ μένῃ καὶ εὐταξίᾳ πολλῇ (*hom. in I Cor.* 34.3 [*PG* 61.289–90]).

539 See chap. III on the force of the terms ἀκαταστασία and εἰρήνη, and for the same argument by appeal to the divine nature in Greco-Roman discourses on concord.

540 14:36. Because "the word of God" comes to many, each person must show some restraint (with Strobel, 225, who takes this verse to construe with 14:31–33a, not 33b–35, which he regards as the extent of the interpolation).

541 "The interesting opposite of 'disorder,' is not quietness or propriety, or even 'order,' but 'peace.' Minimally this refers to the sense of harmony that will obtain in a Christian assembly when everyone is truly in the Spirit and the aim of everyone is the edification of the whole" (Fee, *First Corinthians*, 697).

542 See Dautzenberg, *Prophetie*, 253 on how this concluding section is similar to those in the previous arguments.

543 See chap. III for discussion of the phrase κατὰ τάξιν. The same appeal is made in *1 Clem.* 40.1–2.

544 *hom. in I Cor.* 37.2 [*PG* 61.318].

545 For the same strategy see *1 Clem.* 24ff., 35.2.

resurrection in which all should hope and for which all should strive against the common enemy, death.[546]

The new argument is introduced with γνωρίζω δὲ ὑμῖν. Against those who complain that this opening is too abrupt to follow 14:40, we note that the very purpose of this introductory formula is to change topics,[547] so there is nothing strange about the transition it effects here.[548] Paul names the new topic of consideration at the outset not as the resurrection, but the gospel, showing again that *he* is in control of the subject matter and does not fit his advice into either the Corinthians' framework or the order of events.[549] While the integrity of 15:1–58 itself remains unchallenged, hypotheses have been offered by partition theorists to move 1 Cor 15 to another compositional context which was in their view original. These hypotheses have depended upon three factors:[550] 1) that the section does not begin with περὶ δέ;[551] 2) the exegetical question of whether or not Paul defends himself here and how that squares with his "defense" in 4:1–5 and particularly ch. 9;[552] and 3) the relationship of this argument to 6:14.[553]

---

546 For parallel appeals to mortality in deliberative arguments on concord, see the material collected in chap. III.

547 Allo, 388.

548 With Merklein, 178 (esp. n. 113), against Schmithals, *Gnosticism*, 91–92, who prefers the connection after 11:34; Schenk, 229 (who is aware of this weakness).

549 We simply do not know how Paul learned of this problem at Corinth (as so often in the letter, as we have seen). For scholarly opinion on both sides (orally or written) see Hurd, 91–92 and notes, for whom 1 Cor 15 is a stumbling block because it is not introduced with περὶ δέ, but he wants it to be a response to a question from the Corinthians' letter. Partition theorists have also had difficulties fitting 1 Cor 15 into this imperfect schema based on distinguishing "oral" and "written" topics. In the earlier partition theories 1 Cor 15 was normally placed in the same letter as the περὶ δέ sections regardless of its different opening (Weiss, *Korintherbrief*, xlii, 343–44; Goguel, 76–77, though not without some hesitation). But since Schmithals's *Gnosticism* the restriction of oral and written topics to discrete letters of response on the basis of a rigid application of the observation of the formula περὶ δέ has meant that 1 Cor 15 had to be excised from the *Antwortbrief* and placed in the *Vorbrief* (Schmithals, *Gnosticism*, 91; *idem*, "Korintherbriefe," 269; Schenk, 224–25 [quoted in n. 451 above]; Suhl, 206; Schenke-Fischer, 93–94; Pesch, 90). Sellin, "Hauptprobleme," 2976, has tried to save 1 Cor 15 for the *Antwortbrief* (which, since he holds to the same presuppositions, can only contain Paul's responses to written questions) by reference to the ὅτι *recitativum* in 15:12, but this argument holds no water because that construction can refer equally well to quotations from oral and written sources (see Smyth, §2589–90; cf. BDF §397; this is true without even mentioning the λέγουσιν in 15:12). The problem is not with 1 Cor 15, but with the assumptions governing the exegesis.

550 The arguments are surveyed and critiqued by Merklein, 177–79 and Sellin, "Hauptprobleme," 2975–76.

551 Therefore 15:1–58 "interrupts" the movement from 12:1–14:40 to 16:1 (see n. 549 above).

552 Two contrary positions have in fact been represented. Many argue that Paul's statement in 15:9, οὐκ εἰμὶ ἱκανὸς καλεῖσθαι ἀπόστολος, which seems to innocently concede the very charge against which he must defend himself in ch. 9, is incompatible with that chapter and thus cannot have originally stood in the same letter (Schmithals, *Gnosticism*, 92; *idem*, *Briefe*, 28; Schenk, 224; Senft, 18). But now Pesch, 90–91 has argued that 1 Cor 9 and 15, because they are

Once again, when the argument by reference to περὶ δέ is deleted we see on what little basis such hypotheses assign 1 Cor 15 to either the reconstructed *Vorbrief* or *Antwortbrief*. The argument that Paul's voluntary self-criticism in 15:8–10 is inconceivable in the same letter with his defense in ch. 9 can similarly be defused since, as we have shown above, 1 Cor 9 is no defense of Paul's apostleship.[554] In fact the self-renouncing, self-effacing attitude displayed in 15:8–10[555] is entirely consonant with Paul's use of himself as the example of humility and conciliatory self-sacrifice throughout the letter.[556] To the reverse argument, that 15:9–10 is itself part of a defense argument which runs throughout 1 Cor 15,[557] we must counter that 1 Cor 15 (even more than 1 Cor 9!) hardly constitutes a defense of Paul's apostolate.[558] Paul is not the subject of 1 Cor 15. It

---

both full-fledged rhetorical defenses of Paul's apostolate, cannot have originally been in the same letter.

553 This argument has been discussed above on 1 Cor 6:12–20 (see chap. III n. 267).

554 Merklein's argument (p. 178), that 1 Cor 9 and 15 are part of the same letter because both are apologetic by reference to weakness, is to me far less convincing in both cases.

555 Εἶδες πάλιν ἑτέρας ταπεινοφροσύνης ὑπερβολήν; (Chrys. *hom. in I Cor.* 38.5 [*PG* 61.328]).

556 For the same extreme see esp. 4:9–13. In both places ghastly pictorial images describe the lowest depths of humility: περικαθάρματα and περίψημα in 4:13, and ἔκτρωμα here in 15:8 (for the extensive research on the latter term see Sellin, *Streit*, 246–51).

557 Bünker, 59–72 and Pesch, 170–90 (who appears to follow him) present rhetorical analyses of 1 Cor 15 as a *Verteidigungsrede*. Bünker is unclear on the exact *causa* of this defense – whether Paul's apostolate or the teaching on the resurrection. Pesch, 170, 178 and passim, boldly combines the two – in defending his resurrection teaching Paul defends himself. But Pesch has combined two unlike things: "defense" of a *position* is not the same thing as *self-defense against charges*. If the charge is that Paul is not an apostle, then how can 1 Cor 15 function as a defense when Paul virtually admits the charge in 15:9? If Paul's goal is to "defend" a proper understanding of the resurrection, there are no grounds for why the rhetorical species of forensic rhetoric would be an appropriate medium for that task. A further methodological problem in the analyses of Bünker and Pesch is that they think that if "opponents" can be unearthed, the text must be a defense.

The compositional analyses by Bünker and Pesch of 1 Cor 15, in addition to their incorrect designation of the rhetorical species, are beset by other weaknesses. First, Bünker does not reckon with the fact that 1 Cor 15 is not a separate speech, but is part of a larger rhetorical composition and therefore does not have its own plan of disposition (see chap. I). But Pesch, 177–78 is so convinced by Bünker's analysis that he makes 15:1–58 one single letter, the *Auferstehungsbrief* (as does Schmithals, *Briefe*, 28–33, with 16:13–24, but on the opposite grounds – that Paul *is not* on the defensive here!). But that 1 Cor 15 is one coherent argument does not consequently mean that it is *a separate letter* (these most recent trends in partition theories unhesitatingly make this inference, and thus wind up with more and more individual Pauline letters). Secondly, the analysis of Bünker (followed by Pesch with only minor changes) atomizes the argument in 1 Cor 15 virtually beyond recognition (1–3a exordium, 3b–11 narratio, 12–28 argumentatio I, 29–34 peroratio I, 35–49 argumentatio II, 50–58 peroratio II). In my view it must be regarded as an index of an unsuccessful rhetorical analysis that its prevailing assumptions (in this case that the chapter is a defense argument) fit the text so poorly that large portions of it must be excused as "digressions" or "excurses" as Bünker has (9–10 [extraordinary given his genre designation!], 24b–28, 50–58 "excursartige peroratio").

558 As asserted by Lüdemann, 115–17 ("Paulus verteidigt seinen Apostolat in V. 8ff."). It is

is instead an argument on the resurrection of the dead, aimed at convincing all the Corinthians of the fact and manifestation of human resurrection which all believers can expect. It is therefore appropriately deliberative, not forensic argumentation.[559] While there is no doubt that 1 Cor 15 is a coherent argument on the resurrection, that does not correspondingly mean that it constitutes a discrete Pauline letter.[560] It is rather a sub-argument within the larger compositional whole of 1 Corinthians.

The logical and rhetorical progression of the sub-argument on the resurrection of the dead in 15:1–57 was well schematized by Lightfoot, whose straightforward analysis I shall follow here:

(a) Evidence for the Resurrection of the dead (15:1–34)
  (1) Testimony to Christ's Resurrection (15:1–11)
  (2) Christ's Resurrection involves man's Resurrection (15:12–28)
  (3) Testimony of human conduct to a belief in the Resurrection. Baptisms for the dead. Sufferings of the Apostles. (15:29–34)
(b) Difficulty as to the manner of the Resurrection (15:35–49)
(c) Triumph of life over death (15:50–58).[561]

Although the exegetical and historical questions posed by 1 Cor 15 are myriad, this assessment of the structure of Paul's argument in this chapter is followed, with slight variations in some cases, by many scholars.[562] Here our particular

no accident that he deals with 15:8–11 only in reference to 15:1–11, and never in the context of the whole chapter (as also on pp. 76–84). In this Lüdemann follows P. von der Osten-Sacken, "Die Apologie des paulinischen Apostolats in 1. Kor 15:1–11," *ZNW* 64 (1973) 245–62, who holds that this passage can only be exegeted on its own, apart from its context. The conclusion that 15:1–11 contains (even in part) an apology of the Pauline apostolate must rest on such a methodological standard (cf. Weiss, *Korintherbrief*, 353, who, because he holds 15:9–10 to be apologetic, must consider these verses to be a "digression"). Von der Osten-Sacken's exegesis is rightly critiqued by Sellin, *Streit*, 243.

[559] This is supported by the linguistic analysis of W. Stenger, "Beobachtungen zur Argumentationsstruktur von 1 Kor 15," *LB* 45 (1979) 71–128, who writes of the "*persuasive Ziel*" of the chapter, which is to urge the Corinthians to stand firm in the tradition (pp. 85–86, 127–28).

[560] Contra Schmithals, *Briefe*, 28–33; Pesch, 177–78 (see n. 557 above).

[561] Lightfoot, 141 (his notes do not reach this far, but this is from his tabulated analysis of the whole letter). For the types of proofs in this chapter as compared with ancient rhetoric see Heinrici, *Korinther*, 441–42.

[562] See the representative description of Jeremias, 153: "Das 15. Kapitel des I. Korintherbriefes ist sehr klar aufgebaut. Nach Feststellung der grundlegenden Tatsache der Auferstehung Christi (vv. 1–11) behandelt Paulus erst das OTI (vv. 12–34), dann das ΠΩΣ (vv. 35–57) der christlichen Auferstehungshoffnung; v. 58 ist der paränetische Abschluss." Comparable analyses are made by Godet, 2.321–450; Weiss, *Korintherbrief*, 343–80; Robertson-Plummer, 328–81; Allo, 387–454; Conzelmann, 248–93; Vielhauer, *Geschichte*, 127; Wolff, 147–216; Stenger, 71–128; Klauck, *1. Korintherbrief*, 107–23; and Fee, *First Corinthians*, 713–809. The recent study by Sellin, though more detailed, takes 15:1–34 and 35–58 to be the two sections of the argument, which he then breaks down further (*Streit*, 210–89).

task is to discuss the role of this unfolding argument within the compass of Paul's deliberative argument in 1 Corinthians for church unity.[563]

In 15:1–11 Paul calls the Corinthians to unity in common principles,[564] in this case the Christian gospel. These verses, in which Paul recites anew for the Corinthians the tradition of the witnesses of Christ's resurrection (reminding them that they have believed this),[565] are the basis for the argument to follow on the resurrection of Christians.[566] By first naming the issue as the gospel (and not resurrection) Paul emphasizes the importance of the things all Christians share: a common faith in the same received παράδοσις. In v. 8 Paul names his own resurrection experience as the last in the succession of witnesses. In vv. 9–10 he qualifies even this experience by his own unworthiness, with an openness to self-criticism hardly befitting an apologia.[567] If 15:1–11 (or all of ch. 15) were a defense of Paul's apostolate, then we would expect proof of his contention that he had seen the risen Lord, but here, as also in 9:1, that assertion stands without need of proof. But Paul turns from his self-abasement to his most important point – the way in which he has put his faith into action so that it may not be in vain. This verse (15:10) has not an apologetic, but rather an exemplary function, for it represents the very advice which Paul in his conclusion will urge on the Corinthians.[568] With his fifth εἴτε ... εἴτε construction in 1 Corinthians,[569] in 15:11 Paul relativizes the difference[570] between the competing missionaries (to whom the Corinthians claimed allegiance)[571] in service of the unity which they share in the common tradition: οὕτως κηρύσσομεν καὶ οὕτως ἐπιστεύσατε.[572]

The logic of 15:12–28 is dependent upon the premise[573] established in 15:1–11,

---

563 Barth's famous book focuses on how 1 Cor 15 is the theological crown of the epistle, where our emphasis is on its rhetorical function (though many of his observations are also applicable here).

564 This is on what they stand, the θεμέλιος of the strong building, which is Christ (see Calvin, 348; Weiss, *Korintherbrief*, 346; Stenger, 85–86, 127–28 on the connection between 15:1–3 and 58).

565 Καὶ πῶς τοὺς σαλευομένους ἑστάναι φησί; Προσποιεῖται ἄγνοιαν συμφερόντως (Chrys., *hom. in I Cor.* 38.2 [*PG* 61.323]). See also Barrett, *First Corinthians*, 336, on how these verses come close to flattering the Corinthians with another *captatio benevolentiae* (see above on this rhetorical strategy in deliberative rhetoric).

566 Sellin, *Streit*, 231 calls the section "Die Argumentationsbasis: die Wirksamkeit des Kerygmas." See also Conzelmann, 250; Stenger, 72–85.

567 For the extensive research on these verses see Sellin, *Streit*, 242–45.

568 "v. 8–10 ist schon von daher als eine Illustration der Wirksamkeit des Kerygmas am Beispiel des Paulus aufzufassen" (Sellin, *Streit*, 229 n. 57; also p. 250; on the exemplary function here see also Barth, 147). Sellin points to two parallels between 15:10 and 58: οὐ κενή/οὐκ ἔστιν κενός and ἐκοπίασα/ὁ κόπος ὑμῶν.

569 See n. 392 above for the other places, and for the conciliating force of this construction.

570 Also Conzelmann, 260.

571 Barth, 145–46.

572 See Chrys. on 15:11: ἀλλὰ πάλιν ἑαυτὸν ἐκείνοις συντάττει, τὴν κατὰ Χριστὸν ἐνδεικνύμενος ὁμόνοιαν (*hom. in I Cor.* 39.1 [*PG* 61.332]).

573 See Quint. *Inst.* 5.10.11 (and context) on arguing from common principles: "Conse-

that Christ has been raised from the dead. The purpose of the recital of the tradition becomes clear.[574] It is to prove the necessary consequence of Christ's resurrection – the resurrection of believers – as against "some" Corinthians who deny that there is a resurrection of the dead.[575] As in 15:1–2, 11, Paul continues to use the Corinthians as evidence against their own mistaken impressions, since the resurrection of Christ is the subject of *their* faith (15:14, 17), as it was of Paul's teaching (15:12, 14, 15). Paul argues that for any of the Corinthians not to believe and hope in the resurrection of believers is to hold a position incompatible with their prior commitments and action.[576] His purpose is to convince them that believers, both living and dead, will indeed be raised.

This argument calls all Corinthians to unite in the common kerygma and its shared implications for all Christians as against some who deny it. Here Paul cannot easily conciliate between the two sides because the problem, as he understands it, is proper adherence to the gospel, on which there can be no compromise.[577] He must side with those who have argued against their fellow Corinthian Christians that believers will indeed be raised. But his conciliatory strategy here is evidenced in Paul's emphasis that the promise of resurrection extends to *all* (15:22, 23, 28, 51),[578] perhaps against exclusive positions proffered by those who themselves held to the general resurrection. The common destiny of all Christians is shown definitively in Paul's description of them as οἱ τοῦ Χριστοῦ (15:23), Paul's replacement phrase for Corinthian partisanship (3:23). United in the common ancestor (Adam) and the common savior (Christ), all Christians will share the same fate without distinctions (15:21–22). The real enemy, Paul introduces in 15:25–26, is not in the congregation – it is death, which God has vanquished. The culmination of history in the eschaton involves

---

quently, since an argument is a process of reasoning which provides proof and enables one thing to be inferred from another and confirms facts which are uncertain by reference to facts which are certain, there must needs be something in every case which requires no proof." The constant appeals to "ones" in 1 Cor are such common principles to which Paul appeals, as here from the acceptance of the common tradition.

574 The objection of von der Osten-Sacken, 247–49, to "reading 15:12 back onto 15:1–11" must be overruled. Because this is an argument, we cannot responsibly interpret parts of it in isolation from the whole. While this is true as a general exegetical principle it is even more particularly justified in the case of 1 Cor 15, *because the premise is itself restated* in the syllogisms in 15:12 and 20. Even Barth, 150–51, who for theological reasons does not take 15:1–11 as "proof" of the historical fact of the resurrection of Christ, understands that theologoumenon as the premise of vv. 12–19. See also Chrys.'s praise of Paul's logical reasoning here (*hom. in I Cor.* 40.1 [*PG* 61.333]).

575 For the many hypotheses concerning the possible reasons for this denial, see the literature cited in chap. III n. 678.

576 Barrett, *First Corinthians*, 346–47; Conzelmann, 265.

577 As above on πορνεία and εἰδωλολατρία. Cf. his rebuke in 15:33–34.

578 This emphasis was noted by Barth, 166; Stenger, 91, 94–95.

the submission of all things[579] (15:27–28) – even of Christ – to God,[580] for the sake of cosmic divine unity (ἵνα ᾖ ὁ θεὸς [τὰ] πάντα ἐν πᾶσιν).[581]

In 15:29–34 Paul offers more human evidence for the resurrection of believers, first by appeal to the practice of vicarious baptism. In 15:30–32 Paul turns again to his own example. The apostle endures suffering in this life for the sake of the ultimate ὄφελος – the resurrection. Partisan battles, fighting κατὰ ἄνθρωπον,[582] are wars with no enemy,[583] for there one fights one's own sisters and brothers for no possible reward. The Christian has no time or attention for such earthly power struggles since a real challenge awaits. The proverb from Menander in 15:33 shows again that "associations" (parties?) are also at the heart of the resurrection controversy.[584] The Christian's energies should be consumed in proper eschatological expectation (ἐκνήψατε), not in shameful sin and ignorance of God and the true reward.

15:35–49 logically moves from the fact that Christians will be raised to the question of the type of body the resurrected ones will have. This has clearly been a topic of controversy (among many) at Corinth. Paul now takes up the position of those who deny the resurrection of the dead, agreeing with them that *the dead* are not raised, but demonstrating that the resurrected body will be a transformed body. By the example of the earthly seeds Paul argues (as before when dealing with differentiation in the community) that the subject of dispute is firmly in God's own hands: ὁ δὲ θεὸς δίδωσιν αὐτῷ σῶμα καθὼς ἠθέλησεν, καὶ ἑκάστῳ τῶν σπερμάτων ἴδιον σῶμα (15:38; cf. 15:23). Just as the concordant sun, moon and stars have their individual glories, so also Christians in this life have different glories. This is important for the Corinthians, who pride in the distinctions of glory and power among themselves. In fact the course of humility and self-renunciation which Paul had urged throughout the letter, he now argues, is to be rewarded eschatologically: σπείρεται ἐν ἀτιμίᾳ, ἐγείρεται ἐν δόξῃ. σπείρεται ἐν ἀσθενείᾳ, ἐγείρεται ἐν δυνάμει. σπείρεται σῶμα ψυχικόν, ἐγείρεται σῶμα πνευματικόν (15:43). All Corinthians will be honored, strong, and complete spiritual people in the resurrected life. Present contentions for transient earthly status are

---

579 Interesting in this connection are the two quotations of 15:23 in *1 Clem.* 37.3 and 41.1, to argue for unity in differentiation.

580 See Chrys. *hom. in I Cor.* 39.5–6 [*PG* 61.340] on how in his submission Christ shows ὁμόνοια with the Father.

581 Cf. 1 Cor 8:6; Eph 4:6, and the language of Chrys.'s treatment of this verse: Ὅταν γὰρ οἱ μὲν ἔχθροι ὑπὸ τοὺς πόδας ὦσι κείμενοι τοῦ Παιδός, ὁ δὲ ἔχων αὐτοὺς ὑπὸ πόδας ἐῤῥιμμένους μὴ στασιάζῃ πρὸς τὸν γεγεννηκότα, ἀλλ' ὁμονοῇ μετὰ πολλῆς τῆς ἀκριβείας, αὐτὸς ἔσται τὰ πάντα ἐν πᾶσι (*hom. in I Cor.* 39.6 [*PG* 61.341–42]).

582 See chap. III n. 98 on how this is a *topos* in arguments urging concord.

583 See Lucan, *BCiv.* 1.682 (quoted in chap. III n. 315, with further references to this commonplace).

584 Several scholars have regarded the proverb as addressing associations with those persons within the church community (therefore factionalists) who deny the resurrection (Weiss, *Korintherbrief*, 367; Héring, 173; Conzelmann, 278–79).

therefore entirely trivial. With a second application of the analogy of Adam and Christ, Paul stresses the lowliness of the earthly body but also the necessity for it as all Christians commonly await transformation, by God alone, to higher glory and status.

In 15:50–57 Paul gives a concluding exhortation on the resurrection victory *all* will share in common. The most important ὄφελος toward which all Christians should direct themselves is immortality, the final victory for all Christians over the true enemy, death. With the cosmic battle won, there can be no reason for any other kind of strife. Instead all will share this magnificent victory and transformation. The argument ends on a climax with triumphal Scriptural quotations and a small prayer of thanksgiving to God who will give this victory to those who believe (15:57).[585]

d) 15:58 ἐπίλογος (Conclusion/Summation) to the Argument in the Body of the Letter

The verse 15:58 simultaneously closes the letter body of 1 Corinthians[586] and constitutes the rhetorical ἐπίλογος[587] which concludes the deliberative argument for church unity which that letter body contained. The conclusion is short and to the point,[588] and amounts to a restatement of the central argument of the letter: seek the upbuilding of the church in concord, even when it entails sacrificing what appears to be to your present advantage, because this is the appropriate Christian behavior of love (τὸ ἔργον τοῦ κυρίου) which will lead to eschatological advantage (οὐκ ἔστιν κενὸς ἐν κυρίῳ). This kind of recapitulation (ἀνακεφαλαίωσις) of the argument and final appeal is the very description of a simplified rhetorical ἐπίλογος.[589] 15:58 can be so brief a peroration for several reasons.[590]

---

[585] For the same construction used to end an argument (or letter) see 2 Cor 9:15 (and Betz, *2 Corinthians 8 and 9*, 126–28), and Rom 7:7ff. (Conzelmann, 293). This construction is, however, used in other places in Paul's letters as well (2 Cor 2:14; 8:16).

[586] See White, *Body*, 42–51 on different functions of body closing phrases in Greek letters. One category of those he identifies is "expressions urging responsibility," which "call attention to previous material in the body. Their function is to urge the addressee to be responsive regarding an earlier request" (p. 46). See also White's *Light From Ancient Letters*, 204, 210, on conjunctions which are used to end the letter body (in regard to ὥστε in 15:58).

[587] With Betz, "Rhetoric and Theology," 33. See also the exegesis of Grosheide, 395: "The admonition with which Paul concludes is not a summons to believe in the resurrection of the body, but in close connection with vs. 57, is of a more general nature. Thus it can serve also as the conclusion of the whole epistle."

[588] Compare the example in Arist. *Rh.* 3.19.6.

[589] Throughout the rhetorical tradition the varied functions of the ἐπίλογος are recognized (see Volkmann, 262–71; Martin, 147–66). These recurrent functions to the concluding portion of a speech are recapitulation, emotional appeal and amplification. While many theorists consider these to be three *parts* of the ἐπίλογος (Arist. *Rh.* 3.19.1; *Rhet.Her.* 2.30; Cic. *Inv.Rhet.* 1.52.98–99; cf. *Part.Or.* 15.52; Aps. *Rh.* 1.384 Spengel), others consider them to be different *types* of conclusions (Quint. *Inst.* 6.1.1–2; Anon. *Rh.* 1.453 Spengel; cf. *Rh.Al.* 20.1433b;

First of all, the whole argument in 15:1–57 serves to culminate Paul's appeal throughout 1 Corinthians,[591] so 15:58 need only draw the connections implicit in that extensive argument. Secondly, the ἐπίλογος in 15:58 is single and general because so was the πρόθεσις to the argument in 1:10 to which it corresponds, which did not delve into the specifics of the Corinthian disputes, but subordinated all of them to the overriding concern for unity in the church. The peroration in 15:58 appropriately employs that same strategy. The specific advice which Paul gave in his deliberative proof on each point of Corinthian dispute (sexual immorality, court battles, marriage, status, idol meats, hairstyles, the Lord's supper, spiritual gifts, and the resurrection of the dead) need not be recapitulated here.[592] As throughout his argument for church unity, Paul concludes with a final appeal to the building metaphor for concord[593] and the eschatological advantage,[594] incorporating all the specific concerns into his single focus – the work of the building up of the church.[595]

4. 16:1–24 Epistolary Closing

After closing the body of his letter to Corinth[596] with the conclusion to its deliberative argument, Paul turns to some business relating to the church before

33.1439a–34.1440a on παλιλλογία). In this argument Paul employs only a brief recapitulation of his advice to the Corinthians, without need for emotional appeal (though 15:50–57 serves this function to some degree) or amplification, due to the nature of this case and the deliberative species. Dem. *Or.* 3.36 is a similarly brief recapitulation of a deliberative speech (Volkmann, 264), also with a closing appeal to advantage: Ὑμεῖς δ' ἕλοισθ' ὅ τι καὶ τῇ πόλει καὶ ἅπασι συνοίσειν ὑμῖν μέλλει. For further examples of deliberative recapitulations see Dem. *Or.* 2.31 (Λέγω δὴ κεφάλαιον . . .); Isoc. *Or.* 5.154; *Ep.* 2.24; Pl. *Ep.* 8.357C-D; Aristid. *Or.* 23.80 (with Behr, 2.366); 24.59 (Behr, 2.369), especially the last lines of the two.

590 Brevity in the ἐπίλογος is of course recommended by the handbooks (e. g., *Rh.Al.* 20.1433b; *Rhet.Her.* 2.30.47; Cic. *Inv.Rhet.* 1.52.98–99; Quint. *Inst.* 6.1.2).

591 In this Barth was surely right.

592 This conforms to rhetorical strategy, according to Volkmann, 265: "So kann es auch vorkommen, dass der Redner von der ganzen Beweisführung nur den Haupttheil recapitulirt, worin gerade die Stärke derselben liegt, die andern Theile dagegen unberührt lässt."

593 See chap. III on the proliferation of building terminology in this verse, and its relationship to the problem of factionalism.

594 In this repect and the reference to the building metaphor we see the correspondence of the ἐπίλογος also with the προοίμιον to the argument in 1:4–9.

595 "In the abundance of results they may be equal to Apostles (v. 10); but it must be in work, not in disputation" (Robertson-Plummer, 379–80; cf. Barrett, *First Corinthians*, 385).

596 I follow the majority of commentators who regard 1 Cor 16 as an independent section of the letter (e. g., Schmiedel, 205 ["Geschäftliches und Persönliches"]; Lightfoot, 141 ["Conclusion"]; Heinrici, *Korinther*, 510; Weiss, *Korintherbrief*, 380 [who follows Schmiedel on the title, as does Heinrici]; Allo, 455 ["Epilogue" "Questions personnelles"]; Conzelmann, 294 ["Information and Greetings"]; Klauck, *1. Korintherbrief*, 123 ["Briefschluss"]; among others are Bachmann, 474; Wolff, 217; Lang, 245; Strobel, 264.

This standard compositional conclusion has had two recent competitors. Barrett, *First*

ending the letter.[597] Differently from the body of the letter, here Paul does not so much advise as inform and instruct. 1 Cor 16 contains a variety of epistolary topics and formulae: business (the collection), travel plans, final instructions and greetings, and farewell. In this case these practical matters and epistolary forms are not unrelated to the argument for concord in the body of the letter.[598] In fact in several places they continue and make reference to that argument. Although 1 Cor 16 is made up of a variety of small matters of concern, there is no reason to suspect partition here,[599] for the epistolary closing serves these assorted purposes.[600]

Corinthians, 28–29, 385 and Bruce, 26–27, 157–59, place 16:1–4 in the argument section 7:1–16:4, "Paul Answers the Letter From Corinth," on the sole grounds of the περὶ δέ in 16:1. But to be consistent with that methodological principle, one must also include 16:12 in that same argument section, as observed by Fee, *First Corinthians*, 22–23, 809–25, who does just that (7:1–16:12, "In Response to the Corinthian Letter"). This same presupposition on the περὶ δέ in 16:1 and 12 has led partition theorists to divide up chapter 16 and put 16:1–12 in the *Antwortbrief* (Schmithals, *Gnosticism*, 93–94; *idem*, "Korintherbriefe," 272, 285–86; *idem*, *Briefe*, 28, 34; Schenk, 224, 229; Suhl, 203–13). (See also n. 599 below on partition theories and 1 Cor 16.) But since we have seen (above) that the use of περὶ δέ in itself does not tell us that Paul is answering the Corinthians' letter, and further that 1 Cor does not adhere to the order of "oral" topics followed by "written" topics, the compositional analysis of this chapter cannot depend upon such assumptions about this formula. We must turn to other criteria, in this case to rhetorical and epistolary conventions. Since we have already seen that 15:58 is the conclusion to the argument in the body of the letter, 16:1 ff. stands outside of that and therefore must have a different function. Like the scholars named above, we must conclude that the function of 16:1–24 is that of the epistolary news and closing section.

597 In other deliberative letters see, e. g., Isoc. *Ep.* 7.10–13 and *1 Clem.* 65.1, where the author introduces the bearers of the letter and expresses concern about their proper treatment by the recipients.

598 See the discussion in chap. III.

599 As we have seen, when the argument by appeal to περὶ δέ is removed, there are little grounds for partitioning ch. 16. The argument by appeal to the rhetorical correspondence between 15:58 and 16:13 will be refuted below (n. 607). The other arguments for partition of 16:1–24 are bound up with the travel plans of Paul and Timothy (on which see above on 4:17–21), and the reference to Stephanas in 16:15, who had been named in 1:16. Against those who find unacceptable Paul's lack of reference to the presence of Stephanas when he mentioned him at the beginning of the letter, we must counter that this is based upon an expectation which has never been demonstrated for ancient letters. It is also possible (we can never know) that Stephanas was a member of "Chloe's people" who were already mentioned (1:11). Weiss's proposed division of ch. 16 (*Korintherbrief*, xli-ii, 366), to put 16:8 in a different letter from 15:32, which he considers impossible in the same letter, has received no support. We should also note that many partition theorists do not find these arguments for dividing 1 Cor 16 compelling, but instead retain ch. 16 intact (Dinkler, "Korintherbriefe," 18; Schenke-Fischer, 94, 99; Klauck, *1. Korintherbrief*, 123; Pesch, 91–92; Sellin, "Hauptprobleme," 2968, 2977).

600 Compare, for example, the loose arrangement of topics of business and personal matters in Pl. *Ep.* 2 and 13 (where also the formula περὶ δέ often serves to introduce the next item of treatment; see Mitchell, 239–44 for discussion).

a) 16:1–4 Instructions on the Collection

The business concern which Paul appends to his letter urging concord is on the collection for the saints in Jerusalem. That Paul introduces the collection with περὶ δέ tells us only that he could assume that the Corinthians knew enough about the collection to recognize the topic. We cannot reconstruct how they knew about the collection, nor can we assume that they had asked Paul about it in their letter. The collection may have been another cause of Corinthian divisions since, as we have seen, economic disparity in the church has been a source of conflict. Paul urges that each individual decide what she or he can give and set it aside on their own, perhaps to avoid another public manifestation of the economic differences in the community.

b) 16:5–12 Visit Plans (Paul, Apollos, Timothy)

Upcoming visits of Paul, Timothy and Apollos are taken up next. Paul will come to the Corinthians when he can, and hopes to have a long visit with them (16:5–8). This announcement of an impending visit serves to anchor his epistolary advice in their personal relationship, for which this letter is a substitute, bonded in his personal presence among them (cf. 4:18–21; 11:34). The arrival of Timothy, who will either deliver 1 Corinthians or follow soon after it,[601] is announced by Paul (16:10–11). Behind his concern for Timothy's friendly reception is not Paul's concern about Timothy's youth or shyness, but the epistolary convention that one shows one's acceptance of the message of a letter by the way in which one treats the sender's envoy. The Corinthians will display their concord (their positive response to Paul's advice) in the way in which they treat Timothy, and send him on back to Paul.[602] Paul lastly discusses Apollos' travel plans. As so often in ancient letters, Paul brings up a person whom both he and his addressees know well using the formula περὶ δέ to give news about him.[603] We cannot reconstruct from 16:12 that Paul and Apollos actually were on such good terms, but only that Paul wishes to give that impression to the Corinthians. It is no surprise that that is the same rhetorical strategy he employed in his argument in the body of the letter (3:5–8). On practical terms, it is likely that both Paul and Apollos will stay away from the church at Corinth until it has become reunited. Since they are in some way objects of the controversies, it is best if they keep their distance at this point.

---

601 See the discussion above on 4:17.

602 See chap. III nn. 688–89 on patristic exegesis of Timothy's role which corroborates this.

603 Examples are cited in Mitchell, 241 n. 51; 256 n. 120.

c) 16:13–18 Recapitulation of the Argument. Final Concrete Advice for Unity

After these business matters, Paul returns to his appeal in the argument in the body of the letter for church unity. 16:13–14 is a second recapitulation of that appeal[604] which resounds with the two major emphases of Paul's argument: the image of the concordant strong building,[605] and the appeal to love as the principle of social and political unity.[606] This well summarizes Paul's deliberative argument for church concord in the body of the letter,[607] from which Paul now turns to very concrete advice for harmony in the church. In 16:15–18 he calls upon the church to submit itself freely to the governance of the house of Stephanas. This is a direct response to the discord in the church, which will only be resolved by submission to recognized leadership.[608]

d) 16:19–21 Epistolary Greetings

Following Hellenistic epistolary convention, before closing Paul gives reciprocal greetings to his addressees using the ἀσπάζεσθαι formula.[609] Paul's customary closing command to "greet one another with a holy kiss" has a particular poignancy in the contentious Corinthian situation. It may serve as another way in which Paul urges the church to unity, in a reconciliatory gesture. Paul appends his own greeting in his own hand (16:21).

e) 16:22–24 Final Curse and Prayer Calling for Unity in Love and in Jesus Christ

The Pauline letter customarily ends with a blessing, Paul's uniquely Christian version of the Hellenistic farewell formula ἔρρωσο or εὐτύχει.[610] In 1 Corin-

---

604 Wuellner, "Greek Rhetoric," 183 correctly calls it the *recapitulatio* which restates 1:10. Fiorenza, "Rhetorical Situation," 393, regards 16:15–18 as the *peroratio*, but those verses do not themselves sum up the letter (as 16:13–14 surely do). Neither, however, notes that 15:58 also plays this role.

605 See chap. III for discussion and documentation.

606 The parallel 14:26c shows that Paul equates "building up" with "love." This is also the final appeal to the *topos* of the commonality of possessions in a concordant community (see chap. III n. 171).

607 The correspondence of 16:13–14 with 15:58 was correctly noted by Schmithals (*Gnosticism*, 93–94, and subsequent work), but he drew the wrong conclusion from it – that the two verses must have been originally adjacent. The restatement would make no sense after 15:58 (Wolff, 224 rightly observed that it would be tautological). It performs a clear function, however, to recapitulate, after the intervening business matters and travel plans in 16:1–12.

608 See chap. III.

609 Exler, 111–16; Koskenniemi, 148–151; Doty, *Letters*, 42; White, *Light From Ancient Letters*, 202.

610 Exler, 69–77; Koskenniemi, 151–54; Doty, *Letters*, 39–40. In addition to the examples

thians Paul precedes his blessing with a final curse upon those who do not love the Lord, who divide his church by their self-interests. As throughout the argument in 1 Corinthians, Paul counters such behavior with an eschatological appeal, here the early Christian acclamation μαράνα θά. This is then followed by Paul's customary blessing for the grace of the Lord Jesus.[611] Unique to 1 Corinthians in the Pauline corpus is the final exhortation ἡ αγάπη μου μετὰ πάντων ὑμῶν ἐν Χριστῷ 'Ιησοῦ in 16:24. This is a last call for church unity in the love of the exemplary apostle for *all* the members of the church in the one Lord Jesus Christ, to unity in whom Paul has called the church throughout 1 Corinthians.

---

from documentary papyrus letters cited by Exler and Koskenniemi, see Dem. *Ep.* 1.16; 3.45; Pl. *Ep.* 1.310B; 13.363C; Isoc. *Ep.* 7.13.

611 1 Thess 5:28; Gal 6:18; 2 Cor 13:13; Phil 4:23; Rom 16:20.

Chapter V

Conclusion

This investigation, through an exegetical study of the language and composition of 1 Corinthians, with particular utilization of the method of historical rhetorical criticism, has argued that 1 Corinthians is a unified deliberative letter which throughout urges unity on the divided Corinthian church. First, a summation of the argument presented in support of this conclusion is in order. Chap. II demonstrated that deliberative rhetoric in Greco-Roman antiquity was characterized by four things: 1) concentration on the future as the realm of deliberation; 2) a fixed set of appeals, the most common of which is the appeal to advantage; 3) the use of examples for imitation in the proof; and 4) specific topics of consideration, among which are discussions of factionalism and concord. In that same chapter it was also demonstrated that 1 Corinthians contains those first three characteristics of deliberative rhetoric. The last step in that argument, to demonstrate that 1 Corinthians is indeed a letter which throughout discusses factionalism and concord (a content thus appropriate to deliberative rhetoric) was made in chap. III. Therefore the first conclusion of this investigation is that 1 Corinthians is deliberative rhetoric, a conclusion offered both against those who would assign it to one of the other rhetorical species (forensic or epideictic) and against those who consider the letter to be loosely arranged instruction or paraenesis without adherence to any logical or rhetorical scheme.

In chap. III a detailed examination of the terminology and argumentation of 1 Corinthians was made which focused on the points of intersection between 1 Corinthians and Greco-Roman political texts discussing concord and factionalism. That investigation has issued forth in the conclusion that 1 Corinthians is throughout filled with terms and *topoi* which were of general commerce in the Imperial period for urging divided groups to become reunified. This body of evidence led to several conclusions. First of all, the content of 1 Corinthians, a series of arguments rooted by Paul in the issues of factionalism and concord, is appropriate for the rhetorical species of deliberative rhetoric to which we have assigned it. Secondly, the prevalence of terms and *topoi* derived from politics for responding to factionalism[1] *throughout 1 Corinthians*, and not just in 1 Cor 1–4, as

[1] This part of our investigation illustrates the methodological principle that one cannot

scholars have presumed, lends further support to our argument for the compositional unity of the letter, as against those who partition the letter. Thirdly, this documentation becomes a building block for the compositional analysis of 1 Corinthians, because the significant correspondence between the entire letter and 1:10 demonstrates that 1:10 is the rhetorical πρόθεσις or thesis statement of the argument in the letter.

Chap. IV presented an analysis of the epistolary and rhetorical structure of 1 Corinthians. 1 Corinthians is a letter, the body of which contains a deliberative argument. That argument, centered in the πρόθεσις in 1:10, can be well understood, both in regard to its content and its compositional structure, by comparison with other Greco-Roman discourses which urge unity on divided groups. The composition of 1 Corinthians has here been analyzed in a way different from previous attempts, which were either based solely on content, or were based on the assumption that the letter's composition was to be understood as merely reflecting the course of events which led to its creation, rather than its own rhetorical purpose or coherent plan. Having established that 1 Corinthians is a rhetorical document, in chap. IV the argument of the letter was analyzed according to ancient rhetorical conventions and norms, and found to make sense according to those canons. 1 Corinthians is Paul's own response to the multifaceted situation at Corinth of which he had learned from several different sources. The compositional principle of this letter is not the order of contacts from Corinth, as exegetes have often presumed, for that schema does not account for most of the letter.[2] The argument in the letter is best understood as Paul's own composition, in which he was free to put forward his own diagnosis of the problem at Corinth (factionalism) and his own advice for its resolution (building up in concord through love). In 1 Corinthians we see a Paul himself in control of his material and his medium, not a Paul enslaved to the order or logic of his communiqués from Corinth.

The conclusion that Paul's argument in 1 Corinthians exhibits thematic, rhetorical and compositional unity when seen as a deliberative letter urging

---

simply look for and identify isolated rhetorical *topoi* from Greco-Roman parallels, but must ground that comparative study in the overall argument. It is especially important that one demonstrate the parallel *functions* of the *topoi* in the NT and Greco-Roman parallels. Not only are the terms and *topoi* which Paul uses to describe Corinthian factionalism paralleled in Greco-Roman texts, with the same function (to urge unity), but they are often found in tandem with many other *topoi* we have identified in 1 Cor as well.

[2] Only 5:1; 7:1; and 11:18 can surely be assigned on this basis (cf. also 1:11, though the extent of that reference is much disputed). Of the other argumentative subsections in 1 Corinthians most simply do not say how Paul learned of the subject of controversy (6:1–11; 6:12–20; 8:1–11:1; 11:2–16; 12:1–14:40; 15:1–57; 16). Even in the schema constructed on the basis of 1:10; 5:1; 7:1 and 11:18, 11:18 is an oral report in the midst of Paul's response to written questions, so the view that this was Paul's normal mode of writing, to deal with oral and then written communications, must admit of at least one (large) exception from the very beginning. It also rules out any possible overlap between various communications.

concord is here presented as a direct challenge to partition theories which deny the coherence and thus the original integrity of the letter. This conclusion gains further credence from the witness of the earliest readers of 1 Corinthians, closer to the language and world of this text than we, who read it and understood it as a letter which throughout responded directly to the problem of factionalism at Corinth. We conclude (against Bauer),[3] that this interpretation of 1 Corinthians in the early church was no "peculiar" or unfounded reading, but rather one that is true to the nature and function of the letter itself. The attention to patristic exegesis of Paul's letters throughout this study shows further the significant contribution those interpretive works can make to investigations of Paul's rhetoric and argumentation.

This study has consciously presented a *constructive* argument for the unity of 1 Corinthians, where in the past those who have actually defended the unity of the letter have too often been content to do so mainly by questioning the arguments of the partition theorists. Yet alongside our constructive argument, in the course of this study several of the methodological bases of the partition theories have also been challenged. In particular, we have demonstrated that unproven presuppositions about epistolary conventions govern most of those theories, such as the significance of the formula περὶ δέ, the assumption that one can only discuss possible visits or one's personal presence at the end of a letter, and the assumption that one letter should respond to only one isolated oral or epistolary contact.

Rhetorical analysis of the letter provides a second front of attack on the arguments upon which the partition theories of 1 Corinthians have been based, because it reveals how much those theories have relied on mechanical applications of methodological principles which are not appropriate for rhetorical texts. For example, the standard literary-critical criterion of the doublet, which is so valuable in Pentateuchal and synoptic source criticism, does not function the same way in the analysis of an argument as it does in narrative or other genres. Paul's repeated call "be imitators of me!" in 1 Cor 4:16 and 11:1[4] is in no way similar to the Matthean doublets, or Noah entering the ark twice! Partitions based on mechanistic applications of the "doublet" criterion must be challenged. The same is true of a second methodological common denominator of partition theories of 1 Corinthians. Often a particular division hypothesis will make appeal to the argumentative coherence between parts of the text which are separated by intervening arguments. In this way the excision of the intervening material is proposed, so that those parts which are regarded as coherent will be adjacent to one another in the reconstruction. But in argumentation there can be coherence over a large argumentative whole, with the author returning to prior

---

[3] See chap. I.

[4] Or the repeated slogan in 6:12 and 10:23, the double refrain in 6:20 and 7:23, or the "dual treatments" of idol meats in chaps. 8 and 10, and spiritual gifts in chaps. 12 and 14.

subjects of discussion, repeating appeals, and varying approaches for the sake of diversity and to maintain the attention of the audience. Argumentative coherence does not in itself justify the inference of original adjacency. Thus such arguments may be turned around to support the unity of the letter instead of its partition. While a subjective element is of course inherent in all literary interpretation (for unity as for disunity), the arguments which have been put forward to buttress partition theories of 1 Corinthians have dressed themselves in these "formal" claims which do not hold up on methodological grounds, and therefore must be contested. We are still left, however, with the problem of how to adjudicate the dispute between the interpreter who sees an inclusio where another sees an insertion. In this respect the present investigation is a call for greater methodological precision on both sides.[5]

Toward that end, this study has entered into the current investigation of New Testament texts by rhetorical criticism with a critical distance. While rhetorical analysis is crucial and fruitful for rhetorical documents, and can play an important role in discussion of the unity or fragmentation of a text, it must be done with great care. In this investigation I have set out five mandates for rhetorical criticism of Pauline (and other New Testament) texts: 1) rhetorical criticism is an historical undertaking; 2) actual speeches and letters from antiquity must be consulted along with the rhetorical handbooks throughout the investigation; 3) the designation of the rhetorical species of a text cannot be begged in the analysis; 4) the appropriateness of rhetorical form or genre to content must be demonstrated; and 5) the rhetorical unit to be examined should be a compositional unit, which can be further substantiated by successful rhetorical analysis.[6] These mandates were justified in relation to previous rhetorical analyses in chap. I, but their effectiveness is also to be measured by their employment throughout the course of the present investigation. This attention to the methodology of rhetorical criticism constitutes an overt attempt to keep rhetorical criticism under the

---

5 This study has focused only on the partition theories of 1 Corinthians, and has challenged those particular arguments. This is not intended as a wholesale refutation of partition theories in general (such dismissive arguments as the lack of text-critical evidence for partition, or the superiority of the presupposition of unity over partition, have not been relied upon here, because I do not recognize them as convincing). Arguments for the division of 1 Thess, 2 Cor, Phil or Rom must be evaluated in themselves (though the call for methodological consistency and precision is applicable to all such investigations).

6 The lack of stylistic analysis in this study should not be understood as an implied disparagement of that aspect of rhetorical criticism, but it is simply beyond the scope of this investigation. While rhetorical criticism as here defined and employed is not identical with style criticism, as was earlier the case (see chap. I n. 15), style criticism is important on all rhetorical texts (the recent works of Watson [*Invention*; "1 Cor 10:23–11:1"] are notable in this regard). Some valuable research has already been done on the style of 1 Cor or parts of it (Weiss, "Rhetorik"; Jeremias, "Chiasmus"; Wischmeyer, *Weg*, 175–90; most recently T. Schmeller, *Paulus und die 'Diatribe.' Eine vergleichende Stilinterpretation*, NTAbh n. s. 19 [Münster: Aschendorff, 1987] 332–427, on diatribe style in portions of 1 Cor).

umbrella of the historical-critical method, against those who would move it permanently toward structuralism and other forms of ahistorical interpretation.[7] Because such a plethora of sources is extant for reconstructing the pervasive Greco-Roman rhetorical tradition operative at the time the New Testament documents were composed, we are in an enviable position in which to undertake analysis which subjects itself to the relevant ancient norms and conventions of rhetorical composition, and not merely to those of the modern reader.

In this study much attention has been devoted to the "political" nature of 1 Corinthians. This is not to say, however, that 1 Corinthians is not a "religious" document. Rather, 1 Corinthians represents the fundamental problem of *practical ecclesiology*[8] which Paul chose to treat by employing Greco-Roman political terms and concepts for the society and the interrelationships of its members. This means that Paul in 1 Corinthians presents a viewpoint on the church as *a real political body* (even the local church) to which some Greco-Roman political lore, especially the call for concord, is directly applicable. Paul's intimate conception of the church as a family or household in need of harmony also is consistent with such Hellenistic analogues. Consequently, in the continuing debate on Paul's affinities to Judaism(s) versus Roman Hellenism I have stressed (as did Grant over twenty-five years ago)[9] the extent to which in this letter we see Paul readily drawing upon Hellenistic commonplaces which are well attested in the cities of Asia Minor in the first century. Yet before this is too quickly claimed as another point for the "Hellenistic" side of Paul, we must remember also the extent to which we have seen that Hellenistic Judaism (at least as represented by those unique figures Philo and Josephus) was itself quite at home with many of these commonplaces about social concord in the religious community. Thus the complexity of Paul's dual allegiances remains.

Some of the evidence collected in this study (especially in chap. III) also suggests a fruitful area for further detailed research: ancient sociology. The many recent anthropological and sociological investigations of the New Testament have, not surprisingly, found 1 Corinthians to be a gold mine of resources[10] (though in some works its prescriptive nature is perhaps too readily assigned a descriptive meaning). This is so because contemporary sociological analysis of the New Testament is interested in the very same questions which

---

[7] Those investigations can be valid in their own right. My point is that they must not be considered representative or normative for all rhetorical criticism. To preserve the distinction I refer to "historical rhetorical criticism" (see chap. I).

[8] After the present study was finished, I was delighted to see Bowe, 4 apply this same phrase to *1 Clem.* which I have applied to 1 Cor! It no doubt does suit both, as I have argued throughout this study.

[9] "Hellenistic Elements."

[10] E.g., Schreiber; Meeks, *Urban Christians* (see the index of Scriptural citations under 1 Cor, which fills two pages, 281–82); Theissen (whose work is notable for its detailed incorporation of ancient materials); Neyrey; Barton.

Paul directly faced in 1 Corinthians – group formation, integration, alienation and social structures. What those studies have seen in 1 Corinthians through the synchronic models of social scientific research is by this study at many points confirmed in ancient texts which overtly discuss the problems of social formation and cohesion in their own context. A good example of this correspondence is the body metaphor for concord, which both anthropologists and sociologists have correctly identified as a socially unifying metaphor, a conclusion which is further confirmed in antiquity by the writers who both manifestly regarded and used it in the same way, to forge unity. The insights of modern sociology about the early church can and should be tested against ancient societies, not just in terms of their general behavior, but also their politics. Much as we might assume that in "all societies" to form unity there must be harmony in such things as fashions, dietary habits, and marital practices, as well as careful rules about group membership, to find Plutarch saying the same thing in the late first century[11] provides diachronic substantiation of the position proposed on synchronic grounds via social scientific methodology. This helps us to understand better Paul's difficult task at Corinth on ancient terms as well as in relation to universals of culture. The further explicit investigation into *ancient* sociological reflections (which leads in most cases to political theory and practice) can therefore be worthwhile.

In the final analysis, this study has constituted an interpretation of 1 Corinthians, one which has stressed the extent to which Paul combats Corinthian factionalism (as he describes it) throughout the letter. Seen in this way certain elements of the text come into relief, and the exegesis of specific problem sections is provided with some new directions. This has been the major goal of this exegetical study: to understand this one ancient text on its own terms. But this study has in no way exhausted 1 Corinthians, nor touched on all of the problems posed by its interpretation and its historical location. In particular it may surprise the reader that, in an investigation which so much stresses the factionalism at Corinth, no new comprehensive analysis of the names, composition, socioeconomic background and theological positions of the Corinthian parties is provided. This has been deliberate. My intention here has been to read *Paul's rhetoric of response to factionalism* against the background of Greco-Roman political texts which do the same thing. The tasks of historical reconstruction remain. This study provides some prerequisites, both positive and negative, for further investigations of the Corinthian parties.

Positively, the whole letter is now opened up as a resource for that search (not just ch. 1–4), on the basis of our conclusion that Paul himself sees all of the topics of consideration in 1 Corinthians to be related to the problem of party strife. But negatively for historical reconstruction, we have observed the extent to which Paul caricatures the behavior of the Corinthians, and the extent to which it is *he*

[11] *Mor.* 329C-D, on Alexander's unifying policies (quoted in chap. III n. 305).

who names their problem as factionalism, utilizing very strong terminology derived from ancient politics. In accord with others in Greco-Roman antiquity, Paul's diagnosis of the problem probably exaggerates its intensity and pervasiveness and thus in some way may distort the actual sociological situation. Even more difficult for historical reconstruction, we have observed that in his rhetoric of response Paul does not name the parties individually, but treats "factionalism" itself. The best clue that remains is not a new one: that in his oscillating arguments in 1 Corinthians Paul seeks to conciliate different sides (yet even here he may exaggerate the extent of those positions for the sake of argument). Thus the problem of reconstructing the true nature of the situation at Corinth from Paul's 1 Corinthians alone is beset by the same rhetorical difficulties as with other Greco-Roman texts, severely compounded by the meager information we have outside of the letter about the individual members of the church community and their varied allegiances.[12]

But even as the methodological problems of historical reconstruction of the Corinthian parties remain, this study argues that one must nevertheless begin by reading 1 Corinthians on Paul's own terms. In the letter he undeniably names the problem at Corinth as σχίσματα, factions. This means that Pauline scholarship should not simply talk about Paul's "opponents" in 1 Corinthians in the same way as is done in the case of 2 Corinthians or Galatians, where Paul's own description of the situation justifies such language. This investigation has uncovered the great extent to which Paul's own recurrent rhetorical strategy of appealing to himself as the example of proper behavior to be imitated depends upon his assumed support at Corinth. The present analysis has also concluded on rhetorical grounds that Paul does not defend himself in 1 Corinthians, not even in 1 Cor 9. He may have needed to (as the letters in 2 Corinthians suggest), but he did not, either because he misdiagnosed the situation, was ill-informed, or because he chose to avoid the facts. But when 1 Corinthians is understood as Paul's response to Corinthian factions (because that is how *Paul* diagnosed and treated the problem), not opponents, we see that one cannot methodologically proceed by reconstructing a "Corinthian" position from 1 Corinthians (as one does for 2 Corinthians and Galatians), because several Corinthian positions are represented there. That this is the case may be well illustrated by even a cursory look at the extraordinarily conflicted scholarly literature on Paul's "opponents" in 1 Corinthians, which has named them at one time or another as variously libertines or ascetics, Judaizers or Hellenizers, hyper-sacramentalists or secularists, gnostics or representatives of the Jerusalem church. The present study would suggest that each of those scholarly positions has been defended by extrapolating from one portion of Paul's response to the Corinthian divisions, without due attention to the overall rhetorical strategy of reconciliation of a

[12] The available evidence (mostly about notables in the community) is collected and carefully analyzed by Theissen, 69–119.

divided church in which those portions are embedded. My own suspicion is that, on more common-sensical grounds, at Corinth we probably do not have full-blown representatives of any such clearly defined groups, but rather members of the same community who incline in the direction of the various extremes, their separation fomented and exacerbated by socioeconomic factors. The structure of individual house churches within the Christian community at Corinth also must have played a significant role in the divisions. Paul may have actually been trying to create rather than preserve unity in the church at Corinth, but in his rhetoric of response he presents their factionalism as a deficiency and shortcoming from their theological calling to Christian unity and concord. Further historical investigation of the situation which Paul faced at Corinth and addressed in 1 Corinthians, which takes at some face value his own description of the problem as factionalism (not immediately for historical reconstruction, but in order to read his letter correctly for information toward that end), is therefore justified and necessary.

Lastly, we must ask how we can evaluate the effectiveness of the rhetorical composition which is 1 Corinthians. As much as in this study I have objected to the polemical situation of 2 Corinthians being read back onto 1 Corinthians, that does not mean that 2 Corinthians cannot be used to answer this different question. Paul's rhetoric of reconciliation in 1 Corinthians was a failure.[13] It seems to have failed on at least two grounds. First of all, it is clear from 2 Corinthians that Paul's rhetorical strategy of appealing to himself as the respected example to be imitated was not well received at Corinth, but was instead negatively interpreted as Paul's "self-recommendation."[14] Secondly, as a deliberative argument for concord, Paul's 1 Corinthians was an inherently risky undertaking. Instead of reuniting the Corinthian factions, Paul seems, by his argument in this letter, to have "incurred the enmity of both."[15] So 1 Corinthians was a failure in its original historical setting.

Nevertheless, as we have so often noted in this study, despite its inaugural failure, 1 Corinthians was a very popular and commonly employed letter in the early church for this same purpose: to urge reconciliation of divided factions. The history of Christianity has provided no end of situations to which Paul's argument for unity in 1 Corinthians has been yet again applicable. Once established as an apostolic document, the rhetorical strategy of self-appeal which led to its original failure was imbued with effectiveness. From the grave the person of the apostle Paul could speak the words "be imitators of me," and call upon himself as the example of partisan-free behavior without incurring the enmity

---

[13] Barrett, *First Corinthians*, 5: "The epistle was not a successful document." Cf. differently Koester, *Introduction*, 2.126.

[14] 2 Cor 3:1; 4:2; 5:12; 6:4; 10:12, 18.

[15] This is Aristotle's description of Solon's fate when he tried to reconcile factions (*Ath. Pol.* 5.2; 6.3; 11.2). However, this is not to suggest that 1 Cor alone can account for the different situation we see in 2 Cor (which appears to include the incursion of outside agitators).

(or disbelief!) of both parties. In Paul, for most of the life of the church, all parties were at least ostensibly united.[16] Yet appeals for concord, though commonplace and commonly given lip service, are not nearly so readily enacted (though the concomitant conservatism of 1 Corinthians has always found ready admirers and imitators[17]). Thus 1 Corinthians continues in its place in the Christian canon, its call for Christian unity above all other considerations revered but still largely unheeded, and manifestly unrealized.

[16] Cf. *1 Clem.* 5.

[17] No one has better expressed the ambivalence of this facet of the legacy of 1 Corinthians than Theissen: "If the basic pattern of primitive Christian love-patriarchalism today appears insufficient for shaping our social relationships, it should nevertheless be given its historic due: it was a human attempt to shape social relationships . . . Christianity cannot remain indifferent to this radicalization of ancient democratic traditions which has so irrevocably shaped our ethical and political consciousness" (p. 110).

Bibliography

Reference Works

Balz, H. and G. Schneider, eds. *Exegetisches Wörterbuch zum Neuen Testament.* 3 vols. Stuttgart: Kohlhammer, 1980–83.

Bauer, W. *A Greek-English Lexicon of the New Testament and Other Early Christian Literature.* Trans. and rev. W. F. Arndt, F. W. Gingrich and F. W. Danker. 2nd edition. Chicago: University of Chicago Press, 1979.

Blass, F. and A. Debrunner. *A Greek Grammar of the New Testament and Other Early Christian Literature.* Trans. and rev. R. W. Funk. Chicago: University of Chicago Press, 1961.

Brown, F., S. R. Driver and C. A. Briggs. *A Hebrew and English Lexicon of the Old Testament.* Oxford: Clarendon, 1972.

Galling, K. von, ed. *Die Religion in Geschichte und Gegenwart.* 6 vols. Tübingen: Mohr/Siebeck, 1957–62[3].

Glare, P. G. W. *Oxford Latin Dictionary.* Oxford: Clarendon, 1982.

Hammond, N. G. L. and H. H. Scullard. *The Oxford Classical Dictionary.* Oxford: Clarendon, 1970.

Kittel, G., ed. *Theological Dictionary of the New Testament.* 10 vols. Trans. G. W. Bromiley. Grand Rapids, MI: Eerdmans, 1964–76.

Klauser, T., E. Dassmann, *et al.*, eds. *Reallexikon für Antike und Christentum.* 14 vols. Stuttgart: Hiersemann, 1950–.

Lampe, G. W. H. *A Patristic Greek Lexicon.* Oxford: Clarendon, 1961.

Liddell, H. G. and R. Scott. *A Greek-English Lexicon.* Rev. H. S. Jones and R. McKenzie. 9th ed. Oxford: Clarendon, 1940.

Moulton, J. H., W. F. Howard and N. Turner. *A Grammar of New Testament Greek.* 4 Vols. Edinburgh: T & T Clark, 1906–76.

Moulton, J. H. and G. Milligan. *The Vocabulary of the Greek New Testament Illustrated from the Papyri and Other Non-Literary Sources.* London: Hodder, 1930.

Murray, J. A. H., H. Bradley, *et al.*, eds. *The Oxford English Dictionary.* 2nd edition prepared by J. A. Simpson and E. S. C. Weiner. 20 vols. Oxford: Clarendon, 1989.

Sophocles, E. A. *Greek Lexicon of the Roman and Byzantine Periods.* Hildesheim: Olms, 1983.

Smyth, H. W. *Greek Grammar.* Cambridge, MA: Harvard University Press, 1920; repr. 1980.

Spicq, C. *Notes de lexicographie néotestamentaire.* 3 vols. OBO 22.1–3. Fribourg/Suisse: Editions Universitaires; Göttingen: Vandenhoeck & Ruprecht, 1978–82.

Wissowa, G., W. Kroll, *et al.*, eds. *Paulys Realencyclopädie der classischen Altertumswissenschaft.* Vols. I-XXIV, IA.1-X.A, Supp. I-XV. Stuttgart: Metzler; Munich: Druckenmüller, 1894–1978.

Ancient Sources: Texts, Editions, Translations

Aeschines. Trans. C. D. Adams. LCL. Cambridge, MA: Harvard University Press, 1919.

Aeschinis quae feruntur epistolae. Ed. E. Drerup. Leipzig: Weicher, 1904.

Aeschylus. 2 Vols. Trans. H. W. Smyth. LCL. Cambridge, MA: Harvard University Press, 1922–26.

Ammonius. *De adfinium vocabulorum differentia*. Ed. K. Nickau. BT. Leipzig: Teubner, 1966.

Andocides. *Minor Attic Orators*. Vol. 1. Trans. K. J. Maidment. LCL. Cambridge, MA: Harvard University Press, 1941.

Antiphon. *Minor Attic Orators*. Vol. 1. Trans. K. J. Maidment. LCL. Cambridge, MA: Harvard University Press, 1941.

Apollonius von Kitium. Ed. H. Schöne. Leipzig: Teubner, 1896.

The Letters of Apollonius of Tyana. A Critical Text with Prolegomena, Translation and Commentary. Ed. R. J. Penella. Leiden: Brill, 1979.

The Apostolic Fathers. Ed. J. B. Lightfoot and J. R. Harmer. Repr. edition. Grand Rapids, MI: Baker Book House, 1984.

The Apostolic Fathers. 2 vols. Trans. K. Lake. LCL. New York: Putnam's Sons/Macmillan, 1912–13.

Die apostolischen Väter. Ed. F. X. Funk and K. Bihlmeyer. SAQ n. s. 1. Tübingen: Mohr/Siebeck, 1970[3].

Appian: Roman History. 4 vols. Trans. H. White. LCL. New York: Macmillan, 1912–28.

Aelii Aristidis Smyrnaei quae supersunt omnia. 2 vols. Ed. B. Keil. Berlin: Weidmann, 1898; repr. 1958.

Aristides: Orations. Vol. 1. Trans. C. A. Behr. LCL. Cambridge, MA: Harvard University Press, 1973.

P. Aelius Aristides. The Complete Works. 2 vols. Trans. and ed. C. A. Behr. Leiden: Brill, 1981–86.

Aristophanes. 3 vols. Trans. B. B. Rogers. LCL. Cambridge, MA: Harvard University Press, 1924.

Aristotle. Trans. H. P. Cooke, H. Tredennick, *et al.* 23 vols. LCL. Cambridge, MA: Harvard University Press, 1938–60.

Aristotelis privatorum scriptorum fragmenta. Ed. M. Plezia. BT. Leipzig: Teubner, 1977.

[Aristotle]. *De Mundo*. Trans. D. J. Furley. LCL. In *Aristotle. On Sophistical Refutations, On Coming-to-Be and Passing Away*. Cambridge, MA: Harvard University Press, 1955.

[Aristotle]. *Rhetorica ad Alexandrum*. Trans. H. Rackham. LCL. Vol. with *Aristotle. Problems II*. Cambridge, MA: Harvard University Press, 1937.

Biblia Hebraica Stuttgartensia. Ed. K. Elliger, W. Rudolph, *et al.* Stuttgart: Deutsche Bibelgesellschaft, 1983.

Caesar: The Civil Wars. Trans. A. G. Peskett. LCL. Cambridge, MA: Harvard University Press, 1914.

Catalogus Codicum Astrologorum Graecorum. Vol. 3, pt. 2. "Codices Hispanienses." Ed. C. O. Zuretti. Brussels: Lamertin, 1934.

John Chrysostom. *Hom. I-XLIV in I Cor.* Migne, *PG* 61.9–382.

Cicero. 28 vols. Trans. G. L. Hendrickson, H. M. Hubbell, *et al.* Cambridge, MA: Harvard University Press, 1912–72.

[Cicero]. *Ad C. Herennium De Ratione Dicendi (Rhetorica ad Herennium).* Trans. H. Caplan. LCL. Cambridge, MA: Harvard University Press, 1954.

Clement of Alexandria. Trans. G. W. Butterworth. LCL. New York: Putnam's Sons, 1919.

–, *Stromateis.* Migne, *PG* 8.685–1382.

Corpus Medicorum Graecorum. Ed. I. L. Heiberg, H. Diller, *et al.* Leipzig/Berlin: Teubner, 1908–.

Cramer, J. A., ed. *Catenae in Sancti Pauli Epistolas ad Corinthios.* Oxford: University Press, 1841.

The Cynic Epistles. A Study Edition. Ed. A.J. Malherbe. SBLSBS 12. Missoula, MT: Scholars Press, 1977.

Cyril of Alexandria. *Explanatio in I Cor.* Migne, *PG* 74.855–916.

Demades. "Twelve Years." *Minor Attic Orators.* Vol. 2. Trans. J. O. Burtt. LCL. Cambridge, MA: Harvard University Press, 1954.

Demetrius. On Style. Trans. W. R. Roberts. LCL. In Aristotle vol. 23, *The Poetics.* Cambridge, MA: Harvard University Press, 1927.

Demosthenes. 7 vols. Trans. J. H. Vince, C. A. Vince, *et al.* LCL. New York: Putnam's Sons; Cambridge, MA: Harvard University Press, 1930–1949.

Scholia Demosthenica. 2 vols. Ed. M. R. Dilts. BT. Leipzig: Teubner, 1983–86.

Dio Cassius: Roman History. 9 vols. Trans. E. Cary. LCL. Cambridge, MA: Harvard University Press, 1914–27.

Dio Chrysostom. 5 vols. Trans. J. W. Cohoon and H. L. Crosby. LCL. Cambridge, MA: Harvard University Press, 1932–51.

Diodorus Siculus. 12 vols. Trans. C. H. Oldfather, C. L. Sherman, *et al.* LCL. New York: Putnam's Sons; Cambridge, MA: Harvard University Press, 1933–67.

Diogenes Laertius: Lives of Eminent Philosophers. 2 vols. Trans. R. D. Hicks. LCL. Cambridge, MA: Harvard University Press, 1925.

Dionysius of Halicarnassus: Critical Essays. 2 vols. Trans. S. Usher. LCL. Cambridge, MA: Harvard University Press, 1974–85.

Dionysius of Halicarnassus: Roman Antiquities. 7 vols. Trans. E. Cary, on the basis of E. Spelman's translation. LCL. Cambridge, MA: Harvard University Press, 1937–50.

Elegy and Iambus with the Anacreontea. 2 vols. Trans. J. M. Edmonds. LCL. New York: Putnam's Sons, 1931.

Elephantine-Papyri. Ed. O. Rubensohn. *Ägyptische Urkunden aus den königlichen Museen zu Berlin: Griechische Urkunden.* Sonderheft. Berlin: Weidmann, 1907.

Epictetus. 2 vols. Trans. W. A. Oldfather. Cambridge, MA: Harvard University Press, 1925–28.

Euripides. 4 vols. Trans. A. S. Way. LCL. New York: Macmillan/Putnam's Sons, 1912.

Eusebii Pamphili praeparatio evangelica. 4 vols. Trans. E. H. Gifford. Oxford: Academy, 1903.

Eusebius. Ecclesiastical History. 2 vols. Trans. K. Lake and J. E. L. Oulton. LCL. New York: Putnam's Sons; Cambridge, MA: Harvard University Press, 1926–32.

Eusebius Werke. Achter Band. Praeparatio Evangelica. Ed. K. Mras. GCS. Berlin: Akademie-Verlag, 1956.

Fragmenta Historicorum Graecorum. 5 vols. Ed. C. Müller. Paris: Didot, 1841–70.

Fragmenta Philosophorum Graecorum. 3 vols. Ed. F. W. A. Mullach. Paris: Didot, 1881–83.

Die Fragmente der griechischen Historiker. 3 vols. Ed. F. Jacoby. Berlin: Weidmann; Leiden: Brill, 1923–50.

Die Fragmente der Vorsokratiker. 3 vols. Ed. H. Diels and W. Kranz. Berlin: Weidmann, 1974–75[6].

Fragments from Hellenistic Jewish Authors. Vol. 1: Historians. Ed. C. R. Holladay. Texts and Translations 20. Pseudepigrapha 10. Chico, CA: Scholars Press, 1983.

The Correspondence of Marcus Cornelius Fronto. 2 vols. Trans. C. R. Haines. LCL. Cambridge, MA: Harvard University Press, 1919–20.

Galen. *Opera Omnia*. 20 vols. Ed. C. G. Kühn. Leipzig: Cnoblochi, 1821–33.

Griechische Papyri. Ed. F. Bilabel. Heidelberg: Winter, 1923.

Hellenica Oxyrhynchia. Ed. B. P. Grenfell and A. S. Hunt. Oxford: Clarendon, 1909.

Hennecke, E. *New Testament Apocrypha*. 2 vols. Ed. W. Schneemelcher. Trans. R. McL. Wilson. Philadelphia: Fortress, 1963.

Hermogenis opera. Ed. H. Rabe. Rhetores Graeci vol. 6. BT. Leipzig: Teubner, 1894.

"[Hermogenes] *On Stases*: A Translation with an Introduction and Notes." Ed. and trans. R. Nadeau. *SM* 31 (1964) 361–424.

Herodas. The Mimes and Fragments. Ed. W. Headlam and A. D. Knox. Cambridge: University Press, 1922.

[Herodes Atticus]. ΠΕΡΙ ΠΟΛΙΤΕΙΑΣ. *Ein politisches Pamphlet aus Athen 404 vor Chr.* Ed. E. Drerup. *Studien zur Geschichte und Kultur des Altertums* vol. 2, pt 1. Paderborn: Schöningh, 1908.

Herodian. 2 vols. Trans. C. R. Whittaker. LCL. Cambridge, MA: Harvard University Press, 1969–70.

Herodotus. 4 vols. Trans. A. D. Godley. LCL. Cambridge, MA: Harvard University Press, 1921–25.

Hesiod, the Homeric Hymns and Homerica. Trans. H. G. Evelyn-White. LCL. Cambridge, MA: Harvard University Press, 1914; rev. ed. 1936.

The Hibeh Papyri. Part I. Ed. B. P. Grenfell and A. S. Hunt. London: Egypt Exploration Fund, 1906.

Inscriptiones Graecae. Ed. F. Hiller von Gaertringen. Vol. 12, Fasc. 1. Berlin: Reimer, 1895.

Isocrates. 3 vols. Trans. G. Norlin and L. Van Hook. LCL. Cambridge, MA: Harvard University Press, 1928–1945.

Jebb, R. C. *Selections From the Attic Orators*. London: Macmillan, 1957.

Josephus. 9 vols. Trans. H. St. J. Thackeray, R. Marcus and L. H. Feldman. LCL. Cambridge, MA: Harvard University Press, 1956–65.

Libanius. 2 vols. Trans. A. F. Norman. LCL. Cambridge, MA: Harvard University Press, 1969–77.

Libanius. Opera. 12 vols. Ed. R. Foerster. BT. Leipzig: Teubner, 1903–23; repr. Hildesheim: Olms, 1963.

Livy. 14 vols. Trans. B. O. Foster, F. G. Moore, *et al.* LCL. Cambridge, MA: Harvard University Press, 1919–59.

'Longinus' On the Sublime. Trans. W. H. Fyfe. LCL. In Aristotle vol. 23, *The Poetics*. Cambridge, MA: Harvard University Press, 1927.

Lucan. The Civil War (Pharsalia). Trans. J. D. Duff. LCL. Cambridge, MA: Harvard University Press, 1928.

Lucian. 8 vols. Trans. A. M. Harmon, K. Kilburn and M. D. Macleod. LCL. New York: Macmillan; Cambridge, MA: Harvard University Press, 1913–67.

Lysias. Trans. W. R. M. Lamb. LCL. Cambridge, MA: Harvard University Press, 1930.

The Communings with Himself of Marcus Aurelius Antoninus, Emperor of Rome. Trans. C. R. Haines. LCL. Cambridge, MA: Harvard University Press, 1916, rev. ed. 1930.

Menander Rhetor. Ed. and trans. D. A. Russell and N. G. Wilson. Oxford: Clarendon, 1981.

Midrash Rabbah. 10 vols. Trans. H. Freedman, S. M. Lehrman, *et al.* London/New York: Soncino, 1983.

במדבר רבה (*Numbers Rabbah*). Ed. M. A. Mirkin. Tel Aviv: Yabneh, 1977.

"Musonius Rufus. 'The Roman Socrates.'" Ed. and trans. C. E. Lutz. *YClS* 10 (1947) 1–147.

New Documents Illustrating Early Christianity. Vols. 1–4. Ed. G. H. R. Horsley. New South Wales: Macquarie University Ancient History Documentary Research Centre, 1981–87.

The New Oxford Annotated Bible with the Apocrypha. Revised Standard Version. Ed. H. G. May and B. M. Metzger. New York/Oxford: Oxford University Press, 1973.

Notices et extraits des papyrus grecs du musée du Louvre et de la bibliothèque impériale XVIII. Ed. W. Brunet de Presle. Paris: Imprimerie impériale, 1865².

Novum Testamentum Graece. 26th ed. Rev. and ed. K. Aland, *et al.* Stuttgart: Deutsche Bibelstiftung, 1979; 7th corrected printing 1983.

The Old Testament Pseudepigrapha. Ed. J. H. Charlsworth. 2 vols. Garden City, NY: Doubleday, 1983–85.

Orientis Graeci Inscriptiones Selectae. 2 vols. Ed. W. Dittenberger. Leipzig: Hirzel, 1903–1905.

Origène. Contre Celse. Ed. M. Borret. SC 132, 136, 147, 150. Paris: Cerf, 1967–69.

–, *Fragmenta ex commentariis in I Cor.* Ed. C. Jenkins. "Origen on 1 Corinthians." *JTS* 9 (1907–08) 231–47; 353–72; 500–14; *JTS* 10 (1908–09) 29–51. Supplemented by C. H. Turner. "Notes on the Text of Origen's Commentary on 1 Corinthians." *JTS* 10 (1908–09) 270–76.

The Oxyrhynchus Papyri. Ed. B. P. Grenfell and A. S. Hunt, *et al.* London: Egypt Exploration Fund, 1898-.

Papyrus grecs d'époque byzantine. Vol. 2. Ed. J. Maspéro. Cairo: L'Institute Français, 1913.

Paraleipomena Jeremiou. Ed. and Trans. R. A. Kraft and A.-E. Purintun. Text and Translations 1. Pseudepigrapha Series 1. Missoula, MT: Society of Biblical Literature, 1972.

Philo. 12 vols. Trans. F. H. Colson, G. H. Whitaker, *et al.* LCL. Cambridge, MA: Harvard University Press, 1929–53.

Philostratus: The Life of Apollonius of Tyana. 2 vols. Trans. F. C. Conybeare. LCL. Cambridge, MA: Harvard University Press, 1912.

Philostratus and Eunapius: The Lives of the Sophists. Trans. W. C. Wright. LCL. New York: Putnam's Sons, 1922.

Plato. 12 vols. Trans. H. N. Fowler, W. R. M. Lamb, *et al.* LCL. Cambridge, MA: Harvard University Press, 1914–35.

Plato. Epistulae. Ed. J. Moore-Blunt. BT. Leipzig: Teubner, 1985.

Plautus. 5 vols. Trans. P. Nixon. LCL. New York: Putnam's Sons; Cambridge, MA: Harvard University Press, 1916–38.

Pliny: Letters, Panegyricus. 2 vols. Trans. B. Radice. LCL. Cambridge, MA: Harvard University Press, 1969.

Plutarch's Lives. 11 vols. Trans. B. Perrin. LCL. Cambridge, MA: Harvard University Press, 1914–26.

Plutarch's Moralia. 15 vols. Trans. F. C. Babbitt, W. Helmbold, *et al.* LCL. Cambridge, MA: Harvard University Press, 1927–69.

Polybius. 6 vols. Trans. W. R. Paton. LCL. Cambridge, MA: Harvard University Press, 1922–27.

Procopius. 7 vols. Trans. H. B. Dewing. LCL. Cambridge, MA: Harvard University Press, 1914–40.

Prolegomenon Sylloge. Ed. H. Rabe. Rhetores Graeci 14. BT. Leipzig: Teubner, 1935.

Quintilian. 4 vols. Trans. H. E. Butler. LCL. New York: Putnam's Sons, 1921–1922.

Sallust. Trans. J. C. Rolfe. LCL. Cambridge, MA: Harvard University Press, 1921; rev. ed. 1931.

Seneca: Ad Lucilium Epistulae Morales. 3 vols. Trans. R. M. Gummere. LCL. New York: Putnam's Sons; Cambridge, MA: Harvard University Press, 1918–25; rev. ed. 1943, 1953.

Seneca: Moral Essays. Trans. J. W. Basore. 3 vols. LCL. New York: Putnam's Sons; Cambridge, MA: Harvard University Press, 1928–35.

Seneca, The Elder: Controversiae, Suasoriae. Trans. M. Winterbottom. 2 vols. LCL. Cambridge, MA: Harvard University Press, 1974.

Septuaginta. Ed. A. Rahlfs. Stuttgart: Deutsche Bibelgesellschaft, 1935.

Sophocles. 2 vols. Trans. F. Storr. LCL. Cambridge, MA: Harvard University Press, 1912–13.

Sorani Gynaeciorum. Ed. V. Rose. BT. Leipzig: Teubner, 1882.

Spengel, L., ed. *Rhetores Graeci*. 3 vols. BT. Leipzig: Teubner, 1853–56.

Staab, K. *Pauluskommentare aus der griechischen Kirche*. NTAbh 15. Münster: Aschendorff, 1933.

Ioannis Stobaei anthologium. 5 vols. Ed. C. Wachsmuth and O. Hense. Berlin: Weidmann, 1958.

Stoicorum Veterum Fragmenta. 4 vols. Ed. H. F. A. von Arnim. Leipzig: Teubner, 1905–24.

Strabo: Geography. 8 vols. Trans. H. L. Jones. LCL. Cambridge, MA: Harvard University Press, 1917–32.

Suetonius. 2 vols. Trans. J. C. Rolfe. LCL. Cambridge, MA: Harvard University Press, 1914.

Supplementum Epigraphicum Graecum. Ed. J. J. E. Hondius, *et al.* Leiden: Sijthoff; Amsterdam: Gieben, 1923-.

Sylloge Inscriptionum Graecarum. 4 vols. Ed. W. Dittenberger. Leipzig: Hirzel, 1915–24[3]; Hildesheim: Olms, 1960[4].

Syriani in Hermogenem commentaria. 2 vols. Ed. H. Rabe. Rhetores Graeci 16. Leipzig: Teubner, 1892–93.

Tacitus: Histories and Annals. 4 vols. Trans. C. H. Moore and J. Jackson. LCL. Cambridge, MA: Harvard University Press, 1925–37.

The Testaments of the Twelve Patriarchs. Ed. M. de Jonge. Leiden: Brill, 1978.

Themistii orationes. Ed. W. Dindorf. Hildesheim: Olms, 1961.

Theodoret. *Interpretationes in Pauli epistulas. – I Cor.* Migne, *PG* 82.225–376.

Theognis, Ps.-Pythagoras, Ps.-Phocylides, etc. Ed. D. Young. BT. Leipzig: Teubner, 1961.

Theophrastus: Characters. Trans. J. M. Edmonds. LCL. Cambridge, MA: Harvard University Press, 1929.

Thucydides. 4 vols. Trans. C. F. Smith. LCL. Cambridge, MA: Harvard University Press, 1919–23.

Vettii Valentis anthologiarum libri. Ed. G. Kroll. Berlin: Weidmann, 1908.
Virgil. 2 vols. Trans. H. R. Fairclough. LCL. Cambridge, MA: Harvard University Press, 1918; rev. ed. 1934.
Walz, C., ed. *Rhetores Graeci*. 9 vols. Stuttgart/Tübingen: Cotta, 1832–36.
Weichert, V., ed. *Demetrii et Libanii qui feruntur* ΤΥΠΟΙ ΕΠΙΣΤΟΛΙΚΟΙ *et* ΕΠΙΣΤΟΛΙΜΑΙΟΙ ΧΑΡΑΚΤΗΡΕΣ. BT. Leipzig: Teubner, 1910.
Xenophon. 7 vols. Trans. C. L. Brownson, O. J. Todd, *et al*. LCL. Cambridge, MA: Harvard University Press, 1918–25.

Secondary Literature Consulted

Alewell, K. *Über das rhetorische* ΠΑΡΑΔΕΙΓΜΑ. *Theorie, Beispielsammlung, Verwendung in der römischen Literatur der Kaiserzeit*. Leipzig: Hoffmann, 1913.
Allo, E.-B. *Saint Paul. Première Epitre aux Corinthiens*. EBib. Paris: LeCoffre, 1956[2].
Atkins, J. W. H. *Literary Criticism in Antiquity*. Gloucester, MA: Peter Smith, 1961.
Attridge, H. W. *The Interpretation of Biblical History in the* Antiquitates Judaicae *of Flavius Josephus*. HDR 7. Missoula, MT: Scholars Press, 1976.
Aune, D. E. *The New Testament in Its Literary Environment*. Library of Early Christianity 8. Philadelphia: Westminster, 1987.
–, Review of *Galatians: A Commentary on Paul's Letter to the Churches in Galatia*, by H. D. Betz. In *RelSRev* 7 (1981) 323–28.
Aurenche, O. *Les Groupes d'Alcibiade, de Léogoras et de Teucros*. Paris: Société d'Edition les Belles Lettres, 1974.
Baasland, E. "Die περί-Formel und die Argumentation(ssituation) des Paulus." *ST* 42 (1988) 69–87.
Bachmann, P. *Der erste Brief des Paulus an die Korinther*. KNT 7. Leipzig: Deichert, 1905.
Bailey, K. E. "The Structure of 1 Corinthians and Paul's Theological Method with Special Reference to 4:17." *NovT* 25 (1983) 152–81.
Balch, D. L. *Let Wives Be Submissive: The Domestic Code in 1 Peter*. SBLMS 26. Chico, CA: Scholars Press, 1981.
Baldry, H. C. *The Unity of Mankind in Greek Thought*. Cambridge: University Press, 1965.
Baldwin, C. S. *Ancient Rhetoric and Poetic*. New York: Macmillan, 1924. Repr. Westport, CT: Greenwood, 1971.
Barrett, C. K. "Christianity at Corinth." *Essays on Paul*. Philadelphia: Westminster, 1982. 1–27.
–, *The First Epistle to the Corinthians*. HNTC. New York/Evanston: Harper & Row, 1968.
–, "Things Sacrificed to Idols." *Essays on Paul*. Philadelphia: Westminster, 1982. 40–59.
Bartchy, S. S. Mallon Chresai: *First-Century Slavery and the Interpretation of 1 Corinthians 7:21*. SBLDS 11. Missoula, MT: Scholars Press, 1973.
Barth, K. *The Resurrection of the Dead*. Trans. H. J. Stenning. New York: Revell, 1933. Repr. New York: Arno, 1977.
Barton, S. C. "Paul's Sense of Place: An Anthropological Approach to Community Formation in Corinth." *NTS* 32 (1986) 225–46.

Bauer, W. *Orthodoxy and Heresy in Earliest Christianity*. Trans. Philadelphia Seminar on Christian Origins. Philadelphia: Fortress, 1971.

Baumert, N. *Ehelosigkeit und Ehe im Herrn. Eine Neuinterpretation von 1 Kor 7*. Forschung zur Bibel 47. Würzburg: Echter Verlag, 1984.

Beck, I. "Untersuchungen zur Theorie des Genos Symbuleutikon." Ph.D. diss. Hamburg, 1970.

Behr, C. A., ed. and trans. *P. Aelius Aristides. The Complete Works*. Vol. 2. Leiden: Brill, 1981.

Beker, J. C. "Paul's Theology: Consistent or Inconsistent?" *NTS* 34 (1988) 364–77.

Belleville, L. L. "Continuity or Discontinuity: A Fresh Look at 1 Corinthians in the Light of First-Century Epistolary Forms and Conventions." *EvQ* 59 (1987) 15–37.

Berger, K. "Hellenistische Gattungen im Neuen Testament." *ANRW* 2, pt. 25.2 (1984) 1031–1432.

Best, E. *One Body in Christ. A Study in the Relationship of the Church to Christ in the Epistles of the Apostle Paul*. London: S.P.C.K., 1955.

Betz, H. D. *Der Apostel Paulus und die sokratische Tradition: Eine exegetische Untersuchung zu seiner 'Apologie' 2 Kor 10–13*. BHT 45. Tübingen: Mohr/Siebeck, 1972.

–, *2 Corinthians 8 and 9: A Commentary on Two Administrative Letters of the Apostle Paul*. Hermeneia. Philadelphia: Fortress, 1985.

–, *Der Galaterbrief. Ein Kommentar zum Brief des Apostels Paulus an die Gemeinden in Galatien*. Trans. S. Ann. Munich: Kaiser, 1988.

–, *Galatians: A Commentary on Paul's Letter to the Churches in Galatia*. Hermeneia. Philadelphia: Fortress, 1979.

–, *Lukian von Samosata und das Neue Testament*. TU 76. Berlin: Akademie, 1961.

–, *Nachfolge und Nachahmung Jesu Christi im Neuen Testament*. BHT 37. Tübingen: Mohr/Siebeck, 1967.

–, ed. *Plutarch's Ethical Writings and Early Christian Literature*. SCHNT 4. Leiden: Brill, 1978.

–, ed. *Plutarch's Theological Writings and Early Christian Literature*. SCHNT 3. Leiden: Brill, 1975.

–, "The Problem of Rhetoric and Theology According to the Apostle Paul." *L'Apôtre Paul: Personnalité, style et conception du ministère*. Ed. A. Vanhoye. BETL 73 (1986) 16–48.

–, Review of *New Testament Interpretation Through Rhetorical Criticism*, by G. A. Kennedy. In *JTS* n. s. 37 (1986) 167.

Beyer, H. W. "κυβέρνησις." *TDNT* 3.1035–37.

Bjerkelund, C. *Parakalô: Form, Funktion und Sinn der parakalô Sätze in den paulinischen Briefen*. Bibliotheca theologica Norvegica 1. Oslo: Universitetsforlaget, 1967.

Blass, F. *Die attische Beredsamkeit*. 4 vols. Repr. ed. Hildesheim: Olms, 1962[3].

Blumenthal, A. von. "Τύπος und παράδειγμα." *Hermes* 63 (1928) 391–414.

Boer, W. P. de. *Imitation of Paul: An Exegetical Study*. Kampen: Kok, 1962.

Bonnard, P. *Jésus-Christ édifiant son Eglise. Le concept d'édification dans le Nouveau Testament*. Cahiers Théologiques de l'Actualité Protestante 21. Neuchâtel/Paris: Delachaux & Niestlé, 1948.

Bornkamm, G. "Der köstlichere Weg [1 Kor 13]." *Das Ende des Gesetzes. Paulusstudien. Gesammelte Aufsätze*, vol. 1. Munich: Kaiser, 1961. 93–112.

–, "Lord's Supper and Church in Paul." *Early Christian Experience*. Trans. P. L. Hammer. New York/Evanston: Harper & Row, 1969. 123–60.

–, "The More Excellent Way. 1 Corinthians 13." *Early Christian Experience*. Trans. P. L. Hammer. New York/Evanston: Harper & Row, 1969. 180–90.

–, "On the Understanding of Worship." *Early Christian Experience*. Trans. P. L. Hammer. New York/Evanston: Harper & Row, 1969. 161–79.

–, "Die Vorgeschichte des sogenannten Zweiten Korintherbriefes." *Geschichte und Glaube*, vol. 2. *Gesammelte Aufsätze*, vol. 4. BEvT 53. Munich: Kaiser, 1971. 162–94.

Bowe, B. E. *A Church in Crisis. Ecclesiology and Paraenesis in Clement of Rome*. HDR 23. Minneapolis, MN: Fortress, 1988.

Bradley, D. G. "The *Topos* as a Form in the Pauline Paraenesis." *JBL* 72 (1953) 238–46.

Bratsiotis, P. I. "Paulus und die Einheit der Kirche." *Studia Paulina* in honorem *Johannis de Zwaan*. Haarlem: Bohn, 1953. 28–36.

Braun, H. "περπερεύομαι." *TDNT* 6.93–95.

Bruce, F. F. *1 and 2 Corinthians*. NCBC. Grand Rapids, MI: Eerdmans, 1971.

Brunt, P. A. "'Amicitia' in the Late Roman Republic." *Proceedings of the Cambridge Philological Society* 191 (1965) 1–20.

Bultmann, R. *Faith and Understanding*. Trans. L. P. Smith. New York/Evanston: Harper & Row, 1969.

–, "καυχάομαι κτλ." *TDNT* 3.645–54.

Bünker, M. *Briefformular und rhetorische Disposition im 1. Korintherbrief*. GTA 28. Göttingen: Vandenhoeck & Ruprecht, 1984.

Burgess, T. C. *Epideictic Literature*. Ph.D. diss. University of Chicago. Chicago: University of Chicago Press, 1902.

Cairns, F. *Virgil's Augustan Epic*. Cambridge: Cambridge University Press, 1989.

Calhoun, G. M. *Athenian Clubs in Politics and Legislation*. Austin: University of Texas Press, 1913.

Calvin, J. *The First Epistle of Paul the Apostle to the Corinthians*. Trans. J. W. Fraser. Calvin's Commentaries. Grand Rapids, MI: Eerdmans, 1960.

Campbell, J. Y. "ΚΟΙΝΩΝΙΑ and its Cognates in the New Testament." *JBL* 51 (1932) 352–80.

Cancik, H. *Untersuchungen zu Senecas epistulae morales*. Spudasmata 18. Hildesheim: Olms, 1967.

Chadwick, H. "'All Things to All Men' (I Cor. IX.22)." *NTS* 1 (1955) 261–75.

Church, F. F. "Rhetorical Structure and Design in Paul's Letter to Philemon." *HTR* 71 (1978) 17–33.

Collins, A. Y. "The Function of 'Excommunication' in Paul." *HTR* 73 (1980) 251–63.

Collins, J. J. "Chiasmus, the 'ABA' Pattern and the Text of Paul." *Studiorum Paulinorum Congressus Internationalis Catholicus 1961*. Rome: Pontifical Biblical Institute, 1963. 2.575–83.

Colson, F. H. "Μετεσχημάτισα in I Cor. iv. 6." *JTS* 17 (1915–16) 379–84.

Conzelmann, H. *I Corinthians*. Trans. J. W. Leitch. Hermeneia. Philadelphia: Fortress, 1975.

Conzelmann, H., and A. Lindemann. *Interpreting the New Testament. An Introduction to the Principles and Methods of N. T. Exegesis*. Trans. S. S. Schatzmann. Peabody, MA: Hendrickson, 1988.

Cope, L. "1 Cor 11:2–16: One Step Further." *JBL* 97 (1978) 435–36.

Corsani, B. "L'unità della chiesa nella I. Cor." *Neues Testament und Geschichte. Historisches Geschehen und Deutung im Neuen Testament. O. Cullmann zum 70. Geburtstag*. Ed.

H. Baltensweiler and B. Reicke. Zurich: Theologischer Verlag; Tübingen: Mohr/Siebeck, 1972. 219–22.

Crouch, J. E. *The Origin and Intention of the Colossian Haustafel*. FRLANT 109. Göttingen: Vandenhoeck & Ruprecht, 1972.

Dahl, N. A. "Paul and the Church at Corinth according to 1 Cor 1:10–4:21." *Christian History and Interpretation: Studies Presented to John Knox*. Ed. W. R. Farmer, C. F. D. Moule and R. R. Niebuhr. Cambridge: University Press, 1967. 313–35. Repr. in *Studies in Paul*. Minneapolis: Augsburg, 1977. 40–61.

D'Alton, J. F. *Roman Literary Theory and Criticism*. London/New York/Toronto: Longmans, Green, 1931.

Dautzenberg, G. "Der Verzicht auf das apostolische Unterhaltsrecht. Eine exegetische Untersuchung zu 1 Kor 9." *Bib* 50 (1969) 212–32.

–, *Urchristliche Prophetie. Ihre Erforschung, ihre Voraussetzung im Judentum und ihre Struktur im ersten Korintherbrief*. BWANT 104. Stuttgart: Kohlhammer, 1975.

Deissmann, G. A. *Bible Studies*. Trans. A. Grieve. Edinburgh: T & T Clark, 1901.

–, *Light From the Ancient East*. Trans. L. R. M. Strachan. London: Hodder & Stoughton, 1927.

Delling, G. "στάσις." *TDNT* 7.568–71.

Dibelius, M. *From Tradition to Gospel*. Trans. B. L. Woolf. New York: Scribner's, 1935.

–, *James. A Commentary on the Epistle of James*. Rev. H. Greeven. Trans. M. A. Williams. Hermeneia. Philadelphia: Fortress, 1976.

Dinkler, E. "Korintherbriefe." *RGG*^{3} 4 (1960) 17–23.

–, "Die Taufterminologie in 2 Kor i.21 f." *Neotestamentica et Patristica. Eine Festgabe O. Cullmann zum 60. Geburtstag*. NovTSup 6. Leiden: Brill, 1962. 173–91.

Doty, W. G. "The Classification of Epistolary Literature." *CBQ* 31 (1969) 183–99.

–, *Letters in Primitive Christianity*. Philadelphia: Fortress, 1973.

Dover, K. J. "ΔΕΚΑΤΟΣ ΑΥΤΟΣ." *JHS* 80 (1960) 61–77.

Downing, F. G. "*A bas les aristos*. The Relevance of Higher Literature for the Understanding of the Earliest Christian Writings." *NovT* 30 (1988) 212–30.

Edmunds, L. *Cleon,* Knights, *and Aristophanes' Politics*. Lanham/New York: University Press of America, 1987.

Elliott, J. H. *A Home for the Homeless, A Sociological Exegesis of 1 Peter, Its Situation and Strategy*. Philadelphia: Fortress, 1981.

Ellis, E. E. "Traditions in 1 Corinthians." *NTS* 32 (1986) 481–502.

Exler, F. J. *The Form of the Ancient Greek Letter of the Epistolary Papyri (3rd c. B.C. – 3rd c. A.D.): A Study in Greek Epistolography*. Washington: Catholic University of America Press, 1923. Repr. Chicago: Ares, 1976.

Fascher, E. *Der erste Brief des Paulus an die Korinther*. THKNT vol. 7, pt. 1. Berlin: Evangelische Verlagsanstalt, 1975.

Fee, G. D. "Εἰδωλόθυτα Once Again: An Interpretation of 1 Cor 8–10." *Bib* 61 (1980) 172–97.

–, *The First Epistle to the Corinthians*. NIC. Grand Rapids, MI: Eerdmans, 1987.

Ferguson, J. *Moral Values in the Ancient World*. London: Methuen, 1958.

Fiedler, P. "Haustafel." *RAC* 103 (1986) 1063–73.

Filson, F. V. "The Significance of the Early House Churches." *JBL* 58 (1939) 105–12.

Finley, M. I. *Politics in the Ancient World*. Cambridge: Cambridge University Press, 1983.

Fiore, B. "'Covert Allusion' in 1 Corinthians 1–4." *CBQ* 47 (1985) 85–102.

–, *The Function of Personal Example in the Socratic and Pastoral Epistles.* AnBib 105. Rome: Biblical Institute, 1986.
Fiorenza, E. S. *In Memory of Her. A Feminist Theological Reconstruction of Christian Origins.* New York: Crossroad, 1983.
–, "Rhetorical Situation and Historical Reconstruction in 1 Corinthians." *NTS* 33 (1987) 386–403.
Fisher, N. R. E. "Drink, *Hubris*, and the Promotion of Harmony in Sparta." *Classical Sparta. Techniques Behind Her Success.* Ed. A. Powell. Norman: University of Oklahoma Press, 1988. 26–50.
Fiske, A. M. "Hieronymus Ciceronianus." *TAPA* 96 (1965) 119–38.
Fitzer, G. "'Das Weib schweige in der Gemeinde.' Über den unpaulinischen Charakter der mulier-taceat-Verse in 1. Korinther 14." *Theologische Existenz Heute* n. s. 110. Munich: Kaiser, 1963.
Fitzgerald, J. T. *Cracks in an Earthen Vessel: An Examination of the Catalogues of Hardships in the Corinthian Correspondence.* SBLDS 99. Atlanta: Scholars Press, 1988.
Fitzmyer, J. A. "A Feature of Qumran Angelology and the Angels of 1 Cor xi.10." *NTS* 4 (1957/58) 48–58.
Foerster, W. "ἀρέσκω κτλ." *TDNT* 1.455–57.
Forbes, C. "Comparison, Self-Praise and Irony: Paul's Boasting and the Conventions of Hellenistic Rhetoric." *NTS* 32 (1986) 1–30.
Fougères, G. "Inscriptions de Mantinée." *Bulletin de Correspondence Hellénique* 20 (1896) 119–66.
Fridrichsen, A. "Ackerbau und Hausbau in formelhaften Wendungen in der Bibel und bei Platon." *TSK* Sonderheft (1922) 185–86.
–, "Themelios, 1. Kor 3,11." *TZ* 2 (1946) 316–17.
Friedrich, G. "Christus, Einheit und Norm der Christen. Das Grundmotiv des 1. Korintherbriefs." *KD* 9 (1963) 235–58.
Fritz, K. von. *The Theory of the Mixed Constitution. A Critical Analysis of Polybius' Political Ideas.* New York: Columbia University Press, 1954.
Fuchs, H. "Augustin und der antike Friedensgedanke." *Neue Philologische Untersuchungen* 3. Ed. W. Jaeger. Berlin: Weidmann, 1926.
Fuks, A. "The Jewish Revolt in Egypt (A.D. 115–117) in the Light of the Papyri." *Social Conflict in Ancient Greece.* Jerusalem: Magnes; Leiden: Brill, 1984. 322–49.
Funk, R. W. "The Apostolic Parousia: Form and Significance." *Christian History and Interpretation: Studies Presented to John Knox.* Ed. W. R. Farmer, C. F. D. Moule and R. R. Niebuhr. Cambridge: University Press, 1967. 249–69.
Furnish, V. P. "Fellow Workers in God's Service." *JBL* 80 (1961) 364–70.
–, *II Corinthians.* AB 32A. Garden City, NY: Doubleday, 1984.
Gaiser, K. *Protreptik und Paränese bei Platon. Untersuchungen zur Form des platonischen Dialogs.* Tübinger Beiträge zur Altertumswissenschaft 40. Stuttgart: Kohlhammer, 1959.
Gauthier, R. A. and J. Y. Jolif. *L'Ethique à Nicomaque.* 2 vols. Louvain: University of Louvain Press, 1959.
Gehrke, H.-J. *Stasis. Untersuchungen zu den inneren Kriegen in den griechischen Staaten des 5. und 4. Jahrhunderts v. Chr.* Vestigia 35. Munich: Beck, 1985.
Godet, F. *Commentary on St. Paul's First Epistle to the Corinthians.* 2 vols. Trans. A. Cusin. Edinburgh: T & T Clark, 1889.

Goguel, M. *Introduction au Nouveau Testament*. vol. 4, pt. 2. Paris: Leroux, 1926.

Goldstein, J. A. *The Letters of Demosthenes*. New York: Columbia University Press, 1968.

Goodspeed, E. J. *The Meaning of Ephesians*. Chicago: University of Chicago Press, 1933.

Goppelt, L. "τύπος." *TDNT* 8.246–59.

Gouldner, A. W. *The Hellenic World. A Sociological Analysis*. New York/Evanston: Harper & Row, 1965.

Grant, R. M. *Augustus to Constantine*. New York: Harper & Row, 1970.

–, "Hellenistic Elements in I Corinthians." *Early Christian Origins. Studies in Honor of Harold R. Willoughby*. Ed. A. Wikgren. Chicago: Quadrangle Books, 1961. 60–66.

–, "The Wisdom of the Corinthians." *The Joy of Study: Papers on New Testament and Related Subjects Presented to Honor F. C. Grant*. Ed. S. E. Johnson. New York: Macmillan, 1951. 51–55.

Grosheide, F. W. *Commentary on the First Epistle to the Corinthians*. NICNT. Grand Rapids, MI: Eerdmans, 1953.

Grossmann, G. *Politische Schlagwörter aus der Zeit des Peloponnesischen Krieges*. Diss., Basel. Repr. New York: Arno, 1973.

Hainz, J. *Ekklesia. Strukturen paulinischer Gemeinde-Theologie und Gemeinde-Ordnung*. Biblische Untersuchungen 9. Regensburg: Pustet, 1972.

–, *Koinonia. Kirche als Gemeinschaft bei Paulus*. Biblische Untersuchungen 16. Regensburg: Pustet, 1982.

Hanson, S. *The Unity of the Church in the New Testament, Colossians and Ephesians*. Acta Seminarii Neotestamentici Upsaliensis 14. Uppsala: Almqvist & Wiksell, 1946.

Harnack, A. "Das hohe Lied des Apostels Paulus von der Liebe (I Kor. 13) und seine religionsgeschichtliche Bedeutung." *Sitzungsberichte der königlich preussischen Akademie der Wissenschaften*. Berlin: Königliche Akademie der Wissenschaften, 1911. 132–63.

Hartlich, P. "De exhortationum a Graecis Romanisque scriptarum historia et indole." *Leipziger Studien* 11 (1889) 207–336.

Hauck, F. "κοινός κτλ." *TDNT* 3.789–809.

Heinrici, C. F. G. *Der erste Brief an die Korinther*. MeyerK 7; 8th ed. Göttingen: Vandenhoeck & Ruprecht, 1896.

–, *Das erste Sendschreiben des Apostel Paulus an die Korinthier*. Berlin: Hertz, 1880.

Hellegouarc'h, J. *Le vocabulaire Latin des relations et des partis politiques sous la République*. Paris: Société d'Edition les Belles Lettres, 1963.

Héring, J. *The First Epistle of Saint Paul to the Corinthians*. Trans. A. W. Heathcote and P. J. Allcock. London: Epworth, 1962.

Hilgert, E. *The Ship and Related Symbols in the New Testament*. Assen: van Gorcum, 1962.

Hock, R. F. *The Social Context of Paul's Ministry: Tentmaking and Apostleship*. Philadelphia: Fortress, 1980.

Hooker, M. "Authority on Her Head: An Examination of 1 Cor xi,10." *NTS* 10 (1963/64) 410–16.

Horsley, R. A. "The Background of the Confessional Formula in 1 Kor 8,6." *ZNW* 69 (1978) 130–35.

–, "Wisdom of Word and Words of Wisdom in Corinth." *CBQ* 39 (1977) 224–39.

Hort, F. J. A. *The Epistle of St. James*. London: Macmillan, 1909.

Hübner, H. "Der Galaterbrief und das Verhältnis von antiker Rhetorik und Epistolographie." *TLZ* 109 (1984) 242–50.

Hudson-Williams, H. L. "Political Speeches in Athens." *CQ* n. s. 1 (1951) 68–73.

–, "Thucydides, Isocrates, and the Rhetorical Method of Composition." *CQ* 42 (1948) 76–81.

Hurd, J. C. *The Origin of 1 Corinthians.* London: S.P.C.K., 1965. Repr. Macon, GA: Mercer University Press, 1983.

Jacoby, E. "De Antiphontis Sophistae περὶ ὁμονοίας libro." Diss. Berlin, 1908.

Jaeger, W. *Early Christianity and Greek Paideia.* Cambridge, MA: Harvard University Press, 1961.

–, *Paideia: The Ideals of Greek Culture.* 3 vols. Trans. G. Highet. New York: Oxford University Press, 1939–44.

–, "Tyrtaeus on True Arete." *Werner Jaeger. Five Essays.* Trans. A. M. Fiske. Montreal: Casalini, 1966. 103–142.

Jal, P. "Pax civilis-concordia." *Rev. Et. Lat.* 39 (1961) 210–31.

Jaubert, A. "Le Voile des Femmes (I Cor XI.2–16)." *NTS* 18 (1971/72) 419–430.

Jeremias, J. "Chiasmus in den Paulusbriefen." *ZNW* 49 (1958) 145–56.

Jeske, R. L. "The Rock Was Christ: The Ecclesiology of 1 Corinthians 10." *Kirche.* FS G. Bornkamm. Ed. D. Lührmann and G. Strecker. Tübingen: Mohr/Siebeck, 1980. 245–55.

Jewett, R. *Paul's Anthropological Terms. A Study of their Use in Conflict Settings.* AGJU 10. Leiden: Brill, 1971.

–, "The Redaction of 1 Corinthians and the Trajectory of the Pauline School." *JAARSup* 46 (1978) 398–444.

–, *The Thessalonian Correspondence. Pauline Rhetoric and Millenarian Piety.* Philadelphia: Fortress, 1986.

Johnson, L. T. "James 3:13–4:10 and the *Topos* ΠΕΡΙ ΦΘΟΝΟΥ." *NovT* 25 (1983) 327–47.

–, *The Writings of the New Testament. An Interpretation.* Philadelphia: Fortress, 1986.

Joly, R. *Le vocabulaire chrétien de l'amour, est-il original?* Brussels: Universitaires de Bruxelles, 1968.

Jones, C. P. *Plutarch and Rome.* Oxford: Clarendon, 1971.

–, *The Roman World of Dio Chrysostom.* Cambridge, MA: Harvard University Press, 1978. Press, 1978.

Jones, F. S. *"Freiheit" in den Briefen des Apostels Paulus. Eine historische, exegetische und religionsgeschichtliche Studie.* GTA 34. Göttingen: Vandenhoeck & Ruprecht, 1987.

Jost, K. *Das Beispiel und Vorbild der Vorfahren bei den attischen Rednern und Geschichtschreibern bis Demosthenes.* Rhetorische Studien 19. Paderborn: Schöningh, 1936.

Judge, E. A. "Paul's Boasting in Relation to Contemporary Professional Practice." *AusBR* 16 (1968) 37–50.

Kagan, D. G. *The Great Dialogue. History of Greek Political Thought from Homer to Polybius.* New York: Free, 1965.

Kaiser, O. and W. G. Kümmel. *Exegetical Method.* Trans. E. V. N. Goetschius and M. J. O'Connell. New York: Seabury, 1975.

Käsemann, E. "1. Korinther 6,19–20." *Exegetische Versuche und Besinnungen.* Göttingen: Vandenhoeck & Ruprecht, 1960[2]. 1.276–79.

–, "The Pauline Doctrine of the Lord's Supper." *Essays on New Testament Themes.* Trans. W. J. Montague. SBT 41. Naperville, IL: Allenson, 1964. 108–35.

Kempthorne, R. "Incest and the Body of Christ: A Study of 1 Corinthians VI.12–20." *NTS* 14 (1967/68) 568–74.

Kennedy, G. A. *The Art of Persuasion in Greece*. Princeton: Princeton University Press, 1963.

–, *The Art of Rhetoric in the Roman World*. Princeton: Princeton University Press, 1972.

–, *Classical Rhetoric and its Christian and Secular Tradition from Ancient to Modern Times*. Chapel Hill: University of North Carolina Press, 1980.

–, "The Earliest Rhetorical Handbooks." *AJP* 80 (1959) 169–78.

–, "Focusing of Arguments in Greek Deliberative Oratory." *TAPA* 90 (1959) 131–38.

–, *New Testament Interpretation Through Rhetorical Criticism*. Chapel Hill: University of North Carolina Press, 1984.

Kitzberger, I. *Bau der Gemeinde. Das paulinische Wortfeld* οἰκοδομή/(ἐπ)οικοδομεῖν. Forschung zur Bibel 53. Würzburg: Echter Verlag, 1986.

Klauck, H.-J. "Eucharistie und Kirchengemeinschaft bei Paulus." *Wissenschaft und Weisheit* 49 (1986) 1–14.

–, *Hausgemeinde und Hauskirche im frühen Christentum*. SBS 103. Stuttgart: Katholisches Bibelwerk, 1981.

–, *Herrenmahl und hellenistischer Kult. Eine religionsgeschichtliche Untersuchung zum ersten Korintherbrief*. NTAbh n. s. 15. Münster: Aschendorff, 1982.

–, *1. Korintherbrief*. Die Neue Echter Bibel 7. Würzburg: Echter Verlag, 1984.

Klek, J. *Symbuleutici qui dicitur sermonis historia critica*. Rhetorische Studien 8. Paderborn: Schöningh, 1919.

Koester, H. *Introduction to the New Testament*. 2 vols. Philadelphia: Fortress, 1982.

–, "I Thessalonians – Experiment in Christian Writing." *Continuity and Discontinuity in Church History. Essays Presented to George Huntston Williams on His 65th Birthday*. Ed. F. F. Church and T. George. Leiden: Brill, 1979. 33–44.

Kontorini, Y. "Rome et Rhodes au Tournant du IIIe s. av. J.-c. d'après une Inscription Inédite de Rhode." *JRS* 73 (1983) 24–32.

Koskenniemi, H. *Studien zur Idee und Phraseologie des griechischen Briefes bis 400 n. Chr.*. Suomalaisen Tiedeakatemian Toimituksia, Annales Academiae Scientiarum Fennicae 102, 2. Helsinki: Suomalainen Tiedeakatemia, 1956.

Kötting, B. "Haar." *RAC* 98 (1984) 176–203.

Kramer, H. "Quid valeat ὁμόνοια in litteris Graecis." Diss., Göttingen, 1915.

Kroll, W. "Rhetorik." PWSup 8 (1940) 1039–1138.

Kümmel, W. G. *Introduction to the New Testament*. Trans. H. C. Kee. Nashville: Abingdon, 1975.

Lake, K. *The Earlier Epistles of St. Paul*. London: Rivingtons, 1911.

Lang, F. *Die Briefe an die Korinther*. NTD 7. Göttingen: Vandenhoeck & Ruprecht, 1986.

Larsen, J. A. O. "Freedom and Its Obstacles in Ancient Greece." *CPhil*. 57 (1962) 230–34.

Lausberg, H. *Elemente der literarischen Rhetorik*. Munich: Hueber, 1967.

–, *Handbuch der literarischen Rhetorik*. Munich: Hueber, 1973[2].

Lee, E. K. "Words Denoting 'Pattern' in the New Testament." *NTS* 8 (1962) 166–73.

Lehmann, E., and A. Fridrichsen. "1 Kor. 13. Eine christlich-stoische Diatribe." *TSK* Sonderheft (1922) 55–95.

Lietzmann, H. *An die Korinther I, II*. Rev. W. G. Kümmel. HNT 9. Tübingen: Mohr/Siebeck, 1949[4].

Lightfoot, J. B. *Notes on Epistles of St. Paul from Unpublished Commentaries*. London/New York: Macmillan, 1895.

Lintott, A. *Violence, Civil Strife and Revolution in the Classical City*. Baltimore: Johns Hopkins, 1982.

Loenen, D. *Stasis. Enige aspecten van de begrippen partij–en klassenstrijd in oud-Griekenland.* Amsterdam: Noord-Hollandsche Uitgevers Maataschappij, 1953.
Lohse, E. *Colossians and Philemon.* Trans. W. R. Poehlmann and R. J. Karris. Hermeneia. Philadelphia: Fortress, 1971.
Lüdemann, G. *Paulus, der Heidenapostel. Bd. II. Antipaulinismus im frühen Christentum.* FRLANT 130. Göttingen: Vandenhoeck & Ruprecht, 1983.
Luedemann, G. *Paul, Apostle to the Gentiles. Studies in Chronology.* Trans. F. S. Jones. Philadelphia: Fortress, 1984.
Lührmann, D. "Freundschaftsbrief trotz Spannungen. Zu Gattung und Aufbau der Ersten Korintherbriefs." *Studien zum Text und zur Ethik des Neuen Testaments. Festschrift zum 80. Geburtstag von H. Greeven.* Ed. W. Schrage. BZNW 47. Berlin/New York: de Gruyter, 1986. 298–314.
–, "Wo man nicht mehr Sklave oder Freier ist. Überlegungen zur Struktur frühchristlicher Gemeinden." *WD* n. s. 13 (1975) 53–83.
Lumpe, A. "Exemplum." *RAC* 6 (1966) 1229–57.
Lyons, G. *Pauline Autobiography. Toward a New Understanding.* SBLDS 73. Atlanta: Scholars Press, 1985.
MacMullen, R. *Enemies of the Roman Order.* Cambridge, MA: Harvard University Press, 1966.
Malherbe, A. J. *Ancient Epistolary Theorists.* SBLSBS 19. Atlanta: Scholars Press, 1988.
–, ed. *The Cynic Epistles. A Study Edition.* SBLSBS 12. Missoula, MT: Scholars Press, 1977.
–, "Exhortation in First Thessalonians." *NovT* 25 (1983) 238–56.
–, *Moral Exhortation, a Greco-Roman Sourcebook.* Library of Early Christianity 4. Philadelphia: Westminster, 1986.
Marshall, P. *Enmity in Corinth: Social Conventions in Paul's Relations with the Corinthians.* WUNT 2/23. Tübingen: Mohr/Siebeck, 1987.
Martin, J. *Antike Rhetorik: Technik und Methode.* HAW II, 3. Munich: Beck, 1974.
Marxsen, W. *Einleitung in das Neue Testament. Eine Einführung in ihre Probleme.* Gütersloh: Mohn, 1978[4].
Maurer, C. "Ehe und Unzucht nach 1. Korinther 6,12 – 7,7." *WD* n. s. 6 (1959) 159–69.
–, "Grund und Grenze apostolischer Freiheit. Exegetisch-theologische Studie zu 1. Korinther 9." *Antwort. Karl Barth zum siebzigsten Geburtstag am 10. Mai 1956.* Zollikon-Zurich: Evangelischer Verlag, 1956. 630–41.
–, "σχίζω." *TDNT* 8.959–65.
McCall, M. H. *Ancient Rhetorical Theories of Simile and Comparison.* Cambridge, MA: Harvard University Press, 1969.
Meeks, W. A. "'And Rose Up to Play': Midrash and Paraenesis in 1 Cor 10:1–22." *JSNT* 16 (1982) 64–78.
–, "The Christian Proteus." *The Writings of St. Paul.* New York: Norton, 1972. 435–44.
–, *The First Urban Christians. The Social World of the Apostle Paul.* New Haven/London: Yale University Press, 1983.
–, "The Image of the Androgyne: Some Uses of a Symbol in Earliest Christianity." *HR* 13 (1974) 165–208.
–, "In One Body: The Unity of Humankind in Colossians and Ephesians." *God's Christ and His People: Studies in Honour of Nils Alstrup Dahl.* Ed. J. Jervell and W. A. Meeks. Oslo/Bergen/Tromsö: Universitetsforlaget, 1977. 209–21.

–, Review of *Galatians: A Commentary on Paul's Letter to the Churches in Galatia*, by H. D. Betz. In *JBL* 100 (1981) 304–307.

–, "'Since Then You Would Need to Go Out of the World': Group Boundaries in Pauline Christianity." *Critical History and Biblical Faith. New Testament Perspectives*. Ed. T. J. Ryan. Annual Publication of the College Theology Society. Villanova, PA: College Theology Society, 1979. 4–29.

Meinertz, M. "Σχίσμα und αἵρεσις im Neuen Testament." *BZ* n. s. 1 (1957) 114–18.

Merk, O. "Nachahmung Christi. Zu ethischen Perspektiven in der paulinischen Theologie." *Neues Testament und Ethik. Für Rudolf Schnackenburg*. Ed. H. Merklein. Freiburg/Basel/Vienna: Herder, 1989. 172–206.

Merklein, H. "Die Einheitlichkeit des ersten Korintherbriefes." *ZNW* 75 (1984) 153–83.

Metzger, B. M. *A Textual Commentary on the Greek New Testament*. London/New York: United Bible Societies, 1971.

Meyer, P. W. Review of *Galatians: A Commentary on Paul's Letter to the Churches in Galatia*, by H. D. Betz. In *RelSRev* 7 (1981) 318–23.

Michaelis, W. "μιμεῖσθαι." *TDNT* 4.659–74.

Michel, O. "οἶκος." *TDNT* 5.119–59.

Mikat, P. *Die Bedeutung der Begriffe Stasis und Aponoia für das Verständnis des 1. Clemensbriefes*. Arbeitsgemeinschaft für Forschung des Landes Nordrhein-Westfalen 155. Köln/Opladen: Westdeutscher Verlag, 1969.

Mitchell, M. M. "Concerning ΠΕΡΙ ΔΕ in 1 Corinthians." *NovT* 31 (1989) 229–56.

Momigliano, A. "Camillus and Concord." *CQ* 36 (1942) 111–20.

Moulakis, A. *Homonoia: Eintracht und die Entwicklung eines politischen Bewusstseins*. Munich: List, 1973.

Mullins, T. Y. "Disclosure. A Literary Form in the New Testament." *NovT* 7 (1964) 44–50.

–, "Formulas in New Testament Epistles." *JBL* 91 (1972) 380–90.

–, "Greeting as a New Testament Form." *JBL* 87 (1968) 418–26.

–, "*Topos* as a New Testament Form." *JBL* 99 (1980) 541–47.

–, "Visit Talk in New Testament Letters." *CBQ* 35 (1973) 350–58.

Munck, J. "The Church Without Factions. Studies in I Corinthians 1–4." *Paul and the Salvation of Mankind*. Trans. F. Clarke. Richmond: John Knox, 1959. 135–67.

Murphy, N. R. *The Interpretation of Plato's Republic*. Oxford: Clarendon, 1960.

Murphy-O'Connor, J. "1 Cor. viii,6 – Cosmology or Soteriology?" *RB* 85 (1978) 253–67.

–, "1 Corinthians 11:2–16 Once Again." *CBQ* 50 (1988) 265–74.

–, "Food and Spiritual Gifts in 1 Cor 8:8." *CBQ* 41 (1979) 292–98.

–, "Freedom or the Ghetto (1 Cor 8:1–13; 10:23–11:1)." *RB* 85 (1978) 543–74.

–, "The Non-Pauline Character of 1 Corinthians 11:2–16?" *JBL* 95 (1976) 615–21.

–, *St. Paul's Corinth. Texts and Archaeology*. GNS 6. Wilmington, DE: Glazier, 1983.

–, "Sex and Logic in 1 Corinthians 11:2–16." *CBQ* 42 (1980) 482–500.

Nestle, W. "Die Fabel des Menenius Agrippa." *Klio* 21 (1927) 350–60.

Newman, W. L. *The Politics of Aristotle*. 4 vols. Oxford: Clarendon, 1887- 1902.

Neyrey, J. H. "Body Language in 1 Corinthians: The Use of Anthropological Models for Understanding Paul and his Opponents." *Semeia* 35 (1986) 129–70.

Nock, A. D. *Early Gentile Christianity and its Hellenistic Background*. New York/Evanston/London: Harper & Row, 1964.

–, *St. Paul*. New York/London: Harper & Brothers, 1938.

Oliver, J. H. "The Ruling Power." *TAPA* 43 (1953) 871–1003.

Osten-Sacken, P. von der. "Die Apologie des paulinischen Apostolats in 1. Kor 15:1–11." *ZNW* 64 (1973) 245–62.

Padgett, A. "Paul on Women in the Church: The Contradictions of Coiffure in 1 Cor 11:2–16." *JSNT* 23 (1984) 69–86.

Pearson, B. A. *The Pneumatikos-Psychikos Terminology in 1 Corinthians. A Study in the Theology of the Corinthian Opponents of Paul and its Relation to Gnosticism.* SBLDS 12. Missoula, MT: Society of Biblical Literature, 1973.

Perdue, L. G. "Paraenesis and the Epistle of James." *ZNW* 72 (1981) 241–56.

Perelman, Ch. *The New Rhetoric and the Humanities. Essays on Rhetoric and its Applications.* Dordrecht: Reidel, 1979.

Perelman, Ch., and L. Olbrechts-Tyteca. *The New Rhetoric. A Treatise on Argumentation.* Trans. J. Wilkinson and P. Weaver. Notre Dame/London: University of Notre Dame Press, 1969.

Perlman, S. "The Historical Example, Its Use and Importance as Political Propaganda in the Attic Orators." *Scripta Hierosolymitana VII: Studies in History.* Ed. A. Fuks and I. Halpern. Jerusalem: Magnes, 1961. 150–66.

Pesch, R. *Paulus ringt um die Lebensform der Kirche. Vier Briefe an die Gemeinde Gottes in Korinth.* Herderbücherei 1291. Freiburg/Basel/Vienna: Herder, 1986.

Peterson, E. " Ἔργον in der Bedeutung 'Bau' bei Paulus." *Bib* 22 (1941) 439–41.

Pfammatter, J. *Die Kirche als Bau. Eine exegetisch-theologische Studie zur Ekklesiologie der Paulusbriefe.* Analecta Gregoriana 110. Rome: Gregorian University Press, 1960.

Pfitzner, V. C. *Paul and the Agon Motif. Traditional Athletic Imagery in the Pauline Literature.* NovTSup 16. Leiden: Brill, 1967.

Plank, K. A. *Paul and the Irony of Affliction.* SBLSS. Atlanta: Scholars Press, 1987.

Price, B. J. "Παράδειγμα and *Exemplum* in Ancient Rhetorical Theory." Ph.D. diss., University of California at Berkeley, 1975.

Prümm, K. "Die pastorale Einheit des ersten Korintherbriefes." *ZKT* 64 (1940) 202–14.

Rad, G. von. "Die Vorgeschichte der Gattung von 1. Kor. 13,4–7." *Geschichte und Altes Testament.* FS A. Alt. Ed. W. F. Albright, *et al.* BHT 16. Tübingen: Mohr/Siebeck, 1953. 153–68.

Reinhold, M. *From Republic to Principate. An Historical Commentary on Cassius Dio's* Roman History, *Books 49–52.* American Philological Association Monograph Series 34. Atlanta: Scholars Press, 1988.

Reumann, J. "OIKONOMIA-Terms in Paul in Comparison with Lucan *Heilsgeschichte.*" *NTS* 13 (1966) 147–67.

Richardson, P. "On the Absence of 'Anti-Judaism' in 1 Corinthians." *Anti-Judaism in Early Christianity. Vol. 1: Paul and the Gospels.* Ed. P. Richardson and D. Granskou. Studies in Christianity and Judaism 2. Waterloo: Wilfred Laurier University Press, 1986. 59–74.

Richardson, P., and P. W. Gooch. "Accommodation Ethics." *TynBul* 29 (1978) 89–142.

Roberts, C., T. C. Skeat and A. D. Nock, "The Gild of Zeus Hypsistos." *HTR* 29 (1936) 39–88.

Robertson, A. and A. Plummer. *A Critical and Exegetical Commentary on the First Epistle of St. Paul to the Corinthians.* ICC. New York: Scribner's, 1925.

Rohde, J. "Häresie und Schisma im ersten Clemensbrief und in den Ignatius-Briefen." *NovT* 10 (1968) 217–33.

Roller, O. *Das Formular der paulinischen Briefe. Ein Beitrag zur Lehre vom antiken Briefe.* BWANT 58. Stuttgart: Kohlhammer, 1933.

Romilly, J. de. "Vocabulaire et propagande, ou les premiers emplois du mot ὁμόνοια." Mélanges de Linguistique et de Philologie Grecques offerts à Pierre Chantraine. *Etudes et commentaires* 79. Paris: Klincksieck, 1972. 199–209.

Runnals, D. R. "Hebrew and Greek Sources in the Speeches of Josephus' *Jewish War.*" Ph.D. diss., University of Toronto, 1971.

Russell, D. A. *Greek Declamation.* Cambridge: Cambridge University Press, 1983.

Russell, D. A., and N. G. Wilson, ed. and trans. *Menander Rhetor.* Oxford: Clarendon, 1981.

Sampley, J. P. *Pauline Partnership in Christ. Christian Community and Commitment in Light of Roman Law.* Philadelphia: Fortress, 1980.

Sanders, B. "Imitating Paul: 1 Cor 4:16." *HTR* 74 (1981) 353–63.

Sanders, J. T. "First Corinthians 13, Its Interpretation Since the First World War." *Int* 20 (1966) 159–87.

–, "The Transition from Opening Epistolary Thanksgiving to Body in the Letters of the Pauline Corpus." *JBL* 81 (1962) 348–62.

Sanders, L. *L'Hellénisme de Saint Clément de Rome et le Paulinisme.* Studia Hellenistica 2. Louvain: University of Louvain Press, 1943.

Sänger, D. "Die δυνατοί in 1 Kor 1,26." *ZNW* 76 (1985) 285–91.

Schenk, W. "Der 1. Korintherbrief als Briefsammlung." *ZNW* 60 (1969) 219–43.

Schenke, H.-M. and K. M. Fischer. *Einleitung in die Schriften des Neuen Testaments I. Die Briefe des Paulus und Schriften des Paulinismus.* Gütersloh: Mohn, 1978.

Schlier, H. "αἱρέομαι κτλ." *TDNT* 1.180–85.

–, "βέβαιος κτλ." *TDNT* 1.600–603.

–, "Das Hauptanliegen des ersten Korintherbriefes." *Die Zeit der Kirche: Exegetische Aufsätze und Vorträge.* Freiburg/Basel/Vienna: Herder, 1964[4]. 147–59.

Schmeller, T. *Paulus und die 'Diatribe.' Eine vergleichende Stilinterpretation.* NTAbh n. s. 19. Münster: Aschendorff, 1987.

Schmid, U. *Die Priamel der Werte im Griechischen von Homer bis Paulus.* Wiesbaden: Harrassowitz, 1964.

Schmiedel, P. W. *Die Briefe an die Thessalonicher und an die Korinther.* HKNT vol. 2, pt. 1. Tübingen: Mohr/Siebeck, 1892[2].

Schmithals, W. *Die Briefe des Paulus in ihrer ursprünglichen Form.* Zurich: Theologischer Verlag, 1984.

–, *Gnosticism in Corinth.* Trans. J. E. Steely. Nashville: Abingdon, 1971.

–, "Die Korintherbriefe als Briefsammlung." *ZNW* 64 (1973) 263–88.

Schneider, J. "Brief." *RAC* 2 (1954) 563–85.

–, "μέρος." *TDNT* 4.594–98.

–, "συζητέω κτλ." *TDNT* 7.747–48.

–, "κινέω κτλ." *TDNT* 3.718–20.

Schoedel, W. R. *Ignatius of Antioch. A Commentary on the Letters of Ignatius of Antioch.* Hermeneia. Philadelphia: Fortress, 1985.

Schreiber, A. *Die Gemeinde in Korinth. Versuch einer gruppendynamischen Betrachtung der Entwicklung der Gemeinde von Korinth auf der Basis des ersten Korintherbriefes.* NTAbh n. s. 12. Münster: Aschendorff, 1977.

Schubert, P. *Form and Function of the Pauline Thanksgivings.* BZNW 20. Berlin: Töpelmann, 1939.

Scroggs, R. "Paul and the Eschatological Woman." *JAAR* 40 (1972) 283–303.

–, "Paul and the Eschatological Woman: Revisited." *JAAR* 42 (1974) 532–49.

–, "The Sociological Interpretation of the New Testament: The Present State of Research." *NTS* 26 (1980) 164–79.

Seesemann, H. *Der Begriff* ΚΟΙΝΩΝΙΑ *im Neuen Testament*. BZNW 14. Giessen: Töpelmann, 1933.

–, "παροξύνω, παροξυσμός." *TDNT* 5.857.

Segalla, G. "Struttura filologica e letteraria della prima lettera ai Corinti." *Testimonium Christi. Scritti in onore di Jacques Dupont*. Brescia: Paideia, 1985. 465–80.

Sellin, G. "Hauptprobleme des Ersten Korintherbriefes." *ANRW* 2, pt. 25.4 (1987) 2940–3044.

–, *Der Streit um die Auferstehung der Toten*. FRLANT 138. Göttingen: Vandenhoeck & Ruprecht, 1986.

Senft, C. *La première Epître de saint-Paul aux Corinthiens*. CNT n. s. 7. Neuchâtel/Paris: Delachaux & Niestlé, 1979.

Shanor, J. "Paul as Master Builder. Construction Terms in First Corinthians." *NTS* 34 (1988) 461–71.

Sheppard, A. R. R. "*HOMONOIA* in the Greek Cities of the Roman Empire." *Ancient Society* 15–17 (1984–86) 229–52.

Siegert, F. *Argumentation bei Paulus, gezeigt an Röm 9–11*. WUNT 34. Tübingen: Mohr/Siebeck, 1985.

Simon, M. "From Greek Hairesis to Christian Heresy." *Early Christian Literature and the Classical Intellectual Tradition:* in honorem *Robert M. Grant*. Ed. W. R. Schoedel and R. L. Wilken. Théologie Historique 54. Paris: Editions Beauchesne, 1979. 101–16.

Skard, E. *Zwei religiös-politische Begriffe: euergetes-concordia*. Avhandlinger utgitt av Det Norske Videnskaps-Akademi i Oslo, II. Hist.-Filos. Klasse 1931 no. 2. Oslo: Dybwad, 1932.

Smit, J. "The Letter of Paul to the Galatians: A Deliberative Speech." *NTS* 35 (1989) 1–26.

Soden, H. von. "Sakrament und Ethik bei Paulus. Zur Frage der literarischen und theologischen Einheitlichkeit von 1 Kor. 8–10." *Urchristentum und Geschichte. Gesammelte Aufsätze und Vorträge*. Ed. H. von Campenhausen. Tübingen: Mohr/Siebeck, 1951. 1. 239–75.

Solmsen, F. "The Aristotelian Tradition in Ancient Rhetoric." *AJP* 62 (1941) 35–50; 169–90.

–, "Drei Rekonstruktionen zur antiken Rhetorik und Poetik." *Hermes* 67 (1932) 133–54.

Spicq, C. *Agapè dans le nouveau testament*. 3 vols. Paris: Gabalda, 1958–59.

Staden, H. von. "Hairesis and Heresy: The Case of the *haireseis iatrikai*." *Jewish and Christian Self-Definition*. Vol. 3: *Self-Definition in the Greco-Roman World*. Ed. B. F. Meyer and E. P. Sanders. Philadelphia: Fortress, 1982. 76–100.

Stählin, G. "σκάνδαλον, σκανδαλίζω." *TDNT* 7.339–58.

–, "φίλος κτλ." *TDNT* 9.146–71.

–, "'Um mitzusterben und mitzuleben.' Bemerkungen zu 2 Kor 7,3." *Neues Testament und christliche Existenz*. FS H. Braun. Ed. H. D. Betz and L. Schottroff. Tübingen: Mohr/Siebeck, 1973. 503–21.

Standaert, B. "Analyse rhétorique des chapitres 12 à 14." *Charisma und Agape (1 Kor 12–14)*. Ed. L. de Lorenzi. Rome, 1983. 23–50.

–, "1 Corinthiens 13." *Charisma und Agape (1 Kor 12–14)*. Ed. L. de Lorenzi. Rome, 1983. 127–47.

–, "La Rhétorique Ancienne dans Saint Paul." *L'Apôtre Paul: Personnalité, style et conception du ministère*. Ed. A. Vanhoye. BETL 73 (1986) 78–92.

Stanley, D. "Become Imitators of Me: The Pauline Conception of Apostolic Tradition." *Bib* 40 (1959) 859–77.

Stenger, W. "Beobachtungen zur Argumentationsstruktur von 1 Kor 15." *LB* 45 (1979) 71–128.

Stowers, S. K. *Letter Writing in Greco-Roman Antiquity*. Library of Early Christianity 5. Philadelphia: Westminster, 1986.

Strasburger, H. "*Concordia ordinum*. Eine Untersuchung zur Politik Ciceros." Diss. Leipzig, 1931.

Strobel, A. *Der erste Brief an die Korinther*. Zürcher Bibelkommentare NT 6, pt. 1. Zurich: Theologischer Verlag, 1989.

Suhl, A. *Paulus und seine Briefe. Ein Beitrag zur paulinischen Chronologie*. SNT 11. Gütersloh: Mohn, 1975.

Sykutris, I. "Epistolographie." PWSup 5 (1931) 185–220.

Syme, R. *The Roman Revolution*. Oxford: Clarendon, 1939.

Tarn, W. W. *Alexander the Great*. 2 vols. Cambridge: University Press, 1948.

–, "Alexander the Great and the Unity of Mankind." *Proc. Brit. Acad.* 19. London: Amen, 1933.

Taylor, L. R. *Party Politics in the Age of Caesar*. Berkeley/Los Angeles: University of California Press, 1949.

Theissen, G. *The Social Setting of Pauline Christianity. Essays on Corinth*. Ed. and trans. J. H. Schütz. Philadelphia: Fortress, 1982.

Thraede, K. *Grundzüge griechisch-römischer Brieftopik*. Zetemata 48. Munich: Beck, 1970.

Titus, E. L. "Did Paul Write I Corinthians 13?" *JBR* 27 (1959) 299–302.

Tonneau, R. "L'Inscription de Nazareth sur la violation des sépultures." *RB* 40 (1931) 544–64.

Trompf, G. W. "On Attitudes Toward Women in Paul and Paulinist Literature: 1 Corinthians 11:3–16 and its Context." *CBQ* 42 (1980) 196–215.

Turner, C. H. "Greek Patristic Commentaries on the Pauline Epistles." *A Dictionary of the Bible*. Ed. J. Hastings. New York: Scribner's, 1904. Extra Volume. 484–531.

Unnik, W. C. van. "Is 1 Clement 20 Purely Stoic?" *VC* 4 (1950) 181–89.

–, "Studies over de zogenaamde eerste brief van Clemens. I. Het Litteraire Genre." *Mededelingen der koninklijke Nederlandse akademie van wetenschappen, afd. letterkinde* 33 (1970) 149–204.

Verner, D. C. *The Household of God. The Social World of the Pastoral Epistles*. SBLDS 71. Chico, CA: Scholars Press, 1983.

Vetschera, R. *Zur griechischen Paränese*. Smichow/Prague: Rohlicek & Sievers, 1912.

Vielhauer, P. *Geschichte der urchristlichen Literatur*. Berlin/New York: de Gruyter, 1975.

–, *Oikodome. Das Bild vom Bau in der christlichen Literatur vom Neuen Testament bis Clemens Alexandrinus*. Karlsruhe-Durlach: Tron, 1940. Repr. in *Aufsätze zum Neuen Testament*. Ed. G. Klein. TBü 65. Munich: Kaiser, 1979. 2.1–168.

Volkmann, R. *Die Rhetorik der Griechen und Römer in systematischer Übersicht*. Leipzig: Teubner, 1885^2.

Vollenweider, S. *Freiheit als neue Schöpfung. Eine Untersuchung zur Eleutheria bei Paulus und in seiner Umwelt*. FRLANT 147. Göttingen: Vandenhoeck & Ruprecht, 1989.

Walbank, F. W. *A Historical Commentary on Polybius*. 3 vols. Oxford: Clarendon, 1957–79.

Walker, W. O. "1 Corinthians 11:2–16 and Paul's Views Regarding Women." *JBL* 94 (1975) 94–110.

–, "The 'Theology of Women's Place' and the 'Paulinist Tradition.'" *Semeia* 28 (1983) 101–12.

Wardman, A. *Plutarch's Lives.* Berkeley/Los Angeles: University of California Press, 1974.

Wassermann, F. M. "Thucydides and the Disintegration of the Polis." *TAPA* 85 (1934) 46–54.

Watson, D. F. "1 Corinthians 10:23–11:1 in the Light of Greco-Roman Rhetoric: The Role of Rhetorical Questions." *JBL* 108 (1989) 301–18.

–, *Invention, Arrangement and Style. Rhetorical Criticism of Jude and 2 Peter.* SBLDS 104. Atlanta: Scholars Press, 1988.

–, "A Rhetorical Analysis of Philippians and its Implications for the Unity Question." *NovT* 30 (1988) 57–88.

–, "A Rhetorical Analysis of 3 John: A Study in Epistolary Rhetoric." *CBQ* 51 (1989) 479–501.

Wedderburn, A. J. H. "The Problem of the Denial of the Resurrection in 1 Corinthians XV." *NovT* 23 (1981) 229–41.

Weische, A. *Studien zur politischen Sprache der römischen Republik.* Münster: Aschendorff, 1966.

Weiss, J. "Beiträge zur paulinischen Rhetorik." FS B. Weiss. *Theologische Studien.* Göttingen: Vandenhoeck & Ruprecht, 1897. 165–247.

–, *Earliest Christianity.* 2 vols. Ed. and trans. F. C. Grant. New York: Harper, 1959.

–, *Der erste Korintherbrief.* MeyerK 7. 9th ed. Göttingen: Vandenhoeck & Ruprecht, 1910.

Weiss, K. "συμφέρω." *TDNT* 9.69–78.

Welborn, L. L. "A Conciliatory Principle in 1 Cor 4:6." *NovT* 29 (1987) 320–46.

–, "On the Discord in Corinth. 1 Corinthians 1–4 and Ancient Politics." *JBL* 106 (1987) 83–113.

Wendland, P. *Die hellenistisch-römische Kultur in ihren Beziehungen zum Judentum und Christentum.* HNT 2. Tübingen: Mohr/Siebeck, 1972[4].

Wengst, K. *Pax Romana and the Peace of Jesus Christ.* Trans. J. Bowden. London: SCM, 1987.

Wettstein, J. J. *Novum Testamentum Graecum.* 2 vols. Amsterdam: Ex officina Dommeriana, 1752.

White, J. L. *The Form and Function of the Body of the Greek Letter. A Study of the Letter-Body in Non-Literary Papyri and in Paul the Apostle.* SBLDS 2. Missoula, MT: Society of Biblical Literature, 1972.

–, "Introductory Formulae in the Body of the Pauline Letter." *JBL* 90 (1971) 91–97.

–, *Light from Ancient Letters.* Philadelphia: Fortress, 1986.

Wickert, U. "Einheit und Eintracht der Kirche im Präskript des ersten Korintherbriefes." *ZNW* 50 (1959) 73–82.

Wilckens, U. *Weisheit und Torheit.* BHT 26. Tübingen: Mohr/Siebeck, 1959.

Willis, W. "An Apostolic Apologia? The Form and Function of 1 Cor 9." *JSNT* 24 (1985) 33–48.

Willis, W. L. *Idol Meat in Corinth. The Pauline Argument in 1 Corinthians 8 and 10.* SBLDS 68. Chico, CA: Scholars Press, 1985.

Wills, L. "The Form of the Sermon in Hellenistic Judaism and Early Christianity." *HTR* 77 (1984) 277–99.

Wilson, J. H. "The Corinthians Who Say There Is No Resurrection of the Dead." *ZNW* 59 (1968) 90–107.

Wimbush, V. L. *Paul the Worldly Ascetic. Response to the World and Self-Understanding according to 1 Corinthians* 7. Macon, GA: Mercer University Press, 1987.

Windisch, H. "ζύμη κτλ." *TDNT* 2.902–906.

Wischmeyer, O. *Der höchste Weg. Das 13. Kapitel des 1. Korintherbriefes.* SNT 13. Gütersloh: Mohn, 1981.

–, "Vorkommen und Bedeutung von Agape in der ausserchristlichen Antike." *ZNW* 69 (1978) 212–38.

Wolff, C. *Der erste Brief des Paulus an die Korinther.* THKNT vol. 7, pt. 2. Berlin: Evangelische Verlagsanstalt, 1975.

Wood, N. *Cicero's Social and Political Thought.* Berkeley/Los Angeles/London: University of California Press, 1988.

Wooten, C. "The Speeches in Polybius. An Insight into the Nature of Hellenistic Oratory." *AJP* 95 (1974) 235–51.

Wuellner, W. "The Function of Rhetorical Questions in 1 Corinthians." *L'Apôtre Paul: Personnalité, style et conception du ministère.* Ed. A. Vanhoye. BETL 73 (1986) 46–77.

–, "Greek Rhetoric and Pauline Argumentation." *Early Christian Literature and the Classical Intellectual Tradition:* in honorem *Robert M. Grant.* Ed. W. R. Schoedel and R. L. Wilken. Théologie Historique 54. Paris: Etudes Beauchesne, 1979. 177–88.

–, "Where is Rhetorical Criticism Taking Us?" *CBQ* 49 (1987) 448–63.

Yarbrough, O. L. *Not Like the Gentiles. Marriage Rules in the Letters of Paul.* SBLDS 80. Atlanta: Scholars Press, 1985.

Zillig, P. "Die Theorie von der gemischten Verfassung." Diss. Würzburg, 1916.

Zweck, D. "The *Exordium* of the Areopagus Speech, Acts 17.22, 23." *NTS* 35 (1989) 94–103.

Zwicker, H. "Homonoia." PW 8, pt. 2 (1913) 2265–69.

Indices

Passages Cited

a) Old Testament and Apocrypha

c) New Testament

d) Early Christian Literature and the Ancient Church

e) Greek and Latin Texts

Modern Authors

Hermeneutische Untersuchungen zur Theologie

Alphabetical Index

Printed in the United States
28167LVS00004B/19-27

9 780664 221775

Made in the USA
Las Vegas, NV
02 December 2020

11830743R00231